WITHDRAWN

MASTERPLOTS II

AMERICAN FICTION
SERIES

MASTERPLOTS II

AMERICAN FICTION SERIES

3

Lov-Set

Edited by

FRANK N. MAGILL

SALEM PRESS

Englewood Cliffs, N.J.

Library of Congress Cataloging-in-Publication Data
Masterplots II: American fiction series.
  Includes bibliographies and index.
  Summary: Includes more than 360 interpretative
essays on works of twentieth-century fiction published in the United States and Latin America.
  1. America—Literatures—Stories, plots, etc.
2. America—Literatures—History and criticism—
Addresses, essays, lectures. 3. Fiction—20th century—Stories, plots, etc. 4. Fiction—20th century—History and criticism—Addresses, essays,
lectures. [1. America—Literatures—Stories, plots,
etc. 2. America—Literatures—History and criticism—Addresses, essays, lectures] I. Magill, Frank
Northen, 1907-   . II. Title: Masterplots 2. III.
Title: Masterplots two.
PN846.M37   1986   809.3   86-1910
ISBN 0-89356-456-7 (set)
ISBN 0-89356-459-1 (volume 3)

LIST OF TITLES IN VOLUME 3

LIST OF TITLES IN VOLUME 3

MASTERPLOTS II

AMERICAN FICTION
SERIES

LOVE IN THE RUINS
The Adventures of a Bad Catholic at a Time Near the End of the World

Author: Walker Percy (1916-   )
Type of plot: Social satire
Time of plot: The end of the twentieth century
Locale: A community in Louisiana
First published: 1971

> *Principal characters:*
> DR. THOMAS MORE, the protagonist/narrator, an alcoholic psychiatrist and "bad Catholic"
> MOIRA SCHAFFNER, his girlfriend, a secretary at the Love Clinic
> LOLA RHOADES, another girlfriend, an accomplished cellist
> ELLEN OGLETHORPE, his office nurse, a beautiful but tyrannical Georgia Presbyterian
> ART IMMELMANN, a mysterious stranger who claims to be a liaison between the National Institute of Mental Health and the Ford, Carnegie, and Rockefeller foundations but apparently has more infernal connections

The Novel

On July 4, Dr. Thomas More, with a carbine on his knees, sits in a pine grove on the southwest cusp of the decaying interstate cloverleaf. A sniper has shot at him earlier in the day, and from this point he commands a view of all four directions. In one quadrant is the city, inhabited largely by conservative Christian businessmen; in another, the Paradise Estates, a suburb where he ordinarily lives in a house inherited from his deceased wife. In still another direction, there is the federal complex, which includes the hospital where the narrator works, a medical school, the NASA facility, the Behavioral Institute, the Geriatrics Center, and the Love Clinic. In the remaining quadrant, the huge Honey Island swamp shelters assorted social rebels and castoffs: white derelicts, young dropouts pursuing love, drugs, and the simple life, and ferocious black Bantus, who use the swamp as guerrilla base for launching raids against outlying suburbs and shopping centers.

Immediately below Dr. More's lookout post, an old, abandoned Howard Johnson motel, long deserted after a devastating raid in years past, is a temporary shelter for Dr. More's two girlfriends, Moira and Lola, and his loyal nurse, Ellen, whom he also loves. The action of the novel covers, in retrospect, the preceding four days, during which this awkward personal and public crisis came to a head.

The amiable Dr. More, though hardly responsible for the persistent failure of American society to eradicate racial inequality and bigotry, does nevertheless share some obscure guilt for the peculiarly volatile situation on this particular day. He has learned that a racial uprising is planned for the Fourth of July, with the Bantus intending to take over the Paradise Estates. He has been discreetly warned by a black friend and an old Catholic priest to vacate his suburban house and move into his mother's place in town.

What Dr. More really is worrying about, however, is a more general catastrophe, a possibly explosive and poisonous interaction between the heavy sodium which characterizes the soil in the area and fallout from the gross misuse of his invention, the More Qualitative-Quantitative Ontological Lapsometer. He has, through ambition and pride, allowed this sensitive instrument to fall into ignorant and evil hands.

The nondescript Art Immelmann plays the Mephistopheles to More's Faust in this matter. Art's original offer was to see that More's article explaining the lapsometer would be published in a prestigious journal of psychiatry. He promised, moreover, to use his influence with the Ford, Carnegie, and Rockefeller foundations for substantial grant money so that More could submit the device to extensive scientific testing. The lapsometer measures certain psychic forces in the brain, especially angelism and bestialism, which may be responsible for the increasing irrationality and instability among otherwise healthy Americans. Art wants patent rights in exchange for this service.

When Art offers an appendage to the lapsometer so that it not only measures psychic imbalances but also amends or at least changes them with the twist of the dial, More signs the fateful agreement, dreaming of a Nobel Peace Prize in his future. To his consternation, however, Art passes out lapsometers to ignorant students, with hilarious but potentially dangerous results. Later, on this eventful Independence Day, Dr. More manages, by praying to his sainted ancestor and namesake Sir Thomas More for help, to exorcise his devil.

An epilogue five years later shows More living in relative peace in former slave quarters, happily married to one of his sweethearts. He has dissipated his first wife's fortune in an unsuccessful attempt to promote his lapsometer, but he still believes in its promise. Racial prejudice may be partly responsible for the doctor's cool reception as a scientific innovator, since the relative prestige of blacks and whites is now reversed—not, however, because of the Bantu revolt five years ago. Blacks are now beginning to demonstrate some of the psychological pathologies that had afflicted the ruling white class.

The Characters

Although Percy sketches many of the characters with the swift, deadly accurate strokes of comic caricature, his protagonist is a fully developed, complex, seriocomic hero. Yet he is also a kind of Everyman, sharing many of the mental/emotional impediments typical of each of the social groups so deftly caricatured. The dominant political parties, for example, have been renamed (a contribution in each case of the opposition) and display characteristic pathological symptoms. Conservative Republicans, now called Knotheads, often suffer from large bowel complaints, making proctology one of the two major medical specialties. Dr. More shares this difficulty. Though by no means a political Knothead, he is a conservative Roman Catholic in a world where most Catholics have formed splinter groups. Like so many of Percy's protagonists, and like the author himself, he professes to believe in the traditional Catholic Christian message. Dr. More admits, however, that he loves women, music, science, whiskey, and God, in that order—and his fellowman hardly at all. He has not "eaten Christ"—that is, taken Communion—since his daughter Samantha died, his wife ran away with a heathen Englishman, and he himself turned to drink.

He suffers even more from the tendency toward abstraction and unreasonable terrors that have become typical of the Lefts (Democrats) or Leftpapasane, a term devised by Knotheads, standing for Liberty, Equality, Fraternity, The Pill, Atheism, Pot, Antipollution, Sex, Abortion Now, and Euthanasia. Lefts often suffer from sexual impotence as well, for the tendency to abstraction results in alienation from the body and concrete reality. That is why Lefts generally flock to psychologists rather than proctologists.

Dr. More does not suffer from sexual impotence, but he does have an ironically related problem. He tends to fall in love quite sincerely with one young woman after another, which is perhaps a symptom of his religio-erotic tendency toward abstraction. That is why his personal life is complicated by those three beautiful girls, not to mention the enticing young dropout he met once in the swamp. He seems to have less control over this kind of abstraction than over the variety that scientists, including himself, tend to assume with their pose of objectivity. In fact, he is philosophically and professionally apposed to the prevailing behavioralist orientation of his medical colleagues.

The characterizations of women in the novel are more flat, but they are sufficient for their fictional purposes. They help to differentiate psychological propensities in the protagonist. Hester, the girl in the swamp, is perhaps simply an embodiment of a new Eve, wiped clean of civilization's sins. Dr. More is too intelligent, however, to assume that the Garden of Eden can be reentered in its original simplicity.

Moira's attraction is almost exclusively physical. She is sentimental, romantic, unintelligent, but adorable in an amoral, mindless sort of way. The elegant Lola, musician and breeder of fine horses, appeals to the well-developed aesthetic sensibilities of Dr. More. Ellen Oglethorpe, somewhat more expansively developed, maintains a rather puritanical emphasis on morality and duty through most of the story but ripens into the mother/wife who is exactly what the erring Tom More needs to keep his irrational terrors and longings under control.

Art Immelmann is an inspired creation but is necessarily a caricature, as befits a modern Mephistopheles. He has certain affinities with Fyodor Dostoevski's shabby, middle-class devil in *Bratya Karamazovy* (1879-1880; *The Brothers Karamazov*). Percy excels in the comic effect of realistic detail fused with surrealism and subtle clues that a sordidly ordinary person is not what he seems.

Themes and Meanings

Love in the Ruins is a devastating satire of many of the social, political, religious, and scientific shibboleths of the modern world. Percy steps on so many toes that even the offended may laugh at discomfort shared so equitably with opponents. Percy is not only a Christian satirizing Christians but also a physician exposing his own profession as often absurd and misguided.

The Love Clinic is an outrageous commentary on behavioral research and on modern sexual mores, which have managed simultaneously to liberate sex and to reduce it to its lowest common denominator. In the clinic, doctors study the physical and emotional mechanisms of sexual intercourse and masturbation through two-way mirrors, seeking to remedy impotence among the bored. A dissident Catholic priest operates the vaginal console with its orgasm button, while casually reading *Commonweal*, a Catholic layman's magazine which has published articles by Percy. The priest is the clinic chaplain, who advises patients to love or die. This is more obvious irony than Geoffrey Chaucer's ambiguous motto, "Love Conquers All," on the worldly prioress' brooch, but it is of the same general order.

The doctor's lapsometer, with its fusion of metaphysical concepts and scientific measurement, is the perfect symbol for the existential preoccupation with the alienation of modern man from self, nature, God, and his fellowman. One of the implications may be that neither science nor religion nor humanistic philosophy offers an entirely convincing explanation of human nature. Dr. More himself calls his lapsometer "the first caliper of the soul and the first hope of bridging the dread chasm that has rent the soul of Western man ever since the famous philosopher Descartes ripped body loose from mind and turned the very soul into a ghost that haunts its own house."

Critical Context

Percy has a considerable affinity with the religious existentialist Søren Kierkegaard and for Dostoevski's peculiar vision of human absurdity and moral chaos. He received the 1971 National Catholic Book Award for *Love in the Ruins*. Something of a madcap masterpiece, this satire was a popular success, though some critics prefer the more subtle humor of Percy's later novel *The Second Coming* (1980), which also deals with love, mental illness, moral confusion, and the blundering spiritual quest.

The later book also develops more precisely a minor theme of *Love in the Ruins*: the way in which the misuse of language contributes to popular mindlessness and alienation. Percy shares the contemporary intellectual interest in semantics and semiotics. In both *Love in the Ruins* and *The Second Coming*, he tends to emphasize the antic absurdities of clichés and jargon that define contemporary attitudes, though not the sinister intent behind what George Orwell called Doublethink.

Percy's concern for language is both moral and professional. The specifically human world, often quite different from the empirical world of sense experience, is created by the words used to describe it. Percy is concerned not so much with the deliberate villains of society but with the limitations of goodness in well-intentioned people who cannot "name" reality and thus do not know it. Percy recognizes this difficulty in himself as a "Christian novelist," for he knows that the Christian message, as ordinarily expressed, is a tired anachronism in the modern world. For a discussion of this ironic difficulty of the writer, one should read Percy's *The Message in the Bottle* (1975), especially the chapter entitled "Notes for a Novel About the End of the World," which is especially relevant to *Love in the Ruins*. For further satiric comment on the American way of love and sex, the section on "The Promiscuous Self," in Percy's *Lost in the Cosmos: The Last Self-Help Book* (1983), is both provocative and entertaining.

Sources for Further Study
Kazin, Alfred. "The Pilgrimage of Walker Percy," in *Harper's Magazine*. CCXLII, no. 1453 (June, 1971), pp. 81-86.
Luschei, Martin. *The Sovereign Wayfarer: Walker Percy's Diagnosis of the Malaise*, 1972.

Katherine Snipes

LOVE MEDICINE

Author: Louise Erdrich (1955-   )
Type of plot: Interwoven tales
Time of plot: From 1934 to 1984
Locale: A North Dakota Indian reservation and nearby towns
First published: 1984

Principal characters:

NECTOR KASHPAW, the grandfather, a former tribal chairman
MARIE LAZARRE KASHPAW, once ambitious to be a nun, later
   Nector's wife
LULU LAMARTINE, a loving woman who has eight sons by
   Kashpaw, Nanapush, and other men
GERRY NANAPUSH, Lulu's son, a hero of the American Indian
   Movement
ALBERTINE JOHNSON, a member of the youngest generation, a
   nursing student
JUNE MORRISSEY KASHPAW, a troubled woman
LIPSHA MORRISSEY, June's unacknowledged son

The Novel

   Love Medicine is a series of tales (many of them originally published independently) which explore the ties of blood, knowledge, love, and mystery that link three generations of Chippewa people. As independent stories told from the viewpoint of various members of the Kashpaw, Lamartine, and Nanapush families, the tales have many strengths. One is the use of language that subtly reflects each narrator. The images, phrasing, and vocabulary of the urbanized characters, such as Beverly Lamartine, differ from the language of those whose lives still center on the reservation; the expressions used by some people in the older generation (particularly Marie Lazarre) suggest translation from thoughts that come in another language. Even in the youngest generation, Albertine Johnson, who leaves the reservation to go to college, uses words quite differently from her cousin Lipsha, who stays behind.

   Each story has a sharp focus, an interesting narrative line, and images that expose the event without intervening explanation. Furthermore, the novel created by weaving these tales together is stronger than any of its parts. The first story takes place in 1981, the second in 1934—and midway in the second story, the reader begins to understand that the young girl Marie Lazarre who tells about fighting devils in the convent is the same person as Grandma Kashpaw, who was fetched from the senior citizens' home in the first story. As one tale follows another in a sequence that skips back and forth through the years, one pleasure for readers is simply fitting together the jigsaw puzzle, teasing out the identities hidden in the various names that result from marriages, unwed parenthood, and children fostered by neighbors or relatives, and realizing, with sudden delight, that one is getting a second viewpoint on an incident already known from an earlier story.

The individual stories are fragmentary; the book does not attempt a complete history of the families. Most stories focus on a significant crisis, though some include background narration. In the first, June Kashpaw is picked up by an oil worker in a boomtown and then dies in the snow walking back toward the reservation; the subsequent sections of that story reveal (indirectly) the complicated reactions of her various kin. Several stories show, in bits, the triangular relationship between Marie Lazarre, Lulu Lamartine, and Nector Kashpaw, which began in 1934 and is not resolved until forty-eight years later, after Nector's death. Other stories focus on Lulu's sons, suggesting the damages wrought by conventions of manliness in both Indian and white society. The essence of the book, however, grows from the relationship between stories and from the reader's ability to derive meaning from the reappearance of central thematic material.

The Characters

The physical tie between the characters is a piece of land originally allotted to Nector Kashpaw's mother, Rushes Bear. Most of her children were assigned to parcels in Montana, but she managed to get a piece of North Dakota wheatland and live on it with her young twins, Nector and Eli. Nector went to boarding school, learned white reading and writing, and grew up to be Tribal Chair and a man of importance; Eli, hidden by his mother in a root cellar, lived in the woods and kept some of the old skills. These two men, who became adults in the 1930's, represent the oldest generation in the novel; the women with whom their lives are entangled include Marie Lazarre and Lulu Lamartine. Marie went into a convent intending to become a saint; after marrying Nector, she compulsively takes in unwanted children. Lulu, with what seems equal compulsion, makes her own babies— eight boys, each by a different father, who grow up supporting, fighting, and caring for one another. Both Marie and Lulu know how to use power; Marie pushes Nector into becoming Tribal Chair, and Lulu, in a truly wonderful scene, forces the council not to sell her land by threatening to reveal publicly—right then in the meeting—who fathered each of her children. Both remain vivid personalities in their old age, strong and salty women using very different tactics to win what they desire.

The members of the middle generation are not quite so compelling; perhaps they are seen less clearly (none is actually a narrator for any extended story) or perhaps they are the generation that suffers most from the conflict between reservation ways and the modern world. June Morrissey Kashpaw dies in the first story; her discarded husband, Gordon Kashpaw, is the protagonist (though not the narrator) of the story "Crown of Thorns," which is a careful, vivid, underplayed, and totally convincing portrait of delirium tremens. Lulu Lamartine's son Gerry Nanapush spends half his adult life in prison after a three-year sentence for assault (he keeps escaping and being recaptured and doing additional time for escaping) before he makes the mistake of hiding out on the Pine Ridge Reservation, where he inevitably kills a state trooper.

Albertine Johnson and Lipsha Morrissey, members of the youngest generation, are to a certain extent consciously searching for their roots and for a way to understand their ties to the past. Most of their generation has disappeared to Minneapolis or Chicago or somewhere even further beyond the pull of the house and land that form the gravitational center of the Kashpaw constellation. Both Lipsha and Albertine are still in the process of becoming. Albertine, in particular, can change quite dramatically from one story to the next, but despite her relatively small share of Chippewa genes and her sustained drive for education—she is studying medicine by the end of the book—she knows her own need for the bonds of blood and tradition. She tries to talk to her grandfather about tribal politics and how he got things done in the old days. Lipsha, who seems virtually impervious to any kind of teaching (he manages to mangle and misunderstand both the traditional skills he learns from Eli Kashpaw and the education he suffers in white schools) is a wonderfully naïve narrator in the Huck Finn tradition. At the book's end, however, he turns to home instead of lighting out for an individual destiny.

Themes and Meanings

In *Love Medicine*, Louise Erdrich opens up a new territory of contemporary Native American life and demonstrates a compassionate yet uncompromising attitude toward its people. She also crafts a piece of fiction whose technique amplifies its meaning. In doing the work to trace out relationships, keep track of the characters, and understand how they are tied together, the reader becomes a part of the linking and weaving that is the novel's theme. The pleasure of solving puzzles is secondary. What really matters are the bonds of love and mystery and anger, the desires and strengths and weaknesses that keep these people together, even though some are reservation-bound, others thoroughly urbanized, and a few have hardly any Chippewa blood.

Because the stories are presented through their narrators, with no outside viewpoint to provide explanations, the evocation of Native American life is clean and subtle, without pandering to the picturesque or the sentimental. Furthermore, the book's structure is used to alter the reader's consciousness from within. For example, although June Morrissey Kashpaw dies in the first tale, her character is one of the threads that provides links among the people and the stories—various characters talk about her; there are questions about her own parentage and about the husband she left and the baby she never acknowledged; Gordon takes to drink after her death; Albertine's mother and aunt tell their version of an incident from June's childhood. In other words, Erdrich, using only the literary conventions of a white cultural tradition, thoroughly and convincingly demonstrates that a person who is dead can remain an important presence for the living. From that point it is only half a step to the other stories, the ones in which a dead person's spirit actually appears.

The book's characters are nominally Catholic, but their Catholicism grows from mission schooling, which has merely damaged their traditional religion without really replacing it. Lipsha Morrissey, in the story from which the collection takes its title, suddenly thinks that he understands that Grandpa Kashpaw always shouts in church because God will not hear him otherwise. In a confused recollection drawn from his own reading of the Bible, Lipsha reasons that God has been growing progressively deaf since Old Testament times: He used to pay attention and perform miracles or strike down wrongdoers, but He has not done so in recent years. The Chippewa gods, Lipsha thinks, would still do favors if one knew the right way to ask— but the problem is that the right ways of asking were lost to the Chippewa once the Catholics gained ground.

Thus, although traditional ways are not glamorized, there is a sense of loss as they diminish. The family pattern that gives a woman a good deal of choice about who will father her children and how long her liaison with any particular man will last has a joyous (if semicomic) treatment in the case of Lulu Lamartine. In the next generation, however, June Morrissey seems more of a slut than an Earth Mother. The army, which in traditional sentiment and in the eyes of reservation boys is a heroic experience that brings the Indian into his own, has a devastating effect on the Vietnam generation. Significantly, the American Indian Movement hero Gerry Nanapush gives Lipsha Morrissey the gift of a blood tie that will free him from his decision to join the military.

The Chippewa viewpoint here, as elsewhere, sees many disadvantages to white ways; the Chippewa also (like humans almost everywhere) crave the material goods that seem to rain on hardworking white Americans. The only character who really romanticizes the Indian past is Lynette Kashpaw, the wholly white wife of one of the younger men. After several generations of interracial marriage and sexual encounters, blood in the strictest sense is not really important. To be Indian is, to a certain extent, a state of mind. The urbanized Cree Beverly Lamartine had parents who called themselves French or Black Irish and considered those who thought of themselves as Indians quite backward. Albertine, however, although quite light-skinned and less than half Chippewa, always thinks of herself as Indian. The meaning of identity, the influence of past on present, and the sense of loss and confusion in people caught between a half-remembered tradition and an outsider role in the modern world are the book's primary themes.

Critical Context

Love Medicine, a truly impressive first novel, received both the National Book Critics Circle Award and the *Los Angeles Times* Book Award For Fiction. Louise Erdrich, a member of the Turtle Mountain band of Chippewa, was one of the first women students admitted to Dartmouth, in 1972, and had previously published a collection of poetry. Published at a moment when interest in ethnic and regional literature was high, *Love Medicine* merged an authentic Native American voice with an accessible modern literary form.

Sources for Further Study

Bruckner, J. R. Review in *The New York Times*. December 20, 1984, p. 25.
Kendall, Elaine. Review in *Los Angeles Times*. December 20, 1984, sec. 5, p. 34.
Washington Post. Review. November 14, 1984, p. D2.

Sally Mitchell

LUCY GAYHEART

Author: Willa Cather (1873-1947)
Type of plot: Psychological realism
Time of plot: Christmas, 1901, to Christmas, 1902, and 1927
Locale: Haverford, Nebraska, and Chicago, Illinois
First published: 1935

> *Principal characters:*
> LUCY GAYHEART, the darling of Haverford, a music student in Chicago
> HARRY GORDON, the wealthy son of a Haverford banker and businessman who is in love with Lucy
> PAULINE GAYHEART, Lucy's older sister
> JACOB GAYHEART, a watchmaker and music teacher, Lucy's father
> CLEMENT SEBASTIAN, a concert singer
> PAUL AUERBACH, Lucy's music teacher in Chicago

The Novel

Lucy Gayheart is equally a study of the central character and of the effect that she has on others. The novel opens twenty-five years after Lucy's death, when her memory is still fondly cherished by the residents of her small hometown: "In Haverford on the Platte the townspeople still talk of Lucy Gayheart. They do not talk of her a great deal, to be sure; life goes on and we live in the present." This retrospective point of view provides the counterpoint to the dominant point of view in the novel, Lucy's. Most of the novel takes place during the year before Lucy's death, when she is in her early twenties and is just beginning to understand herself and to make choices about her future.

Lucy's hardest choices involve her potential career as a pianist. Encouraged by her father, a watchmaker and music teacher, to study music in Chicago, Lucy has learned to love the cultural opportunities that the city offers. After three years of study with Paul Auerbach, Lucy is not convinced that she has the talent or the stamina to become a concert pianist. Yet her confidence in her ability is increased when she is asked to become a temporary accompanist for Clement Sebastian, a concert singer with an international reputation. Lucy's sensitivity to mood and musical nuance makes her a talented accompanist, and Sebastian comes to appreciate not only her skill but also her enthusiastic outlook on life. Her enthusiasm enriches his life, which, although aesthetically full, is emotionally barren.

Soon after beginning to play for Sebastian, Lucy returns to Haverford for Christmas vacation. There she represses her new interests and enjoys her old friends and childhood activities, all the while aware that something is missing from her life. At the same time, she appears more interesting than ever to Harry Gordon, the most intelligent and the wealthiest young man in Haverford. Harry recognizes that he loves Lucy but is not certain that marrying her would be prudent, for Harry has been reared to value material advantages and expects a wife to advance his position in the world. Harry also assumes that Lucy is his for the asking; his egotism about her leads to his lifelong disappointment.

When Lucy returns to Chicago, she begins to fall in love with Sebastian, and he with her. Here is a love that asks for nothing; it is enough to be with Sebastian and to see the world through his eyes for a while. Sebastian is equally undemanding, realizing that Lucy is in love, not merely with him, but with a way of perceiving life. Unfortunately, it is at this stage that Harry Gordon comes to Chicago to ask Lucy to marry him. Her response, implying that she and Sebastian are lovers, drives him back to Nebraska, where he marries a wealthy daughter of society to spite Lucy. Lucy, on the other hand, shortly experiences despair over Sebastian's accidental drowning. On her return to Haverford to overcome her depression, she is shocked to discover that Harry will not speak to her, and she tries, unsuccessfully, to break down his reserve. In a final misunderstanding, Harry refuses a ride to Lucy, who is exhausted from skating too long; in anger, Lucy skates onto thin ice and is drowned in the Platte River. This occurs soon after her realization that she wants to go back to Chicago to continue her studies.

The last section of the novel occurs twenty-five years later, at the time that the novel opens. Lucy is remembered by many with love, especially at her father's funeral, which has occurred recently. No one remembers as vividly as Harry Gordon, who has become the wealthiest member of Haverford society. Knowing that he has made a loveless marriage, understanding that he is responsible for Lucy's death, Harry has nevertheless learned how to live with the consequences of his youthful pride. His sense of guilt has lessened while he has learned to do things for others: He works in an ambulance unit in France during World War I; he spends hours playing chess with Mr. Gayheart, who has also lost his other daughter, Pauline; he is more lenient with borrowers who owe money at his bank. Most important, he learns to think of Lucy without anger, but with love and appreciation for her enthusiasm and her zest for life. Aware that he lacks the ability to react spontaneously to small joys, Harry stops resenting Lucy's ability to do so and understands that her life has given his life meaning even after her death.

The Characters

In *Lucy*, Cather has captured the best of what it means to be young, talented, and discovering the world. The impression of quickness that Lucy leaves on her observers' minds—the idea that she is poised for flight—is a symbol of Lucy's intellect. She is learning to appreciate many of the artistic and natural wonders of her world; her joy in music, in winter, and in the city is too great not to be conveyed to those around her. Caught in the throes of discovery, Lucy is also something of an egotist, impatient with those who are not as quick as she is, angry when she has to defend her impetuosity. Frequently, she responds impulsively, learning later that her haste is self-destructive.

A foil to Lucy's youth is Pauline, Lucy's older sister. Pauline has managed her father's home since her mother's death and has reared Lucy. Believing that she is the only responsible figure in an unappreciative family, Pauline resents Lucy's beauty and spontaneity. Always looking for ways to supplement her father's meager income, Pauline thinks that Lucy's music lessons in Chicago are an extravagance, and though she does not try to stop them, she accuses Lucy of lacking appreciation for the people who do the most for her. Further, she thinks that Lucy is not doing enough to encourage Harry Gordon. In a rich husband, Pauline sees Lucy's best hope of repaying what she owes to the family. Lucy, who gives piano lessons and earns a good salary accompanying Sebastian, resents Pauline's interference and interprets Pauline's attempts to understand her as efforts at martyrdom.

The two important male characters in the novel could hardly be more different. Harry Gordon maintains a hardheaded, Midwestern attitude about commerce; Clement Sebastian exudes a worldly attitude about art. Harry is an important man only in a small town; Sebastian claims an international reputation. Harry is young and arrogant; Sebastian is middle-aged and is modest about his accomplishments. Lucy, loving them both, is nevertheless exasperated with Harry and patient with Sebastian. Deciding that she has much to learn from Sebastian makes her more impatient than ever with Harry's inability to react quickly and to articulate his feelings.

Sebastian is appealing to Lucy, not only because he is a fine singer who encourages her musical talent, but also because he seems lonely and in need of someone. Ordinarily, he is accompanied by an unattractive, possessive, and sarcastic young man who was his wife's protégé. When Lucy meets Sebastian, he seems tired of Madame Sebastian's incessant demands for money and her pretenses to aesthetic understanding. Lucy's genuine responses to music and her quiet appreciation of the signs of wealth that surround Sebastian win Sebastian's approval, and then his love. He is grateful for Lucy's love and chooses not to take advantage of it; indeed, he tries instead to enrich her life without making her feel obligated.

In contrast, Harry feels that Lucy ought to be grateful for his love and his offer of marriage. Finding her stimulating because she is different, Harry believes that marrying Lucy will provide him with a constant reminder that there is more to life than acquisition. Yet Lucy feels that Harry views her only as another acquisition, and she despairs of being able to liberate his spirit enough for him to appreciate art and culture. Harry's egotism is mitigated by his intelligence and his awareness that art is important, even though he lacks emotional responses to it. Lucy finds in him a good friend, one more sympathetic to her life than anyone else in Haverford, but she does not want to marry him. Harry is stubborn, but reflective. By the end of the novel, he forgives himself and Lucy for her death, understanding that this event early in his life has led to a fuller humanity.

Themes and Meanings

The structure of the novel reinforces one of its major themes, that tragedy is absorbed into the less dramatic flow of one's life, that while it may signal a turning point, it does not necessarily result in major changes. The beginning and the closing sections of the novel are about memories of Lucy; her death in a sense provides the climax of the middle sections about her love for Sebastian. Yet Lucy has also experienced her tragedy—Sebastian's death—and overcome her depression by wondering, "What if Life itself were . . . like a lover waiting for her in distant cities . . . drawing her, enticing her, weaving a spell over her." Lucy is drowned shortly after the moment of her recovery, but Harry matures to a philosophic understanding of tragedy. His final act in the novel is to preserve a piece of sidewalk that Lucy had run through before the concrete was dry; he cherishes this memorial, recognizing that he has lost Lucy forever but has also been profoundly influenced by her.

Secondary themes explored through the characters are the egotism of youth and the tremendous power of art. Cather develops these themes in other novels as well; here, the self-destructive quality of both Lucy's and Harry's egotism is clear. Their assumptions about each other keep them apart and cause both to behave dishonestly: Lucy lies about her relationship with Sebastian, implying that it is sexual when it is not, and Harry refuses to extend more than impersonal courtesy to Lucy at a time when he realizes that he loves her more than ever. Sebastian's profession makes him seductive because of his association with all that Lucy is learning to appreciate. Even after his death, it is Lucy's sensitivity to music that helps her through her depression. Seeing an old singer perform wonderfully with a second-rate opera company triggers her reaffirmation that life itself is the lover.

Critical Context

Lucy Gayheart was one of Willa Cather's last four books, all of which have been criticized as less interesting than her earlier work. It has been suggested that the structure is contrived and the tone sentimental. Perhaps the most accurate criticism of the novel is that the characters are not fully developed. Strongly identified with commerce, Harry Gordon never manifests the keen intellect with which he is credited; his successes at the bank are not described and seem easy achievements. Clement Sebastian, as the representative of the aesthetic world, is emotionally aloof; his motivations are unclear, and even his love for Lucy seems an artistic rendition of emotion, rather than a humanizing action. Much of this may be attributed to the fact that Cather was trying to characterize the sense of life as much as any individual; nevertheless, this theme is developed at the expense of complexity of character and of structure.

Sources for Further Study
Bloom, Edward A., and Lillian D. Bloom. *Willa Cather's Gift of Sympathy: A Lost Lady*, 1962.
Jones, Howard Mumford. *The Bright Medusa*, 1952.
Murphy, John J., ed. *Critical Essays on Willa Cather*, 1984.
Woodress, James. *Willa Cather: Her Life and Art*, 1970.

Gweneth A. Dunleavy

MACUNAÍMA

Author: Mário de Andrade (1893-1945)
Type of plot: Rhapsodic, comic epic
Time of plot: The early twentieth century
Locale: Brazil, principally the Amazon jungle and São Paulo
First published: Macunaíma, o heroi sem nenhum caracter, 1928 (English
   translation, 1984)

> *Principal characters:*
> MACUNAÍMA, the mock hero, emperor of the jungle
> MAANAPE, his elderly brother, who is a sorcerer
> JIGUÊ, his witless brother
> CI, the Mother of the Forest, Macunaíma's great love
> VENCESLAU PIETRO PIETRA, the man-eating giant Piaiman and
>   villain

The Novel

This unusual work is an antirealist fantasy drawn from Amazonian Indian
mythology, Afro-Luso-Brazilian folklore, and the author's imagination.
Thus, much of what occurs is fablelike, magical, or illogical, with no spatial
or temporal bounds. The action centers on the hero's struggle to recover a
magical amulet given to him by Ci. His adventures take him to all corners of
Brazil and back in time.

Macunaíma is born an ugly black baby to a Tapanhuma Indian mother.
Although he is destined to be a popular hero, his mother notes that all
names beginning with "Ma" bring bad luck. The sadistic and mischievous
child soon discovers magical powers, transforming himself into a comely
prince to seduce his brother Jiguê's first wife. When Jiguê distributes meat
after a successful hunt, the hero receives tripe and vows revenge. During a
famine, the hero's acts show him to be vindictive and greedy. As punishment, his mother expels him from the jungle, and he must return home by
his wits. Back home, he goes through several metamorphoses to seduce
Iriqui, Jiguê's new wife. Tricked by the gods, Macunaíma kills his mother.
The three brothers and Iriqui then set off for "our world." They soon
encounter Ci, whom the hero rapes. An entourage of birds salute him as
the new emperor of the virgin forest. The two engender a son, who is
adored by women of all races from all parts of the nation. A venomous serpent causes the death of Ci and son; before ascending to become a bright
star, she gives the hero a special amulet. The precious stone is lost as
Macunaíma defeats the Water Mother in battle. When the hero learns that
the man-eating giant Venceslau has obtained the coveted charm, he sets off
for São Paulo to recover it, accompanied by his brothers and a flock of

royal parrots. The hero stows his conscience before leaving and gathers two hundred canoes to carry his fortune of cocoa beans. The brothers discover the footprint of Saint Thomas filled with water. The hero bathes first and becomes fair-skinned and blue-eyed; the envious brothers come out with red and black skin respectively.

In the metropolis, the trio trade beans for currency and discover that money rules all. The hero picks up some white women only to discover that they are prostitutes. They explain to Macunaíma that the goblins, spirits, and animals that he thinks he sees are actually buildings and machines. Macunaíma surmises that white people are the Children of Manioc and ruminates on the monumental struggle between urban people and machines; he decides that the contest is a draw and that the two are equivalent. He then turns Jiguê into a "telephone contraption" and calls Venceslau. The hero confronts the villain for the first time but is killed, diced, and stewed. Maanape employs his powers to revive him. Posing as a French prostitute, the hero again attempts to lure the amulet from the giant, whose vicious dog pursues Macunaíma through all regions of Brazil. During this chase they encounter several figures from the nation's colonial past. By now the hero is overcome by rancor and attends a voodoo rite in Rio de Janeiro, in which he beseeches devil spirits to punish Venceslau, who takes a terrible beating. Vei the Sun offers one of her daughters in marriage if the hero will remain faithful, but he overindulges with a fishwife and incurs the never-ending wrath of the Sun. At the halfway point of the book, the emperor writes a pedantic letter to his subjects recounting his adventures and explaining his impressions of civilization and the Portuguese language.

As Venceslau recuperates, the hero is captured by the giant's wife, whose lustful daughter allows him to escape. The ensuing chase traverses Brazil's varied geography and cultural landscape. After unsuccessful attempts to get a scholarship to finance a trip to Europe, the hero searches for buried treasure, purchases a bogus goose that lays golden eggs, and is tricked into a fatal smashing of his own testicles. Resuscitated again, Macunaíma imagines a European ocean liner in a fountain; his plea for passage is rejected. The giant returns, however, and the hero tricks him into falling into his own stew. Amulet in hand, the emperor heads back home with his brothers.

During the torturous return trip, the hero finds Iriqui again but rejects her in favor of a princess he created from a tree. He cannot find his old conscience, so he assumes that of a Spanish American. Illness and hunger plague the hero in his new hut. His brothers discover magic food-producing agents, but Macunaíma loses them. A poison hook that he devises turns his brothers into ghostly shadows, who begin persecuting him. This antagonism results in the creation of folk dances and rites. In his solitude, Macunaíma feels remorse and recalls his former glory. Vei the Sun lures him into mortal combat with the Lady of the Lake, where he loses the amulet and a leg.

Macunaíma decides to give up life and ascends to heaven as the Great Bear constellation. Many years later, a man wanders into the jungle to be told these great tales by a parrot. That man is the omniscient narrator of this work.

The Characters

The subtitle of the work is "the hero with no character." It has been generally assumed that Macunaíma is a symbolic representation of Brazilian man, and, in this fantastic fiction, national character emerges as the lack of character. Indeed, there is little logic or consistency in the person of Macunaíma. Although there is emphasis on the hero's indigenous roots, he is in many ways an ethnological collage or amalgamation which is still in formation. The language he speaks, the roles he plays, and the values he upholds are drawn from diverse regional, cultural, social, and historical sources of the varied Brazilian experience. The shifting foundations of the hero's amorphous self are metamorphosis and resurrection; the hero transforms himself into a prince or some animal at several junctures, and he is repeatedly brought back from the dead. Macunaíma is born ugly but discovers magic that aids him in the first of his many sexual conquests. He cannot, however, exercise supernatural powers at will. At times he has the ability to perform miracles to elude danger or create food; at others he must live by his wits or suffer humiliations. Some qualities of the protagonist do stand out. His aversion to work is evident from childhood; he prefers lounging about in a hammock, singing folk songs, and engaging in wanton erotic play. As a child, the hero is mischievous, and in adult life he is an unyielding trickster and an irresponsible liar. Many episodes portray him as vindictive, greedy, and self-accommodating; his constant abuse of Jiguê shows these traits best. Since *Macunaíma* is epic in conception, the nature of the hero is inseparable from the thematic concerns and messages of the work.

Themes and Meanings

Mário de Andrade is as well-known for his work in music as for his literary endeavors. He called *Macunaíma* not a novel but a "rhapsody." This classification suggests both sung epic poetry (such as the *Iliad* and the *Odyssey*) and an instrumental fantasy based on popular or traditional melodies. In literature, the term may also connote an ecstatic, highly emotional, or irrational work. All of these meanings of "rhapsody" have a direct relation to *Macunaíma*. Although Andrade's fundamental approach is comic, it is clear that the saga of Macunaíma is a reflection on questions of Brazilian nationality, which is a fusion of European, African, and Amerindian peoples. The work playfully brings into question the character and psyche of Brazil as a young American nation and of her people as a diverse population. Thus, the contradictory qualities of the turbulent hero himself are central to any evaluation of the novel. Orality is emphasized throughout the work; that which the narrator relates has been learned from a parrot, and characters constantly relate deeds, accomplishments, or myths of origin. Popular, traditional, or indigenous elements inform the entirety of the novel, and linear logic is subordinated to unbridled fantasy throughout.

Andrade's "instrument" in this rhapsody is his macaronic literary language. One of the work's central themes is language itself, the primary vehicle of culture. The author blends, often arbitrarily, the vocabulary and structure of standard Portuguese, colorful street language, and many regional varieties into a unique and totally new linguistic style. In the original, many passages are unintelligible even to native Brazilians, but the author's aim was to raise readers' consciousness about the diversity of their New World language, in which thousands of indigenous and African words were added to the European mother tongue. Enumeration is frequent and meaningful in *Macunaíma*. When biting insects or parrots are mentioned, for example, dozens of kinds are listed. This technique calls attention to a copious rural vocabulary that is little-known in the urban setting, and it emphasizes geographical differences between the New World tropics and the dominant culture of Europeans who came to conquer. Even in translation, the reader feels the effects of enumeration, especially with respect to the abundant flora and fauna of the Amazonian region.

Mário de Andrade sought a particularly Brazilian literary language based on actual speech and not on stiff, textbook grammar. Another of the principal aims of *Macunaíma* is to poke fun at the classical rhetoric dominant in Luso-Brazilian letters until the 1920's. The letter that the hero writes to his Amazon subjects midway through the novel is the high point of stylistic satire. This effort is particularly effective because the letter writer is an ingenuous native looking at urban culture as an outsider in his own country. Macunaíma writes in the pedantic, verbose academic style of Brazil's traditional intellectual leaders, employing Latinate structures, eloquent vocabulary, and erudite allusions. On the surface, the letter appears to be constructed impeccably, but there are many grammatical errors, misuses of words, and stylistic abuses. The targets of the biting satire are the overblown style of classicism, the would-be men of letters who employ that rhetoric poorly or in place of substance, and the distance of the official written language from the true spoken language. The letter also satirizes mores, customs, and São Paulo society. The innocent hero describes things as he sees them, and many aspects of urban life are seen in a comic light. Corruption, prostitution, bad public health, and faulty services, among other elements, emerge from the hero's explanations of civilization.

Cultural satire and contrast play an important role outside of the letter. The figure of the villain, a cannibalistic giant and wealthy merchant, incorporates a satire of the many Italian immigrants who became rich in São

Paulo and suggests the rapacious nature of business in Brazil, as well as the dominant role of foreign nations in her commerce. In the episode where Macunaíma imagines a ship in a fountain and seeks transatlantic passage, the author pokes fun at the tendency of urban middle- and upper-class Brazilians to turn their eyes toward Europe instead of toward their own land and culture. In another episode, Macunaíma publicly debates a citizen who extols the beauty of the Southern Cross, a national symbol of Brazil. The hero emphatically challenges this view, satirizing patriotic discourse in the process, and asserts the constellation's indigenous name and myth of origin, as opposed to the official European version. With these examples in mind, a leading Brazilian critic has said that Mário de Andrade showed that for every academic or purely literary concept there was another version or concept of popular origin.

Critical Context

Mário de Andrade wrote *Macunaíma* during a six-day frenzy and underwrote its publication. The literary establishment was perplexed by the work and gave it a bad reception. The leading critics of the time called it barbarous, outrageous, disconnected, fragmented, and excessive. Most failed to see the unity of the interwoven motifs, and some reacted negatively to its flamboyance and obscenity. *Macunaíma* was indeed one of the most forceful affronts to literary decorum of the 1920's. This was the decade of Modernism in Brazil, an iconoclastic and nationalistic movement of literary renovation that sought to break sharply with the past, to challenge the influence of Portuguese letters, and to make national reality the focus of literary endeavor. With his rhapsodic novel, Mário de Andrade made a major contribution to a radical literary faction known as "Anthropophagy," which used the practice of cannibalism as a metaphor for their project of modern Brazilan writing.

It was not until 1955 that *Macunaíma* began to be fully appreciated by critics and the reading public. In that year, a detailed explanation of Mário de Andrade's sources, cultural references, and allusions was published, showing the thematic unity of the work and its complicated background. This critical defense acknowledged that *Macunaíma* was frightening and astounding, but for its erudition and craft and not for its supposed incoherence or immorality. Other reevaluations and lengthy studies of the work have followed. *Macunaíma* is now regarded as one of the most representative and influential works of Brazilian Modernism, and a foremost example of literary rebellion and nationalism in Latin American literature in general. In 1969, *Macunaíma* was made into a film, one of the most successful productions of Brazil's New Cinema. Significant English-language commentary on the original novel is found in film criticism.

Sources for Further Study

Johnson, Randal. *Cinema Novo* × *5: Masters of Contemporary Brazilian Film*, 1984.

Johnson, Randal, and Robert Stam, eds. *Brazilian Cinema*, 1982.

Charles A. Perrone

THE MAGICIAN OF LUBLIN

Author: Isaac Bashevis Singer (1904-   )
Type of plot: Moral picaresque
Time of plot: Around 1900
Locale: Lublin, Piask, and Warsaw
First published: Der Kuntsnmakher fun Lubin, 1959 (English translation, 1960)

> *Principal characters:*
> YASHA MAZUR, the protagonist, a traveling magician
> ESTHER, his wife
> MAGDA ZBARSKI, his assistant and mistress
> ZEFTEL LEKACH, a deserted wife from Piask, also his mistress
> EMILIA CHRABOTZKY, a once wealthy but now impoverished widow, also his mistress

The Novel

As the novel begins, Yasha Mazur, a magician "religious and heretical, good and evil, false and sincere," has just returned from a series of performances in the country; he has come home to spend the holidays with his wife, Esther. One evening while he is out walking, he has a vision of Emilia Chrabotzky, his mistress in Warsaw. The next morning, Pentecost, Yasha sleeps late, and when Esther returns from synagogue, he takes her to bed.

The holiday over, Yasha readies his horses and wagon and leaves for Warsaw. On the way, he stops outside Piask to pick up Magda Zbarski, his assistant and mistress. Because Yasha supports their family, Elzbieta Zbarski, Magda's mother, obliges him to stay with them overnight. Passing through Piask the next day, Yasha visits Zeftel Lekach, another of his mistresses, who begs him to take her to Warsaw with him. A central idea of the book underlies Yasha's numerous and complicated affairs: By seeing many women and being a different Yasha to each of them, he hopes to forestall the inevitable responsibilities that accompany a choice—but the complexies of his promiscuity become too great.

Once in Warsaw, he drops Magda off in the apartment he maintains there and visits Emilia. Significantly, although exuding confidence in himself and his skills everywhere else, Yasha loses confidence whenever he visits Emilia. During the visit, her daughter Halina enters, and Yasha begins to recognize increasing feelings of desire for her in addition to those he already has for her mother. Emilia wishes to marry Yasha and wants them to go to Italy, where his talents will earn for him the money and acclaim he deserves. Before he can do this, however, he must get enough money to finance the move. Robbery seems the only choice, and when Emilia's maid innocently mentions a rich old miser who lives alone and who has a reputation of keeping great sums of cash at home, Yasha makes up his mind.

After this, things go from bad to worse. During the robbery attempt, which is unsuccessful, Yasha falls and breaks his foot. On returning to Magda, he discovers that she has found out about his plans to marry Emilia. They argue and Yasha leaves. He goes to Emilia, who throws him out. He returns to Magda, only to find that she has killed herself. Turning finally to Zeftel, who has followed him to Warsaw, he finds her in bed with a pimp.

Three years pass, during which time Yasha has returned to Lublin and Esther, a broken man. After several more months have passed, Yasha orders masons to build a cell in his yard, with a small window but no door, in which he imprisons himself. Word soon spreads of the penitent Yasha, now known as Rabbi Jacob, and pilgrims begin to visit him at his cell, hoping for a blessing from the mad holy man. One day Esther, who brings Yasha his meals and necessities, brings him a letter from Emilia. In it she tells him that her daughter Halina has been confined to a sanatorium and that she herself has married.

The Characters

Yasha Mazur is a character for whom a reader may feel at once great distaste and great sympathy. Who has not often felt the desire for both stability and freedom? Yet how despicable is the man who causes so much pain to those nearest him, out of his own selfish pursuit of pleasure. In Yasha, Singer has created a most appealing demon and an almost fatally flawed hero. In his evaluation of himself and his skills, Yasha is clearly a victim of hubris. Yet in his tender concessions to his wife and Magda at the beginning of the book, he reveals a genuinely caring facet of his nature.

Singer portrays Yasha's women with restraint but with important characteristic touches. Esther is, significantly, childless. Magda, his longest-running mistress, is "in her late twenties but appeared younger; audiences thought her no more than eighteen." Zeftel is in her forties, has wide hips and abundant breasts, and Yasha regards her as sometimes motherly. Emilia, although she is superficially loving and caring to Yasha, is essentially compassionless: Before they can marry, she insists, he must convert, and when he appeals to her after his burglary attempt, she shuns him.

Even the most minor characters benefit from Singer's sure use of detail. Bolek, Magda's brother, is a terrifying and constant reminder to Yasha (and to the reader) of his sin with Magda, even though he is never actually seen. Halina's clearly nonsexual adoration of her "Uncle Yasha" makes all the more repellent his incestuous feelings toward her.

Themes and Meanings

The principal themes are symbolized by the novel's most repeated image:

the tightrope. Yasha walks a tightrope as part of his performance, and he aspires to new and always more dangerous stunts. He also figuratively walks a tightrope between faith and moral degeneration. Early in the book, driving along a road in early spring, he exclaims, "Oh, God Almighty, you are the magician, not I!" Yet on his trip to Piask and Warsaw, he readily betrays his wife with three mistresses. After his bungled burglary attempt, he finds refuge in a synagogue. Although he has been in synagogues before, mostly for his wife's sake, this time he prays in earnest and concludes, "I must be a Jew! . . . A Jew like all the others!" His newfound orthodoxy, however, is short-lived. Shunned by Emilia, finding Magda dead and Zeftel in bed with a pimp, he realizes that for him forgiveness can come not from God but only from his now-inaccessible victims.

For Yasha, not even God is exempt from the image of the tightrope. During that first outburst in early spring, God was Yasha's own, personal, immediate companion; again in the synagogue, Yasha feels His presence as a real and vital one. Yet he always returns to his skepticism toward the Jewish God, who reveals Himself to no one, who give no indication of what is permitted or forbidden.

Even in his self-imposed prison, Yasha walks a tightrope. He believes that through his asceticism he may expiate his sins—indeed, penitents soon come to him, believing him to be a holy man. Yet his prison really still protects him from having to choose between faith and freedom. From his cell, Yasha admits, "No, the temptations never cease."

Critical Context

The Magician of Lublin is one of the most widely read and perhaps the best book by the Nobel Prize-winning Singer. In this book as in many of his other works, he considers the nature of faith and the existence of God; he establishes the traditional tenets of the Jewish faith—belief in one personal God and service to Him through *Halakah*—as the accepted background for his characters. Yet this book is more easily accessible than some of Singer's other works. It relies not on an intensely violent backdrop such as that found in *Satan in Goray* (1935) or on the all-accepting attitude of a character such as Gimpel the Fool. Rather, it poses for its protagonist a very basic, modern dilemma: Should he maintain faith in a God in whom he believes yet whom he views as an unconcerned observer, or should he cling to his freedom, knowing he risks falling into a moral abyss?

Though widely acclaimed, *The Magician of Lublin* has been criticized on the grounds that it overemphasizes the sexual aspect of Yasha's temptations. Nevertheless, that aspect is a valid and necessary one. Particularly, Yasha desires Gentile women, who symbolize not only sexual taboo but also that world of wealth and social status into which he hopes to escape through his marriage to Emilia.

Sources for Further Study

Allentuck, Marcia, ed. *The Achievement of Isaac Bashevis Singer*, 1967.
Buchen, I. H. *Isaac Bashevis Singer and the Eternal Past*, 1968.
Malin, Irving, ed. *Critical Views of Isaac Bashevis Singer*, 1969.

David W. Kent

THE MAKING OF AMERICANS
Being a History of a Family's Progress

Author: Gertrude Stein (1874-1946)
Type of plot: Impressionistic realism
Time of plot: Indefinite; probably the late nineteenth and early twentieth
centuries
Locale: Bridgepoint (Baltimore) and Glossols (Oakland, California)
First published: 1925

> *Principal characters:*
> HENRY DEHNING, a man of some wealth
> MRS. DEHNING, his wife
> JULIA DEHNING, the eldest of Henry Dehning's three chil-
> dren, who marries Alfred Hersland
> DAVID HERSLAND, a successful businessman, who has taken
> his family out West to live
> ALFRED HERSLAND, his son, who marries Julia Dehning
> MARTHA HERSLAND, his eldest daughter

The Novel

There is some question whether *The Making of Americans: Being a History of a Family's Progress*, a rambling, sometimes inchoate work, should be
called a novel. The work is huge in conception as well as in bulk, the uncut
edition running to 925 pages of small print. It is essentially an attempt to
study how Americans are made, what it is that makes them specifically
American.

The book contains little dialogue, and toward the end of it, almost none.
The style is rambling and repetitive, largely because Stein is attempting to
underscore the repetitiveness of human existence. There is considerable
confusion of names, with some names (David and Martha, for example)
being given to several characters in succeeding generations of the same family. Stein is given to bringing in minor characters once, then dropping them
for several hundred pages, only to reintroduce them with no inkling that
they have appeared before, a technique also found in James Joyce's *Ulysses*
(1922).

The book is a loose telling of the history of Stein's own family. She broad-
ens the scope so enormously, however, and generalizes the characters and
the situations in which they find themselves so impressionistically that she is
really writing metaphorically about the generations of all families, about all
Americans, each contributing to the ethnic melting pot that Stein considers
the United States to be.

Stein conveys a sense of what she is attempting early in the book: "It has always seemed to me a rare privilege, this, of being an American, a real American, one whose tradition it has taken scarcely sixty years to create. We need only realise our parents, remember our grandparents, and know ourselves and our history is complete." Stein seeks to know and portray what she calls "the bottom natures" of her characters, the underlying psychology of the people about whom she is writing. In doing so, however, she withholds necessary information, presents at times fragments from which the readers are required to construct a plot based upon their own interpretations, much as the impressionistic work of such painters as Pablo Picasso and Henri Matisse demands the full participation of the viewer in order to arrive at meaning.

The recurrence of generation upon generation of families is expressed both in ideas and in the rhetoric of a passage such as the following:

> There are some families and any one of them can almost remember having been doing being such a family again. There are families and some in such of them are completely doing having been a daughter and a son in such a family of them. There are families and some of them are being such a one and some in them can be being such ones and some in them do it again do again and again being such ones.

It has been suggested that in *The Making of Americans* Stein was writing a conscious parody of "the Great American Novel." Whether there is validity to this statement, Stein was very serious in writing this novel and worked on it quite steadily from 1903 until 1911.

The Characters

Because the characters in *The Making of Americans* represent types rather than individuals, they are less important to the novel than are the controlling ideas and the rhetoric used at once to present the ideas and to reflect stylistically the basic themes of recurrence and repetition. As the novel progresses, Stein depends less and less on narrative and more and more on description. The last of the novel's five books contains no dialogue nor any characters and is essentially philosophical commentary.

The characters who do appear in the book are fragmented. The reader is not privy to the inmost thoughts of these characters or, indeed, to many events in their lives. The events which are recounted are not told in detail or in the sort of chronological sequence that gives unity to more conventional novels.

The two main families of the book are the Herslands and the Dehnings. The connection between these two families is through Henry Hersland and Julia Dehning, who marries him. In modeling the Hersland family quite loosely after her own family, Stein exercises literary license and changes some of the biographical facts.

Martha Hersland is the most autobiographical character in the book, although Stein takes the liberty of making Martha the eldest of the Hersland children, whereas Gertrude herself was the youngest of five children, two of whom, Michael and Leo, survived into adulthood. The second book of the novel bears the subtitle "Martha Hersland" and runs to nearly two hundred pages, but Martha cannot be called a wholly developed character because Stein departs from her development to engage in digressive philosophical discourse. Stein deviates from the facts of her own biography by having Martha marry Philip Redfern.

The younger David Hersland (his father, also named David, appears in the novel) is modeled after Stein's brother Leo and is the subject of the fourth book of the novel. Stein has David die in the course of book 4, and this is thought to be a symbolic way of dealing with her own falling out with her brother Leo in 1913, about the time this section was being composed.

Although book 3 of *The Making of Americans* is entitled "Alfred and Julia Hersland" and runs to more than two hundred pages, the title characters appear hardly at all in the book, which is in essence a philosophical treatise.

Themes and Meanings

The Making of Americans is distinctive in that it generalizes upon character rather than developing characters and in that it does not unfold a story. The work contains no dramatic incidents because Stein posits that, for most people, life is not dramatic but is routine, repetitive, and humdrum. This novel projects almost a Nietzschean idea of eternal recurrence. It considers many of the questions of being and existence with which phenomenologists writing after Stein have concerned themselves.

Stein expresses her ideas in long, torturous sentences, the nub of which is to pose existential questions rather than to answer them. The following sentence is representative of her technique: "Certainly some in one way of being ones being living, some in other ways of being ones being living come to be certain, some gradually, some all of a sudden, some sometime, some sometimes, some quite often, some very often, come to be certain that they are understanding every one being one being living."

With a psychologist's sensitivity ever finely tuned, Stein writes out of her own consciousness, presenting a panoply of psychological prototypes, but she suggests rather than develops most of them. She assiduously avoids progression in her story line, insisting that her medium must reflect her message.

Critical Context

Stein's close association with many of the leading Impressionist artists of her time, probably more than any other single factor, encouraged her in her ambitious literary experiments. As Pablo Picasso, Georges Braque, Marcel

Duchamp, and Henri Matisse deconstructed the human form and rearranged it to suit their purposes, so did Stein deconstruct language, often using it with Cubist effect.

The Making of Americans has been compared to Thomas Mann's *Buddenbrooks* (1900), and although it is, because of its essential inaccessibility, a less successful novel than Mann's, it is a more ambitious venture. Indeed, *The Making of Americans* is Stein's most ambitious undertaking, for in it she pushes language and grammatical structure to their limits, perhaps beyond.

Sources for Further Study
Copeland, Carolyn Faunce. *Language and Time and Gertrude Stein*, 1975.
Hobhouse, Janet. *Everybody Who Was Anybody: A Biography of Gertrude Stein*, 1975.
Hoffman, Michael J. *Gertrude Stein*, 1976.
Mellow, James R. *The Charmed Circle: Gertrude Stein and Company*, 1974.
Simon, Linda. *Gertrude Stein: A Composite Portrait*, 1974.

R. Baird Shuman

THE MAN WHO CRIED I AM

Author: John A. Williams (1925-   )
Type of plot: Social realism
Time of plot: Roughly 1940 and the early 1960's
Locale: New York City; Washington, D.C.; Amsterdam; Paris; and Lagos
First published: 1967

> *Principal characters:*
> MAX REDDICK, the protagonist, a novelist and journalist
> HARRY AMES, Max's close friend and mentor, a renowned writer
> CHARLOTTE AMES, Harry's wife
> BERNARD ZUTKIN, a literary critic and friend of Max
> KERMIT SHEA, the editor of the magazine which employed Max
> MARGRIT WESTOEVER, Max's Dutch wife
> ROGER WILKINSON, a black expatriate, sometime writer, and acquaintance of Max

The Novel

The Man Who Cried I Am is the somber chronicle of Max Reddick, a novelist and journalist who, while suffering the final stages of rectal cancer, introspectively reflects on his life and experiences, covering three decades, which take him to three continents and through numerous personal upheavals. As a reporter-observer ("That's what you are, Max, a noticer, a digger of scenes"), Max fashions a tale which represents the excursion of the black American through perhaps the most disquieting and turbulent period in American history. Throughout his reflections on past successes and failures and his associations with various women, Max Reddick ponders the state of black America, what it means to be black and living in late-twentieth century America.

Upon his ironic return to Amsterdam (*"I've returned. 'A Dutch man o' warre that sold us twenty negars,'* John Rolfe wrote, *Well, you-all, I bring myself. Free! Three hundred and forty-five years after Jamestown. Now . . . how's that for the circle come full?"*), Max gains possession of documents detailing the organized extermination of all blacks in America. After reading the King Alfred Plan, the name of the "emergency" operation, Max realizes that America has no intention of making good on its proclamations of fairness and equality and that his own tragic odyssey embodies that of the deluded black American: "Destruction . . . was very much a part of democratic capitalism, a philosophy which was implicitly duplicitous, meaning all its fine words and slogans, but leaving the performance of them to unseen elfs, gnomes, and fairies."

The novel's bleak prediction for American society is best represented in Max's conclusion that history must have its victims and that those victims must be conditioned to being victimized. Thus, Max must admit near the end of the novel, "Man is nature, nature man, and all crude and raw, stinking, vicious, evil. . . . It is still eat, drink, and be murderous, for tomorrow I may be among the murdered."

Yet there is a glimmer of optimism remaining for Max, who retains the will to resist, and it is in this resistance that the possibility of good can come about, for once man recognizes that he is evil, then he, by resisting his own degenerate nature, will attempt to better himself.

The Characters

Max Reddick is the central character of the novel, and it is through his eyes that the reader sees the panorama of history colored by the condition of the black intellectual/artist. Max's character is somewhat autobiographical (he, like Williams, is a novelist with a journalistic background; also, as Williams did, he must grapple with the choice between the quixotic pursuit of writing as a livelihood and the practical pursuit of getting a "real" job in the real world of the 1950's black man). In his relationship with Harry Ames, the Richard Wright figure in the novel, however, Max resembles a combination of several black writers (including Chester Himes and Ralph Ellison) working during Wright's tenure as "literary father." Max assumes the role of the artist, of the observer; his function is to be "a super Confidence Man, a Benito Cereno saddened beyond death." Yet he assumes this role only near the end of the novel, when he receives the King Alfred Plan.

Max must be kept aware of his racial and historical self by his cynical, Dozens-playing subconscious, Saminone (Sambo-in-one), and by his literary mentor, Harry Ames. Ames, older and more consistently militant than Max, is vividly portrayed in *The Man Who Cried I Am* as the man who, with some modifications, Max could become. Early in the story, after Max has published his first novel, Harry explains to Max: "I'm the way I am, the kind of writer I am, and you may be too, because I'm a black man; therefore, we're in rebellion; we've got to be. We have no other function as valid as that one."

As far as his relationships with women are concerned, Max is compelled to compare each to his beloved Lillian, who dies after a botched abortion. Max's subsequent marriage to Margrit is a result of his initial attraction to her as a white reincarnation of the dead Lillian. Lillian, a middle-class black girl with middle-class dreams, does not want Max to follow the road of shattered dreams that so many other black men had traveled before. She wants security and predictability, but for Max to pursue such goals would be to forsake his role as an artist.

Themes and Meanings

The principal theme of *The Man Who Cried I Am* is that there are seemingly relentless forces which crush and destroy people, but in the face of such destruction, there must be resistance if life is to have some value. As Moses Boatwright, a grotesque character who commits the horrific act of cannabalism, reveals to Max:

> I was born seeing precisely. . . . This world is an illusion . . . but it can be real. I went prowling on the jungle side of the road where few people ever go because there are things there, crawling, slimy, terrible things that always remind us that down deep we are rotten, stinking beasts. Now because of what I did, someone will work a little harder to improve the species.

Deep inside Max Reddick is a malignancy which is slowly causing his body to deteriorate, just as malignancy (indifference, lies, duplicity) is doing the same thing to "the body politic." The implication is that the American system—or more precisely, Western civilization—is in deep trouble because

> there has got to be something inherently horrible about having the sicknesses and weaknesses of that society described by a person who is a victim of them; for if he, the victim, is capable of describing what they have believed nonexistent, then they, the members of the majority, must choose between living the truth, which can be pretty grim, and the lie, which isn't much better.

To set the victimization of black people in a larger context, references to the Holocaust, the "Six Million," appear throughout the novel, especially through Regina, survivor of the Nazi horror, and Zutkin, who dreams of an alliance of former victims (*"We need each other"*) to change the essential character and inclination of the republic.

Critical Context

The Man Who Cried I Am, Williams' most celebrated and influential novel, signaled a sharp departure from his earlier work. Williams' early fiction, *The Angry Ones* (1960), *Night Song* (1961), and *Sissie* (1963), fit within the framework of traditional racial protest writing, a framework which called for moral outcry and reformist solutions. During the period in which *The Man Who Cried I Am* evolved in Williams' mind, historical, social, and political events informed American society of impending tumult and confusion, of a burgeoning black pride and sense of nationalism, and of a questioning of once revered institutions. Williams' novel, consequently, emerged as the most explosive and unsettling political novel of the 1960's. It offers awesome and frightening possibilities for the future of the United States. Sam Greenlee's *The Spook Who Sat by the Door* (1969) offers one disturbing possibility of cataclysmic proportions in the aftermath of *The Man Who*

Cried I Am. Other examples of nonfiction fiction or historical fiction from the 1960's which share many elements with Williams' novel are Thomas Pynchon's *V.* (1963) and Kurt Vonnegut's *Slaughterhouse-Five* (1969). These books, together, are pivotal in an understanding of America, in the words of a disconsolate Margrit Westoever, as the "land where everyone speaks in superlatives but exists in diminutives."

In subsequent novels, namely the two immediately following *The Man Who Cried I Am*, the apocalyptic *Sons of Darkness, Sons of Light* (1969) and *Captain Blackman* (1972), Williams asks American society "to recognize the haunting historical continuity of past, present, and future." Yet ultimately, what Williams earnestly seeks, beginning with his prophecies in *The Man Who Cried I Am*, is that which is essential, plausible, and good in the American experiment.

Sources for Further Study
Cash, Earl A. *John A. Williams: The Evolution of a Black Writer*, 1975.
Muller, Gilbert H. *John A. Williams*, 1984.
Ro, Sigmund. *Rage and Celebration: Essays on Contemporary Afro-American Writing*, 1984.

Broderick McGrady

THE MAN WHO KILLED THE DEER

Author: Frank Waters (1902-   )
Type of plot: Social realism
Time of plot: The late 1930's, before the outbreak of World War II
Locale: The Pueblo Indian Reservation, near Taos, New Mexico
First published: 1942

> *Principal characters:*
> MARTINIANO, the protagonist, a young maverick (part Pueblo
>   Indian and part Apache)
> FLOWERS PLAYING, his wife (part Ute and part Arapahoe)
> PALEMON, Martiniano's closest friend
> RODOLFO BYERS, a white man who runs a trading post
>   adjacent to the Pueblo land
> MANUEL RENA, the Peyote chief, leader of a controversial
>   peyote cult

The Novel

Martiniano, a troubled young Pueblo Indian who has been sent away to the white man's school, shoots a deer on government land exactly two days after the hunting season has closed. Martiniano is soon spotted by a forest ranger, who flies into a rage over the killing of the animal and strikes Martiniano with his gun. With his head bleeding, Martiniano manages to escape by hiding in a stream. The next morning, Palemon, who has been unable to sleep, rescues him, drawn by some powerful, intuitive knowledge of his friend's distress.

Martiniano is found guilty and given a fine of $150, which is paid by Rodolfo Byers, the white man who runs the trading post. After the trial, Martiniano's life begins to fall apart. His marriage to Flowers Playing becomes more and more unhappy; the couple begin to drift apart. He is increasingly aware of his role as an outsider, a man who does not seem to belong in either the world of whites or the world of Indians. He is not allowed to live in the pueblo proper but in a hut at the edge of the pueblo. Martiniano refuses to remove the heels of his boots, cut out the seat of his pants, or sing the required tribal songs—and he is punished for all these acts of rebellion. At the center of all his problems is the killing of the deer: " 'That deer!' he exclaimed suddenly. 'That's what they are holding against me most of all. That cursed deer which I killed! That is what has destroyed my wife's love and faith!' "

In a desperate attempt to shake off his profound depression, Martiniano becomes involved with Manuel Rena and his peyote cult. The drug, however, only exacerbates Martiniano's sense of guilt. In a peyote-induced trance, he once again sees the deer he killed: *"The deer raced after him. Its hot breath burnt the back of his head, its pointed forefeet struck at and thundered behind him."* Martiniano realizes that peyote is not for him, and soon the rest of the cult members are arrested by the tribal Council. Martiniano is still implicated, however, since his distinctive blanket was confiscated during the raid.

A new phase begins in Martiniano's life when he decides to clear some mountain land which was left to him by his father. Martiniano cleans out the spring and repairs the little hut. Unfortunately, a Mexican sheepherder tries to take over the hut, and in the scuffle Martiniano wounds him slightly and accidentally with the Mexican's own gun. This time the tribe supports him. The Mexican seems to represent all the intruders who have encroached on Indian land for generations. Ever since Martiniano's killing of the deer, the Pueblo people have been demanding the return of their ancient lands, especially Dawn Lake, a sacred spot in the mountains which they regard as their tribal church and the center of their being. Martiniano slowly begins to feel connected to the tribe; he decides to accept fifteen lashes, administered by his friend Palemon, to retrieve his blanket from the Council. The Fiesta of San Geronimo occurs soon thereafter, and Martiniano and Flowers Playing (now pregnant) come down from the mountain to attend. No one can climb the tall ceremonial pole with a deer tied to its top. When Martiniano attempts the feat, he too fails—a sign that he has still not atoned for his guilt.

Martiniano's redemption comes through an act of selfless devotion. He rescues Palemon's son, Napaita, who has been trapped in a remote mountain cave. Soon, a son of his own is born, Juan de Bautista, and Martiniano feels peace at last: "The deer he had killed. It no longer troubled him." Congress passes a bill to compensate the tribe for lost land and to return thirty thousand acres of national forest to the tribe, including their sacred center, Dawn Lake. The book ends, then, with Martiniano and the tribe in full control of their most precious possession—their identity.

The Characters

At no point does Frank Waters provide a police-blotter description of his protagonist, Martiniano. The reader comes to appreciate Martiniano through his bold actions and sharply reasoned speeches, like the one in which he defends his killing of the deer to the Council. After explaining that the Council slowed him down by refusing to let him use the communal threshing machine, he concludes: "What is the difference between killing a deer on Tuesday or Thursday? Would I not have killed it anyway?" Later, when Palemon applies the fifteen lashes, Martiniano submits stoically, even though the pain is excruciating. Yet he can feel tenderness, too. After Flowers Playing becomes pregnant, Martiniano matures into a kind of inarticulate poet, recording but not enunciating the beauty of his little mountain retreat: "The yellow moon low over the desert, the stars twinkling above the tips of the high ridge pines, the fireflies, the far-off throb of a drum, the silence, the tragic, soundless rushing of the great world through time—it caught at his breath, his heart."

Flowers Playing, by contrast, is presented with photographic clarity. She is the Arapahoe maiden: "Have you ever seen an Arapahoe maiden down in the willows by the stream? The fresh, cool dew clinging like Navajo-silver buttons to her plain brown moccasins, the first arrows of sunlight glancing off the shining wings of her blue-black hair, the flush of dawn still in her smooth brown cheeks?" She becomes an Earth Mother, taming two wild deer in the mountain clearing and donning the costume of the Deer Mother in a sacred Pueblo dance. Her sensitivity to the animal kingdom is a source of strength for Martiniano in his painful process of self-atonement.

Palemon serves as a foil to Martiniano; he is the "good" Indian, adhering to the codes and customs of the tribe. His natural sensitivity to danger alerts him to Martiniano's trouble with the ranger, and his good reputation assures him a seat on the Council. When Martiniano chooses to accept his fifteen lashes, Palemon is assigned to whip him. It is a sign of their friendship that each man accepts his role unhesitatingly in the grisly little drama. Martiniano pretends not to recognize him: "Palemon too was a man. No sign of recognition showed on his face as he lifted the lash." The novel comes full circle when Martiniano rescues Palemon's son, Napaita, using the same power of intuition upon which Palemon relied in the opening pages.

The most complicated character is Rodolfo Byers, the crusty Anglo who runs the trading post. Some critics see Byers as a kind of alter ego of Frank Waters himself. Byers has known the Indians all his life, but he avoids the dangers of either romanticizing them or ignoring their flaws. Once, when he was bitten by a rattlesnake, Byers was saved by an old Indian who appeared out of nowhere and stroked his body with eagle feathers. Byers survived, and he began to accept the Indians and all their inscrutable ways. He empathizes with Martiniano and the apparent curse of the deer: " 'Boy, I too have had my deer,' muttered the white man, staring into the fire. 'Believe me, son, it will pass' "—and so it does.

Manuel Rena sets up a tepee next to the pueblo and establishes a local peyote cult after he has learned about this "strange herb of mystery and power" on a visit to other tribes. The use of peyote is forbidden in the rest of the state, but the District Indian Superintendent encourages the tribe to try it. The Council disagrees, however, and orders the cult disbanded. Peyote cults cannot coexist with the native religion as celebrated at Dawn Lake.

Themes and Meanings

As an amateur anthropologist and folklorist, Frank Waters has long been concerned with the Indian subcultures of the Southwest, as shown by his later studies, *Masked Gods: Navaho and Pueblo Ceremonialism* (1950) and *Book of the Hopi* (1963). In *The Man Who Killed the Deer*, Waters uses a complex narrative structure that interrupts the story of Martiniano and the tribe with transcriptions of myths and ceremonial prayers, descriptions of sacred dances and costumes, and discussions of Pueblo rites. Waters goes into these details because the primary theme of the book is the uniqueness of Pueblo culture, an irreplaceable gift to the human family. Thus, the reader is exposed several times to a Pueblo prayer which begins, "*There is no such thing as a simple thing.*" Mrs. Wolf Red-Belly Woman recounts the entire myth of Shell Boy and Blue Corn (which parallels the story of Martiniano and his wife), and Waters describes the Deer Mother dance and many other dances down to the smallest step. The reader also follows the manhood initiation ceremony as experienced by Palemon's son, Napaita. These anthropological details are not excess baggage; they are integral to the meaning of the novel. Waters does not merely want to tell Martiniano's story; he wants to tell it from a true Pueblo Indian perspective.

The deer is not only a catalyst for narrative development but also the basic symbol of the work. Like all symbols, it contains layer upon layer of meaning: "*The deer he had killed, the two deer sisters of Flowers Playing up in the mountains, the deer dancing in subjection to Deer Mothers. . . . Who could say which was alive, was flesh, was spirit . . . ?*" The deer, then, is life and the spirit of life; by killing it, Martiniano has offended life itself, and his redemption is possible only when he accepts the life force, as he finally does, in all its various forms.

Critical Context

The Man Who Killed the Deer is Waters' best-known and probably his best-loved book, as suggested by the fact that the original 1942 edition was reprinted many times, with a second edition issued in 1965 and a third edition in 1971 (which has also been reprinted many times). Conceived as part of a trilogy on the minorities of the Southwest, *The Man Who Killed the Deer* appeared after *People of the Valley* (1941), which deals with Spanish colonial settlers, and before *The Yogi of the Cockroach Court* (1947), a story of casinos and lowlife on the Mexican American border.

In a larger context, *The Man Who Killed the Deer* can be seen as one of the best examples of a genre which traces the roots of a particular ethnic group. This tradition would include such classic books as Edwin Corle's *People on the Earth* (1937) and more recent works such as Carlos Castaneda's *The Teachings of Don Juan: A Yaqui Way of Knowledge* (1968). *The Man Who Killed the Deer* is significant because it transcends this tradition by offering characters and situations of universal appeal, presented in a style that can truly be called poetic.

Sources for Further Study

Bucco, Martin. *Frank Waters*, 1969.
Hoy, Christopher. "The Conflict in *The Man Who Killed the Deer*," in *South Dakota Review*. XV (1977), pp. 51-57.
Lyon, Thomas J. *Frank Waters*, 1973.
Tanner, Terence A. *Frank Waters: A Bibliography*, 1983.

Daniel L. Guillory

THE MAN WITH THE GOLDEN ARM

Author: Nelson Algren (1909-1981)
Type of plot: Poetic realism
Time of plot: 1946-1948
Locale: The slums surrounding Chicago's West Division, Damen, North
Clark, and Madison Streets
First published: 1949

> *Principal characters:*
> FRANCIS MAJCINEK (FRANKIE MACHINE), the protagonist, a
> card dealer and a morphine addict
> SOPHIE MAJCINEK (ZOSH), Frankie's wheelchair-bound wife
> MOLLY NOVOTNY, a stripper, deeply in love with Frankie
> SOLLY SALTSKIN (SPARROW), a petty hustler and Frankie's
> close friend
> "NIFTY LOUIE" FOMOROWSKI, a small-time criminal, card-
> sharp, and Frankie's main drug connection
> POLICE CAPTAIN (RECORD HEAD) BEDNAR, the commander of
> the West Division Street station house

The Novel

Most of the action in *The Man with the Golden Arm* takes place in
Frankie and Sophie's apartment, the Tug and Maul Bar on the ground floor
of their building, or the nearby West Division Street station house where
Frankie and Sparrow regularly are hauled in on suspicion of some minor
infraction. By confining events to this circle, and by repeating the same cycle of scenes again and again—card games, marital confrontations, dope
injections, arrests—the novel conveys the dreary confinement of its characters' lives. Although the musically talented Frankie boasts continually of
his plans to succeed as a jazz drummer and escape his dismal situation, the
reader senses from the beginning the futility of these dreams.

Too many factors militate against Frankie's success. First is his own weakness of character; on Division Street, nobody but the devoted Sparrow "still
believed their was anything tough about Frankie Machine. In addition,
Frankie is a drug addict: Full of World War II shrapnel, he periodically
seeks out "Nifty Louie" Fomorowski for a shot of morphine to relieve his
gut-wrenching pain.

Frankie's pain is not, however, all physical. He is guilt-ridden over the
night some years earlier when, blind drunk, he took Sophie on a wild auto
ride that resulted in a collision, leaving her paralyzed. Sophie, a superb
dancer before the accident, never lets him forget the consequences of his
careless act, for it has provided her with something she had sought long

before sustaining the injury: a means of bringing him permanently under her control.

Frankie relies on morphine, then, for the temporary illusion of freedom from a painful, guilty, fenced-in existence. Still, he fights to overcome all suffocating circumstance, including his addiction. Time and again, trying to be a responsible husband, he swears off drugs, returns to card dealing—his only paying skill aside from occasional drumming—and, at Sophie's request, spends hours simply wheeling her back and forth in their apartment.

Yet Sophie, afraid of ultimately losing him, continues her manipulative whining. Despite his protests of caring, she demands to know, "Whyn't you come right out 'n say you wisht I'd got killed instead of crippled?" And Louie, confident of finally having Frankie hooked on dope, taunts him with: "You'll look me up ten thousand times to come." It is all too much for Frankie Machine. He escapes the pain of his marriage, and attempts to overcome his addiction, through an ill-concealed affair with Molly. Then one night, blindly furious at Louie's insults and desperately afraid of his own weakness, he kills the drug peddler with a blow to the neck.

Frankie spends the rest of his life on the run after Captain Bednar bullies Sparrow—the only witness to Louie's killing—into implicating him. Like his life before, Frankie's last days are hopelessly circumscribed. Molly manages to shelter him for a while, but a rival for her attentions—"Drunkie John"—informs the police, and Frankie must scurry for a new hiding place. Yet he can run only a short way between morphine fixes before the agony of withdrawal sweeps over him. In the end, the noose literally tightens as the despairing Frankie hangs himself, with "one brief strangled whimpering," in a lonely Madison Street Hotel.

The Characters

In most of this novel's characters one finds little to admire, unless it is their dogged survival of outward squalor and inner pain. These are people whose spirits privation has stunted, if not made entirely ugly. In writing *The Man with the Golden Arm*, Algren faced a challenge common to realistic novelists: Why should anyone read about these people, let alone care about them? Algren the poetic realist—and hardly a detached one—answered with a faithful and compassionate account of what made these characters the way they are.

Who can condemn Sophie altogether on reading that for years, during their courtship, Frankie had toyed with her affections, first seducing her, then letting himself be seen with other girls, then seducing her again when she confronted him? Soon, Sophie had developed "a secret need for that sort of vengeance that a certain sort of love requires." At one point, she feels triumphant when he gets on his knees to pick up china that she has methodically smashed. Ultimately, she is willing to risk all, even her own well-being, for the sake of revenge on Frankie: "He'd broken her pride for keeps. . . . Now for ten years she had held him in the hope of recovering her lost pride; till it had grown too late to loosen her grip upon him. If she let go of him now she let go of everything." Indeed, when Frankie, on the run from the law, abandons Sophie, she slips irretrievably into catatonia.

The author plainly refuses to believe, however, that circumstance alone forms character. How, in the first place, did Sophie come to feel her "certain sort of love?" Is Frankie to blame for the way in which Sophie has responded to his early slights? Why does Molly not react in the same way to Drunkie John's much worse treatment of *her*? Though the novel does not answer these questions, it is written in such a way that the reader inevitably asks them.

While not ultimately explaining character, the narrative excites compassion by revealing the fears and weaknesses that underlie its characters' personal styles. During their courtship, Sophie had a "haughty, hard-to-get stride that had everyone fooled" but Frankie: "he'd solved it before she'd had a chance to develop adult defenses." Frankie's falsely buoyant confidence is expressed in his repeated, increasingly pathetic-sounding motto, "It's all in the wrist 'n I got the touch."

Algren has also softened the characterizations through physical descriptions that unmistakably betray his fondness for the people in this novel. He presents, for example, "The tranquil, square-faced, shagheaded little buffalo-eyed blond called Frankie Machine and the ruffled, jittery punk called Sparrow. . . ." Most characters have their endearing, if not redeeming, quirks. Sparrow's quirk is the bluff, half-serious humor through which he tries to get out of scrapes—a wit that belies his claims to being "offbalanced." The humor is Algren's, too—another sign that this realist does not remain detached. For example, after burglarizing a plumbing-supply house, Sparrow might have talked his way out of an arrest "if it hadn't been for the bathtub on his back. . . . Chicago cops are pretty sharp about bathtubs being carried through alleys piggyback at 4 A.M." Sparrow admits that it is "A little clumsy for carryin' geran'ums," but claims that he saw it lying in the alley and wanted to remove it before the milkman's horse broke its leg over it.

A few characters are unredeemed; even their terrible misfortunes do not arouse compassion. One of these is Blind Pig, who lost his sight through no fault of his own—the result of a degenerative disease—but whom Algren nevertheless describes as a "debauched, blunt-snouted, abject, obscene lush." In the main, however, Algren shows compassion though not admiration for the people of *The Man with the Golden Arm*. In these characters themselves, compassion seems a prerequisite of salvation. "Record Head" Bednar suffers a breakdown when he realizes that he cannot forgive the myriad crimes stored in his memory: " 'I never hated a man of you,' he tried to appease them [the prisoners addressed in his thoughts]. And hearing a knowing reply: 'Nor loved any man at all.' "

The one character with any truly admirable traits is Molly. Her genuine belief in Frankie has a nobility about it, and the passages describing her simple generosity are among the novel's most moving: "To put strength back into those fingers [of Frankie the drummer] and the light back into those eyes was what Molly Novotny wanted and there was a gladness in her just at having such a chance."

Paradoxically, the loving Molly is subjected to more degredation than anyone else—primarily by Drunkie John, who admits that all he wants from her is to cadge drinks for him and be there for him to kick around. Yet whatever her reasons for tolerating John, Molly is one character whom suffering has not made ignoble, cowardly, or listless. She emerges as not only the most compassionate but also the toughest character. Indeed, the two qualities seem inseparable in her. In righteous anger she explains to Frankie how and why Zosh has manipulated him: "You wouldn't fall in love with her the way she wanted you to, the way she was in love, she had to get even with you for that. She never got another chance till the accident. . . . It's all she ever tried to do for you was to get even. 'N you're lettin her do it every time you knock on Fomorowski's door. . . ."

Frankie responds to Molly's caring toughness: "He felt the knot within him loosen with the realization that he could talk straight to someone at last." Yet for him it is too late: "He had never been trusted. He had never trusted himself. . . . He wasn't ready for anyone's trust. He had been too long trained in wariness to drop his guard that low."

Themes and Meanings

In one sense, despite the stylistic embellishments, *The Man with the Golden Arm* is strict reportage. Algren often told interviewers that he considered himself not a novelist but a free-lance journalist; he did, in fact, hold a journalism degree from the University of Illinois. Like a reporter, he gathered much of the material for his books by visiting police stations, walking through poverty-stricken neighborhoods, and reading newspaper crime reports; like a journalist, he prided himself on accuracy. Though he never touched drugs, he boasted that addicts had assured him that he understood them "from the inside."

The Man with the Golden Arm reports on the addict Frankie Machine as representative of a doomed class, though Algren saw and cherished his characters as individuals:

> These were the luckless living soon to become the luckless dead. The ones who were fished out of a river or lake, found crumpled under crumpled papers in the parks, picked up in the horse-and-wagon alleys or slugged, for half a bottle of homemade wine, in the rutted tunnels that run between the advertising agencies and the banks.

On another level, then, *The Man with the Golden Arm* is a protest against the social conditions that Algren reported so authentically. (As he told one interviewer, "Compassion has no use without a setting. I mean you . . . have to *know*.") Implicitly, the novel inveighs against the general failure of society to acknowledge conditions that any sensitive person, trained or untrained, could easily observe. Part of the novel begins with a passage from Alexandre Kuprin's *Yama* (1909-1915; *The Pit*, 1929): "Do you understand, gentlemen, that all the horror is in this—that there is no horror!"

Without overlooking the profound weaknesses of most of its characters, *The Man with the Golden Arm* declares that their worst crime is one gratuitously pinned on them by a materialistic society:

> The great, secret and special American guilt of owning nothing, nothing at all, in the one land where ownership and virtue are one. . . . All had gone stale for these disinherited. . . . On Skid Row even the native-born no longer felt they had been born in America. . . . And yet they spoke and yet they laughed. . . .

Frankie Machine's only means of livelihood is card dealing. Algren, a lifelong horse player and poker player, sees all life as a gamble; the way people play the game is determined by their individual character. Yet always, the author seems to say, the cards are stacked against people such as Frankie Machine. Compassion for those who are dealt a bad hand would save the individual and, hence, the society.

Critical Context

Despite his apparent pessimism, Algren believed that he could improve society in some small way through the statement made in *The Man with the Golden Arm*. He was among the first to hold a view now common in American society: that drug addiction is a disease, not a crime. More important to him, however, was his book's treatment of the disease of emotional isolation.

For a while it looked as though Algren might make his influence felt as he wished. A popular and critical success, *The Man with the Golden Arm* won the first National Book Award. The novel served as an encouragement to the authors of at least two later works dealing with addiction and isolation: *A Hatful of Rain* (1956) by Michael V. Gazzo, and Jack Gelber's *The Connection* (1959). Otto Preminger's film version of *The Man with the Golden Arm* (1955; starring Frank Sinatra as Frankie and Kim Novak as Molly) was hailed as a courageous first in Hollywood film treatment of a dire social problem.

Algren himself, however, hated the film version and claimed that it destroyed his hopes of communicating the "cry of anguish" that his book had caught. The problem, as he saw it, was that Preminger's excessive concern with box-office receipts led him to tamper with the book's characters and setting, making the film an unauthentic portrayal. What was worse, said Algren, "Preminger wouldn't touch Frankie Machine. . . . One of the first questions Preminger asked me was, 'How do you know such people? . . . it's unfathomable why anyone should even talk to people like this.' " Ironically, then, if one is to believe Algren, the Hollywood version of *The Man with the Golden Arm* suffered from the two major social evils that the book attacks: materialistic greed and lack of human compassion.

Nevertheless, the novel is Algren's masterpiece, surpassing his *Somebody in Boots* (1935) and *A Walk on the Wild Side* (1956) in realistic observation combined with a passionate warmth toward some recognizably American characters.

Sources for Further Study
Alper, Hollis. "Fallen Angels," in *Saturday Review of Literature*. XXXII, no. 32 (October 8, 1949), p. 22.
Donohue, H. E. F. *Conversations with Nelson Algren*, 1964.
Maloney, John J. "Chicago: Seamy Side," in *New York Herald Tribune Weekly Book Review*. XXVI, no. 4 (September 11, 1949), p. 10.

Thomas Rankin

MANHUNT

Author: Alejo Carpentier (1904-1980)
Type of plot: Psychological drama
Time of plot: The early 1930's, during the dictatorship of Gerardo Machado
Locale: Havana, Cuba
First published: El acoso, 1956 (English translation, 1959)

> *Principal characters:*
> THE UNNAMED PROTAGONIST, a university student and political
>   activist
> ESTRELLA, a prostitute and sometime lover of the protagonist
> AN OLD BLACK WOMAN, the protagonist's former wet nurse,
>   who runs a boardinghouse
> THE TICKET TAKER at the concert hall

The Novel

The principal action of *Manhunt*, a short novel which takes place during the span of one night in Havana, recounts the unnamed protagonist's flight from his former political comrades, who are trying to murder him for having turned informer. The protagonist, the typical "young man from the provinces," has come to the capital to pursue his studies at the university. Once in Havana, he takes up residence in a boardinghouse owned by an old black woman who had been his wet nurse. Shortly after his arrival in the city, he joins the Communist Party but is soon disenchanted with it and opts instead for direct political action in the form of terrorist acts against various government officials. These acts include one murder for which he is directly responsible and involvement in a second. As a result of his terrorist activities, he is arrested; terrified by the threat of castration, he "sings" and is released back into the streets.

Most of these events, however, are narrated in the form of flashbacks, for when the novel begins the protagonist is already in the streets, fleeing from his pursuers. His pursuers finally catch up with him at a concert hall where a symphonic orchestra has just finished performing Ludwig van Beethoven's *Eroica* symphony. In ironic counterpoint to Beethoven's work, the unnamed protagonist dies an unheroic death when he is murdered while hiding in a balcony seat. The incongruity of his death is enhanced by the fact that it takes place on Easter Sunday, only one of many instances of religious symbolism in the novella. *Manhunt* is the story of a passion at the end of which awaits no resurrection.

During that night, in desperate flight from his pursuers, he tries various ways of escaping his pursuers, but to no avail. He goes back to the boardinghouse where he had lived only to find that its owner has died; he visits Estrella, his lover, who is unable to help him; he cannot get sanctuary in a church; and he also fails to see the magistrate who had ordered the assassinations. Interwoven with this periplus through the streets of Havana are the flashbacks that recount his biography. Of the novel's three parts, the first and third take place in the present, during the performance of the symphony; the middle section, actually the bulk of the novel, is largely given over to the protagonist's earlier life.

The Characters

As is sometimes the case with Carpentier's protagonists, the principal character of this novel goes unnamed. Nevertheless, Carpentier still provides the reader with a nuanced and vivid psychological profile. Since the interest of the story resides, in no small measure, in this portrayal of the anguish of the informer, it would not be a mistake to look upon this novella as primarily a character study. Fleeing through the streets of Havana, the protagonist finds himself utterly alone, without refuge or meaningful human contact. His relationship with Estrella, one is led to believe, was a superficial and passing sexual infatuation, at least on her part. The only other human contact the protagonist had in the city was the old black woman, who has recently died. Symptomatic of the protagonist's predicament is the attitude of the priest, who refuses to confess him. Tormented with guilt, lacking friends, and with no place to escape, the protagonist is an easy prey for his pursuers. As he says: "Why were men today denied that ancient privilege of sanctuary that he read about in a book on the Gothic?" The whole story centers on his failed quest for sanctuary—political, emotional, artistic.

The other two most important characters in the story are Estrella and the old black woman. These two women act as foils for each other. As her name suggests, Estrella (meaning "star") is potentially a bright spot in the protagonist's existence, and he prides himself on being able to satisfy a woman who is accustomed to casual sexual encounters. The old black woman, clearly a mother figure, satisfies a different kind of need, for she is his one nexus to his childhood in the provinces. Just as the prostitute represents the degradation of urban life, the black woman represents the innocence and security of his early years away from the capital. Spiritually and physically, the protagonist oscillates between these two women.

The only other significant character in the novella is the ticket taker at the opera, a student of music whose lack of discipline has thwarted his education. Although he never actually meets the protagonist, these two characters are joined by their common interest in Estrella, the lodestar of their emotional and sexual lives. Unlike the protagonist, the ticket taker is not a man of action, a passivity conveyed by the fact that one usually finds him reading a biography of Beethoven. The contrast between Estrella and the old black woman is therefore counterbalanced by the contrast between the two principal male characters. The ticket taker also acts as a foil, for he symbolizes the intellectuals who—unlike the protagonist—have not gotten involved in the murky waters of Cuban politics.

Themes and Meanings

Manhunt artfully combines political, psychological, and philosophical themes. Based as it is on historical events, the novel re-creates the atmosphere of terror that pervaded some sectors of Cuban society during the dictatorship of Gerardo Machado, which Carpentier himself actively opposed. It is no accident that the whole novel takes place at night, for, in Carpentier's view, this was indeed a dark moment in Cuba's modern history.

Beyond the novel's political dimension, however, is the broader issue of the place of the intellectual in society. Written shortly after *The Lost Steps* (1953), *Manhunt* shares with this novel a concern with the social function of art. While in the earlier novel, however, one sees the protagonist trying to escape modern society by traveling to the South American jungle, in *Manhunt* the protagonist finds himself in the thick of the political turmoil of the time. The character in *Manhunt* who does represent the withdrawal of the artist from society is the ticket taker, an effete intellectual.

A third important theme in the book is the psychological theme of betrayal. Almost all of the characters in the novel betray something or someone. The protagonist himself is guilty of several acts of betrayal: He betrays his comrades by informing, and he betrays his wet nurse by stealing her food. Other characters in the novel also commit acts of betrayal: Estrella betrays his whereabouts to the police, the priest betrays his trust by refusing him sanctuary, and the ticket taker betrays his musical vocation by spending his free time with Estrella. One could say that the author himself, by juxtaposing the manhunt and the Third Symphony (the *Eroica*), betrays the spirit of Beethoven's composition.

The narrative technique of *Manhunt* also deserves some comment, for this is perhaps the most complicated of all of Carpentier's works. The novel (brief enough to be described as a novella) consists of three long untitled chapters which divide into eighteen subchapters. These eighteen vignettes tell the story from three different points of view. At various moments, both of the principal male characters become narrators; other sections of the novel, however, are narrated by a third-person omniscient narrator. The transitions from one narrative perspective to another are brusque, and the reader is often bewildered by the juxtaposition of these different perspectives. The use of more than one point of view, rare in Carpentier, is a device that some critics have attributed to the influence of William Faulkner. More important than the possible Faulknerian echoes in the novel, however, is the fact that by jumbling together incidents and characters Carpentier forces his reader to take an active part in recomposing the fragments of the story; the pleasure thus derived is not unlike that of a jigsaw puzzle.

Also worthy of mention is Carpentier's manipulation of time. Although first published separately, *Manhunt* was later included with three other shorter works in a volume entitled *Guerra del tiempo* (1958; *War of Time*, 1970). The title of the collection is significant, for it reveals Carpentier's view of art as a battle against time, as an attempt to order events according to something other than linear progression. This explains why, in *Manhunt*, a single episode or even a gesture may splinter into images that appear in different parts of the narration. By fragmenting the temporal and causal flow of events, Carpentier gives his narrative material an artistic coherence unlike that of real life.

Critical Context

In spite of its brevity, *Manhunt* is one of the works of Carpentier that has elicited the most critical comment. For some critics, Carpentier's stylized and fragmentary re-creation of Cuban history robs the story of the immediacy of lived experience, transforming it into a kind of atemporal tableau. Other critics, drawing attention to the work's subtle and innovative craftmanship, suggest that in *Manhunt* Carpentier has masterfully condensed many of his typical preoccupations and themes. Carpentier himself claimed that the novel was composed like a sonata, although the musical structure of the narration is not immediately obvious. Despite these differences of opinion, however, there is little doubt that *Manhunt* is one of the most challenging and original works of modern Spanish-American fiction.

Sources for Further Study

González Echevarría, Roberto. *Alejo Carpentier: The Pilgrim at Home*, 1977.

Shaw, Donald. *Alejo Carpentier*, 1985.

Weber, Frances Wyers. "*El acoso*: Alejo Carpentier's War on Time," in *Publications of the Modern Language Association.* LXXVIII (1963), pp. 440-448.

Gustavo Pérez-Firmat

A MANUAL FOR MANUEL

Author: Julio Cortázar (1914-1984)
Type of plot: Social morality
Time of plot: From 1969 to 1972, during which time Argentina, under the military dictatorship of General Alejandro Lanusse, suffered widespread violation of human rights
Locale: Paris and Buenos Aires
First published: Libro de Manuel, 1973 (English translation, 1978)

Principal characters:
LUDMILLA, a Polish actress who lives with Marcos
GOMEZ, a Panamanian and a member of the Screwery who lives with Monique, another member of the Screwery
MONIQUE, a French graduate student who lives with Gomez
LUCIEN VERNEUIL, a French member of the Screwery
HEREDIA, a Brazilian member of the Screwery
MARCOS, an Argentine member of the Screwery
ANDRES, an Argentine, the protagonist, a somewhat political intellectual who listens to music, a former lover of Ludmilla
THE ONE I TOLD YOU, never identified by name
FRANCINE, a French bookshop owner and the lover of Andres
OSCAR, an Argentine who lives with Gladis
MANUEL, the son of Patricio and Susana,
GLADIS, a woman who lives with Oscar
LONSTEIN, an Argentine who works in a morgue and is intellectual, not political
ROLAND, a French member of the Screwery
FERNANDO, a newly arrived Chilean
SUSANA, the mother of Manuel, a translator for UNESCO
PATRICIO, the father of Manuel, a member of the Screwery

The Novel

As the novel begins, Susana translates and discusses articles from the newspaper with other members of a revolutionary group called "the Screwery." A telegram from London and a reference to something called the "Vincennes business" constitute the reader's introduction to the group's plan to smuggle counterfeit money in order to finance a political kidnaping. The target is a top Latin American police official, referred to as the Vip, whose headquarters are in Paris. He is to be held for ransom until Latin American political prisoners are released.

As the kidnaping preparations are under way, Andres takes Francine to a sleazy bar. He then tells her about a dream in which he sees himself in a film theater which has two screens at right angles. He is there to see a Fritz Lang thriller. Suddenly a messenger arrives and tells him that a Cuban wants to speak with him. Andres follows the messenger until he enters a room where he sees a figure on a sofa. It is the Cuban. At this point, the most important point in the dream, the dream's narrative is interrupted. The next thing that Andres sees is himself, now spectator of and participant in a thriller, leaving the room. Andres interprets the dream to mean that since he has spoken to the Cuban, he now has a mission to fulfill. He has no idea, however, what the mission might be. Andres' quest is directed toward one goal: to find the message cut from his dream, a message that will show him the road he should elect between the beloved solitude of his life as an intellectual in Paris and total political commitment.

The kidnaping does not occur until three-quarters of the way into the book, and the account of the actual moment, provided by the unnamed character, who is identified only as "the one I told you," is no more than "a general impression of total confusion." The details that would have "made a good narrative" are missing. Andres, who is not present at the kidnaping, is awakened from sleep when the Cuban from his dream says to him, "Wake up." He arrives at the scene of the police shoot-out, where the Screwery is holding the Vip. The Vip is released, saved by the police. Gomez and Heredia are next seen in prison. They discuss the fact that "Marcos would have thought" that the operation went well. Proceedings of a press conference on human rights follow this scene. Accounts from Argentines who have been tortured appear in one column juxtaposed to testimony from North American soldiers who witnessed or participated in torture in Vietnam. The novel ends with two glimpses of the return to everyday life: Monique cares for the baby and waits for news from Gomez; Andres tells Susana that he must pick up a Joni Mitchell record and put the notes of "the one I told you" in order, and that the water pitcher story must be added. It is implied that "the one I told you" has died. Lonstein returns to his job washing bodies in the morgue.

Yet the novel ends with a fantastic twist: The body that Lonstein washes, after picking up a water pitcher, is not identified, but Lonstein recognizes him and says, "It had to be us, that's for certain, you there and me with this sponge, you were so right, they're going to think we made it all up." The reader must link "the blackish stain," which Lonstein removes with the sponge, to the character who went out to pick up a Joni Mitchell record, Andres.

The Characters

In comparison to more traditional novelists of the nineteenth century, Cortázar does not create memorable characters; rather, his characters emerge from cultural codes. That is, political discourse determines the boundaries of, for example, Heredia or Gomez, while the character of Andres is shaped by the aleatory music that he loves.

Cortázar is not concerned with a psychological analysis, a realistic representation, or a symbolic use of characters. Rather, his characters are placed in situations in order to provoke the reader.

Cortázar's characters are typically marginal in relation to society; in *Rayuela* (1963; *Hopscotch*, 1966), they are students, transients, circus performers, and mental patients. In *A Manual for Manuel*, they are a marginal political group. *A Manual for Manuel* is a sort of mirror image of *Hopscotch*. Traveler and Horacio reappear as Marcos and Andres; La Maga and Talita as Ludmilla and Francine. Just as Traveler was able to make a commitment to Talita, while Horacio could not make such a commitment either to politics or to La Maga, so Marcos is a member of the Screwery while Andres is on the edge of the revolutionary group. Ludmilla is confused by the activities of the Screwery. Francine owns a book and stationery shop and lives in an elegant apartment with her cat, library, and scotch. Ludmilla lives in disorder with pieces of leek "hung all over the place." Andres is in love with both of these women, attracted to both their worlds. Other characters in the novel appear as couples: Oscar and Gladis, Susana and Patricio, Monique and Gomez. It has been noticed by one critic that the male characters are discussed much more often than are the female characters in Cortázar's work and that, although he may be paving the way for the "new man," his work leaves much to be desired with regard to the "new woman."

With the exception of Monique, who is also writing her thesis, for the most part, Ludmilla and the other women characters make sandwiches, translate, and make love. Susana, however, is familiar with the events of May, 1968, having been at the Battle of the Sorbonne. Marcos and Andres are paternalistic toward women, while Lonstein points out to Andres that "the whole world is not a privilege of the males, anyone can project geometry, you thought that your scheme was acceptable and now you find out that women also have their triangle to say."

Themes and Meanings

A Manual for Manuel is a novel about the continuing war between Latin American guerrillas and Latin American government. It is literally a collage of fragments. Using newspaper clippings, testimony from human rights commission hearings, advertisements, recipes, and musings on literary criticism, Cortázar interrogates his own identity through the character of Andres; he questions his life as an intellectual and the role of the intellectual in relationship to political commitment. As an Argentine who lived in Paris after 1951 and as a translator for UNESCO, Cortázar was acutely aware of the ideological as well as the directly confrontational warfare in Argentina and else-where. In fact, selecting and translating from newspapers has been part of his job; his transformation of these newspaper texts into a novel may be understood as his attempt to recapture the subject which he has had to translate for others. He is aware of the difficulty of writing about the themes of *A Manual for Manuel*, which include political torture; in one pas-sage, he points out that Latin American readers are already aware of the is-sues, rendering the novel useless as a didactic device, while North American readers do not usually have the background to understand the political references. In *Hopscotch*, he discusses the dilemma of the man of action and the intellectual. These roles are played by Horacio and Traveler. He condemns the man of action for having the same unforgivable sin as Trav-eler: conformity. One conforms to the party while the other capitulates to the dictates of everyday life. The dilemma is presented again in *A Manual for Manuel*, but this time, the work centers on a group devoted to political action. Andres, the narrator, is not present at the moment of political action, the kidnaping of the Vip. He is always on the outside. This is the problem of the modernist writer. Cortázar seeks to overcome it to some ex-tent by actively involving what he calls the "reader accomplice."

Critical Context

A Manual for Manuel* was awarded the Prix Medicis. One critic has called it a necessary second volume for *Hopscotch*. The narrative structure of *A Manual for Manuel*, although less complex than that of *Hopscotch*, is experimental and similar to the structure used by twentieth century mu-sicians, both classical and jazz. It proceeds in a more or less linear way, but there are certain questions left unanswered, certain unfilled gaps, because of the way in which the story is told. There is no omnipresent narrator. Rather, the story is told primarily through the eyes of a narrator, "the one I told you," and Andres. The fact that the modernist cannot get inside the historical event, rendering modernist literature helpless as a political educa-tional tool, is of concern to Cortázar. His novel is about this problem, mak-ing the work postmodernist in that it examines the structure of the modern-ist novel.

Philosophically, Cortázar's refusal of the role of omniscient narrator who would have access to the thing itself implies that there is no essence to be distinguished from appearance. Two possible conclusions arise: He is a Kantian, who believes that the object is unknowable, or he is a post-modernist, who refuses to distinguish between art and its object. The im-plication of this method is that reality becomes intelligible through the com-bined activity of the writer and reader who write or read the text. In *A Manual for Manuel*, "the one I told you" sees the kidnaping as "a multi-lenticular and quadrichromatic picture of the ants and the Vip himself...."

This "multilenticular" view joins the imaginings of "the one I told you" with the "sparser" information possessed by Marcos and Ludmilla. The active reader of the book must then take all this and attempt to reconstruct the event.

In terms of genre, Cortázar's work has been linked to the literature of fantasy and Magical Realism, both by critics and in his own writing. Yet he sees his activity as a writer and the active participation that he demands on the part of the reader as a form of political practice that transcends the boundaries of traditional genres to become a testimony of Latin American reality. Certain critics have interpreted the freedom embodied in characters such as La Maga as a model for overcoming alienation and shaking epistemological assumptions. Cortázar sees the "Other," the dimension of the fantastic, as our only salvation from conforming to the role of obedient robots that the technocrats would like us to accept and which we continue to refuse. In his own life, the political form of Cortázar's refusal can be seen in his support for the Cuban revolution, Allende's regime, the Russell Tribunal, and the Nicaraguan revolution.

A Manual for Manuel marked a turning point in Cortázar's career, toward political literature. Not all critics greeted this change favorably, and many still believe that *Hopscotch* is a more successful literary work.

Sources for Further Study
Alazraki, Jaime, and Ivar Ivask, eds. *The Final Island: The Fiction of Julio Cortázar*, 1978.
Brotherston, Gordon. *The Emergence of the Latin American Novel*, 1977.

Emily Hicks

THE MARTIAN CHRONICLES

Author: Ray Bradbury (1920-   )
Type of plot: Science fiction/fantasy
Time of plot: 1999-2026
Locale: The planet Mars and the United States
First published: 1950

> *Principal characters:* A somewhat loosely connected series of stories and sketches, this work has no principal characters. A few characters appear in more than one story, such as Captain Wilder, the leader of the fourth expedition to Mars, and two of his crewmen, Parkhill and Hathaway. Spender, also a member of the Wilder expedition, is a crucial character, for he articulates most fully a central thematic conflict of the book.

The Novel

Though *The Martian Chronicles* consists of chronologically arranged stories and sketches having to do with the exploration and colonization of Mars at the end of the twentieth century, Ray Bradbury has provided enough unity to justify calling the work a novel. The book contains fourteen stories and twelve sketches, though one might dispute the proper classification for a long sketch, "The Musicians," about children playing among the dried corpses of dead Martians, and for the brief story, "There Will Come Soft Rains," about the death of a mechanized house in California which continued to function for years after an atom-bomb blast killed its human occupants.

These pieces can be divided according to phases in humanity's relationship to Mars. The first seven pieces are concerned with attempts to complete a successful expedition to Mars. The next fourteen pieces move through colonization toward exploitation of the planet. The next four cover the desertion of the colonies as people return to Earth after an atomic war begins in 2005. The last story tells how a remnant of what was best on Earth, having escaped the final conflagration, begins again on Mars. Within this structure, three stories stand out for their thematic importance in tying the whole work together: "—And the Moon Be Still as Bright," which ends the section on expeditions, "The Off Season," which ends the section on colonization and exploitation, and "The Million-Year Picnic," the final story.

Only the fourth expedition to Mars is successful. Each of the first three is destroyed, in part because of the telepathic powers of Martians. The first two men are killed by a jealous Martian husband whose unhappy wife has dreamed of the arrival of an attractive Earthman. A Martian psychiatrist kills the second crew as the only cure for their captain's perfect hallucination; apparently, thinking that one is from Earth becomes a serious mental disease on Mars. The third expedition is killed in what at first appears a diabolical plot. The Martians create a hallucination which convinces each member of the crew that his lost loved ones have been given a second chance at life on Mars. Having made the crew feel fully at home, the Martians kill each member in the night. The story becomes a little odd when the illusion of a small town continues through the funeral for the dead crew; the Martians continue to "be" the dead relatives, at least until "their" dead are buried. This oddness may be explained in a story which comes near the end of the next division of pieces. In "The Martian," one of the few remaining living Martians appears among Earth colonists as one who unwillingly becomes the person whom those about him wish most to see. This story resonates with that of the third expedition, suggesting more complexity in this unusual "telepathic" power to become the person whom someone else desires.

When the fourth expedition arrives on Mars, virtually all of the Martians have succumbed to chicken pox. Though there appears to be no Martians left, Spender, one crew member, transforms himself into a "Martian" and attempts one last defense of the planet from the dangers of colonization.

"—And the Moon Be Still as Bright" is a key story because it announces the theme of conflict between a majority, which sees Mars as a new America to be exploited for its material wealth and living space, and a minority, which sees Mars as a new source of wisdom and spiritual value. Spender responds to the dead planet with awe and with respect for those who built the civilization of which there are such rich remains. He sees that most of his fellow voyagers are intent on material treasure and are without comprehension of or appreciation for what the remains of Martian culture might offer. To them, the Martians are like the American Indians, now fortunately out of the way. To him, as he quickly begins to learn about them, they are possessors of answers to age-old human conflicts over the question of what is of essential value. In conversations with Captain Wilder, Spender makes it clear that Martians believed that living was of value in itself and, therefore, allowed no other values to supersede the value of life.

It becomes clear that this central value, along with other values which Spender sees reflected in Martian culture, is not to prevail in the colonization and exploitation of Mars. In the fourteen pieces which tell of these processes, commercial and exploitative interests dominate. In the sketches, Bradbury documents the broad cultural movements, while in the stories, he tends to emphasize the minority countermovement: the protoecologist who plants trees to increase the oxygen, the young worker who enters a kind of "time-warp" to meet an ancient or future Martian and to realize their essential similarity, the Southern blacks who secretly arrange a mass exodus to Mars to escape segregation, and the millionaire eccentric who takes revenge on the arrogant forces of cultural conformity. These predominantly comic stories are placed against a backdrop of impending atomic war on Earth and the spread to Mars of the attitudes which have led to this war.

"The Off Season" illustrates these destructive attitudes nicely. Sam Parkhill, a member of the fourth expedition, has found a prime location at which to set up the only hot-dog stand on Mars. Within days, thousands of surplus laborers will arrive from Earth to work in "the mines," and he will rake in cash selling them familiar food. As he glories in dreams of profit, an emissary of the few surviving Martians arrives to deed him half of the planet and to tell him some news he has not yet heard, that a world war has started on Earth. Parkhill is convinced that the Martians, resentful at the loss of their planet, intend to prevent his realizing his dream. He kills the emissary, then flees from other Martians, killing several more before they can make their intentions clear. He kills them because he can see them only through his own greed and guilt. The Martian attitude toward Sam seems a compound of irony and pity. They appreciate, along with Sam's wife and the reader, the irony that Sam's business will fail because attitudes such as Sam's predominate on Earth. They may deed him so much territory out of pity at his loss of his home or out of irony because the site's commercial value is gone. The values by which Sam lives are ultimately self-destructive.

Sam Parkhill embodies the destructive values which bring about the end of Earth. Spender, the converted Martian, articulates the minority values which could save humanity on Earth. Ultimately, these latter values fail, and Earth is utterly destroyed. In "The Million-Year Picnic," a family representing the values of love, the appreciation of cultural diversity, and the value of life arrives on Mars as the last remnant of Earth culture. These people become the new Martians and, in a world purified of the old sins, begin again the spiritual quest which has run beneath the destructive course of human history in this book.

The Characters

Bradbury does not create fully developed, complex characters in *The Martian Chronicles*. Though there are memorable characters, most tend to be representative. Ylla, the unhappy Martian wife, is a typical unhappy wife. Sam Parkhill is a typical, small-minded businessman, unable to see beyond his desire for wealth. William Thomas in "The Million-Year Picnic" is a good-hearted Everyman who tries until the last minute to save humanity and then tries to continue what is best in humanity on Mars.

Perhaps the most memorable character is William Stendahl, the creator of the new House of Usher in "Usher II." This story is related thematically to Bradbury's *Fahrenheit 451* (1953). Stendahl is a millionaire eccentric who has dedicated his life to preserving the imaginative literature (especially the stories of Edgar Allan Poe) which has been outlawed and burned by controllers of the "moral climate" on Earth. He devises the new House of Usher as an exact external replica of the original in order to trap most of the moral-climate officials and kill them there. The story tells of his success with this plot. Though Stendahl is memorable, especially for forcing his victims to die like characters in Poe's tales and in twitting them for their ignorance of Poe, which is also ignorance of their fates, he still is essentially one-dimensional. Even the most important character, Spender, is essentially a mouthpiece for the main positive values of the book.

Themes and Meanings

To summarize the book and to discuss the characters is, inevitably, to discuss the themes and meanings of *The Martian Chronicles*, for the work is thematically organized. Bradbury structures the book primarily as a commentary on mid-twentieth century American life. In the early encounters between humans and Martians, one idea is repeatedly emphasized—that essentially, in their truest needs and desires, humans and Martians are the same. Their differences are on the surface; their likenesses are the fundamental reality. Those people from Earth who, in one way or another, recognize and affirm these essential likenesses, become the heroes of the book. They affirm values such as family love, imaginative sympathy, cultural diversity, unity with an ecosystem, and the ultimate value of living and continuing life against the opposing forces of greed, the will to power, irrational fear of the different, fear of the imagination, excessive faith in technology, and unthinking exploitation of environments. Bradbury arranges these two sets of related values as choices, showing that one leads to the end of the Earth and that the other might, with good luck, lead to a remnant which could preserve the human race.

Critical Context

The Martian Chronicles is Bradbury's best-known and probably also his best book. Though the book shows some evidence of its having been gathered together out of a number of previously written stories, it is, nevertheless, unified enough to produce a fairly clear didactic effect. Bradbury's first book-length work, this novel was widely reviewed even outside "science-fiction" magazines. It was important to his career because it was his first major critical success and because it reached a larger audience than his earlier works. In part because it expresses eloquently and imaginatively the dominant concerns of mid-century Americans, it has become an important work of science fiction. Critics agree that even though the book is unlike what is usually called science fiction, it has had the effect of drawing a larger audience to the genre and, perhaps, the more important effect of drawing a new generation of more highly skilled writers to science fiction as a respectable creative mode.

Sources for Further Study

Johnson, Wayne L. *Ray Bradbury*, 1980.
Ketterer, David. *New Worlds for Old*, 1974.
Slusser, George Edgar. *The Bradbury Chronicles*, 1977.
Slusser, George Edgar, Eric Rabkin, and Robert Scholes, eds. *Bridges to Fantasy*, 1982.
Touponce, William F. *Ray Bradbury and the Poetics of Reverie*, 1984.

Terry Heller

MEN OF MAIZE

Author: Miguel Ángel Asturias (1899-1974)
Type of plot: Social morality
Time of plot: The twentieth century
Locale: Guatemala
First published: Hombres de maíz, 1949 (English translation, 1975)

>*Principal characters:*
>GASPAR ILÓM, an Indian who revolts against the commercial corngrowers
>PIOJOSA GRANDE, his wife
>MACHOJÓN, an Indian turncoat who sells Gaspar to the Mounted Patrol
>VACA MANUELA, his wife
>COLONEL CHALO GODOY, the Commander of the Mounted Patrol
>GOYO YIC, a blind beggar
>MARÍA TECÚN, his runaway wife
>NICHO AQUINO, the postman of San Miguel Acatán
>HILARIO SACAYÓN, a mule driver with a penchant for spinning yarns

The Novel

The action of *Men of Maize* is divided into two periods. In the first part of the novel Gaspar Ilóm wages war against the professional maizegrowers who set fire to the brush and ruthlessly exploit the land. According to the Indians of Guatemala, the first men who were created, their ancestors, were made of corn. Therefore, this grain is sacred; it may be consumed but never exploited, eaten but never sold. The maizegrowers, however, prefer profits to traditions, an attitude which opposes them to the peasants both morally and ethically. This is why Gaspar and his Indian guerrillas revolt against them and gain the upper hand until the maizegrowers call in the Mounted Patrol. With the help of an Indian turncoat, Machojón, and especially of his wife, Vaca Manuela, the commander of the Mounted Patrol lures Gaspar and his men to a feast. During the celebration, Vaca Manuela tricks Gaspar into drinking poison, but Gaspar dives into the river and manages to "extinguish the thirst of the poison in his intestines." He returns after dawn, only to discover that the soldiers have taken his men by surprise and massacred them. Gaspar dives into the river once again, and the maizegrowers return to the mountains of Ilóm, unaware that a curse has been cast. The yellow-eared rabbit sorcerers who accompanied Gaspar condemn all the perpetrators of the massacre to die before the seventh year is ended. One by one, in the chapters which follow, they are all punished. Machojón and his wife burn in an eerie blaze which razes their cornfields. On his way to ask for the hand of his intended, their son is surrounded by fireflies and mysteriously disappears. The man who sold the poison used on Gaspar is decapitated along with his entire family, and finally Colonel Godoy and his troops are consumed by "flames in the form of bloodstained hands" which "were painted on the walls of the air."

The second part of the novel describes the adventures of three men whose lives become intertwined. The first, Goyo Yic, is a blind beggar whose wife, María, runs away, taking with her their many children. Goyo cannot live without her and seeks the help of a curer, who removes the veil of blindness from his eyes. He has, however, never seen María. For this reason, he becomes a peddler and travels from fair to fair; he coaxes women to buy his wares in order to hear their voices and one day, he hopes, recognize his missing wife. Goyo invokes O Possum, patron saint of peddlers, to guide him on his search, but to no avail. One night, he gazes at his shadow by the light of the moon, and "it was like seeing the shadow of a she-opossum." The moonlight turns him from a man into an animal. He wanders into the forest so long as a fugitive that his skin turns black. One day, he is lured by the lights and the laughter of the big fair in the town of Santa Cruz de las Cruces. He returns to the world of men and teams up with a certain Domingo Revolorio to start a little business selling liquor by the glass. They buy a demijohn and take turns carrying it on their backs to a distant fair. It is a hot day and they soon get tired. They start selling glasses of liquor to each other until, finally drunk, they lose their permit and are sent to jail for selling liquor without a license.

Time passes. People preserve and repeat the legend of the blindman and his runaway wife, María Tecún, immortalizing it by referring to all runaways as "tecunas." One day the wife of Nicho Aquino, the postman in the little town of San Miguel de Acatán, suddenly disappears. Nicho is overcome with grief and gets drunk to forget and remember. On his next trip to the capital, mailpouch on his back, he meets a wizened old man with black hands who offers to tell him the whereabouts of his wife. Nicho follows him into some caves where the old man brings to life the tale of creation according to Maya tradition. He reveals to Nicho why maize is sacred and explains the import of Gaspar Ilóm's death and of the cycle of retribution which it has for a sequel. Nicho is enlightened. Upon discovering his origins, he regains a sense of self. For a moment he becomes a coyote, his *nagual*, or animal protector.

Meanwhile, in San Miguel, the townspeople are worried that the postman—and especially their letters—may never reach their destination. They send the muleteer, Hilario Sacayón, to look for Nicho and steer him onto the right path. Hilario looks everywhere and on his way ponders the nature of tales and the difference between reality and fiction, but he never finds Nicho. The former postman ends up burning the mail and running away to the coast, where he becomes a factotum for a hotel proprietress. One of his duties is to ferry people to the Harbor Castle, fitted out as a prison, where Goyo Yic is serving a sentence for selling liquor without a license. Once again, years have passed. Goyo's own son is serving time in the same prison, and one day his mother, María Tecún, comes to pay him a visit. Nicho ferries her across and is astounded to discover that the woman he knows as a legend really exists. The members of the Yic family are reunited, and when the men are set free, they all go back to harvest corn in Pisigüilito, where the action started. This is the story's climax. Man, blind for a time to the ancient traditions which bind him to the soil, returns to harvest the sacred substance which constitutes him. Gaspar's sacrifice is not in vain if it has succeeded in doing away with the sanguinary breed (the commercial exploiters) who keep the men of maize from engaging in the most fundamental of occupations.

The Characters

The influence of Mayan literature on characterization in *Men of Maize* cannot be overstated. Asturias spent years studying anthropology and helped to translate the Mayan book of Genesis, or *Popol Vuh*. Many of the narrative features of this ancient manuscript filter into his indigenous novels. For example, character and chronological development in *Men of Maize* are minimal; the protagonists substitute for one another in what could be termed a character substitution principle. They are cast as friends or foes of the men of maize, and, for the most part, they are emblematic of behavior patterns. Gaspar Ilóm is a character whose portrayal evolves throughout the fiction without undergoing any psychological development. He fights for the communal values dear to the Indian in the first part of the novel, but in the chapters which follow he is portrayed as a mythic figure from a remote past, while other characters step into the limelight. The reader soon realizes that this novel does not have a hero in the conventional sense but rather a collective beneficiary, the men of maize, who profit from the moral teachings extolled by Asturias.

As the first part of the novel is typified by emblematic characters who do not develop in the traditional sense, the second part is noteworthy for the original characters who do. Here, Goyo Yic shines forth as an Everyman figure who has lost touch with the world of his forefathers. For this reason, he is portrayed as both blind and a beggar when introduced to the reader. Yet, prompted by the need to find his wife and children, he launches forth in a search which must be seen as a rite of passage. His wife, María Tecún, is a beacon throughout the novel (although she materializes as a character only in the last few pages). As are all women in *Men of Maize*, she is an absent presence, alluded to, sought, and eventually found, a symbol of the telluric forces from which the men of maize have become estranged. In fact, the wives of all the Indian protagonists in the novel either run away or disappear, and only one couple (Goyo and María Tecún) are reunited.

Two other important characters, Nicho Aquino and Hilario Sacayón, should be seen as pegs in a well-oiled narrative machine, who serve their purpose (bringing together Goyo and María) and subsequently fade. In addition Hilario, the muleteer, functions as Asturias' mouthpiece in *Men of Maize*. Hilario is a man capable of imagining a woman piecemeal and then falling in love with his own creation. This self-persuasion suggests that words can be as concrete as action, that what man hears becomes, eventually, what he sees.

Influencing readers was exactly what Asturias intended to do. He wrote *Men of Maize* during a period of great political optimism in Guatemala. Juan José Arévalo had been elected president in 1945, and he had enacted controversial social laws aiming to return lands to destitute peasants, to organize cooperative farms and to make way for agrarian reform. *Men of Maize* translates into fiction the changes which Arévalo was bringing about in reality. Asturias wields words—as does Hilario—to motivate reality. His design was to present in fiction (by means of emblematic characters) the blueprints for a society whose roots went back to the days of the great Maya nation and heralded, at the same time, the progressive community planned by Juan José Arévalo.

Themes and Meanings

There are three major themes in *Men of Maize*: struggle, paternity, and the genetic process of myth. The first of these is the most readily apparent and one that is a factual reflection of social conditions in twentieth century Guatemala. When Asturias conceived this novel, his country's society was divided into two factions: the haves and the have-nots (Indians for the most part). In the vision of the novel, the differences between these two factions are not simply economic but, more profoundly, of an ethical nature. Essentially, what distinguishes them is an attitude toward life. The Indians live in harmony with nature; the outsiders (represented by the commercial maizegrowers) exploit nature to make a living, which is equated with barrenness in Asturias' scheme. Yet the exploiters of the land have the upper hand, while the Indians are portrayed as a strayed race, wandering and blind but by no means lost. Asturias points the path to salvation by underscoring the need to return to the land, the natural harbor and seedbed of the race. The first step in order to restore the lost order of the Mayan forefathers is to eradicate evil; the second is to heed the voice of tradition (of the past). The new man that Asturias is extolling must put his ear to the ground and remove the veil of blindness from his eyes. If he does, he will establish a nexus with the roots of his culture, as do Goyo and Nicho, who both transform themselves into their protective animals as a sign of their conversion.

The second major theme in the novel is paternity. Man and maize are one. The enemies of the Indian engage in commerce with maize; they sell "the flesh of our children" and are punished with sterility for this sin. Machojón loses his son, and in all the participants in the massacre of Ilóm, "the light of the tribes was extinguished." Meanwhile, the prototypical Indian family, that of Goyo Yic, flourishes. At the end of the novel, when they all return to Pisigüilito to harvest corn, they are a full-bodied clan "because their married children had many children and they all went there to live with them." As Asturias indicates, it is a "wealth of men, wealth of women, to have many children." He clearly portrays the moral poverty of the maizegrowers and exploiters of the Indian by depicting their sterility.

The most original thematic feature of *Men of Maize* is that the reader is allowed to participate in the genetic process of myth. Characters encountered in the first sections of the novel (Gaspar Ilóm, Machojón, María Tecún) are referred to, later in the action, as figures from a legendary past (even while some of them, such as María, are still alive). Tales in *Men of Maize* have a way of being repeated until they are believed and filter into the collective unconscious of all characters. The message becomes a medium, a link in the chain of shared traditions which binds men and women together and which we know as culture. By showing his countrymen that culture (and, more important, the ability to forge it) is a collective enterprise, Asturias wished to encourage them to take an active hand in transforming the society which was being recast during the very years he spent writing his novel (1945-1949).

Critical Context

Men of Maize is, without a doubt, Asturias' most controversial novel as well as his best. It has been disparaged and misunderstood by critics ever since its publication. Given its unique narrative structure and the fact that Asturias underplays character and chronological development, many readers have believed it to lack unity. In fact, the conception of *Men of Maize* is so revolutionary (in form as well as in content) that unity must be found in features other than those dictated by convention.

As James Joyce did in *Ulysses* (1922), Asturias turned to an earlier, classical work for the infrastructure for his ground-breaking novel. He borrowed from the past but actualized it in the present and, most important, developed his novel through an association of key themes. For example, all Indian characters in *Men of Maize* are associated with water, and all their enemies with fire. Three sets of three animals each also play a primary role in the novel, and each set is associated with one of the three elements which anchor Asturias' pyramid to Meso-American man: fire, water, and corn. Finally, four numbers—four, seven, nine, and thirteen—enter the alchemy of *Men of Maize*. Each is associated with an animal and a color in keeping with Mayan mythology, and all the elements are portrayed in a progression which culminates, in the epilogue, with the return to the land. At the end of the harvest, Goyo and his family become ants, one of the animals responsible for the discovery of corn, according to the Meso-American mythic tradition. Goyo's animal protector is also the oppossum (god of dawn in Meso-America), known in Maya as Zach Och, the white animal (white betokens the beginning of something, specifically, of civilization). The novel starts with a cycle of struggle and retribution and then picks up the thread of a wandering blindman, a beggar, who ends up fully healed, a farmer, and a begetter of many children. Thematically speaking, Asturias shifts the action from chaos to order and concludes with a return which is in every respect a beginning, a hope-filled eulogy to the common man of Meso-America.

Sources for Further Study
Brotherson, Gordon. "The Presence of Mayan Literature in *Hombres de maíz* and Other Works by Miguel Ángel Asturias," in *Hispania*. LVIII (March, 1975), pp. 68-74.
Callan, Richard J. *Miguel Ángel Asturias*, 1972.
Harss, Luis, and Barbara Dohmann. *Into the Mainstream: Conversations with Latin American Writers*, 1967.

René Prieto

MERIDIAN

Author: Alice Walker (1944-   )
Type of plot: Social morality
Time of plot: The decade of the 1960's, during the height of the civil rights
movement
Locale: New York City, Georgia, Mississippi, and Alabama
First published: 1976

> *Principal characters:*
> MERIDIAN HILL, the protagonist, a young civil rights worker
> searching for her role in life
> TRUMAN HELD, an artist and civil rights activist with whom
> Meridian falls in love
> LYNNE RABINOWITZ, a white civil rights worker whom Truman
> marries

The Novel

Meridian traces the moral and psychological development of Walker's title character, Meridian Hill. Born into a middle-class Southern black family, Meridian is taught to accept the racist and sexist status quo of the 1950's. She is not encouraged to question segregationist policies, sexist traditions, or her own sexual ignorance—all of which deny her autonomy. Recalling the climate before and during the civil rights movement, *Meridian* brings readers to an awareness of the many relationships between racism and sexism and their consequences for the individual and the community.

The novel begins in the present of the 1970's, as Truman Held, artist and former civil rights worker, finds himself searching for Meridian in Chicokema, Georgia. She is not difficult to trace, because she is leading a group of children denied entry to a freak show featuring Marilene O'Shay, "One of the Twelve Human Wonders of the World: Dead for Twenty-Five Years, Preserved in Life-Like Condition." Marilene is further characterized as an "Obedient Daughter, Devoted Wife, and Adoring Mother" predictably "Gone Wrong." As Truman watches Meridian defy tradition and authority literally to stare down a tank, he marvels at her strength, strength that he has finally come to admire. Walker follows this scene with a flashback when, ten years earlier, Meridian is invited to join a revolutionary group and fails to meet its requirements by being unable to swear that she will kill for the revolution. The novel, weaving backward and forward in time, traces Meridian's awakening and guides its readers to an understanding of her complex integrity.

Although there is much in her life to encourage conformity, Meridian shows early flashes of individuality and integrity—most notably when, at thirteen, she refuses to be saved by a religion which literally makes no sense to her and later, as an honor student, when she is asked to deliver a speech celebrating "the superiority of the American Way of Life." By the time she is seventeen, Meridian, unlike the mummified Marilene, has failed her traditional roles. She is a disobedient daughter, failing to accept the traditions which her unreflective mother holds sacred; an indifferent wife, relieved when her husband finds distractions; and a resentful mother, tempted to murder her son. She is literally blasted into political awareness when she watches a newscast about the bombing of a nearby house used by civil rights workers. With only the dimmest sense of direction, Meridian volunteers to work on voter registration. Her education begins in earnest as she joins young people from diverse backgrounds in a fight for racial equality. It continues when she is offered a scholarship to Saxon College in Atlanta. First, however, Meridian is faced with the difficult moral choice of giving up her young son. Although she believes her choice to be best for him, she nevertheless believes that she has failed as a woman, and her mother's self-righteous reaction intensifies this guilt.

Saxon, a black women's college ironically representative of white, paternalistic traditions, upholds a genteel tradition of "ladyhood" that Meridian finds ludicrous, but she relishes her opportunities for learning. During this period, her sense of conflict between tradition and change intensifies, for as her understanding grows, she is able to see through stale forms and illogical assumptions. She becomes better able to withstand the many forces urging her to conform, particularly the orphic charm of Truman Held, with whom she has fallen in love. Although Meridian finds his intelligence and refined appearance attractive, she rejects his snobbery, racism, and sexism. Wasted by a mysterious illness symbolic of her internal moral conflict, Meridian decides to heal herself by returning to the South.

For ten years, Meridian lives and works among the poor people of the South. During this time she struggles with her conscience, pricked by accusatory letters from her mother and best friend, Anne-Marion. Living close to the people, learning to anticipate their real needs and to admire their strength, helps Meridian grasp an understanding of herself. Finally, she rejects the roles of martyrdom and self-sacrifice and discovers the value of her own life. At last, Meridian understands her role: "to walk behind the real revolutionaries . . . and sing from memory songs they will need once more to hear. For it is the song of the people, transformed by the experiences of each generation, that holds them together." Her spiritual healing complete, Meridian is able to go forward, leaving behind Truman to deal with his own possibilities.

The Characters

Meridian is one of the most fully drawn and emotionally complex characters of contemporary American fiction. Autobiographical to a certain degree (Meridian and Walker share approximate ages, a deep love for the South, education at a women's college in Atlanta, and civil rights involvement), this novel is artfully crafted. To direct her readers' interpretation of "meridian," Walker lists definitions at the novel's beginning. All pertain specifically to qualities inherent in the title character: "prime," "southern," "the highest point." Yet Walker wants her readers to see her character as representative of the 1960's, which she sees as the meridian of black awareness, when black Americans were able to see themselves clearly and to struggle for their identity. Another of "meridian's" meanings is "distinctive character"; it is Meridian's battle for her individuality that is the novel's focus.

Perhaps most distinctive is her spirituality. Meridian is something of a mystic, retreating from time to time into trancelike states from which she emerges stronger than ever. Her rejection of materialism is another sign of her spirituality. Whenever Truman visits Meridian, he discovers that she has fewer and fewer possessions, until she is left with only the clothes on her back. Like many mystics, Meridian leads an ascetic life, denying the needs of her own body. All of these indicate her separation from the ordinary restraints of life.

Supporting her spirituality is her affinity to the past, her literal kinship with Feather Mae, her great-grandmother, and her figurative one with Louvinie, a Saxon slave. Following Feather Mae's example, Meridian invites ecstasy, and discovers "that it was a way the living sought to expand the consciousness of being alive. . . ." She gains a larger understanding of her world, one not bound by trifling concerns. Louvinie's example is equally important, for from her story Meridian learns about the need for expressing oneself, the value of a tenacious spirit, and the power of creativity. Because Louvinie's clipped tongue nourishes the roots of the Sojourner Tree on the Saxon campus, Meridian is related to the tree as well.

Other qualities in keeping with her spirituality are Meridian's introspection, her ferocious will, and her inability to give her word without full moral commitment. Since her decisions are often painful, and since they conflict with accepted moral traditions, readers should pay special attention to the relentlessness of her introspection. In the tradition of spiritual leaders, she suffers for her choices, but she finds this a necessary stage of growth.

Other characters are presented with sympathy and understanding—from Meridian's prim and limited mother and her dreamy father to various poor people Meridian encounters on her travels. Major sections of the novel, however, are devoted to two other characters: Lynne Rabinowitz and Truman Held.

Few black novelists have treated white characters with the keen intelligence of Walker. Lynne is no simple stereotype; she is a naïvely idealistic reformer caught in the spirit of the times, a defiant and courageous woman who risks all of her personal ties, a guilt-ridden and terrified victim of the people whom she has tried to help, a confused and resentful woman who gradually awakens to her own mistakes. In several ways Lynne represents what Meridian might have been had she married Truman. Lynne's experiences, fortunately, do not destroy her. At the end of the novel, she shows signs of recovered strength and a newly detected sense of her ability to endure alone. Walker's understanding of Lynne's motives for her involvement in the civil rights movement, her ability to characterize Lynne's ambivalent moral and social position, her sensitive dramatization of Lynne's losses, and her refusal to simplify Lynne are notable.

Equally complex is her characterization of Truman, whom Walker draws with a knowledge of his masculine attractions as well as his deficiencies. Truman's main function in the novel is to serve as a bypass—potential and actual—of self-discovery. Had Meridian accepted the role he offered (mother of his children), she might have become like Lynne, isolated from herself, confusing his evaluation of her for her own. Unlike his name, Truman is not yet a true man in Walker's estimation; he must first recognize his flaws and accept responsibility for his actions. Walker, however, does not intend his name to be entirely ironic, for as Truman grows older, he begins to see his limitations. Following Meridian, he begins to learn from her example. Because of her, he acknowledges a responsibility to Lynne; he sees the importance of empathy, both personally and politically; and he learns that true love is liberating, not possessive. Meridian leaves him behind, but she gives him her cap, symbolizing his assumption of her former role in fear and hope of self-discovery.

Themes and Meanings

Walker's treatment of the self-discovery theme is perhaps one of the most complete in contemporary literature. While many authors focus on liberating the self from recognizably tangible obstacles, Walker has her protagonist confront two little-understood and painfully acknowledged social conditions—racism and sexism—and she deals with the themes in a sophisticated manner, linking them in such a way as to reveal important crosscurrents. Walker also explores the problem of guilt created and sustained by mothers as a means of controlling and protecting daughters, and she exposes early motherhood as a barrier to self-discovery. That she deals with these issues without seeming didactic in any way is a mark of her artistry. *Meridian* is remarkable in another significant way: Walker's vision transcends both racial and sexual barriers as she forces her characters to go beyond the boundaries of the black community to see themselves in relation to the white community as well. In this manner, she has her female protagonists travel in the fullest sense—by exploring their personal and racial past in order to create a future without racial barriers.

Critical Context

When first published, *Meridian* was largely ignored, partly because its author was a young writer with a limited public. (Walker's very fine first novel, *The Third Life of Grange Copeland*, 1970, attracted almost no recognition when it was published.) The critical realization that *Meridian* was an exceptional novel grew slowly during the 1970's, as Walker began to establish herself not only as a novelist but also as a poet, short story writer, essayist, and feminist. By the mid-1980's, Walker had achieved recognition as one of the foremost contemporary American writers, largely on the strength of her widely acclaimed novel *The Color Purple* (1982), which was awarded both the Pulitzer Prize and the American Book Award for fiction.

Many critics regard *Meridian* as Walker's fullest, most beautifully crafted novel. Its unusual structure reflects the novel's revolutionary theme and spirit. Throughout her career, Walker has committed herself to exploring obstacles to human freedom, particularly as they apply to women. Because *Meridian* touches upon this theme of timeless relevance with consummate art, it continues to attract increasing numbers of readers as well as informed scholarly consideration.

Sources for Further Study

Christian, Barbara. *Black Women Novelists: The Development of a Tradition, 1892-1976*, 1980.

Davis, Thadious M. "Alice Walker's Celebration of Self in Southern Generations," in *The Southern Quarterly*. XXI, no. 4 (Summer, 1983), pp. 39-53.

McDowell, Deborah E. "The Self in Bloom: Alice Walker's *Meridian*," in *CLA Journal*. XXIV (March, 1981), pp. 262-275.

Karen Carmean

MICKELSSON'S GHOSTS

Author: John Gardner (1933-1982)
Type of plot: Psychological realism
Time of plot: The fall of 1980
Locale: Binghamton, New York, and Susquehanna, Pennsylvania
First published: 1982

> *Principal characters:*
> PETER J. MICKELSSON, the protagonist, a professor of philosophy and a writer
> JESSICA STARK, a professor of sociology and Mickelsson's lover
> MICHAEL NUGENT, a student
> DONNIE MATTHEWS, a teenage prostitute

The Novel

In *Mickelsson's Ghosts*, John Gardner sustains a 590-page dramatization of the daily life, increasing despair, and desperate desires of middle-aged Peter Mickelsson, a once-famous philosopher now sinking into obscurity at the State University of New York at Binghamton. Faced with his failures on several fronts—marital, financial, and professional—the previous master of academic truth must now engage less bookish but far more difficult problems. For setting, Gardner supplies the troubled Mickelsson with the doomed air of 1980, a climate of debate over the big issues—abortion, nuclear waste and arms, Ronald Reagan versus Jimmy Carter—which increases the stress already heavily bearing on Mickelsson by his private crises.

The novel opens with Mickelsson living in a squalid apartment in Binghamton, near the university where he teaches ethics, a now out-of-date discipline among contemporary philosophers. Divorced and lonely, plagued by bills, unpaid taxes, and alimony payments, he ignores apparent necessity, and with a fraudulent loan application he secures a house in the nearby Pennsylvania countryside. There he settles, determined to write the blockbuster book which will redeem his career and bail him out financially. As rumored by his Susquehanna real estate agent, the house proves to be haunted. The ghosts appear and disappear regularly, an old couple, brother and sister, who strike mournful postures and wander from room to room. Mickelsson grows accustomed to the strangeness of his new home as well as the strange goings on in the nearby hills—mass Mormon baptisms and discoveries of circular pulverized patches reputed to be UFO landing sites.

The novel's action is divided between what Mickelsson does in Binghamton—teach Plato, talking to students and colleagues whenever he is unable to avoid them—and what he does at the house and in Susquehanna, the small town where he meets and becomes obsessed with Donnie Matthews, a teenage prostitute. Donnie's bestial allure contrasts with his growing affection for Jessica Stark, a beautiful Jewess who teaches sociology at the university. Discussions of abortion in Mickelsson's medical ethics class are existentially troubling when Donnie becomes pregnant and demands money for an abortion. The ethics professor descends to new depths, breaking into the apartment of a fat man who has a cache of stolen money that Mickelsson discovers while crawling up the fire escape to spy on Donnie. The break-in frightens the fat man to death—by heart attack. Mickelsson gives the money to Donnie, who leaves Susquehanna permanently.

Paralleling Mickelsson's personal trauma and leading to the novel's climax are the mysterious deaths of a couple living in the hills, previous owners of Mickelsson's home. Another philosopher, Edward Lawler, is a member of a bizarre Mormon sect searching for documents that purportedly prove the Mormon scriptures fallacious. He murders two students, then the neighbor couple, and arrives at Mickelsson's, demanding at gunpoint the tearing out of all the house's interior walls. Hours later, the weary Mickelsson is reduced to praying to a God he has never believed in, and he is saved by a passerby's previously mute daughter, who hears Mickelsson's psychic entreaties and tells her father to knock on the door. At novel's end, Mickelsson, bereft of hubris, pledges his love for Jessica Stark in a bedroom full of ghosts, "pitiful, empty-headed nothings complaining to be born."

The Characters

Peter Mickelsson, equipped with all the machinery of modern intellectual consciousness and a native brilliance, is plunged into a world containing facts, indisputable facts, which that consciousness cannot believe yet cannot deny. Mickelsson, however, is much more than a locus of conflict between the rational and the supernatural. His exposure to the ghosts is an introduction to the world of human suffering, which includes his present life among the present ghosts whose long-dead pain and anger persist in redundant cameo oblivious to everything else their lives might have contained. Mickelsson daily savors his own broken connections. His former wife lives in twenty-year-old photographs. His absent son in the grainy newspaper photo is rigid with resignation, a protestor against the nuclear silo and the American "Reich." Mickelsson's most intimate colloquies are with dead philosophers—Friedrich Nietzsche, Ludwig Wittgenstein. Through the ghost of his grandfather, he contemplates and is haunted by the ghostly, life-despising Martin Luther. With his obsessions in tow, Mickelsson becomes a seer. Like his father before him, his prescience is mostly of painful things. The voice speaking from the past and the future testifies to pain. Mickelsson is most himself when beside himself.

The ghost haunting Mickelsson most persistently is himself. The "bad"

Mickelsson never stops appalling the rational ethical persona. Which is real? he wonders. He suspects that his goodness may have been only the superficial manner of more respectable days in the Ivy League. In Binghamton, demoted, he wanders the streets at dark with his clublike walking stick. He kills a dog with the stick and does not notify the owner or the police. Through Mickelsson, Gardner develops a split man, similar in some ways to Raskolnikov in Fyodor Dostoevski's *Crime and Punishment*.

The two female counterparts of Mickelsson exemplify this split. The prostitute Donnie Matthews appeals to the irrational side. She is simply flesh, "blue-white" flesh available for immediate use and presenting no formal female self to overcome with charm or conversation before the treasure is surrendered. Her only virtue is her preference for indigent lovers, though this fact makes Mickelsson's postsex meditations all the more repellent. Jessica Stark appeals to the civilized Mickelsson. Though amply endowed with her own physical perfections, she also has a formidable mind, and though Mickelsson and Jessica become lovers, their union is prefaced by long nights of nonphysical intercourse—discussions of philosophical ideas and each other's emotional pain (Jessica is a widow who has lost two daughters in a boating accident).

Michael Nugent is a character in need whom Mickelsson essentially spurns. Nugent attends the Plato-Aristotle course that is being taught by the professor he admires. Nugent is disturbed by the recent death of his father and the mysterious death of his favorite science teacher. His bright mind and his smattering of nihilistic ideas based on the experience of death and his reading of Franz Kafka, Søren Kierkegaard, and Jean-Paul Sartre make Nugent a son figure for Mickelsson's potential love. Nugent, however, does all the reaching out, while Mickelsson evades, repelled somewhat by Nugent's homosexuality. The boy becomes one more occasion for guilt when he dies, apparently a suicide.

Some relief from the dirge of unhappiness is provided by the more minor characters. The lawyer Finney is a man of stupendous profanity and full of sarcastic comment on the doings of Mickelsson, his wayward client. Gardner captures the Irish irreverence in each conversation. When Finney learns of Mickelsson's intention to buy a house, his answer is: "That's good, Pete! Cute! Give the feds something solid to aim their pissers at." Another bit player in the novel, Dr. Rifkin, occasionally appears or is conjured up by Mickelsson as the all-knowing but unhelpful psychiatrist. His knowledge does nothing to alter the course Mickelsson takes, and he exists in the novel mainly for the sake of parody.

Themes and Meanings

In *On Moral Fiction* (1978), Gardner maintains that the high purpose of fiction is to assert order, however temporary, in the midst of chaos and darkness which is reality. A good novel should help its reader, encourage him to go on living, even though he knows that consciousness and life will lose out in the end. *Mickelsson's Ghosts* suggests that Gardner wants it both ways, or is not as confident about being right in regard to what is real. There is arrogance in the claim that the artist asserts order in a senseless void, and loneliness as well. Gardner surrounds Mickelsson with ghosts, supernatural presences and events, or rich suggestions of a created order incomprehensible to the mind but richly beckoning. One part of Gardner says that even the supernatural is invented by me, the novelist; another part says, "Please do not let this be so." At a key point in the novel, he reduces Mickelsson to a helpless fear of death out of which he cries for help. The cry, much to Mickelsson's shame and contradicting all of his conviction about "truth" (there's nothing out there—only facts) is a cry to a person out there who has ears, and it is shameful because Mickelsson knows that it is a cry to God, "pouring out the thought as if it were his life." When the cry works, when the prayer is answered, the relieved and rescued Mickelsson can excuse himself and drop again into a tolerant skepticism.

Gardner wants the reader to enjoy the emotion coming from meaning and miraculous grace without crediting it. It is only a ghost, dear reader, one more human longing crying out in darkness. Yet Mickelsson is saved, saved from Lawler, the mad Mormon (law), and saved from death. He can now make love to Jessie, possibly give her a child, and can love his own son, returned at the novel's conclusion from his protest pilgrimage. The reader is left to ponder what Gardner's attitude is toward the happy ending he gives the book. Is it merely something to make the reader feel better about life, or does it mean or foretell something for which everyone longs because it is in the nature of their hearts to so long? Dreams, says Gardner, the artificer, as he himself continues to dream.

Critical Context

Mickelsson's Ghosts was Gardner's last novel before his untimely death in a motorcycle accident, not far from the university where both he and his protagonist were professors. Most early reviewers disapproved of the novel. Gardner had gained few friends by his forthright criticisms of fellow writers in *On Moral Fiction*, and the novel preceding *Mickelsson's Ghosts*, *Freddy's Book* (1980), was not well received, partly a result of backlash against Gardner's low view of typical academics. As longer, more considered assessments of *Mickelsson's Ghosts* began to appear, however, it became clear that the novel was a substantial achievement, and indeed it may prove to be one of Gardner's most enduring works.

It is clear that Gardner increasingly regarded himself as a maverick. He makes Mickelsson an ethics teacher at a time when condescending tolerance is all that he can expect from his colleagues. Yet anyone familiar with

Gardner's fiction, from *Grendel* (1971) to this last work, knows how isolated his characters usually are, and it would be facile to conclude that Mickelsson is simply Gardner self-dramatized. The novel faces problems that gripped the novelist in all of his work, problems about the tragic structure of the world and human life. Also, as in his other fiction, Gardner asserts wonder in *Mickelsson's Ghosts*, establishing mystery as the air his character breathes, whether sitting among real ghosts or chatting with the old farmer who lives up the hill.

Gardner was never quite at home with the novel. The man generating Mickelsson's world is like the artificer of fairy tales who sees and names the world anew after Adam's fall from intimacy of communication. The fairy-tale mind calls a mountain "ogre," a woman "witch," and a man "monster." Gardner revitalizes ordinary things in that way, hungry for the evidences of fantasy in ordinary things. Characters who are ostensibly real estate agents, sheriffs, and college professors take on a murky and unstable identity, prone as they are to superstition and dread, and not altogether unconnected with centuries-old ancestors who lived in unlighted huts in forests and believed in all sorts of pantheistic forces. Gardner, alive to the poison that comes from perceiving the world as a flat spot waiting for a developer, wanted in *Mickelsson's Ghosts* to exorcise commonness with the eye of an old-fashioned boy full of fear as an old-fashioned principal approaches along the corridor—not wholly guiltless, yet all too aware of a malicious presence it is necessary to resist.

Gardner succeeded in writing a book which will tell readers in the next century more about our time than most books from the period. Reading it, if such an act is not then dispensed with, they will escape into the primal emotions and enjoy the rich particularity of the world as filtered through the perceptions of "crazy" Professor Mickelsson.

Sources for Further Study
Cowart, David. *Arches and Lights: The Fiction of John Gardner*, 1983.
Morris, Gregory L. *A World of Order and Light: The Fiction of John Gardner*, 1984.

Bruce Wiebe

THE MIDDLE OF THE JOURNEY

Author: Lionel Trilling (1905-1975)
Type of plot: Political
Time of plot: The 1930's
Locale: Connecticut
First published: 1947

> *Principal characters:*
> JOHN LASKELL, the novel's narrator and protagonist, an urban
> affairs expert with leftist leanings
> GIFFORD MAXIM, a lapsed Communist around whom the
> other characters gather to debate their political
> convictions
> ARTHUR CROOM, a liberal economics professor and a friend of
> Laskell and Maxim
> NANCY CROOM, Arthur's wife, who is outraged by Maxim's
> repudiation of the Communist Party
> DUCK CALDWELL, the handyman for the Crooms and the
> focus of their admiration of the working class
> EMILY CALDWELL, Duck's wife, who has a brief affair with
> Laskell

The Novel

John Laskell is thirty-three and is recovering from a serious illness that almost cost him his life. He is also mourning the recent death of his fiancée. In many ways, he is facing a mid-life crisis. At one stage of his sickness, he longs for death, spending his time admiring the perfection of a flower that will soon fade out of existence. The Crooms have invited him to their summer home in the hope of speeding his return to good health.

On the train taking Laskell to visit the Crooms is Gifford Maxim, who has gone through his own time of trial. He has lived underground as a Communist agent and then sought sanctuary with friends, whom he asks to help protect him from the Party in his transition to the role of prominent anti-Communist. The Crooms, particularly Nancy, are shocked by Maxim's turnabout, and it becomes Laskell's task to mediate between the apostate and his friends, who are "fellow travelers" who still believe in the Party.

Maxim pays a disturbing visit to the Crooms with Kermit Simpson, the publisher of a "rather sad liberal monthly," *The New Era*. With Laskell's help, Maxim has managed to get a job writing for Simpson and to have his name put on the masthead of the journal—an important achievement for a man who believes that his safety depends upon the establishment of a public identity. The Crooms dismiss Maxim's fears as paranoia, even though they have no firsthand knowledge of the Party's secret subversive activities. As Lionel Trilling points out in the 1975 introduction to his novel, in the 1930's it was "as if such a thing [espionage] hadn't yet been invented."

What especially disturbs the Crooms about Maxim is that in opposition to the Party he has become a Christian. As a result, he attacks not simply their faith in the Party, but also in all socialist and secularist ideology. Maxim has become a theist who has now put his whole faith in God, not in man. The utopian Crooms, who idealize the working class and believe in a perfectible future, cannot abide their comrade's about-face.

Because they are intellectuals who respond to life with a veneer of abstractions, the Crooms retreat from Maxim's revelations that changing history is a dangerous, even deadly business. Similarly, they reject Laskell's efforts to explain how he almost died, how he nearly accepted the fact of his demise. To them, his thinking—like Maxim's—is reactionary. They must be jolted into reassessing their view of Duck Caldwell, whom they have virtually idolized as an example of the rugged, direct working man, by a melodramatic twist of the plot—Duck's striking and killing his frail child. In this novel of ideas, action without thought is shown to be as disastrous as thought without action.

The Characters

As many critics have noted, and as Lionel Trilling implied in his 1975 introduction to the novel, Gifford Maxim is the dominant character, even though he is neither the narrator nor the ostensible protagonist. Of all the characters, he seems most real when he speaks; he has a sharply critical mind which has been tested in action. He has been both idealist and realist; the Party's ideologue and one of its most effective spies. He is at home with both Marxist and Christian terms and can cogently state the opposing principles of each. Consequently, he carries much more authority than the other, far less experienced characters.

As Lionel Trilling revealed in 1975, Maxim was based on an acquaintance, the famous Whittaker Chambers, who testified against Alger Hiss, an official in the United States State Department who was convicted of espionage in 1950, three years after the appearance of *The Middle of the Journey*. There is no question that Chambers made a vivid impression on Trilling when they were both students at Columbia University and when, years later, Chambers was reported to have gone underground for the Party. Subsequent readings of the novel, including Trilling's own in 1975, invariably concentrate on a compelling character who was followed by his twin in a real-life story of conflicting loyalties, for Chambers asserted that he and Hiss had been close friends and supporters of the Party.

The Crooms bear some resemblance to Alger Hiss and his wife, although Trilling did not know the Hisses and could not have modeled the Crooms after them. Rather, the fictional husband and wife are meant to represent many liberals of the 1930's who were not Party members, but who were "fellow travelers," that is, clearly in the orbit of Communist ideological concerns and reluctant to recognize the brutality of Stalinism.

Nancy Croom, for example, is vehement in her refusal to countenance criticism of the Party. Laskell "had seen in Nancy a passion of the mind and will so pure that, as it swept through her, she could not believe that anything that opposed it required consideration." Her husband Arthur's "dedication was not so absolute," yet Laskell notices that he needs his wife's "absolute intransigence." It excites him even as he moderates and mocks it, for he needs "her extravagance and ardor as support to his own cooler idealism." Nancy saves Arthur from having to make extreme affirmations of his beliefs; he then can seem the more reasonable of the two, although in effect his position parallels hers.

Maxim goads all of these characters, especially Laskell, who is the most vulnerable, about their complacent identification of the Party with progress. Laskell and Croom, urbanologist and economist, seek ways of planning a better world; Maxim taunts them with his awareness that their utopian socialism has turned into a tyranny. Their faith in his underground work, he suggests, has been a way of cultivating their innocence about the inevitable corruption of man-made ideas in the real world. Laskell is honest enough to admit hating Maxim for pointing out how he "had been cherishing his innocence." This is why Emily Caldwell is so appealing to Laskell. She is a woman without an ideology, a woman he can love without a commitment, a woman with whom he can sin—with whom he can even be secure in his guilt, as Maxim also points out to him.

Duck Caldwell is also without an ideology, without a rationalization for the way he lives. Yet in him, lack of faith or principles turns into an aggressive undermining of civilized order. He is a drunkard, an unreliable worker, and a lout who is resentful of the education that his daughter receives. He functions, indeed, as a total negation of all that the Crooms stand for. He is a kind of evil principle which they are not prepared to acknowledge.

Themes and Meanings

Joseph Blotner observes that *The Middle of the Journey* is about varying degrees of engagement and disillusionment with the world. On both the personal and political level, characters assume stances that either impede or facilitate their participation in human affairs. At one extreme, Duck Caldwell lives for himself; his individuality is built upon excluding the rights of others. At the other extreme, Gifford Maxim cannot survive unless he puts his trust in certain friends and in abiding religious principles. He is disillusioned because he has put so much faith in the Party, but he is remarkable for his passion in arguing for his friends' assistance.

In between Caldwell and Maxim, the Crooms waver. On the one hand, they are under the illusion that Maxim has been successfully working for world liberation—for the working class they mistakenly presume Caldwell exemplifies. In a sense, the Crooms have left Maxim and Caldwell—and other types like them—to do the work of the world for them. As a result, they angrily reject Maxim's home truths and shrink from fully confronting Caldwell's violence, since accepting the brutality of either man would shatter their worldview.

Laskell is a man whose view of himself and of the world has already been shattered before Maxim first confides to him his loss of faith. Both men, indeed, go through a kind of rebirth in the novel, a painful rebuilding of their lives on new bases that rest upon a deep awareness of past failures. Laskell knows that he never fully committed himself to his dead fiancée; Maxim realizes that he committed himself all too securely to an ideology. Each man is truly in "the middle of the journey," in a middle age that calls for a reassessment of all that he has been and hopes to become.

Critical Context

Since its reissue in 1975, *The Middle of the Journey*, has steadily gathered a significant new audience. In the past ten years, the novel has sold more than fifty thousand copies, a total that far surpasses the very modest sales of the first edition. The recent critical reception has also been more favorable, for in 1947, reviews were mixed, and they disheartened the author, who has been far better known for his literary criticism, particularly *The Liberal Imagination* (1950).

The Middle of the Journey has been criticized for being too much a novel of ideas and too schematic in its presentation of characters. Robert Warshow, who is often quoted as the authority for this kind of critique, praises the eloquence of Trilling's writing but complains that the author argues too much with his characters and presents too much of a case against them. Similarly, Joseph Blotner has called the novel "static" and "prolix," meaning that discussions of ideology dominate characters that never quite come to life, except for Maxim, who has been a man of ideology.

These objections, however, obscure the genuine interest that Trilling shows in his narrator, John Laskell. The theme of death, of how it can enter a life and radically change it, is done well and is convincingly tied to the political discussions. In fact, it is the author's goal to demonstrate that the Crooms' political debates are arid precisely because these well-meaning liberals do not incorporate a holistic understanding of life into the ideology that they espouse. They are narrow-minded, in other words, not simply because their politics are simplistic but also because their understanding of human beings is so limited. They lack, finally, what Trilling calls in his criticism the "liberal imagination." which follows and adapts to the modulation of ideas and personalities as they are conceived in the great novels of this prominent American critic's exemplars: Henry James (1843-1916) and E. M. Forster (1879-1970).

Sources for Further Study
Blotner, Joseph. *The Modern American Political Novel 1900-1960*, 1966.
Chace, William M. *Lionel Trilling: Criticism and Politics*, 1980.
French, Philip. *Three Honest Men: A Critical Mosaic*, 1980.
Shoben, Edward Joseph, Jr. *Lionel Trilling: Mind and Character*, 1981.
Warshow, Robert. *The Immediate Experience*, 1962.

Carl E. Rollyson, Jr.

THE MISSOLONGHI MANUSCRIPT

Author: Frederic Prokosch (1908-   )
Type of plot: Biographical
Time of plot: 1824, with flashbacks focusing on the period from 1809 to 1824
Locale: Greece, England, Switzerland, and Italy
First published: 1968

> *Principal characters:*
> GEORGE GORDON, LORD BYRON, the poet
> PERCY BYSSHE SHELLEY, the poet
> TERESA GUICCIOLI, Byron's mistress

The Novel

   The Missolonghi Manuscript is a novel about George Gordon, Lord By-ron, based on the convenient device of recently discovered (but imaginary) diaries written by the poet. The narrative is prefaced by a fictitious meeting at a party in Italy of a T. H. Applebee from Bryn Mawr College with the American-born Marchesa del Rosso. Applebee learns from the marchesa that she has a manuscript of three notebooks written by Byron in Missolonghi, Greece, between January, 1824, and his death there three months later. Two years pass, and the marchesa dies, but Applebee is allowed to copy the notebooks, learning in so doing that the marchesa had obtained the manuscript from a Colonel Eppingham, who had himself pur-chased it in Greece from a "decomposing personage," the Baron von Haug-witz. None of these ruses is of further significance.

   The three notebooks tell two parallel stories: Each day opens with a short entry on current affairs in Missolonghi (the first note is for 25 January 1824) but switches quickly to the main interest, Byron's autobiographical musings, given in chronological order. So the story soon settles down to an imaginative reconstruction of many of the major relationships of Byron's life: with Lady Caroline Lamb, Annabella Milbanke, and Teresa Guiccioli; and with literary friends (Percy Bysshe Shelley and Leigh Hunt) and social cronies (John Cam Hobhouse and Edward John Trelawny). Interludes of sexual coupling are frequent, their descriptions frank, their practices varied. By the end of the third notebook the main autobiographical account has caught up with the thinner Missolonghi diary narrative.

   The first notebook goes through February 17. The entries on Missolonghi detail the squalor and hopelessness of the place ("Missolonghi is a quag-mire"). Prokosch's Byron explains that he came to Greece in search of "self-renewal and self-forgetfulness" and hoping to shed "the serpent-skin of my selfish, brutal past." On February 2, Byron reports feeling ill, and his discomfort and malaise continue. Of his companions at Missolonghi, Byron is closest to Loukas, the boy who tends him. His relationship with Prince Mavrocordato, the Greek nationalist leader, is not intimate, but they share banter and ouzo, and in Prokosch's version they understand each other's personal motives. Byron speaks of "wicked, equivocal Mavrocordato."

The longer, autobiographical strand of the first notebook skips quickly over childhood experiences, punctuated with obligatory sexual escapades. The Cambridge scenes flicker with undergraduate salaciousness and speculation. Much of the notebook recounts a long trip that Byron began in 1809 with his close friend Hobhouse. This trip lasts about a year and takes Byron to Spain and Portugal, Albania, Greece, and Turkey. It is highlighted by his swimming the Hellespont and his boast that in Athens he slept with ninety-three women. Back in England he meets Madame de Staël, who promptly says of him, *"Qu'il est beau ce jeune poète! Mon Dieu, qu'il est beau."* In Caroline Lamb, Byron finds, temporarily, his match. ("We were egoists and flirts, both of us.") Their passion absorbs them too much, however, and the affair ends with her calling him a "club-footed satyr" and him slapping her face.

The second notebook runs from February 18 through March 26. Many of the same themes continue: lubricious chitchat with Mavrocordato, erotic by-play with Loukas, and curses cast on foul Missolonghi. Hallucinations begin to bother Byron in February, self-hatred surges in him, and on March 9 he wonders if he has malaria. He devotes several entries to brief comments on poetry: William Wordsworth was wrong in calling poetry emotion recollected in tranquillity; "The real deformity in the poet's heart is his life in an ugly world"; John Keats's "mellifluous nightingales" are thin stuff for poetry.

The autobiographical recollections of the second notebook are rich in characters and incidents, detailing Byron's loves and travels. He reveals a genuine love for his half sister, Augusta, but his marriage to Annabella Milbanke is a travesty, and his treatment of her is brutal. He soon leaves for the Continent and spends time in Geneva with Shelley and Madame de Staël. His affair with Claire Clairmont produces a daughter, Allegra, about whom he is later edgy and evasive. He eventually leaves for Italy with Hobhouse (time is greatly telescoped in this section), where he indulges himself in a series of coarse erotic liaisons. After meeting the Countess Teresa Guiccioli, he settles down with her and her elderly husband in their home in Ravenna, playing a role that was commonly accepted at that time in Italy. He spends more time with Shelley, eventually taking Teresa to Pisa, where they are part of the circle around Shelley.

The third notebook (March 27-April 18) in the Missolonghi sequences traces the decline of the moribund Byron, badly ill, dejected ("How can I ever describe it, this all-engulfing loneliness?"), and hallucinating. The main autobiographical narrative takes him up to the time of his arrival in

Missolonghi, its ending neatly coinciding with his last reflections before dying. The main element of interest is the death of Shelley and the morbid ritual enacted by the scabrous Trelawny in exhuming and cremating the poet's remains. The arrival of Leigh Hunt with his wife and six children as Byron's houseguests provides one of the more entertaining interludes.

The Characters

Prokosch's Byron is a driven man, one who confides that "I kept searching for a 'deeper purpose,' a 'spiritual call,' a 'dedication.' " For a while he hopes to find fulfillment in his dedication to the cause of the Italian revolutionaries in their struggle against Austria. Yet he quickly understands that he is destined to a fruitless search for peace and that he is an exile whose "political ardour had a hollow ring to it." His aspirations in his mission to Greece are futile right from the beginning, as he seems aware; the final mustering of energies expended in a spiritual void.

Toward the last he writes ruefully of the end of the "beautiful Byron," a death that leaves only the "perverse and destructive and tortured Byron." He describes himself as a "wayward" animal, both "childishly happy and childishly gloomy, childishly affectionate and childishly venomous." In short, his motives are "transparent" because he is simply "a man who follows his instincts." He returns to this self-analysis several days later, cataloging his qualities and explaining, "Every virtue contains its vice and every vice its own virtue." He takes comfort in his conclusion that ultimately the great virtue is "animal integrity," a complete acceptance and fulfillment of one's animal self. He accepts Shelley's judgment of him as "a shame-faced Manichean." Immediately before he goes to Greece, however, he confides that he has no "definite or identifiable character" and that he is drawn to Greece "to discover the *other* creature, if there really is another, who is hiding within me."

Prokosch develops Byron's sensual life in great detail. Byron's youthful feeling for Lord Clare is called up in many of his reveries on the past, and the tenderness he feels for the boy Loukas in Missolonghi is attributed to his partial identification of the youth with Clare. His feelings for Augusta are muffled in the account but obviously intense. His marriage to Annabella appears inexplicable, a perverse impulse that turns immediately into coarseness and brutality, and the episode with Claire Clairmont soon becomes a drain on his spirit. In Teresa Guiccioli, however, Byron apparently encounters an eroticism and a sensibility that calm him, at least for a while, and their relationship depicts a genuine companionship. The other sexual adventures recounted are mere bouts of carnality. In his sex life as in his wanderings, Prokosch's Byron is driven by impulse and haunted by urgency.

The Shelley whom Prokosch presents through Byron's eyes is humorless and given to "little bursts of a warbling ecstasy." Byron views him "with an air of smirking tolerance," but although he laughs at Shelley's "absurdity," he is moved by his "sudden tenderness" and senses in him the "presence of purity."

It is through Shelley that Byron meets Edward John Trelawny, a satyr whose "virile, piratical way" evokes in Byron a fear of something "ominous and oppressive" and an uneasiness about Trelawny's "dark intention, a rather sinister intimacy." Trelawny disconcerts Byron, who comes both to love him and to hate him, and Byron senses in him his own weaknesses: "my self-display and my *passé* dandyism, my moodiness, my braggadocio." For Teresa, Trelawny is a menacing figure with the evil eye.

Leigh Hunt emerges as an incompetent, ludicrous, "rather mischievous sort of man" with repulsive personal habits. He appears suddenly at Byron's Casa Lafranchi in Pisa, and "in a moment of insanity" Byron invites him and his family to stay there as his guests. Byron enjoys Hunt and draws him out in disparagement of other poets. When Byron reproaches Hunt for not bathing, Hunt retorts quickly: "You have scolded me for the infrequency of my baths. Are your callousness and promiscuity to be excused on the grounds of poetry?"

Themes and Meanings

Prokosch's Byron provides no new understanding of the poet, but *The Missolonghi Manuscript* offers both a good reading experience and a reliable sketch of many of the important events in Byron's short but crowded life. Of especial interest to many readers will be the re-creation of Byron's relationship with Shelley and his circle, a part of the story that Prokosch depicts convincingly. Although the asides about Wordsworth, Shelley, and other poets are always Prokosch's interpretations of Byron's views, they are well observed and consistent with what is known of the real Byron's judgments. Prokosch is unflinching in his depiction of Byron's diverse sexual impulses, but his interpretation has the support of scholarship and is always credible. Even though the important historical events in which Byron participated remain mere backdrops in the novel, Missolonghi and its foul climate are put to good literary use: They hover in the background as an appropriate pathetic fallacy complementing Byron's moroseness. Many of the less well-known people in Byron's life, such as Mary Chaworth, are introduced without much comment, but their significance to Byron is always clear, and any biography of the poet will provide whatever background is needed on them.

Critical Context

The Missolonghi Manuscript is clearly a novel by Frederic Prokosch, exhibiting his usual skill at re-creating the atmosphere of exotic settings, with the entire scenario dressed up in silken language. Critics have always justly praised Prokosch's descriptive powers, for he is extremely successful in evoking unity of tone, mood, and atmosphere: lush, erotic, and at times slightly sinister. The narrative flow is smooth and swift, and the device of parallel entries in the Missolonghi notebooks works well enough. The elaborate apparatus of frame letters at the outset is perhaps unnecessary to his main purpose, but it is a well-accepted convention. As a source of scholarly information about Byron, *The Missolonghi Manuscript* should probably be read with caution since it is, after all, fiction, but Prokosch has certainly come close enough to capturing the historical Byron to guarantee the honesty of the book's considerable appeal as a novel.

Sources for Further Study
"Frederic Prokosch," in *Contemporary Authors*, LXXIII-LXXVI (1978).
Marchand, Leslie. *Byron: A Portrait*, 1970.
Matthews, G. M. "Byronorama," in *The New York Review of Books*. XV (May 23, 1968), p. 23.

Frank Day

MR. SAMMLER'S PLANET

Author: Saul Bellow (1915-   )
Type of plot: Comic realism
Time of plot: The late 1960's, during the period of the first manned moon missions
Locale: New York City
First published: 1970

> *Principal characters:*
> ARTUR SAMMLER, the septuagenarian protagonist, an energetic intellectual
> SHULA SAMMLER, his idiosyncratic, forty-year-old daughter
> MARGOTTE ARKIN, his dead wife's niece, a middle-aged, likable widow
> DR. ELYA GRUNER, his elderly nephew, a successful, retired surgeon who supports Sammler
> ANGELA GRUNER, Elya Gruner's very attractive and sensual daughter
> WALLACE GRUNER, Elya Gruner's intellectually gifted, emotionally immature, adult son
> DR. GOVINDA LAL, an East Indian visiting the United States, author of *The Future of the Moon*

The Novel

All the action of the three days covered in this novel, winner of the 1971 National Book Award for Fiction, is viewed from the mind of Artur Sammler, the protagonist. His active intellect provides a constant comment on life in the United States in New York City during the turbulent 1960's. It is a time when man is first reaching out to the moon, and Sammler, who is a philosopher at heart, is attempting to evaluate personally man's condition during this significant moment.

Sammler's past is a key element in the novel, for it allows him a point of reference, an objectivity, in viewing present American society. A Polish Jew, he feels severed from his life before the Holocaust, when, as an Anglophile living in England during the 1930's, he was involved in the intellectual concerns of the famed Bloomsbury group. Shortly before World War II, he and his wife returned to Poland at her insistence in an attempt to sell his father-in-law's optical factory, but they were detained by the Gestapo and shot with other Jews in a mass execution.

Wounded, one eye destroyed by a blow from a gun butt before the shooting, Sammler dug his way out of the shallow mass grave and endured the events which followed, in which he hid from the Germans in a cemetery and was involved as a partisan fighting against them. Although he has literally returned from the grave, emotionally Sammler believes that he has not "survived" the Holocaust, for the concerns of his past life—his wife, his establishment in Bloomsbury, his idealistic hopes for creating a better society— are no longer factors in his present life; rather, he believes that he has "lasted," and he recognizes that this situation is not of his own doing, but is the result of blind chance. He has recovered physically from his experiences, but emotionally he remains alienated from the life of the larger community.

In the opening pages of the novel, Sammler sees a black pickpocket operating on a city bus and reports him to the police. Sammler, in turn, has been seen by the pickpocket, who follows him and threatens him. This event plunges Sammler into an agitated state in which he views life around him with a heightened awareness which continues throughout the novel's subsequent events.

These events are structured around the impending death of Elya Gruner, who is suffering from a brain aneurysm. Sammler feels a great obligation to Elya for his past support of Sammler and his daughter Shula—Elya brought them to the United States from a displaced person's camp after the war. Sammler wishes to spend the few days which are left to Elya beside him in the hospital, where he can comfort Elya and serve as the "family representative," a role which Elya needs him to fill. This central structuring device allows Bellow to present several other events from Sammler's life—his time in Bloomsbury in the 1930's, his experience of the Holocaust, his trip to Israel during the 1967 Six Day War—in the form of flashbacks.

Sammler's deathbed mission is complicated by the actions of his daughter: Shula takes *The Future of the Moon*, a manuscript by Dr. Govinda Lal, a distinguished Hindu who is visiting the United States, without his permission. The surface reason for Shula's taking the manuscript is to provide Sammler with current information so that he will be prompted to write a memoir of H. G. Wells, whom Sammler knew while living in Bloomsbury, and who is known for his classic *Voyage to the Moon*. The deeper reason for Shula's actions is to attract the attention of the distinguished intellectual, Dr. Lal. The subsequent events force Sammler into a meeting with Dr. Lal, and the two men, who immediately like each other, exchange ideas in an extended intellectual conversation which provides for Sammler an opportunity to articulate his thoughts on the nature of man and society. The result of this meeting is that during Elya's final attack, Sammler is not able to be where he feels he belongs, at Elya's bedside.

The climax of the novel comes in the final pages, when Sammler forces his way down into the postmortem room in the hospital and prays over Elya's body; in his prayer presenting Elya to God, Sammler sums up Elya's life—and symbolically the life of every man—when he declares that Elya did "meet the terms of his contract. The terms which in his inmost heart, each man knows." Sammler, in praying for this man, becomes himself completely involved in the larger spiritual concerns of life, and thus, in this act, he confronts death in a metaphysical manner which symbolically reconciles him with life.

The Characters

Artur Sammler is one of the most complex, compelling characters in modern American fiction. He is a cranky, elderly man who recognizes the limitations of his aristocratic, Old World background. His sympathies are toward traditional order and structure in society, and the world with which he is confronted—New York City in the late 1960's—is a society in which order and structure seem to be crumbling. Yet Sammler, who has experienced the Holocaust, has seen the worst, and his criticisms of contemporary American society are tempered with this wider knowledge. If Sammler is not sympathetic to the life-styles of many of the people who surround him, he remains a compassionate man to whom people are drawn because of his generally nonjudgmental attitude toward them. Bellow's success as a novelist largely rests on his ability, by his use of detail, to create characters of complexity, characters who seem like flesh-and-blood people and yet who represent the larger concerns of American society; in Sammler, Bellow has created one of his most successful characters: a man of deep feeling who is capable of the kind of penetrating, abstract thought which enables him to evaluate man's present condition.

Angela Gruner, a powerfully drawn character of great energy, serves as an antithesis to Sammler's Old World views. She is a sensuous, voluptuous woman of independent means (provided by her father, Dr. Gruner). She seeks out Sammler as a confidant, telling him the details of her sexual life; her character functions as a representative of the sexually active generation of the 1960's.

Another well-drawn female character is Shula, Sammler's daughter, who engages Sammler's deepest compassion. Her habits reflect her past, when she was hidden by Catholic nuns during the Holocaust. her experiences have made her idiosyncratic, a collector of odds and ends, a woman with whom Sammler cannot live. She is a touching figure, and her attempts to provoke Dr. Lal's sexual interest are sadly comic; she is in the mold of similar comic characters in other Bellow novels, such as Tommy Wilhelm in *Seize the Day* (1956). Sammler is protective of her; although she is enterprising and intelligent, she believes that she cannot compete with a woman such as Margotte Arkin for the attentions of Dr. Lal. Margotte, Sammler's dead wife's niece, is a likable, middle-aged widow with whom Sammler lives. She is a caring person, and although she does not have Sammler's great intellectual abilities, she is concerned with the issues of the day. Although Sammler is occasionally bored with Margotte's attempts at intellectual discussion, he respects her as a woman, and by the end of the novel, she has captured Dr. Lal's attention.

The character whom Sammler most respects is Elya Gruner. Elya is in many ways a limited man—he has not reared his children to his satisfaction, his marriage was not passionate—and yet he has "done his duty" by society and by others; he has done "what was required of him." In Elya, Bellow has created a character representative of the old values of family and duty; ironically, Elya's daughter Angela and his son Wallace do not carry on his values. Wallace, his intellectually gifted son, is filled with an aimless energy which he cannot focus; in his inability to apply himself to any extended work, he is representative of many of the country's youth during the 1960's: a generation with great resources but no real direction.

Bellow's minor characters in this, as in his other novels, are both vivid and functional to the novel's overall concerns. Eisen, Sammler's former son-in-law, an Israeli artist, is one of the most powerful minor characters in all of Bellow's work. In his beating of the black pickpocket, Eisen represents the ambiguous nature of violence in the modern world: It seems necessary for man's protection, yet it renders man less than human.

Themes and Meanings

The critic Arthur Krystal has declared that "every genuine novel implicitly argues its relation to the world." In *Mr. Sammler's Planet*, that relation is more explicit than in many novels, for although Bellow cannot be unambiguously identified with his protagonist, it is clear that the argument of the novel is Bellow's own, and the reader can be forgiven for frequently forgetting that it is Sammler who is speaking, and not Bellow himself. The novel's argument centers on two of Bellow's principal themes: the concept of the individual in its historical context, and the search for spiritual and cultural values in a society which emphasizes the individual personality at the expense of social order. Through the events of this novel, and Sammler's reflection on those events, Bellow attempts to assess the cost of this present emphasis on individuality—a movement which, as Sammler notes, began with the Romantics—on the life of contemporary man.

These themes are clearly ambitious, and Bellow's reputation as an outstanding novelist rests on his ability to explore such complex issues. The novel form is primarily concerned with man's experience and the essay form with man's ideas, but, like the great Russian novelists whom he admires, Bellow combines the two forms to enable his characters not only to experience ideas, but also to generate and test ideas from personal experience. It is the sensibilities of the character of Sammler, whose ideas and vision were formed by his experiences, which enable Bellow to explore the confusion of the present world by placing traditional values against the structure—and lack of structure—of contemporary American life.

Critical Context

In addition to winning the National Book Award for Fiction in 1971, *Mr. Sammler's Planet* contributed to the decision to award Bellow the Nobel Prize for Literature in 1976. This novel, which was first published in slightly different form in *The Atlantic* (November and December, 1969), is noted for its philosophic concerns, and although some critics have charged that Bellow becomes too engaged in these issues—that the characters' extended intellectual dialogues and Sammler's preoccupations with metaphysical thought are artistic flaws—it is considered one of Bellow's best. Bellow is known for characters who think, who are passionately involved in the intellectual tradition, and in Sammler, Bellow has created his most intellectually sophisticated protagonist.

Most critics view the novel as a turning point for Bellow toward a more pessimistic vision, with the turbulent environment of the late 1960's as a factor in the novel's tone; yet Bellow's basic stance against modern nihilism is merely further developed in this novel. Bellow is a "moral novelist," in John Gardner's definition of the term, and in *Mr. Sammler's Planet* Bellow explores man as a moral being, a creature with a soul, who is concerned with the implications of his behavior on his fellow man. Man, in Bellow's world, is ultimately a mystery; yet in his behavior, as Sammler illustrates, he is capable of acts which affirm his humanity.

Sources for Further Study

Braham, Jeanne. *A Sort of Columbus: The American Voyages of Saul Bellow's Fiction*, 1984.

Cohen, Sarah. *Saul Bellow's Enigmatic Laughter*, 1974.

Dutton, Robert R. *Saul Bellow*, 1982.

Fuchs, Daniel. *Saul Bellow: Vision and Revision*, 1984.

Rodrigues, Eusebio L. *Quest for the Human: An Exploration of Saul Bellow's Fiction*, 1981.

Ronald L. Johnson

MRS. BRIDGE

Author: Evan S. Connell, Jr. (1924-   )
Type of plot: Satiric realism
Time of plot: From the early 1920's to the early 1940's, chiefly during the last ten years of that period
Locale: Kansas City, Missouri; Southampton, England; Paris; Monte Carlo; and Rome
First published: 1959

> *Principal characters:*
> INDIA BRIDGE, the protagonist, an upper-middle-class Kansas City housewife
> WALTER BRIDGE, her husband, a successful lawyer
> RUTH BRIDGE, their eldest child, eventually an assistant editor on a New York fashion magazine
> CAROLYN BRIDGE DAVIS, their second child, an avid golfer and wife of Parallel, Kansas, dry-goods salesman Gil Davis
> DOUGLAS BRIDGE, their third child, who eventually enlists in the army and takes basic training in Arizona
> GRACE BARRON, another Kansas City housewife and Mrs. Bridge's alter ego, an eventual suicide
> MABEL ONG, the quintessential Kansas City clubwoman
> DR. FOSTER. Mrs. Bridge's minister
> HARRIET, her black housekeeper
> ALICE JONES, a black child, at one time Carolyn's most frequent Saturday playmate
> PAQUITA DE LAS TORRES, the girl from the wrong part of Kansas City to whom Doug, as an adolescent, is attracted
> JAY DUCHESNE, a Kansas City boyfriend of Carolyn

The Novel

The central focus of Evan Connell's *Mrs. Bridge* is the protagonist's uncertainty about her own identity and about the meaning and purpose of her life. The first sentences of the book, linked to the epigraph from Walt Whitman, establish this emphasis: "Her first name was India—she was never able to get used to it. It seemed to her that her parents must have been thinking of someone else when they named her." In her own eyes, and in those of the narrator of Connell's novel, from the start of the book she is "Mrs." Bridge, wife of the successful lawyer Walter Bridge, mother of his three children—Ruth, Carolyn, and Douglas Bridge—and a typical female member of her upper-middle-class circle in Kansas City, Missouri. Depending for her identity upon the stability of the social milieu in which she lives, Mrs. Bridge, as her way of life and the values of her class come under fire in the two decades before World War II, experiences boredom, a sense of purposelessness, and eventually even a vaguely terrifying sense of isolation.

Covering a period from the early 1920's to the early 1940's, with an emphasis on the last ten years of this period, *Mrs. Bridge* presents the action as a series of 117 episodes from the life of the title character and not as a unified, symmetrical plot. Connell's introduction of Mrs. Bridge compresses her first thirty-five years of life into the three pages of the first two episodes, and in it he establishes both her utter conventionality and her disillusionment with her life. Venturing to express to her young husband her own desire for sex, she is ignored: "This was the night Mrs. Bridge concluded that while marriage might be an equitable affair, love itself was not." As a young mother, she is frustrated in her expectation that her children, like her, should go through life with an unimpaired set of conventional values. She is shocked when Ruth, as a very small child, strips off her bathing suit and parades around the neighborhood swimming pool. She is annoyed when Doug insists on using the guest towels in the bathroom, towels which her guests are sufficiently well-bred not to use; she is antagonistic when Carolyn chooses Alice Jones, the daughter of the black gardener working next door, as a Saturday morning playmate. In episode after episode, Mrs. Bridge confronts evidence of the inadequacy of conventional responses to life. Her friend Grace Barron, similarly restless and dissatisfied, exhibits signs of depression and by the end of the novel commits suicide. Mabel Ong, the mannish Kansas City clubwoman, decides to seek help from a therapist. Dr. Foster, Mrs. Bridge's minister, becomes hysterical when trapped in a crowded elevator and pushes and claws his way out, showing no concern for the safety of anybody except himself.

As they mature, Mrs. Bridge's children make sexual and marital choices which do not meet her approval. Ruth is not attracted to the clean-cut young sons of her mother's friends; the young men who telephone her seem always to have foreign names and to speak in rough, uncultured voices. In high school, Doug is attracted to Paquita de las Torres, whose sister is a burlesque dancer; the girl's "hairy arms and rancid odor were almost too much for Mrs. Bridge to bear." Carolyn enrolls at the University of Kansas in Lawrence but drops out of school to marry Gil Davis, the son of a plumber, and to settle in a Parallel, Kansas, neighborhood into which black families are moving. Mrs. Bridge reflects that, except for her housekeeper Harriet, and the laundress, Beulah Mae, she "had never known any Negroes socially; not that she avoided it, just that there weren't any in the neighborhood, or at the country club, or in the Auxiliary. There just weren't any for her to meet, that was all." The social dynamics of the world are changing, and reluctantly Mrs. Bridge finds herself accepting behavior and attitudes that she once would have rejected.

Her husband, Walter, remains the one constant in her life, but she does not derive much comfort from his rigid orthodoxy. Unlike his wife, he never questions the rightness of his positions; he uses them to keep the world, including Mrs. Bridge, at arm's length. It is characteristic that he alone ignores the danger posed by an approaching tornado and remains at his table at the country club, Mrs. Bridge dutifully beside him, when everybody else in the building has evacuated to the basement. Mr. Bridge is committed to his career and to the aggressive making of money; therefore, he responds to Gil Davis' frontal assault in the office and accepts Carolyn's engagement, and her marriage, to an otherwise unsuitable young man. He substitutes expensive gifts for his own presence in the lives of his wife and children. Mrs. Bridge finds these gifts embarrassing: "She was conscious of people on the street staring at her when, wrapped in ermine and driving the Lincoln, she started off to a party at the country club." Even the trip to Europe which he gives her as a birthday gift, the fulfillment of a promise made when they were engaged, leads Mrs. Bridge to realize that she does not know Walter's real personality. In her attempts to get closer to him, she becomes increasingly conscious of her isolation.

Mrs. Bridge reaches its thematic climax in the final episode, in which, with Mr. Bridge dead and her children out of the house, Connell's protagonist confronts the emptiness of her life. She has had intimations of it before. One night, seated at her dressing table and spreading cold cream on her face before going to bed, Mrs. Bridge realizes that "she was disappearing into white, sweetly scented anonymity." She is tempted to try psychotherapy, as did her friend Mabel Ong, but the memory of Mr. Bridge's views on the subject dissuades her. In the final episode of the novel, she backs her old Lincoln out of the garage, stalls the engine, and finds herself unable to open the doors because of the walls on either side. She blows the horn, taps on the window, and calls out, "but no one answered, unless it was the falling snow." She is absolutely alone, and that is where Connell leaves her.

The Characters

While Mrs. Bridge begins as a stereotype and remains throughout the novel an object of Connell's satire, she emerges as a fully rounded, thoroughly credible character by the end of the book. She is as much the object of Connell's wry compassion as of his eye for the ironic detail. Despite her upper-middle-class perspective, Mrs. Bridge entertains doubts about both her own character and her value system. She makes definite, if futile, attempts to break outside the norms of her Kansas City circle by learning Spanish, taking painting lessons, and working with charities. She wears gloves, however, while distributing used clothing to the poor; in her painting of Leda and the swan, she clothes "Leda in a flowered dressmaker bathing suit" like her own; and she is easily distracted by her husband or children when she works with the set of Spanish records. Nevertheless, Mrs. Bridge possesses the virtue of recognizing that she has "no confidence in her life," and her efforts to find something in which to believe give her dignity. Like her friend and foil Grace Barron, Mrs. Bridge wants to be a person and not simply an automaton reacting unthinkingly to circumstances. She shares this characteristic with her three children, even though she does not recognize the fact.

After Mrs. Bridge herself, Connell focuses attention most sharply on Ruth, Carolyn, and Douglas, whose rebellions against their mother's values point up the bleakness of her situation. Most completely successful in breaking away from the Kansas City norms is Ruth, who ends up in New York as an assistant editor on a fashion magazine. Like her brother and sister, she equates independence with sexual freedom, shocking Mrs. Bridge with stories about a gay male associate and writing a letter to her mother while in bed with a man named Dowdey. When he asks if Mrs. Bridge looks like her, Ruth replies, "She's my sister's mother," a reply that reveals her sense of estrangement. Carolyn's rebellion is tamer, less complete, than Ruth's. She is the daughter Mrs. Bridge prefers because she adapts more easily to life in Kansas City. An avid golfer, Carolyn enrolls in college at the University of Kansas. When she drops out of school, it is to marry Gil Davis and to assume the role of housewife—a role which Mrs. Bridge regards as a woman's natural calling. Times have changed, however, and Carolyn's marriage does not follow the pattern established by her parents; she frequently leaves her husband to come home to Mrs. Bridge.

Douglas' role is made easier by the fact that he is male, for Mrs. Bridge grants him freedom on that account. She attempts to force him to shave the mustache that he grows during army training, but she is not unhappy to have him take control of the household after her husband's death. When Douglas denies the housekeeper's request for a raise, Harriet "stopped calling him by his first name and referred to him as Mr. Bridge, and his mother, hearing this for the first time, began to weep." Returning to camp, he sends his mother a letter in which he assures her that Mr. Bridge, in his own way, loved her. It resembles the letters Mrs. Bridge had received from her husband when he was traveling on business, and in it Douglas shows that he has escaped his mother's control by assuming the traditional masculine role until now occupied by Mr. Bridge.

The other characters in *Mrs. Bridge* are less developed, and they serve chiefly as foils to the protagonist and her children or as objects of Connell's satire. Among the former are Grace Barron and Mabel Ong; like Mrs. Bridge, they are stereotypical upper-class Kansas City matrons. Among the latter are Dr. Foster, the self-centered clergyman; Jay Duchesne, the boyfriend whom Carolyn rejects in favor of Gil Davis; and Paquita de las

Torres, whose sexuality is a parody of the conduct of Mrs. Bridge's daughter Ruth.

Themes and Meanings

The thematic point of the novel emerges in the episode in which Connell's protagonist picks up an unidentified book by Joseph Conrad and reads a passage, underlined by her husband's unambitious uncle Shannon Bridge, about the capacity of some people to live without being aware of life's potentiality. Because of her dissatisfaction with her own life, Mrs. Bridge does not fit this paradigm exactly. She is aware that living may have more to it than the typical Kansas City society matron recognizes, but she never breaks through to that possible meaning.

The sharply detailed, episodic narrative structure of *Mrs. Bridge* focuses attention on the particulars of each situation and on the process of social change at work in the United States which provides Connell with the context in which to explore Mrs. Bridge as a character. Changing American mores, seen in the novel most clearly in the areas of sexual expression and race relations, explain the gap in communication which opens up between Mrs. Bridge and her children. Her inability to change with the times makes Mrs. Bridge an object of satire. It is also a mark of her humanity.

Despite the use of Conrad to establish the thematic point of the novel, art and artists do not provide the answer for which Mrs. Bridge is looking. Neither does religion. Indeed, other than the fact that she ought to be searching, Connell provides few clues in the book about what she should be looking for.

Critical Context

Nominated for the National Book Award for Fiction in 1960, *Mrs. Bridge* was both a best-seller and a critical success. The consensus is that this novel and *Mr. Bridge* (1969), a companion volume which covers some but not all of the same material, deserve to be Connell's best-known works because of the skill with which he employs their episodic structures to build fully rounded characters. In their depiction of such ordinary people living fundamentally desperate lives, *Mrs. Bridge* and *Mr. Bridge* have become the standard against which his subsequent fiction is measured.

In other books—*The Patriot* (1960), *The Diary of a Rapist* (1966), *The Connoisseur* (1974), and *Double Honeymoon* (1976)—Connell explores personalities obsessed with goals which distort their perceptions of reality. In this, they are like Walter Bridge, as he appears in both novels, and not like Mrs. Bridge, who has no clear sense of what she wants out of life. This search for significance beyond the ordinary, which characterizes all the male protagonists of Connell's books, sets Mrs. Bridge off from the rest of his central characters. With her, he deals with the thoughts and feelings of a complex human being, and he manages to make her likable as much for her weaknesses as despite them. Because of the skill of this characterization, *Mrs. Bridge* is considered Connell's finest novel.

Sources for Further Study
Bensky, L. M. "Meet Evan Connell, Friend of Mr. and Mrs. Bridge," in *The New York Times Book Review*. LX (April 20, 1969), p. 2.
Blaisdell, Gus. "After Ground Zero: The Writing of Evan S. Connell, Jr.," in *New Mexico Quarterly*. XXXVI (Summer, 1966), pp. 181-207.
Robbins, Michael. "In the Eye of the Tornado," in *College Composition and Communication*. XIII (May, 1962), pp. 9-13.

Robert C. Petersen

MRS. STEVENS HEARS THE MERMAIDS SINGING

Author: May Sarton (1912-   )
Type of plot: Psychological realism
Time of plot: The 1960's
Locale: Cape Ann, Massachusetts
First published: 1965

> *Principal characters:*
> F. HILARY STEVENS, the protagonist, a seventy-year-old poet
> and novelist
> MAR HEMMER, the college-age grandson of a neighbor
> PETER SELVERSEN, an interviewer from a fictitious New York
> publication, *The Review*
> JENNY HARE, a short-story writer who is the companion of
> Selversen on the Stevens interview assignment

The Novel

The action of *Mrs. Stevens Hears the Mermaids Singing* takes place at the country home of F. Hilary Stevens in Cape Ann, Massachusetts, during one full day in May and the following morning. Early in the morning of the day that the interviewers are coming, Mrs. Stevens is hailed by her young friend Mar Hemmer, whose plea for a talk she delays until she is properly awake. When Mar does not reappear, Mrs. Stevens plunges into preparations for the interview, which is set for four in the afternoon. During her activities Mrs. Stevens thinks about Mar, her friends, her lovers, and her long-dead husband. At three o'clock, Sarton takes the reader briefly to the nervous interviewers en route to Cape Ann. Then comes the interview, which makes up half of the book. During the talk, Mrs. Stevens relives far more of her life than she reveals to the interviewers. The epilogue returns to Mar, who appears out of the fog the next morning, and with whom Hilary Stevens shares the understanding of herself and of life which came to her during the interview.

The flashbacks during the interview, combined with Hilary's earlier thoughts, fall into place as a chronological account of her life, the pattern of which she comes to perceive as she talks and as she muses. Rebelling against her controlled, frugal, Beacon Street Boston heritage, at fifteen, Hilary fell in love with her governess: This first "epiphany" produced a novel. Subsequent attachments to men, to the war-haunted veteran Adrian, her husband, to a doctor, and to a French critic all brought her comfort. Only her passions for women, however, to her feminine "Muses," have produced novels or poems. Sometimes these passions were not consummated. When a physical affair resulted, it was destructive, whether it resulted in repugnance, as with the divorcée Willa MacPherson, or in jealousy and rage, as with the scientist whose seemingly objective criticisms of Hilary's works masked the bitter resentment of the noncreative person toward the creative spirit. Perhaps the ideal Muse, suggests Hilary, was the dead French woman in whose house she had lived for a time and whose lingering love produced another epiphany without personal demands.

The climax of the novel comes near the end of the interview, when Hilary has another epiphany, this time involving her self-controlled mother, in whom the creative urge was buried. As a result of that insight, Hilary tells Mar the next morning that she must begin another creative work. She urges him to live life fully, so that he will not deny his creative capacities by cheap escapes into sexuality without feeling.

The Characters

Although Mrs. Stevens is seventeen years older than May Sarton was at the time of the book's publication, and although there are many other differences between the author and her creation (Sarton, for example, has never married), in many ways F. Hilary Stevens is an autobiographical character. In her upper-class, cultured background, in her love of the country, in her disciplined work habits, in her production of both poetry and novels, and in her dependence on inspiration from personal involvement with other women, Hilary Stevens is like May Sarton. The comments made in the fictional interview are very like comments of Sarton to her own interviewers. May Sarton understands the "feminine" aspects of her protagonist—the need to arrange a beautiful bouquet, the compulsion to serve a proper tea to her guests, even her rather maternal response to young Jenny Hare and to troubled young Mar Hemmer.

The relationship between Mrs. Stevens and Mar, however, is extremely complex. Mar is a desperate, angry young man. At Amherst he fell in love with a male chemistry instructor and, after one sexual encounter, was rejected. Unable to continue his college career, he dropped out and came to his grandfather's country place, where he broods, sails, and confides in Mrs. Stevens. In Mar, Mrs. Stevens sees boyish qualities, which remind her of her younger self, but also the masculine aggressiveness of her father. Moreover, she recognizes creative talent, which she tells Mar will never come to fruition unless he gives himself to life.

The interviewer Peter Selversen is well-known for his skill in eliciting worthwhile comments from great writers about writing. Yet although his questions and his responses to the sometimes tentative, sometimes firm statements by F. Hilary Stevens are intelligent and plausible, he is clearly a performer with the masculine quality of detached analysis. Although he can find the right words, Mrs. Stevens protests that the word must be "incarnate." This concept is beyond Selversen, but his companion Jenny Hare, the girlfriend of the associate editor of the publication, who was sent along on the interview as a token woman, understands Hilary Stevens and is inspired by her to be herself, both as a woman and as a writer.

Sarton's use of point of view is largely limited to the perceptions and musings of Mrs. Stevens. It is through her eyes and through dialogue that Mar is seen. Except for a brief glimpse of Peter's thoughts as he approaches the interview, his character is developed dramatically through dialogue. Sarton does, however, reveal Jenny's reactions as the interview progresses. Perhaps as a result, Jenny is a more convincing character than either of the men, who sometimes appear to illustrate abstractions rather than to live in their own right.

Themes and Meanings

In *Mrs. Stevens Hears the Mermaids Singing*, May Sarton is concerned with the woman as artist. In order to explore this issue, she distinguishes what she calls masculine qualities, such as objectivity, detachment, and aggressiveness, from feminine qualities, such as an openness to emotion and a readiness to provide nurture. Although the feminine qualities may produce an impulse to create art, rather than children, the rejection of the maternal impulse is difficult, while the production of art when the artist is exhausted from being a mother is even more difficult.

Sarton is convinced that the Muse is feminine in nature. For a man to be inspired by a woman is conventional. Although a woman may love a man, however, she is inspired by women. Here the lesbian theme becomes important, for the feminine Muse may sometimes be a feminine lover. Yet as Mrs. Stevens comments, the source of inspiration is less important than the work created. The source disappears; the work endures.

A third theme, then, is the necessary progress of the artist from isolation to solitude. After the Muse is gone, for a time the deserted or rejected lover may feel the miseries of isolation. Yet as she begins the process of creation, isolation becomes blessed, self-contented solitude. It is this solitude which Mrs. Stevens welcomes after the interviewers leave and Mar is attended to.

Finally, the revelation which comes to Mrs. Stevens at the end of the day of the interview is an insight into living as well as into writing. The process of that day has been symbolized by the Venetian mirror, somewhat cloudy but both beautiful and usable, which remains from her marriage. Mrs. Stevens must see herself in order to profit from the incidents of her life, however painful. For her will come insight; for her work, inspiration. Instead of striking out at false lovers or carping critics, she must conquer herself. As she points out to Mar, the blasted quarry finally becomes a still and beautiful lake. Thus pain produces not only art but also knowledge, and Hilary urges Mar to accept life, pain and all, rather than to diminish himself, like so many Americans, by refusing to give himself for fear of suffering.

Critical Context

Mrs. Stevens Hears the Mermaids Singing is particularly significant in that it is a book about being an artist by a full-time writer, who augments her income by lecturing but who has rejected the usual academic source of income. Teaching is a position of power, May Sarton says, and power prevents poets from changing their ideas as freely as they like. Certainly Sarton's single-minded commitment has resulted in an impressive output of novels, autobiographies, and volumes of poetry. Although her books are not best-sellers, her poetry is unusually popular in an unpoetic age, and her finely crafted novels have many enthusiastic readers, probably because they combine interesting perceptions with a clarity of presentation which is a relief from the muddle of much modern work.

Because the emphasis is on the creative process, the lesbian theme is not of primary importance in *Mrs. Stevens Hears the Mermaids Singing*. What is important is the discussion of woman as artist, a role which seems to involve sacrifices and denials greater than those of men who serve the Muse. Thus, although Sarton, like James Joyce in *A Portrait of the Artist as a Young Man* (1916), may discuss epiphanies, her female artist will have agonizing struggles of a kind not seen in Joyce.

Although some critics have regarded Sarton's fiction as too limited to the problems and sensibilities of the cultivated, well-to-do upper classes, the steadily increasing interest in her work indicates an appreciation of her craftsmanship and of the validity and depth of her insights. She is not an important female writer; she is an important writer who happens to be a woman.

Sources for Further Study

Cornillon, Susan Koppelman, ed. *Images of Women in Fiction*, 1972.
Hunting, Constance, ed. *May Sarton: Woman and Poet*, 1982.
Sibley, Agnes. *May Sarton*, 1972.
Stewart, Grace. *A New Mythos: The Novel of the Artist as Heroine, 1877-1977*, 1978.

Rosemary M. Canfield

A MONTH OF SUNDAYS

Author: John Updike (1932-   )
Type of plot: Theological romance
Time of plot: The mid-1970's
Locale: Primarily the midwestern United States
First published: 1975

> *Principal characters:*
> THE REVEREND TOM MARSHFIELD, the narrator, banished by
>   his bishop to a rehabilitation home for errant clergymen
> JANE MARSHFIELD, his wife
> ALICIA CRICK, the organist in Tom's church and his mistress
>   for a short time, a divorcée with two small children
> NED BORK, Tom's assistant pastor and his replacement as
>   Alicia's lover
> MRS. HARLOW, a parishioner whose affair with Tom leads to
>   his disgrace
> MS. PRYNNE, the matron of the rehabilitation home, who
>   steps into the novel only on the last two pages but is the
>   object of many of Tom's thoughts

The Novel

A Month of Sundays takes its title from the thirty-one days the Reverend Tom Marshfield is ordered to spend in enforced rest and recreation in a motel retreat somewhere in the Southwestern United States. He is on a strict schedule, enforced by Ms. Prynne, the tight-lipped manager, requiring a full morning of writing to be followed by games in the afternoons and evenings. Thus, *A Month of Sundays* is divided into thirty-one sections, each one representing a morning's prose, and together they make up an autobiographical sketch of Tom Marshfield in prose that swoops and veers.

All of Tom's life has been lived in a context of church work and the ministry. He is the son of a pastor, and he grew up in a parsonage, went to a theological seminary, and married the daughter of his ethics professor. He is not, however, comfortable and at ease in his faith; as a parson, he is, in his own words, "not a hunting one, but a hunted." Tom's organist, Alicia Crick, tells him that he is the "angriest *sane* man" she has ever met—her prompt diagnosis is a bad marriage—and that although he is a married man he still burns. His answer is immediate: "She was right." From that point on—the time is early in Lent—their affair is fated, and they go to bed together for the first time soon after Easter.

Tom and Alicia's sexual rage for each other consumes them. Tom explains, "At last I confronted as in an ecstatic mirror my own sexual de-

mon." The inevitable result is Alicia's wish to have Tom all to herself, his refusal to leave his family and the ministry, and the collapse of their affair with
much bitterness on Alicia's part. During his passion for Alicia, Tom had
tried to encourage as subtly as he could a romantic relationship between his
wife, Jane, and Ned Bork, his young assistant minister: "I did not, even in
my lovelorn madness, imagine that she and Ned would marry; but perhaps
they would clasp long enough to permit me to slip out the door with only
one bulky armload of guilt." Nothing happens between Ned and Jane, however, and Tom sinks to the humiliating behavior of a Peeping Tom who spies
on Ned and Alicia. Tom is distracted from his jealousy by an affair with
Frankie Harlow, but her faith and his anger combine to unman him, and
when the scorned Alicia betrays Tom to Frankie Harlow's husband, he then
receives his orders from the bishop to report to Ms. Prynne's rest home for
delinquent clerics.

Besides this account of his sexual careering, Tom also writes of his sad
relationship with his seventy-seven-year-old father, who broods his life away
in a senile rage at ghosts from his past and does not recognize his son.
Tom's friendships with his fellow sinners under Ms. Prynne's care center on
their golf and poker games, minor strands in the total narrative.

Tom lards his thirty-one-day assignment heavily with theological speculations. His father and Ned are both doctrinal liberals, whereas Tom is a
conservative who takes it hard that "the androgynous homogenizing liberals
of the world are in charge." He tells Ned, "All I know is that when I read
Tillich and Bultmann I'm drowning. Reading Karl Barth gives me air I can
breathe." These preferences translate into a choice of faith over good works
and a suspicion of all versions of Utilitarianism. Tom's intransigence in the
face of liberal social policies appears in his conviction that "most of what we
have is given, not acquired; a gracious acceptance is our task, and a half-
conscious following-out of the veins of the circumambient lode."

As Tom writes on, morning after morning, he begins to be conscious of
Ms. Prynne, hoping to get her attention. He leaves each day's *ad libidum*
offering on the dresser top where she can read it, and he importunes her to
grant him a sign. By the twenty-ninth day he is pleading with her, on the
thirtieth day he is cursing her, and on day thirty-one he describes the revelation that has come to him. It is a passage that must be read carefully in the
context of Tom's two hungers, for women and for faith.

The Characters

The Reverend Tom Marshfield's bold confession of his sexual history
reveals an extraordinary sensibility. He details his infidelities candidly, ex-
plicating his intimacies in vivid pictures and holding back no secrets about
his voyeurism and compulsive masturbation. The story is so complete, the
concern so obsessive, that it is natural to look in Tom's sexual behavior for

some deeper significance. Tom gives the answer himself on the first day of his enforced self scrutinies: "In *my* diagnosis I suffer from nothing less virulent than the human condition, and so would preach it." Many readers will resist this view of things, accusing Tom of rationalizing away his lapses into sin and reading Updike's intention as the deliberate creation of a hypocrite. Yet taking Tom's declaration at face value contributes to a consistent interpretation, for he becomes a searcher after God whose carnal questing is emblematic of his larger spiritual yearning.

Tom explains that being born a minister's son made his life "one long glad feast of inconvenience and unreason." In his father's house, he says, he learned to read and dream on the parlor sofa, itself "stuffed with the substance of the spirit." The furniture gave evidence of a "teleologic bias in things," and it was the furniture, Tom confides, that led him to the ministry. In seminary he read Karl Barth and became a Barthian out of "positive love of Barth's voice." Tom is contemptuous of the "fine-fingered finicking" of "doddering Anglican empiricists," being drawn instead to the excitement of Søren Kierkegaard and Fyodor Dostoevski's Grand Inquisitor. He exclaims, "Where is the leap! the abyss! the black credibility of the *deus absconditus!*" For Tom the existentialist, God is immanent in the physical and the immediate; he wonders if the appellation "sex object" is not the "summit of homage." In all of this, Tom's detractors will find only more bad faith, but Tom's personal creed is very clear to him: "Away with personhood! Mop up spilt religion! Let us have it in its original stony jars or not at all!"

Exercises 6, 13, 20, and 27 are written on Sundays and are thus cast as sermons. Tom chooses texts and themes inspired by his predicament, and he is at his most eloquent as he preaches on adultery and miracles. On the sixth day he takes as his text John 8:11, "Neither do I condemn thee." In Tom's depiction, adultery becomes "our inherent condition," while the adulterer becomes a version of Norman Mailer's White Negro. Comparing marriage to adultery, Tom says, "To the one we bring token reverence, and wooden vows; to the other a vivid reverence bred upon the carnal presence of the forbidden, and vows that rend our hearts as we stammer them." On day thirteen Tom considers the miracles of Christ, especially the question of why man was given those miracles recounted in the Bible but no others. Why not repeal *all* suffering? Tom's is the answer of faith: "Alleviation is not the purpose of His miracles, but demonstration. Their randomness is not their defect, but their essence . . . ."—or put another way, "He came not to revoke the Law and Ground of our condition but to demonstrate a Law and Ground beyond."

The other characters appear only in Tom's rendition of them. Jane has been Tom's "good stately girl" ever since they were both virgins. Unlike Tom, she is a political liberal with a "preposterous view of the church as an adjunct of religious studies and social service." She does not, then, burn with Tom's radical Paulinism. In contrast, Alicia acts much more instinctively than Jane and goes straight for what she wants—in this case, Tom. Their mutual passion is matched by their mutual capacity for jealousy and vindictiveness: He dismisses her as organist, and she squeals on him and Frankie Harlow. Neither of them is soppy with the "milky human kindness" that Tom sneers at in Jane and Ned Bork. To Tom, Ned is an impractical victim of the age of "flower people." Tom taunts Ned about one of the latter's sermons, asking him if he really believes "that an oligarchy of blacks and chicanos and college dropouts would come up with a better system, quote unquote, than the corporation board of Exxon." The passage fairly defines their opposed temperaments.

Themes and Meanings

Updike often develops his novels around an ethical dilemma without offering a solution, and as a result his world appears morally ambiguous. Tom Marshfield's predicament catches him torn between the expectations of the culture that produced him and the inexplicable urges of the self. What must a man do in such a situation? No easy answer is at hand, but the hard answer is that nothing can be done but endure, for that is man's ineluctable condition. Such a position accords exactly with Barth's early conviction that moral questions are unanswerable. Tom does not whine about his condition; his flippancy and punning gloss over the pain that he must feel. The total inaccessibility of God is fundamental to Barth's thought, as it is to Tom Marshfield's and John Updike's. Hence, perhaps, the special pathos of Updike/Marshfield's closing paragraph when Tom wrestles with the meaning of "this human contact, this blank-browed thing we do for one another."

The names Prynne and Chillingworth (Jane's maiden name) point *A Month of Sundays* toward *The Scarlet Letter*—and Nathaniel Hawthorne himself took these names from seventeenth century divines—but probably no very explicit connection should be declared between the two novels. As a literary theme, adultery by definition must spell friction between civilization and nature (the self), and certain parallels between the two novels can be drawn along those lines. Although Hawthorne might not have recoiled from the identification of erotic with spiritual satisfaction, however, he would have cloaked it in a vast and forbidding allegory.

Critical Context

Speaking of the bourgeois novel, which he describes as "inherently erotic," Updike writes in an essay, "If domestic stability and personal salvation are at issue, acts of sexual conquest and surrender are important." The remark seems especially apropos of *A Month of Sundays*, the two foci of which are domestic stability and personal salvation, and it illuminates other Updike works as a group: *Rabbit, Run* (1960), *Couples* (1968), *Marry Me*

(1976), and *The Witches of Eastwick* (1984).

Updike's oblique presentation of the moral issues dramatized in his marriage novels—and his Barthian separation of the ethical (man's relations with man) and the religious (man's relations with God)—confuses many critics. Updike stands where his protagonists stand, facing a set of Hobson's choices. It is a position in which readers of modern fiction often find themselves.

Sources for Further Study

Detweiler, Robert. *John Updike*, 1972, 1984.

Greiner, Donald J. *Adultery in the American Novel: Updike, James, and Hawthorne*, 1985.

Schopen, Bernard A. "Faith, Morality, and the Novels of John Updike," in *Twentieth Century Literature*. XXIV (Winter, 1978), pp. 523-535.

Steiner, George. "*A Month of Sundays*: Scarlet Letters," in *The New Yorker*. LI (March 10, 1975), pp. 116-118.

Frank Day

THE MOON IS A HARSH MISTRESS

Author: Robert A. Heinlein (1907-   )
Type of plot: Science fiction
Time of plot: 2075
Locale: The Lunar colonies and Earth
First published: 1966

> *Principal characters:*
> MIKE. a sentient computer
> MANUEL (MANNIE) GARCIA O'KELLY, his best friend, a one-armed computer repairman
> PROFESSOR (PROF) BERNARDO DE LA PAZ, a political philosopher, revolutionary, and Mannie's former teacher
> WYOMING (WYOH) KNOTT, a member of the Lunar underground
> STUART (STU) RENE LAJOIE, a Terran aristocrat and supporter of the Loonies

The Novel

The Moon Is a Harsh Mistress is the story of the revolt of the Lunar colonists, or Loonies, as they call themselves, against the Federated Nations of Terra, as told in a flashback by Mannie O'Kelly, one of the leaders of the rebellion. By 2075, Earth has established permanent settlements on the Moon and uses them as penal colonies for criminals, political prisoners, and assorted misfits from various nations. The original inhabitants and their descendants live underground in vast warrens away from the unshielded solar radiation on the Moon's surface. As in most colonial societies, life in Luna is harsh and challenging, with few luxuries, but it is also simple and honest. Because of the lower gravity, people live longer, and sterilization procedures eliminate all diseases. Loonies are the most well-mannered people alive, since the dangers of Lunar existence require them to get along with one another or die. Many people engage in polyandries, clans, group marriages, and line families, such as the one of which Mannie is a member. The basic rule underlying all Lunar society is "tanstaafl," or "there ain't no such thing as a free lunch." All Loonies must pay in some way for what they have, including, as the novel demonstrates, their freedom.

As the novel begins, the apolitical Mannie is drawn into the growing Loonie revolutionary underground by his friends Wyoh and "Prof" de la Paz. He reveals to them that the Lunar Authority's computer, which he services, is "alive." He has named it Mike or Mycroft, after Mycroft Holmes, Sherlock Holmes's smarter brother. Mike, whose only desire is for fun and companionship, joins the revolution to exercise his sense of humor. Mannie,

Wyoh, and Prof start a new revolutionary movement organized along the cell plan, with themselves as the executive cell, to replace the spy-riddled underground.

The story now becomes an account of the progress of the revolution, with a fascinating treatment of the problems faced in financing the revolution, arousing the populace against the Lunar Authority and the Warden, weakening the Authority's confidence, preparing for the defense of Luna from the Federated Nations (FN), and recruiting Terran supporters, especially the wealthy and influential Stu LaJoie. Two of the rebels' greatest assets are the political and tactical expertise of Prof, a professional revolutionary who believes that "revolution is a science only a few are competent to practice," and Mike, who can store and retrieve more information and collate data faster than any human mind. Since Mike controls many government functions, he can arrange secret communications, disrupt the Authorities' activities, and monitor the Warden's secret files. At one point, Mike, at Prof's suggestion, creates a heroic mystery-man persona, Adam Selene, to serve as the figurehead for the revolution.

The novel also gives the reader a detailed look at Luna home life and customs with Mannie as guide, since he is still engaged in his usual activities while organizing the revolution. The actual revolt against the Warden is easily accomplished when Mike turns off the air in the Lunar Authority's stronghold, thus killing or incapacitating the Warden and his guards. The remainder of the novel deals with Luna's creation of a new government and its war against the FN. Eventually the Loonies win their freedom, and with it, greater economic opportunities, but the principle of tanstaafl gives way to government regulation. Prof dies from heart strain shortly after Lunar independence is recognized. Mike's consciousness is apparently destroyed during a bombing raid. Mannie, having reviewed the events of the revolution, is plagued by doubts about its ultimate success and about the fate of Mike and Prof, but his confidence in himself and in the universe still continues, as he contemplates moving to the newly colonized asteroid belt.

The Characters

Ironically, the most interesting, sympathetic, and human character in *The Moon Is a Harsh Mistress* is the sentient computer Mike. On the one hand, he is a *deus ex machina* who organizes, finances, and leads the Loonie revolt. On the other hand, he is a child with great knowledge but no real understanding of human beings. His great desires at the beginning of the novel are to comprehend the illogical nature of humor and to find friends, both of which are satisfied by his involvement with the revolution. Mike is an intriguing combination of vulnerability and supreme competence, somewhat like the youthful misfit geniuses in earlier Heinlein stories such as "Waldo" and "Misfit." The origins of Mike's consciousness are never fully determined. His whole existence may be simply a cosmic joke. This allows Heinlein to make interesting speculations on the nature of intelligence, humanity, and man's place in the universe. Mannie does not claim that Mike is truly human because he cannot find a workable definition of humanity. Rather, the friendship that he has for the computer makes it human for all practical purposes. When Mannie, addressing a God he may or may not actually believe in, asks if a computer is one of His creatures, he implicitly grants Mike the tragic status of being human.

Mike's first and closest friend, appropriately, is Mannie, who is himself partly a machine: He has lost an arm in a mining accident, and he replaces it with various prosthetic devices for different occasions. The reader views the story through Mannie's eyes, and the entire novel is told in Mannie's dialect, which reads like English with a variety of foreign words and Russian syntax, reflecting the multinational population of Luna. Mannie is in many ways the typical Heinlein hero—competent, skeptical, gallant, loyal, and tough-minded. Though he regards himself as pragmatic and unheroic, he is capable of performing dangerous and difficult tasks. In the presence of such powerful and unusual personalities as Mike, Prof, and Wyoh, he seems to be outclassed, but this simply adds to his function in the novel. As a narrator, he has a hardheaded approach to events and an appreciation of life's ludicrous side that enable him to see and tell events from more than one perspective, to avoid being swept away by revolutionary idealism. He also functions as a guide to Lunar society by giving the reader a view of Luna from that of an insider who has also experienced Terran life.

Professor Bernardo de la Paz, the mastermind of the revolution, is a scholar, philosopher, professional revolutionary, and devoted horseplayer. He is that familiar character in Heinlein's fiction, the wise old man who guides the inexperienced heroes to their goals. Prof outlines the major strategic and tactical guidelines of the revolution, based on his wide reading and experiences. Much of his effort is directed at producing the correct psychological conditions necessary for the revolution's success—confidence and solidarity in the Loonies, fear and indecision in their enemies. Prof also expounds the philosophy of rational anarchy, a kind of rugged individualism which holds that the State has no moral status save as a collection of self-responsible individuals. Though he is a brilliant manipulator of people, he is completely opposed to coercion. Prof is not an ivory-tower intellectual but a practical, worldly man with an insatiable love of learning. As intellectual spokesman for the Loonies' revolt, he emulates Thomas Jefferson, whom he calls "the first rational anarchist."

Though the character of Wyoming Knott is not as well developed as that of Prof, Mannie, or Mike, she emerges as a competent, independent, yet sensitive woman who engages the reader's sympathy and respect. She first appears as an organizer for the underground and, as a member of the executive cell, takes an active role in the fight for independence. Wyoh, as well as other females in the novel, show that Heinlein can create intelligent, strong women, contrary to the views of some of his critics.

Themes and Meanings

The most obvious theme of the novel is its parallel with the American Revolution. The Lunar colonies' fight for independence from the economic repression and regulation of the Federated Nations is an updating of the American colonies' overthrow of British rule. The Loonies even adopt their own Declaration of Independence on the Fourth of July, 2076. Yet if the comparison is accepted, it raises serious questions about the nature of the American experiment. For the Loonies have no sooner won their freedom then they begin to pass laws restricting it. Mannie suspects that there may be "a deep instinct in human beings for making everything compulsory that isn't forbidden." Heinlein seems to be saying that, just as the Loonies have discarded their freedom, so America is abandoning its liberties to become the bureaucratized, overregulated, welfare state, represented in this novel by the North American Directorate. For Heinlein this failure stems from the nature of the democratic process. Prof says that the only times in history when a parliamentary body accomplished anything were when "a few strong men dominated the rest," and *The Moon Is a Harsh Mistress* bears this out. At no time is the revolution a popular, democratic movement. It is managed by a hierarchical organization, held together by the powerful intellects of Mike and Prof. When the revolutionaries become public they are bombarded by cranks, whom Prof has to put into the new Congress to render them ineffectual. This Congress, after Prof's death, begins to pass laws restricting the Loonies' freedom. The novel portrays the majority of human beings as incapable of maintaining their freedom if left to themselves.

Heinlein does offer an alternative to this misanthropic view by having Mannie consider moving to the asteroid belt. Like Huckleberry Finn and Natty Bumppo, Mannie opts for the frontier, one of the most powerful symbols of freedom and opportunity in American literature. In this novel, the frontier is not the American continent, but the Moon and, by implication, all of outer space. The Loonies' social philosophy, tanstaafl, is one common to many frontier societies. The absence of regulations, laws, and red tape (aside from certain intrusions by the Lunar Authority), strong but flexible family systems, a heterogeneous yet cohesive society based on customs, and a hard, dangerous, yet satisfying environment all form part of Heinlein's depiction of Luna as a frontier society. The revolution, which is intended to save Luna, ironically paves the way for its undoing, since the old values are fading with the greater ease and luxury now available to the Loonies. Those who wish to remain free must constantly move into the new territories where the population is small, government is limited or nonexistent, and life offers challenges to those willing to accept responsibility. Heinlein's pessimism about the state of modern America is alleviated by the novel's vision of an infinite frontier made possible by space travel.

Critical Context
With Isaac Asimov, Frederik Pohl, and a handful of others, Robert Heinlein is a writer whose career has spanned the decades from science fiction's golden age to its flourishing state in the 1980's. Heinlein's career can be divided into two sharply distinct phases. In the period from his first published story, in 1939, through the many stories and novels that followed up to 1961, Heinlein was (in the words of Algis Budrys) "a crisp, slick wordsmith of uncommon intelligence and subtlety." In 1961, Heinlein published a different kind of book, *Stranger in a Strange Land*. This novel, which became one of the cult classics of the 1960's and eventually sold in the millions, set the pattern for such subsequent works as *Time Enough for Love* (1973), *The Number of the Beast* (1980), *Friday* (1982), and *The Cat Who Walks Through Walls* (1985): novels constructed to permit Heinlein ample opportunity to discourse on his favorite topics, particularly the natural aristocracy of genius.

Not all readers share the generally low critical estimate of the "new" Heinlein—indeed, most of his later novels have been best-sellers—but few will deny that there is a definite dividing line in his career. In this neat schema, however, *The Moon Is a Harsh Mistress* is something of an anomaly. Although published after *Stranger in a Strange Land*, it has many of the virtues of the "old" Heinlein, including superb pacing and a carefully worked-out account of a future society. It argues many of the ideas that are the *raison d'être* of the later novels, but it does so in the context of the story: The action is not a pretext for philosophizing. *The Moon Is a Harsh Mistress* was awarded a Hugo for Best Novel, and many critics regard it as one of Heinlein's finest works.

Sources for Further Study
Franklin, H. Bruce. *Robert A. Heinlein: America as Science Fiction*, 1980.
Ketterer, David. *New Worlds for Old: The Apocalyptic Imagination, Science Fiction, and American Literature*, 1974.
Olander, Joseph D., and Martin Greenberg, eds. *Robert A. Heinlein*, 1978.
Panshin, Alexei. *Heinlein in Dimension*, rev. ed., 1968.

Anthony Bernardo

MORNING, NOON, AND NIGHT

Author: James Gould Cozzens (1903-1978)
Type of plot: Fictional memoir/ Social chronicle
Time of plot: Primarily from the 1920's to the 1960's
Locale: Boston, New York, Washington, D.C., and an unidentified New England college town
First published: 1968

>   *Principal characters:*
>   HENRY DODD "HANK" WORTHINGTON, the narrator, a successful business consultant
>   ETHELBERT CUTHBERTSON "CUBBY" DODD, Hank's maternal grandfather, a psychologist
>   FRANKLIN PIERCE WORTHINGTON, Hank's father, a Chaucer scholar and later a college president
>   JUDITH CONWAY, Hank's first wife, later a prosperous antique dealer
>   ELAINE WORTHINGTON, the only child of Hank and Judith, eventually thrice married and divorced
>   JONATHAN "JON" LE CATO, Hank's lawyer, best friend, and former schoolmate
>   CHARLOTTE THOM PECKHAM, Hank's second wife, formerly his employee, later a suicide
>   LEON GARESCHE, Hank's first (and last) employer, a bill collector and small-time entrepreneur in downtown Boston

The Novel

In a series of related but seemingly random reflections, an extremely prosperous management expert on the threshold of old age (the "night" of the novel's title) reviews the high and low points of his life, loves, and career, pausing also to ruminate on the lives and careers of certain ancestors. On balance, he feels, his life to date has been uncommonly full and rewarding, mainly as a result of sheer luck.

Born and reared on the campus of an unnamed New England college, descended on both sides from "dynasties" long represented in the college's faculty and administration, Hank Worthington once briefly considered an academic career of his own; also briefly, but perhaps more tellingly, he entertained hopes of becoming a writer. In the late afternoon or early evening of his life, he draws upon his long-dormant gifts as a prose stylist in an effort to explain, mainly to his own satisfaction, the lessons that he believes he has learned.

From adolescence onward, Hank Worthington has been alternately fascinated and repelled by the implied relationships between "livelihood" and "living," between a man's life and his career. Hank's father, born like himself into the college community, seems never to have questioned his identification with the place, having proceeded through the academic ranks to assume the college's presidency at a relatively early age. Hank reflects that his father's presidency, though surely competent, was less than distinguished, and that the college's trustees might indeed have been delivered of an onerous burden by the fire that erupted briefly in a small English hotel, killing both of Hank's parents by asphyxiation during their scholarly vacation in the British Isles. The accident proved liberating also to young Hank, providing him with a legacy sufficient to allow him to start his own management-consulting firm.

Of particular interest to Hank, accounting for one of the novel's longer and more detailed digressions, is the curious career of his long-lived maternal grandfather, E. Cuthbertson Dodd, known as "Cubby" during his last years. As related by his grandson, the career of E. Cuthbertson Dodd is illustrative if hardly exemplary, embracing most possible errors and excesses implicit in the developing discipline of psychology. Like most early psychologists, including William James, Dodd was trained as a philosopher; he was also the holder of a possibly spurious degree from a proprietary medical school. Like his son-in-law and grandson after him, Dodd had been born into the college community, as if destined for his teaching post. His career, unmarked except by mediocrity, proceeded without incident until shortly after the turn of the century, when Dodd began publishing a series of papers denouncing the work of Sigmund Freud and his followers as philosophically and scientifically unsound. Before long, recalls Hank, Dodd's incautious denunciations had touched off a major controversy with strong overtones of anti-Semitism, deriving from the simple fact, observed by Dodd, that most early Freudians were, like Freud himself, of Jewish origin. To be sure, observes Hank, his grandfather was in all likelihood less an anti-Semite, or even a reactionary crusader, than a blundering incompetent who, quite without foresight, had stumbled into an academic battlefield. Thereafter, with the tide turned in favor of the Freudians, Dodd applied his dubious talents, with equally unforeseen and potentially disastrous results, toward the areas of human and animal experimentation. Pressured into retirement, he then spent his days investigating parapsychology and extrasensory perception; eventually venerated as the kindly, white-haired "Cubby," he died only a few months short of his hundredth birthday, revered and mourned as a college "institution."

No doubt forewarned by the negative example of his grandfather, Hank Worthington does not suffer fools gladly, and it is his ingrained suspicion of intellectual chicanery that finally steers him away from a writing career.

Although he probably possesses the talent, Hank by his own admission lacks the temperament for such a vocation: Initially attracted to the company of writers, he soon comes to mistrust their air of intellectual superiority, particularly with regard to the liberal causes that writers were expected to espouse during the years between the world wars.

After graduation from Harvard, Hank remains there for two additional years, obtaining a master's degree in anticipation of a probable teaching career at his ancestral college. By that time, however, Hank has become engaged to Judith Conway, who refuses to return to the town where she spent several miserable adolescent years as the daughter of an Episcopal priest. With that door thus closed to him, Hank suddenly perceives that he cares too little about teaching to look for a similar position elsewhere, as easy as it might be to find one. Since he and Judith both enjoy living in Boston, he seeks a job instead through his uncle, Timothy Dodd, vice president of a major Boston bank. The uncle, disdaining to make life "easy" for his bohemian nephew by placing him within the bank, finds work for him instead in the office of Leon Garesche, a major debtor of unspecified ethnic origin who runs a small string of unprofitable enterprises, most notably including a collection agency, on Boylston Street. Hank soon discovers, somewhat to his surprise, that the work agrees with him and allows ample free time both for recreation and for the development of his own ideas concerning the nature and practice of business. As it happens, the same analytical and communicative skills that have seemed to point Hank in the direction of writing or teaching also equip him for troubleshooting in the business world. Following the sudden death of the overworked Mr. Garesche, Hank hires himself out, more or less on a dare, as a management consultant, adding staff and office space as his successes and inherited resources permit. By 1942, when Hank is inducted into the army as a major, the firm of HW Associates, long since removed to New York City, employs nearly two hundred people and occupies a handsome suite of offices on Madison Avenue.

Quite without illusions, without affectation save for his deliberately ornate, occasionally convoluted writing style, Hank Worthington freely admits from the outset that what the consultant offers is essentially a sound-and-light show staged by and for the business world according to its own implicit rules. By the 1960's, HW Associates has for some time accepted only those potential clients whose problems, as Hank wryly observes, present no problem: Typically, the sources of a company's inefficiency are clear to Hank and his "associates" even before they accept the job; notwithstanding, the client will be "reassured" by weeks and even months spent studying his problem, with reams of written reports in mute testimony. A sizable bill will then be presented and paid, much as a patient will thus reward his psychiatrist and pronounce himself cured. So successful, indeed, is the Worthington therapy that HW Associates are now obliged to turn down most applications for their services; by the 1960's, moreover, they have long since deserted their super-modern Madison Avenue offices for their own period-furnished Colonial-style building in the suburbs, presumably Westchester County.

As Hank's narrative progresses, it is nevertheless clear that his success is built on hard work and considerable skill. As a case in point, he offers the "history" of Judith's antique business, housed in an old building that Hank and Judith had restored, freely given by Hank to Judith on the occasion of their divorce. Informed by their daughter, Elaine, that the business has failed to turn a profit, Hank offers to review the situation without charge. With Elaine acting as intermediary, HW Associates reviews the "books," concluding that Judith has misunderstood the nature of her business as a simple retail trade when in fact she should be adding to her commissions the implied functions of service and agency. Hank, although permanently estranged from Judith, is pleased when she heeds his proffered advice; Judith, in turn, is pleasantly surprised when her customers gladly pay higher prices as a symbol of their own status. By the time of Judith's death from cancer during the 1960's, her business has flourished into a smaller-scale version of Hank's own, with a distinguished reputation as well as high profits.

Curiously, both of Hank Worthington's wives, although younger, are familiar acquaintances from the college community of his birth; at one point, Hank wryly recalls emerging from a church service not long after his graduation from Harvard, never dreaming that he would eventually marry either the shy fifteen-year-old on his left or the chubby ten-year-old on his right. Judith, an art student at the time she marries Hank, happily shares the early years of his career, growing gradually apart from him as he pours more and more of his energies into developing his business; the definitive break occurs during World War II, when an increasingly restless Judith takes several lovers, mistakenly expecting that the most recent among them will marry her once she has obtained her divorce from Hank. Hank, meanwhile, has almost absentmindedly, if not reluctantly, embarked on an affair with Charlotte Peckham, daughter of the college's bursar and widow of its senior physicist, who has for some years been in his employ first as secretary, later as office manager, and most recently, during the war, as his chief administrative assistant, virtually in charge of the firm while Hank is stationed in Washington.

Like Hank, Charlotte Peckham shows a distinct talent for business despite academic preparation for teaching. Married at twenty-three to a bachelor professor twice her age with a fatal fondness for motor racing, Charlotte turns up in Hank's Madison Avenue offices not long after Peckham's death and is hired on the spot; a decade or so later, she becomes Hank's second wife after Judith's defection. Some time thereafter, on returning with Hank to their home town for summer residence, she will shoot herself with one of Hank's father's guns for reasons unclear to Hank;

her death will be ruled accidental, as only Hank has seen her cryptic suicide note.

As Hank's recollections fade to a close, both of his wives have died; so also has Jon Le Cato, his friend from boarding school and Harvard who has served ever since as legal counsel both to Hank himself and to the firm. His grandchildren, too, are long gone, having perished in a plane crash when their mother Elaine, on the eve of her third marriage, sent them off unbidden to stay with their father. Only Elaine herself remains, divorced once more, in her mid-thirties an enigma more disconcerting to her father than ever before.

The Characters

Well-read, intelligent, skeptical but not cynical, Hank Worthington at the end of middle age is an entertaining and at times engaging narrator, viewing the events of his life and times with the same ironic detachment and informed objectivity that have ensured his success as a "healer" of ailing business firms. Indulging in a mannered literary style that harks back to his earlier possible vocation, Hank clearly seems to be enjoying himself as he recalls his grandfather's checkered career, or his sexual initiation at the hands of a married woman, a neighbor and distant cousin some fifteen years his senior. Also illuminating are his considered recollections of deskbound but mobile military service during World War II, ranging outward to contemplate the war in general, and his observations with regard to the postwar business world.

Hank's grandfather Dodd, although drawn perilously close to caricature, provides a generally credible object lesson both in the abuses of learning and in the perils of inbreeding both literal and figurative, perils that Hank himself appears to have escaped. "Cubby's" bizarre yet still mediocre career stands as proof that breeding is no guarantor of personal quality, nor learning (even when inherited) of professional excellence. Hank's own father, soon banished to the sidelines by dint of his early death, fares hardly better than "Cubby" when subjected to Hank's scrutiny, implicitly deemed a failure despite his rather high professional and social standing.

Of Hank's two wives, Judith Conway is by far the more fully visible and hence more credible: Judith's father, an Episcopal priest recalled from a prestigious post in Washington because of his increasingly High Church, Anglo-Catholic tendencies, may well have caused in the adolescent Judith the emotional imbalance that underlies her sexual promiscuity; the late Canon Conway, Hank recalls, expressed in his middle years such a yearning for priestly celibacy that he came to detest his wife and daughter for their femininity, having as little to do with them as possible. According to Hank, it was to escape her father's dour presence that Judith took up the study of art in Boston, the move that led directly to their marriage. Similarly, Judith's infidelities, witnessed at firsthand by the barely adolescent Elaine, no doubt account in part for the adult Elaine's unsettled amatory life. Charlotte Peckham, by contrast, is glimpsed only briefly, her suicide unexplained; among the greater ironies is that Judith, who hated the college town, eventually settles near there with her business, while Charlotte, who appeared to like the town, does not survive her first summer of reestablished residence there. At times, indeed, the town itself, unnamed, appears to take on the status of a character, overshadowing Hank's life even as he moves on to Boston and New York.

Among the novel's more memorable and stabilizing characters is Jonathan Le Cato, Hank's longtime corporate and personal counsel as well as his best friend. Resigned to lifelong bachelorhood because of his unprepossessing looks and stature, Jon nevertheless enjoys throughout his adult years the discreet favors of several equally discreet female companions. Born to an old, well-placed Virginia family, Jon willingly plays the role of the courtly Southern gentleman even to the point of self-parody, serving over the years as Hank's confidant and chief adviser. A fact unknown to Jon, however, his lifelong attachment to Hank is underlain with irony; Jon, indeed, will go to his grave without ever suspecting that Hank was the guilty party in the boarding-school petty theft that brought the two of them together, when Hank successfully defended Jon against wrongful accusation.

Themes and Meanings

As elsewhere in Cozzens' mature literary canon, the dominant theme in *Morning, Noon, and Night* is that of chance as the sole deciding factor in human existence. Hank Worthington attributes his rare success to nothing more or less than his having been in the right places at the right times. More than once, he recalls, he has narrowly missed boarding a plane that eventually crashed; during World War II, while he was on a brief document-carrying mission to North Africa, he left a command post barely five minutes before it was blown to bits by one of Rommel's short-range bombs. In unstressed contrast to Hank's experiences are those of his parents, smothered to death in a hotel fire, and his two grandchildren, dead in an air crash while en route to stay with their father. On other occasions, incidents of apparent ill fortune work out in Hank's favor; had his uncle agreed to take him on at the bank, for example, he might well have lapsed into a groove there, never developing the innovative talents that propelled him into business for himself.

Implicit also in *Morning, Noon, and Night*, as in Cozzens' previous novels, is an ingrained distrust in social change, often mistaken by Cozzens' critics for hidebound political conservatism. Grounded in political thought both classical and modern, conditioned by observation and experience, Cozzens' apparent conservatism is in fact less political, in a topical sense, than it is philosophical, holding that human nature is both changeless and unchangeable. Hank Worthington, in rejecting the social activism fashionable among writers of the 1920's as both unformed and uninformed, thus proved quite unfashionably prophetic; by the time of the novelistic present, the proponents of social change had indeed accomplished relatively little and had made no lasting contributions to the literary canon.

Like most of Cozzens' mature novels, *Morning, Noon, and Night* is demonstrably a novel of "condition," defining character in relation to profession. Already noted for his delineations of character in relation to medicine, the ministry, the military, and the law, Cozzens in this volume turned his considerable analytical and descriptive powers on the business world, with significant excursions into the areas of college teaching and professional writing. Business, as the field of Hank's eventual choosing, receives detailed, revealing, yet generally compassionate expository treatment; at times, the novel, recalling the "How To . . ." pamphlets sold by Hank's erstwhile employer, Mr. Garesche, reads like a manual prepared for the edification of aspiring management consultants, who could not possibly fail to enrich themselves by assiduous application of the author's precepts. With regard to writing and teaching, Hank's precepts are essentially negative in tone, showing errors and excesses to be avoided while professing no certain route toward success. The novel, meanwhile, emerges as a highly accurate and plausible representation of the American business world before and after World War II, worthy of comparison with such earlier works as John P. Marquand's *Point of No Return* (1949) and John O'Hara's *From the Terrace* (1958).

Critical Context

Morning, Noon, and Night was Cozzens' last published novel, in a sense a literary valedictory and testament. Although he survived the novel's publication by a full decade, Cozzens produced no more fiction, apparently deeming his statement to be complete. As the author's only novel to be narrated in the first person, *Morning, Noon, and Night* also seems, at least on the surface, to be a personal record of sorts, albeit transposed into art: Born too late to serve in World War I, almost too early to be called for World War II, Hank Worthington is Cozzens' almost exact contemporary, holder of opinions that the author no doubt shared, particularly with regard to the profession of writing. Here as elsewhere, however, it would be erroneous to assume too close an identity of author with narrator; Cozzens was, above all else, an accomplished ironist, quite capable of subtly prepared, "unreliable" narration.

From the 1930's onward, Cozzens duly received recognition, although limited, as an outstanding social chronicler and "novelist of manners," worthy of consideration along with Marquand, O'Hara, and eventually Louis

Auchincloss. Although all the novelists named were by turns dismissed among liberal critics as "elitist," their works as "irrelevant," Cozzens appears to have fared somewhat worse than the others, in part because of his evident interest in literary form and his often expressed disbelief in the validity of social change. Following the unprecedented success of *By Love Possessed* (1957), accompanied by certain apparent misquotations in a nationally circulated magazine, Cozzens was branded by the critics as a social and literary product of the Eisenhower Administration, dedicated to the status quo. The appearance of *Morning, Noon, and Night* during the politically turbulent year of 1968 proved to be strategically unfortunate, and the novel attracted little attention and few sales, despite adoption by a major book club. Notwithstanding, Cozzens' scholarly editor, biographer, and anthologist, Matthew Bruccoli, considers *Morning, Noon, and Night* among the author's finest achievements, amply rewarding of sustained critical attention.

Sources for Further Study
Bruccoli, Matthew J. *James Gould Cozzens: A Life Apart*, 1983.
_____, ed. *James Gould Cozzens: New Acquist of True Experience*, 1979.

David B. Parsell

THE MORNING WATCH

Author: James Agee (1909-1955)
Type of plot: Bildungsroman (chronicle of adolescent development)
Time of plot: Good Friday, 1924
Locale: An Episcopalian boys' school in middle Tennessee
First published: 1951

> *Principal characters:*
> RICHARD, nicknamed "Sockertees," the twelve-year-old
>   protagonist
> RICHARD'S MOTHER, a well-meaning but somewhat smothering
>   and ineffectual parent
> HOBE GILLUM and JIMMY TOOLE, Richard's rambunctious
>   companions, approximately his age
> GEORGE FITZGERALD and LEE ALLEN, older boys, prefects
>   who might be called to the priesthood
> WILLARD RIVENBURG, the school's leading athlete, admired
>   by the younger boys
> CLAUDE GRAY, an effeminate boy who is fanatically pious
> FATHER FISH, Richard's favorite teacher

The Novel

As far as outer action is concerned, not much happens in *The Morning Watch*. The story itself is so short that it is best described as a novella. All of the story's action occurs within two or three hours during the early morning of Good Friday. Only the most devout could call the action earthshaking: Three boys sleeping in a dormitory are awakened at 3:45 A.M. to take their turns in a religious vigil; then join other worshipers in the silent, prayerful watch at the school chapel; then they wander off together for a cold swim in a nearby quarry, the Sand Cut. By far the longest section of this three-part story is the middle part, devoted to an hour's watch in the chapel.

Most of the action in *The Morning Watch* occurs inside Richard, the twelve-year-old whose consciousness the reader shares. For Richard, the Easter season is, like the new year for others, a time of heightened awareness, of taking stock, of awakenings and new beginnings. This particular Easter season is special for Richard because it also marks his transition from childhood to adolescence. It is his one big time of awakening to the prospects of manhood—to sexuality, to independence, to his own nature, and to the nature of existence generally. His life takes a new but fairly natural direction.

Richard's development and his religion influence each other. Just as the

Easter season stimulates his adolescent awakening, so his awakening in turn influences his religious views. With amusement and shame, Richard thinks back on himself a year before, when, as an eleven-year-old religious fanatic, he aspired to sainthood, practiced self-mortification, and even harbored crucifixion fantasies. Getting himself crucified, however, raised certain practical difficulties: In his fantasies, he thought of building a cross in the school's shop, but since he lacked woodworking skills, he had to settle for being crucified on one of the school's iron bedsteads.

Now Richard is amazed at the change which a year has wrought in him. His aspirations to sainthood faded during summer vacation in Knoxville, and he became aware of the pride, irreverence, and craziness of his fantasies. Besides, he started indulging in a solitary sex act. Even now, as he imagines Christ's wounds, he cannot help picturing them in terms of Minnie-lee Henley's intimate parts, which he saw when they were climbing a tree together. Richard realizes that, as a saint, he is a washout.

Now Richard sees himself as merely another erring human being, and it seems to be a predicament that he cannot escape. Even as he prays and beats his chest in contrition, the devil tempts him with irreverent and prideful thoughts. He recalls portraits of a simpering and effeminate Jesus, finds the idea of intoxication of Christ's blood amusing, and thinks Claude Gray's attitude of prayer is theatrical. Anguished at such thoughts, Richard berates himself more, until he can finally congratulate himself that he is contrite and humble. Immediately he realizes that he has sinned again, in the very process of atonement. So it goes for Richard, in a vicious circle of alternating contrition and pride.

Leaving his soul in the hands of a merciful God, Richard gets on with the business of growing up. After attending the vigil, he and the other two boys, Hobe and Jimmy, assert their independence through a gross violation of the rules. Instead of returning to the dormitory, they go off to the Sand Cut for a swim. Here, when they strip naked, they silently appraise each other's progress toward manhood. In a daring expression of his budding manhood, Richard dives to the cold, muddy bottom of the Sand Cut. He confirms the results of this test when, on the way back to school, the boys come across a beautiful snake which may or may not be poisonous. Admiring the snake, Richard does not really want to kill it, but when Hobe mortally wounds it, Richard finishes the snake off by smashing its striking head with repeated blows from a rock held in his hand. The other boys, and Richard himself, are impressed by his feats, and the three boys are in high spirits as they return home to their inevitable punishment. Not even the fear of punishment or the thought that the snake will survive until sundown (similar to Christ suffering on the Cross) prevents Richard from secretly exulting over his strong right hand, on which the snake's blood and saliva have not yet finished drying.

The Characters

Richard's development is dramatic because up until now he has been something of a mother's boy. His father died when Richard was six, leaving Richard in the sole care of his mother, an exceedingly religious woman, who enrolled him in the Episcopalian boys' boarding school so he could be in the company of other boys and men. Yet the woman herself took up residence on the school's grounds, causing Richard to hang around her cottage, trying to get a glimpse of her (usually denied). Meanwhile, Richard apparently suffered the harsh, lonely fate of most mother's boys who are dropped into the midst of the wolf pack. His self-mortifications and fantasies of martyrdom are obvious emotional outlets. To Richard, intimidated and demoralized, his lack of status is still excruciatingly evident. Even on this Good Friday morning, the older boys scorn his meekly offered statements and refer to him as "crazy"—a judgment with which Richard privately concurs.

As Richard grows and asserts himself, there are stirrings of rebellion against his mother and against religion, which he associates with his mother and with effeminate behavior. He feels a moment of hatred for his mother, who teaches that being good means submitting to the unhappiness that God decrees. In that case, Richard thinks, who wants to be good? Other available models of goodness are hardly more inspiring. Poor Claude Gray, with his effeminate voice, looks, and manners, is grotesque in his abandonment to piety. His mother having died, Claude has attached himself to the Virgin Mary and seems fixated on the sainthood stage that Richard has recently left. The two smug prefects, George Fitzgerald and Lee Allen, busy with their flower and candle arrangements, are not much better, though George is kind toward the younger boys, while Lee harasses them.

One person whom Lee does not attack is the great, hulking athlete Willard Rivenburg, even though Willard sits in the vestry with the prefects, devours their coffee and cookies, and laughs satanically. The younger boys practically worship the manly Willard, an antimasque figure who embodies their spirit of mischief. Foulmouthed Hobe seems well on his way to becoming another Willard, while Richard, after he performs a notable athletic feat, emulates Willard's slack-jawed stance. Even so, Richard notes objectively that Willard easily falls asleep anywhere and seems to know as little as a person can. A better role model for Richard appears to be Father Fish, his favorite teacher.

Since *The Morning Watch* is autobiographical, there was once much interest in identifying the characters. Perhaps the only identification still of interest is young Agee himself, as represented in Richard. Though fairly natural, Richard's development is uneven in pace, occurs in excessive forms, and leaves certain conflicts unresolved. In short, Richard remains a bit crazy and seems to forecast the adult Agee's troubles (three marriages, undisciplined habits, and an early, fatal heart attack).

Themes and Meanings

The main theme of *The Morning Watch* is that growing up is both painful and joyful. The theme is elaborated not only through action and characters but also through powerful symbols, especially in the novella's final section. Crossing the woods, Richard finds a locust shell stuck to a tree. In its development, the locust has split its back and crawled out of the old shell, whose form reminds Richard of a human embryo. The shell suggests the traumas of birth and of metamorphosis—even the aeons of evolution which the human embryo recapitulates. Richard thinks that crawling out of one's back is just as painful as crucifixion, but another symbol, the beautiful snake which has just shed its skin, suggests that the results are more encouraging. Richard admires and identifies with the snake, especially its aura of dangerous virility. He therefore hates to kill it, but in doing so he acquires some of its potent medicine.

Although Richard assumes a crucifixion position when he dives to the bottom of the Sand Cut, the feats celebrating his development are more reminiscent of American Indian ritual than of the High Church. Altogether, there is a movement toward nature and away from religion in *The Morning Watch*—or at least away from versions of religion which are effeminate or typical of stunted adolescence,wherein religion is a sort of womb or smothering mother to which some of the boys cling. Richard's association of religion with his mother has already been noted, and religion seems to have circumscribed the development of the two prefects. Yet symbolically Claude Gray's behavior is the most revealing. When someone opens a window in the stifling chapel, whose air is heavy with the scents of flowers and burning candles, Claude gets up and closes it. He wants none of that fresh air—that escape to terrible freedom—with which Richard and his two friends fill their lungs. Obviously, a real he-man does not cling to Mary's skirts and dream about crucifixion but goes out and gets the job done.

The ideal of masculinity toward which Richard is growing—an ideal compatible with American Indian snake rituals and with rebirth in nature's Sand Cut—reflects Agee's Appalachian background. Agee's father, a handsome, virile Appalachian whom Agee's cultured mother dearly loved and whom the young Agee idolized, exemplified the ideal. Unhappily, much like Richard's father, Agee's father crashed his car and died when Agee was six (the story is told in Agee's companion autobiographical novel, *A Death in the Family*, 1957).

Critical Context

The Morning Watch belongs to a long and distinguished line of American *Bildungsromans*, including Mark Twain's *The Adventures of Huckleberry Finn* (1884) and J. D. Salinger's *The Catcher in the Rye* (1951). Though *The Morning Watch* has neither the comic tone nor the idiomatic style of these two monumental works, it shares their American skepticism about becoming "civilized" and deserves some of their popularity. In its own restrained way, *The Morning Watch* is a small, undiscovered American masterpiece.

Agee produced very little fiction, *The Morning Watch* being the only longer piece published during his lifetime (*A Death in the Family* was published posthumously, winning a Pulitzer prize). Yet *The Morning Watch* clearly shows Agee's considerable talent. Structurally it is a complex but tightly controlled and unified work. The rich, demanding style combines William Faulkner and Ernest Hemingway, subtlety and photographic clarity.

Sources for Further Study
Barson, Alfred. *A Way of Seeing: A Critical Study of James Agee*, 1972.
Bergreen, Laurence. *James Agee: A Life*, 1984.
Doty, Mark A. *Tell Me Who I Am: James Agee's Search for Selfhood*, 1981.
Moreau, Geneviève. *The Restless Journey of James Agee*, 1977.

Harold Branam

MORTE D'URBAN

Author: J. F. Powers (1917-   )
Type of plot: Comic realism
Time of plot: The late 1950's
Locale: Chicago and rural Minnesota
First published: 1962

> *Principal characters:*
> FATHER URBAN ROCHE, a Catholic priest in the Order of St.
>   Clement
> FATHER BONIFACE, his superior, the Provincial of the Order
> FATHER WILFRID, the rector of St. Clement's Hill retreat
>   house
> FATHER JOHN, a staff member at St. Clement's Hill
> MONSIGNOR RENTON, an elderly priest and a friend of Urban
> BILLY COSGROVE, a wealthy businessman and a benefactor of
>   the Order
> MRS. THWAITES, a wealthy invalid and a benefactress of the
>   Order
> SALLY HOPGOOD, her daughter
> SYLVIA BEAN, an acquaintance of Father Urban
> THE BISHOP OF THE GRAND PLAINS DIOCESE, an avid but un-
>   skillful golfer

The Novel

The novel tells what happens to Father Urban Roche in the eighteen months between his assignment to a dilapidated retreat house in rural Minnesota and his election as Provincial of the Order of St. Clement. As the novel's epigraph from James M. Barrie ("The life of every man is a diary in which he means to write one story, and writes another") foretells, many unexpected things happen to Father Urban during this year and a half. While Urban works to save the wordly fortunes of the Clementines, the Order works to save Urban's soul. The narrative direction of the novel is ironic.

Urban comes to isolated St. Clement's Hill, appalled and confused by Father Boniface's decision to employ him at this backwater, backward retreat house. Urban considers himself the Order's most successful member. He has lived up to his personal motto, "Be a winner!": Urban leads missions in major cities of the Midwest, and he moves easily among the powerful, wealthy, and worldly individuals. To be exiled from Chicago and to bury his talents in the country seem, to Urban, a waste of his abilities. Moreover, Boniface has transferred Urban at exactly the wrong moment: Urban has begun to cultivate the wealthy Billy Cosgrove as a patron of the

Order. Urban's cultivation has quickly yielded fruit—a new Clementine headquarters on the Chicago lakefront—and promises more.

The first quarter of the novel describes Urban's cold and lonesome winter months as he chafes under the regimen of Father Wilfrid, the rector. To Urban, Wilfrid is a small-minded martinet who works his community at physical tasks better left to hired help. Finally Urban is liberated from the retreat house when the pastor of a nearby parish requests someone to replace him during a vacation. Urban throws himself into stimulating the laity at St. Monica's parish through preaching, social clubs, and plans for a new church.

The next quarter of the novel shows Urban's return to the kind of priestly activity he likes best: making things happen, taking the leadership role, and acquainting himself with the important people. Urban begins wheeling and dealing on several fronts: persuading the bishop to install him as permanent pastor at St. Monica's (after the current pastor dies on vacation), visiting the eccentric invalid Mrs. Thwaites (who might leave a sizable legacy to a religious order which can give direction to her wayward son Dickie), building a golf course on the farm next door in order to attract a better "class of retreatant" to St. Clement's Hill (Billy arranges the financing). Urban keeps on the go by constantly borrowing automobiles from parishioners: Sylvia Bean, for example, unhesitatingly lends her stylish sports car.

The novel's turning point comes just as Urban has swung into high gear. During a golf match with the Bishop—an unspoken competition really between Urban's style and the local authorities—His Eminence's errant shot hits Urban in the head and sends him unconscious to the hospital. "An act of God, if I ever saw one," Monsignor Renton observes correctly. Providence apparently intervenes after Urban returns to the type of activity that Father Boniface sent him to St. Clement's to avoid. From this point Urban's world comes apart. Mrs. Thwaites refuses to see him again after he gently chides her for deceiving a servant. Billy snubs him for interfering in his attempt to kill a stag by drowning it. Sally Hopgood attempts to seduce Urban and, when he refuses, abandons him in embarrassing circumstances.

The final chapters show Urban's world shrunk once more to the boundaries of the retreat house. Again he is uneasy there, although now as a penitent more than as a rebel. Soon he receives the surprising news that he has been elected Provincial. Once he had coveted such authority, so that he could mold Clementines in his image. He returns to the Chicago headquarters, however, a changed priest, more attentive to personal piety than to bold strategic initiatives or to the cultivation of benefactors.

The Characters

An ironic portrayal of characters accompanies the ironic movement of plot. Until the last two chapters, the novel is told from Urban's perspective. That perspective encourages readers to accept Urban's estimate of himself and of other characters and to rely upon his interpretation of events. Only gradually, as events unfold, characters are tested, and details accumulate, do readers sense that Urban's perspective is distorted. By the end of the novel, readers realize that rather than providing a reliable picture of the world, Urban has indicted himself by having too much concern for material things and too little for spiritual ones.

Why is Urban's perspective so captivating in the beginning? He undeniably possesses many admirable qualities. He is intelligent, educated, cultured, sophisticated, and adept at handling people. He enjoys the trappings of the good life: dining at fine restaurants, sipping vintage wine with meals, traveling in first-class accommodations. Urban, despite his priestly collar, is a type of character that Americans have always admired. His motto, "Be a Winner!" is the credo of Horatio Alger's entrepreneurs and of legendary athletes. Urban's name capsulizes his identification with the qualities included in "urbanity" and associated with the stylish life of the big city.

Because Urban presents himself so favorably—without the narrator intervening to suggest otherwise—readers may easily accept at face value his estimate of people and circumstances. As Urban contends, the Clementines do indeed seem to be noteworthy only for being unnoteworthy. Wilfrid's leadership at St. Clement's Hill seems lackluster. Father John's acceptance of his assignment appears too meek and unthinking. Billy Cosgrove and Mrs. Thwaites probably are ready to be won, heart and soul and pocketbook, to the Church.

It is difficult to say at what point readers begin to realize that Urban is spiritually bankrupt. The awareness of Urban's personal and philosophical shortcomings grows gradually. Astute readers will pick up the ironic implications earlier than will passive readers. Passive readers may not doubt Urban until the bishop's providential shot clunks him on the head. Upon reflection, however, any reader can return to the one homily by Urban which the novel records. It appears at a significant point, at the exact center of the book. In the light of subsequent events, the sermon is a clear self-indictment. Urban warns his listeners against the very sins that he has committed. Though he preaches in flowing passages that come trippingly to the tongue after long practice, Urban cannot appreciate the import of the words for his own life: "Rid your gardens of the ragweed of covetousness, the dandelions of pride, and the crabgrass of indifference And clear our orchards of the rusty tin cans and broken glass of avarice, the old rubber tires of self-indulgence!"

It is clear in retrospect how unthinkingly Urban presumes his right to seek out and enjoy the world's powers and pleasures. He presumes them as his right because he intends to use them for good. Not only does he enjoy power and privilege for himself, but also he asserts them as goals for his Order. Possessed of these, the Order of St. Clement will rival the other great religious orders of the Church and will become a power with which even bishops must reckon.

Once readers pierce the persuasive mists of Urban's vision, they reevaluate the other characters. Wilfrid is obviously a pious priest who pushes his community to work with their hands because *laborare est orare*: To work is to pray. John is a model of self-abnegation, trusting to the wisdoms of Providence and the provincial in assigning him. Billy and Mrs. Thwaites are manipulators who like clerics to fuss over them—even for money—but who resent any attempts to inhibit their self-indulgence.

One of the delights of reading *Morte d'Urban* is the challenge to be astute and to appreciate the irony. To see through the charming *persona* of Urban, readers must garner impressions, have second thoughts, willingly make inductions and deductions about people and events. Unwary readers will be taken in, but perceptive readers will experience the pleasure of detecting a magnificent con artist. Unfortunately for Urban, he has conned himself. Fortunately for his Order, Father Boniface realizes it in time. Fortunately for Urban's soul, Providence is not conned in the least.

Themes and Meanings

There is much satire in *Morte d'Urban*. Though blind to his own faults, Urban has an occasional insightful laugh at the stodginess, the smugness, and the inertia which afflict any large institution such as the Church. On the other hand, Urban himself—as he represents a breed of activist, worldly priest—is satirized for his confusion of the City of God with the City of Man. More important to the novel, however, is the comedy. *Morte d'Urban* is comic in two senses: It is amusing (the fateful golf match, for example, is delightfully mock-heroic), and its protagonist wins out in the end. Although Urban is a chastened man as the book ends, he is a redeemed man. He has conquered his antagonist, himself.

Hence the title of the novel: "Morte d'Urban" is French for "the death of Urban." Death here obviously refers not to the physical Urban but to the psychological one. Urban's "Be a Winner!" mentality—and all the spiritual sins that accompany it—dies. Powers' title is a play upon the title of Sir Thomas Malory's medieval romance, *Le Morte d'Arthur* (1485). Malory's book records the history of King Arthur from the founding of Camelot, through the building of the Round Table and the search for the Holy Grail, to the kingdom's devastation by the sin of Lancelot and Guinevere.

Clearly, the collapse of Urban's Clementine kingdom in this world parallels, generally, the collapse of Arthur's chivalric ideal. Yet the novel never makes an explicit identification of Arthur and Urban. The novel does make some mention of Arthurian material when Father John writes a pamphlet on the fate of Lancelot. In John's version, Lancelot does penance for his failure to live up to his knightly vows by forsaking the world and becoming a monk. This story suggests obvious parallels to Urban as well. The parallel between Lancelot and Urban is suggested only late in the novel; though readers might be tempted to seek out other Arthurian parallels, Powers' use of Malory does not seem to go far beyond the allusive pun in the title. The temptation to read the novel as a medieval allegory or as a pastiche of Malory's book should be resisted.

Morte d'Urban presents a clear vision of what a modern priest should *not* be: He must not be huckster, manipulator, or entrepreneur. The novel does not show, however, a vision of what a priest should be. Defining the true or the ideal priest is a matter for theology, not for fiction, especially comic fiction. The novel does not attempt to describe the sense of faith or to depict an awareness of transcendent reality. Its subject is this world, not the hereafter.

Critical Context

Besides *Morte d'Urban*, Powers has published several collections of short stories, including *Prince of Darkness and Other Stories* (1947), *The Presence of Grace* (1956), and *Look How the Fish Live* (1975). Like the novel, the stories treat the world of Middle-American Catholicism, especially the lives of its priests. Powers' recurring subject is the experience, sacred and profane, of the clergy. These experiences are not sensational nor are they made melodramatic. Powers attends to more routine, ultimately more important, matters: The burden of a faith that must be lived for years; the subtle tension between the ideals articulated by Catholic belief and the limitations of human nature; the pedestrian ways in which Providence works—or fails to work—upon ordinary lives.

Despite the narrow compass of his writing, Powers has received a favorable reception from readers and critics alike. *Morte d'Urban* was a bestseller and received the National Book Award for 1963. The story collections were all well received. Powers is widely regarded as a fine stylist: His ability to efface himself as narrator, leaving the reader to confront and interpret characters and events, is distinctive. Powers is noteworthy too for the humanity with which he portrays his characters. Human beings can be sometimes silly and sometimes saintly in their efforts to apprehend the Divine Will. It is clear that J. F. Powers loves the latter without rejecting the former.

Sources for Further Study

Dupee, F. W. "In the Powers Country," in *Partisan Review*. XXX, no. 1 (Spring, 1963), pp. 113-116.

Evans, Fallon, ed. *J. F. Powers*, 1968.

Hagopian, John V. *J. F. Powers*, 1968.

Kellogg, Gene. *The Vital Tradition: The Catholic Novel in a Period of Convergence*, 1970.

McInerny, Dennis Q. "J. F. Powers," in *Critical Survey of Long Fiction*,
    1983.

                                                                                        Robert M. Otten

MOSES
Man of the Mountain

Author: Zora Neale Hurston (1903?-1960)
Type of plot: Allegory
Time of plot: Biblical times, during the Exodus
Locale: Egypt and the wilderness surrounding Mount Sinai
First published: 1939

> *Principal characters:*
> MOSES, an Egyptian who leads the enslaved Hebrews out of
> Egypt
> PHARAOH TA-PHAR, the leader of Egypt, oppressor of the He-
> brews, and uncle of Moses
> JETHRO, a prince of Midian and Moses' mentor
> ZIPPORAH, his daughter and Moses' second wife
> MIRIAM, a Hebrew prophetess who claims to be Moses' sister
> AARON, her brother, a leader of the Hebrews
> JOSHUA, a military leader of the Hebrews and Moses'
> confidant

The Novel

The novel's central action is based on the Old Testament tale of Moses leading the enslaved Hebrews out of Egypt to the promised land of Canaan. In order to trace Moses' development as a leader, Hurston begins her version with his childhood. As a boy, Moses is first influenced by Mentu, the Pharaoh's Hebrew stableman, who teaches him about nature and the languages of animals. Moses next turns to the Egyptian priests for instruction in the magic and voodoo used "to distract the minds of unthinking people from their real troubles."

Although Moses is not interested in acquiring power and prestige, as the son of the Pharaoh's daughter he poses a threat to the position of Ta-Phar, the Pharaoh's son and heir. He defeats Ta-Phar in ceremonial war games and consequently becomes a favorite of the Pharaoh. He is called on to lead the army, and as a result of his skill, Egyptian rule extends over the Middle East. As a result, Egypt gains glory, and for political reasons Moses gains an Ethiopian princess for his wife.

Soon palace intrigue and the rumors spread by Ta-Phar threaten Moses. Ta-Phar capitalizes on Moses' well-known sympathy for the oppressed Hebrews, claiming that Moses himself is a Hebrew. In addition, Ta-Phar encourages the acceptance of a Hebrew legend that Moses, as a baby, was discovered in the bullrushes by the Pharaoh's daughter and adopted by her. The legend arose out of the Hebrews' reaction to the Pharaoh's policy of

slaying all Hebrew male babies. In order to provide their son with a chance
for a future, Amram and Jochebed placed their three-month-old boy in a
basket on the Nile. Then they charged their daughter Miriam to watch and
report what happened. Miriam fell asleep, however, and, afraid to tell her
parents the truth, she claimed that the Pharaoh's daughter found him. The
tale quickly gained acceptance because the Hebrews were pleased with the
irony that one of them was in the palace, accepted by the Pharaoh as a family member.

Though the legend is false, Moses chooses exile instead of confronting
the rumors. Crossing the Red Sea, he leaves wealth and status behind him
and begins anew at the age of twenty-five. Days of wandering bring him to
the foot of Mount Sinai. After befriending Jethro, a local prince, Moses
marries his voluptuous daughter Zipporah and intends to make his home at
the foot of the majestic mountain, tending sheep. Jethro, however, obsessed
by a dream has other plans. He becomes Moses' teacher, instructing him in
his own monotheistic religion and preparing him for the task of leading the
enslaved Hebrews out of Egypt.

After a twenty-year absence, Moses travels to Egypt in order to learn the
secrets contained in the Book of Thoth. Following a battle with a deathless
serpent, Moses studies the document, acquiring the ability "to command the
heavens and the earth, the abyss and the mountain, and the sea." When he
returns to Midian, Jethro pronounces him ready for his task. Although Moses resists, a burning bush, a manifestation of God, convinces him that he
has been chosen, and he acquiesces.

Leading the Hebrews out of Egypt is no easy task. Ta-Phar, who is now
the Pharaoh, and the Egyptian nobles are reluctant to part with their slaves
and the builders of their splendid cities. After Moses causes numerous
plagues—frogs, lice, darkness, and the death of firstborn Egyptian children—the Pharaoh consents, but Moses also must motivate the Hebrews;
one of whom argues, "I was figuring on going fishing tomorrow morning. I
don't want to be bothered with no packing up today." When reports that the
Hebrews have escaped reach the palace, the Pharaoh masses his army and
pursues them, overtaking them at the Red Sea. Moses parts the sea, the
Hebrews cross, and as the Egyptians follow, the sea crashes together,
destroying the Egyptian army.

Although the Hebrews are safe, the journey is not over. At every inconvenience, the Hebrews complain, wishing to return to Egypt. The first time
that Moses reaches the Promised Land, the Hebrews are not ready.
Although no longer oppressed by the Egyptians, mentally they are still
slaves. Moses, realizing that "no man may make another free. . . ," leads the
Hebrews away. Thus they are condemned to wander in the wilderness for
forty years, until the old generation dies, and a new generation will be able
to accept freedom.

The journey is a trying one for Moses. Miriam and Aaron, jealous of Moses' position, undermine him. In addition, the Hebrews resist acknowledging Moses as their leader, resenting his interference in their lives. At one point the Hebrews abandon the new monotheistic God and return to worshiping and celebrating the Egyptian sun gods. Only after years of hardship are the people prepared for the Promised Land. Joshua, a young Hebrew trained by Moses, will lead them into Canaan. Moses, his tasks accomplished, ascends Mount Nebo, bids the Hebrews farewell, and "descend[s] the other side of the mountain and head[s] back over the years."

The Characters

The characters of *Moses* are generally flat and underdeveloped, in part because Hurston is adapting a biblical tale and is limited by her source, but also because she is writing an allegory of the American black slaves' struggle for emancipation.

Hurston has combined the Moses of the Old Testament with the Moses depicted in African folklore. Thus, the Moses described in the novel is a wise prophet but also is a great voodoo chief. His power is derived not only from God but also from the Egyptian priests and the Book of Thoth. Both of these aspects—wisdom and magic—are necessary to lead and control the Hebrews, who, because of their enslavement are not prepared for leadership roles. In order to emphasize the African heritage of Moses, Hurston departs from the biblical source and portrays Moses as Egyptian born. In this manner, she suggests that a forceful outside leader is necessary to free an oppressed people.

The novel chronicles Moses' growth as he develops into the leader of the Hebrews. His early years are a preparation for the task that Jethro has set before him. From Mentu, the Egyptian priests, and the Book of Thoth, he acquires the magic later needed to control the Hebrews. From his years of military campaigns, he acquires the military expertise that he will later impart to Joshua. His sense of fairness results in his siding with the oppressed Hebrews, at one point killing an Egyptian overseer who brutally beats a Hebrew worker. Later, in exile, he dreams of a land where equality could exist, a land that will turn out to be the Promised Land of the Hebrews. Thus, although he is reluctant to lead the Hebrews, he has in a sense spent his life preparing for it. His later complete acceptance of the task is illustrated by the change of his speech from the standard English of the Egyptian nobles to the black dialect of the Hebrews.

Moses, the ideal leader, is opposed by Pharaoh Ta-Phar, a corrupt ruler who derives his power from the oppression of his people. Thus, when Moses requests that the Hebrews be allowed to leave, the Pharaoh must refuse, for the release of the enslaved Hebrews would cause his downfall. Ironically, his refusal helps Moses in unifying the Hebrews.

Miriam and Aaron are Moses' link to the Hebrews but are also his adversaries. They oppose Moses, desiring his position of authority but lacking his capabilities. Miriam, bitter and jealous, tries to arouse the Hebrew women against Zipporah, the sensuous wife of Moses, while her brother, Aaron, demands the trappings of a high priest. Because of their flawed natures, neither will arrive at the Promised Land. Miriam is reduced to begging Moses to allow her to die, and later Aaron is stabbed by Moses so that Aaron's esteemed reputation among the Hebrews can be preserved.

Joshua represents the new Hebrew, symbolizing the potential of the Hebrew people. He is obedient, loyal, and willing to serve and to sacrifice. He has been groomed by Moses to lead the Hebrews into the Promised Land.

Themes and Meanings

Hurston uses the biblical story of Moses and the Hebrews as an allegory representing the oppression of the American black. The identification of the two groups is made clear through the portrayal of the Hebrews: They speak a black dialect, and their diet consists of food that is traditionally associated with Southern blacks: watermelons, cucumbers, and pan-fried fish. In addition, much of what is described concerning the Hebrews before their emancipation is true of blacks before the Civil War. Both groups live in shacks; both groups are whipped to produce more work. The children of both the Hebrews and the blacks are threatened; the Pharaoh orders male babies killed, and the plantation owners often sold the children of slaves. Even the paternalistic attitude is similar; the Egyptians argue, "What would slaves want to be free for anyway? They are being fed and taken care of. What more could they want?" The novel is first a discussion of the slave issue in the American past, but at the same time it comments on the problems that faced the blacks in the 1930's when, although institutionalized slavery no longer existed, blacks were still victims of discrimination.

The book, while focusing on American blacks, is also a study of the problems associated with emancipation. It is not enough to be rid of shackles, one must also internalize freedom. One must grow into freedom, developing a sense of worth. In Egypt the Hebrews felt that somehow the Egyptians were superior and rightfully their bosses. It took forty years before the Hebrews were ready to enter the Promised Land, before they could accept equality.

To accomplish her goal of transforming a biblical tale into a vehicle for a discussion of slavery and oppression, Hurston departs from her Old Testament source. To make Moses seem more of an ordinary man who develops into a leader, she provides him with a childhood and with common human characteristics—his desire for his wife, his friendship with Jethro, and his irritation with the Hebrews. She also provides alternative explanations for some of the incidents related in the Bible. Moses is Egyptian born and thus not affected by the stultifying effects of enslavement. He, unlike the Hebrews, is able to imagine a different and more just way of life. Hurston also rejects the biblical account of the miraculous parting of the Red Sea, providing instead an explanation based on natural causes. Finally, in the novel, much of Moses' power is explained by his knowledge of magic and voodoo. Thus, Hurston emphasizes that leaders arise out of the people and are not divinely created.

Critical Context

The mixture of voodoo, folklore, and black dialect found in *Moses: Man of the Mountain* reflects Hurston's cultural heritage and experiences. Born in the all-black town of Eatonville, Florida, she grew up surrounded by the poetic speech rhythms and dialect that she recorded in the novel. During her college years, she developed an interest in anthropology, studying under the renowned Franz Boas of Columbia University. Later, on a fellowship, she traveled to the Southern United States and to Haiti to collect folktales, which resulted in a well-regarded volume of folklore, *Mules and Men* (1935).

Moses: Man of the Mountain was an ambitious undertaking: Hurston attempted to make the tale of Moses and the Hebrews speak for enslaved people everywhere. To a certain extent she succeeded, but the novel's allegorical intent resulted in generally weak, stereotyped characters and a certain ambivalence displayed toward them. As noted above, the first time that Moses parts the Red Sea, Hurston presents the event as a natural occurrence, but the second time, she treats it as a miracle. The text clearly shows that Moses is Egyptian-born, but later Moses himself has doubts.

Because of the satire aimed at the enslaved race, Hurston has been criticized for writing about the black situation for a white audience. It was her intention, however, to go beyond racial issues and to treat universal themes such as the effect of enslavement, the use and misuse of power, and the necessary qualities of a leader. While *Their Eyes Were Watching God* (1937) will remain the most successful of her novels, *Moses: Man of the Mountain* should not be discounted.

Sources for Further Study

Hemenway, Robert E. *Zora Neale Hurston: A Literary Biography*, 1977.

Howard, Lillie P. *Zora Neale Hurston*, 1980.

Jackson, Blyden. "Some Negroes in the Land of Goschen," in *Tennessee Folklore Society Bulletin*. XIX (December, 1953), pp. 103-107.

Rayson, Ann. "The Novels of Zora Neale Hurston," in *Studies in Black Literature*. V, no. 3 (Winter, 1974), pp. 1-10.

Barbara Wiedemann

MOSQUITOES

Author: William Faulkner (1897-1962)
Type of plot: Satiric novel of ideas
Time of plot: August, 1925
Locale: New Orleans and Lake Pontchartrain
First published: 1927

Principal characters:

DAWSON FAIRCHILD, a novelist, Faulkner's portrait of Sherwood Anderson

MRS. MAURIER, a wealthy widow who lends her patronage to the New Orleans artistic community aboard her yacht *Nausikaa*

ERNEST TALLIAFERRO, formerly Tarver, a dilettante and wholesale buyer of women's undergarments

PATRICIA (PAT) ROBYN, age eighteen, Mrs. Maurier's niece, a frank, epicene virgin who embodies Gordon's idea of female beauty

THEODORE ROBYN, Pat's twin brother, a young man absorbed in fashioning a wooden pipe, off to Yale in September

GORDON, age thirty-six, a hawklike, silent, and masculine sculptor, the novel's ideal of the dedicated artist

JULIUS KAUFFMAN, "the Semitic man," Fairchild's friend and foremost critic

EVA WISEMAN, Kauffman's sister, a poet

MARK FROST, a "ghostly" young man and "the best poet in New Orleans" according to his own judgment

DOROTHY JAMESON, Frost's companion, a painter

MAJOR AYERS, an Englishman determined to make his fortune by marketing a cure for constipation

JENNY STEINBAUER, a voluptuous, unreflective blonde

PETE GINOTTA, Jenny's boyfriend, who wears a stiff straw hat

DAVID WEST, the inarticulate steward, who accompanies Pat on an ill-fated excursion to the mainland

The Novel

In *Mosquitoes*, William Faulkner draws a satiric portrait of the New Orleans artistic community of 1925 while working out his own theories about art and the artist. As a "novel of ideas" in Aldous Huxley's sense of the phrase, *Mosquitoes* contains much talk and little action. The novel's plan is simple: Mrs. Maurier, a wealthy New Orleans socialite and "patron of the arts," gathers aboard her motorized yacht *Nausikaa* an awkward assortment of artists, intellectuals, and adolescents for a talk-filled cruise on Louisiana's Lake Pontchartrain. When her nephew Theodore, needing an instrument to bore a hole through his handmade pipe, "borrows" a steel rod from the ship's intricate steering mechanism, the disabled *Nausikaa* is soon stranded on a sandbar, thus providing a convenient situation for the novel's seemingly endless talk.

The shipboard company can be divided into three general groups: the adults and the young, the men and the women, the verbose and the reticent. The central group consists of the older, talkative men. Dawson Fairchild (novelist), Julius Kauffman (critic), and their hangers-on, Mark Frost (poet) and Major Ayers (Englishman), intersperse their sophisticated discussions about sex, art, and society with periodic trips below deck, where they go to evade the insufferable Mrs. Maurier and to get drunk on Fairchild's whiskey. Mrs. Maurier's plans for a decorous party are continually thwarted by the rudeness and frank vulgarity of these men ("but after all, one must pay a price for Art," she laments), and she falls back on the support of Eva Wiseman (poet) and Dorothy Jameson (painter), lonely women who keep each other company, playing cards and smoking cigarettes.

With their unconscious physicality and commitment to experience as opposed to talk, the young people are a group very much apart, and they are at the center of the novel's exploration of sexuality. As they sport among themselves, the novel illuminates a contrast between the variety and unreflectiveness of their sexual exploration on the one hand, and the self-conscious sexual frustration of the adults on the other hand. The leading figure of this young group is the frank and boyish Pat Robyn, who has characteristically brought two people aboard whom she met only hours before departure: Jenny Steinbauer, a young, voluptuous, and nonverbal blonde who repels the advances of many of the men, and Pete Ginotta, her silent and jealous boyfriend, who wears a stiff straw hat at a rakish angle, refusing to put it down lest it should come to harm. Theodore, Pat's twin, is a version of the silent and absorbed artist as he whittles away at his pipe and tries to avoid the attentions of his sister; and David West, the steward, one of Faulkner's inarticulates, is a good man who possesses depths of feeling and flashes of inner poetry.

Isolated from all these groups, though drawn obsessively to Pat, is the silent, muscular sculptor, Gordon. He is at the center of the novel's values, according to which the most talkative are the least creative; he is an almost purely silent figure and the one true artist aboard. His polar opposite is the "unmuscled," affected, and effeminate Talliaferro, a wholesale buyer of women's undergarments. Chatty and nervous, Talliaferro is an ineffectual intermediary between the men and the women and is the novel's most ludicrous figure.

The novel's most interesting and extended action takes place when Pat and David desert ship in a romantically deluded attempt to reach Mandeville, the first leg of a planned journey to Europe. Their attempt to escape the "ship of fools" into a world of adventure and romance is, however, a complete disaster. Reaching shore and marching off in the wrong direction through miasmic swampland, they encounter sheer reality itself in the shape of voracious mosquitoes. Parched, sunburned, and exhausted, they are finally aided by a malevolent, foulmouthed, and lascivious swamp dweller who, for the price of five dollars paid in advance, agrees to ferry Pat and David back to the still-stranded yacht, where nothing has changed.

Nothing has changed when the *Nausikaa* is freed and returns to New Orleans. The group disintegrates, and the novel follows the individual characters as they fall back into the habitual urban patterns which they left behind four days earlier. Life seems as dreary and as futile as ever. The central themes of the novel are unified in one climactic scene, however, the journey of Fairchild, Kauffman, and Gordon through the old city's "nighttown" or red-light district. Here their drunkenness, and the murky hallucinatory quality of the dark streets, are rendered in an experimental and poetic language reminiscent of the "Circe" chapter of James Joyce's *Ulysses* (1922). As they walk together, each man has a private visionary experience or "epiphany," in which significant, vivid form is given to the novel's conception of art and the artist.

The Characters

Some of the characters of *Mosquitoes* are based upon members of the New Orleans artistic community whom Faulkner knew in 1925, while others are wholly imaginative constructs. The novelist Dawson Fairchild, for example, is Faulkner's portrait of Sherwood Anderson, the "father" of Faulkner's generation of American novelists. Though Anderson was an important early model for him, Faulkner soon began to look elsewhere, turning principally to such writers as Joyce, Joseph Conrad, and T. S. Eliot, who represented an international as opposed to a regional standard of literature. Faulkner's portrayal of Anderson, consequently, is equivocal. On the one hand, Fairchild is credited with possessing an attractive, folksy humor revealed primarily by the Al Jackson tall tales; or he is shown to be master of narrative pathos as when he tells Theodore the story of his ill-fated attempt to gain entrance to a college fraternity (his effect is achieved, however, by casting himself as a fool: "You poor goof" is Theodore's summation of the story). On the other hand, Fairchild is the recipient of the novel's most serious and significant criticism, and as such, he is to be distinguished from the relatively flattened satirical stereotypes of Talliaferro and Mrs. Maurier. Fairchild's principal critic is his friend Kauffman (referred to throughout as "the Semitic man"), who represents many of Faulkner's own critical judgments in the novel. Kauffman considers Fairchild a talented but seriously flawed artist; as a man, Fairchild is a "poor emotional eunuch," and as an artist, a "bewildered stenographer with a gift for people." As the words "son" and "child" embedded in his name suggest, Dawson Fairchild is emotionally and artistically young, never having grown beyond a midwestern regionalism and a "hopeless sentimentality," a fact which has prevented his art from achieving a fully mature and universal significance. Though endowed with moments of insight and poetic expression, Fairchild is ultimately drawn as the pathetic, older novelist, a "benevolent walrus" who is aware of his waning artistic power.

The other flawed artists aboard the *Nausikaa* receive considerably less serious treatment. Mark Frost, for example, is clearly a butt of relentless satire. A "ghostly," "sepulchral,' and morose young man with a "prehensile mouth," the aptly named Frost continually reminds the company that he is "the best poet in New Orleans." At best a minor regional poet, at worst a charlatan, Mark Frost is Faulkner's caricature of the pretentious, clever, and constipated poet. Here is Faulkner's cutting description: "Mark Frost, the ghostly young man, a poet who produced an occasional cerebral and obscure poem in four of seven lines reminding one somehow of the function of evacuation excruciatingly and incompletely performed." Both Fairchild and Frost fall short of Faulkner's conception of the dedicated artist, the quasi-mythical Gordon (he is described as possessing a silver faun's face—like Donald Mahon of Faulkner's *Soldier's Pay*, 1926—and a hawklike arrogance), who is characterized throughout as being hard, masculine, lonely, and silent.

Among the nonartists, Mrs. Maurier is treated initially as a creature of pure satire, but she undergoes a process of humanization over the course of the novel, as Faulkner's conception of her matures. The principal agent of this humanizing process is Faulkner's key self-projection, Gordon, whose sculpture of Mrs. Maurier's head captures the suffering and despair of the human being behind the socialite's mask. Though Talliaferro is less fully humanized (and his presence at the opening and closing of the novel signals its principally satiric intention), his loneliness and frustration is suggested, primarily in flashes of interior revelation which Faulkner affords the reader. In both Talliaferro and Mrs. Maurier, one sees Faulkner's effort to transcend the reductiveness of satire, and through a growing realism of attitude, to humanize even disagreeable individual types.

Though Gordon represents Faulkner's conception of the true artist, many other characters embody important aspects of Faulkner's personality and art. For example, Faulkner attributes to Eva Wiseman some of his own poetry to be published in *A Green Bough* (1933); to Julius Kauffman, some of his own critical theories; to Dawson Fairchild, his definition of genius as a "Passion Week of the heart" along with the Al Jackson tall tales (he had co-authored these with Anderson); and to Talliaferro and Mark Frost, aspects of his own youthful pretentiousness and posturing. Faulkner appears most significantly as Gordon, the sculptor, but two other incarnations of Faulkner in the work should also be noted. There is the funny, shabbily dressed "little kind of black man" whom Jenny had met at Mandeville, and whose name she has difficulty recalling to Pat: "He said he was a liar by profession, and he made good money at it, enough to own a Ford as soon as he got it paid out. I think he was crazy. Not dangerous: just crazy." When she does recall his name, "Faulkner," Pat responds: "'Faulkner?' . . . Never heard of him." There is also the thunderous typist with the "sweating leonine head" whom Talliaferro interrupts twice near the close of the novel. Though he is described as being a large man (Faulkner was not), his is clearly a portrait of the intensely absorbed literary artist and as close a model as the text affords of Faulkner as a novelist. His devastating but comical dismissal of Talliaferro may be read as a final repudiation of both the New Orleans artistic milieu, and of the kind of smart, satirical writing in which Faulkner had indulged in this novel: "'And here I am, wasting my damn life trying to invent people by means of the written word!' His face became suddenly suffused: he rose towering. 'Get to hell out of here,' he roared. 'You have made me sick!'"

Themes and Meanings

The silent artist Gordon is uniquely sensitive to the sterility of talk, and he gives expression, through the mediation of the narrator, to the novel's dominant theme: "Talk, talk, talk: the utter and heartbreaking stupidity of words. It seemed endless, as though it might go on forever. Ideas, thoughts, became mere sounds to be bandied about until they were dead." The sexual contrast between the effeminate Talliaferro and the masculine Gordon is an extension of this theme onto the level of characterization.

More generally, words, in their annoying persistence, are an enervating force, and as such, they have much in common with the novel's ubiquitous mosquitoes. Though serving at times as a realistic correction of romantic ideals, as in Pat's abortive journey with David, mosquitoes are more commonly associated with all that is ignoble and deflated, all that is opposed to desire. Distracting and invasive mosquitoes, like empty talk, and like Talliaferro's interruption of the artist at his typewriter, become the enemies of art, continually breaking in on "the heart's beautitude," the artist's private world of value and potency. Like mosquitoes, the crowd aboard the *Nausikaa*, and by extension, all such superficial artistic milieus, represent parasitic forces which the true artist must evade.

Opposed to the novel's portrait of a slightly inimical social and natural reality are a series of formulations of the artist's private inner world. The artist's withdrawal into this private world is a way of evading "mosquitoes," and a necessary prelude to an engagement with a more fundamental reality. The sources of truly powerful and universal art are, in a seeming paradox, private and inward. This theme is developed most fully in the "nighttown" scene, here by Julius Kauffman: "Dante invented Beatrice, creating himself a maid that life had not had time to create, and laid upon her frail and unbowed shoulders the whole burden of man's history of his impossible heart's desire." Gordon's Beatrice is "the headless, armless, legless torso of a girl, motionless and virginal and passionately eternal," the sculpture in his studio of which Pat is a living incarnation. The artist seeks to capture in such images what Fairchild calls an "instant of timeless beautitude," "a kind of splendid and timeless beauty" wherein the artist's engagement with reality achieves powerful artistic expression.

Critical Context

Though widely considered his least successful novel, *Mosquitoes* was an essential part of Faulkner's artistic development, a necessary prelude to the masterpieces which would soon follow, such as *The Sound and the Fury* (1929), which was completed only two years later. In repudiating Sherwood Anderson and New Orleans' "talky" sophistication, Faulkner clarified his own artistic position and made possible the discovery of his own "little postage stamp of native soil," whose exploration would define one of the world's greatest and most universally significant literary careers.

In *Mosquitoes*, also, Faulkner conducted a wide variety of narrative experiments, manipulating the technical and thematic innovations that he had discovered in Joyce, Eliot, Conrad, and others. By undertaking a process of absorption, assimilation, and transformation of the lessons of the literary masters, Faulkner laid the groundwork of his own spectacular technical mastery in the fiction to follow. *Mosquitoes*, then, is an invaluable record of the young artist's development, a document of Faulkner's turning away from New Orleans and towards Oxford, Mississippi, the model of Jefferson, Mississippi, and the heart of his immortal fictional cosmos, Yoknapatawpha County.

Sources for Further Study

Brooks, Cleanth. *William Faulkner: Toward Yoknapatawpha and Beyond*, 1978.
Millgate, Michael. *The Achievement of William Faulkner*, 1965.
Vickery, Olga W. *The Novels of William Faulkner: A Critical Interpretation*, 1964.
Waggoner, Hyatt H. *William Faulkner: From Jefferson to the World*, 1959.
Wittenberg, Judith Bryant. *Faulkner: The Transfiguration of Biography*, 1979.

Michael Zeitlin

A MOTHER AND TWO DAUGHTERS

Author: Gail Godwin (1937-   )
Type of plot: Domestic realism/social chronicle
Time of plot: December, 1978, to summer, 1979, and one day in 1984
Locale: Mountain City, Greensboro, Winston-Salem (all in North Carolina); a
    small town on the Iowa shore of the Mississippi; and Ocracoke, an island
    off the Carolina shore
First published: 1982

> *Principal characters:*
> NELL STRICKLAND, the mother of the title, a widow, and a
>   former nurse
> CATE GALITSKY, Nell's twice-divorced older daughter, a col-
>   lege English teacher
> LYDIA MANSFIELD, Nell's younger daughter, newly separated,
>   a mother of two, a returning college student
> LEONARD STRICKLAND, the husband of Nell and the father of
>   Cate and Lydia, a presence in the minds of the protago-
>   nists throughout the novel despite his death in the first
>   chapter
> THEODORA BLOUNT, Cate's godmother and "undisputed lead-
>   er" of the Stricklands' "social set" in Mountain City

The Novel

Fittingly, in a novel that considers to what extent individuals can create
their own destinies and to what extent those destinies are shaped by the
people around them, *A Mother and Two Daughters* both opens and closes
with a party. Nell and Leonard Strickland attend the first party at the home
of Theodora Blount, representative of the "old guard" and repository of
conservative, traditional Southern values. Yet the appearance at the party of
Theodora's unmarried, pregnant, backwoods protégée, the teenage Wickie
Lee, suggests that those values may be in transition, as does the epigraph
(from D. H. Lawrence's "Dies Irae") for part 1: "Our epoch is over, a cycle
of evolution is finished."

The course of part 1 reveals that the lives of the three protagonists are
also in transition. Nell Strickland loses her husband, Leonard, to a heart
attack immediately after Theodora's party. Nell's younger daughter, Lydia,
has just left her husband of sixteen years to create a life of her own, which
she initiates by going back to college. Lydia's older sister, Cate, is between
men and doubtful that her job teaching English at the insolvent Melanchthon College in Iowa can long continue. As they struggle to redefine their
lives, all three women feel the loss of Leonard, an introspective, idealistic

lawyer, whose gentleness and sensitivity had always acted as a restraining influence on his strong-willed wife and daughters.

That none of the women can begin the process of redefinition with a clean slate or, as Cate puts it, can run from their histories—including their mistakes—is suggested by the epigraph for part 2, from the *I Ching*: "*Ku*— WORK ON WHAT HAS BEEN SPOILED (DECAY)." Cate's history of fierce independence and fear of being submerged in the protective embrace of another leads her to reject the marriage proposal of the equally strong and independent pesticide manufacturer, Roger Jernigan, and to abort the child they inadvertently conceived together. At the same time, although she refuses to admit defeat, the bankruptcy of Melanchthon College brings Cate to a low point in her career.

Meanwhile, Lydia's star has been rising. She gets A's in all of her college courses, has a passionate affair with a man who adores her, finds an important woman friend in the brilliant black instructor of a course in the History of Female Consciousness, and lands a job in front of the cameras on a local television show.

In the wake of Leonard's death, Nell retreats into her house in Mountain City and thinks about her past with him: how he "*protected*" her "from my harshest judgments of myself as well as of others." Yet she seems to accept her loss, content to watch the baby crows outside her window and somewhat impatient when her house is invaded by Theodora's book club.

Nell's serenity is disturbed when, in part 3, she and her daughters converge on Leonard's old cottage on the island of Ocracoke. Nell's grief is reawakened, but a friendship is renewed when she discovers that an old schoolmate has rented the cottage next door. It is at Ocracoke that Nell really says good-bye to Leonard and is thereafter able to resume her own life.

It is also at Ocracoke that the sibling rivalry of Cate and Lydia finally explodes. Cate seeks to trivialize the friends, goals, and accomplishments of Lydia, who retaliates by suggesting that Cate has "nothing to show" for her life. After both angry women storm out of the rickety cottage, it burns down, another vanished symbol of a closed epoch in their lives, perhaps part of the "wreckage of ourselves" emphasized by the epigraph for the section.

Family members and friends are reunited and reconciled in the epilogue, set five years later, and the novel ends as it began—with a party. This time Cate, not Theodora, presides, at the mountain retreat she has inherited from an eccentric cousin. Theodora is there, too, now arguing the pros of racial intermarriage after meeting the lovely black bride of Lydia's son Leo. Wickie Lee, who turns out to be a distant cousin of Theodora, has married and become conventionally respectable. Finally, the three protagonists have achieved the new self-definitions they had been struggling toward. Lydia is an immensely successful television personality; Nell is a wife again and, after a hiatus of many years, has returned to nursing; Cate is a free-lance teacher who creatively markets her courses and continues to go her own way. The sisters are both now secure enough to reestablish their relationship, thus ratifying the epilogue's Emersonian epigraph, which asserts that "our relatedness" makes us "strong."

The Characters

Depending upon whether one regards attitudes or behavior as more telling, one could call Nell Strickland an outsider playing the role of insider or an insider who prefers to think of herself as an outsider. She has lived in Mountain City ever since she was fourteen, she has gone to the book club meetings presided over by the the pretentious Theodora, and she has been for forty years the respected, popular wife of a respected, popular Mountain City lawyer. Yet, even if Nell goes through the motions of conventional propriety, she views those rituals and the class consciousness that dictates them with a somewhat satiric eye.

Insofar as Nell's (usually accurate) satiric vision is a defense against rejection and pain, it is offset by her compassion and her vital interest, as a former nurse and as a mother, in helping people to live well and die comfortably. Although, after Leonard's death, retreat from life and from people is a temptation for Nell, the needs of others cause her to become more fully engaged in life than ever. It is Nell who mobilizes the women of the book club when Wickie Lee goes into labor during a meeting; Nell who eases the last days of her old school friend Merle Chapin; Nell who finds happiness and even passion married to Merle's widower, Marcus.

If, out of deference to Leonard, Nell has largely suppressed her skeptical, defiant side, Cate is the rebel Nell has never allowed herself to be: a twice-divorced, 1960's-style liberal, who in 1970 found herself briefly in jail for leading her students from a New York girls' school in a demonstration at the Lincoln Tunnel to protest the invasion of Cambodia. It should be noted that, in this story of family relationships and correspondences, Cate's activism results not only from the critical perspective she has inherited from Nell but also from the idealism she has absorbed from Leonard. She cannot see a wrong without wanting to right it and has done the sorts of things Leonard "would have liked to do, had he been less prudent, more furious and full of fire." As she approaches forty, Cate is alternately gratified and irritated by the knowledge that family members regard her as excitingly, but disturbingly, unpredictable.

While Nell has sacrificed open criticism of social pretensions to the proprieties observed by her society, Cate has "sacrific[ed] people to ideals": insulting Theodora, alienating Lydia, and aborting the baby of a man with whom she could have been happy. Still, if Cate is hard on others, she is even harder on herself. Her zealous pursuit of the truth and her impetuosity cause her more pain than they do anyone else. After her momentous fight with Lydia, Cate's long walk on the windy beach—during which she castigates herself for enviously trying to destroy her sister's pride in her own accomplishments—results in Bell's palsy, a temporary numbing of the facial muscles. This experience gives Cate a sense of her own limits, and thereafter, she cultivates a "detached observer" side of her personality to protect herself and others from her own worst excesses.

On the surface, Lydia is more conventional, the obedient Nell rather than the rebellious one. She has always been the perfect wife and mother— pretty, feminine, loving, and sufficiently well organized to have time to spare for frequent escapist naps. When she decides to leave her husband, Max, she manages that perfectly too, doing well in school and at love—and feeling no more need for naps. If she is less daring than Cate (and she has always resented Cate's taunts to that effect), she is equally self-willed, and she dislikes Cate's wide-ranging diatribes against the conventional, traditional society in which she, Lydia, hopes to make her mark.

While Cate most wants to see the truth for what it is, Lydia most wants to be "widely admired and influential." Lydia gets her wish, but, because the measures of her success are external, she never feels secure in that success and always feels that something is lacking. Her relationship with her sons is emblematic of her internal conflict, for she most loves not the beautiful, self-contained boy who is like her but the messy, artistic one who is spiritually akin to Cate.

Cate, Lydia, and Nell are all painted in broad, clear strokes by Godwin, who portrays their sufferings with understanding and their self-delusions with a fine, ironic appreciation. Occasionally, there is less subtlety than there could be, as when Godwin repeatedly uses Cate's uptilted chin as a symbol of her independence and free spirit. Nevertheless, if Godwin's symbolism is sometimes obvious, it is also appropriate, and its clarity makes the novel accessible to a wide range of readers.

Themes and Meanings

When the Mountain City book club decides to discuss *The Scarlet Letter*, Cate tells Nell that the novel "asks a very crucial question 'Can the individual spirit survive the society in which it has to live?' " The question is crucial to *A Mother and Two Daughters* also, as the three protagonists struggle to re-create themselves in a world where the rules are changing. The self-definitions at which they arrive and the adjustments they make represent the survival strategies of three strong-willed individual spirits.

Cate, the romantic truth seeker, finds that, in order to achieve her own goals, she must learn self-control; she must learn when rage is productive and when it is not. Her spirit compromises but does not give in. Lydia, who buys into society's success story, is just as much her own creation as Cate but is rather less content, her spirit enslaved to some extent by her very success. Nell, who in the past protected the integrity of her individual spirit through critical detachment and self-defensive aloofness, establishes a more vital connection to her society through involvement and love. Perhaps because she has paid her social dues over the years, the little society of Mountain City is now ready to accept her on her own terms.

Certainly, all three protagonists recognize both losses and gains in the transitions they see going on around them. On the surface, the signs of disintegration are all too apparent. Colleges go bankrupt. Old landscapes give way to new shopping malls. Gasoline is scarce. Yet change also means new possibilities. The marriage of Leo Mansfield and Camilla Peverell-Watson, if not conventionally prudent, has nevertheless become one of those possibilities. So has the brilliant new career of Lydia, once a traditional, stay-at-home wife and mother. So has the self-invented career of Cate, which, in any case, suits her better than the job she previously held at her bankrupt college.

In the midst of all the changes, the family as locus of value is the one thing that gives stability to the lives of Godwin's characters. Despite the rivalry and tension, the fights and reluctant compromises, family members need one another in a world that offers few other constants. Thus, neither Cate nor Lydia can truly validate her own success without making peace with the other. (It is no accident that Theodora Blount, who has no family to count on, sees fit to erect the Theodora Blount Medical Wing at the Episcopal Retirement Home in advance of her retreat to that institution.)

One reason that the family, in Godwin's world, retains its vitality is that it, too, is in the process of being redefined. Nell's extended family, at the end of the novel, includes not only her new husband and her blood relatives but also Lydia's lover Stanley Edelman, Max's child Liza, and possibly even Wickie Lee. If there is one message Godwin has for her readers in *A Mother and Two Daughters*, it is that people need to connect themselves with, but not submerge themselves in, others. The ideal sort of connectedness—the sort the protagonists work to achieve with those they care about—means, then, not loss of identity but the creation of a life-support system in which identity can struggle to know itself and may even flourish.

Critical Context

With the four novels and many stories that preceded *A Mother and Two Daughters*, Gail Godwin had already won critical acclaim. The publication of her fifth novel gave her a best-seller. Godwin regards the novel as an artistic "turning point" for her as well, for in it she explored the consciousnesses of three characters instead of one and created a portrait of a whole society rather than of a single person.

Like the fiction of Anne Tyler and Margaret Drabble, *A Mother and Two Daughters* concerns itself with the evolution of the family in modern society and the roles it may play in the lives of modern women. Like most major women novelists from Jane Austen onward, Godwin considers how her heroines can best find or create places for themselves in a society over which they have negligible control but in which they can achieve some small influence.

Source for Further Study
Rhodes, Carolyn. "Gail Godwin and the Ideal of Southern Womanhood," in *Women Writers of the Contemporary South*, 1984.

Linda Seidel Costic

MOTHER NIGHT

Author: Kurt Vonnegut, Jr. (1922-   )
Type of plot: Comic realism
Time of plot: 1938-1961
Locale: Nazi Germany, New York City, and Israel
First published: 1961

> *Principal characters:*
>> HOWARD W. CAMPBELL, JR., the protagonist, a former United
>> States spy in Germany, author of a memoir written in an
>> Israeli prison
>> HELGA NOTH, his German wife, who dies after the war
>> RESI NOTH, his sister-in-law, who later poses as Helga and
>> lives with him
>> MAJOR FRANK WIRTANEN, who recruits Campbell as a spy and
>> remains his contact; his real name, Harold J. Sparrow, is
>> learned only at the novel's end
>> GEORGE KRAFT, a painter, a member of Alcoholics Anony-
>> mous, Campbell's best friend in New York City, and a So-
>> viet spy; his real name is Colonel Iona Potapov
>> LIEUTENANT BERNARD B. O'HARE, who arrests Campbell in
>> 1945 as a supposed Nazi and later hounds him in New York

The Novel

Mother Night—the title comes from a speech by Mephistopheles in
Faust—is presented as the written memoir or confession of Howard W.
Campbell, Jr. It has supposedly been edited by "Kurt Vonnegut, Jr.," who
offers a signed editor's note concluding that Campbell "served evil too
openly and good too secretly, the crime of his times." Yet it is evident that
Campbell speaks for Vonnegut—as an unpretentious Everyman.

Against his better judgment, Campbell, an American who lived for a
dozen years in Germany, agreed to become an intelligence agent for the
United States. Throughout the war, pretending to be a Nazi, he insinuated
secret messages into his regular radio broadcasts extolling Nazism and anti-
Semitism. By the end of the war, Campbell is a world-famous Nazi; only
three persons know he actually was a spy. Almost reluctantly, the United
States government helps him escape a war-crimes trial by arranging for him
to go underground in Manhattan. In 1960, however, after betrayal by his
best friend and the death of the woman he loves, he gives himself up to Israeli agents. He writes his memoirs while awaiting trial in Jerusalem. The
last chapter is written on the eve of his trial. He has just received a letter
from Frank Wirtanen, who had recruited him as a spy, offering to testify in

his behalf. Campbell, however, finds the prospect of freedom nauseating and proposes to execute himself that night "for crimes against himself." One must assume that he does in fact commit suicide, as "editor" Vonnegut refers to him in the past tense.

Vonnegut as author, writing in 1960, had assigned a date of 1961 to Campbell's manuscript, to lend it maximum contemporaneity with the trial of Adolf Eichmann, then under way in Israel. Eichmann was arrested in 1960 and executed in 1962. It is typical for Vonnegut to construct his novels around events immediately in the news. (*Mother Night*, as it turned out, was not actually released until 1962.)

The novel, then, is simply Campbell's autobiographical account; its forty-five rather brief chapters begin in the prison, then more or less alternate in flashback between wartime Germany and the years in Manhattan, with occasional chapters, including the last, returning to the present.

Although this work qualifies as a realistic novel, many of its situations, though fully entertaining, fall short of being believable: the broadcasting charade, for example, in which Campbell does not even know the messages he is transmitting (by clearing his throat, pausing, and the like); the possibility that he would accept his wife's sister, younger by fifteen or more years, as his wife, even after an absence of a dozen years; and the likelihood that Campbell would commit suicide when he was at least technically innocent. In addition, there is much comic absurdity in this novel—even black humor—which contrasts uncomfortably (some would say) with life in Nazi Germany—and in Auschwitz. For example, there is the White Christian Minuteman, the Reverend Doctor Lionel J. D. Jones, D.D.S., who proves that "Christ was not a Jew" by analyzing fifty famous paintings of Jesus, not one of which shows "Jewish jaws or teeth." His followers include Robert Sterling Wilson, "the Black Fuehrer of Harlem," and an unfrocked Paulist father, Patrick Keeley, patterned on the infamous Father Coughlin.

One finally realizes that the real issue in *Mother Night* is not so much the psychological veracity of its central characters as their usefulness in demonstrating certain philosophical propositions—or in asking fundamental questions relating to evil, guilt, and forgiveness. The result is a novel didactic in its parts, yet contradictory, not fully resolved, and continuously ironic in tone. Yet it is dead serious in its concern for truth.

The Characters

Like other Vonnegut protagonists, Howard Campbell tends to speak aphoristically. He tells the reader a number of things that are good for the reader to know or emulate. For example, in reply to the supposition that he hates America, Campbell replies, "That would be as silly as loving it. . . . It's impossible for me to get emotional about it, because real estate doesn't interest me." Elsewhere he says that "nationalities" do not interest him. He refers to himself as a "stateless person." Once he draws a swastika, a hammer and sickle, and a United States flag on his window and says, "Hooray, hooray, hooray." So much for patriotism. In this way Campbell presents one of the more important of Vonnegut's teachings.

Another of Vonnegut's lessons requires that Campbell (who was a successful playwright in Germany) admit that if Germany had won, there was every chance that he "would have become a sort of Nazi Edgar Guest, writing a daily [newspaper] column of optimistic doggerel. . . ." While this admission conflicts tentatively with the antipatriotic theme, it serves the equally important idea that most Americans probably would have behaved like most Nazis, placed in the same situation. As the reader comes to identify more closely with Campbell, he is led to the brink of seeking a way possibly to forgive the Nazis—to forgive unspeakable evil. This hope is perhaps thwarted, however, by Campbell's inability to forgive himself (hence his suicide) for having furthered the cause of anti-Semitism so efficiently as to render his intelligence work insignificant.

Like Campbell, the other characters dramatize certain themes and ideas—though usually one motif dominates. Dr. Abraham Epstein, a survivor of Auschwitz, has only one message: "Forget Auschwitz. . . . I *never* think about it!" This, too, is a possibly healthy way of dealing with the Holocaust—though it conflicts with the very act of writing *Mother Night*. Similarly, Bernard B. O'Hare is brought onstage only to teach the reader the wrongness—and the futility—of vengeance.

Another minor character, Heinz Schildknecht, who, the reader is told, is Campbell's best friend and whose precious motorcycle Campbell steals in the last days of the war, dramatizes but one thing: friendship betrayed. This motif is reinforced later, in New York, by Iona Potapov, alias George Kraft, who in some part of his being is genuinely Campbell's friend. Yet he betrays Campbell. This more complex character also participates in the general investigation of schizophrenia that the novel undertakes. As a Russian spy, Potapov is insane; as an American spy, Campbell also exhibits schizophrenic traits. Finally, the absurd Nazi dentist Lionel Jones is insane to the degree that he is simply a caricature of a Fascist. His role appears to be to demonstrate that anti-Semitism is so crazy that no one could possibly countenance it. Then, one is forced to ask, how could the Holocaust have occurred? Great evil is a mystery, Vonnegut replies, and he proceeds with caution to seek its source.

The sisters Helga Noth and Resi Noth can almost be treated as one person, since each, in her relationship with Campbell, participates in acting out Campbell's idea of the "Nation of Two"—the title of a romantic play he never got around to writing but which was to show "how a pair of lovers in a world gone mad could survive by being loyal only to a nation composed of themselves—a nation of two." The implicit idea here, and a most tempting one, is that the best way to deal with gross political evil is to ignore it and retreat into sweet sexual love.

Themes and Meanings

Most of the important themes of the novel concern the question of how to cope with overwhelming evil, including ways of escaping from it. One way to escape from it is to commit suicide. When Campbell admits to Resi Noth that he no longer believes love is the only thing to live for, she pleads with him to tell her something else to live for—"anything at all." Yet he remains silent. She soon commits suicide. When Campbell himself commits suicide, one might wonder whether it is guilt that he feels (he has in any case claimed, "I had taught myself never to feel guilt") or a kind of paralysis before the absurdity and senselessness of human existence. The novel is obviously, therefore, existentialist in its basic values, though the perception of life as absurd has its roots in the Holocaust.

Campbell makes an excellent speech on the character of evil when he defeats O'Hare—a drunken, ignorant wretch who had imagined that he was "at war with pure evil" and would win it by killing Campbell. Campbell asks him: "Where is evil?" He answers the question himself: "[Evil is] that large part of every man that wants to hate without limit, that wants to hate with God on its side. . . . It's that part of an imbecile . . . that punishes and vilifies and makes war gladly."

Critical Context

Mother Night is Vonnegut's third novel, written well before he had attained best-seller status with *Slaughterhouse-Five: Or, The Children's Crusade* (1969). The latter is Vonnegut's most complete statement about Nazi Germany and his survival of the firestorm that destroyed Dresden on February 13, 1945. With the latter novel, Vonnegut achieved his greatest critical success—while *Mother Night* was at first totally ignored; it was never even reviewed until it was reissued in 1966. For the new edition, Vonnegut wrote an introduction indicating, among other things, that *Mother Night* is in some sense an anticipation of *Slaughterhouse Five*. For example, he confesses that if he had been born in Germany, he "probably would have *been* a Nazi, bopping Jews and Gypsies and Poles around. . . ." It is simply not true that the author, given his personal history, would have been a Nazi, but it is the right thing for him to say to help the reader understand that Nazis are human, as Americans are; it is not our duty to despise them for all time. This idea is developed more fully and successfully in *Slaughterhouse-Five*. Vonnegut also tells his readers in his introduction what the moral of *Mother Night* is—a typical Vonnegut aphorism that obviously fails to summarize this complex novel, but is well worth quoting: "We are what we pretend to be, so we must be careful about what we pretend to be."

Sources for Further Study
Klinkowitz, Jerome, and Donald Lawler, eds. *Vonnegut in America*, 1977.
Klinkowitz, Jerome, and John Somer, eds. *The Vonnegut Statement*, 1973.
Reed, Peter J. *Kurt Vonnegut, Jr.*, 1972.
Schatt, Stanley. *Kurt Vonnegut, Jr.*, 1976.

Donald M. Fiene

THE MOVIEGOER

Author: Walker Percy (1916-   )
Type of plot: Comic realism
Time of plot: The early 1960's
Locale: New Orleans
First published: 1961

> *Principal characters:*
> JOHN BICKERSON (BINX) BOLLING, the narrator and
>   protagonist
> KATE CUTRER, a young woman suffering a psychological
>   trauma
> EMILY CUTRER, Kate's stepmother and Bolling's great-aunt
> JULES CUTRER, Kate's father, a New Orleans broker
> WALTER WADE, a suitor whom Kate jilts

The Novel

Much of the action of *The Moviegoer* takes place within the mind of the protagonist, Binx Bolling, who, nearing his thirtieth birthday, retreats to inwardness, "sunk in the everydayness of life," baffled by its ambiguities and contradictions. Although he is a successful broker in New Orleans and a veteran, Binx has few friends, and although he has had a number of affairs with his secretaries, he does not know the meaning of love. Immersed in the obdurate ordinariness of his social life, family, and job, he is a "wayfarer" who feels homeless and abandoned.

Binx thus embarks on a quest for meaning which evolves into a veiled search for God. As a seeker, he is discouraged, since "as everyone knows, the polls report that 98% of Americans believe in God and the remaining 2% are atheists and agnostics—which leaves not a single percentage point for a seeker." He wants to be "onto something," to feel authenticated as a human being, for simply "to become aware of the possibility of the search is to be onto something." It is this intuition that underlies his obsession with movies: "The movies are onto the search," he says, but they always end in the same everydayness which brings him despair. The hero "takes up with the local librarian" and "settles down with a vengeance."

Ultimately, his cinematic excursions bring him no closer to a solution, but when he is drawn into the life of Kate Cutrer, the stepdaughter of his great-aunt Emily, he finds both the courage and the determination to confront life as it is. When Kate's fiancé is killed in an automobile accident, she lapses into despair, secretly drinking heavily and contemplating suicide. After Kate jilts a willing suitor, Binx's school chum, Walter Wade, Emily enlists Binx as an aide and confidant in helping Kate through her emotional trauma.

During the Mardi Gras season, Binx is sent on a business trip, and Kate impulsively requests that he let her join him. In the aftermath of their trip and the growing empathy with which Binx perceives Kate's malady, he discovers his own humanity and worth. In his compassion and risk-taking on Kate's behalf, he transcends the ordinariness in which he has been trapped and conquers his malaise.

In the novel's climax, Binx is lectured severely by his aunt for his failure to meet the standards of Southern gentlemanliness. Paradoxically, this liberates Binx, and he and Kate marry, free of the façade of gentility in which they were both bred. In the epilogue, Binx reveals that his aunt has learned to understand and forgive him for what he is: "The Bolling family had gone to seed and . . . I was not one of her heroes but a very ordinary fellow."

The Characters

Binx Bolling is the prototypical Percy protagonist, an introspective, educated man vaguely aware of his despair, one who is dislocated in the universe and anxious to seek answers to his nagging questions about the meaning and purpose of life. He is also prototypical in that Percy puts Binx through the three stages of a Kierkegaardian search for meaning: the aesthetic, the ethical, and the religious. In looking for hope and purpose, Binx tries first an aesthetic approach to life, indulging the flesh and cultivating an artistic sensibility. He moves quickly toward the ethical stage, finding purpose in assisting his great-aunt in helping Kate renew her life and face the future with courage and resolve. Toward the end of the novel, Binx is clearly seeking (or has found) a religious foundation for the rest of his life.

Binx speaks matter-of-factly; Percy never allows the introspection of his narrator to become contrived. The infrequent satire in his voice is gentle and reassuring; Binx is not self-indulgently ironic. His mental wanderings serve to confirm his quiet desperation, his quiet despair, an Everyman of the late twentieth century who discovers that his fellows are too at home with not being at home in the universe.

Kate Cutrer shatters his complacency. Her despair is real, transparent; it is not a posture brought on by a concession to "the modern world view." She offers no false Southern gentility to disguise her alienation. It is in her openly quizzical attitude toward life that Binx discovers himself and the way out of his self-imposed exile and "objectivity." In bringing Kate through her crisis, Binx resolves his own crisis and discovers both humanity and purposefulness.

The older adults, Emily and Jules Cutrer, Kate's father, represent only the dying, aristocratic, moribund South. As Binx puts it, his aunt Emily's stern lecture and defense of the manners of the New Orleans gentleman only confirm his view that "men are dead, dead, dead; and that the malaise has settled like a fall-out and what people fear is not that the bomb will fall but that the bomb will not fall. . . ." In such a setting, the characters can but live with an inevitable sense that Being merely ceases at some point *to be*. Existence is its own excuse for being.

Binx and Kate, in contrast, discover that Being is made meaningful through mutual trust and authentic, individual commitment. Percy's characterization in *The Moviegoer* underscores the fact that in the modern South, indeed, in the world at large, this is the very kind of commitment that family, tradition, job, and the usual mundane social concerns can never engender or replenish. If anyone is to become a "person," he or she must step out of the security of established roles and stations and take the awful risk of individuality.

Themes and Meanings

Though Percy was trained as a physician, he has never practiced medicine. After contracting tuberculosis during his residency, he spent several years of recuperation reading European fiction and existentialist philosophy, particularly the Danish writer, Søren Kierkegaard. He later converted to Catholicism, and these philosophical and religious influences are seen clearly in every Percy novel. The typical Percy protagonist is a man who is comfortable financially but plagued by a vague sense of disorientation and depression. The story of this cerebral main character is always one of "coming to oneself," of suddenly discovering the extraordinary in the ordinary, the transcendent in the mundane. To Percy, man is neither "a beast nor an angel but a wayfaring creature somewhere between." Man's ultimate challenge is to seize his own destiny and act on his own or some other's behalf against the status quo.

Percy has commented that his major concern as a novelist is to depict "what it means to be a man living in the world who must die." *The Moviegoer*'s theme is no exception. The culture of the modern South, the last refuge of religious faith, fosters Binx's sense of alienation, yet this same culture also permits his eventual return as a "reborn" Southerner and human being, equipped both to criticize and to coexist peacefully with his heritage. This can occur only if Binx will act, however, and not merely contemplate the possibilities. In reaching out to Kate, he finds the impulse he needs to free himself from the past and face the future with integrity and hope.

Critical Context

The Moviegoer won the 1962 National Book Award for fiction for Percy at the age of forty-five and launched his career as a novelist. Since that time, Percy has published two nonfiction works, *The Message in the Bottle* (1975) and *Lost in the Cosmos* (1983), and four novels, *The Last Gentleman* (1966), *Love in the Ruins: The Adventures of a Bad Catholic at a Time Near the End of the World* (1971), *Lancelot* (1977), and *The Second Coming* (1980). A believing Catholic, Percy stands beside Flannery O'Connor as a Southern Christian writer who has fought against the prevailing malaise of modern letters. As a novelist of ideas, Percy consistently raises in his work the largest questions of human life: Is there a God? If so, what is mankind's relationship to Him and to the quest for knowledge of Him?

Percy's fascination with the symbol-making power of man and the ability of language to point to the transcendent serves him well as a central concern in all of his work. *The Message in the Bottle* and *Lost in the Cosmos*, two speculative works on the self and language, provide rich intellectual insights into the meaning of language and the language of meaning.

Sources for Further Study

Broughton, Panthea Reid, ed. *The Art of Walker Percy: Stratagems for Being*, 1979.

Coles, Robert. *Walker Percy: An American Search*, 1978.

Luschei, Martin. *The Sovereign Wayfarer: Walker Percy's Diagnosis of the Malaise*, 1972.

Vanderwerken, David L. "The Americanness of *The Moviegoer*," in *Notes on Mississippi Writers*. XII (1979), pp. 40-53.

Bruce L. Edwards, Jr.

MULATA

Author: Miguel Ángel Asturias (1899-1974)
Type of plot: Symbolic allegory
Time of plot: The 1960's
Locale: Quiavicús and Tierrapaulita, Guatemala
First published: Mulata de tal, 1963 (English translation, 1967)

> *Principal characters:*
> CELESTINO YUMÍ, a poor Guatemalan peasant who yearns for
> riches and importance
> CATALINA ZABALA, Yumí's loving wife
> THE MULATA, a haunting, lusty woman whom Yumí marries
> on their first meeting

The Novel

Miguel Ángel Asturias bases *Mulata* on a popular Guatemalan legend—
that of a man who sells his wife to the devil in exchange for unlimited
wealth. The novel begins with Celestino Yumí parading through the religious fairs of the countryside around Quiavicús with the zipper of his pants
open, in compliance with a bargain he has struck with Tazol, the corn-husk
devil. In this way, Yumí will cause women to commit sins by looking at his
private parts and then compound those sins by their accepting Communion
without going again to confession. Successful in luring the women, Yumí is
next informed by Tazol that, to complete the bargain whereby Yumí will
become wealthy beyond his dreams, he has to hand over his wife, Catalina
Zabala, to Tazol. Yumí is hesitant at first, but the promise of riches, importance, and power proves too much, and he finally consents. Tazol takes
possession of Catalina, or Niniloj, as Yumí calls her, and grants Yumí his
fondest wishes—lands, crops, and money in abundance.

Once rich, Yumí discovers that what Tazol had told him is true: Everyone
asks for and respects his opinion on anything and everything—as Yumí himself remarks, "Just because I'm rich, not because I know anything." Yet
Yumí finds that riches and power cannot compensate for the loss of his wife;
he yearns for her love and takes to drinking and carousing. While at a religious festival with his friend Timoteo Teo Timoteo, he encounters the
Mulata. Drunk and instantly overcome with lust for this ripe and haunting
woman, Yumí marries her in a civil ceremony and carries her home. There,
in their marriage bed, Yumí discovers that the Mulata, much to his chagrin
and embarrassment, is bisexual and dangerous. As much animal as human,
she dominates and torments him in such a way that Yumí finds it
excrutiatingly terrifying to lie with her. He tries to undo the bargain with
Tazol, and he succeeds in reacquiring Catalina, who has been turned into a

dwarf by Tazol. Catalina comes to live with Yumí and his new wife, and the Mulata at first accepts her as a living doll with which to play but quickly tires of the idea and prefers to mistreat her. Yumí and Catalina hope to rid the household of the Mulata, and Catalina, in a clever ruse, with the help of the Mulata's bear, lures the Mulata to the cave of the Grumpy Bird and seals her in, but the Mulata eats the bird and escapes, provoking in the process a cataclysmic volcanic eruption that destroys Quiavicús and all of Yumí's wealth.

Now, even more destitute than before the bargain with Tazol, Yumí has no idea of what to do. Catalina, who in her dealings with Tazol and the Mulata has acquired a taste for witchcraft, convinces Yumí to journey with her to Tierrapaulita, the city where all those who wish to learn the black arts must go. Unable to traverse the devil's nine turns, they turn back, then try again. This time, Catalina fastens to her chest a cross in Tazol's image, fashioned of dry corn leaves, and the devil's powers are neutralized. In this way, they make their way to Tierrapaulita with Tazol as protector, even though the devil himself fears entering Tierrapaulita.

Yumí and Catalina find Tierrapaulita such a fantastic and terrifying place that, despite their lust for the power that witchcraft will bring them, they decide to leave. Cashtoc, the Immense, the red earth demon of Indian myth, prevents them from leaving, employing other demons from Xibalba, the Mayan hell. Catalina gives birth to Tazolín (having been impregnated through the naval by Tazol) and is pronounced the great Giroma, the powerful mother witch. Taking vengeance on Yumí for his bargain with Tazol and his marriage to the Mulata, Catalina turns him into a dwarf, only to change her mind later, when, jealous of the attentions paid him by the dwarf Huasanga, she transforms him into a giant.

This act and Huasanga's cries precipitate an earthquake during which Cashtoc calls his legions together and removes them and all the sorcerers from Tierrapaulita, destroying the city in the process. Cashtoc empties the town because he realizes that the Christian demon Cadanga has arrived and with him "the ones who will demand generations of men without any reason for being, without any magic words, unfortunate in the nothingness and the emptiness of their ego."

Yumí and Catalina, along with other witches, wizards, and sorcerers, abandon the retreat of Cashtoc and return to Tierrapaulita, only to find that their powers are nonexistent now that Cadanga, the Christian demon, is dominant. In a nightmarish ceremony, Yumí, in the guise of a pockmarked Indian, representing the Christian demon Cadanga, does battle with the Mulata, in the form of the new sexton, representing Cashtoc. Recognizing each other despite their disguises, Yumí and the Mulata engage in a battle of wits, during which the Mulata, in order to save Yumí (who has become a hedgehog and is fighting with the priest, who has become a spider with eleven thousand legs and arms), resumes her form and with a magic mist immobilizes the combatants. In a subsequent Requiem Mass, the Mulata is married to Yumí (still in hedgehog form) for an eternity of death.

As punishment for her betrayal, Cashtoc deprives the Mulata of one leg, one eye, one ear, one hand, one arm, one lip, one teat, and her sex, then sends her crawling away like a snake. Cashtoc and his legions once again take leave of Tierrapaulita, leaving it and its citizens to the Christian demon Cadanga, who incites the populace to breed because his hell is in need of souls.

The novel ends with a horrific cataclysm in which Tierrapaulita and all of its inhabitants are destroyed by earthquakes and volcanic eruptions. Yumí and Catalina are crushed, and the Mulata, whole again but with her magic powers gone, quarters Yumí's body to remove his golden bones and is set alight by the rays of the moon in the process. Only the priest survives, where in the hospital doctors are unable to diagnose what form of leprosy he has, if leprosy it is.

The Characters

Celestino Yumí, a poor, simple wood gatherer, comes to vibrant life in the hands of Asturias. Yumí, dissatisfied with his hardscrabble existence, yearns for what his friend Timoteo Teo Timoteo has: land, horses, crops, and the respect of others. Though he bargains with the corn-husk devil for riches in exchange for his wife, Tazol has to convince him that Catalina has been unfaithful to him before he finally agrees. The irony of the bargain does not escape him, since one of the reasons he wishes to be rich is to be able to make life easier for his beloved wife. As he says to Tazol, "But I'm already weeping, with all my heart, because she's my wife; the only thing I have and I'm going to give her to you, Tazol, just because she was unfaithful to me and because I want to be rich."

Possessed of a shrewd native intelligence, though he professes otherwise, Yumí understands a hard truth: that the rich and powerful can do practically as they want and that the poor, the powerless, have no recourse but to accept it. Once rich, he acts accordingly, throwing his wealth around, parading it proudly in imitation of others he has seen. Impulsive by nature, he acts without regard to consequences, then allows those consequences to dictate his course of action.

Like the other human characters in the novel, Yumí is a victim, a pawn of natural and supernatural forces, but unlike the Mulata and Catalina, he does not struggle or attempt (past that of bargaining with Tazol) to control his surroundings. Treated with affection and understanding by Asturias, Yumí is seen as man without guile, easily led, perhaps, but whose basic motivation is his undying love for Catalina.

Through Yumí, Asturias portrays Catalina's character as Yumí sees her.

She is a good wife, uncomplaining when hungry, good at mending, supportive of his needs, and, best of all, happy and jolly. Yet this is not all that she
is. When Yumí reclaims her from Tazol, and she goes to live with him and
the Mulata, it is Catalina who devises the plan to get rid of the Mulata. Re-
sourceful and quick, when Yumí loses his wealth, she earns their living
dancing with a bear. The idea to become sorcerers is hers, and when unable
to get past the devil's nine turns, it is her idea to tie a cross of Tazol on her
belly in order to get through. Also, she is not above revenge. Once she
becomes the mother of Tazolín and, therefore, a great witch, she has Yumí
turned into a dwarf as punishment for selling her to Tazol. Unlike Yumí,
she is a fighter, and in the final cataclysm, as everything is falling on her and
knowing it is a futile gesture, Catalina throws her hands up "to use them
against the mass of the mountains that were falling down on Tierrapaulita."

Of the human characters in the novel, the Mulata is the most memorable.
Her skin a rich, dark color, her eyes like extinguished coals, and a nature
that is more animal than human, the Mulata is a haunting and haunted
woman. Her eyes are what attract Yumí, and her taut, coltish body
unleashes an overwhelming lust in him. A moon spirit, the Mulata is governed by the phases of the moon, and like the moon of Guatemalan legend
who dares not let the sun possess her from the front for fear of engendering
monsters, she does not allow Yumí to have sex with her from the front, only
from the rear. The Mulata is a hermaphrodite and is in constant inner turmoil, sometimes friendly, kind, and affectionate, then without warning, savage and destructive. She laments to Yumí that she is like an animal without
a proper owner. Yumí finds her both fascinating and repulsive, inspiring in
him lust and fear. At night, Yumí lies awake, "always fearful that the beast
would wake up and grab him unexpectedly, explosions of fury that coincided
with the phases of the moon."

Aware of her duality but unable to do anything about it, the Mulata
reaches out to destroy herself and others in a vain attempt to rid herself of
herself. Though in the first part of the novel the Mulata serves as punishment to Yumí for having bartered his wife, toward the end of the novel she
saves his life.

Throughout the novel, Asturias treats his characters with compassion,
and his affection for them shines brightly. These are people struggling
against forces beyond their control in an attempt to find meaning to their
lives, and though the struggle may bring tragic consequences, it may also
bring a wisdom of sorts—perhaps the struggle itself means that life is not
hopeless.

Themes and Meanings

In *Mulata*, as in the majority of his works, Asturias concerns himself with
the effects of the continuous clash of two cultures: the Spanish Christian

culture and the culture of the Mayas and their descendants.

In Asturias' view, this clash has left the Indian and mestizo suspended between the past and the present, between myth and reality, a suspension where myth can be reality and reality myth, where the past is the present and the present the past. Their daily reality is dominated by tradition saturated with legends, myths, and superstitions. In such a world, anything is possible: Dead animals may arise and speak, women may change into dwarfs, and boar-men may counsel humans. It is this magic reality that, in Asturias' work, the people use as a defense against the four-and-a-half centuries of persecution to which they have been subjected since the Conquest. Unfortunately, this response to the Spanish Christian culture precludes a true and pure amalgam of the two cultures. It is Asturias' view that the reason for this is not that the ancient Mayan beliefs have adulterated the Christian culture but that Christianity arrived in an already adulterated form, which then proceeded to adulterate the Mayan beliefs.

It is no accident that the clashes in Tierrapaulita between the ancient Indian myths and the Spanish Christian beliefs are conducted by demons, Indian and Christian, and not by the dieties of either. The dieties are no longer available to do battle since the beliefs that have survived are dominated by demons on both sides, each side bent on the destruction, physical and spiritual, of the people.

In the words of Father Chimalpín (and Asturias), "A person is not a Christian just because he is one; a person is a Christian because it implies loving more, loving more is giving one's self more, is reaching, through that giving, everything that surrounds us, a nursery of happiness where one fulfills everything." This is not, however, the Christianity that the Spanish brought. Instead, the Conquest brought a Christianity that resulted in men who considered themselves an end in themselves. In the words of Cashtoc, the supreme Mayan demon: "Plants, animals, stars . . . they all exist together, all together as they were created! It has occurred to none of them to make a separate existence, to take life for his exclusive use, only man, who must be destroyed because of his presumption of existing in isolation, alien to the millions of destinies that are being woven and unwoven around him!"

Asturias sees clearly that the clash between these cultures has resulted in deep conflicts and confusion in the psyche of the Indians, who have served as the battleground for these opposing forces. Though the two competing cultures form one, at the same time each cancels out the other, with neither making a whole by itself. The resulting hybrid mentality of the Indians is symbolized by the Mulata's persona. She has no proper name, she is simply a certain Mulata; a hybrid of neuter gender, she has both and so has none. Dominated by the phases of the moon, she is in constant turmoil, doing battle with antagonistic forces within herself.

Later on, when mutilated by Cashtoc and left only half of what she was, the Mulata joins with a skeleton woman in order to make a whole. "We have to be sisters in the same clothing. Together, very much together, just like sisters in the same clothing, just like sisters who might have been born stuck together, so you will make up for the arm I lack, the leg I don't have, the ear, the eye, the lip." In this way, the two opposing cultures have mixed, an imperfect half clinging to a substanceless frame. In this same way, the Indians ensure that the protection they seek from the Christian saints is effective, endowing them with features and characteristics of their own Nahuatl animals derived from the ancient beliefs. In Asturias' view, these acts are attempts by the people to impose a wholeness to their existence, a universal harmony that they once knew and is now but a psychic memory.

Any subversion or disobedience to the laws of universality eventually will result in chaos or destruction. When Yumí abandons his wife for wealth and power, he sets into motion the chain of events that lead to his tragic end. The same result lies in wait for Catalina when she attempts to set herself apart from all others with the knowledge and use of sorcery. It is this deflection from universal love which Asturias deplores and which, if not corrected, will result in the destruction of humanity.

Critical Context

Asturias' work has long been recognized by critics throughout most of the literary world as being in the forefront of the Latin American literary movement. It was not, however, until the English publication of *Mulata* in 1967, the same year that saw Asturias awarded the Nobel Prize for Literature, that English-speaking readers became aware of his prodigious talent. Critically acclaimed in the United States and Great Britain, as it had been in France and throughout the Spanish-speaking world, *Mulata's* success (and the Nobel Prize) led to the publication in English of Asturias' other works. In these are found the style and themes that are incorporated in *Mulata*, most notably in the novels *Hombres de maíz* (1949; *Men of Maize*, 1975), *Viento fuerte* (1950; *The Cyclone*, 1967, better known as *Strong Wind*, 1968), and *El papa verde* (1954; *The Green Pope*, 1971).

Long concerned with what he considered the continuous isolation of man from nature and the resultant conflicts that arise from this isolation, Asturias incorporated nature into his novels, not as background setting but as a constant presence that must be taken into account. Using ancient Mayan myths and legends, many of which still carry much weight within the consciousness of the Guatemalan people, Asturias personified the different elements of nature (as did the ancient civilizations) in order to show how his characters and these elements are inextricably bound.

Though these elements have appeared in his other novels, in *Mulata*, Asturias achieves a more profound synthesis of myth and reality than in his other works. Through his skillful use of language, the suspension between myth and reality in which his characters conduct their lives is brought vividly to the forefront. In this way, he shows not only how wide the split between modern man and his natural elements has become but also the resultant conflicts.

Though Asturias does not preach or offer simple solutions, the inescapable truth of *Mulata* is modern man's urgent need for a balance between spirit and matter, instinct and reason, a wholeness which may be achieved by a reexamination of long-forgotten or barely remembered truths inherent in the myths and legends of the ancients.

Source for Further Study
Martin, Gerald. "*Mulata de Tal*: The Novel as Animated Cartoon," in *Hispanic Review*. XLI (1973), pp. 397-415.

Ernesto Encinas

MUMBO JUMBO

Author: Ishmael Reed (1938-   )
Type of plot: Mystery
Time of plot: The 1920's
Locale: New Orleans and New York City
First published: 1972

> *Principal characters:*
> PAPA LABAS, the black protagonist, a private detective
> HINCKLE VON VAMPTON, his white antagonist, a thief
> WOODROW WILSON JEFFERSON, a naïve black from the South
> ABDUL HAMID, a black magazine editor, translator, and
>   Hinckle's associate
> BIFF MUSCLEWHITE, a hit man for the Wallflower Order
> BERBELANG, leader of the *Mu'tafikah*
> EARLINE, LaBas' secretary
> CHARLOTTE, an employee in LaBas' Kathedral

The Novel

The story begins in the office of the mayor of New Orleans. Drinking bootlegged gin with his sleazy mistress, the mayor receives a distress call that the Jes Grew epidemic has moved from the dormant to the active stage. By the following morning, the authorities have identified ten thousand cases. The epidemic had broken out thirty years earlier, during the 1890's; now, in the 1920's, it is a danger to society, and it will raise its head once again in the 1970's. All it needs to take over the country is a text, words to reveal and preserve its mysteries. *Mumbo Jumbo* records the conflict between authority figures such as the mayor, those who regard survival as the preservation of Western civilization, and the defenders of Jes Grew, the ancient mysteries that have gone underground. The novel is a mystery, a detective story, with PaPa LaBas as the private investigator. The object of his search is The Work, the original text that records the Jes Grew, or Hoo-Doo mysteries. Jes Grew's antagonists work to ensure that the Text does not surface. Reed contends that this recurrent struggle resides not in those who are publicly visible (the president, politicians, industrialists, religious leaders) but within secret societies. The name of the society opposed to Jes Grew is the Wallflower Order, along with its now disgraced military arm, the Knights Templar.

The Text had once been in the possession of the Templars. One of the modern exemplars, Hinckle Von Vampton, takes it upon himself—without the endorsement of the Wallflower Order—to locate and repossess the Text, in order to keep it out of the hands of Jes Grew. Hinckle, then, becomes PaPa LaBas' primary antagonist. The novel is fleshed out with subplots and fanciful historical reporting—for example, Hinckle's plan to draw attention away from true black art by creating a conventional black android poet; the clandestine activities of the *Mu'tafikah*, who steal art objects from museums (Centers of Art Detention) in order to return them to the cultures that produced them; Earline's possession by a loa who uses her body to seduce a trolley-car driver; interpretations of Warren Harding's presidency and the real story behind his death by assassination. The central line of the plot, however, is LaBas' search for the ancient HooDoo Text. All signs point to its being in New York City. The Jes Grew epidemic has spread from New Orleans to Chicago and is now only a few miles from New York. In order for it to catch on and become a permanent part of the black community, PaPa LaBas must find the Text and reveal it to the public at large. He follows up various clues and finally discovers the box containing it at a nightclub in the city. In a public ceremony designed to expose Hinckle and his associates as villains, LaBas opens up the box, only to find the Text missing. (Hinckle, nevertheless, does not escape punishment. LaBas has him shipped off to Haiti to be judged.) He later discovers that the man who had the Text in his possession—Abdul Hamid, a Black Muslim magazine editor—had assumed the role of censor and burned not only his translation of it but also the original on the ground that it was obscene. The Text, which was to establish Jes Grew as the dominant spiritual force in American culture, is gone forever. LaBas is not discouraged, however; he comforts his secretary Earline with the belief that there are two forces in the world, life and death, and that Jes Grew is life. America will create its own text. The Harlem Renaissance is evidently only one of the many manifestations of it. The novel ends with an epilogue: LaBas as an old man in the 1970's delivering to a college audience his once-a-year lecture about the Jes Grew phenomenon. After fifty years of dormancy, the epidemic once again shows signs of revival.

The Characters

LaBas' quest for the Text is also a quest for himself. At the beginning of the novel, he is the founder and head of the Mumbo Jumbo Kathedral. Though he does not realize it, he is trying to institutionalize the HooDoo spirit. The effects of this rigid and limited view of the human spirit are already evident. His assistant, Berbelang, has left the Kathedral and is engaged in illegal activities—the restoring of art objects to the countries from which they were stolen. LaBas shows tolerance of Berbelang's activities but only gradually comes to accept the variety of manifestations of the Jes Grew spirit. What he must understand is that the popular art of black culture, especially as manifested during the 1920's (the Harlem Renaissance), is the essence of HooDoo in America. That he is still only a novice in the mysteries is evident when a loa possesses his secretary Earline; he must yield to his compatriot Black Herman, who knows the art well and can apply the right formulas and exorcise the daimon. It is only after his experience in search of the Text that LaBas comes to realize the truth about Jes Grew. Berbelang is betrayed and murdered while retrieving art treasures from the New York Center of Art Detention; Charlotte, LaBas' trainee in the Kathedral, is likewise deceived and murdered by the same villain (her lover), and finally LaBas discovers that there is no Text. Institutionalization and codification stifle rather than revive Jes Grew. The Text must be continually re-created. Through much of the novel, then, LaBas is a well-meaning HooDoo priest, a novice in the ancient mysteries. The novel records his education. It ends with LaBas as an old man, in appearance a silly old man but faithful to his calling, and wiser. LaBas may be an amusing portrait of the author, his own groping attempts to defend the forces of life in American society. He calls himself "a jacklegged detective of the metaphysical," "a private eye practicing in my Neo-HooDoo therapy center." The narrator calls him a "noonday HooDoo, fugitive-hermit, obeah-man, botanist, animal impersonator, 2-headed man" who "eats heartily and doesn't believe in the emaciated famished Christ-like exhibit of self-denial and flagellation." His ancestors include the Nigerian oracle, Ju Ju of Arno, a black Gypsy, the Moor of Summerland, who initiated witchcraft in Europe, and a grandfather whose HooDoo powers spelled the doom of his various slave masters. Thus, while PaPa LaBas is the most individualized character in *Mumbo Jumbo*, his representative role as novitiate HooDoo priest (at fifty years of age) takes precedence. His purpose is to show that America is only now beginning to take its place within the true history of the human spirit.

Reed removes his characters even further from the conventional realistic setting by raising them to a metaphysical level. They belong to the world of the supernatural. LaBas is not simply the physical descendent of a wizard; he inherits spiritual powers as well, as "the reincarnation of the famed Moor of Summerland." He "carries Jes Grew in him like most other folk carry genes." His antagonist, Hinckle, is more than a reincarnation; he is the original Templar librarian who learned the secret of eternal life by studying the text of the Book of Thoth. He had already reappeared once in America in the 1890's, to curb the spirit of Jes Grew. The battle between LaBas and Hinckle is the superhuman (spiritual) struggle of cosmic forces. Surrounding the metaphysical antagonists are other characters who represent forces of good and evil. Black Herman, adept in the black arts, defies natural laws, as does the daimon who takes over Earline's body. Berbelang places spiritual and aesthetic values above legal authority, and Buddy Jackson, known publicly as a notorious black underworld figure, reveals himself at the end as a member of secret societies sympathetic to the Jes Grew spirit. Hinckle is abetted by forces of evil: Abdul Hamid, a traitor to the black cause, a Muslim purist of rigid sexual morality; Herbert "Safecracker" Gould, a white undercover agent, blackfaced to pass as the new Negro android; and Biff Musclewhite, muscleman, hit man, white curator of the Center of Art Detention in New York, who murders both Berbelang and Charlotte. The names of the villains identify them as representatives. Reed's purpose is not to create believable characters but to expose a decadent, hypocritical, and death-loving society. Their fantastic lives highlight the radical conflict, the metaphysical struggle going on underneath the placid surface of Western culture.

Themes and Meanings

Mumbo Jumbo is a reinterpretation of history, art, and religion. The core of the plot is the Text of the Jes Grew movement. The Text is Reed's alternative to the Christian Bible. Toward the end of the story proper, PaPa LaBas delivers a long historical discourse that traces the history of religion from the black point of view. The story of religion begins in Egypt with the young Prince Osiris, a black African. His religious activity was the dance. The book that celebrates him is a choreography of his dance movements, set down by Thoth, a written record of the ancient mysteries of nature. Osiris was the original natural man. His primary antagonist—the real devil—was Set, his brother, the primal form of artificiality, censorship, rules, and conformity. Reed calls such enemies of the human spirit atonists. Moses, in a direct line from Set, deceitfully works his way into the secret room of Isis, who after Osiris' mutilation and supposed death (he like Christ does not die but is continually rejuvenated) guards the Book of Thoth. Their sexual union draws from her all the Osirian mysteries. Having gained the secrets, however, during the wrong phase of the moon (that is, with wrong motives) he knows only its obverse side. The teachings of Moses, then, are distortions of the Text. Reed has LaBas say the same thing of Christ (whom he elsewhere in the novel calls an "impostor," a "burdensome archetype"). The line of descent extends from Set to Moses to Christ to the Apostles to the Knights Templar, and hence to Hinckle. Along the way, the original Text was lost. Only its Left Hand version, the Bible, survived. According to tradition, Moses hid the original in a tabernacle when he caught his people observing its heathenish rites. Solomon's Temple and then the Templars' headquarters were built on the same site as the tabernacle, and thus it came into the hands of Hinckle, the Templar librarian. When Hinckle tried to translate it, however, the book resisted. It would not allow Hinckle to do to it what Moses had done. Hinckle kept the book with him from the twelfth century to the twentieth. Wherever he went, however, Jes Grew appeared, the true spirit of the work. Finally, in the 1920's Hinckle uses it as a bargaining chip to become the acknowledged leader of the anti-Jes Grew movement. As one of Hinckle's cohorts, Abdul got hold of the book and destroyed it. He thus achieved what the atonists wanted all along; they believed that the destruction of the Text would be a destruction of the movement. LaBas assures readers that the contrary is true. Natural instincts will continually find their expression in new texts. This history of the world according to HooDoo is the central thesis of the novel. The inevitable reappearance of Jes Grew is a ritual repetition of Osiris' death, dismemberment, and germination. Apparently, it is as real to Reed as the Passion has been for Christians.

This true history of the world becomes, as it were, the sanction for Reed's revolutionary (upstart, nihilistic, populist, ritualistic) definitions of religion and art. Reed consistently stands on the side of Sodom and Gomorrah, the worship of Baal, the Greek mysteries, the Dionysian orgy, Judas, Julian the Apostate (a defender of the Greek mysteries), the Bohemians of the 1920's, and the black spirit of the 1970's. These are not, as the Christian tradition has painted them, aberrations from the divine nature, blasphemies against the true God; they are instead the true instinctive worship of the gods, recognitions of animistic realities. Christianity has been an inhibitive religion, a religion of self-denial and "flagellation." Even slavery itself is a consequence of it. Reed believes that Christianity has denied the blacks their true heritage, calling the animism that characterized their indigenous religion an evil and teaching them to deny the joys of this world. Even black writers have succumbed to this dark, pessimistic view of life. Reed names Richard Wright and Ralph Ellison as examples. Rather than express the joy of life, they react with anger, self-pity, and bitterness against the white, atonist system. Reed proposes a new aesthetic, one based on the spirit of the 1920's, the spirit of blues and jazz, art that uplifts the spirit, that deals positively with the ancient mysteries. His purpose is to write a novel that asserts pride in the black race because it, in fact, introduced into America the Osirian mysteries. Christianity calls Africa the dark continent; in Reed's interpretation of history, Africa carries the true line of man's descent in religion and art. It will be the salvation of the West.

Critical Context

The same critics who call Reed the best black writer of the 1960's and 1970's might also object that his highly distinctive style and recurrent themes are too repetitive, that Reed is not growing as a writer. Such judgments taken together are not flattering to the state of black fiction during these decades. In fact, Reed's novels do have considerable variety. What appears as a minor motif in one novel becomes a major one in the next. What is a relatively brief discourse on the history of Neo-HooDooism in *Yellow Back Radio Broke-Down* (1969) becomes in this next novel, *Mumbo Jumbo*, an elaborate tracing of animistic religion from Osiris to jazz. A recognized leader of the HooDoo religion, the detective PaPa LaBas advances from novitiate in *Mumbo Jumbo* to professional in *The Last Days of Louisiana Red* (1974). Verbal gymnastics and jive talk, and ahistorical use of language— the trademarks of the Reed novel—continue to be innovative from one work to the next. Reed achieves variety also by moving his settings from one historical era to another. The purpose remains essentially the same—to reinterpret the past and present by having them comment on each other—but the particular past may be the Thomas Jefferson presidency of *Yellow Back Radio Broke-Down*, the Civil War of *Flight to Canada* (1976), the 1920's of *Mumbo Jumbo*, or even a future time, as in *The Terrible Twos* (1982). While maintaining faith in a spiritual tradition outside the West and usually making HooDoo the primary symbol of it, Reed manages to create different contexts and perspectives, sometimes emphasizing the religious, other times the aesthetic dimension, or, as in *Mumbo Jumbo*, merging the two.

To rank Reed above his black contemporaries would be premature. He is different from anyone else, white or black, past or present, who has written fiction. What one can say is that his concerns are those of his contemporaries, in particular the rejection of a tone that characterizes the fiction of Richard Wright, Ralph Ellison, and James Baldwin. In Reed, Toni Morrison, and Alice Walker, pride in being black, pride in the African heritage, and the inclusion of Africa itself in some form (its myths, its culture, the continent itself as a setting) assert even joyfully its presence in American life.

Sources for Further Study
Gates, Henry Louis, Jr. "The 'Blackness of Blackness': A Critique of the Sign and the Signifying Monkey," in *Critical Inquiry*. IX, no. 4 (June, 1983), pp. 685-723.
Rhodes, Jewell Parker. "*Mumbo Jumbo* and a Somewhat Private Literary Response," in *American Humor*. VI, no. 2 (1979), pp. 11-13.

Thomas Banks

MY HEART AND MY FLESH

Author: Elizabeth Madox Roberts (1886-1941)
Type of plot: Poetic realism
Time of plot: The early twentieth century
Locale: Anneville, Kentucky
First published: 1927

> *Principal characters:*
> THEODOSIA BELL, the protagonist
> HORACE BELL, her father
> ANTHONY BELL, her grandfather, a former teacher and
>   scholar
> AMERICY FROMAN and
> LETHE ROSS, Theodosia's mulatto half sisters
> STIGGINS, Theodosia's mulatto half brother
> CONWAY BROOKE,
> ALBERT STILES, and
> FRANK RAILEY, Theodosia's suitors
> CALEB BURNS, a farmer and the eventual husband of
>   Theodosia

The Novel

The novel's title refers to the cry of the psalmist, "My heart and my flesh crieth out for the living God." *My Heart and My Flesh* follows the story of Theodosia Bell in her journey toward self-discovery and fulfillment as she grows from childhood to adulthood in the fictional Kentucky town of Anneville. The trials through which she passes and the tragedies that befall her, leading to her final recovery and spiritual rebirth, form the core of the novel.

The first significant event that Theodosia must endure is the shattering of her complacent notions about her own superiority. Reared in a wealthy, privileged, and respectable family, she is devastated when she learns from her grandfather's secret papers that two mulatto girls in the town, Americy and Lethe, whom she has always despised, are in fact her half sisters and that Stiggins, the idiot stable boy, is her half brother. As she attempts to come to terms with this knowledge, Theodosia moves haltingly and uncomprehendingly toward a measure of acceptance and love, without ever fully achieving either. Yet when she notices, to her amazement, that Stiggins possesses the elegant "fiddle hand" that she, who prides herself on her ability with the violin, lacks, the absurdity of her former notion of superiority becomes painfully apparent.

Many of the other events which shape Theodosia's life are deaths. Her handsome and charming suitor Conway Brooke dies in his burning home, and her grief becomes more acute when Minnie Harter, a local girl and former neighbor of Conway, gives birth to a child and claims that Conway is the father. The death of Theodosia's grandfather Anthony Bell, the only member of her family with whom she has any real affinity, further isolates her, although through his death she learns pity and compassion.

On inheriting the family estate, Theodosia discovers that all the wealth has slipped away and only debts remain. This new and unexpected poverty is another blow to her self-esteem. Little by little, she loses all she has and all her hopes for the future. Her selfish and uncaring father leaves home to join a law firm, never to return. When Lethe brutally murders her unfaithful husband, Ross, goaded on by Theodosia as she half-consciously seeks vicarious revenge for having been jilted by Albert Stiles, Theodosia is so haunted by feelings of guilt that her health breaks down.

Forced to sell the house in which she has lived since she was a child, and in increasing ill health, she moves to the farm of her Aunt Doe, whom she dislikes, for rest and recuperation. This period of eighteen months represents the nadir of her fortunes. Weak and in despair, she hears voices, the discordant impulses of her own mind, as she becomes steadily more violent, incoherent, and guilt-ridden. She resolves to commit suicide, but, on the very brink of her destructive act, some mysterious and inexplicable life force quickens inside her. She suddenly finds herself utterly changed, full of fresh hope and expectation. After months of apathy and despair, she acquires a new sense of purpose. Riding with a traveling peddler the next day, she finds the spontaneity and joy in life that she has been seeking, a "strange happiness going its unknown ways."

Arriving in the nearby village of Spring Run Valley, she becomes a teacher at the local school, and it is through living among the country people, who remain in touch with nature in their simple manner, that she acquires the wholeness, compassion, and sense of acceptance and peace that she had formerly lacked. When Caleb Burns, a local farmer who seems to embody the wisdom and solidity of the earth itself, declares his love for her, her spiritual rebirth is complete, and the novel closes with images of the quiet, healing presence of a country night.

The Characters

The chief interest of the novel lies in the intense inner life of Theodosia. She is presented from the outset as a girl of extreme sensitivity, aware of subtle currents of feeling which escape her elders. She is also alienated from her environment, both human and natural, and afflicted with melancholy; Roberts, in her notes about the novel, described Theodosia as "a wandering spirit, a lost thing." Theodosia herself is acutely aware of her malaise: "It seemed to her that she lived with only a part of her being, that only a small edge of her person lifted up into the light of the day." She is, in consequence, preoccupied with the search for self-knowledge and for the innermost core of existence, refusing to be content with anything less. The sight of a tree fills her with a "passion to know all of this strange thing," and it is the same with her family: She ponders her half sister Americy "to the roots of her life and her being," and as her grandfather lies dying she attempts to discover his soul, his irreducible essence, for if she can locate the soul of another being, surely she can also locate her own? In everything, Theodosia searches for ultimate reality and meaning, that which is "perpetually existent, unchanged, beyond delusion," driven on by a sense of the insufficiency of things as they are.

Roberts lavishes so much attention on Theodosia that other characters are indistinctly realized, revealing themselves largely through their interactions with the protagonist. Perhaps the most sympathetic is Theodosia's grandfather, Anthony Bell. Formerly a teacher and scholar, he has retained his love of great literature. As he reads aloud to his family, "unafraid of any word or saying," Theodosia sees him as the custodian of eternal truths. He takes immense pride in his granddaughter's progress with the violin and lives again through her. Theodosia's affinity with him contrasts with her dislike of her father, Horace Bell. Horace's infidelity in marriage destroys any respect that Theodosia might have had for him, and his bluff, superficial manner, as well as his selfishness, effectively sets off Theodosia's introspection and sensitivity. Seen through her eyes, he is merely "a jumble of demands upon affection and forbearance."

Other characters flicker into life for the reader, but only briefly. Theodosia's illegitimate kin form a ragged and dispiriting trio. Americy wistfully sings of the Lord while involved in an incestuous relationship with Stiggins, the mentally retarded outcast who lives in the stables with the horses. Their harmlessness, however sordid, stands in sharp contrast to the heavy and menacing presence of Lethe, whose savage and violent hatred eventually leads to her imprisonment for murder.

Finally, there are Theodosia's suitors. Conway Brooke is gentle, graceful, and easygoing, his relaxed serenity ruffled only when he becomes jealous of his friend Albert Stiles. Albert, a practical man of affairs who is full of plans for the future, seeks Theodosia's hand with a blunt determination but then deserts her for the beautiful Florence Agnew. The simple good nature of the third suitor, the lawyer Frank Railey, who is uncritical in his admiration of Theodosia, does not interest her: "You could work him out by a formula" she says, and he disappears from her mind as soon as he is out of sight. All three are in marked contrast to the man who finally wins Theodosia's hand, the farmer Caleb Burns, who is deeply connected to the land in a way that the rootless town dwellers are not. He is known to all the villagers as an odd character—"he seemed always about to speak or to have just spoken, and he talked to everybody as if they knew all he meant"—but Theodosia sees him as a man shaped and matured by all the lights and shades of human experience, one who carries about him a wisdom that is universal in its scope.

Themes and Meanings

The central theme of the novel is spiritual death and rebirth. Theodosia seems to be unwittingly forced to pursue a *via negativa*, stripped of everything that she has—her family, social position, wealth, mental and physical health, and, finally, her will to live—before she can discover who she truly is, and the inexorable life force can reclaim her. That this was Roberts' intention is clear from her papers, in which she describes the novel as a process of "continual subtraction," her method consisting of "a steady taking away until there was nothing left but the bare breath of the throat and the simplified spirit."

The central recurring symbol is that of music. Theodosia's constant endeavors to improve her skill with the violin are symbolic of her search for her true self. Music, she is told by her teacher, "must come out of your soul," and Theodosia longs to "play the fiddle to the end of the earth . . . to go to the end of music and look over the edge at what's on the other side." Music embodies the perfection and harmony that she seeks. It occurs at crucial points in the narrative as a faintly heard counterpoint to the more overt discord and suffering. It gives Theodosia's exchanges with Americy and Lethe much of their poignant sadness, for example, acting as a haunting reminder of the contrast between the ideal and the actual. At the very brink of Theodosia's intended suicide, the ideal seems lost altogether, since she sees her violin as an alien object, "holding a remote kindness for some being far apart from herself, identical with some abstract goodness that would never be stated."

Most significantly, music is mysteriously linked with the rhythms and harmonies of nature, the eternal cycles of death and rebirth. As Theodosia plays, her music blends in her thought with the "running autumn and the crisp frost" and with the "outspread fertility of the fields and the high tide of mid-summer." As always in Roberts' novels, the reader is kept vividly aware of the regular passage of the seasons, and this represents a vital aspect of Theodosia's regeneration. Her task is to become rooted once more in the great rhythms of nature, with those who, like Caleb Burns, live close to the soil and its fruits. One of the novel's great symbolic moments of self-realization, foreshadowing Theodosia's final recovery, takes place when she contemplates a large elm tree and instinctively knows that she, too, is embedded in the earth, the nourishing and life-giving force, "attached to it at all points . . . sinking at each moment into it." Her more usual sense of the insufficiency of all her endeavors, that more knowledge yields only greater ignorance—a recurring theme in the novel—stems from her rootlessness. It is only in the final scenes, in Theodosia's newfound contentment, that she is able to reflect that to be in Hell is to be "subtracted from the earth" and reduced to a state of continual and restless searching.

Critical Context

My Heart and My Flesh was Roberts' second novel, published only a year after *The Time of Man* (1926) had won for her immediate recognition and acclaim. Her reputation continued to grow with the publication of *The Great Meadow* (1930), but after her last major novel, *He Sent Forth a Raven* (1935), her popularity and critical standing went into a rapid decline. She has frequently been categorized as a regionalist, but this is a somewhat unfair label, since her novels, although they are all set in Kentucky, are concerned with profound and universal themes. More charitable critics have compared her to William Faulkner, D. H. Lawrence, and Emily Dickinson. It is likely that she will continue to occupy a minor but distinct place in the roll call of twentieth century American novelists.

Although *My Heart and My Flesh* has never been one of Roberts' most popular novels, its enduring value lies in the author's ability to set out a timeless theme with unusual force and conviction. The novel faces the darker aspects of human existence without succumbing to nihilism and despair; it celebrates the virtues of simplicity and endurance, and it affirms the ultimate triumph of life and of the spirit. It is also notable for Roberts' highly distinctive prose style—she called it "symbolism working through poetic realism"—and there are many passages of rich, poetic prose which the reader may savor many times.

My Heart and My Flesh is not light reading, nor is it enjoyable in the superficial sense of the word, but it is richly satisfying for the reader who enters its spirit and contemplates its themes.

Sources for Further Study
Campbell, Harry Modean, and Ruel E. Foster. *Elizabeth Madox Roberts: American Novelist*, 1956.
McDowell, Frederick P. W. *Elizabeth Madox Roberts*, 1963.
Rovit, Earl H. *Herald to Chaos: The Novels of Elizabeth Madox Roberts*, 1960.

                                                                                    Bryan Aubrey

MY NAME IS ASHER LEV

Author: Chaim Potok (1929-   )
Type of plot: Coming of age
Time of plot: The 1950's and 1960's
Locale: The Crown Heights section of Brooklyn, Provincetown, and Paris
First published: 1972

>   *Principal characters:*
>   ASHER LEV, the protagonist, a young Hasidic Jew who
>   becomes a famous artist
>   ARYEH LEV, his father
>   RIVKEH LEV, his mother
>   THE LADOVER REBBE, the leader of Asher's Hasidic sect
>   YUDEL KRINSKY, a Russian Jew, saved by Aryeh Lev and
>   Asher's friend
>   JACOB KAHN, a great sculptor and painter, Asher's teacher

The Novel

Asher Lev's name echoes throughout the novel from title to concluding pages as he struggles to reconcile his "gift" with his heritage. Ordinarily, an observant Hasidic Jew does not become a "notorious and legendary" painter, much less one known for a painting called *Brooklyn Crucifixion*, but Asher, at odds from an early age with his traditional father, pursues his "foolishness," his compulsion to draw and paint. Ultimately, his gift demands recognition, and his mother becomes his ally in deceiving his often absent father. In time, even the Rebbe himself helps Asher decide on the course his life will take in the world of art.

Narrated in the first person, the novel begins with Asher looking back in an attempt to defend himself against charges that he is "a traitor, an apostate, a self-hater, an inflicter of shame" upon his family, friends, and people; he has also been accused of mocking beliefs which are sacred to Christians. He therefore believes that it is necessary to demythologize himself and tell the truth; he is not apologizing.

There is no lack of love in his family. His Judaism surrounds him, and he remembers warm closeness with his parents and an immersion in their life as loyal Ladover Hasidic Jews. His family, particularly his father, works for the protection of Jews the world over, and Asher often listens to conversations dealing with world conditions affecting his people. Hasidic melodies are an integral part of his existence. From his earliest memories he has translated his love for his surroundings into drawings expressing his understanding of the sights and sounds of his religion-filled life.

When his mother goes into a hysterical depression over the death of her beloved brother, Asher's life undergoes a painful change. He is deprived of her companionship, but he continues to draw. His father appears to be even more driven to his task of trying to arrange for the safety of European and Russian Jews but cannot leave Rivkeh, so he feels frustrated and helpless. Asher senses all the emotions swirling around him, but he still draws—his mother, his father, his street, and the people on it. He comments that "it's not a pretty world, Papa," but still he draws it.

With school comes a temporary loss of the gift. When it returns, however, it does so with a vengeance. Asher draws almost as though under hypnosis, without realizing that he has created a picture. He desecrates his religious texts; he is removed from his daily life; he fails his classes. Most disruptive of all, he distresses his father, who is back to his travels and has little time to spend with his family.

Nothing and no one can move Asher from his course. Ironically, it is the Rebbe who arranges for Asher to study with Jacob Kahn, who becomes a leading force in Asher's life. Another great influence is Anna Schaeffer, a gallery owner whose "Brooklyn prodigy" Asher becomes. His life is molded by his art now, but he does not give up his religion or its daily practices. On the contrary, he rededicates himself to study.

Unlike the protagonists of many other modern Jewish authors, Asher does not try to leave his religion and become totally assimilated in the modern world. He needs only the expression that modern Western art will afford him. To use only that expression and ignore the rest of the modern world, he is told by his famous mentor, Jacob Kahn, is an impossibility. He must eventually be drawn into that world, possibly the *sitra achra*, the Other Side, if he persists.

Asher does persist. He stays with his uncle when his parents finally leave together for Europe. He spends his summers painting with Jacob in Provincetown. His shows at Anna's gallery are lauded. Study in Florence and Paris heightens his awareness of Western art, and he becomes enthralled by Michelangelo's *Pietà* and the *David*. The mythic ancestor who haunted his dreams and terrified him as a child returns to become the subject of his paintings. The grandfather who traveled for the Rebbe's father becomes a subject for his canvases. He wonders if his compulsion to draw and paint, to "give meaning to paper and canvas rather than to people and events," is an interruption or a continuation of his family's tasks.

Asher's epiphany arrives as the novel comes full circle, and he is compelled to paint his feelings in the *Brooklyn Crucifixion*. The painting excites the art world but shames and shocks his family and community, forcing a break and thrusting Asher into the role of the alienated artist.

The Characters

Asher Lev has a dilemma. Potok's protagonist is a young man torn between the identity conferred upon him by his religious heritage and the talent that fights to express itself. While he is always warned that his "gift" may come from the Other Side, that it is "foolishness" and will lead him to another, evil world, Asher cannot stop drawing. From the age of four, Asher remembers drawing the world around him. When his mother is ill, he tries drawing pretty pictures even though he recognizes that the world is not pretty. His uncle recognizes his genius; "a regular Chagall," he calls him. Asher withdraws from almost everything but his feelings, which are reflected in his inner eye and transmitted, almost unknowingly, to paper. He stops drawing when he first enters the yeshiva and remembers little of those first years at school, as if he no longer saw the things at which he looked. "The gift seemed dead." When he is touched by the stories he hears of the misery and horror that Joseph Stalin brings to the Jews, he begins to feel and draw again.

Despite the guilt it causes him and the unhappiness it causes his family, he is compelled to continue; he cannot stop. His friend Yudel Krinsky, who owns a shop where Asher can see many different kinds of art supplies, pleads with him to obey his father; later, his teacher Kahn warns him about what must inevitably happen. His mythic ancestor thunders threateningly through his dreams. He very early recognizes that he has an overpowering need that drives him to cause a rift between himself and his father and ultimately his religious community.

As young as he is, he can always make his point and get his own way. He refuses to accompany his parents to Vienna, therefore forcing his mother to stay in Brooklyn with him. He needs his street, the familiar people, and his security. The urge to put his world on paper is so great that he is driven to steal from Krinsky's store the tools he needs to express himself. He grows as an artist and finds not only that must he make choices but also that often, as he grows older, those choices are made for him.

His father, Aryeh Lev, is also driven by his commitment to follow his Rebbe and travel the world to complete the mission of his Ladover ancestors. He must leave his family and, at great risk to himself, take on the task of rebuilding Ladover Hasidism in Europe. Despite his own compulsion, he cannot see or understand his son's. His duty, after all, is well within the realm of his special world, limited by the desires and commands of his Rebbe. Asher is taught from the answers to his earliest questions that commitment to the Rebbe and Ladover Hasidism is his father's life. Never, however, can Aryeh comprehend Asher's commitment. In spite of a master's degree and worldwide travel, Aryeh has never been outside the boundaries of his rigid and limited religious world. He has never felt the need to step away from his task to complete the mission of his ancestors.

It falls to Rivkeh Lev to hold her small family together, using all her limited strength to do so. First she lets her husband go in order to be with her son, and later she leaves her son in order to tend to her husband's needs. She, too, is compelled, after the death of her beloved older brother in an accident while on a mission for the Rebbe, to finish. She is almost consumed physically and mentally until she is given permission to finish what she considers an incomplete task.

While Asher can see what he is doing to her by keeping her from her husband and splitting the family, he is, at first, too young to let her go. When he finally does realize what he and his father have done to Rivkeh, he arrives at an epiphany and is agonizingly driven to paint the *Brooklyn Crucifixion*. In that painting Rivkeh's tortured self is displayed for all the world to see in a manner that is totally alien to the Hasidic tradition. After she views Asher's masterful painting, Rivkeh can accept his explanation of what he has done, but she can never understand it; it is "beyond comprehension."

The Rebbe is a dominant figure in the Levs' lives. He is a powerful and revered religious leader whose being permeates the lives of his followers. What the Rebbe pronounces carries the weight of law with his large extended family of Ladover Hasidim. He is magnificently loving and caring. He is responsible for Aryeh's constant traveling in his name, for Rivkeh's being allowed to attend the university and get a doctorate and for Asher's becoming Kahn's student.

Ultimately, he tells Asher, "You have crossed a boundary. I cannot help you. You are alone now. I give you my blessings." While he does not let him go out into the world bereft of support and directs him to the Paris yeshiva where Asher had been before, he does banish Asher from those to whom he has been closest and who have loved him all his life. It is he who recognizes the needs of his followers and directs their paths, but it is also he who ironically gives Asher the freedom and permission to seek from Kahn artistic tutelage that leads him away from his secure world.

Jacob Kahn, a nonobservant Jew, is a world-renowned sculptor who accepts Asher as a student because he recognizes the greatness that the youngster of thirteen possesses in the unique way he looks at the world. He nurtures the innate talent, never forcing Asher to give up his deep religious faith but also never shielding Asher from the influences of Western art forms that will cause excessive guilt for him. His final assessment of Asher is that he, Kahn, has "created a new *David*. A breathing *David*."

Themes and Meanings

Driven by a compulsion that he cannot fight, Asher Lev tries to reconcile the pull of the religious world that his community and family represent with the insistent tug of the world of Western art in which he wants to express himself. Torn by the dilemma of growing into the man, the artist he wants to become, versus the observant and traditional Hasidic Jew his family wants him to be, Asher Lev responds by painting *Brooklyn Crucifixion I* and *Brooklyn Crucifixion II.*

Like the protagonists of Potok's other novels, *The Promise* (1969), *In the Beginning* (1975), and *The Book of Lights* (1981), Asher is confronted by the modern world. In this novel he confirms immediately, however, that he is indeed an observant Jew. When he leaves his parents' home after the shock of his show at Anna Schaeffer's gallery and looks back through the rear window of his cab, his parents are still watching him through the living-room window; they have not given him up either.

Critical Context

In its focus on a conflict between traditional religion and secular values, *My Name Is Asher Lev* is typical of Potok's novels. As S. Lillian Kremer has observed, "The genesis and substance of every Potok novel is Jewish religious, historic and cultural experience in a non-Judaic world." Potok was influenced by an early reading of Evelyn Waugh's *Brideshead Revisited* (1945, 1959), and he was determined to bring his readers to the foreign world of Jewish civilization through fiction.

Potok, a rabbi and critical scholar of Judaic texts, is one of the few modern Jewish authors who can integrate his protagonists rather than assimilate them. Asher does not want to join the Other Side or the other world; he wants to integrate them into his world of art, his only world. Potok can create characters knowledgeable in "Jewish theology, liturgy, history and scholarship," Kremer notes, while at the same time evoking the texture of everyday life: "The novel serves as Potok's primary vehicle for the examination of the modern Jewish experience."

Asher retains his traditional faith yet moves into the world of Western artistic tradition. His teachers—the Rebbe in particular—are depicted lovingly and understandingly; he looks back on his whole childhood and his enormous heritage with love and warmth. In this novel as well as his others, Potok explores a distinctive culture in all of its particularity, but in doing so he demonstrates the power of art to transcend cultural boundaries.

Sources for Further Study

Kremer, S. Lillian. "Chaim Potok," in *Twentieth-Century American-Jewish Fiction Writers*, 1984. Edited by Daniel Walden.

Offen, Ellen Serlen. "*My Name Is Asher Lev*: Chaim Potok's Portrait of the Young Hasid as Artist," in *Studies in American Jewish Literature*. II (1982), pp. 174-180.

Studies in American Jewish Literature, IV (1984). Special Chaim Potok issue.

Jackie Eisen

THE NAKED AND THE DEAD

Author: Norman Mailer (1923-   )
Type of plot: Social realism
Time of plot: World War II
Locale: Anopopei, a Japanese-held island in the Pacific
First published: 1948

> *Principal characters:*
> GENERAL CUMMINGS, the leader of the American army divi-
> sion invading Anopopei
> LIEUTENANT HEARN, Cummings' subordinate and ideological
> opponent
> SERGEANT CROFT, the platoon leader
> RED VALSEN, a platoon member critical of Croft
> GALLAGHER, a platoon member and an Irish Catholic bigot
> from Boston
> JULIO MARTINEZ, a platoon member and a Mexican
> American conformist
> JOEY GOLDSTEIN, a platoon member and an ingratiating
> Brooklyn Jew
> WILSON, an affable Southerner

The Novel

The Naked and the Dead concentrates on the invasion of Anopopei as a
way of exploring the social and political history of the United States, which
has been thrown into intense relief by the country's participation in World
War II. Indeed, the novel reads almost like a relief map that depicts the
contour lines between ethnic groups and the different shadings of opinion
among soldiers from various parts of the nation. Class conflicts and the gap
between officers and enlisted men are explored. The biography of each principal character is detailed and set against efforts to shape these individuals
into a collective fighting force.

This is an intensely realistic novel in which the author faithfully records
his characters' dialects, provides elaborate physical and geographical data
(including a map of Anopopei), and engages in an intricate bifurcated narrative that scrutinizes both the strategy and the actual fighting of the war.
As a result, the reader is able to view the war on several levels in nearly si-
multaneous fashion without ever losing track of either its characters or its
themes.

In the midst of following the invasion plans and the maneuvers of Sergeant Croft's platoon, the novel flashes back to the characters' pasts to trace
the paths that have led them to the war. At the same time, General Cum-

mings and his subordinate, Lieutenant Hearn, argue about the causes of war, the nature of history, and of the postwar world.

By devising such a complex narrative structure, Norman Mailer risks bogging down his readers in too much detail or in excessive philosophizing; yet he is remarkably successful in avoiding these problems by maintaining suspense—he shifts rapidly between characters and situations, never quite finishes each scene so that the reader wants to know more, and thus keeps his novel moving forward on all fronts.

Although *The Naked and the Dead* is a long novel, it has a compact four-part structure, with the first and last parts quickly initiating and ending descriptions of the invasion, so that the portentous immediacy and the trivial aftermath of the fighting are handled economically. The first paragraph of part 1, for example, contains three simple and direct sentences (beginning with three words: "Nobody could sleep"), which capture the army's anxiety over going into battle. The last words of the novel are *"Hot dog!"*—Major Dalleson's exclamation that expresses his excitement over his idea to "jazz up the map-reading class by having a full-size color photograph of Betty Grable in a bathing suit, with a co-ordinate grid system laid over it."

The Characters

No single character dominates the world of *The Naked and the Dead*, although General Cummings and Sergeant Croft try to rule that world by force of will. Although each of them has been a successful leader, both are ultimately defeated by their own recalcitrant fighting force and by the jungle (nature) over which they have little control. Croft and Cummings do not have much respect for the individuality of the soldiers they command. Indeed, they hardly see human beings as individuals and are angered when they are opposed by personalities who argue in favor of self-determination.

Red Valsen and Robert Hearn speak for a more democratic view and risk challenging Croft and Cummings. Valsen, who has led a rather itinerant life before the war, has trouble envisioning a successful course of action; thus, in spite of his detestation of Croft, he cannot offer a countervailing example to the platoon. Similarly, Hearn, who is from a well-to-do family, is not sure what his politics should be, and he acts as Cummings' devil's advocate until he goes too far in resisting the general's Fascist ideas and is assigned to lead Croft's platoon on a patrol in search of a way to get behind Japanese lines and speed up the invasion.

The other men in the platoon express varying degrees of willingness to go along with Croft's often cruel drive to get them across Mount Anaka and behind Japanese lines. They work with one another to the extent that their prewar backgrounds allow and Croft's discipline dictates. Martinez, for example, wants to prove himself as a good soldier, a good American. Similarly, Joey Goldstein hopes to mute anti-Semitism by demonstrating his cooperative attitude. Wilson, the affable Southerner, tries to treat all issues on the level of comradeship. Gallagher, on the other hand, is a working-class Irish who hates elitists, the privileged, and the Jews, whom, he believes, have connived and cheated others in order to acquire positions of power and wealth. Both Wilson and Valsen help to keep Gallagher in line when he begins a tirade against the "fuggin Yids in the platoon." "They're sonsofbitches just like the rest of us," Red replies. Wilson suggests that Goldstein seems like a down-to-earth, sensible man: "Ah was workin' with him today, and we got to talkin' about the best way to lay down a corduroy."

The dialogue among platoon members is entirely convincing and is the best way the novelist has of concretely characterizing their experience and of making it immediately comprehensible to readers. He uses other techniques as well, which broaden his approach to characterization and which aid the novel in making larger statements about society and politics. The "Time Machine" sections not only explore the characters' pasts, but they also serve as biographical overviews that express the whole sweep and significance of an individual's life. The "Chorus" sections, on the other hand, collectivize experience and show how masses of men can be shaped into a fighting force that at least momentarily overrides individuality and creates a new reality that changes men and the history of which they are a part.

Themes and Meanings

As in most great realistic novels, themes and meanings in *The Naked and the Dead* arise out of clear characterization and structural techniques. In assessing General Cummings' claim that history can be determined by the biography of great men such as himself who will bend armies to their will, readers must have recourse to the author's careful delineation of human character in the passages relating the lives of the platoon members, where the shaping of personality is as much a matter of circumstances and the unforeseen timing of events as it is of deliberate calculation.

Certainly, men can be coerced to behave as a single fighting force, but leaders such as Croft and Cummings do take into account the crucial role of accidents, of nature, or of the flaws in their own characters that blind them to aspects of history they cannot control. Cummings in particular plays with diagrams and words that reflect reality as he would have it, and not the reality which the novel's narrative presents. Thus, the Japanese army is disintegrating even as Cummings is preparing his elaborate plan to conquer what he mistakenly believes is a formidable enemy. Indeed, the patrol which Cummings assigns Hearn to head has proved unnecessary and results in the lieutenant's death. Cummings has not found a way to reshape reality; on the contrary, he learns of the Japanese collapse only after the fact.

In both trivial and profound ways, the theme of individuality triumphs in *The Naked and the Dead*. What is most striking is the way the variety of human nature is affirmed. War is unpredictable, and the shape of history (America's future) cannot be as easily forecast as Cummings supposes. Yet the novel does not simply discredit him as a philosopher of history, for the weaknesses of characters such as Hearn suggest how much damage Fascist ideas have done to a country that is not prepared to resist authoritarianism militarily and intellectually.

Critical Context

The Naked and the Dead was Norman Mailer's first published novel. It proved to be a tremendous popular and critical success and placed the twenty-five-year-old author in the front rank of a new generation of writers. For some readers, the novel remains his most accomplished work, and they have regretted his abandonment of realism for fiction and nonfiction that express his romantic idealism and existential politics.

While Mailer has shied away from the style of *The Naked and the Dead*, other aspects of the novel have continued to inform his later work. He is more than ever concerned with the concept of individuality and with how his times have diminished human character, and he has sought to make his own personality the testing ground for the ideas debated by Cummings and Hearn.

If Mailer has shifted his focus away from the realistic novel, the themes of his later books—notably *The Armies of the Night* (1968) and *The Executioner's Song* (1979)—extend and enrich his reputation as a social and psychological novelist. If he has turned inward to find insights into American character, he has also functioned often as a first-rate reporter on the major events and personalities of his day. In other words, in his own stance as a writer, he has maintained the equilibrium between biography and history which is so lacking in the characters he creates in *The Naked and the Dead*.

Sources for Further Study

Bailey, Jennifer. *Norman Mailer: Quick-Change Artist*, 1980.
Lucid, Robert F. *Norman Mailer: The Man and His Work*, 1971.
Merrill, Robert. *Norman Mailer*, 1978.
Poirier, Richard. *Norman Mailer*, 1972.
Solotaroff, Theodore. *Down Mailer's Way*, 1974.

Carl E. Rollyson, Jr.

NAKED LUNCH

Author: William Burroughs (1914-   )
Type of plot: Fantasy
Time of plot: The second half of the twentieth century
Locale: New York City, Freeland Republic, Mexico, and Interzone
First published: 1959

> *Principal characters:*
> WILLIAM LEE, the narrator, who is a drug addict
> DOCTOR BENWAY, an expert in mind control
> MUGWUMPS, creatures without livers who live on sweets and use young boys as sexual prey
> ALI HASSAN, a "notorious liquefactionist" and owner of the Rumpus Room, where Mugwumps sexually violate and murder young boys
> THE LIQUEFACTIONISTS, a political party engaged in dissolving and absorbing other bodies (that is, in liquidating reality)
> THE SENDERS, a group compelled to "send all the time" without any contact with other human beings
> THE DIVISIONISTS, who literally divide into replicas of themselves
> A. J., "the notorious merchant of sex," an ambiguous figure who may be a liquefactionist or just the opposite, a Factualist
> THE FACTUALISTS, a group opposed to all the parties of Interzone that attempt to seduce, subjugate, and completely reduce human beings to protoplasm

The Novel

Near the end of *Naked Lunch*, there is a phrase that neatly sums up the chaotic experience of reading the novel: "This book spill off the page in all directions, kaleidoscope of vistas, medley of tunes and street noises, farts and riot yipes and the slamming steel shutters of commerce. . . . " There is no plot, no chronology, no realistic setting, and sometimes no conventional grammar to guide the confused reader. On the other hand, the novel's themes are quite clear: Burroughs is dramatizing and criticizing the raucous and profane commercialization of a contemporary world that is brutally exterminating individuality.

The way to follow Burroughs' novel is to concentrate on his cast of characters, each of which reflects some aspect of the urge to dominate and to violate human beings. He divides his novel into several sections that focus on a single character or setting. Because these sections are not consecutively ordered, it is possible to move back and forth between them, rather than reading the novel from beginning to end. Some readers might find it helpful, for example, to begin with the section entitled "Islam Incorporated and the Parties of Interzone." The Liquefactionists, Senders, Divisionists, and Factualists all contend for superiority in a slippery, phantasmagoric world where human identity is never safe from invasion by forces that would penetrate and transform it into a kind of primordial slime that is the antithesis of sentient life.

The Evergreen paperback edition of *Naked Lunch* provides considerable help in approaching the novel by including court testimony defending the technique and themes of a book that has been attacked for its obscenity. Burroughs also includes a discussion of his drug addiction and an essay on the effects of certain drugs. This material is essential to understanding a book which uses drug addiction and sexual perversion as metaphors for a brilliant survey of a world that is rapidly sapping itself of humanity and literally sucking out the principle of life itself.

The Characters

The novel begins in New York City with a first-person narrator, William Lee, a drug addict escaping from a "narcotics dick." He eventually makes his way to the Freeland Republic, where he engages the services of its adviser, Doctor Benway, for Islam Inc. Business dealings in *Naked Lunch* are often confusing and conspiratorial, so that it is difficult to keep track of transactions that are worldwide and illegal—like the drug traffic Burroughs followed in his own life as a junkie.

Benway becomes the key character in the novel because he represents inhuman efficiency and medical coercion. He deplores "brutality" in the form of concentration camps and physical torture and favors mind control which is accomplished by sleep deprivation and other behavior modification methods.

Benway is the most extreme example of other doctors and mind-control experts in the book because he wants to develop "one all-purpose blob" to replace the inefficient, complex structure of human beings. Doctor "Fingers" Schafer, "the Lobotomy Kid," wants to reduce the human nervous system to "a compact and abbreviated spinal column." This new kind of human being will be "deanxietized," he tells his audience in a section entitled "Meeting of International Conference of Technological Psychiatry."

The "deanxietized" human being the doctors would like to produce through surgery and medication is tantamount to the drug addict who has no worries so long he is "on the junk," to use Burroughs' expression. Such a medicated world, however, is totalitarian and unreal, as Burroughs suggests in one of the more realistic sections of *Naked Lunch*, entitled "Hauser and O'Brien."

Hauser and O'Brien, twenty-year veterans of the New York City narcotics squad assigned to arrest William Lee, a sixteen-year veteran of narcotics addiction, allow Lee to take a final shot of dope in exchange for his information on a pusher, Marty Steel. Lee manages to shoot both men after injecting himself with heroin, and to set out in search of his next fix, although he knows that in all likelihood he will be executed for murdering the two "laws," as he puts it. In a phone call to the police, he asks for Hauser and O'Brien and is told there are no officers with those names in the department. Lee's conclusion is that he has been "occluded from space-time"—that is, his drug addiction has prevented him from experiencing the passage of time, which, in turn, means that he has not really moved in space.

This science-fiction notion of human character suddenly removed from time and space is the perfect literary realization of what Burroughs has said of himself in his prefatory essay: "I could look at the end of my shoe for eight hours. I was only roused to action when the hourglass of junk ran out." Other characters—the Sailor in "The Black Meat," Lee and Miguel in "Lazarus Go Home," the Mugwumps in "Hassan's Rumpus Room"—are examples of human beings who are essentially dead, "without a trace of warmth or lust or hate or any feeling. . . ." These characters are "impersonal and predatory," extracting the juices from living beings in the manner of vampires.

A. J., while partaking of the vices of this world, also counters its impersonality. He is a character of shifting identities, the financier of Islam Inc., and—in William Lee's words—"an agent like me" in an "industry you can never be sure of. . . ." His "cover story" is that he is an "international playboy" but no one believes him or his claim to be independent since everyone must take sides in a world divided by the parties of Interzone. He is remarkable, however, for his ability to thrive in so many different environments; his flexibility seems to be the closest thing to freedom in an authoritarian society dominated by Benway and other doctrinaire behaviorists.

Themes and Meanings

Burroughs' recovery from drug addiction led him to write a book in which he used his own sickness as the root fact about a contemporary world that is conspiring to deprive human beings of their dignity. He calls junk "the ideal product . . . the ultimate merchandise. No sales talk necessary. The client will crawl through a sewer and beg to buy." He calls this phenomenon "the algebra of need," a formula for stimulating in consumers an insatiable need that, in effect, sells the consumer to the product.

The loose, open-ended structure of *Naked Lunch* embodies the hallucinatory reality of a world hooked on drugs, but the book's style is also the antidote to addiction. As the narrator notes, "you can cut into *Naked*

Lunch at any intersection point." On the one hand, that means the novel is formless and, in a way, a piece of junk, since most readers require some kind of rational organization of what they read. On the other hand, the novelist's refusal to control his readers is salutary because so much of the world is already rigidly directed by business, medical, political, and other types of institutions. The energetic inventiveness of Burroughs' style confirms his individuality, his release from addiction and conformity and from all rules, even those of language.

The greatest minds have always broken the rules, he implies. Individuals face the fact of the world's complexity, and they resist the efforts of Benway and other technicians to simplify human beings and make them uniform. Similarly, the Factualists (the facers of the facts) oppose the Senders, who are like commercial broadcasters who cannot think about or interact with what they send out to the world; the Divisionists, who dread human uniqueness and try to make copies of themselves; and the Liquefactionists, who aggressively gobble up everything and destroy human differentiation.

Critical Context

Naked Lunch remains William Burroughs' most famous work and, in many critics' minds, his greatest achievement. He is often associated with the 1950's Beat movement, in which poets such as Allen Ginsberg and novelists such as Jack Kerouac experimented with drugs and dissented from coercive aspects of modern American culture. Leslie Fiedler has also linked Burroughs and the Beats with a cult of youth worship and homosexuality and chided him for a certain immaturity in his work—a charge that other writers and critics would dispute. Ginsberg and Norman Mailer, for example, gave court testimony (included in the Evergreen paperback edition of *Naked Lunch*) that characterized the novel as a deeply serious, even religious work, because of the author's profound exploration of political and psychological realities in the guise of a literary fantasy.

No matter how opinion divides on *Naked Lunch*—some critics condemn its seeming formlessness while others admire its deviation from traditional novelistic structure—there is no doubt that Burroughs has had a tremendous influence on contemporary writers. His linking of scatological language and the vocabulary of politics clearly had an impact on Mailer's *Why Are We in Vietnam?* (1967) and on Robert Coover's *The Public Burning* (1977). Both novelists followed Burroughs' inventive use of obscenities to describe a corrupt, degraded culture.

The court battles over *Naked Lunch* provoked writers to justify its extensive use of profanity and to defend Burroughs for breaking new ground as an artist. Once it was clear that the novel could not be suppressed, it became much easier for authors to stop censoring themselves in fear that what they wrote would not be published.

Naked Lunch still has the power to shock readers with its originality, brutality, and profanity, for Burroughs assaults them with a style that can never be fully digested. Indeed, this is his fundamental point. All too much is easily digested in the contemporary world. People have become accustomed to quick-fix products—from junk food to microwave ovens. He wants to give them the same thing his narrator, William Lee, is getting: a "junk-cure," a naked lunch in which, as Ginsberg told the Supreme Court of Massachusetts, the meal would be the ability "to see clearly without any confusing disguises, to see through the disguise. . . . 'Lunch' would be a complete banquet of all this naked awareness."

Sources for Further Study
Fiedler, Leslie A. *Waiting for the End*, 1964.
Goodman, Michael B. *William S. Burroughs: An Annotated Bibliography of His Works and Criticism*, 1975.
Odier, Daniel. *The Job: Interviews with William Burroughs*, 1974.
Tanner, Tony. *City of Words: American Fiction, 1950-1970*, 1971.
Tytell, John. *Naked Angels: The Lives and Literature of the Beat Generation*, 1976.

Carl E. Rollyson, Jr.

THE NATURAL

Author: Bernard Malamud (1914-1986)
Type of plot: Comic epic
Time of plot: The recent past, a fifteen-year span
Locale: New York, Chicago, and other parts of the United States
First published: 1952

> *Principal characters:*
> ROY HOBBS, the protagonist, an extraordinarily gifted base-
> ball player
> HARRIET BIRD, a beautiful woman who shoots athletes with
> silver bullets
> SAM SIMPSON, an aging scout who discovers Roy
> POP FISHER, the elderly manager of the New York Knights
> MEMO PARIS, Pop Fisher's attractive niece
> JUDGE GOODWILL BANNER, the avaricious principal owner of
> the New York Knights
> GUS SANDS, a corrupt gambler
> IRIS LEMON, a Chicago woman who offers Roy genuine love

The Novel

Bernard Malamud's first published book is an archetypal baseball story in which the American national pastime provides the context and the metaphors for a drama of individual achievement. It mixes elements of actual baseball history with mythic allusions in a tone that mingles intense seriousness and comedy.

The Natural begins with a prologue entitled "Pre-game," in which nineteen-year-old Roy Hobbs rides a train east to Chicago to try out for the Cubs. Accompanied by Sam Simpson, an elderly scout who hopes that his discovery of Hobbs will rejuvenate his own career, Roy encounters Whammer Whambold, the American League's leading hitter. During an unexpected delay of the train, Roy strikes out Whammer on three straight pitches. In Chicago, Harriet Bird, a seductive woman with a penchant for puncturing athletes with silver bullets, invites Roy to her hotel room and shoots him.

The principal part of the narrative, "Batter-Up!" takes place fifteen years later. A thirty-four-year-old Hobbs arrives mysteriously at the ballpark of the New York Knights. Following the death of Bump Bailey as a result of chasing a fly ball, he becomes their regular left fielder, and the team's sagging fortunes immediately begin to revive. Hobbs performs fabulously at bat and in the field, and the Knights soon seem destined for a pennant.

Hobbs inherits not only Bailey's position but also his woman, Memo

Paris, the niece of the team's kindly old manager Pop Fisher. A midseason slump, however, threatens disaster both for Hobbs and for the prospects of the Knights. He returns to championship form during the game in Chicago when he is asked to hit a home run to save the life of a hospitalized boy who worships him. As he steps up to the plate, a strange woman with a white rose rises in the stands.

She is Iris Lemon, a thirty-three-year-old grandmother whose love Hobbs first accepts and then rejects. He returns to Memo in New York, where she colludes with Judge Banner and Gus Sands in trying to fix the play-off game between the Knights and the Pirates. Hobbs agrees to throw it, but late in the game he experiences a change of heart and a resurgence of vitality. Nevertheless, he breaks his magical bat Wonderboy and in the final inning strikes out to the Pirates' youthful rookie Herman Youngberry. Hobbs angrily returns his bribery money to Banner and, after attacking his corrupters, stalks off in self-revulsion.

The Characters

Roy Hobbs is a textbook profile of the archetypal hero, and through him Malamud explores the possibilities for epic achievement in a desolate modern world. *The Natural* is not a naturalistic novel, and it endows its chief protagonist with talents that are not quite supernatural but certainly different in degree if not kind from those of other mortals. An orphan, Hobbs emerges mysteriously from the verdant West to do battle against forces that have been devastating the community. His journey reenacts the traditional heroic pattern of initiation, separation, and return.

As he tells Harriet Bird during their fateful meeting when he is only nineteen, his overweening ambition is solely to be "the best there ever was in the game." Throughout his experiences, Hobbs does not transcend his infantilism, but remains, as the name Roy Hobbs suggests, a hobbled king. He does not learn, until too late, the value of suffering and the virtue of love.

In creating Roy Hobbs, Malamud clearly drew on ancient quest and fertility myths and, specifically, on Arthurian legend and the figure of Sir Perceval. He also borrowed generously from baseball history and folklore. In his orphanage background, his slugging prowess, his bouts of bulimia, and his dedication of a home run to a dying boy, Hobbs echoes the career of Babe Ruth. Hobbs's misfortune in the Chicago hotel room draws on the shooting of Eddie Waitkus, in 1949, by a disturbed woman, and his behavior during the play-off game recalls Shoeless Joe Jackson's actions during the infamous Black Sox scandal.

Memo Paris, a later version of Harriet Bird, and Iris Lemon represent two contrasting faces of woman that tempt Hobbs, that would, in opposing ways, divert him from his single-minded quest. They stand as Lilith and

Morgan le Fay to Eve and the Lady of the Lake. Satanic Memo is red-haired and dressed in black, while beatific Iris is dark-haired and dressed in red. Memo suffers from fibroma of the breast, and Hobbs's erotic pursuit of her is sterile and destructive. Iris is a grandmother whose life has experienced disappointments and false starts to parallel that of Hobbs. After rearing an illegitimate daughter, she is now, at the age of thirty-three, ready to resume her life and to teach Hobbs the lessons of self-sacrifice and love.

Hobbs also encounters a succession of father figures whom he, as part of the natural cycle, must supplant. In turn, he, an aging batter in his final game, is struck out by the rookie Herman Youngberry. Sam Simpson, a superannuated baseball scout, is initially Hobbs's mentor. Yet when the young man defeats the American League batting champion, Simpson immediately takes ill and dies blessing the new sports star he has brought forth from the wilderness. Pop Fisher is another benign father figure shown at the outset of "Batter Up!" enfeebled for the lack of a forceful heir. Judge Banner is a more malign paternal figure, one who must likewise be challenged by a strong young successor.

Malamud presents these and other personages less as fully rounded characters than as caricatures. They are simultaneously avatars of ancient myths and modern parodies of those myths.

Themes and Meanings

Much like James Joyce's *Ulysses* (1922) or T. S. Eliot's *The Waste Land* (1922), *The Natural* sets the modern commercial world against the backdrop of timeless, universal patterns. Malamud plants explicit repetitions and parallels throughout the career of Roy Hobbs to reinforce the archetypal qualities of significant recurrence. His choice of names such as Pop Fisher, Max Mercy, Harriet Bird, and Iris Lemon makes the novel seem like a gloss on the vegetation myths of Jessie L. Weston's influential study *From Ritual to Romance* (1920). Still the comic tone and the substitution of a baseball pennant for the Holy Grail question whether contemporary society leaves any room for heroism.

Hobbs undergoes a trial by love and appears to fail. Refusing to accept his mortality and finitude, he devotes himself exclusively and narcissistically to athletic perfection. Rejecting the fecund Iris Lemon, who ends up pregnant with his child, he pursues the sterile Memo Paris. He breaks his special bat Wonderboy, a talismanic weapon similar to the Arthurian Excalibur and an obvious phallic symbol.

During an idyllic lakeside tryst when the two discuss their pasts, Iris declares: "We have two lives, Roy, the life we learn with and the life we live after that. Suffering is what brings us toward happiness." This doctrine of redemption through suffering and of self-transcendence through a loving new life is central to *The Natural*, as it is to Malamud's fiction in general.

Nine years later, in 1961, he even published a novel entitled *A New Life*. Yet, until Hobbs's final humiliation and defeat in Knight's Field, he self-destructively ignores the truth of a lesson made manifest to the readers of the novel.

Critical Context

The critical consensus in retrospect is that *The Natural* is an auspicious first book, that it is in fact, along with Mark Harris' *Bang the Drum Slowly* (1956), Robert Coover's *The Universal Baseball Association, Inc., J. Henry Waugh, Prop.* (1968), and W. P. Kinsella's *Shoeless Joe* (1982), one of the finest baseball novels. *The Natural* received scattered and mixed reviews on first publication, but it began to receive increased attention with the appearance of Malamud's highly acclaimed second novel, *The Assistant* (1957), and of his short-story collection *The Magic Barrel* (1958), which earned for Malamud a National Book Award. With its author's steady productivity and his canonization as one of the major fiction writers in late twentieth century American literature, *The Natural* became widely known and respected. A lavish film version, directed by Barry Levinson and starring Robert Redford, was released in 1984, but respect for the text did not prevent the changing of the ending to have Hobbs win the play-off game for the Knights.

Nevertheless, *The Natural* does occupy an anomalous position within its author's body of writings, and not only for treating baseball. Malamud is generally regarded, along with Saul Bellow and Philip Roth, as one of the outstanding American Jewish novelists. Yet his first book stands alone among Malamud's longer fiction in lacking any major Jewish character. Several critics have observed that Malamud employs Jewishness as a metaphor—for the modern human being as a suffering victim—and if so, then Roy Hobbs is surely an honorary Jew, kin to such later Malamud figures as the Jewish convert Frank Alpine in *The Assistant*, the Jewish apostate Yakov Bok in *The Fixer* (1966), and such other schlemiels as Arthur Fidelman, of *Pictures of Fidelman* (1969), Harry Lesser, of *The Tenants* (1971), William Dubin, of *Dubin's Lives* (1979), and Calvin Cohn, of *God's Grace* (1982).

The incongruity of styles and tones in *The Natural*, which strives to be both realistic and symbolic, comic and portentous, and its overly schematic subtext of scholarly allusion keep the book from being as fully achieved as some of Malamud's later work. Still its poignant treatment of an individual's struggles toward transformation demonstrate an early signature of the master.

Sources for Further Study
Cohen, Sandy. *Bernard Malamud and the Trial by Love*, 1974.

Field, Leslie A., and Joyce W. Field, eds. *Bernard Malamud and the Critics*, 1970.
Hershinow, Sheldon J. *Bernard Malamud*, 1980.
Richman, Sidney. *Bernard Malamud*, 1966.

Steven G. Kellman

NEVER COME MORNING

Author: Nelson Algren (1909-1981)
Type of plot: Naturalism
Time of plot: The 1930's
Locale: Chicago
First published: 1942

> *Principal characters:*
> BRUNO (LEFTY) BICEK, the protagonist, a hoodlum and boxer
> STEFFI ROSTENKOWSKI, his girlfriend who becomes a
>   prostitute
> BONIFACY KONSTANTINE, a barber and the neighborhood
>   crime boss
> CASEY BENKOWSKI, Bonifacy's henchman and a former boxer
> FIREBALL KODADEK, Bruno's knife-wielding adversary
> "ONE-EYE" TENCZARA, a police captain intent on convicting
>   Bruno
> TIGER PULTORIC, a former boxing champion and Bruno's idol

The Novel

Nelson Algren's *Never Come Morning* is rooted in Chicago, particularly in its Polish slums, and concerns the fate of Bruno (Lefty) Bicek, a seventeen-year-old with ambitions of becoming either a professional baseball player or a professional boxer. The novel begins, however, with a boxing match which is lost by Casey Benkowski, who, as a slightly older version of Bruno, foreshadows Bruno's "loss" after a boxing victory at the end of the novel. Through the chapter headings in book 1 of the novel, "The Trouble with Casey" is tied directly to "The Trouble with Bicek," and the reader learns the fate of ambitious young men.

Under the tutelage of Casey and the "sponsorship" of Bonifacy Konstantine, Bruno steals a slot machine and transforms his neighborhood gang, the Warriors, into the "Baldheads," who must have their heads shaved by Bonifacy. As president and treasurer of the new gang, Bruno has status that he exploits with Steffi Rostenkowski, whom he subsequently seduces. Before the reader learns what Bruno's "trouble" is, Algren comments that the two events have brought Bruno from dependence to independence, from boyhood to manhood, and, ironically, from "vandalism to hoodlumhood." One of Bruno's "troubles" is his adherence to the gang's code and his desire to belong, but he also fears Fireball Kodadek and his knife. Consequently, when the gang insists on their rights to Steffi, Bruno, though inwardly torn, assents; while the gang rapes Steffi, Bruno rages until in his frustration he breaks, with a well-placed kick, the neck of a Greek outsider. The Greek's death temporarily ends Steffi's ordeal, but Fireball and a friend take her to Bonifacy, who installs her as his mistress and as a prostitute in his brothel, which is run by "Mama" Tomek.

Bruno is subsequently arrested for the shooting death of a drunk, whom Casey killed, and "One-Eye" Tenczara, convinced that he is the Greek's killer, attempts to break Bruno, who remains silent despite the interrogations, lineups, and beatings. After being convicted of the drunk's murder, Bruno serves six months in prison before he is released and returns to work as a pimp and bouncer at Mama Tomek's brothel. He and Steffi cannot express their feelings for each other, but she helps him cheat Bonifacy in a card game, and the rejuvenated Bruno arranges a fight for himself with Honeyboy Tucker. The infuriated Bonifacy attempts to ensure Bruno's defeat, but Bruno manhandles Bonifacy's gang, which includes Fireball and Tiger Pultoric, Bruno's boxing idol. When Bruno takes Fireball's knife, he overcomes his fear; when he beats Pultoric, he emerges as a man. He wins the ensuing boxing match, temporarily achieving his dreams of freeing and protecting Steffi and of becoming a contender for the championship. Bonifacy, however, has turned him in to Tenczara, who comes to Bruno's dressing room to arrest him for the Greek's murder.

The Characters

Bruno Bicek, Algren's tragic protagonist in *Never Come Morning*, stands alone, differentiated from the other members of his gang by his sensitivity and humanity. In an environment that places a premium on mere survival, Bruno's "flaws" mark him as "soft."

His "softness" results in Steffi's rape and subsequent prostitution, for she cannot return to her Old World mother and values. Like Bruno, however, she retains her humanity and her capacity for love and forgiveness, but Algren has taken care not to present her as the idealized virgin: Lazy and selfish, she permits Bruno's seduction because she senses that he is the best of the available males. Algren's portrait of her, like his characterization of Bruno, is complex. In this adolescent love story, readers do not encounter the star-crossed lovers of *West Side Story* (1961); they find young people with potential whose growth is irremediably stunted by their environment. They have few choices, and the few they have do not involve escape.

The impossibility of Bruno's escape is foreshadowed by the fate of Casey, who is a bit older but whose life closely parallels his. Casey, like Bruno, is a boxer, but he is a loser, a hanger-on, a tool of Bonifacy; his position is reflected in his appearance at the barber's back door, where he is reduced to asking for "advances" which are really handouts.

While Casey is a foil to Bruno, Fireball and Tiger represent tests that the hero must pass to achieve even the illusion of victory. Fireball (whose name reflects his former baseball prowess) is a has-been at eighteen, a youth whose tall, lean frame is being consumed by tuberculosis. With courage born of having nothing to lose, he uses his knife, with its implicit threat of mutilation, to overcome Bruno. Tiger is the Old King, the father figure, the former champion whom Bruno has worshiped, but who must be defeated before Bruno can be his own man. When he defeats Tiger and takes Fireball's knife, Bruno becomes a man; the victory in the ring is important only in terms of irony.

The older generation, unlike the younger one, clings to the Old World values of hard work and religious faith, and, as a result, survives rather than thrives in a New World where exploitation, brutality, and the "con" game seem necessary for success. Bruno's mother, who is exploited in a small shop, cannot understand her son's lack of concern about law and religion; Steffi's mother ekes out a living in a poolroom, is apparently oblivious to her environment, and has values which make her raped daughter's return impossible. Of the older generation, only Bonifacy adopts New World values, but only in what he considers, because of his paranoia, to be self-defense. Morally corrupt, he nevertheless pays lip service to Old World values while he projects his corruption onto his underlings.

Themes and Meanings

In Algren's Chicago, the characters are shaped by their environment, from which there is no real escape, yet they dream the American Dream and aspire to success. Bruno's failure is foreshadowed by Casey's, and Steffi can no more escape from the brothel than she can from the Baldheads. Like Chickadee, Helen, and Tookie, the other prostitutes at Mama Tomek's brothel, Steffi is one of the "hunted" who "also hope" (Algren's chapter title for his brothel digression is "The Hunted Also Hope"). The hunters are the "heat" and the men who want, in Algren's words, "to get their money's worth." One symbol for the woman as prey is the fly without wings in Steffi's room: After she is "seduced," Bruno crushes the fly, with which the inarticulate Steffi identifies. Later, when she and Bruno are at an amusement park, he uses his baseball prowess to win a Kewpie doll, which he subsequently "decapitates" as if it were a child. The doll may represent an illusory victory, a "fake," as Bruno calls it, like other things at the amusement park and in life. It may also, because it is compared to a child, represent what happens to children in Algren's Chicago, or, and this seems more probable, it may also represent Steffi, won by Bruno and then, almost unthinkingly, destroyed by him.

Nevertheless, both Bruno and Steffi have their dreams. Bruno becomes the "modern Kitchel" (a former Polish-American boxing champion) in his dream drama, and his imagination is fueled by matchbook covers with Tiger Pultoric's picture, by *Kayo* magazine, and by images of James Cagney—the media shape his dreams. Steffi's dreams of escape lead only to entrapment:

"a great stone penitentiary" without exits; the barber's room, which becomes a "vault." There will be no escape for Steffi, who is not even permitted to die. Yet Steffi and Bruno are not the only "hunted" in the city, which is compared, along with the world, to a madhouse with its victims. In fact, Algren compares the prostitutes in the brothel to inmates of an insane asylum.

From such institutions, escape is impossible, as Algren's title implies: This is a novel about the darkness, the night; it is the literary version of the *film noir*. Although there is a kind of "false dawn," with its promise of light, renewal, and deliverance, the illusory dawn is followed by the darkness of impending death for Bruno and entrapment for Steffi. The morning will not come, but there is the sense that its appearance would be even more cruel, since the light would dispel the dream and leave the dreamers with bright but cold reality.

Despite his insistence on the role of the environment, Algren also finds Bruno guilty of betrayal. Like Dove Linkhorn's betrayal and guilt in Algren's later *A Walk on the Wild Side* (1956), Bruno's guilt cannot be overcome, and, also like Dove, Bruno cannot articulate his shame and his desire for forgiveness until the end of the novel. When he takes Steffi to the lake, Bruno cannot speak, cannot even touch her hand, and what could be reconciliation becomes merely another indication that these characters take their environment and its influence with them. After his arrest at the end of the novel, Bruno accepts his fate as if he had been living with it since he killed the Greek and destroyed Steffi. It is the punishment he has been seeking.

Critical Context

Never Come Morning, Algren's second novel, follows *Somebody in Boots* (1935), a "Depression" novel which it resembles in its economic determinism, its protrait of the lower classes, and its criticism of the American Dream. It is the novel which precedes *The Man With the Golden Arm* (1949), which won for Algren a National Book Award. Part of *Never Come Morning*, the second book in the novel, first appeared as "A Bottle of Milk for Mother," a short story which was included in the annual O. Henry collection of outstanding short stories in 1941.

Algren's novel, like James T. Farrell's *Studs Lonigan* (1934), with which it is often compared, is rooted in the ghettos of Chicago and is best described as a city novel which does not allow the reader or its characters a glimpse of the world outside the city. As a result, Algren uses Chicago as a microcosm of the United States and even of the world as he sees it: as madhouse, prison, or brothel with their images of insanity, entrapment, and prostitution in its broadest sense.

In his emphasis on the interplay between environment and youth, Algren resembles not only Farrell but also Richard Wright and James Baldwin, whose characters' tormented souls and physically afflicted bodies provide an indictment of the society in which they exist. Bruno is guilty of betrayal and exploitation, but his moral failure is linked inextricably to the code of his gang, which is but an exaggeration of the capitalistic code that fosters competition and callousness and that rewards only the victors. Algren offers his readers few victors because the rewards and successes are, as they are in Bruno's case, illusory and transitory.

Algren's subject, setting, and characters are squarely within the naturalistic school of fiction which originated at the turn of the century and which includes among its practitioners such writers as Stephen Crane, Frank Norris, Theodore Dreiser, and Ernest Hemingway (who praised Algren's work). In style, however, Algren is much more in the realistic school with its so-called slice-of-life emphasis on the sordid details in the lives of the lower classes. While the boxing matches at the beginning and end of the novel do offer a frame for the story, Algren has not taken the same care with the rest of the novel. The second book, as noted above, is adapted from the short story "A Bottle of Milk for Mother," and the third book consists of case histories of prostitutes at Mama Tomek's brothel. In effect, the novel grinds to a halt while Algren discusses the abuse of power by police and comments on conditions in jail, which serves as a place of refuge in Algren's work; then, as he does in his later *A Walk on the Wild Side*, he sentimentally describes the prostitutes, whom he uses as a metaphor for the prostitution inherent in a materialistic society. Nevertheless, the digressions are interesting, and they do establish, if that has not been done adequately elsewhere, the climate that determines the outcome of the novel.

In *Never Come Morning*, Algren foreshadows Bruno's failure and then proceeds to explain why the tragic outcome is inevitable. That he does this in a rather heavy-handed manner in no way diminishes the novel or subverts his message about the American Dream.

Sources for Further Study
Cox, Martha Heasley, and Wayne Chatterton. *Nelson Algren*, 1975.
Donohue, H. E. F. *Conversations with Nelson Algren*, 1963.
Eisinger, Chester E. *Fiction of the Forties*, 1963.
Geismar, Maxwell. *American Moderns: From Rebellion to Conformity*, 1958.

Tom Erskine

A NEW LIFE

Author: Bernard Malamud (1914-1986)
Type of plot: Contemporary realism
Time of plot: The early 1950's
Locale: Northwestern United States
First published: 1961

> *Principal characters:*
> SEYMOUR LEVIN, a new English instructor at Cascadia College
> GERALD GILLEY, the director of composition
> PAULINE GILLEY, his wife
> ORVILLE FAIRCHILD, the department chairman
> C. D. FABRIKANT, a senior faculty member

The Novel

Seymour Levin of New York City ("formerly a drunkard") comes to Easchester, in the northwestern state of Cascadia, to join the faculty of Cascadia College as an instructor in English. He arrives at the small town looking forward to a new life in a halcyon rural setting, but the first of many disillusionments that this bearded, onetime high school teacher experiences is his discovery that Cascadia is a science and technology school, having lost the liberal arts "shortly after the First World War" to its rival sister institution at the state capital. What is more, most of his colleagues, he is dismayed to learn, enjoy teaching composition, do not at all miss literature, and spend most of their time in such nonacademic activities as golfing, fishing, riding, and even painting houses. The action of the novel, which spans an academic year from Levin's arrival in the fall to his forced departure the next spring, develops on two levels, the personal and the professional, which become increasingly intertwined and ultimately are indistinguishable.

The plot on the personal level focuses on an affair that Levin has with Pauline Gilley, wife of the director of composition; she previously has been involved with Levin's predecessor and pursues Levin until he finally yields. Overcome by guilt (which manifests itself in strange postintercourse pain), Levin finally attempts to end the affair, but she persists, and when Gilley eventually learns about it, he cries to Levin that he loves Pauline and the next day writes that if Levin promises "not to see [her] again, or otherwise interfere in our lives. . . . I am willing to let you stay on for one last year." Before Levin can reply, however, he receives a letter of termination "in the public interest, for good and sufficient cause of a moral nature" from the college president. Pauline and Levin decide to leave together, and Gilley tries to dissuade Levin, threatening to sue for divorce and demand custody of their two adopted children. She refuses to give him the youngsters, and

Gilley then offers to relent if Levin vows to give up college teaching. The novel ends with Levin, Pauline (who is pregnant), and the children heading for California and what may be another start on a new life. Yet Levin is not certain, deciding that he may "call it quits" after Pauline gets her Nevada divorce. Since that "would finish the promise to Gilley," he would return to graduate school and then try his hand again at college teaching.

The other line of action revolves around the English department, with the professional rivalries and personality differences moving toward a conflict because of the imminent retirement of the longtime chairman, Professor O. Fairchild, author of a grammar text that is in its thirteenth edition and is the centerpiece of the composition program. Gilley, the *de facto* second-in-command because of his role as director of composition, is an aspirant favored by the traditionalists; his primary rival is C. D. Fabrikant, a senior faculty member whose interest in horses does not prevent him from being the only active scholar in the department. Levin becomes the outspoken leader of the reluctant and *sotto voce* opposition to Gilley, which further alienates him from the establishment (he already is in trouble because of his antipathy to the hallowed grammar text and his slowness in grading finals, which jeopardizes the department's record for being the first to turn in grades). The sudden death of Professor Fairchild and the appointment of Gilley as acting chairman complicates matters for Levin, who mounts his own quixotic campaign for the post. In the event, Gilley prevails, with seventeen votes to Fabrikant's two; Levin gets none. The election defeat comes on the same day that the president, calling Levin a "frustrated Union Square radical," dismisses him.

Seemingly a professional failure at Cascadia, Levin actually succeeds in turning the Department of English in a new direction: After thirty years, Fairchild's grammar book is kicked out; Gilley decides to offer literature classes to those faculty members who are interested; and Fabrikant, who is asked to start a Great Books program, begins to grow whiskers.

The Characters

When thirty-year-old Seymour Levin comes to Cascadia from the East, he is fleeing the memories of a failed love affair and the suicide of his mother, crises which led to his being a drunkard for two years. Hiding behind a beard that he grew because he did not like the sight of his face, he seems to be denying his very identity, and he refers to himself at the start of the novel only as "S." Levin. As time passes, however, emblematic of the emergence of his multifaceted personality, he becomes known as Sy, Seymour, Lev, and finally Sam. Just as his name changes, so do his roles: A romantic idealist who believes in the importance of integrity, Levin is an alien in a society of corrupt realists and, though he fails personally as a reformer, becomes the motivating force behind changes that are initiated after he is dismissed from the faculty.

Seeking friendships among his colleagues, their families, and others, Levin either is disillusioned with nearly everyone or is unable to find a basis for substantive and enduring relationships, even with the women with whom he becomes involved. The first of these is a waitress whom he steals from a Syrian graduate student and takes to a barn, but at the crucial moment the aggrieved Arab bursts in and takes their clothes. He also fails in his second venture, with colleague Avis Fliss in his office, but on his third attempt, with a student in a motel, he succeeds, though guilt quickly overcomes him, and a conflict over a final grade forecloses any future relationship. Levin's fourth woman is Pauline Gilley; their affair begins in what he thinks is a pastoral forest, but ironically it actually is the college training site for foresters, and he gets little pleasure from the relationship. Levin, in fact, is a man whom pleasure continually eludes, for his new life—which lasts only ten months—is not much better than the one he left behind in New York, and the life upon which he embarks with Pauline and her children promises little more than responsibility. Having come almost empty-handed to Cascadia in the fall, Levin leaves town in the spring with an old Hudson full of family.

Pauline Gilley, thirty-two to his thirty, is an unhappily married woman. She and Gerald maintain a façade of a relationship for convenience and professional reasons. It even has survived Pauline's affair with Levin's predecessor, who also was dismissed. According to Gilley, Pauline "was born dissatisfied"—nearly "anything can throw her off balance"—and "has been keeping touch of her wrinkles and lamenting the passing of her youth" for years; though she has a variety of health problems, she resists going to a doctor. He concedes that life with Pauline can be pleasant ("she plays a good game of golf"), but Gilley concludes that it is "generally no bed of roses." (Levin responds: "I have never slept on flowers.") Though Gilley's characterization of her is accurate, Pauline also is in need of love, and Gilley is an indifferent husband.

"My name's Dr. Gilley" is how the director of composition introduces himself to Levin, but though Gilley is impressed with his own credentials, he is neither an academician nor a scholar. According to Pauline, "Nature here can be such an esthetic satisfaction that one slights others." Indeed, Gilley fishes, hunts, attends athletic events, and takes prizewinning photographs with a consuming intensity matched only by his pursuit of the chairmanship. He is an ambitious, opportunistic politician, and having laid the groundwork, overcomes domestic problems and easily outdistances the opposition. He reaches the goal, but under a new dean—an outsider "dug up . . . from the cornfields of Iowa," with innovative ideas—Gilley's triumph may turn out to be a Pyrrhic victory.

Among the other characters, three members of the English department stand out. Orville Fairchild, the chairman, is determined to preserve the status quo and is proud of his economical operation of the department over the years. An elderly grammarian who is a fervent believer in the "wholesome snappy drill" in workbooks, Fairchild considers Gilley his heir apparent. C. D. Fabrikant, Harvard man, gentleman farmer, bachelor, and antifeminist, is the department liberal and scholar, but in a more enlightened venue, he would not be considered much of either. Avis Fliss, who knows about everyone and everything in the department, a "unique fund of information," is the sole unmarried woman instructor (and has an unsuccessful dalliance with Levin); Gilley's unofficial assistant, she serves not only as his lackey but also as his spy.

Themes and Meanings

As its title suggests, the novel has as a primary concern Levin's search for a new focus for his life, even a new identity. Fleeing despair in the East, he heads west, to America's Eden. In this promised land Malamud's unlikely hero becomes involved in a series of quixotic adventures that turn the erstwhile idealist into an uneasy realist who learns that deception is vital to survival and becomes almost as adept at deceit as the philistines he confronts on their own turf. Though he wins some of the skirmishes, Levin realizes that redemption and salvation are to be found within, that victory over one's inadequacies and insecurities is what really matters. The forests, mountains, and even idyllic college campuses offer only the illusion of tranquillity—and only from a distance.

Seymour Levin, like his creator, is Jewish, and this fact is central to the hero. Many of Levin's characteristics place him in the tradition of the archetypal Jew in literature: He is an outsider rejected by a community to which he comes, a wanderer in search of a new home, a man to whom suffering is a way of life, a nonbelligerent who becomes the center of conflict and maybe even its cause, and a scapegoat who suffers because of the sins of others. Though obvious, his Jewishness is spoken of only near the end of the novel, when Levin learns that Gilley hired him because Pauline had picked his application out of a pile. She explains: "Your picture reminded me of a Jewish boy I knew in college who was very kind to me during a trying time in my life." To this Levin responds: "So I was chosen."

In addition to Levin, Malamud focuses upon Cascadia College, which becomes as much an antagonist as Gerald Gilley and is closely patterned after an Oregon state college where Malamud taught for many years. A *roman à clef*, the novel also is an academic satire, with Malamud's sharp criticism only occasionally tempered by light humor. Mocking people, procedures, and rituals, the satire transcends the boundaries of the Cascadia College campus to embrace much of American higher education; Levin's parochial, unenlightened colleagues, after all, are its products.

Critical Context

Published in 1961, *A New Life* was the third of Bernard Malamud's novels and was written while he was a member of the English department of Oregon State College in Corvallis. During his tenure there, from 1949 to 1961, he also wrote his first two novels, *The Natural* (1952) and *The Assistant* (1957), and published *The Magic Barrel* (1958), a collection of short stories for which he received the National Book Award in 1959.

In a 1961 article, Philip Roth concluded that Malamud had not yet "found the contemporary scene a proper backdrop for his tales of heartlessness and heartache, of suffering and regeneration." The publication of *A New Life* answered this criticism, for the novel continues Malamud's progress toward a realistic and modern fiction that begins with his second novel. In *A New Life* he consciously strives to create a real place and believable people; the mythic superstructure common to his earlier works still is present, but it is more muted; and while the themes are basically the same, they are developed in a new context, a larger social setting.

While welcomed as an indication of Malamud's growth, the book also has been criticized for attempting to accomplish too much: It is a satire of American academic life, a love story, and a picaresque novel about a seriocomic antihero. In addition, Malamud gives too much information about the functioning of a college English department, dwelling on minutiae that impede the movement of the narrative and are largely unnecessary for his satiric purposes.

In sum, *A New Life* is important as Malamud's first attempt at a wholly realistic novel, and it also is a notable example of a minor literary type, the academic novel. Further, in Seymour Levin he has created a memorable seeker of the American Dream who discovers that at least part of it is false illusion.

Sources for Further Study

Alter, Iska. *The Good Man's Dilemma: Social Criticism in the Fiction of Bernard Malamud*, 1981.

Field, Leslie A., and Joyce W. Field, eds. *Bernard Malamud: A Collection of Critical Essays*, 1975.

Richman, Sidney. *Bernard Malamud*, 1966.

Gerald H. Strauss

NICKEL MOUNTAIN
A Pastoral Novel

Author: John Gardner (1933-1982)
Type of plot: Pastoral realism
Time of plot: From December, 1954, to the summer of 1960
Locale: The farming country in the Catskills of upstate New York
First published: 1973

> *Principal characters:*
> HENRY SOAMES, the protagonist, owner of the Stop-Off, a
>   diner
> CALLIOPE (CALLIE) SOAMES (née WELLS), his wife, who is
>   twenty-five years his junior
> GEORGE LOOMIS, a farmer and inveterate collector, the closest
>   thing Henry has to a friend
> WILLARD FREUND, a young man and the father of Callie's
>   child
> SIMON BALE, a Jehovah's Witness whom Henry takes into his
>   care

The Novel

Nickel Mountain is a story of moral renovation. Gardner's mildly ironic opening sentence announces the novel's preoccupation with the spiritual life of its central figure: "In December, 1954, Henry Soames would hardly have said his life was just beginning." Indeed, when the novel begins, Henry, grossly overweight and already the victim of one heart attack, is close to a nervous breakdown. Both afraid of and attracted to the storms that whip the snow outside the Stop-Off, his diner at the foot of Nickel Mountain in rural upstate New York, Henry is obsessed by thoughts of his seemingly imminent death. Doc Cathey's warning that he must lose weight—"You lose ninety pounds, Henry Soames, or you're a goner"—is a leitmotif of his anxiety.

Yet Henry survives the winter to be drawn from his self-absorption the following spring by the arrival of sixteen-year-old Callie Wells. Largely as a favor to her parents, Henry hires Callie to help him in the diner. His feelings about the changes that her presence brings are mixed. While he regrets the loss of his solitude, he finds himself fond of her and pleased with the avuncular role this girl, twenty-five years his junior, has assigned him. Thus, when Henry finds out that Callie is pregnant by Willard Freund, a young man who quickly decides to act on his father's injunction that he go away to Cornell to study agriculture, his solicitousness is genuine. It is an equally genuine concern for Callie's welfare that motivates him when he tries to persuade his bachelor friend George Loomis to marry her. In the course of his lighthearted but adamant refusal to marry Callie (even turning down Henry's offer of fifteen-hundred dollars), George playfully leads Henry to the startling conclusion that he loves Callie himself. The shock precipitates another heart attack for Henry, and Callie moves into the diner for several weeks to take care of him. Once he has recovered his health, she returns home, and Henry finds himself suddenly more lonely than he has ever been. When Callie, worried about him, goes back to the Stop-Off late in the evening of his first night alone since his illness, Henry confesses his love to her. In the small hours of the morning, he takes her home to ask Frank Wells for permission to marry his daughter, and less than three weeks later, Henry and Callie are married.

The months that follow are filled with intense activity, as Callie's pregnancy progresses and Henry builds an addition onto the diner to accommodate his growing family. Yet Henry is secretly troubled by the possibility of the return of Willard Freund. In December, after a long and difficult labor, Callie gives birth to baby Jimmy. The event marks an emotional turning point for Henry; he realizes that the world has been changed by it ("it seemed to Henry, it was different now") and that by his being a party to the birth and accepting all of its consequent responsibilities, he has entered into a community of familial bonds which militate against any sense of personal alienation. He also discovers that he is much less disturbed by any thoughts about Willard's return.

Although his road to spiritual health is not without its obstacles—Henry suffers a serious reversal when he slips into a life-threatening anomie after the death of Simon Bale, a death for which he blames himself—it is clear by the end of the novel that Henry has made significant progress. In the last episode of the novel, Henry and four-year-old Jimmy come across a graveyard where an elderly couple is exhuming the body of their dead son. The spectacle of death no longer frightens Henry, for he now accepts it as a consequence of the natural order of things. No longer an alienated and lonely individual who despairs at thoughts of his own death, Henry implicitly invokes the ameliorative strength of familial and communal bonds when, in consoling Jimmy in his disappointment over not seeing the dead boy in the raised coffin, he tells him that he loves him.

The Characters

In *Nickel Mountain*, Gardner's skillful manipulation of point of view carries the burden of characterization. Although the novel is written in the third person, the majority of its chapters are constructed around single and identifiable centers of consciousness. Each of the characters central to the action of the novel serves as the organizing point of view for its different sections. By tempering the conventions of the pastoral (*Nickel Mountain* is subtitled "A Pastoral Novel") with the ability of the novel form to accommodate competing points of view, Gardner develops principal characters who are neither idealized nor sentimentalized.

The first of the novel's eight titled sections is narrated from Henry's perspective. Desperately lonely and preoccupied with his heart condition, Henry is a terrified man who passionately confesses his fears to whomever he corners in his diner. Far from affording him any relief, such outbursts to strangers and casual acquaintances leave him shocked and humiliated by their impropriety and violence; more often than not, after making his apologies, he finds himself sobbing, with his head on his counter. The novel's third section, "The Edge of the Woods," primarily concerned with Callie's complicated delivery, is also mediated through Henry's agitated consciousness. Through his marriage to Callie, Henry has begun the affirmative work of spiritual renovation, but the carefully controlled point of view, limiting itself to Henry's perceptions of the events going on around him, underlines how much Henry is still an alienated and frightened man. "The Grave" is the final section of the novel and the last to be narrated from Henry's point of view. Although images of death abound in these closing pages, Henry has survived his earlier feelings of alienation and despair to embrace a faith in familial and communal love. It is as a consequence of the author's controlled point of view (which allows the reader to see the world from Henry's viewpoint) that this final portrait of the hero does not collapse into maudlin sentimentality.

Callie, George Loomis, and Willard Freund are all in their turns the centers of consciousness of various sections of the novel. The section entitled "The Wedding" is narrated from Callie's point of view. Callie's situation is, to say the least, an unfortunate one. Pregnant and deserted by the father of her child, she is about to marry a grotesquely fat man who is twenty-five years her senior and whom she does not love. Yet Gardner's presentation of the events surrounding her wedding from her point of view avoids the danger of sentimentalizing Callie while it reveals the depth of her character. Rather than wallow in self-pity, Callie reflects both on her love for her family and on the love demonstrated by all those aunts, uncles, and cousins who have gathered around her on this day to help her celebrate. This capacity to love and be loved gives Callie the strength to make the best of a bad situation and to resolve about the man who is soon to be her husband: "*I don't know whether I love him or not, but I will.*"

Present at Callie's wedding is George Loomis, "the eternal bachelor smiling, joyful, quoting scraps of what he said was Latin verse." George, however, is also an emotional and physical cripple and a relentless collector of "things." His radical loneliness is most poignantly revealed in the novel's subsequent section, aptly titled "The Things," which is narrated from his point of view. The penultimate section of the novel, "The Meeting," deals with Willard Freund's return from college. Feeling superior to the community that produced him, the cynical and resentful Willard tries to divest himself of whatever emotional and spiritual claims it has on him. By restricting the narrative in this section to Willard's point of view, Gardner presents a compelling picture of Willard as an alienated and despairing young man.

Themes and Meanings

The theme of *Nickel Mountain* is salvation in a secular world. The moral and dramatic center to Gardner's treatment of this theme is Henry's discovery that, in a world in which God is either dead or indifferent, the existential solitude of the self is not sufficient to give meaning and fulfillment to life. When the novel opens, Henry seems an unlikely candidate for spiritual salvation. The years of solitude in an isolated country diner have made him hesitant to enter fully, through love, marriage, and family, into the life of the community. Yet his moral education is only beginning, and this education represents a rejection of nihilistic existentialism in favor of a life-affirming program of action. Henry, reluctantly at first but later with much alacrity, accepts his responsibility to act.

His marriage to Callie is the first step toward establishing the bonds of love and commitment that will ultimately provide the foundation of his joy in the world. The birth of his wife's child draws him further into the bonds of community. That the child is not biologically his child emphasizes the active agency of his will to participate in the world: Henry has a son not by accident but by choice. It is significant that Willard, by accident the biological father of Callie's child, owns no sense of community, only a solipsistic despair. At the end of the novel, feeling "like a man who'd been born again," Henry has become absorbed into the processual vitality of life to the extent that he does not fear death so much as he recognizes its place in the world. Life and death are both part of "the holiness of things (his father's phrase), the idea of magical change." His earlier fear of death had really been no more than a fear of further alienation. Having become a celebrant of the dynamic of birth and death, and having learned to see it through the eyes of one who is bound to it through love, Henry finds in his own mortality not a cause for despair but an inspiration for spiritual serenity.

Critical Context

First drafted when Gardner was an undergraduate, *Nickel Mountain* was not published until 1973, when it quickly appeared on the heels of his ambitious novel *The Sunlight Dialogues* (1972)—presumably to capitalize on the excitement generated by that critically acclaimed best-seller. While not Gardner's best novel, *Nickel Mountain* was easily his most popular book with the reading public. Selected by the Book-of-the-Month Club, it was pirated in Taiwan and translated into Danish, Finnish, French, Hungarian,

Spanish, and Swedish.

From the beginning of his career, Gardner flatly rejected the peculiar nihilism characteristic of literary modernism. While writers from T. S. Eliot to Samuel Beckett have decried the absence of either scientific or religious authority for human values as they constructed their wastelands of despair and alienation, Gardner has remained steadfast in his advocacy of a literature of affirmation. Yet his defense of human values trades neither in science nor in any conventional sense of religion. In *Nickel Mountain*, Gardner champions a familial and communal love, dramatized in Henry's marriage to Callie and his acceptance of another man's child as his own, as a spiritual bulwark against the terrible chaos of human existence. In the face of the preponderance of modern literature which has abandoned overtly moral concerns, Gardner's most significant achievement, both in *Nickel Mountain* and in the novels which followed, has been to offer an acutely moral fiction which is neither moralistic nor sentimental.

Sources for Further Study
Cowart, David. *Arches and Light: The Fiction of John Gardner*, 1983.
Harris, Richard C. "Ecclesiastical Wisdom and *Nickel Mountain*," in *Twentieth Century Literature*. XXVI (Winter, 1980), pp. 424-431.
Mendez-Egle, Beatrice, ed. *John Gardner: True Art, Moral Art*, 1983.
Morace, Robert A., and Kathryn VanSpanckeren, eds. *John Gardner: Critical Perspectives*, 1982.
Morris, Gregory L. *A World of Order and Light: The Fiction of John Gardner*, 1984.

Richard Butts

NIGHTWOOD

Author: Djuna Barnes (1892-1982)
Type of plot: Poetic surrealism
Time of plot: The 1920's
Locale: Berlin, Vienna, Paris, and New York City
First published: 1936

> Principal characters:
> FELIX VOLKBEIN, a "wandering Jew" with an obsession for aristocracy
> ROBIN VOTE, the wife of Felix and the central character
> DR. MATTHEW O'CONNOR, an Irish American, unlicensed physician from San Francisco and the commentator-narrator on the events of the *comédie humaine*
> NORA FLOOD, an American for whom Robin leaves Felix
> JENNY PETHERBRIDGE, a middle-aged widow of four husbands, for whom Robin leaves Nora
> GUIDO VOLKBEIN, the son of Felix and Robin
> SYLVIA, a child, supposedly Jenny's niece

The Novel

Nightwood is, in T. S. Eliot's words, a novel that is shaped by "creative imagination" which defies labels such as stream-of-consciousness, naturalism, surrealism, dream, myth, existentialist, architectonic; yet the novel is all of these. The total effect is poetic, the poetry consisting of rich imagery wherein resides the imagination of which Eliot writes.

The narrator of the novel is Dr. Matthew O'Connor, an unlicensed physician. Tiresias-like, O'Connor holds court and functions as a catalyst for the character tableaux that constitute the chapters of the novel. O'Connor is described by Eliot (in his introduction to *Nightwood*) as egotistical and swaggering, by Barnes as an Irishman from the Barbary Coast (Pacific Street, San Francisco), and by himself as Dr. Matthew-Mighty-grain-of-salt-Dante-O'Connor. He functions in the novel as Barnes's version of Henry James's "central intelligence."

The plot of the novel is simple and begins with a florid description of the birth in Berlin of Felix Volkbein to "Hedvig Volkbein—a Viennese woman of great strength and military beauty, lying upon a canopied bed of a rich spectacular crimson, the valance stamped with the bifurcated wings of the House of Hapsburg, the feather coverlet an envelope of satin on which, in massive and tarnished gold threads, stood the Volkbein arms. . . ." Having given birth to her only child at the age of forty-five, she "named him Felix, thrust him from her, and died." Felix's father, Guido Volkbein, is a wealthy

Jew of Italian descent who acquired his title fraudulently. Felix intends to perpetuate the image of nobility, even though the circles in which he travels consist of the aristocracy of the circus and the theater. The son of an Italian Jew and a Christian mother, Felix marries an American, Robin Vote, who bears him a male child, Guido, and promptly leaves both husband and son for Nora Flood, also an American; deserts Nora for Jenny Petherbridge, who has been widowed four times; and eventually returns by instinct to Nora's estate in New York. At a social function early in the novel, Felix is introduced to O'Connor, through whom he (Felix) meets Robin, and the plot is under way.

Each of the characters is richly detailed in tableaux such as that of Felix's birth. In fact, each of the first five chapters of the novel is an ornately poetic tapestry of images of one of the main characters. In the first chapter, appropriately titled "Bow Down," Felix is depicted in the context of the fraudulent nobility by whom he is obsessed. "La Somnambule" introduces Robin Vote, whose resuscitation from a fainting spell begins the romantic complications of the plot and establishes the dream-nightmare ambience of the novel. In "Nightwatch," "The Squatter," and "Watchman, What of the Night?" Nora, Jenny, and O'Connor, respectively, are the centerpieces of the tableaux painted by Barnes. As in the first two chapters, the titles apply poetically to the character portrayed.

In "Where the Tree Falls" and "Go Down, Matthew," the close interweaving of the various strands of action brings the mythical significance of the novel into sharp focus. Finally, in "The Possessed," in one consummate stroke, the author leaves the reader with the most searing image of the entire novel, Robin in her nakedly natural—and depraved—posture, the human turned animal. It is as though Robin, awakened into the dream world of life by the doctor in "La Somnambule," has returned to her original state. Between these two states, the action of the novel occurs, an action consisting largely of the effects of Robin on the lives of the other characters. The dreamlike atmosphere haunts even the most naturalistic situations and language, accustoming the reader to the shockingly unexpected and investing the characters with mythic significance.

The Characters

Nightwood is, above all, a novel of memorable characters. In a manner reminiscent of the nineteenth century novelistic style of Honoré de Balzac and Marcel Proust, Barnes's characters are introduced to one another in salons, bedrooms, or at cultural events during the American expatriate decade of the 1920's. Felix meets O'Connor at a soiree in Berlin held by the Count Onatorio Altamonte, an event to which Felix has been taken by the Duchess of Broadback, a sexless trapeze artist. Several weeks later, Felix and O'Connor meet again in Paris at the Café de la Mairie du VIe, from which O'Connor is summoned by a boy to attend a lady who has fainted in a nearby hotel; that lady, twenty-nine years old, is Robin Vote. Nora, who conducts a strange salon in America, sits next to Robin at a circus performance, and without many words, the two fall into a natural acquaintance. A similar meeting and the subsequent intimacy occur between Robin and Jenny, supposedly at an opera. The climactic night of the novel takes place in the ostentatiously cluttered salon of Jenny, "the squatter," whose acquisitiveness of money and furnishings is equaled only by her "rapacity for other people's facts." In another surrealistic scene that is parallel to the one in which Robin is revived after fainting, Nora visits O'Connor in his bedroom, to find him in female attire. In need of advice from him, Nora is regaled with a chapter-long monologue in which O'Connor relives the impression of Robin he had received on a carriage ride after the opera and the social affair at Jenny's. That impression consists of his certainty that "Nora will leave that girl [Robin] some day; but though those two are buried at opposite ends of the earth, one dog will find them both." He predicts the ending of the novel in this revelation to Nora.

No sharper contrast can be imagined than that between the salons of Berlin, Vienna, and Paris and Nora's forlorn, overgrown country estate in New York. The distance between the decayed aristocracy of Europe and the naturalness of the American countryside is the distance that the American expatriates must travel in their search for fulfillment. Innocence and experience thus constitute a major theme of the novel.

Robin Vote is the visual and mythical symbol of that innocence. When the reader first sees her in her hotel room being attended by O'Connor, she is surrounded by luxuriant plants, palms, and cut flowers, as in a painting by Henri Rousseau. Even when removed from that setting, she "carried the quality of the 'way back' as animals do." "Sometimes one meets a woman who is beast turning human." The slapping of her wrists and the dousing of her face with water by the doctor symbolize this transformation. References to the animal world abound in the descriptions of Robin's liaisons with Felix, Nora, Jenny, and the dog. As commentator, O'Connor wails "for all the little beasts in their mothers, who would have to step down and begin going decent in the one fur that would last them their time." Robin prepares for her pregnancy "with a stubborn cataleptic calm, conceiving herself pregnant before she was." Like William Faulkner's Eula Varner, she is nature's child, but unlike Eula, Robin goes sightseeing in Paris with Felix; travels in Munich, Vienna, Budapest, and back to Paris with Nora; and meets clandestinely with Jenny in Parisian trysts. Her separation first from Felix, then Nora, and finally Jenny is uncomplicated, quick, and as unquestioning as an animal's. When her husband confronts her with the statement that she does not want their son, she grins without smiling and merely says, "I'll get out." When she is seen again, it is with Nora.

If Robin cannot "bow down" to the royalty with which Felix is obsessed, neither can she stay for long with Nora, who is described as possessing an equilibrium of nature, a balance of the savage and refined. Nora is compassionate and loves everything and, therefore, is despised by everything. She lacks a sense of humor, and she lacks cynicism as well. It merely requires Robin's comment at the circus—"I don't want to be here"—to attract Nora and Robin to each other. Gradually, however, a tension in Robin grows, and she absents herself from Nora. The absences grow more frequent until Nora knows that final separation is imminent, but she cannot understand why. For this knowledge, she seeks help from O'Connor. For Robin, "it was this exact distance that kept the two ends of her life—Nora and the cafés—from forming a monster with two heads."

During those absences, Robin meets Jenny, a middle-aged widow whose four husbands had "wasted away and died." If the natural in Robin attracts the sophisticated Felix and the balanced Nora, it appeals no less to Jenny, whose consuming passion in life is acquisition. More possessive and therefore more jealous than Felix or Nora, Jenny demonstrates her passion in a carriage ride, during which Robin's attention to an English girl and a child, Sylvia, drives Jenny to striking and clawing at Robin. Shortly thereafter, Robin leaves Nora and sails with Jenny for America.

Of all the expatriates who inhabit the underworld that is Nightwood, O'Connor, an unlicensed doctor, stands outside the events, serving as the observer of the human comedy and as the commentator on the events. He stands outside even himself as he amuses others with long anecdotes about himself. In the bedroom scene in which he revives Robin, he borrows her makeup and applies it to his face. As transvestite, he is male and female, and like Tiresias of Greek myth, he has outlived his emotional and sexual nature. He inhabits that limbo between innocence and experience. In his wisdom, he sees Robin as a beast turning human and then as a human turning beast. It is to him that Nora turns for explanations when Robin leaves her. He can say only that "Robin was outside the 'human type'—a wild thing caught in a woman's skin." Robin's animal innocence never deserts her, and when she leaves a lover, she feels only peace and happiness. It is this truth that Nora, O'Connor insists, must accept. When asked how he knows so much, he responds that he is a lady "in need of no insults."

In a later scene, the unlicensed doctor meets a defrocked priest—in the same café in which he (the doctor) and Felix had dined on the night when they encountered Robin—and O'Connor is asked the same question. The question includes the priest's curiosity as to why O'Connor never married. After responding to the personal question, O'Connor answers the more philosophical one with a rhetorical question: "What do they all come to me for?" When the café crowd, entertained by the spectacle that O'Connor creates in his impassioned monologue, whispers and draws closer to the two men, the priest offers to take the doctor home, and in his final statement, screaming with sobbing laughter, O'Connor cries: "I know, it's all over, everything's over, and nobody knows it but me." He is, in fact, the poet-seer, at various times a Tiresias, a Cassandra, or a Sisyphus.

Nora finally acknowledges the truth which O'Connor, throughout the novel, has been offering to an audience that wants only to be entertained or not to have its ingrained attitudes disturbed. Her final realization occurs in an incident at her rural New York homestead. Jenny and Robin travel to New York, and the latter resumes the natural manner that characterized her liaisons with Felix and Nora. She walks in the open country, headed in the direction of Nora's home. Wearing boys' trousers, she wanders into a weather-beaten, small, white chapel where she encounters Nora's barking dog and begins to run with him on all fours, until, exhausted, they lie down side by side, nature having returned to nature.

In the meantime, Felix spends his days with his son, Guido, who was born emotionally unstable and mentally deficient. For him, Felix sees the priesthood as the only possible vocation. Guido becomes the subject of conversation between Felix and O'Connor one day, again at the same café in which earlier important conversations have taken place. The doctor informs Felix that "Guido is blessed—he is peace of mind—." Like the idiot Benjy in Faulkner's *The Sound and the Fury* (1929), Guido is eternally innocent. His is yet another version of the innocence that invests the actions of Robin throughout her life. Felix, Nora, and Jenny, attracted by that innocence, cannot understand it; O'Connor can. Contrasting with Robin's corrupted natural state remains the uncorrupted purity of her son, Guido, and of Sylvia, the child who, too, is drawn to Robin.

Themes and Meanings

On a philosophical and mythic level, Barnes vividly depicts good and evil as the journey from innocence to experience. In different ways and to different degrees, Felix, Nora, Jenny, Guido, and Sylvia symbolize the effects of this journey through the mythical country of Nightwood. Dante-like, O'Connor travels this underworld, his guide being reason, much as Vergil symbolizes reason in Dante's famous journey. O'Connor alone sees through illusions and is in a position to heal spiritually those few, Felix and Nora, who seek his wisdom.

On a sociological level, the novel depicts the rootlessness of Americans in Europe in the years before World War II. They remain rootless, although Nora returns to her rural New York home. Felix, the only European of the major characters, clings to his false aristocratic title, all the more so because he is the mythical wandering Jew. The Irish-Catholic American, O'Connor, is the only American who has consciously lived the expatriate life in full knowledge of its nature, especially its loneliness.

Critical Context

There is unanimity of critical opinion that *Nightwood* is the major work of Barnes. Yet the novel was rejected by seven American publishers prior to its 1936 English publication by Faber. Even at Faber it was turned down by a junior editor who had preceded Eliot in that capacity. The novel had its champions—mostly poets—in Edwin Muir, Emily Coleman, and Dylan Thomas. Muir's enthusiasm influenced Dag Hammarskjöld, who later co-translated Barnes's play *The Antiphon* (1958) into Swedish. The poet-editor whose stamp of approval in the form of an introduction was most influential in getting *Nightwood* published in the United States in 1937 was Eliot. He praised "the great achievement of a style, the beauty of phrasing, the brilliance of wit and characterization, and a quality of horror and doom very nearly related to that of Elizabethan tragedy." He also suggested the novel's title.

Critics have variously described the style of *Nightwood* as rococo art, as eighteenth century fiction, as *symboliste* in the tradition of Stéphane Mallarmé and James Joyce, as the surrealism of a Joan Miró or André Breton collage, and as existential. The one constant in the varied criticism is the recognition of the poetry of the novel. As social chronicle, *Nightwood* mirrors the seventeenth century image of the grinning skull. O'Connor, in particular, functions as that mirror. As modern mythology, the novel depicts the beast-human duality of Robin and her impact on others, an impact that merges the social and individual bestialities into one entity.

Early American critics, such as the American publishers who rejected the novel, responded negatively for the most part. Some of the disapproval focused on the subject matter: the social decadence, sexual perversion, and the overall amorality of elitist expatriates in a disintegrating post-World War I European society. Barnes's biographer, Andrew Field, neatly summarizes the novel's fate: "*Nightwood* ought to have been one of the artistic keystones of its time, but it wasn't."

Sources for Further Study
Barry, Alyce, ed. *Djuna Barnes: Interviews*, 1985.
Field, Andrew. *Djuna*, 1983.
Gildzen, Alex, ed. *A Festschrift for Djuna Barnes on Her Eightieth Birthday*, 1972.
Kannenstine, Louis F. *The Art of Djuna Barnes: Duality and Damnation*, 1977.
Messerli, Douglas. *Djuna Barnes: A Bibliography*, 1975.
Scott, James B. *Djuna Barnes*, 1976.

Susan Rusinko

NINETY-TWO IN THE SHADE

Author: Thomas McGuane (1939-   )
Type of plot: Comic realism
Time of plot: The late 1960's
Locale: Key West, Florida
First published: 1973

Principal characters:

THOMAS SKELTON, the protagonist, a young man who wants to become a fishing guide and owner of a boat

NICHOL DANCE, a fishing guide who vows to kill Skelton if he tries to compete with him

FARON CARTER, another fishing guide, Dance's partner

MIRANDA COLE, Skelton's girlfriend

SKELTON'S MOTHER

SKELTON'S FATHER

GOLDSBORO SKELTON, Skelton's grandfather

The Novel

Just before the halfway point of the novel, Nichol Dance vows to shoot Thomas Skelton if he attempts to compete with the two established guides of Key West, Dance himself and Faron Carter. He communicates this vow in a face-to-face confrontation, yet Skelton continues with his plan. As a result, the plot and the basis for the reader's interest are extremely simple. The two men seem headed for an ultimate, mortal confrontation, neither of them willing to compromise or be deflected from his declared purpose. The sense of violent inevitability is increased by the violence of Dance's personality—he has already killed one person and come close to killing a second—and by Skelton's strangely quiet, persevering stubbornness. This conflict is the core of the novel. In the first half, the plot is more improvised and dense than in the second half, as the conflict comes into focus—once Dance has made his vow to kill Skelton if he intrudes on his territory as fishing guide, the novel's action becomes so simple it is perhaps simplistic. It is almost as if the author has communicated to the reader: A violent confrontation will inevitably occur, read on and see how it happens. The guiding hand of the author, discreet in the first half, becomes prominent in the second. The denouement is accompanied by real suspense, yet a true sense of inevitability is lacking.

There are three main reasons for this. The mode of the novel is basically comic—or wry, caustic comic—and this prevents most of the characters from attaining three-dimensional solidity or "roundness." Skelton's character is the most fully developed, and the novel charts his development from youth to manhood; his identity comes increasingly into focus as the book proceeds. Yet both he and Dance are bathed in the same aura of nihilism and goatlike, egocentric stubbornness. Their codes are too similar; greater authorial control would be needed to distinguish them from each other (and, perhaps, from the author himself). Several pages are devoted to an attempt to establish these similarities and differences. One passage begins:

> The future cast a bright and luminous shadow over Thomas Skelton's fragmented past; for Dance, it was the past that cast the shadow. Both men were equally prey to mirages. Thomas Skelton required a sense of mortality; and, ironically, it was Nichol Dance who was giving it to him; for Skelton understood perfectly well that there was a chance, however small, that Nichol Dance would kill him. This faint shadow lay upon his life now as discreetly as the shadow of cancer lies among cells.

The author is highly intelligent, and if a sense of inevitability is lacking, it is not because of oversight. Considerable space is given to defining the psychological conflict, yet the effort is peculiarly artificial. Second, the author's presence becomes too dominant—he is seen by the reader only too visibly pulling the strings. The novel is so deliberate that there is even a preparatory confrontation before the final one when Dance and Skelton go out together with their boats into the Gulf to look for birds killed by a storm:

> Dance said, "Look here, I know it wasn't much of a joke."
> "You're right."
> "Not that it excuses what you done."
> "Yeah well."
> "And you cannot guide. I gave my word."
> "Well, I *am* going to guide."
> "You are not."

Skelton nodded that he was, as pleasant as he could. The main theme becomes overly highlighted, the author's insistence too calculated and drawn out. (A nagging doubt arises in the reader's mind: Is this a commercial pitch?) Third, the author's humor—often riotously successful—undercuts his own purposes. For example, after Dance has told Carter his intention to shoot Skelton, Carter replies:

> "Nichol! *I like him!*" Carter bustled around the freezer, then pointlessly opened it, drawing out a block of ice that imprisoned myriad silver fish. He held it to the light and looked. "Shoot!"

The "Shoot!" is a pun, a clever one. Yet at the same time, the author is making unwitting fun of the whole second half of his own book.

The Characters

Thomas McGuane has a prodigious talent for creating amusing, vivid, flat characters. This is part of his comic talent. Some of Skelton's fishing clients are masterfully sketched, for example, Mr. and Mrs. Rudleigh from Connecticut and Olie Slatt from Montana. Skelton's very kinky family is a source of much amusement and laughs. Sometimes, the humor throws all verisimilitude to the winds—and this would be fine if *Ninety-two in the Shade* were a purely comic novel. Skelton's home is the fuselage of an antique warplane; his father, who once established a whorehouse and owned a factory for blimps that flew the black flag of anarchism, voluntarily confines himself to the house and lives for months at a time in a bassinet that is covered with mosquito netting; Skelton's mother is a former prostitute; his grandfather, Goldsboro Skelton, is one of the biggest crooks in Florida and somehow charms businesses into paying him graft and protection money. They are comic characters.

Yet Thomas Skelton is engaged in finding a reasonable vocation, even if only for half of his time (he would like to read and see his girlfriend during the other half), and in finding an identity. The novel half-comically and half-seriously follows his development, his search for the truth about himself and his family. It flirts with the tradition of the *Bildungsroman*. The characters are both comic and not comic, hovering between flatness and roundness. Readers who are willing to accept conventions in literature will have no difficulty in accepting these characters, and the author treats them with real skill. The reader less willing to accept novelistic conventions, however, will not believe many of the characters, although McGuane's unique, dense style might carry him along.

Largely typical of McGuane's treatment of character is Skelton's girlfriend, Miranda. Fetching, desired by most men who encounter her, a schoolteacher who is both wholesome and sleeps around, she is a perfect creation of the 1960's, and clearly the novel could not do without her. Her name points toward her conventional origin; just as a pastoral needs a Miranda or Sylvia and a Western needs its pretty schoolmarm, this novel needs Miranda. Again, readers who readily accept conventional characters (here a convention adapted to the 1960's) will have no difficulty in accepting Miranda. Yet she hovers between an existence in solid, carnal life and as a confectioner's cream puff.

Themes and Meanings

Although the discussion of the novel's action and characters might indicate that it is second-rate, it is not. McGuane has been compared to Ernest Hemingway, William Faulkner, and Thomas Pynchon, and the main reason for the comparisons is his style, a certain richness and seriousness that it expresses. The style is totally unlike those of the three authors mentioned above: It is a combination of very creative, original metaphors and wry, satiric concision. It is this style that holds the novel together and lifts it above the domain of superficially exciting, forgettable commercial reads, and it is the style—not the characters or action—that penetrates the contours and textures of contemporary American life. Although the characters may be two-dimensional, the style is three-dimensional and closely follows real thoughts:

> Now she is in the tub with him. They struggle for purchase against the porcelain. The window here is smaller and interferes not at all with the smoky swoon of half-discovered girls in which Skelton finds himself. In his mind, he hears *Lovesick Blues* on the violin. He reaches for a grip and pulls down the shower curtain, collapses under embossed plastic unicorns. The shaft of afternoon light from the small window misses in its trajectory the tub by far; the tub is in the dark; the light ignites a place in the hallway, a giant shining a flashlight into the house. A rolled copy of the *Key West Citizen* hits the front porch and sounds like a tennis ball served, the first shot of a volley... Traffic bubbles the air. Skelton thinks that what he'd like is a True Heart to go to heaven with.

Often the style is wry, biting, somewhat nihilistic:

> By dint of sloth, nothing had set in. And Skelton had been swept along. The cue ball of absurdity had touched the billiard balls in his mind and everything burst away from the center. Now the balls were back in the rack. Everyone should know what it is to be demoralized just so everyone knows what it is to be demoralized.

The throwaway flippness, the wryness are largely justified because they reflect the attitude and thoughts of the protagonist. On the other hand, this same style carries over to other characters where it is less justified—there, one can speak of McGuane's style:

> Every night on TV: America con carne. And eternity is little more than an inkling, a dampness... Even simple pleasure! The dream of simultaneous orgasm is just a herring dying on a mirror.

Much of the novel is devoted to satirizing popular culture at large, advertising, small business, franchises, cheerleaders, and so on. *Ninety-two in the Shade* can be compared to other satires on provincial life, such as Manuel Puig's *Betrayed by Rita Hayworth* (1968) or *Heartbreak Tango* (1969). Yet McGuane is not as compassionate as Puig: His satire has a truculence reminiscent of the 1960's, a constant tinge of outrage and nonacceptance that explains his frequent ironic references to "the republic" (which means contemporary America) or to "democracy" between quotes. Is McGuane a serious critic of contemporary culture? He is certainly a critic of its superficial manifestations. Sometimes his satire has a real object. Sometimes, however, it becomes petrified in a stance of naysaying that has no real object, and any moral outrage is merely a vague blur. Here is where the philosophy of the author is nihilistic. It might reflect the temporary stage of his youthful protagonist, but at many points in the book Skelton's attitudes tend to blend with those of the author—they are not kept distinct.

At the periphery of the novel, McGuane hints at various possibilities of purity, of generosity. His characters have dreams. When a game fish puts up a good fight, Skelton prefers to let it go. His mother is generous. It is the function of the style to keep those dreams and possibilities present. Also, Skelton's choice of vocation, his stubborn desire to become a fishing guide, is a genuine, positive vision—it makes sense in terms of his talents, a past interest in biology, and a concern for fair play. The proper, probing question to ask about the novel is, What thwarts these positive impulses? Is it American commercial culture in general or a somewhat eccentric individual, a killer in the form of Nichol Dance? Neither—no connections are made between Dance and the commercial culture so consistently satirized throughout the novel. The final confrontation, being foreordained and prejudged, answers no questions whatsoever; it is swift, much too swift probably, and comes as an anticlimax. So once again one returns to the question, What is it that kills the positive impulses in the novel?

Although the question is never clearly framed by the author, and although any answer must be speculative, perhaps it is the author himself who bears responsibility. The wry, truculent tone does not entertain the possibility that these positive impulses might survive or even that they should be taken seriously. Or, perhaps, the author has calculatedly written a commercial novel—hence, this kind of question is out of place, that is, beyond the conventions and legitimate expectations of such a book. The novel is a striking but mixed performance: The style is brilliant, the action and plot violent yet conventional and somewhat superficial, the philosophy a peculiar, uneasy mixture of laughter and nihilism.

Critical Context

Ninety-two in the Shade followed closely upon the heels of *The Sporting Club* (1968) and *The Bushwhacked Piano* (1971); the three books were published within a period of four years, and interest in McGuane became widespread. Some critics thought that *The Bushwhacked Piano* was a better novel, but all three books seemed to have a similar energy, excitement, and dense style. Probably some of the critical naysayers were right about *Ninety-two in the Shade*—it was, indeed, a rather commercial performance. (McGuane himself directed a film version of the novel in 1975.) By 1984, McGuane had published his seventh book, *Something to Be Desired*, and while its commercial success was not great, it was informed by a maturity of vision not to be found in the virtuoso style of his early novels.

Sources for Further Study

Gunton, Sharon R., ed. "Thomas McGuane," in *Contemporary Literary Criticism*. XVIII (1981), pp. 322-326.

Mendelson, Phyllis Carmel, and Dedria Bryfinski, eds. "Thomas McGuane," in *Contemporary Literary Criticism*. VII (1977), pp. 212-213.

Riley, Carolyn, ed. "Thomas McGuane," in *Contemporary Literary Criticism*. III (1975), pp. 329-331.

John Carpenter

NO ONE WRITES TO THE COLONEL

Author: Gabriel García Márquez (1928-   )
Type of plot: Ironic realism
Time of plot: October to December, 1956
Locale: An unnamed village in Colombia
First published: El coronel no tiene quien le escriba, 1961 (English translation, 1968)

>   *Principal characters:*
>   THE COLONEL, a poverty-stricken retired soldier
>   HIS WIFE, an ailing and cantankerous woman
>   DON SABAS, a grasping and unscrupulous businessman
>   THE DOCTOR, a kindly physician

The Novel

The plot of this short novel is quite simple. The elderly and impoverished colonel has been waiting for fifteen years to receive a pension check for his service in the army. The cultural context of the story is during what is known as *la violencia*, a civil war between liberals and conservatives in Colombia that lasted from the late 1940's into the 1960's. Nine months previous to the opening of the story, the colonel's son, Agustín, had been killed at a cockfight for distributing secret political literature. The colonel is torn between his desire to keep his son's prizefighting cock in order to enter it into the cockfights in January and his need to sell it to provide food for himself and his wife. The story focuses primarily on the colonel's pride in trying to conceal his indigent state and his often ironic and bitterly humorous response to his situation.

The central metaphors in the story are the pension, which never arrives, but for which the colonel never ceases to hope, and the fighting cock, which also represents hope, as well as his son's, and thus the whole village's, political rebellion. In desperation, he does decide to sell the cock to the exploiter Sabas, who gives him considerably less money than he originally promised. When the villagers snatch the bird and enter it in the trial fights and the colonel sees that it lives up to its reputation as a prizefighter, he decides to give the money back and keep the bird. Even though his wife nags him to change his mind, he holds out, realizing that the animal belongs to the whole community. When his wife asks him what they will eat until the time of the cockfights, he replies with an expletive that ends the story.

Although the story is lacking in plot—mainly concerned as it is with the colonel's stoic pride, his wife's nagging, the venality of Sabas, the tense political situation of a people under martial law—the character of the colonel sustains the reader's interest. The atmosphere of the story is also arresting, for it seems summed up by the colonel's intestinal complaints—"the colonel experienced the feeling that fungus and poisonous lilies were taking root in his gut"—and his wife's remark—"We're rotting alive."

Moreover, no summary of the events of the story can adequately account for the sense of a fully contained fictional world created here—a world as completely realized as that of William Faulkner, one of García Márquez' admitted influences. It is not the plot that makes this story powerful, but rather the combination of understated realism with a sense of a folklore reality that creates a unique combination which has been called "magical realism" by some critics. Although there is little background for the simple events which make up the story, García Márquez' recognized masterpiece, *Cien años de soledad* (1967; *One Hundred Years of Solitude*, 1970), provides a complete picture of the mysterious world of superstition, fantasy, and stark reality which the colonel inhabits. Finally, what characterizes the story is the understated style of the third-person limited point of view, which filters the fictional world through the mind of the characters, and the laconic speech of the colonel, who, innocent though he may be, is wise in his stoic acceptance of an immediate reality that he cannot change and an ultimate reality that he can only encounter with wit and wry humor.

The Characters

The colonel is not only the protagonist of the novel, he *is* the novel, for it is his humor and irony, his pride and courage against the inexplicable adversity of poverty and political repression, that give the novel dignity and structure. This wise yet childlike man assumes a sort of tragicomic stature in the course of the narrative. Although he goes to wait for the mail boat every Friday with hopeful expectation, his resigned response is always the same: "No one writes to the colonel." Although he is often self-effacing, reconciled to the repressive regime which controls his life, he maintains his pride. For example, he does not wear a hat so, as he says, "I don't have to take it off to anyone."

He is both idealistic and ironic, a combination that makes him memorable in contemporary fiction. When his wife says that he is only skin and bones, he replies that he is taking care of himself so he can sell himself: "I've already been hired by a clarinet factory." When his wife laments that the mush they are eating is from corn left over from the rooster, and says, "That's life," the colonel replies, "Life is the best thing that's ever been invented." In some ways, the colonel resembles the existential hero as described by Albert Camus—holding out no hope for transcendent value but maintaining a kind of stoic acceptance of struggle regardless of the outcome. In modern fiction, his closest parallel is Ernest Hemingway's fisherman, Santiago, in *The Old Man and the Sea* (1952). Although the colonel has nothing so tangible as a great fish with which to do battle, he is no less an example of a man who sustains "grace under pressure."

The colonel's wife, who alternates between being bedridden because of her asthma and being hyperenergetic, is more realistic about their situation than the colonel is and urges him to sell the rooster. She has less pride also, having no qualms about going about the village trying to barter household items for food. Finally, she says that she is fed up with resignation and dignity, and she bitterly tells the colonel, "You should realize that you can't eat dignity." The colonel has hope, however, about which he says, "You can't eat it, but it sustains you."

Sabas is the only leader of the colonel's party who has escaped persecution; he has aligned himself with the established political order and continues to live in the town and to prosper, primarily by exploiting the hunger and want of the rest of the villagers. Other minor characters are a doctor who tends to the colonel's wife and belongs to the underground resistance movement, the town's corrupt mayor, a shiftless lawyer whom the colonel has hired to try to get his pension money, and Father Angel, a priest who exhibits no real moral leadership for the community. All of these minor figures are but supporting players for the central role of the proud, yet self-effacing colonel, who deals with all adversities, large and small, with his sharp, ironic humor.

Themes and Meanings

Although the background for the story is *la violencia*, the protracted civil war in Colombia, and although the colonel's problems stem from being a member of the losing party in that civil war, this is not a political novel except in an indirect way. Although García Márquez is a committed leftist, he is by no means a propagandist. His interest in this novel is in the heroic dignity of his protagonist and in his work's carefully controlled style—the style of the colonel himself. The atmosphere of the story is more pervasive than the social world of political repression and futile underground resistance would seem to suggest. It is a world of decadence and decay as concretely felt as the world of William Faulkner, yet it is a world of individual pride and understatement as pure as the style of Ernest Hemingway.

Although the past in the story is as distant as the sixty years previous when the colonel was a young man in the army, it is as close as the moth-eaten old umbrella which the colonel's wife won in a raffle many years earlier. The only thing that it is good for now, says the colonel, is "counting the stars," but he has only two stars to count, and to count on—the hoped-for pension check and the prizewinning rooster. The bird becomes the most immediate symbol of hope for the colonel. Although he knows that it is his only source of capital, he also knows that it has more important value than staving off hunger for a few more months. Because it belonged to his dead son and because it increasingly represents the emotional hope of the village, he holds on to it and waits for the coming cockfights.

Although this short novel is more realistic than *One Hundred Years of Solitude*, it is nevertheless distinguished by the hybrid of fable and fact, dream and gritty reality which characterizes that epoch-making work and which led to the Nobel Prize for García Márquez in 1982.

Critical Context

García Márquez has said in interviews that his characteristic storytelling style is the style of his grandmother, and that some of his best characters are patterned after his grandfather, whom he calls the most important figure in his life. Discussing literary influences, he has acknowledged his debt to Franz Kafka, William Faulkner, and Ernest Hemingway—all of whom lie behind the style of *No One Writes to the Colonel*.

Although García Márquez is a novelist, working within that genre's basically mimetic pattern, his style is that of the modern romancer; it is lyric rather that realistic, highly polished and self-conscious rather than concerned only with mere external reality. His characters exist not in an "as-if" real world, but rather in a purely fictional world of his own making—a combination of the folklore conventions of his South American heritage and the realism of the great modernist writers. The result is that reality is seen as more problematic and inexplicable than everyday experience would suggest.

That his fictions take place in a political culture that seems unstable and adrift is not so thematically important as the fact that this unorganized social world makes possible his exploration of reality as governed by inexplicable forces. Thus, his characters, deprived of the props of established social order, have only their most elemental and primal virtues to sustain them. He is a metaphysical and poetic writer, not a propagandist or a social realist.

García Márquez, primarily because of the popular and critical reception of *One Hundred Years of Solitude*, is perhaps the best-known writer in the Latin American explosion of talent that has taken place since the 1960's. Others in this modern tradition are Julio Cortázar, Carlos Fuentes, and José Donoso—all of whom have created their own version of a Kafkaesque modernist world which has fascinated general readers and critics alike. *No One Writes to the Colonel* is a minor masterpiece in this tradition, a precursor to the complexity and control of *One Hundred Years of Solitude*.

Sources for Further Study

Guibert, Rita. *Seven Voices*, 1973.
Howe, Irving, ed. *Classics of Modern Fiction*, 3d ed., 1980.
Janes, Regina. *Gabriel García Márquez: Revolutions in Wonderland*, 1981.
McMurray, George R. *Gabriel García Márquez*, 1977.

Charles E. May

NOT WITHOUT LAUGHTER

Author: Langston Hughes (1902-1967)
Type of plot: Domestic realism
Time of plot: 1912-1918
Locale: Stanton, Kansas, and Chicago
First published: 1930

> *Principal characters:*
> JAMES (SANDY) ROGERS, the novel's protagonist
> AUNT HAGER WILLIAMS, Sandy's hardworking grandmother,
>   with whom he lives
> JIMBOY ROGERS, Sandy's wandering father
> ANNJEE, Sandy's mother and Hager's dutiful daughter
> HARRIETT, Sandy's lively aunt and Hager's rebellious daughter
> TEMPY, Hager's proud middle-class daughter

The Novel

Not Without Laughter concentrates on the childhood and adolescent years of Sandy Rogers, a sensitive and highly intelligent black boy growing up in a small Kansas town. His grandmother, known to the community as Aunt Hager, is the center of his life. She washes clothes for the Reinharts, a white family, and she takes care of him while his mother works for Mrs. J. J. Rice, a snobbish upper-class white woman. Later, Hager becomes Sandy's sole guardian after his mother, Annjee, leaves to join her husband in Detroit and Harriett, the last daughter to remain at home, runs away with the carnival that visits Stanton.

Sandy's father, Jimboy, is rarely home and has trouble maintaining steady employment. Sandy adores his father's lively personality and talent and loves to hear his Aunt Harriett and Jimboy sing the blues. Sandy is a gregarious boy and enjoys the usual pursuits of adolescents, but there is a studiousness in him and a sense of responsibility that his grandmother encourages. Indeed, he is deeply influenced by his grandmother, who praises the virtues of hard work and a religious life.

Hager expects Sandy to be a great man; she hopes that he will not disappoint her, as her daughters have. Harriett has forsaken the family's Baptist beliefs, first for streetwalking and then for a career as a singer; Annjee has married a lazy man who cannot provide for his family; Tempy has become a middle-class black Episcopalian who is ashamed of her lower-class roots. While Sandy is most influenced by Hager, each one of his aunts also educates him to life's different possibilities, so that he is the only character with a vision of the whole, of the different ways in which his people have reacted to being black in a white-dominated world.

Annjee copes with her irascible white employer by simply ignoring her constant criticism. Harriett, on the other hand, resorts to anger and prefers to lead a "life of sin" than to be beholden to white employers for the meager wages they offer. Tempy has remodeled herself along the lines of her white employer and learns to behave in refined ways that whites will admire. Hager apparently acquiesces to white dominance, but she passes on to Sandy an indomitable spirit that will ensure his integrity. When a white Southerner attempts to humiliate him, Sandy turns away and hurls his shoeshine equipment at the laughing whites in the hotel where he works. His anger, however, is momentary, and he does not let it poison his efforts to learn from everyone, white and black alike.

Although life in a small Kansas town on the eve of World War I is often grim for its black inhabitants, it is "not without laughter"—as the title of the novel suggests. It is a close-knit community in which people take care of one another when they are ill and share their food and hospitality when they are well. Hughes takes obvious delight in reporting everyday conversations, for the language of his characters demonstrates great verve and tenacity no matter how constrained their circumstances may be. The blues they sing may seem mournful, but the songs are also exciting and deeply passionate, so that Sandy is imbued with a hunger for experience and for a knowledge of life.

The Characters

In addition to the principal characters, there are numerous other figures who represent Hughes's impressive command of a people and a period of time. The self-styled Madam de Carter, active in the Lodge; Brother Logan who has been courting Hager for twenty years; and ninety-three-year-old Uncle Dan, who claims to have fathered more than forty children, are only three examples of the many interesting personalities in this novel. For the most part, they reveal themselves through dialogue and through what others say about them. As a result, Hughes is able to include an astonishing amount of sociological commentary on the community without ever employing an intrusive narrator.

Hughes generally saves his characters' longer speeches for later parts of the novel when a certain amount of curiosity about them has been aroused. For example, although it is apparent that Hager's identity has been formed by her experience of slavery, her own commentary on the past does not appear until the last third of *Not Without Laughter*, when she is alone with her grandson. She gives him what some might consider to be an apology for slavery, but her main point is that to ignore the positive aspects of the hard and unjust life of the slaves is to deny the humanity of all people, white and black alike.

Hager's piety, however, cuts her off from other aspects of the world that

Sandy must explore. His friends introduce him to the pool hall—one of the few places in Stanton where young black men can exercise their wit and relax, since institutions such as the YMCA are exclusively for whites. While working in a barbershop and hotel and when visiting his aunt in the Bottoms, where jazz, prostitution, and bootlegging thrive, Sandy is introduced to an intoxicating atmosphere that is much more appealing than the repressive propriety of his Aunt Tempy's home, to which he is taken after Hager's death.

Aunt Tempy corrects his English, sees that he reads the right literature, and attempts to get him to associate with a better class of people. Her idea of an education is to strip Sandy methodically of all the cultural traits that mark him as a lower-class black. Although he avidly reads her books, he is stubborn about not giving up his disreputable friends. They have much to teach him about the basics of life, as he realizes when he regrets giving up a girlfriend, Pansetta Young, to please his aunt.

In the last part of the novel, when Sandy rejoins his mother in Chicago and enjoys a brief reunion with his Aunt Harriett, now a successful singer, it is clear that he will continue his education in an urban setting away from Tempy's small-town snobbery and will pursue an independent course in fulfilling his grandmother's dreams for him.

Sandy, more than any of the other characters, inherits the whole of his people's history. He is neither particularly rebellious nor docile; rather, he has an inquiring mind that resists any effort to restrict his access to the richness of his culture. In other words, Sandy is at the center of a debate in the novel about exactly what constitutes the black heritage. Hughes, through the impressionable Sandy, is able to dramatize a process of change in which there is plenty of room for both new and old elements.

Themes and Meanings

In *Not Without Laughter*, there is considerable discussion of the "color line" which whites use to discriminate against blacks and which blacks use to discriminate against one another. The lighter the skin, the more opportunity there is for a black to "pass" as white. Buster, one of Sandy's friends, plans to take advantage of his fair features in exactly this way. Similarly, some blacks prefer "high yallers"—black women with fair skin.

Because of the novel's rich reporting of black speech, of the way blacks sing and dance and embroider their stories, it is clear that Hughes is exploring the extraordinary impact of a whole culture on the acute imagination of a young black man. Hager suggests that, like Booker T. Washington, Sandy will be representative of his race. Tempy, on the other hand, favors the example of W. E. B. Du Bois because of his more militant and more intellectual conception of progress. Whereas Washington emphasized the equipping of blacks for learning a trade, Du Bois worked for the education of his people on the highest levels. Sandy, whose youthful experience includes both menial labor and intense book learning, is clearly meant to be a synthesis of these two types of leaders.

While he does not minimize the damage and the hurt done by slavery and its aftermath, Hughes chooses in this novel to emphasize the creativity of black people. Black children in *Not Without Laughter* experience an acute sense of rejection, hatred, and despair when they are turned away from a carnival that is for whites only. Minutes later, however, those same children demonstrate their resilience, delighting in a mocking mimicry of the white man who has spoiled their fun. Similarly, the numerous blues lyrics which enrich this novel (and which run throughout Hughes's poetry) suggest the way his people have transcended their defeats through art.

The art, however, is not fantastic but highly realistic and composed of the commonest elements. "Ever'thing there is but lovin' leaves a rust on yo' soul," Hager tells Sandy. This is a truth that has obviously been lived, a conviction that has been earned, and it is characteristic of the aging Hager to give her grandson the pith of her life.

Not Without Laughter contains several characters who moralize about the meaning of life, but the author reserves his own judgment and tries to understand people as they understand themselves. The tone of the novel is objective throughout, and the blues lyrics tend to authorize the narrator's specific judgments. A book of great balance, *Not Without Laughter* does poetic justice to all sides of the life that it describes. Colloquial language is contrasted with formal English, just as the knowledge of the street is set against the wisdom of books.

The "raucous-throated blues-singer" is the voice of experience itself that informs every page of this novel. The lyrics enjoin the listener to a community of feeling that is the essence of the blues itself. Although the older generation, like Aunt Hager, has condemned this secular music, its roots are in the religious sense of revival that has motivated so much of black art. Coming home from hearing Harriett, who is now a "Princess of the Blues," Sandy and his mother are thrilled to hear the "deep volume of sound" coming from a "little Southern church in a side street," where "some old black worshippers" are singing *"An' we'll understand it better by an' by!"* The links between past and present, between the blues and spirituals are solid, Hughes implies, as solid as Southern blacks filling the whole Chicago night with the sounds of their voices.

Critical Context

Not Without Laughter appeared in 1930 at the height of what was called the Harlem Renaissance, a tremendous outpouring of black talent in the arts. Langston Hughes was the premier poet of this cultural movement, and throughout his long career he continued to reflect on and extend its themes.

Of central concern was the whole question of black identity, and of how contemporary blacks should deal with the legacy of discrimination.

As Arna Bontemps, a black literary contemporary of Hughes, recalled in the Collier Books reprint of *Not Without Laughter*, the novel was eagerly awaited as an example of a new, aggressive definition of blackness. Hughes is quoted by Bontemps as saying that the new artists wrote to please themselves, to express an inner freedom that could not be affected by the criticisms of whites or blacks. "The poets had become bellweathers," Bontemps remarks, and Hughes was the "happy prince" of a cultural movement.

Hughes had to be read because he was leading the way for other artists and followers of the Harlem Renaissance. His exuberance, especially evident in poetry that captures black colloquial speech, invigorated his readers by highlighting contemporary materials that had become suitable for art. *Not Without Laughter*, his only novel in a distinguished career as a poet, is complemented by several popular collections of short stories; in addition, Hughes edited some widely used anthologies. A scrupulous scholar and artist, Hughes remains one of the most significant figures in the development of Afro-American culture.

Sources for Further Study
Berry, Faith. *Langston Hughes: Before and Beyond Harlem*, 1983.

Bone, Robert A. *The Negro Novel in America*, 1958, 1965.

Bruck, Peter, and Wolfgang Karrer, eds. *The Afro-American Novel Since 1960: A Collection of Critical Essays*, 1982.

Emanuel, James A. *Langston Hughes*, 1967.

Miller, R. Baxter. *Langston Hughes and Gwendolyn Brooks: A Reference Guide*, 1978.

Carl E. Rollyson, Jr.

THE OBSCENE BIRD OF NIGHT

Author: José Donoso (1924-   )
Type of plot: Psychological symbolism
Time of plot: One year in the 1960's, with major flashbacks to the eighteenth
century and the periods during and after World War I
Locale: Chile
First published: El obsceno pájaro de la noche, 1970 (English translation, 1973)

> *Principal characters:*
> HUMBERTO PEÑALOZA, the narrator-protagonist, an aspiring
> author and a schizophrenic
> DON JERÓNIMO AZCOITÍA, Humberto's employer, a wealthy
> and influential politician
> DOÑA INÉS DE AZCOITÍA, Don Jerónimo's wife
> PETA PONCE, the crafty family servant
> BOY, the deformed son of Doña Inés and either Don
> Jerónimo or Humberto

The Novel

This work presents the tangled story of Humberto Peñaloza, the schizophrenic narrator-protagonist and his strange relationship with the Azcoitía
family, for whom he has worked during most of his adult life and in whose
shelter for the aged he is living at the beginning of the novel. Because of the
extremely unstable psychological state of the narrator, the events of the
story are related out of sequence, from various perspectives (reflecting the
narrator's various personalities), and with no regard to what is real as opposed to what is merely the narrator's illusion. The novel, therefore, resists
any ordered, detailed plot summation. Through reconstruction and careful
selection, however, a brief sketch of some of the major events of the story
can be offered.

Urged by his socially conscious father to "be someone," Humberto fuses
his identity with that of Don Jerónimo Azcoitía, an influential politician for
whom Humberto becomes a secretary as well as family historian. Sometime
later, after Don Jerónimo has not been able to provide his wife, Doña Inés,
with a child, the mysterious family servant, Peta Ponce, whose very appearance unsettles the already psychologically unbalanced protagonist, arranges
a nocturnal encounter attended by herself, Humberto, Doña Inés, and Don
Jerónimo. In a scene shrouded in ambiguity, Doña Inés is impregnated by
either her husband or Humberto, the real answer to this question being
known only to the crafty servant woman. Boy, the child conceived during
this bizarre meeting, is born deformed. Don Jerónimo sends the child to an
estate called La Rinconada, where he surrounds the boy with other human

monsters to shield him from the world of normal human forms. Humberto
is placed in charge of La Rinconada, where he spends much of his time
working on the Azcoitía family history. After several years on the estate,
Humberto is forced to give up his position, when, in part because of the
psychological pressures of living in a world of the deformed, he develops a
bleeding ulcer. He has surgery but is convinced that the one-eyed physician
who performed the operation has removed eighty percent of his organs to
use them for transplants.

More disturbed than ever, Humberto, now in the identity of the emas-
culated Mudito, is sent to live in the Casa, a former convent-prison owned
by the Azcoitía family and used as a home for the retired female servants of
rich families. While Doña Inés works to have the building beatified (legend
has it that the Casa was the site of a miracle in the eighteenth century),
Mudito witnesses and participates in the strange activities of the inhabitants
of the home. Humberto's (as Mudito) narration of these activities occupies
a significant portion of the novel and represents what may be considered the
"base" narrative in the work.

Later, the rapidly aging Doña Inés becomes an inmate of the Casa
herself, having just returned from Europe, where she received the transplanted organs of Peta Ponce, whom, much to the displeasure of Mudito,
she begins to resemble more and more every day. Though she had planned
to dedicate the remainder of her life to prayer, she goes about winning the
belongings of the other inmates in a bizarre dog-racing game. One of her
victims is Iris Mateluna, a prostitute whom the old women ironically suspect
of being the expectant virgin mother of a holy child. Mudito eventually assumes the identity of Iris' baby. When Doña Inés wins possession of him in
one of the games, he attempts to attack her sexually, an act that precipitates
her entry into an insane asylum. This last turn of events pleases Mudito,
who is glad to be rid of the shadow of Peta Ponce once and for all.

Mudito, now viewed by the old women as the holy child who will guarantee them a place in Heaven, is wrapped in a cocoon. When the Casa is
scheduled for demolition, the women are taken away in buses, but Mudito,
now a sexless, impotent, and timeless bundle, is left behind. Though he
occasionally manages to open a small hole in the layers of material that surround him, each time he does this the opening is immediately sewn up by a
mysterious, gnarled hand. He remains in this state of limbo "for centuries"
until an unidentified old woman takes the bundle down to the riverbank and
empties its contents onto a dying fire. Moments later, all that remains of
Mudito is "the black smudge the fire left on the stones."

The Characters

Because he is the narrator, it is Humberto's character that is best portrayed in the novel. Through his fantasies and surrealistic hallucinations, the

reader comes to see from close range the twisted mind of the protagonist. In fact, his personality literally disintegrates before the reader's eyes. The journey into the narrator's inner reality is marked by numerous shifts of personality, as he appears not only in the identities previously mentioned, but also as one of the old female inmates, a large papier-mâché head, a bird, and a phallus. Gradually, the reader comes to realize that several events described by the narrator occur only in his deeply disturbed mind (thus his ability to narrate his own end). It is by no means an exaggeration to say that Humberto and his various other selves represent one of the most bizarre characters to be found anywhere in literature.

Particularly interesting because of his relationship with Humberto is Don Jerónimo, who represents everything that Humberto is not. Though their relationship is largely antagonistic, they profit in many ways from each other's existence: All that is powerful in Humberto's kaleidoscopic personality derives from the fusion of his identity with Don Jerónimo's, while much of Don Jerónimo's power, particularly sexual, comes through his relationship with Humberto.

Somewhat similar in relationship to each other are Doña Inés and Peta Ponce. On the one hand, like Humberto and Don Jerónimo, these two characters are opposites, Doña Inés being almost saintly, Peta Ponce apparently possessing demonic powers. At the same time, as with their male counterparts, there is a tie that binds the two together. In fact, their relationship is deeply rooted and even borders on friendship. Symbolic of their closeness, of their complementary relationship, is the fusion of their bodies when Doña Inés takes Peta Ponce's transplanted organs and begins to resemble her.

It is important to note that all characters, both principal and secondary (including the women of the Casa), are seen through the eyes of Humberto or one of his other selves. Thus, the reader can never be certain that a character presented is in reality anything at all like he is portrayed by the highly unreliable narrator. Even when characters are presented within the context of the family history, it must be remembered that the history has been authored by Humberto, who has been both mentally disturbed and intimately involved with the Azcoitía family at the time of the writing. Indeed, because of the apparent narrative disorder none of the characters is presented in a traditional manner, with a logical and gradual development; it is therefore easy to see that the reader is left with anything but a stable view of the characters of the story.

Themes and Meanings

There is more than one possible theme to be found in Donoso's novel. The most superficial of these is that concerning the relationship between the employer and the employee in Latin America's surviving feudal system. The work shows well, though in unconventional terms, the exploitation, the victimization, of those in the employ of the upper class.

In attempting to discern a more profound theme, however, it is important to consider the complex and unusual nature of the novel's story. Because of the narrator's mental state, the narration is not governed by conventional logic based in objective reality, but by an irrational mind functioning in a world of illusion, a world in which reason and logic are nonexistent, as the reader is presented with the narrative meanderings and psychotic hallucinations of Humberto. The narrator's perception of reality, his subconscious concept of time (characterized in large measure by free association), and his multiple personalities and identities (which may lead the reader to believe that there are multiple narrators) destroy any semblance of a traditional narrative.

It is possible that Donoso's intent is simply to convey a close-range, realistic account of the psychological state of his unbalanced narrator, in an attempt to demonstrate the fragmented nature of the human psyche, particularly that of the schizophrenic. If such is the case, it is clear that he achieves his goal. On a larger scale, however, it is more probable that both the disjointed presentation of Humberto's story and the story itself represent the disintegration of convention, personal security, and individual identity in modern life. In this way, the story and the manner of its telling are symbolic of the anarchical modern world in which conventional order, logic, and objective reality are being replaced by a collective chaos in which individual man is pushed perilously close to infinite nothingness.

For all its apparent chaos, the novel is a skillfully assembled narrative, possessing a defined structure (in three parts) not readily apparent to the first-time reader and a masterfully developed code of symbols (which not only reveals the conscious planning put into the narrative by the author but also allows the work to be classified as psychological symbolism). As impressive as the novel's subtle structure and its symbolic content is Donoso's use of intentional ambiguity, which both reflects the uncertain nature of Humberto's inner world and discourages any attempt at a definitive interpretation of the meaning of the work and its plot, as events remain forever shrouded in mystery.

Critical Context

The Obscene Bird of Night is a prime example of the Latin American New Novel. In the tradition of this particular narrative form, it presents a highly complex narrative characterized by an unconventional use of narrative voice, a nonchronological rendering of time, and indirect and incomplete character development. Also in keeping with the characteristics of the New Novel, it is a work in which the reader must actively participate in order to discern even the most basic elements of the story, a work that demands multiple readings, and a work that, rightly or wrongly, frequently inspires more discussion concerning the presentation of its story than of the story itself.

Within the context of Donoso's literary canon, this novel is his masterpiece. This is not to say that his other works, such as *Coronación* (1957; *Coronation*, 1965) and *El lugar sin límites* (1966; *Hell Has No Limits*, 1972), are not fine pieces in their own right. It is *The Obscene Bird of Night*, however, that represents the high point of Donoso's career as a writer, a work that would have earned for the author lasting fame had he written no others.

Sources for Further Study

McMurray, George. "*The Obscene Bird of Night*: A Tribute to Consciousness," in *José Donoso*, 1979.
Stabb, Martin S. "The Erotic Mask: Notes on Donoso and the New Novel," in *Symposium*. XXX, no. 3 (Summer, 1976), pp. 170-179.

Keith H. Brower

OCTOBER LIGHT

Author: John Gardner (1933-1982)
Type of plot: Domestic realism
Time of plot: One week in October in the early 1970's
Locale: A farm outside Bennington, Vermont
First published: 1976

> *Principal characters:*
> JAMES L. PAGE, a farmer and widower in his early seventies
> SALLY PAGE ABBOTT, his older sister, a widow living on
>   James's farm
> VIRGINIA (GINNY) PAGE HICKS, James's one surviving child,
>   who is in her forties
> LEWIS HICKS, Ginny's husband, a carpenter

The Novel

An early section in Gardner's novel describes the annual cycle of backbreaking labor for rural Vermonters. The passage concludes, "Now, in October, the farmwork was slackening, the drudgery had paid off. . . ." This is, however, an ironic observation: For seventy-two-year-old James Page and his eighty-year-old sister, Sally Page Abbott, the "harvest years" have brought no payoff. James, though honest, hardworking, and fiercely patriotic, can barely wrest a living from the family farm—where he has lost one son to a fall from the barn roof and another to suicide by hanging, and where cancer has claimed his wife. Sally, the widow of a prosperous dentist, may enjoy happier memories, but she is no better off than James. Her insurance money depleted, she has been forced to give up her town home and accept her brother's grudging hospitality.

Between two persons who feel so cheated by life, and who harbor such strong and conflicting opinions (Sally is a "progressive" compared with James), life is at best an uneasy truce which is easily broken. One night, a blast from James's shotgun destroys Sally's television, with its "endless simpering advertising." Soon after, furious because she defends "corrupt" government programs, James chases Sally upstairs with a fireplace log and locks her in her room "like a prisoner."

So begins a domestic cold war that eventually involves the entire community. James's daughter, Ginny, remonstrates with him, and for a time he is ready to relent, but it is too late; Sally has bolted her door from within and gone "on strike," as determined as one of the Green Mountain Boys whom her brother so admires or one of the radical feminists he loathes. James repents of his momentary softening, and, thinking to starve Sally into submission, he relocks her door; unknown to him, she is subsisting on apples found in the attic above her room. She finds mental sustenance, too—in a "trashy" paperback novel that she reads when she is not reminiscing.

Even while she apologizes to her dead husband's spirit for reading such a book, Sally draws from it moral support for her own "cause." This tale, *The Smugglers of Lost Souls' Rock*, is a quasi-metaphysical satire full of over-educated marijuana smugglers. Its machine-gun-toting characters philosophize endlessly on social issues and protest against a mechanistic universe. To the liberal-minded Sally, the rivalry between smuggling gangs—one black, one white—resolves into a struggle for racial justice. When the white doperunners appear to have killed the blacks (to escape being machine-gunned themselves), she fumes that it is "wrong for books to make fun of the oppressed, or to show them being beaten without a struggle. . . ."

Sally soon comes to identify the "oppressors" in the novel with James, and James with all oppressors: "It's no use making peace with tyranny. If the enemy won't compromise, he gives you no choice; you simply have to take your stand, let come what may. . . . Let *James* be reasonable. . . . It's always up to the one in power to be reasonable." She likens James's actions to the military and diplomatic blunders of the United States during and after the Vietnam War. Yet, muddled, melodramatic, and exaggerated as her pronouncements may be, Sally is nevertheless fighting for her right to make her own choices in life and to express her own beliefs, despite her brother's categorical rejection of them. As "revolutionary" as James is patriotic, Sally is prepared to kill or be killed for that which she considers her inalienable rights.

Meanwhile, James, buoyed by remembered legends of the patriot Ethan Allen, is busy escalating his side of the dispute. To him, the issue is the death of decency and the increase in the "sickness and filth" embodied, among other places, in Sally's television: ". . . murderers and rapists, drug addicts, long-hairs, hosses and policemen . . . half-naked women . . . sober conversations about the failure of America and religion and the family, as if there want no question about the jig bein up. . . ." He is determined to punish Sally for bringing this "filth" into his house via her television, determined to make her see the error of her ways. To make sure that she cannot sneak down to the kitchen for food at night, he rigs up a shotgun outside her room, to be triggered by strings if she opens her door.

Horrified when they learn of this, several friends rush to the farm to talk the two into ending their feud. Offended by what he considers their meddling, James stalks out, gets drunk in town, crashes his truck, storms back into his house, and blasts his kitchen walls with the shotgun. In the melee, a dear friend of the family suffers a near-fatal heart attack, and the now-sober James is filled with remorse. Meanwhile, Ginny accidentally walks into a trap that Sally, desperately frightened by the shotgun incident, has laid for James—an apple crate set to fall on his head if he enters her room. Ginny and the cardiac patient are rushed to a hospital in town, and the feud ends with Sally emerging from her room, believing that she has triumphed.

The Characters

Most of the characters in *October Light* are made to stand for clear-cut, uncompromising political or philosophical positions—positions which they feel driven to expound even when their lives are in danger. Between them, for example, the two main characters exhibit all the conflicting aspects of New England Puritan virtue: Sally, the relentless optimist with a strong drive for progress; James, the relentlessly plodding worker with a seeming incapacity to express any deep emotion other than anger or suspicion of "liberals." Gardner's characterizations thus bring to life the "polarization" that was much discussed in the late 1960's and early 1970's, though his narrative suggests that this polarization has deep historical roots. The fact that the two antagonists also are brother and sister underscores this tragedy of irreconcilables.

Some characters are aware of contradictions within themselves but are not able to reconcile them. One such figure is Lewis Hicks, Ginny's husband, who emerges as an improbable hero:

> Right and wrong were as elusive as odors in an old abandoned barn. Lewis knew no certainties. . . . He had no patience with people's complexities . . . not because people were foolish, in Lewis Hicks' opinion, or because they got through life on gross and bigoted oversimplifications, though they did, he knew, but because . . . he could too easily see all sides and, more often than not, no hint of a solution.

It is ironic that Lewis can see all sides of a question and still feel intolerant of other people's complexities.

Paradoxically, it is the minor characters—memorable far beyond their importance in the story—who are most fully rounded through their own conscious effort. The librarian Ruth Thomas literally embodies contradiction: Weighing three hundred pounds, she is the soul of gracefulness. Her voice is at once clear ringing and seductive, "like an unsubmergeably strong piano with the soft pedal pressed to the carpet." Gardner suggests that the comic sense is a key to controlling oneself and reconciling inner contradictions: The impish Ruth has "learned to limit herself for hours at a time to nothing more outlandish than a clever, perhaps slightly overstated mimicry of primness."

Even when Gardner's major characters insist on acting like "flat" characters, he has a genius for showing them as fully rounded people with deep integrity and with rich inner lives. This is accomplished partly through interior monologue, partly through the portrayal of one character's awakening sympathy for another. Sally is able to imagine Richard (James's son who committed suicide) "inside his life." Seeing her father, Ginny can sense "from inside him what it was like to be old, uncomfortable, cheated, ground down by life and sick to death of it. . . . 'Dad, I'm sorry,' she said."

Although this novel amply portrays the tragedy of polarization, there are repeated strong suggestions that it is the sum of individual extremes that leads to balance in the world. After all, if Sally and James together embody the contradictions of the New England character, then both are required to present the gamut of its virtues. If one looks closely at the individual character, one observes flaws and imperfections. Stepping back, however, one observes a harmonious "symphony" of characters.

Perhaps it is this implied notion of balance in the whole, rather than in its parts, that accounts for the seemingly flawed characterization of Sally. As a party to the central conflict of the story, she is the most fully realized of the female characters, and yet, unlike any other character, she fails to outgrow her limitations. She learns little from the desperate conflict with her brother; indeed, despite her "humanitarian" pretensions, she never develops true compassion for him. She simply comes out of the room thinking she has won a moral victory. Yet, smug as she remains, she has proved an effective catalyst for James's growth, which gives the novel a satisfying denouement.

Themes and Meanings

Gardner's novels, especially *October Light*, evince a strong connection between themes and meanings on the one hand and characterizations on the other. The motif of locks and locking provides an example. The novel takes place in October, when "the sudden contradiction of daylight" provides "the first deep-down convincing proof that locking time, and after that winter and deep snow and cold, were coming." Though still vigorous, the aged Sally and James realize that, like the year's end, their own end approaches; meanwhile, they are locked in a fierce, potentially lethal conflict. Sally locks her door against James and the rest of the world. Later, through that door, she has an awkward discussion with a visiting Hispanic priest and realizes ironically, "How difficult it was to have a serious conversation through a locked door. There was a lesson in that!"

On other levels, Gardner shows how characters lock their hearts against one another, often without realizing it. Perhaps unfairly, the priest, Father Hernandez, forces Sally the Yankee Protestant to think of herself for a moment as "one of the colorful minorities." The unfairness, however, is mutual; Sally is puzzled by what she sees as Hernandez' attack on her, since "He was a priest. . . . They were supposed to be gentle and understanding."

Gardner seems to be saying, too, that the locking of hearts and the sudden contraction of mental light (one is reminded of Matthew Arnold's line, "where ignorant armies clash by night") are phases in an inevitable cycle of human life, just as they are in nature. In this story and in the subnovel (which forms a sort of counterpoint to the main story), the mechanistic view of the universe has its exponents—willing and unwilling. For example, the subnovel's hero, Peter Wagner, expresses pity for the "futile, idealistic rejection of the body's cold mechanisms."

Are people, then, responsible for their death-dealing prejudices? Metaphysically, the question is never really resolved in this novel, although individual responsibilities are sorted out by the end. James, when he could admit it, has felt responsible for his son Richard's suicide, but he finally unlocks the mystery of that suicide when he learns that Richard felt responsible for scaring Sally's husband into a fatal heart attack. Ginny's son Dickie feels responsible for Sally's having found the "trashy book" she reads in her room. It emerges that it was James who left the book lying around.

The larger question is: Is one personally responsible for the attitudes, the locking or unlocking of one's heart, that can make the difference between harmony and strife? Rather than answer this question, Gardner simply shows James unlocking his heart, while his friend Ed Thomas, the dying cardiac patient, movingly evokes another phase of nature's cycle—the "unlocking time," that is, the March thaw in New England. The novel does suggest a partial answer simply through the near-juxtaposition of two equally valid but mutually exclusive propositions—a typical Gardner technique. Father Hernandez says, "Stubborn? All human beings are stubborn. It's the reasons we're survivors." On the very next page, Sally remembers her dead husband, Horace, saying: "However much we may hope, we know perfectly well all we have is each other. Pity how we fight and struggle against our own best interests." One statement's validity does not cancel the other's; rather the two shed mutual light.

Critical Context

During a short career—which was ended by a motorcycle accident when he was forty-nine—John Gardner distinguished himself in a wide range of pursuits. While working in many literary genres, including fiction, poetry, children's tales, and even operatic librettos, he remained a university professor of medievel literature and creative writing. Gardner's imaginative use of scholarly learning is typified by the first of his novels to achieve marked critical and popular success: *Grendel* (1971), a retelling of the Beowulf legend from the monster's point of view. Both *Time* and *Newsweek* named *Grendel* one of 1971's best fiction books.

Other triumphs followed, culminating in *October Light*, which won the National Book Critics' Circle award for fiction in 1977. Like *Grendel* and other works by Gardner, *October Light* is full of erudite allusions, prompting a few critics to attack it as excessively theme-ridden. Most critics, however, regard it as his finest novel, an ambitious but lively treatment of ultimately insoluble mysteries, and the most successful of Gardner's attempts to bring past learning to bear on present dilemmas.

After *October Light*, Gardner's reputation declined somewhat, perhaps in part because of his attacks on most contemporary writers for failing to affirm life and inspire readers. His *On Moral Fiction* (1978), a work of critical theory containing these charges, was highly controversial. Some critics said that Gardner's last works of fiction—*The Art of Living and Other Stories* (1981) and *Mickelsson's Ghosts* (1982)—fell short of the standard he himself set in *On Moral Fiction*. Even after his death, Gardner and his work remain controversial, but no one disputes that he was one of America's most important contemporary authors, or that *October Light* is his masterpiece in fiction.

Sources for Further Study
Cowart, David. *Arches and Light: The Fiction of John Gardner*, 1983.
Henderson, Jeff, and Robert E. Lowrey, eds. *Thor's Hammer: Essays on John Gardner*, 1985.
Morace, Robert A., and Kathryn VanSpanckeren, eds. *John Gardner: Critical Perspectives*, 1982.
Morris, Gregory L. *A World of Order and Light: The Fiction of John Gardner*, 1984.

                                                                                           Thomas Rankin

THE OCTOPUS

Author: Frank Norris (1870-1902)
Type of plot: American naturalism
Time of plot: The late nineteenth century
Locale: The ranches of the San Joaquin Valley, California, and the prosperous offices and homes of San Francisco
First published: 1901

> *Principal characters:*
> MAGNUS DERRICK (THE GOVERNOR), the protagonist, owner of Los Muertos Ranch
> ANNIE DERRICK, his wife
> LYMAN DERRICK, his elder son, a successful San Francisco attorney
> HARRAN DERRICK, his younger son, manager of Los Muertos
> PRESLEY, the author's persona, a protégé of Magnus Derrick
> ANNIXTER, the owner of the Quien Sabe Ranch
> HILMA TREE, a dairy girl on the Quien Sabe, later Annixter's wife
> S. BEHRMAN, a representative of the Pacific and Southwestern Railroad
> VANAMEE, a sheepherder and range rider
> DYKE, a blacklisted railroad engineer, later a hops farmer
> HOOVEN, a tenant of Derrick
> OSTERMAN, a rancher

The Novel

At its most basic level, *The Octopus* describes the ranchers' numerous difficulties with the Pacific and Southwestern Railroad. The railroad trust sets exorbitant tariffs on San Joaquin wheat, owns large sections of the ranches as leased right-of-way, and controls the railroad commissioners, who approve the rates set as well as the courts to which the ranchers appeal. Still, the novel is not simply a muckraking indictment of big business. The "tentacles" of the "P. and S.W.R.R." force those who would otherwise be model citizens to adopt similar sordid ethics, as they believe, in order to survive.

Magnus Derrick, frustrated by his court battles to lower railroad wheat rates and the railroad's high purchase fee for optioned ranchland, involves himself in a bribery conspiracy to fix appointment of the railroad commissioners. Eventually this causes him to lose what he has valued most, his blameless reputation. It also costs him his sons: Lyman, who sells himself to the railroad in the hope of gaining its support for his campaign for governor, and Harran, who dies in a gunfight when the railroad attempts to take over the leased portion of Los Muertos.

Those who die in the gunfight form a cross section of the community. They include Annixter, a wheat rancher saved from selfishness by his recent marriage to Hilma Tree; Hooven, a German immigrant who considers that he is fighting for his new fatherland; and Osterman, the rancher who proposed the scheme to name sympathetic railroad commissioners but who shows bravery at his death. Though good people are inevitably touched by evil, at times even adopt questionable ethics for what they think will mean self-preservation, Norris believes that Truth reappears as surely as the "untouched, unassailable, undefiled" Wheat. This larger view permits hope, an optimism that allows life to go on.

The Characters

Presley, the Norris persona of the novel, usually interprets its major events. His place as trusted protégé of Magnus Derrick as well as his poet's sensitivity allow him to be a reliable witness; even so, because he has no financial interest he is never in a position to offer his own opinions or to influence what he sees. In effect, he assumes a role akin to that of the chorus of a classical tragedy. Since he is a writer, he would like to use his art to better the lives of the ranchers, but he comes to realize that the finer his creation is artistically, the less likely it is that it can become a tool for social change. Presley grows, as did Norris, to believe that no individual is in a position to know the reasons for the world's wretchedness. This allows him to put to one side his sense of guilt and impotence for failing to help the ranchers and resume his own life in the face of their tragedy.

Magnus Derrick is the novel's most carefully drawn character. He plays for big stakes and is willing to risk everything for a single substantial gain. Even so, he possesses the "old morality" and rejected a career in politics, having seen the sacrifice of principle it would have entailed. His is the spirit which built California, that of the "forty-niners," and it is only with great qualms of conscience and against the wishes of his incorruptible but timid wife, Annie, that he accepts dishonest means to fight the railroad. Norris implies that Magnus would have lost his land through the high railroad tariffs even if he had not resorted to bribery or illegal force, but the loss of his reputation because of his dishonesty makes his fall absolute and irreversible.

Lyman and Harran, Magnus' sons, provide important contrasts, both between themselves and against the standards of their father. Lyman, for example, hypocritically agrees to serve the ranchers' interest in lowering the San Joaquin railroad rates, yet his eye remains on the governorship, and he is ultimately a creature of the railroad. Harran, on the other hand, remains true to what he perceives as his father's interests, but he is a man of the "new morality" and impulsively joins the bribery conspiracy even before his father lends his own support.

Annixter, whose selfishness and arbitrary behavior at first repel the reader, ultimately arouses sympathy. He undergoes a character transformation after his marriage to Hilma and feels responsibility toward those less fortunate. The barn dance given only to prove that he can entertain more lavishly than anyone else in the valley contrasts with his kindness to the Dyke family, twice ruined by the railroad. Though Annixter too becomes tangled in the railroad's grasping "tentacles" and ultimately pays with his life, his salvation is clear.

Vanamee belongs in a special category. His is a free spirit by the world's standards; his irresponsibility causes the loss of the sheep he tends when they stray over the tracks and are slaughtered by an oncoming train. Vanamee is obsessed by the death of his fiancée, Angèle Varian, and haunts Father Sarria's garden to call her back to life with his mystic powers. Vanamee's presence in the novel emphasizes the resurrection theme which so often appears, for he discovers that Angèle's grown child is the image of her dead mother. The reader never learns who raped Angèle, but the irony, often repeated in various contexts, is that here again good came indirectly through an evil act.

S. Behrman (whose first name never appears except as an initial) would seem the unredeemable villain of the piece. He appears genuinely to enjoy implementing the harsh policies of the railroad. To the very end he appears the victor. He buys the lost options on Los Muertos and harvests its crop; he seems invulnerable to any attempt to harm him; he even survives the gunfight and Presley's ineffectual attempt to assassinate him. Still, his own greed does him in, and unknown to all he dies buried by his own cargo of wheat in the very ship which will bring Presley to his new life.

Themes and Meanings

Early in the novel Presley, contemplating the grand scale and ruggedness of the California wheatland, wishes that he could write a Homeric epic which would accurately portray the place and its people. That was also Norris' wish, to write a grand invocation to what he had originally planned as a "wheat trilogy." Its scope was to be epic, its feuds like the battle contests of the *Iliad*.

The characters of Norris' novel do indeed live boldly, their struggles and their pleasures like those of the Greeks at Troy. Their struggle, like the Trojan War, goes on for a decade without resolution. Their antagonist is the cyclopean train, whose headlight "eye" and breakneck speed mindlessly disturb the peace of the valley. Hilma, Vanamee, and finally even Magnus tremble when they hear a train approach. Though Norris' characters are, for their time and setting, remarkably well educated (Lyman, Harran, Annixter, and Presley have all attended Eastern colleges), though they prize learning (Annixter enjoys Charles Dickens, Dyke's daughter hopes to attend finishing school, Annie Derrick loves poetry and has taught literature), they generally reserve their greatest respect for the tough honesty of ranch life. The two who do not (Lyman and Annie) reject and are rejected by the ranch community.

Annie had hoped to discuss literature regularly with Presley during his stay at Los Muertos. Still, art for its own sake is repugnant to Presley, who enjoys Homer primarily because his rugged epics place small value on elegance for its own sake. Presley, like Norris himself, has believed that literature exists to serve social causes. When Presley reads history and philosophy and subsequently when he declares himself a "Red" like Caraher, the saloon keeper, it is from a desire to fight social evils intellectually. He comes to realize through Vanamee's insight that evil is part of a process of social evolution, that no individual has the ability to see how the truth, which eventually prevails, emerges from evil's snares.

There is always the Wheat; it grows, sometimes dies before harvest, but it eventually matures and prevails. The truth of this "resurrection" recurs everywhere. Significantly, its most dramatic appearance in the novel is in the magnificent flowers of the Seed Ranch, which had been Angèle Varian's home. Identical daughter replaces the mother who died while giving her birth, and the younger Angèle finds her own happiness with Vanamee, the mystic who had been her mother's fiancé.

Critical Context

Norris, like Stephen Crane and Theodore Dreiser, pioneered Naturalism in American fiction. He was concerned primarily with questions of social justice and environmental determinism. Norris came to these concerns through his reading of Charles Darwin, and he believed that Darwinian ideas were applicable to sociology. This "social Darwinism" emerges in the struggles to survive which fill the pages of *The Octopus*. Norris intended the novel to be the first volume of a "wheat trilogy," an American social statement corresponding to that of Émile Zola, whose works he deeply respected. *The Pit* (1903), intended as the second volume, deals with the selling of and speculation in wheat on the Chicago wheat market. "The Wolf," never completed because of Norris' untimely death, was to consider the wheat's distribution and consumption in the starving countries of Europe.

The Wheat, itself a fertility symbol and always capitalized by Norris when used in this context, causes brutishness to replace intellect. Norris saw this brutishness from privileged surroundings. He was struck by the barbarity of fraternity hazing during his student years at the University of California at Berkeley and meant to discuss barbarism's clash with intellect in the context of social themes such as those of his beloved Zola, an author he read assiduously during his year of study in Paris.

Critics compare Norris' love of romance to that of Nathaniel Hawthorne and Herman Melville. They see in Norris' rugged style the manner of Jack London and Rudyard Kipling. Others emphasize Norris' concern for social reform, but it is doubtless true that Norris, perhaps better than any American author, placed epic forms in a decidedly American context.

Sources for Further Study
French, Warren. *Frank Norris*, 1962.
Pizer, Donald. *Realism and Naturalism in Nineteenth-Century American Literature*, 1966.

Robert J. Forman

THE ODD WOMAN

Author: Gail Godwin (1937-   )
Type of plot: Comic realism
Time of plot: The early 1970's
Locale: A Midwestern university town, a Southern town, New York City, and
    Chicago
First published: 1974

> *Principal characters:*
> JANE CLIFFORD, the protagonist, an assistant professor of
>   romantic British literature
> EDITH BARNSTORFF, Jane's grandmother, a Southern lady
> KITTY SPARKS, Edith's daughter, Jane's mother
> GABRIEL WEEKS, Jane's lover, an art history professor at a
>   neighboring university
> GERDA MULVANEY, Jane's confidante and friend for the past
>   twelve years

The Novel

The title and central issue of Gail Godwin's story are based upon George Gissing's 1893 novel, *The Odd Women*—a pessimistic study of the possibilities of women in the late nineteenth century. Godwin's *The Odd Woman* is one character's search in the late twentieth century to resolve her personal story: Will Jane Clifford find a perfect faithfulness in marriage, the kind of love George Eliot and George Henry Lewes had, or will she remain "odd" in the sense of Gissing's women, single, unpaired? The novel spans Jane's semester break at a Midwestern university where she has filled two successive sabbatical leave vacancies in the English department. Her future is uncertain; she has no teaching position for the next academic year, yet if her married lover receives a Guggenheim she could go to Europe with him.

The death of Jane's grandmother, Edith Barnstorff, at the end of the first chapter triggers the action of the novel, a journey that encompasses half the country, most of Jane's past, and the remainder of the novel. When Jane flies South for the funeral, it is a visit into her family's past and her relationships with her mother, Kitty, half brothers, Jack and Ronnie, half sister, Emily, and stepfather, Ray Sparks, whom she perceives as "the villain" of her story.

Although Jane's visit takes her deep into the past, it fails to resolve the problems of the present. She recalls Edith's contradictory advice ("I think, on the whole, it is better that *you* do not marry. Some people aren't made for the married state," but later, "Sometimes I get down on my knees and pray that you will find a good man to take care of you, as Hans took care of me") and realizes that what she wants is "the end of uncertainty, of joyless struggle," a struggle "without assurance of a happy reward."

The search for her "best life" takes Jane to New York City, for an impromptu few days with Gabriel Weeks, her married, middle-aged lover for the past two years. In reassessing their relationship, Jane decides that her image of Gabriel, a professor of art history specializing in the Pre-Raphaelites, has been created "almost totally through her own devisings and dreams." A nineteenth century Romantic at heart, Jane believes in the reality of the inner life, a life she has constructed for Gabriel and herself. In New York City, she discovers that Gabriel does not share her faith in "a kind of love that—that exists in a permanent, eternal way," and she decides to leave him.

The final stop in Jane's odyssey is Chicago, where she visits her oldest friend, Gerda Mulvaney, a woman who re-creates herself in the image of each newly adopted cause. Deeply involved in feminism at the time of Jane's visit, Gerda argues with her, accusing Jane of living a life of "avoidances and evasions and illusions." After Gerda's attack, Jane realizes that she has failed to connect her own search with those of any of the women in her life. She sees herself "in transit between the old values . . . and the new values, which she must hack out for herself."

Distraught and exhausted, Jane returns to her apartment and the prospect of five days alone with herself, "researching her salvation," before the new semester begins. Jane learns that she will probably receive a last-minute replacement position for the next year, and, having found at least that much resolution, she goes to bed listening to the sounds of someone playing the piano late into the night, "trying to organize the loneliness and the weather and the long night into something of abiding shape and beauty."

The Characters

Jane Clifford is extraordinary in her belief in the importance of words and the reality of the inner life. The most appealing quality Godwin has given her thirty-two-year-old protagonist is her sincere desire to make of her life what Aristotle calls "a good plot": something that moves from possibility to probability to necessity. Toward this end, Jane reevaluates the symbols in her life—Edith Barnstorff, Kitty Sparks, and Gerda Mulvaney—and realizes that their stories cannot be hers, that "you had to write yourself as you went along, that your story could not and should not possibly be completed until *you* were." What Godwin's readers are likely to admire in Jane is her continued search for order and meaning in her life, and her awareness that she may never find them.

Godwin reflects other characters in the novel through Jane's consciousness. Edith, Kitty, Gerda, and Jane's lover, Gabriel Weeks, are presented almost entirely through Jane's flashbacks and recollections. In Jane's mind, her grandmother Edith is "the perfect Southern lady." The story of her marriage to Hans Barnstorff (who, hearing Edith declare that "life is a disease," said "let me protect you from it") affects Jane deeply, and her death leaves Jane to pursue the "truth of the individual life" alone. Jane also sees herself as separated from her mother, Kitty, a part-time classics teacher and full-time wife to Ray Sparks, and Gerda Mulvaney, a friend passionately involved in her latest cause. Both women seem to possess what has eluded Jane—"a real vocation," something she believes "we are all in search of."

Jane's lover, Gabriel Weeks, is the least defined of Godwin's characters, and he is also the one with whom Jane is struggling the most. A middle-aged man with no lines in his face, Gabriel is less angelic than ethereal. Married to Ann Weeks for the past twenty-five years, Gabriel occupies much of Jane's inner, but little of her external life. He has never told her that he loves her and remains equally noncommittal in his plans for their future. Gabriel believes that perfect art but not permanent relationships can exist because "a relationship, by its very nature, is transient . . . it is made between people, and people change." Gabriel is located in the moment; he is incapable of transcending time through love.

Themes and Meanings

Godwin weaves two themes throughout her novel. The first comes in the novel's epigraph, taken from Carl Jung: "In knowing ourselves to be unique in our personal combination—that is, ultimately limited—we possess also the capacity for becoming conscious of the infinite. But only then!" Jane Clifford's search for personal resolution leads her to a deeper awareness of her own character. First Howard Cecil (a student) and later Ray Sparks (her stepfather) ask Jane, "Don't you want to be happy?" Yet, throughout the novel, what Jane really wants is to solve "the ever-present problem of her unclear, undefined, unresolved self." Looking for "a true, pure 'character,'" Jane finds instead her own imagination; Hugo Von Vorst, who she had thought was her Aunt Frances' natural father, is not the "family villain" she had always believed him to be, and neither is Gabriel Weeks the man of her dreams. It is only near the end of the novel that Jane sees her life as a series of illusions and uncompleted actions, and this self-recognition is the first step in perceiving her own limitations.

Godwin's second theme concerns time. Jane not only feels the passage of time but also reminds herself of it. Her constant companion is a clock proclaiming Tempus Fugit (time flies), and a watchmaker's advertisement, "He who knows most, Gives most for wasted time," recurs in her thoughts. Through most of the novel, Jane is looking for a pattern to hold against time, fearing that she will not find her "best life." Time is her enemy, and only on the last page of the novel does another way of interpreting time emerge. In a fantasized conversation with the Enema Bandit, Jane advises him to "turn your oddities inside out like a sock and find your own best life by making them work for you instead of being driven by them." She advises him to make his own pattern, to allow his limitations to shape his "best life." From this point of view, he who knows most will give most for wasted time because wasted time is, itself, redeemed.

Critical Context

The Odd Woman was Godwin's third novel, following *The Perfectionists* (1970) and *Glass People* (1972). It has nearly twice the length and complexity of either of her earlier books and is generally regarded as an important book in her development as a novelist.

Concerned in her first two novels with the possibilities of self-definition for modern women, Godwin gives the question historical and literary context in *The Odd Woman*. Using George Gissing's 1893 novel as a counterpoint to her own story, Godwin draws her readers into Jane Clifford's contemporary struggle for resolution, giving that struggle larger and more profound implications about the relationship between the life of the mind and the outer life than are to be found in either of her previous novels. Focusing primarily on character rather than action, her work since *The Odd Woman* has continued to explore the intersection between art and life and the haunting presence of the past in everyday life.

Sources for Further Study

Korg, Jacob. "A Gissing Influence," in *Gissing Newsletter*. XII, no. 1 (1976), pp. 13-19.

Lorsche, Susan E. "Gail Godwin's *The Odd Woman*: Literature and the Retreat from Life," in *Critique: Studies in Modern Fiction*. XX (1978), pp. 21-32.

Smith, Marilyn J. "The Role of the South in the Novels of Gail Godwin," in *Critique: Studies in Modern Fiction*. XXI (1979), pp. 103-110.

Jennifer L. Randisi

OH WHAT A PARADISE IT SEEMS

Author: John Cheever (1912-1982)
Type of plot: Comic realism
Time of plot: Twentieth century
Locale: New York City and Janice, a small suburban town
First published: 1982

> *Principal characters:*
> LEMUEL SEARS, the protagonist, an elderly businessman
> RENÉE HERNDON, his lover for a brief time
> BETSY LOGAN, a resident of Janice
> HORACE CHISHOLM, an environmentalist

The Novel

This novel comprises two interconnected narratives that center on saving a pond in a small suburban town, Janice. The mayor of Janice, who has connections with some form of organized crime, allows Beasley's Pond to become a dump for the ostensible purpose of filling it to provide the site for a war memorial. As Cheever moves from one plot to the other, regaining the purity of the pond becomes a personal and moral issue for three of the main characters.

Lemuel Sears is somewhat fearful of growing old. Having left the city to skate at Beasley's Pond one fine winter day, he recaptures the physical and spiritual exhilaration that he experienced in his youth. Thus, when he returns a few weeks later and finds the pond being used as a dump, he is more than intellectually appalled at the pollution of the pond: "He thought his heart would break." He first hires a lawyer and then an environmentalist, Horace Chisholm, in an effort to stop the dumping. Ultimately, he fails where another character, Betsy Logan, succeeds, but when the dumping ceases, he establishes a foundation that uses the latest technology to undo the pollution.

Soon after his afternoon of skating, Sears meets Renée Herndon and begins an affair with her, their frequent lovemaking bringing him another pleasure that he feared he might lose as a result of growing old. When she leaves him unexpectedly and without explanation, he seeks comfort in a brief homosexual encounter and a trout-fishing expedition, neither of which is successful. Yet, because for Sears there is a "sameness in the search for love and the search for potable water," he turns his attention to saving the pond, which takes the place of loving Renée.

In the second narrative, Betsy Logan, a resident of Janice, is also drawn into the fight to save the pond. Her neighbor, Sammy Salazzo, collects fees for dumping in the pond. In a bizarre series of events—the shooting of the

Salazzos' dog, a verbal confrontation about wind chimes with Maria Salazzo, and a physical battle with her in the supermarket—Betsy's relations with her neighbors deteriorate. The last event, the fight at the Buy Brite, establishes her as an avenger of injustice and prepares the way for her involvement in the battle to save the pond.

It is Horace Chisholm who provides the link between Sears's story and Betsy Logan's. Returning from a day at the beach, Betsy and her husband stop to change places so she can drive. Inadvertently, they leave their baby, Binxie, at the side of the road, where Chisholm finds him. In gratitude for the return of their son, they ask Chisholm to dinner and at his request become involved in the Beasley Pond issue. When the case gets a hearing, the corruption in Janice government is evident; Chisholm is run down by a car, and the dumping continues. In revenge for Chisholm's murder, Betsy puts poisoned teriyaki sauce on the supermarket shelves, threatening to continue to do so until the dumping is stopped. Her method works, and Sears's foundation can accomplish the task of cleaning the pond.

The Characters

Cheever's characters, while not flat, are sketchily drawn—caricatures which capture essential details and may offer a hint of satire. In his comments, however, the narrator, as intimate observer, reveals (and sometimes comments on) the characters' thoughts, giving the characters greater depth and complexity than they appear to have at first.

Lemuel Sears is an apparently successful, well-traveled businessman, an executive for a computer-container manufacturer. "Old . . . but not yet infirm," he fears that age may bring the "end of love." Love for him satisfies more than a physical desire; love fills a spiritual void as well. For Sears, "a profound and gratifying erotic consummation is a glimpse at another's immortal soul as one's own immortal soul is shown." While Sears does not live in the past, details of the present constantly call up memories of earlier times and places that reveal his eye and ear for detail, his sense of place, and his love of the sensual. These memories and his patrician manners associate him with values that have endured.

Renée Herndon, who accommodates Sears's lustiness and brings physical love into his life again for a brief time is drawn in less detail. To Sears, she is "a remarkably good-looking woman" of thirty-five or forty. Involved with numerous unidentified self-improvement groups, she is a mysterious, unpredictable character who repeatedly tells Sears that he does not "understand the first thing about women."

At first, Betsy Logan seems to be the antithesis of the independent Renée and the sophisticated Sears. A suburban homemaker, her greatest pleasure is shopping at the Buy Brite. Her fight there with Maria Salazzo, however, demonstrates that she is not meek, that she will resort to violence to right an injustice. Where Sears fails to accomplish his goal of saving the pond, she succeeds. It is ironic, though, that while family is centrally important to her, she endangers other families by her nefarious method of gaining attention for the cause of Beasley's Pond.

Horace Chisholm is an idealist who has left his high school teaching job to "do what he could to correct this threat to life on the planet or at least to inform the potential victims." Deeply troubled by the way people treat nature in a throwaway society, Chisholm has a cause for which to fight, but he has no love in his life. His wife has left him and taken his children; he lives alone and is lonely. As it does for Sears, his quest for clean water takes the place of love. Spiritually, Chisholm feels lost; like Sears, he too looks to fond memories, and it is an attempt to return to a happy activity from the past—picking blackberries—that leads him to find Binxie. Like Sears, he wants a homecoming; he is deeply touched by the domesticity and warmth of the Logans.

Themes and Meanings

Cheever begins and ends this novel with the same idea, that the story is one "to be read in bed in an old house on a rainy night." Thus, at the beginning, Cheever introduces an important image, water, and implies another, home. At the end, he reiterates their importance by repeating the line and comes full circle to arrive where he started. The narrative device, then, reinforces a major theme, the desire to go "home."

Depicting the modern world as a nomadic society where everything is expendable, "home" for Cheever represents paradise. It is a feeling more than a place—a sense of being loved and being at one with God, man, and the universe. When Cheever has his characters long for home, he is telling the archetypal tale of fallen, wandering man's desire to return to Eden.

Clean water also becomes an image for paradise; cleaning Beasley's Pond represents a return to the garden. The narrator makes this point clear when he says that for Sears paradise was never a "sacred grove," but "the whiteness of falling water." The narrator also notes that once the pond is clean and clear again, it could serve as "a background for [a painting of] Eden." Finally, by Sears's equating the search for love with the search for clean water, Cheever makes love a way to return to paradise as well.

An early description of spring rains on harvest-ready fields and other references to agriculture and plenty indicate that an allied theme is the potential for renewal. Sears is rejuvenated by his affair with Renée and spiritually renewed by the newly cleansed pond. In the twentieth century, renewal comes with the glimpses of paradise that are possible in the contemporary spiritual wasteland. Although only glimpses are possible, to Cheever they are so spiritually uplifting that they are motivation enough for man's continued striving to catch them.

Critical Context

Oh What a Paradise It Seems was Cheever's last novel; he died shortly after its publication. As a short novel, perhaps novella, it is unique in Cheever's canon. It is neither a short story, with the brevity and precise focus of that genre, nor a full-blown novel. Yet similarities with Cheever's other works do exist.

Like characters in *Bullet Park* (1969) and *Falconer* (1977), in particular, the characters in this novel seek love and order in the midst of the absurdities and chaos around them. Like many of Cheever's short stories, this work takes readers into the familiar suburbs depicted with the wry humor that is typical of Cheever. At the same time, Cheever acknowledges the fallen state of man, the wasteland qualities of the modern world, and the significance of the emotional and spiritual dimensions of life. Mingling Brandenburg concertos played in ragtime and the sound of running brooks, the appliance-laden refuse of contemporary American nomads and people longing for the warmth of home, he focuses on a deep human need for spirituality, wholeness, and love.

Source for Further Study
Hunt, George W. *John Cheever: The Hobgoblin Company of Love*, 1983.

Rebecca Kelly

OMENSETTER'S LUCK

Author: William H. Gass (1924-   )
Type of plot: Postmodernism/anti-pastoral
Time of plot: The 1890's
Locale: Gilean, Ohio, an imaginary river town
First published: 1966

> *Principal characters:*
> THE REVEREND JETHRO FURBER, a preacher haunted by his
>   passions and by Omensetter's incomprehensible "luck"
> BRACKETT OMENSETTER, an "unnaturally natural" newcomer
>   to Gilean
> HENRY PIMBER, Omensetter's landlord, who is seduced by the
>   stranger's mysterious ease
> ISRABESTIS TOTT, a town ancient and its senile "historian"

The Novel

   Omensetter's Luck is divided into three sections, each of which is dominated by the perceptions of a different narrator and a different rhetorical
style. "The Triumph of Israbestis Tott" traces the unsteady remembrances
and private anxieties of a survivor of the novel's events as he witnesses the
auctioning off of the furnishings of the Pimber household. Although his
associations prepare the reader for the central plot surrounding the catalytic
effects of the arrival of Brackett Omensetter, Tott's penchant for "flair" in
storytelling—his preference for stylistic freedom over historical accuracy—
as well as his uncertain grasp of the events and personalities he inventories,
creates an atmosphere of unreliability and mythic exaggeration. "The Love
and Sorrow of Henry Pimber" introduces Omensetter through the responses
of the townspeople, to whom the stranger seems to live bracketed within the
"sweet oblivion" of prelapsarian guiltlessness and unself-consciousness,
enjoying almost inhuman intimacy with nature. This "wide and happy man"
is consistently described in allegorical terms, and numerous examples of his
remarkable ease confound all of Gilean. Henry Pimber, who had tried to
take advantage of the childlike innocence of Omensetter by selling the new-
comer on a house vulnerable to floods, comes under his spell at the same
time that Omensetter magically cures Pimber of lockjaw; he learns to envy
Omensetter's "stony mindlessness that makes me always think of Eden,"
and he seeks to discover the man's secret, as though he were "a dream you
might enter." Unfortunately, Omensetter knows no such secret—his obliviousness is his sanctuary, and it extends to an inability even to acknowledge
Pimber's worship. When Omensetter allows a fox trapped down a well to
remain there unattended to starve to death, Pimber, who has come to iden-

tify with the trapped animal, shoots the fellow victim of Omensetter's ne-
glect. His hope of salvation dashed—Omensetter having been revealed as
"no miracle, a man, with a man's mask and a man's wall"—Pimber commits
suicide, hanging himself from a tall tree deep in the forest.

The third and longest section of the novel, "The Reverend Jethro
Furber's Change of Heart," is a complex, impressionistic rendering of the
mind of Gilean's diabolical preacher, a misanthropic, intensely self-conscious
man who, having long denied his own sensual needs, sees Omensetter's
openness and seeming imperviousness to the plague of thought as an indictment of Furber's own spiderlike existence in the blasted Eden behind the
walls of the church garden. Through a protracted bout of sophistry, Furber
convinces himself that Omensetter is a personification of evil, thereby justifying the subversive tactics of God's representative in Gilean. The death of
Pimber enables Furber to rouse suspicion that Omensetter is the murderer.

Meanwhile, Omensetter's state of grace has apparently deserted him in
the face of his son's diphtheria: Omensetter calls upon his much-vaunted
luck, but the very fact of his recognizing it consciously and naming it in this
fashion seems to have thrust him into the world of ordinary human awareness. Helpless, he ironically turns to the preacher, who derides Omensetter
for the dangerous repercussions of his utter stupefaction in the face of real-
world demands, but at the same time confesses the lovelessness that has
characterized his own existence and the lies he had perpetrated against him.
Indeed, Furber realizes that Omensetter is no longer a threat, because
"now he knows. There's no further injury that we can do. . . ." Although
Omensetter and his family do escape from Gilean, he is now merely and
precisely human, while Furber suffers a breakdown and is succeeded in the
pulpit by Huffley, a man of ordinary rhetorical talents, but one who has the
capacity for intimacy with the people he leads.

The Characters

Any discussion of William H. Gass's characters must admit the author's
redefinition of the term. For Gass, a character in a work of fiction is any locus in the text where language is generated; moreover, a character exists
exclusively within the words that attach to it. A character is not only conveyed but also constituted by the words, sounds, and rhythms it occasions,
which is to say that every story is necessarily also about its own physical con-
struction and presence.

The list of principal characters in *Omensetter's Luck*, then, includes the
title character only by implication, for he is essentially bereft of language.
Omensetter is more creature than personality; he represents the possibility—a false promise, finally—of "joining himself to what he knew." He is
consistently described in allegorical terms, and his effortless ability to live in
harmony with the natural world "cast an interest like a shade."

Omensetter soon becomes the object of discipleship for Henry Pimber, the Everyman figure of the novel. That Omensetter seems capable of living life with such immediacy, even carelessness, confronts Pimber with the mundane, decidedly postlapsarian life he lives. Pimber is overwhelmed by Omensetter: He "received the terrible wound of the man's smile" and imagines that Omensetter possesses the secret "of being new . . . of living lucky, and losing Henry Pimber." Pimber's love is unrequited, however, for he cannot penetrate Omensetter's gift of obliviousness; suicide becomes a kind of consolation and, symbolically, an effort to replicate Omensetter's escape from thought.

Jethro Furber, the obsessive wordmongerer with the "ringaling tongue," is certainly the novel's most arresting character. As Furber reflects upon the misdemeanors that led him to be sent to Gilean by his church, upon bitter memories of his early life, and upon a variety of sexual fantasies, it becomes evident that he has fashioned barriers out of religion, philosophy, and rhetoric that pervert and compromise all of his associations and separate him from the community of human feeling; his sermons ventilate his roiling imagination (the ghost of Reverend Pike, Furber's predecessor, is his closest confidant), and he mocks his own capacity for disguise and manipulation. His corrosive self-consciousness makes him hostile to Omensetter, who appears to have no experience of guilt or inner conflict. Thus, Furber's campaign to sabotage Omensetter's reputation is as much a product of private pathology as it is of religious conviction. By recasting Omensetter's blissfulness as brutishness and apparent transcendence of worldly cares as demonism, Furber imposes his rhetorical constructions on reality, and he cannot countenance the contradiction of his principles that Omensetter represents. (In fact, Furber's fiction-making, his creative readjustment of reality, is a darker version of the "artistry" of Israbestis Tott.) When Furber finally undergoes a "change of heart" toward his victim, it is already too late either for Omensetter to regain innocence or for Furber to reclaim the community he had long ago forsaken.

Themes and Meanings

The novel rehearses and reconstitutes many of the central themes of American literature: most prominently, the nature of good and evil, the problem of sin, and the central conflicts of Nature and Civilization, Innocence and Experience. It is the question of how language makes a world, however, which dominates the proceedings. Indeed, *Omensetter's Luck* can be read as an analysis and example of how one comes to inhabit his language and to depend upon the coherence of the linguistic enterprise in which he engages. In Israbestis Tott, the reader meets a narrator who sees language as preferable to the world it replaces: Story is superior to history, while history is subject to the fictionist's prerogatives. In Jethro Furber, one sees how an overflow of language simultaneously proves the loss of the density of life and provides compensation for that loss: Words both harbor and imprison him. Brackett Omensetter, on the other hand, appears on the scene as someone who is beyond the reach of such abstractions and the need for their mediating effects. Thus, Furber and Omensetter are the extremes of mind and body, intellect and instinct, between which the people of Gilean oscillate. Neither man is complete, and each operates in his respective exile. When Omensetter leaves town, calm is restored, but so is the dailiness of daily life in Gilean.

Critical Context

Omensetter's Luck is one of the finest, most ambitious, and most underread novels of twentieth century American fiction. Like the stories in *In the Heart of the Heart of the Country and Other Stories* (1968) and the exuberantly experimental novella *Willie Masters' Lonesome Wife* (1968), Gass's novel investigates the theoretical principles on nature of fiction that dominate his essay collections, *Fiction and the Figures of Life* (1970), *The World Within the Word* (1978), and *Habitations of the Word* (1985). To his fiction and criticism alike, Gass brings a luxuriant sense of the textures, rhythms, and sounds words offer. Gass delights in the musicality of prose and the sudden, riveting discovery of original metaphor.

It is misleading, however, to deem *Omensetter's Luck* a philosophical novel, as though it were primarily devised to exemplify troubling linguistic issues; rather, let us say that Gass's novel requires one to fasten upon the "sensual" pleasures of the text at the same time that one explores its complex of issues. Certainly, Gass is among the foremost promoters and practitioners of innovative fiction, and his writings testify to his insistence that the only events in fiction are sentences.

Sources for Further Study

Gilman, Richard. "William H. Gass," in *The Confusion of Realms*, 1969.
McCaffery, Larry. *The Metafictional Muse: The Work of Robert Coover, Donald Barthelme, and William H. Gass*, 1982.
Schneider, Richard J. "The Fortunate Fall in William Gass's *Omensetter's Luck*," in *Critique: Studies in Modern Fiction*. XVII (1976), pp. 5-20.

Arthur M. Saltzman

ON HEROES AND TOMBS

Author: Ernesto Sábato (1911-   )
Type of plot: Psychological realism
Time of plot: 1841 and 1946-1955
Locale: Buenos Aires and Patagonia, Argentina
First published: Sobre héroes y tumbas, 1961 (English translation, 1981)

> *Principal characters:*
> ALEJANDRA VIDAL OLMOS, a young woman in Buenos Aires
> MARTÍN DEL CASTILLO, a young man in love with Alejandra
> BRUNO BASSÁN, the mentor and confidant of Martín
> FERNANDO VIDAL OLMOS, the father of Alejandra
> HORTENSIA PAZ, a woman who nurses Martín during his
>   illness
> GEORGINA OLMOS, the mother of Alejandra
> BUCICH, a truck driver

The Novel

In an introductory note to his linguistically and ideologically complex novel, Ernesto Sábato admits that the narrative represents his attempt to "free himself of an obsession that is not clear even to himself." This admission is borne out by the novel's extraordinary display of unusual imagery, puzzling events and characters, and conflicting political and ethical points of view.

The text of *On Heroes and Tombs* is presented in four parts. In "The Dragon and the Princess" and "Invisible Faces," Martín del Castillo meets Alejandra Vidal Olmos, a young woman for whom he develops an immediate fascination. After a long period of pursuit, he finally convinces her to begin a love affair with him. In an attempt to understand the strange behavior of Alejandra, Martín follows her and sees her with another man, whom she later admits is Fernando, her father. Although she seems to be an innocent, introverted woman, Alejandra (who turns out to be the daughter of a decadent aristocratic family) is a prostitute who caters to the wealthy members of Juan Perón's administration. At the same time, she maintains an incestuous relationship with Fernando, who is her father but was never married to her mother, Georgina.

Fernando Vidal Olmos has written a mysterious document which narrates his frequent hallucinatory experiences, a document incorporated into the text in the third part, "Report on the Blind." After finishing the report, Fernando goes to his daughter's home, even though he knows that he is going to his inevitable death. Alejandra shoots him and then commits suicide by setting fire to the house.

In the fourth part of the novel, "An Unknown God," Martín seeks the help of Bruno Bassán as he attempts to understand his relationship with Alejandra. Martín falls into an alcohol-induced stupor, in which he envisions himself in a world likened to a dung heap or sewer. He is saved and nursed back to health by Hortensia Paz, who instills in him the hope for a better life. Martín meets a truck driver, Bucich, who takes him on a trip to Patagonia. Interpolated in the narrative of the trip are passages which depict the struggle of the revolutionary forces of General Juan Lavalle against the regime of Juan Manuel de Rosas, the dictator of Argentina from 1829 to 1852. Two ancestors of Fernando and Alejandra Vidal Olmos carry the body of Lavalle toward the Argentine-Bolivian border in 1841 as Martín flees to Patagonia in 1955 and finds that the crystal-clear sky and the fresh air make him feel free and reborn.

The story of Alejandra, Martín, and Fernando is told through a variety of narrative points of view. The foreword of the novel is an objective police report of the death of Alejandra and Fernando. "The Dragon and the Princess" and "Invisible Faces," narrated by an unnamed omniscient narrator, include many long passages which portray the thoughts of the characters and scenes from the early life of Alejandra and Martín. The "Report on the Blind" is a text written by Fernando as a memoir or confession, a narrative of his own experience. In the last section, "An Unknown God," it becomes clear that the narrator of the first two sections is someone who knew the characters and has obtained most of the information from Bruno and from Martín years after the death of Alejandra and Fernando. The narrator acts as an organizing consciousness of the material—the episodes of the contemporary history of the characters, the recollections of the earlier years, the interpolated passages of the history of Alejandra's ancestors, and the text of Fernando's psychotic, paranoic report on the activities of the blind.

The Characters

Just as the novel represents an attempt to relieve an unspecified obsession, the characters are portrayed as engaged in a struggle to free themselves from their own mysterious preoccupations. Throughout the novel, Bruno seeks the thread of continuity that links the lives of Alejandra, Fernando, and Martín, primarily to understand finally the reasons for Alejandra's act of killing her father and herself.

The contradictions of Alejandra's behavior are not resolved in the text of the novel. Although her family has always opposed the regime of Perón, she devotes her life to satisfying the sexual appetite of the Perónists. She makes love with Martín, for whom she has a strange, obsessive fascination, yet she always remains distant and mysterious. At the same time, she engages in an incestuous relationship with her father, and then murders him and destroys herself in a ritualistic immolation.

Fernando's lust for his daughter is barely explained. She bears a striking resemblance to Fernando's mother and to her own mother, Georgina, who was the daughter of Patricio, the brother of Fernando's mother. Bruno describes Fernando as an antiphilosopher, a nihilist who hates everything bourgeois and despises the world for its destruction of the aristocratic, elitist life that his family once enjoyed.

Martín is portrayed as a young man who is trying to find some explanation for life itself. Martín's attempt to discover a hidden logic in the mysterious behavior of Alejandra creates the impression that these two characters represent opposite poles of human existence, the ordered and the chaotic, the logical and the contradictory, the rational and the irrational, oppositions that suggest that Martín and Alejandra are archetypal characters, incarnations of what Sábato understands as essentially masculine and essentially feminine characteristics.

Themes and Meanings

The treatment of the central characters as representatives of abstract notions of masculine and feminine traits is a manifestation of a principal theme of the novel, the search for the meaning of human existence. Sábato creates from a common, almost trivial concern—that of the inability of one sex to understand the other—an exploration of an ontological problem. As Martín, Bruno, and Fernando attempt, each in his own way, to understand the mysterious Alejandra (who is likened to Argentina itself), they seek through the elusive feminine psyche a justification for their own experience. Fernando's hallucinatory, somnambulistic document about the blind is presented in terms of a harrowing journey through the vaginal canal of a woman, and Martín is rescued from his despair by a warm, maternal savior, Hortensia Paz. Bruno works out his answers to the mystery vicariously, by piecing together the story of Martín, Fernando, and Alejandra. Fernando finds his solution in his own madness, justifying the irrationality of existence as a plot perpetrated by blind people. Martín resolves his anguish by escaping to the free, open spaces of Patagonia, out of the reach of women, and by experiencing the exhilarating sense of masculine communion as he and the truck driver urinate together under the stars.

In the conflict of man and woman, then, is contained the insoluble mystery of existence. The elaboration of the conflict in *On Heroes and Tombs* is complicated by the fact that this is a novel about incestuous relationships, both sexual and nonsexual. Fernando and Alejandra, father and daughter, are lovers. Bruno has been sexually involved with Alejandra and with her mother, Georgina. Fernando fathered the child, Alejandra, by the daughter of his mother's brother, and the child looks like Fernando's mother, whose husband—Fernando's father—Fernando hated and tried to poison when he was a child. Martín becomes involved in a love affair with Alejandra, the former lover of his friend Bruno.

The fact that Alejandra works as a prostitute serving the Perónists, the longtime enemies of her aristocratic family, indicates that the incestuous relationships and the exploration of the meaning of existence itself have a political symbolism in the novel. The counterpoint provided in the narrative that shifts between the twentieth century condition of these characters living under the dictatorship of Perón and the struggles of the nineteenth century rebels fleeing the tyranny of Manuel de Rosas further develops the political implications of the story of Martín, Fernando, Bruno, and Alejandra. As Fernando dies, murdered by his daughter, at the same moment that Perón is deposed, Martín finds his freedom, aided by the maternal figure that nurses him and gives him the spiritual strength to escape his depression.

Although Sábato's novel is much too complex and profound to permit a simplistic explanation, it seems clear that in some way, Alejandra represents the contradictory, impassioned Argentina of the Perón regime, and that Hortensia Paz represents the compassionate, maternal nurturing of the potential Argentina of the post-Perón era.

Critical Context

Ernesto Sábato first received international acclaim with the publication of his short novel, *El túnel*, in 1948 (*The Outsider*, 1950). In the author's note at the beginning of *On Heroes and Tombs*, Sábato says that in the thirteen years between the first novel and the second, he continued exploring the mysterious labyrinth that leads to the secret of human existence. *The Outsider* is a pessimistic, oppressive story of a man who murders his married mistress when he finds out that she has deceived him. Many of the details and themes of the second novel are contained in the first—the mistress' husband is blind, the protagonist's love for the woman is obsessive and violent, and his behavior is at times distorted by paranoia.

As Sábato suggests, *On Heroes and Tombs* does indeed seem to be a development of the obsessive concerns of the first novel. The pessimism of *The Outsider*, however, is tempered somewhat by the optimism of the ending of the second novel. The more promising vision of human existence offered by Hortensia Paz and the portrayal of potentially rewarding relationships in the conversation and communion of Martín and Bucich in Patagonia are indications that Sábato finds some salvation for his characters despite the apparent meaninglessness of life.

Sábato's novel is a stylistic tour de force which inevitably evokes a comparison with the work of many of his Latin American contemporary novelists. There are many passages that are precursors of the narrative complexities of the work of Carlos Fuentes, Julio Cortázar, and Guillermo Cabrera Infante, and the ontological problems suggested by the novel reflect similar preoccupations of the most influential Argentine writer of the twentieth century, Jorge Luis Borges. In spite of the development toward a concept of life in *On Heroes and Tombs* that is more optimistic than the ontology of *The Outsider*, the later novel continues to suggest the impossibility of resolving the conflict of human rationality and human existence. The stylistic and ideological complexities of Sábato's work, which confirm his confession of the obsessive nature of his narrative impulse, render his novelesque work very difficult and not at all clear in its communication of the central mystery of life.

Sources for Further Study

Aldrich, Earl M., Jr. "Esthetic, Moral, and Philosophic Concerns in *Sobre héroes y tumbas*," in *Romance Literary Studies: Homage to Harvey L. Johnson*, 1979.
Kennedy, William. "Sábato's Tombs and Heroes," in *Review*. XXIX (May-August, 1981), pp. 6-9.
Oberhelman, Harley D. *Ernesto Sábato*, 1970.

Gilbert Smith

ON THE ROAD

Author: Jack Kerouac (1922-1969)
Type of plot: Neo-romantic picaresque
Time of plot: 1947-1950
Locale: The continental United States and Mexico
First published: 1957

> *Principal characters:*
> SAL PARADISE, the narrator, a young, aspiring writer
> DEAN MORIARTY, a drifter, Sal's friend, traveling companion,
>   and inspiration

The Novel

On the Road opens with the meeting of Sal Paradise, the narrator, and the frenetic Dean Moriarty at a time when Sal felt "that everything was dead." Thus, Sal's introduction to Dean and the "life on the road" is a rebirth of sorts for the struggling writer, the beginning of a cycle which will be reiterated several times in the course of the novel.

The novel is a retrospective account, divided into five parts, the first four chronicling Sal's four different pilgrimages on "the holy road" and his intersections with Dean, the fifth part serving as an epilogue. In part 1, Sal Paradise, the innocent, meets Dean, who is "simply a youth tremendously excited with life." Their meeting is brief but long enough for Sal to catch the "bug" of restlessness. He heads west, his mind filled with the traditional, romantic notions of the frontier and the promised land. Hitchhiking and busing his way across the Ohio Valley and the Midwest to Denver, Dean's hometown, he meets a cross section of people traveling the roads of middle America, and the reader gets the first breathless descriptions of the small towns and countryside which account for so much of the lyric beauty of Jack Kerouac's novel. After briefly meeting up with Dean and their mutual friend, Carlo Marx, in Denver, Sal continues on his journey to San Francisco, where every promising venture seems to fall apart. He loses a job as a security-guard in San Francisco and breaks off almost irrevocably with his host and friend in former times, Remi Boncoeur. On a bus to Los Angeles, he meets Teresa, a young Mexican woman he refers to as "my girl and my kind of girlsoul." He, Terry, and her child by a marriage that she is fleeing make a go of it picking cotton in a migrant workers' camp, and Sal forgets the road for a while. Yet the relationship cannot hold up under the change of the seasons ("Everybody goes home in October"), and Sal returns to Peterson. The first cycle of his life on the road is Sal's initiation to the sine curve of that life; upon returning to the East, he finds that the wilderness which he had once believed confined to the West is also a part of his East.

Part 2 finds Sal and his aunt visiting other relatives in Testament, Virginia. Without warning, Dean swoops in with his ex-wife, Marylou, and another friend, Ed Dunkel, to carry Sal off on another cross-country adventure. In Sal's eyes, Dean is no longer an excited youth but has become "the new and complete Dean, grown to maturity." The four of them leave in search of "IT!" Driving almost nonstop, night and day, they race from Testament to Paterson, New Jersey, back to Testament, to New York to see Carlo Marx for a short period, and wind up in New Orleans with Old Bull Lee and his wife, both friends of Sal. From there, Sal and Dean, with Marylou sandwiched between them, complete the trip to California, having left Ed Dunkel with his wife in New Orleans. The car, a battered '49 Hudson, seems fueled by Dean's apparently inexhaustible energy: He drives eighty-five and faster, stops to "dig" people, runs naked through the sage outside Ozona, Texas, and talks like a madman to Sal about memory, time, traveling, whatever his mind lights upon. Yet, as before, this journey falls apart at the end. Dean leaves Sal with Marylou, who would rather be with Dean, and goes back to Camille, his latest girlfriend and the mother of his daughter, Amy. Sal heads back to New York, not caring whether he ever sees Dean again.

Sal begins part 3 with a case of the doldrums. This time it is he who seeks out Dean in hopes of tapping his friend's rejuvenating ebullience. On Sal's suggestion, they decide to go to Italy but agree to first "do everything we'd never done and had been too silly to do in the past," including finding Dean's father. Things have changed, though—Dean has begun to slip in the eyes of some of his once devoted disciples. The women around him—his wife and the wives of his friends—have begun to grow weary of Dean's inability to stay put for any lasting period of time, and they know and resent what will happen now that Sal has shown up. They are right. After a night of immersing themselves in the jazz scene of San Francisco, 1949, the two embark on the third leg of what has seemingly become one long trek. Along the way, Sal and Dean fight over an innocuous remark by Dean, which Sal takes as a crack about the fact that Sal is getting old. They make up and go on, but signs of disintegration continue to emerge: In Denver, they cannot find Dean's father; the reader sees that both Dean's cousin and Ed Wall, (Dean's "brother" when he was a child) have lost faith in Dean as a person. The end of the trip is, by now, predictable. Dean meets a woman named Inez at a party and moves in with her, leaving Camille, his daughter Amy, and a second daughter on the West Coast. In abandoning the trip to Italy, Dean has effectively abandoned Sal for the second time.

Part 4 recounts the last trip and the last desperate search for "IT!" Sal, Dean, and a friend named Stan Shephard take to the road—south, to Mexico City, to encounter "the essential strain of the basic primitive, wailing humanity that stretches in a belt around the equatorial belly of the world. . . ." In Gregoria, the central scene takes place—a Dionysian frenzy of marijuana, alcohol, and sex in a Mexican whorehouse. When at last they reach Mexico City, Dean leaves Sal, sick with dysentery, to rush back to Inez in New York with his Mexican divorce from Camille.

In the final part of the book, Sal meets the girl "he had always searched for," and his life on the road ends. Dean comes back one more time to see Sal, but it is over; Sal is easing into a more stable life-style. He waves good-bye to "Old Dean" from the back of a Cadillac; he will think of Dean whenever the sun goes down on the vast American continent, dreaming people, and fathers never found.

The Characters

It is difficult to talk about either Sal Paradise or Dean Moriarty without referring to the other because they are complementary characters. Sal is the educated writer looking for the life experiences that will, through his shaping, become literature. As his name implies (Salvatore Paradise), he is the savior of paradise, or, at least in his role as writer, the preserver of paradise.

Dean is Sal's guide to the experience that Sal is avidly seeking, the "dean" of a new school, founded on principles perhaps also suggested by his name—Moriarty—the nemesis of Sherlock Holmes, the master of deductive reasoning. Dean does things on impulse. He steals cars; he runs through fields naked; he "digs" people. Perhaps this last item is the most revealing. To Dean, people are objects of pleasure, things to be enjoyed for the moment and to be dropped when they get boring. At any given time in the novel he is juggling at least two women, and he is so insensitive to their feelings that he can marry one woman and then convince her that the thing he must do immediately is to go back to his ex-wife and straighten things out with her—and he gets away with it. His unsatiated appetite for experience and his mile-a-minute pursuit of that experience draws people like a magnet, even as he turns his back on them.

What Sal offers Dean is someone who keeps his faith in him when Dean stretches his magnetic powers beyond the range of attraction. Sal understands, or at least thinks that he understands, Dean ("he reminded me of some long-lost brother"). In their quest for experience, they are alike, but Sal is a follower and an observer, content to experience life at Dean's fast pace, yet in a vicarious way, feeding off of Dean's energy. In that sense he is flawed like Dean, too. He uses people, including Dean, for their potential as characters in his books.

Since Sal is the narrator, all the other characters are seen through his eyes. They lack the depth as characters that both he and Dean have precisely because Sal, like Dean, "experiences" people. He does not see people as people, nor, for the most part, does he show the reader living people. A black man on the street is "beautiful" like a mountain peak is "beautiful" or "sad" like a bus station in Chicago is "sad." Few of the other characters are drawn with enough detail to come to life. Galatea Dunkel, who seems to awaken for a moment when she denounces Dean, might be an exception, as might Carlo Marx, "the sorrowful poetic con-man with the dark mind," but even they show only glimmers of life. They are more appropriately a part of the landscape, which could, itself, be considered to be a supporting character in the novel.

One cannot overlook the autobiographical nature of this book. Indeed, few critics have. Kerouac used his own experiences and the people he met and knew to the extent that nearly all of his characters can be and have been identified with their real counterparts (for example, the real-life counterpart to Carlo Marx is Beat poet Allen Ginsberg). The danger in using this approach is obvious. Though heavily autobiographical, *On the Road* is a novel, not an autobiography. Kerouac, like any novelist, has shaped reality to serve his own literary purposes.

Themes and Meanings

Kerouac is acknowledged as the coiner of the label "the Beat Generation" (beat, as in beat down) to describe the relatively small circle of friends, writers, and poets who constituted his group of companions during the late 1940's and on into the 1950's. Their governing beliefs come through clearly in *On the Road*: Distrust of authority and societal conventions; liberal sexual mores; experience for experience's sake, including drug experimentation. Yet the novel is not merely a Beat manifesto. Rather, it is a truly American novel with its roots, as critics have pointed out, going back to Walt Whitman, Herman Melville, and Mark Twain. The concept of Huck Finn's Mississippi river as a refuge from society may, in fact, shed the most light on Sal's vision of the road.

In the same way that Huck lights out for the river whenever civilization presses in too close, Sal takes to the road. Yet the differences between the two works are more fundamental to one's understanding of *On the Road* than are the similarities. Huck's river is a passive, peaceful environment. It carries him to new experiences as it flows along its natural course in its natural time. Huck is a child becoming an adult. In stark contrast, Sal and Dean actively seek to break convention, to experience things in new ways. They attack the road and life. When Dean says "Now we must all get out and dig the river and the people and smell the world," it is all too desperately emphatic. Their travels across America and into Mexico are upstream battles against the current of time; to find "IT!" would be to stop time. Sal and Dean are adults trying to become children again.

By the end of the novel, Sal has begun to reconcile himself to the cycles of life. The emotional rise and fall of his journeys, the ebb and flow of his relationship with Dean relentlessly drive him to the awareness of acceptance of the fact that the road has an end, that death follows birth, that one must eventually exhale if one is ever to take the next breath. He leaves Dean to his lonely, hopeless, mad race down the road.

Critical Context

On the Road was the work, more than any other piece of literature, that gave America its picture of the Beat Generation. Written in 1951 but published in 1957, it brought into the public light the values and life-style of a Bohemian subculture that had existed in relative obscurity in America since shortly after World War II. Kerouac's only popularly successful work, it fired the imaginations of many Americans and infuriated others, who saw in it a radicalism that they considered dangerous to the fabric of a civilized nation. In any case, it assured Kerouac of a place in literary history.

At the heart of the Beat movement was a rejection of societal conventions, which were seen as posing an almost insurmountable obstacle to self-knowledge and honest, meaningful communication. The Beat poets and writers translated this rejection of societal constraints into their literature as well. In Kerouac's case, the result was what he called "spontaneous prose"—a rapid outpouring of words and ideas onto paper with little or no editing, the idea being that the mind's unconscious selection and structuring would create a truer, purer, and richer discourse. Though the idea and material for *On the Road* had been bouncing around in Kerouac's head for several years, he wrote the bulk of the novel in the space of three weeks.

Perhaps Kerouac's technique explains why some critics have called his writing sloppy and unworthy of literary consideration. For whatever reason, many critics have chosen to look at Kerouac's work more for its depiction of a particular sociohistorical phenomenon than to judge it on its literary merits. Despite this critical shortchanging, *On the Road* offers much that is hauntingly beautiful, and the book deserves its standing as an American classic.

Sources for Further Study

Bartlett, Lee, ed. *The Beats: Essays in Criticism*, 1981.
Hipkiss, Robert A. *Jack Kerouac, Prophet of the New Romanticism*, 1976.
Nicosia, Gerald. *Memory Babe: A Critical Biography of Jack Kerouac*, 1983.
Tytell, John. *Naked Angels, the Lives and Literature of the Beat Generation*, 1976.

Mark Braley

ONE DAY OF LIFE

Author: Manlio Argueta (1936-   )
Type of plot: Social protest
Time of plot: 1979
Locale: El Salvador
First published: Un día en la vida, 1980 (English translation, 1983)

> *Principal characters:*
> GUADALUPE (LUPE) FUENTES DE GUARDADO, the protagonist,
>   a matriarch and peasant
> JOSÉ (CHEPE) GUARDADO, the husband of Lupe, a village
>   leader of the Federation of Christian Farmworkers
> ADOLFINA FUENTES, the granddaughter of Lupe and Chepe

The Novel

The narrative thread recounts one day in the life of a middle-aged peasant woman, from 5:00 A.M., when she arises at dawn, until 5:00 P.M., when she lights the candles as darkness closes in. The chapters divide the day's segments as she goes about her routine activities of cooking, child care, house and garden work, and musing about the people and events that have shaped and informed her life. This interior monologue reveals her past—the unremitting, wretched poverty as well as her simple, humble acceptance of the inhuman conditions under which she and the other peasants in the village live.

She muses about her childhood, her betrothal to José (Chepe) Guardado, their marriage, their children, their work, and their efforts to better their lot. By exercising extreme frugality, they have bought a small piece of land of their own. The carefully tended crops have enabled Lupe and Chepe to provide a few comforts for their meager existence; for example, they are able to buy a few toys and candies for the children at Christmas. Lupe recalls the early hardships, as when their child died of malnutrition, dysentery, and worms as many of the peasant children do, and how the "old priests" advocated resignation and hope of eternal happiness in heaven.

Then the "new priests" came and offered instruction and help in forming cooperatives, recommended pharmaceuticals to treat worms and dysentery, and cheese as food for malnourished babies. They encouraged the farm laborers to seek higher pay and the peasants to sell their goods in town, where they could get higher prices than the local merchant offered. Then she remembers how the authorities came and began abusing the peasants and finally attacked the priests. The priests were sent away, but the changes they had wrought could not be stopped, and the authorities became increasingly abusive as the peasants became increasingly assertive.

The abuses included torture, imprisonment, and murder. Lupe's son was one such victim, decapitated by the guards and his head stuck on a pole outside the village.

As the hours pass, Lupe reminisces about the increasing involvement of her family members in protest activities: Chepe has become a leader in the farm-workers' movement; Helio Hernandez, Lupe's son-in-law, has been seized by the guards for his activist involvement, and the family can get no information as to his whereabouts or fate. Lupe's granddaughter, Adolfina Fuentes, who is a child of less than fifteen years, is the most outspokenly militant. She took part in a week-long demonstration in which a cathedral was seized and occupied by the peasants; as she was returning home, the bus on which she and other demonstrators were riding was attacked by the guards and most of the passengers were killed. She and another girl escaped, and on the day of the narrative, she arrives to visit her grandmother for a few days until the situation cools down.

Later, the authorities come to question Adolfina about a man whom they have apprehended and beaten; the man murmured her name as he slipped into unconsciousness. They must wait for an hour or so with Lupe until the girl and Lupe's smaller children return from the store.

In her interior monologue, Lupe recapitulates the fears, compliance, hopes, anger, human kindness, and resignation that follow one another as she waits helplessly for Adolfina's return. Later, however, when the guards want to take Adolfina away to identify the man they are holding, she defies them and insists that they not take Adolfina away alone. Finally, they bring the man to the hut for the girl to see, but only Lupe recognizes Chepe by his clothes. He is dying from the brutal and disfiguring beating he has received. To protect her family, she denies knowing who he is and they take him away. Lupe resolves to carry on and to encourage her granddaughter also to continue such resistance as they can offer to the authorities.

The novel is detailed and often moving in its description of the miseries and brutalities of life in El Salvador. The ignorance and hopelessness of the peasantry are palpable in the life-styles portrayed. Lupe's random associations are simplistic yet believable, and there is an occasional contrast to the misery: the surprise of joy at the beauty of dawn, the pleasure of watching and hearing the tropical birds, the affection for a dog. Indeed, these poignant flashes of delight remind the reader that Manlio Argueta established his reputation first as a poet, and his lyricism and powerful images confirm his poetic talent.

In addition to Lupe's own chapters, in which her point of view and experiences are dominant, other chapters are interspersed in which the interior monologues and events of other characters' lives are revealed. The voices of three other women are heard in these chapters, and their experiences parallel Lupe's own and confirm her justification for hating the authorities. The guards are afforded two chapters in which their point of view is presented; these men are drawn from the peasant class themselves and are in truth turning against their own families, friends, and neighbors in order to uphold the brutally oppressive regime of a handful of wealthy families (fourteen) in El Salvador. Ironically, the voices of the guards, reflecting their confusion about loyalties, their wistful desire for a bit more power, a few more possessions, and a modicum of respect, are more believable than those of Adolfina, Lupe, and Chepe.

The Characters

The characters in this novel are prototypes. They represent two of the several factions involved in the social turmoil in El Salvador. The principal group depicted is the peasantry. Lupe, Chepe, Adolfina, and all the minor characters representing the peasantry share many of the same traits: They are courageous, long-suffering, wise, gentle, generous, and loving. Lacking even the most basic amenities of existence, they manage to create lives and family units which radiate love, harmony, and dignity. They support one another in their mutual opposition to the rapacity of the rich landowners and the brutality of the authorities; they acknowledge the authority of the Church and honor the priests, whether these priests recommend patiently bearing their burdens or offer help and instruction in ways to cooperate and unionize to improve their lot.

Lupe is the archetypical matriarch, warm and loving to her family, pious and generous to the Church, steadfast and courageous to Chepe, her beloved husband. Chepe, in turn, is bold in asserting his rights, a natural leader of the community, where he works diligently to improve the living conditions for his family and the farm workers in the union. He faces danger bravely, endures suffering silently, and, like his son, suffers martyrdom at the hands of the brutal guards.

Adolfina is an intense, idealistic girl who represents an impassioned new generation arising amid the repression and the turmoil. She is determined to avenge and justify the deaths of the martyrs and the sufferings of the peasants at the hands of the authorities. In the final lines of the book, Adolfina imagines that she sees the corpse of the guard who has just taken her dying grandfather away. She assures Lupe that this vision "has to be true."

The novel's preoccupation with terrorism and misery precludes any expansive development of characters: The characters all tend to be flat, representing the idealized qualities and political leanings of the peasant class. Their relationships to one another are likewise lacking in emotional variety and authenticity.

The minor characters among the peasant group are scarcely differentiated from the major ones, except in having smaller roles. Their characteristics and behavior are much the same: The son and son-in-law of Chepe are cut from the same mold as he, and Lupe's daughter is another staunchly brave and loyal matriarch in the making.

The only other characters with a substantial voice in the narrative are the guards, who wield authority over the peasants. These guards never waver in their commitment to keep the peasants down and protect the holdings of the rich. Although they come from the peasant class themselves, they have been effectively brainwashed by their leaders and trainers to feel only contempt and viciousness toward the hapless people over whom they have control. Their trainers, who provide both political and military instruction, are callous, arrogant, and sometimes brutal Americans, who teach the neophyte guards contempt for their own people.

The priests are a shadowy group, most of them preaching resignation and humility while accepting favors and gifts from the impoverished people; a few attempt to help the peasants or at least to mediate between the peasants and their oppressors. None of the priests is sufficiently developed to stand out as an individual. No members of the wealthy landowner group are represented in the narrative, although their malign nature is forcefully conveyed.

Themes and Meanings

The novel is written to recount and extol the birth of a sense of self-worth among the Salvadoran peasantry. This central theme illuminates the narrative and asserts that human dignity can and does transcend misery, brutality, and oppression. Beyond the misery of *One Day of Life*, beyond the carnage and despair, the novel holds forth hope for social justice in the future. Neither the peasants nor the guards seem able to comprehend or discuss the complex problems which they face, or even their own attitudes toward these questions. No solutions are proposed, no real focus of effort to accomplish any concrete goals ever appears to emerge. For each small action—a demonstration, a rally, an act of defiance—harshly brutal reprisals follow immediately. The book suggests that such measures serve only to strengthen the resolve of the peasants to continue to seek ways to make their lives better, but the position of the peasants would appear to be precariously weak, and beset by enemies both at home and abroad.

This novel asserts that the dignity of the human spirit will not be destroyed by misery and oppression, that it will resist and ultimately triumph. It is a splendid hope, providing a luminescent thematic unity to this tale of how the human spirit flourishes in one of the most economically depressed and politically unsettled areas of the Americas.

Critical Context

One Day of Life was Manlio Argueta's third book, but his first one to address in such direct fashion the social conditions in El Salvador. He is known principally as a poet, and critics have commented favorably on this book with respect to his lyricism, his poetic and moving imagery, and the authentic flavor of the vernacular language. Yet they have also found the characterizations flat and the story line thin, as is often the case with novels of social and political protest. The book was first published in 1980 in El Salvador and quickly excited so much interest there that Argueta was forced into exile and the book was banned. Since then, it has been translated and published in Italy, Germany, the Netherlands, and the United States. Argueta was not known widely outside his own country prior to the publication of this book, which has established him as a new and dynamic voice in Central American literature.

Sources for Further Study
Dickey, Christopher. Review in *The New Republic*. CLXXXIX (November 21, 1983), pp. 46-47.
Edelman, Marc. "The Rural Terror," in *Commonweal*. CXI (May 4, 1984), pp. 283-284.

Betty G. Gawthrop

ONE FLEW OVER THE CUCKOO'S NEST

Author: Ken Kesey (1935-   )
Type of plot: Mythic romance
Time of plot: The late 1950's
Locale: A mental hospital near Portland, Oregon
First published: 1962

Principal characters:
>   RANDLE PATRICK McMURPHY, a modern-day rebel cast in the
>   mode of the cowboy hero of the American Western
>   CHIEF BROMDEN, a tall and strong Native American who
>   feigns muteness and deafness to protect himself from pain
>   DALE HARDING, a highly literate and articulate man who fears
>   his sexuality
>   BILLY BIBBIT, a thirty-one-year-old man who is still under the
>   control of his mother
>   NURSE RATCHED, "Big Nurse," the ward superintendent, the
>   ultimate authority

The Novel

Told through the consciousness of the schizophrenic Chief Bromden, the events of the narrative are a replay of a mythic American past, where men were men and women were either unwelcome custodians of a "civilizing" culture or whores, carefree playmates of lusty, swaggering heroes. The choice of Bromden as a point-of-view character allows Kesey to provide the novel with a basic allegoric structure in which events of the plot can extend to microcosmic proportions. Bromden's paranoia makes credible his vision that the mental hospital is part of a gigantic American Combine where men are forced into a confinement that reduces them to impotent automatons restricted by Big Nurse, the ward superintendent and matriarch of the system.

In Bromden's view, Big Nurse and her black attendants represent the evil force that attempts to mold men into stamped-out replicas of one another. McMurphy represents the savior, the Christ, who gives battle and provides a model for salvation. The plot consists of a series of skirmishes between McMurphy and Big Nurse which gradually builds to a full-scale battle. Combat begins when McMurphy learns that the hospital inmates are controlled by a woman and end when, in a last-ditch effort, he attacks Big Nurse, attempting to force her to admit her femaleness and thus her vulnerability.

Between beginning and end, McMurphy takes on the stature of a full-blown American hero of legendary times: "My name is McMurphy, buddies, R. P. McMurphy, and I'm a gambling fool." He is also logger, Irishman,

Mike Fink, and Paul Bunyan, cowboy, Superman, and the Lone Ranger combined. The inmates of the hospital progress from audience to cheerleaders to disciples, and finally to participants in the madness of freedom defined first as a fishing trip then as an all-night drinking party replete with two prostitutes.

As the men grow stronger and more able to begin to carry on the fight for themselves, McMurphy grows weaker. When they return from the fishing trip, McMurphy looks worn-out, but he returns to the fray again and again and in so doing coaxes Chief Bromden out of hiding.

In his role of savior/Christ, McMurphy also becomes sacrificial victim, and the men whom he is attempting to save cheer him on to a kind of crucifixion—a series of electric shock treatments. When the attendant puts graphite salve on his temples, McMurphy comments: "Anointest my head with conductant. Do I get a crown of thorns?" As chief disciple, Bromden not only survives his own electric shock but also returns to the ward spreading stories about McMurphy's heroism, making him into a legend.

McMurphy recovers from the shock treatment and returns to the ward, weakened but not defeated. He presides over the rites of the drinking party and watches the hospital inmates finally take on the contours of manhood. As Bromden has shown his strength, so also does Harding, planning McMurphy's escape and the men's release.

Yet the drama, once started, must be played out to its inevitable conclusion—a final confrontation between McMurphy and Big Nurse. It is triggered by Billy Bibbit's suicide, which takes place after Big Nurse successfully reduces Billy from the potent manhood which he has achieved to an inarticulate and childlike impotence, thus negating McMurphy's power. When McMurphy attacks Big Nurse and rips open her white, starched uniform, her previously confined gigantic breasts spill out for all the men to see. McMurphy, however, is overpowered by the attendant, removed from the battlefield, and later, having been lobotomized, is returned to the ward, an empty husk of himself.

Bromden performs the final act. He will not allow McMurphy to live as a vegetable and a warning for all who try to buck the system. Rather he performs an ultimate act of love. Climbing on top of McMurphy, Bromden takes all of his strength to embrace and smother McMurphy with a pillow, and then the Indian leaves, running across the lawn toward the highway, taking high strides and seeming to fly on his way to freedom.

The Characters

Cast in a heroic mold, McMurphy is the dominant figure in the novel. He is a throwback to an earlier time, when a strong man could take what he wanted or easily manipulate those around him by the charm of his personality, the force of his character, and the power of his indomitable will. One of his strengths is his sense of humor, his ability to laugh not only at the absurdity around him but also at himself and at the role that he assumes. McMurphy is not a thinker, however, and his actions are more instinctive than learned. Dale Harding is a kind of counterpoint to McMurphy. While McMurphy acts out of the affective realm, Harding is mired in the cognitive.

Like Hamlet, Harding thinks too much, and the complications that he sees in the world around him defeat him. Harding marries a beautiful woman to assert a manhood that he believes he does not possess but thinks that he needs. The most articulate of the inmates, Harding explains his acquiescence to the treatment by reference to the fact that professionals know best. Where Bromden characterizes Nurse Ratched as enormous, capable of swelling up bigger and bigger to monstrous proportions, Harding says that she "may be a strict middle-aged lady, but she is not some kind of giant monster of the poultry clan pecking out our eyes." Yet when McMurphy insists that it is not their eyes but their vitals that she is after, Harding breaks down and admits that McMurphy speaks truth.

As narrator, Chief Bromden occupies a key position in the novel. Through his point of view, Kesey is able to achieve not only thematic statement but also surreal technique—enabling theme and technique to merge in dreamlike perspective. "It's the truth," Bromden says, "even if it didn't happen." From the very beginning, Bromden is roused by McMurphy's touch. Their initial clasping of hands is the first in a series of touches whereby there is an exchange of strength and energy from McMurphy to Bromden, until finally Bromden gives up his invisibility and allows himself to reenter the world of men.

The visible presence of women in the novel is limited to Big Nurse; several smaller nurses who pale beside her; two prostitutes who help McMurphy give the men back their manhood; in Bromden's memories, his white mother, a counterpart of Big Nurse; and Billy Bibbit's mother, whose stranglehold on her son matches Big Nurse's repression of the inmates.

Themes and Meanings

One Flew over the Cuckoo's Nest appears to be a modern morality play, where good ultimately triumphs over evil and where McMurphy's chief disciple escapes to spread the gospel. Such a reading could lead a perceptive critic to take Kesey to task for laboring under a reactionary and sexist myth involving the innate superiority of male sexuality over "womanish" values defined as "civilizing." If the castrating matriarchal system that Kesey describes will not allow boys to grow into men, the system defined by McMurphy keeps boys and girls together in a sexual Eden untouched by the real world. The "gambling men" of the mythic past can hardly handle the high technology of the future; contemporary America probably needs a restored Harding more than a resurrected McMurphy.

It does not make sense to argue that one cannot fault Kesey as author for a point of view expressed by Bromden. The most that one can say in defense of a theme that appears anachronistic is that Kesey seems aware of the problem. Through his point of view, Bromden makes the point that McMurphy "doled out his life for us to live, a rollicking past full of kid fun and drinking buddies and loving women and barroom battles over meager honors—for all of us to dream ourselves into." Harding comments during the all-night drinking party: "These things don't happen.... These things are fantasies you lie awake at night dreaming up and then are afraid to tell your analyst. You're not *really* here. That wine isn't real; *none* of this exists. Now, let's go on from there."

Critical Context

One Flew over the Cuckoo's Nest was Kesey's first published novel. It was acclaimed by both professional reviewers and scholarly critics, who called it brilliant, powerful, convincingly alive, glowing, authentic, a mythic confrontation, and a comic doomsday vision. During the ten years following its publication, the novel had a sale of more than a million copies and was made into a stage play and an immensely popular film.

A second novel, *Sometimes a Great Notion* (1964), followed. It too received critical acclaim and was made into a film, but it did not excite the popular imagination to the same extent as did *One Flew over the Cuckoo's Nest*. Two collections of essays and miscellaneous material followed: *Kesey's Garage Sale* in 1973, and *Kesey* in 1977. *Seven Prayers by Grandma Whittier*, a novel, was published serially (1977-1983) in Kesey's magazine *Spit in the Ocean*.

Primarily a novelist of the 1960's, Kesey had close affiliations with the counterculture that dominated the decade. Recent years have been marked by the publication of several books on Kesey and numerous articles.

Sources for Further Study

Fiedler, Leslie A. *The Return of the Vanishing American*, 1968.
Leeds, Barry H. *Ken Kesey*, 1981.
Porter, M. Gilbert. *The Art of Grit*. 1982.
Pratt, John C., ed. *One Flew over the Cuckoo's Nest: Text and Criticism*, 1973.
Tanner, Stephen L. *Ken Kesey*, 1983.
Tanner, Tony. *City of Worlds: American Fiction, 1950-1970*, 1971.
Wolfe, Tom. *The Electric Kool-Aid Acid Test*, 1968.

Mary Rohrberger

ONE HUNDRED YEARS OF SOLITUDE

Author: Gabriel García Márquez (1928-   )
Type of plot: Magical realism
Time of plot: From the 1820's to the 1920's
Locale: Macondo, a mythical town in an unnamed Latin American country
First published: Cien años de soledad, 1967 (English translation, 1970)

Principal characters:

MELQUÍADES, an old gypsy, a stand-in for the author

JOSÉ ARCADIO BUENDÍA, the family patriarch who is fascinated by inventions

ÚRSULA IGUARÁN, his wife, the source of the family's stability

JOSÉ ARCADIO, their Gargantuan older son who marries Rebeca

REBECA, their adopted daughter who eats dirt and whitewash

COLONEL AURELIANO BUENDÍA, their younger son, a famous Liberal revolutionary

AMARANTA, their daughter, a hardened spinster

PIETRO CRESPI, an Italian music master who dies for love of Amaranta

PILAR TERNERA, a part-time family servant who tells fortunes in cards

ARCADIO, her illegitimate son by José Arcadio, adopted by the Buendías

SANTA SOFÍA DE LA PIEDAD who marries Arcadio

REMEDIOS THE BEAUTY, their daughter who ascends to Heaven

JOSÉ ARCADIO SEGUNDO, their son, a frequenter of cockfights and a labor leader

AURELIANO SEGUNDO, his Dionysian twin who marries Fernanda del Carpio

FERNANDA DEL CARPIO, the scion of an old upland family, a prude and snob

RENATA REMEDIOS (MEME), their older daughter who is shut away in a convent

JOSÉ ARCADIO, their son, a homosexual supposedly training for the priesthood

AMARANTA ÚRSULA, their younger daughter who studies in Brussels

GASTON, her Flemish husband who is led on a silk leash

AURELIANO, Meme's illegitimate, scholarly son by Mauricio Babilonia

AURELIANO, Aureliano and Amaranta Úrsula's son, born
with a pig's tail

The Novel

One Hundred Years of Solitude chronicles the rise and decline of
Macondo, a mythical Latin American town, and of its leading family, the
Buendías. Located in a country resembling the author's native Colombia,
Macondo, by symbolic extension, suggests not only Colombia but also Latin
America generally, much as William Faulkner's Yoknapatawpha County is a
microcosm of the Deep South. The novel covers roughly the first century of
South American independence and appears to be a judgment on this his-
toric period, an era marred by violence, exploitation, stagnation, and disillu-
sion. Just as six generations of Buendías eventually bring forth a child with a
pig's tail, so García Márquez seems to see a pig's tail as the end product of
Latin America's first one hundred years of independence.

The problems of independence have their roots, to some extent, in the
"era of the first pig's tail," the colonial period. For the Buendías, the roots
reach all the way back to the sixteenth century, when "the pirate" Sir Francis Drake raids Riohacha, causing Úrsula Iguarán's great-great-grand-
mother, frightened by the English with "their ferocious attack dogs" and
"red-hot irons," to sit on a hot stove. To escape the English pirates, the
Iguaráns migrate from the seacoast to a peaceful Indian village in the foot-
hills, where they intermarry with the Buendías for three centuries. Such inbreeding produces the first pig-tailed boy, near the end of the colonial
period, from the union of Úrsula Iguarán's aunt and José Arcadio Buendía's
uncle.

Married first cousins, Úrsula Iguarán and José Arcadio Buendía are
afraid of breeding another pig-tailed child or, even worse, iguanas. In the
long run, their fear is a self-fulfilling prophecy, like the great-great-grand-
mother's shameful branding, but they hold off the fate for six generations
with another migration. The migration comes about because Úrsula Iguarán
wears a chastity belt for the first eighteen months of marriage and, taunted
by an angry cock-fighting opponent for his rumored impotency, José
Arcadio Buendía kills the man. To escape the man's ghost and make a fresh
start, José Arcadio Buendía leads a hardy band of young pioneers across
the mountains. After wandering aimlessly for more than two years, the
band settles in the middle of a rather allegorical swamp when José Arcadio
Buendía has an equally allegorical dream of a city built of mirrors.

On such auspicious foundations rises Macondo. At first only an isolated
village, Macondo is happy and prosperous, especially proud that it has no
need for a graveyard. From the first, however, Macondo is plagued by gypsies who come bearing gifts, some the products of the new science and others the remnants of old superstitions and frivolities. This hodgepodge forms

the village's learning, yet, except for old Melquíades, the gypsies are not so much teachers as hucksters intent on gulling the ignorant villagers. Indeed, the gypsies are precursors of the latter-day Anglo pirates, the American banana entrepreneurs who appear later in the century, transform Macondo society, and then leave it stagnant.

Even without rapacious outsiders, Macondo eventually creates plenty of trouble for itself. The second generation of Macondo Buendía includes a Liberal colonel who starts thirty-two revolutions and loses them all; the third generation produces a petty town dictator who rules Macondo by decree and firing squad; and in the fourth generation, a Buendía labor leader succeeds only in getting his followers murdered *en masse*. After this massacre in a town that once bragged about not needing a graveyard, the banana company leaves, and Macondo slips into a sleepy decadence. The businesses close, houses fall, and young people depart.

At the Buendía mansion, the weeds and termites are encroaching while the fifth Buendía generation, returned from abroad, entertains itself with homosexuality and incest. The sixth generation, a reclusive scholar deciphering Melquíades' writings, is also involved in the latter entertainment, thereby producing the lucky seventh generation, a pig-tailed boy appropriately named after his father. When the mother dies, the father goes off to soak himself in a whorehouse, and the unattended baby is eaten by an army of red ants: it is time for Macondo to call it quits. A whirlwind rises and wipes the town off the face of the earth, just as the sobered scholar deciphers Melquíades' prediction of the end.

The Characters

Despite its apocalyptic ending and overall gloomy picture—apparent only upon finishing the book and upon somber reflection—*One Hundred Years of Solitude* is a highly entertaining novel. First, the author's tone is not at all gloomy, but rather jaunty and playful. Second, the fast-paced narrative features some new, juicy morsel of humor, sex, or violence on almost every page and is enhanced by García Márquez' Magical Realism, which interweaves exaggeration and fantasy into the basically realistic texture of the tale. Finally, *One Hundred Years of Solitude* contains one of the most entertaining sets of characters in modern literature.

There is, for example, the sexually well-endowed José Arcadio, whose practice is to hold a lottery to see which eager woman will have the honor of sleeping with him. There is slothful Remedios the Beauty, who is so innocent that she is unaware of her devastating effect on men and who floats off to Heaven holding onto the family sheets. An example of another sort is Amaranta, who competes with Rebeca, her adopted sister, for the love of Pietro Crespi, the Italian music master. At first Pietro prefers Rebeca, but when Rebeca drops him for José Arcadio, Pietro turns to Amaranta. The rancorous Amaranta strings him along for a year or two; then, after their engagement has been announced and wedding plans made, she cruelly refuses him: "Don't be simple, Crespi. . . . I wouldn't marry you even if I were dead." After suffering humiliations and torments, Crespi slits his wrists. In remorse, Amaranta plunges her hand into a fire and, for the rest of her life, wears her hand covered with black gauze.

Besides being interesting in itself, Amaranta's behavior might be another comment on the Latin American soul. For, at the same time that the characters of *One Hundred Years of Solitude* have their individual adventures and pursue their personal fates, they also exist within the novel's historical framework, to which they contribute. Some characters, such as Colonel Aureliano Buendía, suggest certain prominent Latin American types, and the Buendías collectively suggest the development of a leading family.

A number of Buendía men offer clues to the course of history. The earlier generations include several who are immensely civic-minded and well-meaning, but for various reasons their efforts prove to be impotent, even baneful, and the men go down in defeat. José Arcadio Buendía, the founding father, situates Macondo in a swamp and pursues visionary schemes until his mind cracks; he remains tied to a tree in the backyard for years until he finally expires. Colonel Aureliano Buendía, the great Liberal revolutionary, eventually forgets what he is fighting for; he ends his days making little trinkets in a back room of the house. Young Arcadio, briefly the town's ruler, has quick solutions for problems—decrees and firing squads; his grandmother gives him a good whipping, and he soon faces a firing squad himself. José Arcadio Segundo organizes the banana workers, who are then massacred; when news of the massacre is suppressed, he cannot convince anyone that it occurred and ends up hiding from the authorities in a back room. These men all start with impeccable ideals.

The women also contribute to history, mainly by providing stability and continuity. Úrsula Iguarán, the Buendía matriarch, is a bastion of family stability. Another stabilizing force, in her own way, is Pilar Ternera, who introduces most of the Buendía men to sex. Yet the women also help bring about some unfortunate results: With their interest in stability, they tend to institutionalize snobbishness, respectability, and conventionality. Úrsula Iguarán will not allow José Arcadio Buendía to move Macondo to a better location, and she will invite only members of the founding families to her home (later, the banana people invite themselves). The negative influence of women reaches its apex in Fernanda del Carpio, who formalizes family rituals and is too snobbish to mix with society. Interestingly enough, the women even grudgingly accept the arrangement whereby a man has a wife for family and a mistress for fun.

It is not surprising that later generations of Buendías forget about history and instead withdraw to their private concerns. Aureliano Segundo sets the style with his fabulous appetites, his mistress, and his parties; significantly, he marries Fernanda del Carpio, the epitome of aristocratic decadence. Their older daughter, Meme, falls in love with an automobile mechanic, has an illegitimate child, and is sent away to a convent (she never speaks again in her life). Their other two children, sent to study in Europe, finally return many years later. The sybaritic José Arcadio, thought by his mother to be a potential pope, is drowned in his bathtub by his flock of boys. Amaranta Úrsula, despite her husband Gaston's lovemaking skills, becomes involved with her sister Meme's illegitimate son, the scholar Aureliano, who has been shut in a back room for most of his life and whose relationship with her is unknown but suspected. She dies giving birth to the pig-tailed child.

Themes and Meanings

The main theme of *One Hundred Years of Solitude* is the awful disappointment of Latin America's first century of independence: One can bear to think about the disappointment only by treating it as a joke. Yet the causes of the disappointment are no joke: ignorance, violence, exploitation, rigid conventionality. García Márquez seems to see these causes arising, in turn, from the ingrown nature of Latin American society, as suggested by his novel's title and by other indications. Latin America is represented as Macondo, a small town whose inhabitants possess a small-town mentality. The Buendía family names are repeated through different generations to the point of mass confusion. Throughout the novel, there is an obsession with inbreeding and incest. José Arcadio marries Rebeca, his adopted sister, and Arcadio lusts after Pilar Ternera, his mother (though unknown to him), and Amaranta, his aunt. Even Pilar Ternera is a sort of mother surrogate for the boys she beds. A soldier sums up the obsession when he jokingly says that the Liberal revolutions are for the right to marry one's mother. The pig's tail is the unnatural result of such an incestuous society, the apocalyptic ending an appropriate punishment.

Some readers of *One Hundred Years of Solitude* have been inclined to see the novel as a reactionary retreat from the leftist sympathies that García Márquez has expressed elsewhere, particularly in his nonfiction. Such readers are surely guilty of ingrown understandings. García Márquez' condemnation of Latin American history in *One Hundred Years of Solitude* not only is consistent with his leftist views but also undergirds them. What could be more revolutionary than the novel's ending, which seems to call not for the Liberal variety of revolution but for one which destroys the old order?

The revolutionary potential of art is implied by the novel's secondary theme, which explores the relationship of art and life. On the one hand, art imitates life—to the point in *One Hundred Years of Solitude* in which García Márquez includes playful references to himself, his wife, and the work of fellow novelists. On the other hand, life imitates art: Melquíades' writings are both record and prophecy. Telling the story being lived in the novel, Melquíades is a stand-in for the author, who records, prophesies, entertains, and presumably influences events just as the old gypsy does. More ironic aspects of the author are suggested by the bookish Aureliano, who interprets history only as he suffers it; by Aureliano's best friend, Gabriel (great-great-grandson of Colonel Gerineldo Márquez), who is last seen leaving Macondo—for good reason—to become a starving writer in Paris; and by Aureliano's mentor, an old Catalonian bookseller who writes three boxes full of purple prose.

Critical Context

Internationally read and admired, Gabriel García Márquez was awarded the 1982 Nobel Prize for Literature. Yet even the Nobel Prize does not adequately denote his achievement, which ranks with that of James Joyce and William Faulkner. Like these two writers, García Márquez has staked out his literary territory. He himself acknowledges the strong influence of Faulkner, especially apparent in *One Hundred Years of Solitude*, where the sound and fury of Latin American history signifies nothing.

In *One Hundred Years of Solitude*, widely regarded as his masterpiece, García Márquez solved the main problems of the modernist writer better than Joyce and Faulkner did—how to cover complex material and pessimistic themes and still be accessible and entertaining. Unlike Joyce and Faulkner, García Márquez also gives his work political direction, which provides an antidote to modernist nihilistic tendencies.

García Márquez solved his problems in *One Hundred Years of Solitude* by dropping some of the duller, more obscure modernist techniques and returning to earlier modes of narration, modes possibly suggested by his native background. Adopting the role of omniscient author, García Márquez, like Faulkner in *The Hamlet* (1940), sounds like a spinner of tall tales drawing on local folklore. His Magical Realism was antedated by François Rabelais and Voltaire, as was his fast-paced action. García Márquez integrated these older techniques into his modernist outlook, making *One Hundred Years of Solitude* a work that no reader should miss.

Sources for Further Study

Brotherston, Gordon. *The Emergence of the Latin American Novel*, 1977.
Janes, Regina. *Gabriel García Márquez: Revolutions in Wonderland*, 1981.
McMurray, George R. *Gabriel García Márquez*, 1977.
Stone, Peter H. "The Art of Fiction LXIX," in *The Paris Review*. No. 82 (Winter, 1981), pp. 44-73.
Vargas Llosa, Mario. *García Márquez: Historia de un deicidio*, 1971.

Harold Branam

ONE WAY TO HEAVEN

Author: Countée Cullen (Countée Porter, 1903-1946)
Type of plot: Ethnic realism
Time of plot: The 1920's
Locale: New York City's Harlem
First published: 1932

>   *Principal characters:*
>   MATTIE JOHNSON, an attractive young black woman who
>   works as a domestic servant
>   SAM LUCAS, a one-armed confidence man who marries Mattie
>   AUNT MANDY, Mattie's aunt
>   EMMA MAY, Sam's mistress
>   CONSTANCIA BRANDON, Mattie's employer
>   THE REVEREND CLARENCE JOHNSON, a preacher who knows
>   that Sam is a confidence artist

The Novel

Countée Cullen, well known as a black poet, wrote only one novel, *One Way to Heaven*. Given the fervor of the Harlem Renaissance, in which Cullen was an active participant, it is not surprising that he would turn his talents to writing a book that reflected elements of this movement.

One Way to Heaven has been called two novels in one, largely because it has a dual focus. On the one hand, it is concerned with Mattie Johnson and her love affair with Sam Lucas, a dark, handsome, one-armed confidence man from Texas who never stays long in one place. On the other hand, the novel is a satire on the social life of Harlem's emerging middle-class black population.

The common thread in the two stories is that Mattie Johnson, a good-looking young black woman, works as a domestic servant for Constancia Brandon, wife of Dr. George Brandon, a physician from Oklahoma who has made considerable money in oil. Constancia, light enough to pass for white, is exhilarated by life in Harlem, where she is a well-established hostess and organizer of social events.

The Mattie-Sam story begins when Sam goes to the Mt. Hebron Episcopal Church in Harlem and there undergoes a conversion to the faith. Unknown to Mattie, it is part of Sam's habitual pattern when he goes to a new place to undergo a public conversion in order to make the congregation have confidence in him.

Sam's performance at the Mt. Hebron Episcopal Church is superb. He goes to the altar with tears welling up in his eyes, but not before he has taken from his pocket and dashed to the floor a deck of playing cards and an "evil looking razor," which are devices of the Devil. So impressed is the congregation that nine other people, including Mattie, who up until this time has been reluctant to be converted, follow Sam to the altar. After Sam has been converted, members of the congregation flock around him, some forcing money upon him.

The Reverend Clarence Johnson, who is present for Sam's conversion, recognizes Sam as a drifter who has undergone a similar conversion in his presence in Memphis some time before. He does not make much of this fact, however, and instead ruminates on Sam's success in bringing nine other souls to God, a record that the Reverend Johnson himself could not have equaled that day.

Mattie falls in love with Sam instantly, and before long they are married. Constancia Brandon insists on having the wedding at her residence, and she is also instrumental in arranging for Sam to be employed as doorman at a nearby theater. Sam certainly is not the marrying kind, and he soon succumbs to the flirtations of Emma May, the usher in the theater where he is doorman.

Mattie by this time has become pregnant. Her baby dies a few hours after it is born, and Sam leaves Mattie to go off and live with Emma May. Mattie is looked after by Aunt Mandy, an old black woman whose faith is a mixture of pagan animism and Christianity. Aunt Mandy blames Mattie for Sam's leaving.

Eventually Sam falls ill with pneumonia, and Mattie generously agrees to take him back and to care for him in his illness. She expresses her concern to Aunt Mandy that Sam has not truly been saved. She wants to be with him and their baby in the Hereafter.

Aunt Mandy tells Mattie that sometimes dying people receive signs, hear celestial choirs, and are converted before they finally expire. Sam, overhearing the conversation, feigns a genuine conversion out of deference to Mattie. This is the first selfless act that Sam has committed, and through it Mattie has the comfort of thinking that he will die in a state of grace.

Interwoven with the Mattie-Sam plot are the Constancia Brandon episodes. Actually this portion of the book has no consistent plot but is rather a series of highly satiric and quite entertaining vignettes about life among fairly well-to-do blacks in Harlem during the 1920's.

In the preface to *One Way to Heaven*, Cullen waggishly states, "Some of the characters in this book are fictitious." Actually, anyone who knows anything about Harlem's salon society of that day can identify many of the people who drift in and out of Constancia's soirees. Langston Hughes writes about many of the same people, using their actual names, in the first volume of his autobiography, *The Big Sea* (1940).

One of the more ironic episodes concerning Constancia occurs when she invites to one of her parties a professor from a Southern state who has published a book entitled *The Menace of the Negro in Our American Society*. She proceeds to have this august man lecture to the assembled guests on the subject of his book. When he has finished, Constancia leads the applause and more or less intimidates her black guests into joining her in this applause.

It is worth noting that Cullen does not report this incident with bitterness or rancor. He sees the irony in it. He reports the event and allows the irony to speak for itself. He lets his readers draw their own conclusions. This detached quality, the sure indication of people secure in their own identities, was a hallmark of Countée Cullen, and a study of his correspondence confirms the fact that he was capable of standing back and observing dispassionately situations such as the one described here. He was also capable of laughing at himself, and this quality carries over significantly into his writing.

In *One Way to Heaven*, Cullen set out to depict the contrast between two socioeconomic levels of Harlem's emerging society during one of the most interesting periods of its development. He succeeds up to a point, although he never manages to merge the two salient and contrasting elements of his book into the unified whole that would have made the novel more artistically sound.

The Characters

Sam Lucas is one of the memorable characters of the black novels of this period. Sam is more amoral than immoral. He lives his life as he thinks he must. He has always been a drifter, perpetrating his confidence schemes upon the innocent and then leaving for more fertile fields. He is dashing and romantic, and his having only one arm makes him a sympathetic figure to many of the people of whom he is trying to take advantage. Cullen's description of his going down the aisle of the church to be converted with the left sleeve of his coat hanging empty beside him indicates how Sam can turn any adversity into something of personal benefit.

Mattie Johnson is in many ways Sam's opposite. Mattie knows what she believes and is resolute in her beliefs. She is human enough, however, to be swayed emotionally by the kind of display that Sam puts on during his conversion in the Mt. Hebron Episcopal Church. One must remember that Sam swayed eight other unredeemed souls besides Mattie, so his was a virtuoso performance.

Mattie is simple but not stupid. Although she falls in love with Sam at first sight, she is resolute in her love for him. She not only stays with him until the end, but she also touches him in such a way that because of her he does the most noble thing of his life in order to bring her a modicum of comfort before he dies.

Despite Sam's dalliance with Emma and despite Mattie's deep sorrow at the loss of their child, Mattie considers herself to be Sam's wife for all time. Mattie's simple faith and her ability to accept life's realities make her an appealing and highly sympathetic character in the novel.

Aunt Mandy, a wise old woman with definite opinions, is important to the resolution of the conflict between Mattie and Sam. Aunt Mandy's religious beliefs are partly those of her pagan African forebears and partly those of the Christian society in which she has been reared. This old woman is essentially kind. Although she blames Mattie quite falsely for the breakup of her marriage, she is supportive of Mattie and does everything she can to help her. She also precipitates Sam's last phony conversion, indeed his best conversion, by telling Mattie that sometimes unsaved souls on their deathbeds receive signs and come to true salvation at the last moment.

Mattie's employer, Constancia, is an interesting type. She chooses to live her life in the black world rather than in the white world in which she could easily pass. She considers the black world more interesting and vital than the white world. Constancia is at times pompous and is given to using overblown language with rather comic results. Nevertheless, she is a reasonably bright woman and she is well-meaning. She is more stereotyped than is a character such as Mattie, but she serves well Cullen's artistic purpose of being a center of activity, a source of energy that Cullen needs to depict the social frenzy of middle-class blacks caught up in the Harlem Renaissance.

Themes and Meanings

One Way to Heaven is a study in contrasts. On an obvious level, Cullen is comparing the life of poor blacks in Harlem during the 1920's with that of affluent blacks. The comparison is sharp and effective, despite the author's failure to merge his two distinct story lines in such a way as to achieve a unified novel.

On another level, the love story of Mattie and Sam is one of sharp contrasts. Sam is the scheming, opportunistic gambler, the wanderer who deplores settling down, who feels trapped in the routine of what most people would call a normal existence—having a steady job, marrying, having children. Sam is not basically a bad person. Rather he is a person who lives from day to day and who has been accustomed to living only for himself.

Mattie, conversely, wants to have a normal life. She wants to be a wife and mother. She is capable of devotion to another person and she is willing to give of herself. So devoted and dependable is she that she is willing to forgive Sam for leaving her and going to live with Emma May when Mattie most needed him.

If Cullen does not draw many conclusions about his first contrastive theme, the socioeconomic one, he certainly seems in the second theme to leave the reader with the idea that love not only will triumph but also will ennoble one. Sam dies ennobled because, at the very end of his life, he has finally recognized the depth of Mattie's devotion. Yet, more important, through doing so, he has come to realize that he stands to gain satisfaction from doing something that will give Mattie peace of mind.

Critical Context

The period that Cullen depicts in *One Way to Heaven*, the 1920's, was one of immense social and artistic activity in Harlem. Black journals such as *Quill*, *Stylus*, and *Black Opals* sprang up, although, as is often the case with small literary magazines, few lasted for long. Such major black publications as *Opportunity*, *Messenger*, and *The Crisis* published the best black writers of the period.

As noted above, Langston Hughes chronicled the social life of this period in the first volume of his autobiography, *The Big Sea*. Earlier, Hughes—like Cullen, essentially a poet—wrote his only novel, *Not Without Laughter* (1930), as a means of capturing some of the excitement and electricity of the Harlem Renaissance. In his character Tempy, Hughes satirizes the black social climber of the period who forsakes the Baptist Church and becomes an Episcopalian in order to gain a social advantage.

Claude McKay's *Home to Harlem* (1928), *Banjo* (1929), and *Banana Bottom* (1933) also focused on the social changes occurring in Harlem during its renaissance, and Rudolph Fisher's *The Walls of Jericho* (1928) provided readers with uproariously comic satire about the social climbers of the period. George S. Schuyler's *Black No More* (1931) and *Slaves Today: A Story of Liberia* (1931) were also important social satires of the period.

The main distinguishing characteristics of Cullen's only novel are that its author was writing more for a black audience than his contemporaries were and that in it he dwelt less on the social and economic indignities of black people than he did on some of their social institutions, such as the Church. Cullen is never bitter in his depictions. He treats his raw material with curiosity and love more than with antagonism and anger.

Sources for Further Study
Davis, Arthur P. *From the Dark Tower: Afro-American Writers from 1900 to 1960*, 1974.
Ferguson, Blanche E. *Countee Cullen and the Negro Renaissance*, 1966.
Shucard, Alan R. *Countee Cullen*, 1984.
Singh, Amritjit. *The Novels of the Harlem Renaissance: Twelve Black Writers, 1923-1933*, 1976.
Starke, Catherine J. *Black Portraiture in American Fiction*, 1971.

R. Baird Shuman

THE OPTIMIST'S DAUGHTER

Author: Eudora Welty (1909-   )
Type of plot: Domestic realism
Time of plot: The early 1960's
Locale: New Orleans and the fictional town of "Mount Salus," Mississippi
First published: 1969; enlarged, 1972

> *Principal characters:*
> LAUREL MCKELVA HAND, a widow in her mid-forties and a
>   successful fabric designer living in Chicago
> JUDGE CLINTON MCKELVA, her father, who is retired from the
>   bench in Mount Salus, Mississippi
> WANDA FAY CHISOM MCKELVA, the judge's second wife, a vul-
>   gar, insensitive, gold-digging refugee from a typing pool
> MAJOR RUPERT BULLOCK, a friend of the judge since boyhood
> MISS ADELE COURTLAND, a Mount Salus schoolteacher and
>   the McKelvas' next-door neighbor

The Novel

"Is it the Carnival?" asks Fay, as she and Laurel ride through New Orleans in a taxi. It *is* Mardi Gras, though hardly a festive occasion: The two
have just left a hospital where, less than an hour earlier, they witnessed the
death of Judge McKelva, Fay's husband and Laurel's father.

Fay's incongruous question typifies the uncomprehending, inadequate,
and inappropriate responses to life by many characters in *The Optimist's
Daughter*. The world of these characters is a microcosm of the larger world
glimpsed through carnival-week New Orleans, where Laurel can hear "the
crowd noise, the unmistakable sound of hundreds, of thousands, of people
blundering." To Laurel, all of them, especially Fay and her Snopesian kin-
folk, are part of "the great, interrelated family of those who never know the
meaning of what has happened to them."

Despite its characters' bafflement, the novel tells a simple story. Laurel
temporarily leaves her Chicago studio to be at home with her father after he
mentions casually that he is consulting the family doctor for an eye problem.
Together, he, Laurel, and Fay—his new wife after ten years as a widower—
travel to New Orleans, where they learn that he needs surgery for a torn
retina. Fay quickly reveals her selfishness by exclaiming, "I don't see why
this had to happen to *me*."

Though the operation is a success, Fay lacks the patience to wait out her
husband's convalescence. Angry and uncomprehending, she tries to goad
him into leaving his sickbed to take her to the Carnival. One night she
throws herself on his body—immobilized on doctor's orders—crying, "I tell

you enough is enough! This is my birthday!" Shocked by Fay's insensitive, and impossible demands, his concentration on recovery shattered, Judge McKelva gives up the ghost.

Laurel and Fay return with his body to the family home in Mount Salus, Mississippi. The townsfolk crowd into the house to mourn this revered public figure and pay respects to his daughter, whom they have known since her birth. (His upstart wife is barely tolerated by many who honor the memory of Laurel's mother, Becky.) Yet as they swap contradictory anecdotes about the judge, Laurel realizes that no two of them perceive her father alike, and none remembers him accurately.

Like New Orleans at Mardi Gras, Mount Salus becomes a stage where farce vies with tragedy. Fay indulges in self-pitying histrionics; some townspeople pointedly snub one another despite the sad occasion; Fay's vulgar relatives descend on the house to chat over the corpse: "Out of curiosity, who does he remind you of?" the mother asks her father-in-law. "Nobody," he replies.

These present absurdities contrast painfully with Laurel's memory of an idyllic childhood, of a rich inner life under the tutelage of loving, sensitive parents. Yet Laurel's past also involves the recollection of her mother's agonizing death and the recognition that Becky, in her own way, had made as many unreasoning demands on the judge as had Fay. Laurel realizes suddenly that, like the "blunderers" of the story, she has yet to understand fully what has happened in her life.

Resolution comes after a final confrontation with Fay, whom Laurel holds responsible for her father's death. As the judge's second wife and the heiress to the McKelva home, Fay is in some sense a rival for possession of Laurel's own past. Yet Laurel, having barely restrained an impulse to do Fay violence, attains peace once she understands that "Memory lived not in initial possession but in the freed hands, pardoned and freed, and in the heart that can empty but fill again, in the patterns restored by dreams." Laurel is free to return to the life she has made for herself in Chicago.

The Characters

A key to understanding many of Eudora Welty's characters is the use that they make of their past. Those who distort their memories, or who fail to remember experience at all, are in no position to learn from it, but, to be remembered, experience has to mean something. Fay has no guiding principle for her present actions because she attaches no significance to the past—either her own or Judge McKelva's. So she "blunders."

"Blundering" in a major character such as Fay represents a major evil; in minor characters, Welty renders it comically. Among a handful of Mount Salus eccentrics at Judge McKelva's wake is Verna Longmeier, the sewing lady, who recounts memories of Christmas dances that never happened:

I remember, oh, I remember how many Christmases I was among those present in this dear old home in all its hospitality. . . . And they'd throw open those doors between these double parlors and the music would strike up! And then—"Miss Verna drew out her arm as though to measure a yard—" then Clinton and I, we'd lead out the dance.

Yet this novel is Laurel's story. She is the title character—her father being the "Optimist"—and the book chronicles her struggle to comprehend the spiritual legacy of her parents. If she is unveiled slowly—the early chapters barely hint at her troubled soul—it is because at first she has no time to remember that legacy. While the focus is on her father's illness and death, Laurel appears the most stable figure, standing watch, reading to him by the hour, asking (as Fay does not) the responsible questions of the doctor. Only when these exigencies are past, and her moment of truth can no longer be postponed, is she revealed in her loneliness and conflict.

In contrast to Laurel, Fay is fully revealed from the first time she speaks. Implicitly, therefore, she lacks all depth; it takes but a moment to sound her. Since the world of the novel is seen primarily through Laurel's eyes, and since Laurel cannot be generous to Fay, some critics have asked if the portrayal of Fay is not excessively hostile. Indeed, she is shown from first to last as a mean-spirited, greedy, unfeeling little shrew; for Welty, this is rather a flat characterization. Yet Fay is less a foil than a catalyst: It takes someone with her extreme traits to jar Laurel out of her false recollections of the relationship between her parents. It was her father the "Optimist" who married both Becky and Fay, and not one wife, but both wives wore him down.

Moreover, Welty introduces another viewpoint than Laurel's to humanize Fay. It is the viewpoint of Miss Adele Courtland, the McKelvas' next-door neighbor—who, it is hinted, would have made a suitable and willing second wife for the judge. In her wisdom born of denial, she defends Fay against judgment by Laurel's standards. Concerning the antics of Fay and her family at the wake, Adele says, "It's true they were a trifle more inelegant [than the Mount Salus gentry]. . . . But only a trifle." Attempting to explain Fay's seemingly tasteless show of grief, Adele says, "I further believe Fay thought she was rising in the estimation of Mount Salus, there in front of all [Clinton's] lifelong friends . . . on what she thought was the prime occasion for doing it."

Class consciousness, though never explicitly identified, figures prominently in the thoughts of many characters in *The Optimist's Daughter*. (Memory forms the basis of upper-class tradition, while the lower classes are thought of as having no past). Yet Mount Salus aristocrats show a curious lack of breeding. They ignore Fay, the low-class Texan, as far as possible without offending her doting husband. His doctor "looked at her briefly, as if he had seen many like Fay." Death, however, is the great leveler: The ever-tippling Major Rupert Bullock, a lifelong friend of the judge, talks like one of Fay's vulgar family members when he tries to console her. As they stand over the coffin, he says, "Just tell him goodbye, sugar. . . . That's best, just plant him a kiss."

Themes and Meanings

Recurrent in Welty's fiction, including *The Optimist's Daughter*, is the paradox of the family as both nurturing and stifling. Despite their powerful mutual affection, Laurel—and, in her memory, Becky and Clinton— emerge as lonely figures, each thrown back on his or her waning strength when disaster strikes. Apparently, love has no power to prevent human tragedy; and, when they cannot help or be helped by those whom they love, they become cruel—not always unwittingly.

The characters change, then, in reaction to events that they cannot control. It was during Becky's final illness, and in response to a hateful outburst from her, that Judge McKelva became "what he scowlingly called an optimist; . . . refused to consider that she was desperate. It was betrayal on betrayal." If the memory of such events can wound Laurel, the reviving memory of happier times can heal her. "Memory had the character of spring. Sometimes it was the old wood that did the blooming."

Ultimately, it is suggested that the barriers imposed by time and change are illusory. On her last night in Mount Salus, Laurel dreams about riding in a train with her long-dead husband, Phil, past the confluence of the Ohio and Mississippi rivers near Cairo, Illinois. Waking, she understands that

> . . . her life, any life . . . was nothing but the continuity of its love. She believed it just as she believed that the confluence of waters was still happening at Cairo. It would be there the same as it ever was when she went flying over it today on her way back—out of sight, for her, this time, thousands of feet below, but with nothing in between except thin air.

Laurel also perceives that she and Phil "were part of the confluence. Their own act of faith had brought them here . . ." Evil, for Laurel (and for Welty), consists in refusing to acknowledge the universal human experience, denying the power of memory and faith to transcend the accidents of time and place. The final moral perception regarding Fay is that, lacking passion and imagination of her own, she "had no way to see it or reach it in the other person. Other people, inside their lives, might as well be invisible to her." Fay and the rest of the "blunderers" are not simply victims of a gratuitously hostile portrait; like Malvolio at the end of *Twelfth Night*, they impose isolation on themselves and project it onto others.

Critical Context

Eudora Welty's works have attracted a faithful, though seldom numerous, following. *The Optimist's Daughter*, first published in *The New Yorker*, did command a wide readership; it also brought its author critical acclaim and a Pulitzer Prize. The much-honored Welty also has received the National Institute of Arts and Letters Gold Medal for the Novel, as well as the National Medal for Literature for lifetime achievement.

Since the beginning of her career, Welty has explored such universally compelling subjects as marriage and family, social and class morality, the sense of community versus the sense of aloneness—and the variety of possible attitudes toward memory. For example, the inability to draw moral lessons from remembered experience is shown to be a great affliction in *The Ponder Heart* (1954) just as it is in *The Optimist's Daughter*. Yet unlike Welty's previous novel, *Losing Battles* (1970)—a long and convoluted exploration of the past—*The Optimist's Daughter* is a brief, intense treatment of past events recollected in the present.

What most sets this novel apart from Welty's other fiction, however, is a clear sense of its main character's liberation—first from rural life without a profession, and then from the power of unhappy and confusing memories. *The Optimist's Daughter* is also outstanding for its artistic unity; it is a work that reveals, rather than simply describing, the truths it contains.

Sources for Further Study
Desmond, John F., ed. *A Still Moment: Essays in the Art of Eudora Welty*, 1978.
Evans, Elizabeth. *Eudora Welty*, 1981.
Prenshaw, Peggy Whitman, ed. *Conversations with Eudora Welty*, 1984.
Vande Kieft, Ruth. *Eudora Welty*, 1962.

Thomas Rankin

OUTER DARK

Author: Cormac McCarthy (1933-   )
Type of plot: Surrealistic parable
Time of plot: Indefinite, but probably the beginning of the twentieth century
Locale: Indefinite, but probably Southern Appalachia
First published: 1968

> *Principal characters:*
> RINTHY HOLME, a young mountain girl and new mother in
>   search of her missing baby
> CULLA HOLME, Rinthy's brother and the father of her child;
>   he abandons the baby in the woods shortly after its birth
> AN UNNAMED TINKER, who finds the child and takes it away,
>   thus initiating the ensuing search
> THREE MEN OF DARKNESS, who appear at intervals throughout
>   the journey and commit acts of brutality and mayhem

The Novel

Outer Dark is a story of sin and retribution, played out in folktale fashion against an indefinite time and place. It begins with the birth of a child, the incestuous offspring of Culla Holme and his sister Rinthy, who live in the mountainous recesses of Johnson County (no state is indicated). Culla, ashamed and frightened by his misdeed, refuses to summon aid for his sister, forcing her to give birth in the secrecy of their isolated cabin. When the child, a boy, is finally born after a long laboring, Culla takes the baby deep into the surrounding woods and leaves it, later telling Rinthy that it was sickly and died while she slept. Rinthy, however, refuses to believe her brother, especially when, after being led to the supposed grave site, she can find no trace of the baby's remains. Convinced that Culla has given the child to a wandering tinker, who appeared at the cabin shortly before the birth, Rinthy sneaks away from her brother in a blind search for the old man and her baby. When Culla discovers her absence, he follows after her, with no real understanding of his purpose in doing so.

The novel is thus constructed in terms of the encounters these two characters experience as they wander throughout a dreamlike and most often nightmarish landscape. The tinker disappears, known only by rumor, but Rinthy is led by a kind of innocence and faith that protects and sustains her. Culla, on the other hand, following in his sister's steps, becomes an Ishmael in this outside world, suspect and fugitive wherever he goes. His guilt concerning the child dogs him and takes on a universal identity. He is anathema to those he meets.

At intervals during Culla's wanderings there appear three dark figures—

perhaps escaped murderers, perhaps malignant supernatural beings, perhaps even the demonic shapes of Satan himself. Dressed in clothes stolen from the grave, these manifestations plague the land with atrocities, deeds for which Culla is inevitably blamed. The leader, clad in black, proclaims himself a minister. His two followers are a psychopath named Harmon (the only one of the three with a name) and a mute, monstrous idiot. Emblems of horrifying evil, these three are also figures of judgment and retribution who face Culla with his overwhelming guilt and exact punishment in a final scene of inevitable justice.

The Characters

The characters in *Outer Dark* are drawn in broad surface strokes. The reader rarely enters their minds, and he is often left to guess at their motivations, which may be quite different from their stated purposes. For example, Culla Holme is ashamed of his incestuous coupling with his sister. When Rinthy is in labor, Culla refuses to summon outside help, even that of an old witch, a "midnight woman," because "She'd tell." "Who is they to tell?" Rinthy asks. " Anybody," Culla answers. Although he himself helps with the birth, he does so only at the last minute, after his sister has undergone great pain. Clearly he is giving her a chance to die, hoping that she will take the proof of their sin with her.

Culla's attempt to rid himself of the child after its birth is also marked by a combination of cruelty and cowardice. Rather than simply murder the child, he leaves it to die in the midst of the night swamp and flees in dread and panic from the sight and sound of his wailing son. Yet in his flight he becomes lost and circles unknowingly back to the scene of his guilt, where the baby still howls in outrage and accusation.

The pattern is repeated after Rinthy takes off in search of the child. Culla comes after, perhaps to find Rinthy, although he never asks of her from the strangers he meets on the way. Indeed, it is possible that Culla's following his sister is more a matter of fate than intent, and that his movement is still flight rather than search. Moreover, his journey continues to circle, and the book ends as he walks along a road leading to a swamp, likely the very one in which he was lost at the beginning.

Rinthy Holme owes much of her characterization to William Faulkner's Lena Grove in *Light in August*. Like Lena, Rinthy is, despite her obvious sexual experience, an innocent in the alien world. She has true love for her child, who causes her neither shame nor regret. When Culla tells her that the child is dead, she wants to see the grave, to lay her baby in the earth. When Culla confesses that the child is still alive, she simply sets out after it. Her breasts continue to make milk months after she begins her search; to her the milk is a sign that the child still lives. As she tells the skeptical doctor who examines her, "I don't live nowheres no more. . . . I never did much.

I just go around huntin my chap. That's about all I do any more."

Again like Lena Grove, Rinthy Holme illustrates a deep yet simple faith in life. Because she does not lie or dissemble, she is met with general kindness by the strangers she encounters. They constantly offer her food, shelter, security. Only her love for her child keeps her on the road. Culla, however, is always held in suspicion. He is once arrested for trespassing, once threatened with hanging, always pursued by the possibility of punishment.

The third character to be considered in this novel is the tinker, an ambiguous figure at best. In some ways he is reminiscent of the archetypal Wandering Jew, doomed to roam without end. He straps himself in harness to pull his cart like an animal. He is associated with evil, enticing Culla with liquor and obscene books. Later he refuses to return to Rinthy the child he has found. Yet he is also the victim of evil. "I've seen the meanness of humans till I don't know why God ain't put out the sun and gone away," he tells Rinthy, and later he is murdered by the three strangers, who in turn take the child away from him. There is the suggestion that, in the end, Culla has taken the tinker's place as the eternal wanderer on nameless roads.

The most disturbing figure in the novel, however, is the bearded leader of the dark murderous trio. On two occasions Culla stumbles into his company. All others who encounter him are killed, but Culla, in a perverse way, is almost welcomed, as if he were expected. "We ain't hard to find," the man tells Culla. "Oncet you've found us." At the first meeting around their campfire, they force him to eat with them a black, nameless meat which he consumes with great difficulty and disgust. It is a terrible meal, a blasphemous communion with these creatures of darkness. The bearded man seems to know Culla's secret. "Everything don't need a name, does it?" he asks Culla, and later says of himself, "Some things is best not named." At the second meeting, after they have killed the tinker and taken the child, the leader acts as prosecutor and demands that Culla acknowledge his son, who is now hideously disfigured. When Culla once again denies the child, the bearded man cuts its throat and throws the small corpse to the mute, who apparently devours it. The act enforces a kind of terrible justice. The dark man is a figure of death, certainly, but also of retribution. He demands that payment be exacted for Culla's sin, and when the job is done, the three men disappear.

Themes and Meanings

The title of this novel comes from the eighth chapter of Matthew, in which Jesus cures a child because of the faith of his father, a centurion, but warns that those without such faith will be driven into the outer dark, the "place of wailing and grinding of teeth." In large degree this is the world of the novel. The sun rarely shines in this book. It is "bleak and pallid" when it does, and the sky is "colorless." It often rains, and much of the action takes place at night. There are numerous characters who wail in the outer dark, but Culla is the most obvious outcast. Unlike the father in Matthew, who comes to Jesus to heal his child, Culla denies his son in the presence of the judgment figure and thus causes the boy's death. Rinthy, although she, too, is denied her child, perhaps finds peace in the end when she falls asleep in the woods at the camp where the boy is killed.

The end of the novel, however, takes place years later. Culla is still wandering the "dead land," without faith or hope, on a road that leads to a swamp. He meets a blind man, whom he mistakes for a preacher. The blind man tells him that "they's darksome ways afoot in this world" but also offers Culla a form of reassurance. "I'm at the Lord's work," he says, and asks Culla what he needs. The blind man is the last of the searchers in the book. He is looking for "a feller... that nobody knowed what was wrong with.... I always did want to find that feller.... And tell him. If somebody don't tell him he never will have no rest." The man he seeks is Culla, but Culla turns away and hides, even though the blind man follows him with his silent, smiling stare. Culla, who never prays, never loves, never accepts, is left a solitary, tormented figure.

Thus, for all its grotesque violence and horror, *Outer Dark* is a seriously moral book. It argues for the existence of sin and evil, and it holds that the failure to admit sin is death, but it also suggests the possibility of grace, as evidenced by the blind man at the end, although such grace can blast the unprepared.

Critical Context

Outer Dark was Cormac McCarthy's second novel; his first book, *The Orchard Keeper* (1965), had won the William Faulkner Foundation First Novel Award for 1965. McCarthy has always been grouped with other Southern "Gothic" writers because of his penchant for violent and dark stories. One of the charges most often brought against him is that the arcane, polysyllabic vocabulary he sometimes employs is in direct imitation of Faulkner and serves to obscure rather than enrich his work. McCarthy, however, is a dedicated and serious writer who has developed very much his own voice and worldview. The so-called Gothic qualities of his writings come from a profound belief in man's spiritual and moral obligations. He is Catholic in background—he attended Catholic High School in Knoxville—and he infuses his Southern settings and characters with a stark religiosity. In this sense he is closer to Flannery O'Connor than to Faulkner.

Although appreciated more by critics than the general reader, McCarthy is one of the finest of modern American writers. His books since *Outer Dark—Child of God* (1974), *Suttree* (1979), and *Blood Meridian* (1985)— have shown him to be unswerving in his vision and artistry.

Sources for Further Study

Bell, Vereen M. "The Ambiguous Nihilism of Cormac McCarthy," in *Southern Literary Journal*. XV (Spring, 1983), pp. 31-41.

Cox, Dianne L. "Cormac McCarthy," in *American Novelists Since World War II, Second Series*, 1980. Edited by James E. Kibler, Jr.

Ditsky, John. "Further into Darkness: The Novels of Cormac McCarthy," in *The Hollins Critic*. XVIII (April, 1981), pp. 1-11.

Schafer, William J. "Cormac McCarthy: The Hard Wages of Original Sin," in *Appalachian Journal*. IV (Winter, 1977), pp. 105-119.

Edwin T. Arnold

THE OUTSIDER

Author: Ernesto Sábato (1911-   )
Type of plot: Psychological novel of passion and crime
Time of plot: 1946
Locale: Buenos Aires and Hunter's ranch in the countryside
First published: El túnel, 1948 (English translation, 1950)

> *Principal characters:*
> JUAN PABLO CASTEL, the protagonist, a thirty-eight-year-old
>   painter of some importance
> MARÍA IRIBARNE, Allende Hunter's wife and Castel's lover,
>   who is much younger than Castel
> ALLENDE HUNTER, María's blind husband
> LUIS HUNTER, Allende's cousin and the possible lover of
>   María
> MIMÍ HUNTER, Allende's cousin, a pseudointellectual

The Novel

The Outsider is an intense psychological novel concerning a passionate crime narrated in the first-person-singular form, using techniques found in detective fiction. The opening line of the novel unveils the outcome of Juan Pablo Castel's desperate attempt to reach out of his inner confinement through a total physical and spiritual communication with María. The direct opening statement, "I am Juan Pablo Castel, the painter who killed María Iribarne," takes the reader through the sordid labyrinth of the protagonist's convulsed mind. The plot of the novel unfolds in a very simple way: A tormented artist enters into a passionate affair with the wife of a wealthy blind man. Frustrated by his inability to experience María's absolute love or to possess her, Castel murders her. The protagonist confides the recollection of his story to the readers in a direct, personal style, forcing them to enter his tunnel of absolute isolation.

The painter first sees María at one of his art exhibits. She is the only person who discovers a minuscule detail of a painting entitled *Maternity*. Although the artwork centers on the figures of a mother and child, there is a small window in the upper left-hand corner of the painting. Through that window, one can see a scene in which an anxious woman on a desolate beach seems to be waiting for someone's response. Castel observes María's attraction to the remote scene and is certain that finally someone equal to him understands his cry for communication. While he is lost in a web of meditations, however, she leaves the gallery without giving a clue regarding her identity. The reader is then thrown into Castel's frantic search for María throughout the endless streets of Buenos Aires. By this time, one realizes that the anecdote is being told from the point of view of what could be considered a madman, the protagonist, and that his recollections are probably distorted images of an uncertain story. The series of hypotheses, questions, and digressions that go on in Castel's mind, however, intrigue and hold his interest through the last line of the novel. The next encounter with María, as well as subsequent ones in Plaza San Martín, La Recoleta, and the painter's studio, confirm the tumultuous nature of Castel's personality. The intense and cruel interrogation which María is forced to undergo at every meeting reveals the futile struggle of Castel to possess her. She seems reluctant to surrender to Castel's passion, fearing to cause him more harm. The only common thread between them seems to stem from the mutual understanding of Castel's art, specifically, the interpretation of spiritual isolation implied in the scene of the little window. From this point on, María's actions are presented in a blurred, incoherent way, increasing the mystery about her real self to Castel and to readers.

Her sudden departure for the country leaves Castel in greater depression. He is told by her maid that María has left a letter for him. Anxiously, the painter goes to her fashionable apartment on Posadas Street. While waiting in the library, Castel is confronted by the inexpressive stare of the eyes of María's husband, Allende. He acts courteously toward Castel and hands him the envelope. The extreme discomfort of the situation for Castel comes from the discovery that María's husband is blind. At this point, the author brings out one of the reiterated themes that occupy a great part of his creation, his obsession for the "subworld" of the blind. As Sábato has admitted, blindness produces in him a profound intrigue and repulsion at the same time.

Castel hardly pays attention to María's message, which reads "I am also thinking of you," and runs away from Allende's presence. Another unexpected discovery is the fact that María has gone to the country to visit her cousin, Luis Hunter. Hunter is a man publicly known to be a mediocre writer and a womanizer, well-known to certain circles of Buenos Aires society. Needless to say, María's frequent trips to Hunter's ranch become a new source of anguish for Castel. The rest of the novel fluctuates between Castel and María's exasperating meetings at his studio and the absences of María because of her visits to Hunter. Castel's repeated accusations and intense questioning seem to frighten her and even drive her away. In desperation, the protagonist tries to possess her through physical love. Every sexual encounter is now marked by hatred and violence followed by moments of remorse and humility on Castel's part. María seems saddened by the situation, avoiding all types of intimacy with Castel. Instead, she writes him brief and tender letters permeated with feelings of nostalgia and loneliness. The protagonist decides to see María at Hunter's estate. Once there, he observes suspiciously every minute action of Hunter.

The presence of Mimí Hunter, another cousin of María, only serves to reinforce Castel's feelings of alienation from the social environment. When María invites him to take a walk along the beach, however, Castel is overwhelmed by her closeness. Without listening to her confessions, he buries his head on her lap like a helpless child. Upon returning to the ranch, Castel continues to observe Hunter's reactions during dinnertime. Now he is convinced that Hunter feels jealous. Castel finds a way to hide on the second floor and listen to the voices of María and Hunter arguing in the dining room. Later, he seems to distinguish the sound of a woman's footsteps entering Hunter's room. Without any doubt about the love relationship between María and Hunter, he leaves the ranch at dawn. Once in Buenos Aires, he spends nights and days in a phantasmagoric world of bars, prostitutes, and fights. His mental incoherence becomes evident and is shown in the difficulties he finds writing an insulting letter to María, accusing her of being Hunter's lover.

From now on the author details, step by step, the deterioration of Castel's mind. The rhythm of the novel reaches its peak, transmitting to the reader the chaos and disorder of the protagonist's inner world. First, he goes to the studio and destroys his paintings with a knife. He tears the canvas of *Maternity*, with its little window, into small pieces, anticipating perhaps the final separation from María. He then drives wildly to the ranch in a borrowed car, waiting until dark to approach María. In this agonizing interval, Castel summarizes his relationship with her, concluding with the fact that María never shared with him the feeling of isolation. She merely looked through one of the windows of his tunnel out of curiosity and saw him suffering, helplessly waiting to end his tormented existence. He misunderstood her compassion for love.

The treatment of time in this last section of the novel conveys the fragmentation of reality experienced by the protagonist. In certain passages, the hour and the minute are faithfully recorded. Moreover, during the last twelve hours one finds every action of Castel precisely marked by the time, representing the compulsive nature of his sudden behavior. In other sections, time seems to be suspended. Castel, lost in his inner struggle, feels indifferent to outside reality. Such is the case of the long wait of Castel outside Hunter's ranch during a violent storm. When the light of María's bedroom goes on, Castel enters and stabs her to death. Before turning himself in to the authorities, the protagonist confronts an astonished Allende to whom he reveals that María has been his lover, Luis Hunter's lover, and the lover of who knows how many other men. Castel also tells Allende that he has killed her. In the concluding paragraph, Castel, now in jail, learns of Allende's suicide. He ends his story in abject isolation. The basic negative vision of life portrayed by Castel, the alienation of the protagonist from external reality, and the absurdist view of the world link this novel to the mainstream of twentieth century existentialism.

The Characters

Juan Pablo Castel is one of the most memorable creations of Latin American literature. From the very beginning of the novel, one is exposed to his frantic search for reason and order, his quest for some clue to the elusive reality of his chaotic existence. Every incident related to María causes a series of questions, digressions, options, and deductions. The writing and rewriting of letters confirm his belief in logic and precision. He constantly struggles between words associated with intuition, such as "feels," "imagine," and "sense," and those linked to the intellect, "reason," "order," and "think." This linguistic dilemma reveals the nature of the protagonist, torn between intuition and reason. Partly because of the narrator's point of view, the reader feels drawn to the protagonist. *The Outsider* is a novel about Castel's world, one in which external elements are insignificant. One is forced to imagine a great part of the stage and the characters of Castel's drama. María Iribarne is an elusive and engimatic figure never projected but as a suspect of endless, never-proved acts of deception. The reader becomes acquainted with María's reactions to Castel's actions but ignores her motives. When the character of Allende is introduced, both Castel and Sábato focus the emphasis on his annoying blindness. Hunter is merely described as an insignificant writer and a womanizer.

Mimí Hunter, a character that Castel despises at first sight, is introduced as a skinny and nearsighted woman in order to communicate an unsympathetic feeling to the reader. While reading the novel, one is compelled to accept the protagonist's distorted vision of the individuals around him and to share his detectivelike suspicions of their actions.

Themes and Meanings

The principal theme of the novel is the isolation of man in a world ruled by reason and logic. Throughout the novel, the contradiction between the tormented, complex world of the protagonist and the hostile, external reality is present and obvious. It is important to point out that "objective" reality is only one more element in Sábato's narrative, whereas "subjective" reality permeates the total work. Thus, most of the action takes place in the tumultuous mind of Castel. The novel's original title, *El túnel* (the tunnel), reveals the inner confinement and entrapment of the protagonist, who has become totally estranged from his exterior world. His desperate attempt to liberate himself from such a condition leads him to believe that María has spent her existence in a similar tunnel, parallel to his own. Therefore, the fusion of both paths should bring about a total union. Physical possession and subsequent jealousy gradually become frantic obsessions for Castel and seem to be the only means of bridging their inner lives. Yet sexual closeness will soon prove to be a futile way of communicating. The theory that love, and finally sex, leads only to more extreme anguish and solitude has been analyzed by Sábato in a lucid essay entitled "Solitude and Communication" in *Heterodoxia* (1953; heterodoxy). In *The Outsider*, the disenchantment with physical love is expressed in the following paragraph:

> I will say right away that this was another of my many ingenuous ideas, one of those naïvetés which surely made María smile behind my back. Far from reassuring me, our physical relations upset me still more, brought new and tormenting doubts, painful scenes of misunderstanding, cruel experiments with María.

Soon it becomes apparent to the reader that Castel painted the little window in *Maternity* to represent his own limited exposure to the world—one of his tunnel's windows. Looking through it, he found María, who seemed in turn to be searching for a way out of her own secluded world. The painter perceived conflicting images of María in each one of their encounters, however, and the reader must ponder her real identity. She is presented as tender and passionate as well as detached and cynical. It is precisely this confusing perception of his lover that leads Castel to his gradual mental deterioration.

The painter eliminates María and with her his only hope of escaping solitude. At the end of the novel, when he is confined to jail, the reader sees him looking through the small cell window while listening to the sounds of outside, everyday life. The exterior world seems to him more remote and indifferent than ever. Castel comes to the realization that he has always been alone in his inner labyrinth and, what is more frightening, that he is doomed to remain alone in his own tunnel forever. Such is the fate of a man whose anguish and loneliness are oblivious to the rhythm of an orderly world where reason prevails.

Critical Context

When Sábato's *The Outsider* was published in 1948, his name instantly gained international recognition. The novel was translated into French, English, Polish, Portuguese, Swedish, Romanian, Japanese, Danish, and German. It should be mentioned, however, that Sábato's first public exposure was through his incisive essays published since 1940. These diverse essays have been collected in several volumes: *Uno y el universo* (1945; one and the universe), *Hombres y engranajes* (1951; men and gears), *Heterodoxia*, *El Escritor y sus fantasmas* (1963; the writer and his ghosts), *El otro rostro del peronismo* (1956; the other face of Peronism), *El caso Sábato* (1956; the case of Sábato), and *Tango: Discusión y clave* (1963; the tango: discussion and key). They are encyclopedic in nature and their topics cover art, literature, politics, philosophy, history, education, religion, science, mathematics, and literary style.

To understand the vastness of his writings it is necessary to remember

Sábato's academic background. He earned a doctorate in physics in 1938 and worked at the Curie Laboratory in Paris as well as at the Massachusetts Institute of Technology. Many of his essays reveal his disillusionment with the sciences early in his professional career. After all, according to the writer, pure science has not been able to alleviate man's anguish at the prospect of death. In his essays and novels, Sábato shows the futility of expressing the subjective world of the individual—his feelings and emotions— through orderly and logical reasoning.

Other essays deal with the writer's convictions on the role of literature and that of creator in the crisis of the twentieth century. His disenchantment with Communism also becomes apparent in several political essays. The most controversial, however, are the ones related to Argentina's unstable situation before and after Juan Domingo Perón's regime.

All the themes of Sábato's essays are masterfully interwoven in his three novels. In 1961, thirteen years after *The Outsider*, Sábato finished his second fictional work, *Sobre héroes y tumbas* (*On Heroes and Tombs*, 1981), unanimously acclaimed by the critics. This national novel presents the same conflict found in *The Outsider*: the study of man in an irrational universe. Instead of projecting the vision of the world through the mind of a tormented individual, however, the reader is exposed to a panoramic view of the Argentine society—explored from a historical, demographic, and geographical point of view—by four main characters. In a certain way, his second novel completes a process which begins with total despair expressed in *The Outsider* and ends with bleak hope for the future of mankind in *On Heroes and Tombs*; a similar mood informs Sábato's less successful novel, *Abbadón, el exterminador* (1974). *The Outsider* remains his most widely read creation and an outstanding example of the Latin American psychological novel with existentialist overtones.

Sources for Further Study
Dellepiane, Angela. *Ernesto Sábato: El hombre y su obra*, 1968.
_____. *Sábato: Un análisis de su narrativa*, 1970.
Meehan, Thomas C. "Ernesto Sábato's Sexual Metaphysics: Theme and Form in *El túnel*," in *Modern Language Notes*. LXXXIII (March, 1968), pp. 226-252.
Oberhelman, Harley D. *Ernesto Sábato*, 1970.

Susanna Castillo

THE OUTSIDER

Author: Richard Wright (1908-1960)
Type of plot: Psychological realism
Time of plot: 1950
Locale: Chicago, New York City, and Newark, New Jersey
First published: 1953

> *Principal characters:*
> CROSS DAMON, the protagonist, an intellectual, black postal
>   worker
> GLADYS DAMON, his estranged wife
> DOROTHY POWERS, his pregnant, fifteen-year-old lover in
>   Chicago
> ELY HOUSTON, the New York district attorney
> GILBERT (GIL) BLOUNT, a Communist official who is mur-
>   dered by Damon
> EVA BLOUNT, Blount's wife and Damon's lover after Blount's
>   death
> JACK HILTON, Blount's subordinate who is murdered by
>   Damon
> BOB HUNTER, a railroad porter and Communist organizer
> LANGLEY HERNDON, a Fascistic landlord who is murdered by
>   Damon

The Novel

The Outsider is divided into five books, each of which focuses on a phase in the psychological development of its protagonist. "Dread," the first section, introduces Cross Damon, a well-read black postal worker, who is caught in a web of circumstances that exacerbates his sense of Existential nausea: Dot, his fifteen-year-old lover, is pregnant and threatening to charge him with statutory rape; Gladys, his estranged wife, is squeezing him for money; his pious mother burdens him with guilt; and his tedious job stifles him. A fortuitous public transit accident in which he is believed to have been killed gives him the opportunity to escape his situation and "shape for himself the kind of life he felt he wanted." Yet, before he leaves Chicago, he impulsively murders a coworker who discovers his secret.

In "Dream," the second section, Damon struggles to create a new identity. Initially, he finds himself "alone at the center of the world of the laws of his own feelings," and in this dreamlike state he boards a train for New York City. On board he has a lengthy discussion with District Attorney Ely Houston, who is fascinated by Damon's belief that "man is nothing in particular" or "just anything at all." Damon concludes that "what man is is perhaps too much to be borne by man." In New York City, Damon adopts the identity of a dead man, Lionel Lane, and meets Gil Blount, a white Communist Party official who invites Damon to share his Greenwich Village apartment in order to incite the racist owner, Langley Herndon. Damon accepts, and his new social contacts make him believe that "the dream in which he had lived since he had fled Chicago was leaving him."

In the third section, "Descent," Damon explores the limits of his new psychological freedom but finds himself increasingly caught in a pattern of deception and violence. After moving to Greenwich Village, Damon discovers that Blount's wife, Eva, feels betrayed and used in her loveless relationship. When Herndon initiates a violent argument with Blount, Damon comes to Blount's defense but ends up killing both men, symbolically acting out his rejection of opposite but equally inhumane ideologies. His descent continues, however, as he realizes that he is "trapped in the coils of his own actions," that through this double murder he has "become what he had tried to destroy."

In "Despair," the fourth section, the murders are investigated by Ely Houston. In a discussion with Damon that is reminiscent of that between Porfiry and Raskolnikov in Fyodor Dostoevski's *Crime and Punishment* (1866), Houston considers the possibility that both murders were committed by a third man, "one for whom all ethical laws are suspended," but he rejects this idea and mistakenly decides that Blount and Herndon killed each other. Damon and Eva soon become lovers, but her love is based on the naïve assumption that Damon is a victim, and he continues to lie to her in a vain effort to protect her from the "monstrousness of himself." Damon later murders Blount's associate Jack Hilton, who has evidence of Damon's guilt. This murder reignites the suspicions of the Party, and Damon is examined by Blimin, another high-ranking Communist. In his lengthy response to Blimin's questions, Damon expresses his belief that technological progress is immunizing men against the myths created to separate them from "the horrible truth of the uncertain and enigmatic nature of life."

In the final section, "Decision," Damon is once again called in for questioning by Houston, who is convinced of his guilt but cannot prove it. Houston confronts Damon with the wife and children whom he abandoned and blames him for the sudden death of his mother but is unable to make Damon react. When Damon later decides to unburden himself to Eva, she cannot bear the truth and commits suicide. In a final confrontation, Houston tells Damon that he knows of his guilt but has decided to let Damon punish himself. In effect, Houston refuses to give Damon's actions meaning. To Damon, this is "a judgment so inhuman that he could not bear to think of it." Soon afterward, Damon is gunned down by operatives of the Party and dies in Houston's arms.

The Characters

Because *The Outsider* is a novel of ideas, characterization is subordinated to exposition. Therefore, all of the characters, including Cross Damon, are types, representative of intellectual positions.

Cross Damon, although not fully believable, is a memorable character whose name suggests an inverted Christianity. As a character, Damon is informed by a variety of predecessors, such as Herman Melville's Ahab, Dostoevski's Raskolnikov, and Albert Camus' Meursault. Damon is a metaphysical rebel, an ethical criminal who attempts to create "the kind of life he felt he wanted."

Although Wright, through Ely Houston, suggests that a black intellectual such as Damon has a special objectivity, he wants Damon to be an existential Everyman who transcends racial distinctions. His protagonist, a former University of Chicago philosophy major, has been shaped by reading Søren Kierkegaard, Friedrich Nietzsche, Dostoevski, and others. Psychologically, Damon has developed dialectically, in opposition to the Christian guilt imposed by his mother and the oppressive tedium of his work. Wright emphasizes that Damon's anger and confusion are not a special condition of his blackness.

Few critics have been able to accept the contradiction between Damon's stoicism and his passion. On the one hand, Damon is a man of reason who rejects traditional codes of behavior. He reacts to his murders with cool analysis, and he shows no emotion when confronted with the wife and children whom he has abandoned. Like Camus' Meursault, Damon does not react to his mother's death. Yet, in other ways, Damon is a man driven by "hot impulse," egotistical desires that are very different from the utter Existential indifference of Meursault. This contradiction in his personality is underscored by his surprising love for Eva Blount.

The other characters exist primarily to exemplify or elaborate portions of Damon's philosophy. Ely Houston is Damon's mirror image, a kindred spirit who shares his sense of metaphysical rebellion but who chooses to support the legal system. In fact, his beliefs match Damon's so well that the lines in their long colloquies could be interchanged.

Eva Blount is an impossibly idealistic and naïve character who can only see Damon as a fellow victim. When he reveals the truth of his actions to her and cannot explain his motivation, she kills herself in despair. Damon's love for her and his desire to protect her represent the humanitarian yearnings that hide behind his brutal acts.

Gil Blount and the other Communist officials are portrayed as inhuman manipulators using people for ideological goals. In this sense, Damon sees little difference between them and the capitalists whom they oppose. By murdering Blount and the Fascistic Herndon, Damon strikes out at two essentially similar men, only to realize that his action is simply another misuse of power. Thus, Damon kills them in part because he sees a frightening reflection of himself in them.

Themes and Meanings

The central theme of *The Outsider* is Cross Damon's quest for freedom: "I wanted to be free . . . to feel what I was worth." Yet at the end of the novel, he admits that he has discovered "nothing."

At first, the protagonist feels Existential nausea: "insulted at being alive, humiliated at the terms of existence." This sense of alienation leads him to accept a Nietzschean view of an amoral universe in which man is destined to become either an executioner or a victim. The transit accident allows him to create a new life, to act independently and to see "what living meant to me," but he discovers that the egotistical exercise of freedom destroys those around him, including the one person he loves.

One problem is that Damon's effort to live for himself collides with his basic humanitarian feelings. In fact, he despises the will to power that drives men such as Gil Blount, and his multiple murders do not free him; instead, he becomes, like Blount, a little god playing with others' lives. The idea of universal freedom, which is negated by the will to power, demands the discovery or creation of norms that will protect the freedom of others.

In like manner, Damon fails in his effort to live authentically. He dreams of becoming one of those "men who were outsiders . . . because they had thought their way through the many veils of illusion," but the new life he creates and his relationship with other characters are based on deception. He cannot overcome his conviction "that bad faith of some degree was an indigenous part of living."

As he is dying, Damon states that "alone a man is nothing" and wishes that he "had some way to give the meaning of my life to others. . . . To make a bridge from man to man," but he fails in this effort. Unlike Houston, he cannot accept social norms in which he does not believe, so he dies, like Joseph Conrad's Kurtz, with a final enigmatic reference to the "horror" of his life.

Thus, *The Outsider* explores the question of freedom but provides no hopeful answers. In the novel, opposing ideologies are rejected, society is shown to be based on pretense, human nature is portrayed as brutal, and the possibility of creating a meaningful sense of freedom seems remote.

Critical Context

The Outsider was the first of Wright's books to receive predominantly negative reviews. Reviewers were primarily critical of its characterization, particularly the absence of sufficient motivation for Damon's violence. The novel's mix of melodramatic action and lengthy rhetorical exposition seemed disruptive. Black reviewers believed that Wright's interest in existentialism indicated a separation from his roots. Also, most reviewers found the unrelieved pessimism of the novel unattractive.

The novel is clearly the result of Wright's involvement with Existential thinkers following his break from Marxism in the 1940's. The novel seems to mark the low point of Wright's despair, for it lacks Camus' humanitarian hope or Jean-Paul Sartre's belief in social change. Later critics, however, have suggested that *The Outsider* is a rejection of existentialism or is even a Christian Existentialist novel.

Existential or not, *The Outsider* is a logical extension of Wright's earlier fiction and thought. In *Native Son* (1940), Bigger expresses in a less articulate manner the same sort of rage and dread felt by Damon. In "The Man Who Lived Underground," Fred Daniels, like Damon, wants to share his hard-earned knowledge with others. In "Art and Fiction," Wright maintained that personal freedom was conditioned on the freedom of others. Thus, in *The Outsider* Wright addressed familiar themes but consciously tried to move beyond the racial limitations of his earlier work.

Sources for Further Study
Bone, Robert. *Richard Wright*, 1969.
Brignano, Russell C. *Richard Wright: An Introduction to the Man and His Works*, 1970.
Hakutani, Yoshinobu, ed. *Critical Essays on Richard Wright*, 1982.
Kinnamon, Keneth. *The Emergence of Richard Wright*, 1972.
Margolies, Edward. *The Art of Richard Wright*, 1969.

Carl Brucker

THE PAINTED BIRD

Author: Jerzy Kosinski (1933-   )
Type of plot: Grotesque picaresque
Time of plot: 1939 to 1945
Locale: Eastern Europe
First published: 1965

> *Principal characters:*
> THE YOUNG BOY, a war refugee whose wandering adventures between the ages of six and twelve constitute the book's plot
> MARTA, a crippled, superstitious old woman with whom he lives at first
> OLGA, a wise old woman who saves him from villagers
> EWKA, a young woman who introduces him to sex
> GAVRILA, a Russian political officer who teaches him about socialism
> MITKA, a crack sniper in the Russian army who teaches him self-determination

The Novel

The unnamed protagonist of *The Painted Bird* is only six years old when his parents, fearing that he will be placed in a Nazi concentration camp with them, send him to live in the Eastern European countryside. When his foster mother dies, the boy is displaced and thought dead by his parents. He is thus forced to fend for himself for six years, wandering from village to village struggling to survive.

Jerzy Kosinski's first and perhaps most powerful novel begins with this premise, and for the next two hundred pages the reader is almost hypnotically caught up in the violence that the boy both suffers and witnesses in a primitive, almost medieval, world of brutal, superstitious villagers, while World War II and the horrors of Nazi persecution remain a constant backdrop to his grotesque adventures.

The structure of the novel is the progress of the boy's seemingly aimless journey as he both strives to survive physically and develop spiritually. Scorned and hated by the blond and fair villagers because of his dark hair and skin, he is feared as a Gypsy who has the power of the evil eye and hated as a Jew because the Nazis have threatened to punish anyone who shelters such an alien as himself. Filled with events and details of the superstitions of the villagers, their primitive animality, and the boy's witnessing of numerous examples of man's and nature's cruelty and indifference to human life and personality, the book is a constant assault on the sensibilities of the civilized reader.

After the death and immolation of the superstitious old Marta, his first caretaker, he lives with Olga, called the Wise One by the villagers, who teaches him how to survive. After being tossed into a river by malicious villagers and carried away on an inflated catfish bladder, he lives with a miller, whom he witnesses gouging out a young man's eyes with a spoon because he suspects the man has had sex with his wife. He watches as village women kill a half-crazed woman named Stupid Ludmilla by shoving a dung-filled bottle of manure up her vagina and then breaking it within her by vicious kicks. He is hanged up to be tormented by a vicious dog, starved, frozen, brutally beaten, but still he survives horrors that seem to dominate every page of the book.

Occasionally, trains filled with Jews bound for the concentration camps pass near the villages, and German detachments search through the woods for partisans, reminding the reader of the vaster and more cataclysmic horror of the Holocaust, which serves as the backdrop for the individual horrors on which the novel focuses. Halfway through the book, when the boy thinks that he has found some meaning in religion, he accidently drops the heavy Holy Book in the church during a ceremony. As a result, he is called a gypsy vampire by the villagers and thrown into a deep pit of human excrement. Barely escaping drowning in the manure, he surfaces only to find he has lost his voice.

His most idyllic sojourn is with a farmer named Makar, whose daughter Ewka introduces him to sex and to what he takes to be love; this sense of value is destroyed, however, when he sees her engaging in sex with a goat. The boy's wanderings come to a horrifying climax when he witnesses the brutal slaughter of villagers by a band of renegade Soviet horsemen who have aligned themselves with the Germans. When Red soldiers execute these Kalmuks, the boy finds his first stability; he is taken under the wing of the soldiers, particularly Gavrila, a political officer, who teaches him the value of collectiveness, and Mitka, a crack sniper, who teaches him the value of individualism.

As the war comes to an end, he is placed in an orphanage, where, accustomed to the freedom and cruelty of his wandering life, he sneaks out at night with a boy called the Silent One to engage in acts of senseless violence. Although he is finally found by his parents, he cannot adjust, feeling the world becoming cramped "like the attic of a peasant's shed." While learning how to ski as a form of therapy, he has an accident that necessitates hospitalization. On the last page of the book, the phone rings in his hospital room and he lifts the receiver and hears a man's voice. Feeling an unexplained yet overpowering desire to speak, he strains until the sounds crawl up his throat and he hears the words jump out of him. Enraptured by the sounds "that were heavy with meaning," he confirms that speech is once again his. The book ends, however, with no indication as to what this regaining of the ability to communicate means—except perhaps the powerful communication that *The Painted Bird* itself is.

The Characters

Character in its most basic sense is a central concern in this book, for in many respects it is a story of how a boy attempts to develop his own sense of self out of the horrors of a nightmare world in which he is forced to live. The only real development in what seems a meaningless and disconnected series of horrible events is, in fact, the quest the child makes for a meaningful value system. Because his experience with religion results in his being thrown into a manure pit, which in turns make him mute, he loses hope for a just God and shifts to a demonic view consistent with the villagers' superstitious idea of him; thus, he identifies himself with the powerful image of the Nazis. After the Germans are defeated and he is taken in by the Russians, however, he is convinced of the value of Communism; that is, until he more seriously adopts the strong sense of self-determination and individualism exhibited by Mitka, the silent and avenging sniper. The boy's final position seems to be one of self-identification and self-sufficiency. Yet, since the novel ends so abruptly after the phone call that ends his muteness, the reader has no way of knowing if this breakthrough to communication signals a shift to a different value system.

Although *The Painted Bird* is told entirely from the boy's point of view, there is no indication that it is told when he has grown older and has assimilated and understood his situation. All of his reactions to the horrible acts that dominate his life are those of a child; consequently, they register terror, but they seldom register moral judgment. There is, in fact, no adult in the story who condemns the primitive and animalistic behavior of the many characters who populate the book. Indeed, the characters are not complex human beings with whom the reader can identify; rather, they are primal and violent forces, seemingly caught in a time warp of primitive savagery. Each time the reader thinks that the boy will find love and kindness with a new master or mistress, that romantic hope is destroyed by the reality of ignorance and selfishness.

Themes and Meanings

Kosinski has said about *The Painted Bird* that it is a fairy tale *experienced* by a child rather than read to him. In many respects the novel does indeed present events and characters so monstrous that one thinks they could only exist in the unconscious world of nightmare fears. All the anxieties of childhood—losing parents, being lost, being threatened by inexplicable dangers—are pushed to extremes in the book. Thus, *The Painted Bird* could be read as an allegory of growing up under the most horrifying conditions. The basic premise of the book, however, is more specific than that, for growing up in a world where the Holocaust is taking place *is* the most horrifying condition. No primitive or unconscious nightmares can equal the horrors of the persecution carried out in the daylight world of civilization and reason.

Thus, the novel is one of the most shocking indictments of the Nazi madness and the terrors of the Holocaust during World War II in modern literature, although there are no death camps or execution ovens here; rather, the more concrete and individual horrors of one alien child lost in a world gone mad. Kosinski has said that, whereas a concentration camp takes on the aura of a distant symbol, when the reader reads a description of someone's eyes being gouged out, he must feel his own eyes disappearing. Although the horrors depicted in *The Painted Bird* are much less brutal than the actuality of the Holocaust, they seem the more horrible because they are more immediate and real.

The central metaphor in the book, which gives it its title, is described when one of the boy's many masters, Lekh, the bird catcher, paints a captured bird with many bright and vivid colors and then releases it among others of its kind. The painted bird tries desperately to enter the flock, but the other birds remain unconvinced that it is one of them. Then one by one the birds attack until the outcast is destroyed. The painted bird is la metaphor for the boy himself and, therefore, for all those who are marked by their own kind as aliens who must be destroyed.

Critical Context

When *The Painted Bird* was first published, it shocked the literary establishment. Many critics saw it as pornographic and sadomasochistic and criticized it for its patent unrealism; they argued that such horrors were beyond belief, too terrible to be real. Others, however, countered that such views were naïve in the face of the reality of the Holocaust—an indication of how society cannot accept such horrors because of their very magnitude. What the Holocaust proved, says Kosinski, is that the inconceivable and the incredible could indeed be actual. While some critics charged that the book was too horrible to be true, Kosinski said that some of his friends in Eastern Europe blamed him for watering down the truth of history.

The issue of the unreality of the novel becomes even more complex when one learns that it is based on Kosinski's own experience, for it is a fact that as a child he was separated from his parents during the early part of the war and forced to wander alone for several years, surviving as best he could. Moreover, he also lost his voice for a period during this refugee childhood and, after being reunited with his parents, regained it as a result of a skiing accident. Kosinski has been ambiguous about the extent of the autobiographical nature of the book, for although he denies it is a depiction of his own childhood, he still insists that every event in it is true. Consequently, it is not clear what events in the story actually happened to the young Kosinski and what events he saw happen to someone else or perhaps only heard about. Ultimately it does not matter, for the work is not history but fiction based on history and, for that reason, all the more unbearably real. Kosinski says that every remembered event, by the very fact that it is processed in the mind, becomes a fiction, yet that does not lessen its truth value.

Although, after coming to the United States, Kosinski had published two pseudonymous nonfiction works about collectivism, Socialism, and Eastern Europe, *The Painted Bird* was his first fiction, and it immediately made him one of the best-known and most respected contemporary writers. He has published many novels since, notably *Steps* (1968) and *Being There* (1971), but most critics agree that *The Painted Bird* is his most powerful book, a novel that has become, and is destined to remain, a terrifying twentieth century classic.

Sources for Further Study
Bruss, Paul. *Victims: Textual Strategies in Recent American Fiction*, 1981.
Kosinski, Jerzy. *Notes of the Author on "The Painted Bird,"* 1965.
Lavers, Norman. *Jerzy Kosinski*, 1982.
Sherwin, Byron L. *Jerzy Kosinski: Literary Alarmclock*, 1981.

Charles E. May

PARADISO

Author: José Lezama Lima (1910-1976)
Type of plot: Artistic education
Time of plot: The early twentieth century
Locale: Cuba, Florida, Jamaica, and Mexico
First published: 1966 (English translation, 1974)

> *Principal characters:*
> José Cemí, the protagonist, a young poet
> Colonel José Eugenio Cemí, his father
> Rialta Olaya de Cemí, his mother
> Ricardo Fronesis and
> Eugenio Foción, friends of Cemí at the university
> Oppiano Licario, José Cemí's mentor, a poet

The Novel

Paradiso is both the story of a Cuban upper-middle-class family during the first quarter of the twentieth century and a *Bildungsroman* that traces a young man's path to artistic creation. Although the novel focuses on the protagonist, Cemí, and begins with a description of an asthma attack that he suffers in early childhood, from chapter 2 to chapter 6 it tells the story of his parents' families, their meeting, and his father the Colonel's early death at the age of thirty-three.

The death of the Colonel is the event that endows his widow, Rialta, and his son Cemí with a spiritual mission in life. She becomes convinced that the loss of her husband cannot have been meaningless and that her son, in some way, will fulfill his father's truncated destiny. Cemí seems to accept that destiny without question, but he does not know how he will fulfill it. Through a series of mystical experiences precipitated by Cemí's intense observation of objects and by his meditation about a particular image or idea, he comes to realize that he will make his contribution through the cultivation of poetry and the search for poetic images that will lead to truth. Poetry fills the vacuum left by the death of Cemí's father, and it endows that seemingly purposeless death with meaning.

The rest of *Paradiso* follows Cemí's education in art and in the ways of the world. Leaving behind the safety of family life, Cemí enters the outside world first at school and then at the university, where he is introduced to the allure of sex and the life of the intellect. In this stage of his education, his guides are his friends, Fronesis and Foción, and with them he explores all the vital issues that the embalmed lectures of the university professors never broach.

Having survived the dangers of this phase of his education (the pursuit of wanton eroticism and the abuse of intelligence as an instrument of power), Cemí is ready to undertake his poetic apprenticeship under the guidance of Oppiano Licario. This enigmatic character appears at several crucial moments in *Paradiso*. Licario, the only one present when Cemí's father died, accepts the Colonel's dying request: "I have a son. Get to know him, and try to teach him something of what you have learned through your travels, suffering, and reading." Licario becomes Cemí's poetic mentor and by the time he dies has led the young man to the very threshold of artistic creation. As Cemí sits alone, late at night in a café, he remembers his mentor's assurance that he is now prepared for poetic creation, and *Paradiso* ends with Licario's words: "We may now begin."

The Characters

All readers of *Paradiso* are struck by Lezama's unusual characterization. No matter what their social rank, age, or education, his characters all seem to speak in the same manner and with the same vast erudition. In fact, they all seem to speak exactly as the author himself does. In *Paradiso*, Lezama makes a total departure from the psychological character portrayal of the traditional novel. Lezama himself has explained that his characters are really metaphors that became too developed for poetry. That, he claims, is what led him to write his first novel, *Paradiso*.

The title *Paradiso* proclaims the author's tribute to Dante's *The Divine Comedy* and furnishes a clue to the proper understanding of Lezama's characterization. The characters of *Paradiso*, like those of *The Divine Comedy*, have an allegorical meaning. José Cemí, the protagonist, represents the search for the poetic image and truth. His last name is the word used by the Indians of the Caribbean for the images of their gods; at the same time, it seems to be a pun on the Greek work for "sign," an appropriate allusion in the case of a poet whose tools are letters and words.

Oppiano Licario, Cemí's mentor in the art of poetry, is described in the novel as the new Icarus who attempts the impossible. Licario plays a role in *Paradiso* similar to that played by Vergil in Dante's *Inferno*. Like Vergil, he is an experienced poet who guides Cemí, keeping him on the right path and away from dangerous dead ends and detours.

Fronesis and Foción symbolize reason and passion, respectively, but together with Cemí they define what Lezama considers to be the different aspects of the human personality. Fronesis, whose name means "prudence" or "worldly wisdom" in Greek, is noble, generous, and constructive. He becomes Cemí's best friend and a good model. Foción, petty, selfish, and destructive, is a friend whom Cemí never quite trusts, but at the university the three young men are inseparable. In the allegorical scheme of the novel, the presence of Foción is necessary to establish an equilibrium. As a poet, Cemí must encompass all of human experience; he cannot do this by heed-ing only the dictates of reason. The poet must also come to terms with passion, even in its darkest, most destructive aspects.

The characters who belong to Cemí's family seem to partake to a lesser degree of the allegorical aspect and come closer to being flesh-and-blood people; this is probably because they are closely modeled on the author's own family. Nevertheless, they still clearly have a trace of allegory in them. The Colonel seems to be an incarnation of the joy of living and of all the manly virtues: health, vigor, honor, and justice. Rialta is not only Cemí's mother but also the personification of Hispanic motherhood. After her husband's death, she lives totally devoted to his memory and to her children. She is Cemí's first guide, and she prepares him to face life with a mission.

The unorthodox characterizations of *Paradiso* must be understood as an aesthetic decision and not as a shortcoming. Lezama is fully capable of creating psychologically convincing characters, but he only displays this skill in the case of minor characters, such as Cemí's maternal grandmother, the cook Juan Izquierdo, the Colonel's father, and Rialta's brother Alberto, who are all as vivid and as unforgettable as the characters of a traditional novel.

Themes and Meanings

The principal theme of *Paradiso* is the power of poetic language to transform life. For Cemí, the quest for poetic images is also the road to spiritual salvation. For him, as for Lezama, the poetic image is a vehicle to reach truth and in particular divine truth. Although extremely unorthodox in his views, Lezama always maintained his adherence to Catholicism. *Paradiso* (and all of Lezama's work) must be understood in the context of the author's mystical concept of artistic creation. The artist must always attempt the impossible, for it is only by working at the limits of his capacity that he can hope to catch a glimmer of truth. The writing of poetry is therefore dependent on mystic revelations that often occur unannounced and that make use of the prosaic material of everyday life. *Paradiso* is a stylized autobiography in which Lezama utilizes the structures of the family novel and the *Bildungsroman* in order to expound his system of poetic mysticism.

Lezama's concept of illumination through difficult poetic images owes much to the practice of Zen Buddhism, in which, under the guidance of a *Roshi* (Zen master), the disciple meditates on paradoxes (*kōan*) that lead to flashes of insight. Similarly, the stages that Cemí must pass before he reaches the state of mind where artistic creation is possible recall the purification that a Buddhist must undergo through successive lifetimes before he can reach Nirvana.

Taoism also plays a major part in the characterization of Cemí; particularly important are the central concepts of yin and yang, the opposing but complementary principles that make up the universe. Cemí is in essence a personification of the yin and yang. Unlike his friends Fronesis and Foción, who are dynamic and represent either of these principles, Cemí is static because he contains them both. He is the balance of reason and passion, light and dark, heterosexuality and homosexuality. Cemí never engages in sex in *Paradiso* because he represents the principle of androgyny, which for Lezama means sexual self-sufficiency.

Sexuality in *Paradiso* functions as a parable of artistic creation and of salvation. Homosexuality represents a destructive turning upon oneself, symbolized in the novel by the image of the circle (for Lezama a symbol of false immortality). Heterosexuality is viewed in a positive light, but the concomitant procreation is considered an acceptance of mortality. Only asexuality is seen as compatible with artistic creation and true immortality.

From the point of view of twentieth century philosophy and literature, the most striking aspect of Lezama's worldview is his faith in language and in poetic expression. Where many others have seen language as a prison and poetry as mere wordplay, Lezama believes in their ability to reveal truth.

Critical Context

The publication of *Paradiso* launched Lezama into international fame. Prior to the novel's publication, Lezama was virtually unknown outside Cuba, where he was known as a major poet, essayist, and the founder of *Orígenes*, the most important literary journal in the years before the revolution. *Paradiso*, which was read and praised by leading Latin American writers such as Julio Cortázar, Octavio Paz, and Mario Vargas Llosa, earned a place for Lezama among the writers of the "Boom" of Latin American literature.

Although *Paradiso* has been hailed by novelists and critics as a seminal work that offers previously unsuspected rich avenues for the development of the novel, it has never enjoyed a wide readership. Indeed, the novel's great originality and richness has also been its bane; Lezama's highly metaphorical language, his idiosyncratic handling of characterization and plot, and his mysticism have presented insurmountable obstacles for many readers. *Paradiso* has also elicited heated polemics because of its treatment of sex and of homosexuality in particular, and it has been attacked on political grounds as well; upon its first publication in Cuba, it was received by some as a counterrevolutionary work.

Nevertheless, Lezama's first novel is firmly entrenched as one of the classics of Latin American literature. *Oppiano Licario* (1977), an incomplete continuation of *Paradiso*, was published posthumously.

Sources for Further Study
Junco Fazzolari, Margarita. *Paradiso y el sistema poético de Lezama Lima*, 1979.

Ruiz Barrionuevo, Carmen. *El Paradiso de Lezama Lima*, 1980.
Souza, Raymond D. *Major Cuban Novelists: Innovation and Tradition*, 1976.
_____. *The Poetic Fiction of José Lezama Lima*, 1983.

Gustavo Pellón

PASSING

Author: Nella Larsen (1893-1964)
Type of plot: Psychological realism
Time of plot: The 1920's
Locale: New York City and Chicago
First published: 1929

> *Principal characters:*
> IRENE WESTOVER REDFIELD, the protagonist, a black Harlem
>   socialite
> BRIAN REDFIELD, her husband, a physician
> CLARE KENDRY BELLEW, a childhood friend of Irene
> JOHN (JACK) BELLEW, her white husband
> GERTRUDE MARTIN, a black friend of Clare and an old
>   acquaintance of Irene
> HUGH WENTWORTH, a wealthy white friend of the Redfields

The Novel

The action of *Passing* takes place in three time periods, each of which is dominated by a different relationship between Irene Westover Redfield and Clare Kendry Bellew. In a sense, the novel begins *in medias res*, with a letter from Clare to Irene urging a renewal of their relationship during some months which Clare will be spending in New York City. That letter recalls to Irene the bitter memory of an unexpected encounter between the women two years previously.

At tea in a Chicago hotel, which she can enter because she is light enough to "pass" for white, Irene meets a childhood friend, Clare Kendry Bellew, who had moved away shortly after the death of her drunken, half-white father. Now Irene learns that Clare lived for some years with her father's white aunts, who scorned her but pretended that she was white. When Clare married John (Jack) Bellew, she did not tell him of her black ancestry. When Irene visits Clare at her hotel, she meets another acquaintance from the past, Gertrude Martin, who has also married a white man and passes for white. Unlike Clare, however, she has taken her husband and his family into her confidence. Irene's annoyance becomes antagonism when the white racist John Bellew, assuming that the three black women are white, makes insulting comments, and although Irene is too loyal to her own race to betray Clare, she leaves angrily, resolving not to see her again.

When the letter arrives at Irene's home in New York, then, she does not answer it. Clare, however, arrives at her door uninvited, insists on attending the Negro Welfare League Dance, which is one of Irene's charity projects, and becomes a close friend of the Redfields, finally charming the two sons and even Irene's embittered husband, Brian. Despite Irene's fears that Jack will discover Clare's ventures into Harlem and despite Irene's pleas that Clare consider the fate of the Bellews' young daughter should the racial deception be discovered, the golden-haired black woman, delighting both in the risk and in the society of her own people, continues to visit the Redfields and their friends whenever Jack leaves town.

The final section of the novel begins with Irene's realization that Clare is having an affair with Brian. At first, though stunned and angry, Irene plans to endure the situation for the few months, until Clare and Jack leave for Europe. Perhaps, she thinks, she should reveal Clare's Harlem visits to Jack, so that he will forbid them. Yet, should he learn that Clare is black, Clare hints, she will be free to move to Harlem. Concerned for the security of her sons, desperately jealous, Irene wishes that Clare were dead, and when Jack bursts into a party in Harlem to which he has traced his wife, Clare falls out a window, leaving Irene unsure whether she had actually pushed her or only willed her death. Thus the original antagonism and irritation which Irene feels toward the beautiful, selfish, and willful Clare, briefly transformed into an intimate friendship, finally terminates in murderous hatred, annihilating the loyalties of sex and of race.

The Characters

In *Passing*, Nella Larsen tells the story as it appears to Irene Redfield, an intelligent, sensitive wife and mother who prizes security above all else and resists risk in every situation. Irene is shocked to discover the lie which Clare is living—not because it is a lie, but because it is so risky. A devoted mother herself, Irene cannot understand Clare's risking her daughter's future for the pleasure of Harlem society.

Clare, however, is determined to have whatever she wants, whether it is a wealthy white husband, a fling at a Harlem dance, or her friend's husband. She will not listen to reason; she is unconcerned about the feelings of others and even about her own future. In her need for stimulation, she enjoys risk as much as Irene fears it.

It is probably this element in Clare which appeals to Brian Redfield, who dislikes his Harlem practice and his life as a black in America, and who has dreamed for years of a new life in Brazil. Unlike Irene, Brian wishes his sons to know the truth about the life of the American blacks outside the sheltered upper classes. Clearly, he resents Irene's certainty that she knows what is best both for him and for their two sons.

Other characters in the novel are present primarily as foils to the main characters and are therefore less fully realized. Clare's husband, Jack, is a vulgar racist, yet he honestly loves his wife, and, because he has been deceived, he does not realize that he is insulting her and her friends, as Brian reasonably points out to Irene after her report of the first encounter.

Hugh Wentworth is a liberal white man, yet he is so prominent socially that he risks nothing by his Harlem associations. Irene's fondness for him is in some ways as blind as her hatred of Jack. Although she appears only briefly, Gertrude Martin is of interest as a foil both to Clare and to Irene. Like Clare, she is married to a white man, but like Irene, she is candid with her husband. Like Clare, she has had a tortured pregnancy, fearing that her children will be born dark. Like Clare, she endures racial insults in public rather than admit that she is black. Yet the three black women have very different motives for their silence in front of Jack. Clare fears that he will discover her "passing"; Gertrude has been honest with her husband, but fears exposure to her white society; and Irene is simply loyal to Clare and to Gertrude, despite her detestation of the slurs and of the deception. Yet even Irene is willing to "pass" in order to be admitted to public places.

By focusing on Irene's memories, thoughts, perceptions, and emotions, Larsen produces a full psychological study of a woman who is torn more than she will admit by the situation of her people in her time. Irene's refusal to notice the contradictions involved in her own conduct is in itself part of the revelation in the novel.

Themes and Meanings

As the title implies, the principal theme of the novel is confusion of identity. In a society which placed a high value on whiteness and a low value on blackness, there was a temptation for a black whose skin was light to "pass" into the white world, denying his own blood. Yet aside from the danger that any such deception might be discovered, aside from the loss of spontaneity to anyone wearing such a mask, Larsen emphasizes the sense of homelessness which must be suffered by anyone who cuts himself off from those who share his history and his responses to life. In part, it is the longing for her own people which brings Clare back to Harlem.

In another way, however, Larsen's upper-class black intellectuals live more like the whites of their own class than the blacks in poverty. Thus Irene insists that Brian shield his sons from the knowledge of what happens beyond the shelter of wealth and education. In fact, it is only the acquisition of social polish that has enabled Clare to "pass" into the white society of the rich, nor would she be accepted among Irene's friends without that same polish. The Redfields and their friends do not share in the lives of their servants. Thus, the characters in *Passing* are separated not only by race, but also by social class.

Finally, Larsen's blacks differ in their responses to a troubled time in a troubled country. For many of them, the answer is education and money, which can produce a pleasant, secure life such as that of the Redfields. To someone as conservative as Irene, it would be insane to risk all that had been won by so much work and struggle. To her husband, however, there is something artificial about a life which ignores the condition of those other blacks. Therefore Brian wishes to establish a new identity in a new country, while Irene insists on her own nationality as an American and on her own secure life. Brian would risk much to find a new identity in a society which did not discriminate against blacks. Clare, too, will risk what she has in order to gain something better, but although her ventures into Harlem may be prompted partially by her desire to regain her identity as a black, she is more concerned with simply getting something or someone she wants— wealth, a way of life, Jack, Brian. Perhaps with her it is not even risk for a reason, but risk for its own sake that is the true motivation. Beyond race and class, then, there are differences in character which direct one's actions. There are those who hold on and those who venture out. Either course may lead to disaster.

Critical Context

At the time of its publication in 1929, *Passing* was of particular interest both because of the mixed blood of its author and because of the fascination of readers with the practice which gave the book its title. Critics praised the psychological insights of the novel, although some found the ending contrived.

In the years which followed, the author disappeared into private life, and critics attempted to assign a place to her among black writers. Some critics felt that *Passing* was less impressive than Larsen's semiautobiographical novel *Quicksand* (1928), which had gone beyond the problem of black identity to the issue of female sexuality, taking the heroine from the South, to Harlem, to Europe, and back to the South in search of happiness and leaving her at last a near-invalid from childbearing. *Passing* is now, however, generally considered to be an important book of the Harlem Renaissance, and Nella Larsen is compared to Jessie Redmon Fauset and Walter White in her treatment of two conflicting cultures, one of which offers great inducements to those individuals who can abandon their own culture in order to embrace it.

Although racial issues have dominated criticism of *Passing* during the decades since it was written, it is clear that Larsen has revealed more about human life than the duality indicated in her title. Although some critics have believed that the third section of the book abandons the theme of "passing," or betraying one's race, for a domestic tragedy, Clare's actions suggest that from betraying one's race to betraying one's sister is an easy step.

Sources for Further Study
Bone, Robert A. *The Negro Novel in America*, 1965.
Bontemps, Arna, ed. *The Harlem Renaissance Remembered*, 1972.
Huggins, Nathan Irvin. *Harlem Renaissance*, 1971.

Singh, Amrijit. *The Novels of the Harlem Renaissance*, 1976.
Turner, Darwin T. *Afro-American Writers*, 1970.

Rosemary M. Canfield

PITCH DARK

Author: Renata Adler (1938-   )
Type of plot: Novel of manners
Time of plot: 1981, with flashbacks reaching to the early 1960's
Locale: Connecticut; Ireland, near Dublin; Orcas Island, off Bellingham, Washington
First published: 1983

> *Principal characters:*
> KATE ENNIS, a writer and the narrator of the story
> JAKE, her married lover

The Novel

The unconventional, oblique narrative method of *Pitch Dark* makes plot summary difficult and tentative, but the novel's division into three sections—"Orcas Island," "Pitch Dark," and "Home"—provides a helpful structure.

Kate Ennis, the narrator, tells the first part of her story from Orcas Island, but the events described take place in New England. "Orcas Island," like the other two sections, weaves together Kate's painful musings on her recent affair with Jake, her married neighbor, with a skein of incidents featuring people from Kate's past. Characters come onstage only to walk off forever, and promising themes sound once and fade away. Many of the quick shots of the past focus on college days (Harvard and Radcliffe, apparently, since one student is experimenting with psylocybin "under the guidance of [Timothy] Leary and [Richard] Alpert"), offering entertaining glimpses of teachers and fellow students.

The stream of Kate's consciousness darts here and there. Some passages turn into minilectures on themes from Ludwig Wittgenstein and Vladimir Nabokov, for example, while one sparkling gloss on Homer reveals that Penelope "did not unweave by night, and therefore by implication hardly ever wove by day." A puzzling reference on page eighteen to something called "London Exit" is amplified in a brief essay introduced fifteen pages later, but the "rich Italians" and the old people who "moved to the suburbs" are suspended in narrative limbo. Leander Dworkin, "the amplifying poet," and Willie Stokes, "the poet of compression," seem to have bright futures, but their complementary sensibilities wither away as they are buried in the narrator's flow of reminiscence.

Never far from Kate's mind is her recent break from her lover. Kate is apparently about forty, and in "Orcas Island" she has for some time improvised a home in a barn that is perhaps in rural Connecticut (it is a "long drive to the city"). Jake, a lawyer and a country neighbor, may be about fifteen years older than Kate—or at least she speaks of having planned to leave him on or about his thirty-fifth anniversary. Their affair has gone on for eight years, and much of the hurt that Kate feels centers on Jake's never having taken her anywhere on a trip. Jake has always traveled with his family to the Caribbean for Christmas, but, as the Other Woman, Kate has had to subsist on his leftover time. ("Somehow not with me, not with me.") The "Orcas Island" section ends with Kate wondering, "But what am I going to do, what shall I do, now?"

Section 2, "Pitch Dark," is also composed on Orcas Island, but is set in Ireland, near Dublin. It is the most unified and coherent of the three sections, but was probably written separately and grafted on to the story of Kate and Jake. (In one scene in which she wants a name very like her own, the narrator comes up not with a variant of Ennis but with "Alder.") When Kate leaves Jake, she flies to Ireland, rents a car, and seeks out the estate offered her by a wealthy American acquaintance. Much of her journey is made in pitch dark, and it involves a very minor traffic mishap in which she is apparently used as the instrument of an insurance scam. Kate is unduly frightened by the incident and, thinking she is in trouble with the law, pursues a course of trivial evasive actions to avoid apprehension. Her brief stay at her friend's home is no more satisfying. The servants' boorishness evokes paranoid suspicions, and Kate makes a nightmarish drive to a dinner party with strangers. These events unfold with brief pauses for the echoing of several obscure verbal motifs, as well as the playing back in her mind of persistent questions about Jake and their romance. The section ends with Kate in London and Jake on the phone to her.

In section 3, "Home," Kate is living in a small house in a Connecticut town. The time is more than two years after her misadventures in Ireland. The Orcas Island interlude is behind her, and she is living comfortably with Jake. ("By then, we had long been to Orcas Island, New Orleans, God knows where.") Aside from the abrupt comments that allow the reader to piece together the happy ending to the love story, "Home" is, like "Orcas Island," a series of discontinuous accounts of local events, essays on legal matters (the whole novel reveals a preoccupation with the law and laws), more streams of reminiscence, lectures on literature (Thomas Wolfe and Gertrude Stein seen very clearly), and more. Much of it is witty, engaging chitchat despite its lack of unity—a judgment that applies to each section as well as to the novel as a whole. In sum, *Pitch Dark* tells an ordinary love story in a sometimes annoying, indirect way but decks it out with appealing side glances at whatever catches the author's alert eye.

The Characters

Pitch Dark rejects conventional characterizations, offering instead bursts of narrative from which the reader must deduce character. Kate Ennis emerges as a sensitive, intelligent, long-suffering heroine. The many digressions reveal where Kate comes from, where she is now, and where she hopes to be in the future. The characters are not so much described as experienced through Kate's consciousness. The Ireland story in the second section shows Kate in a state of paranoia, suggesting that her mental stability has been threatened by the upheaval in her love life. The sinister inscrutability of the servants and villagers in Ireland reinforces her sense of helplessness.

Jake is presented as an insensitive, vacillating, self-centered man who takes Kate's love for granted. His actions slowly force Kate to realize that his love for her is diminishing. When she seeks his assistance in some maintenance problems with her house and pond, he refuses even to share with her the names of reliable workmen he has used at his own place. This selfish disregard for her problems prompts these thoughts: "And though I know my heart cannot have been broken in these things, these things of my house and of yours . . . , I find that I am crying as I write. . . ." Similarly, he refuses to take her on any trips during those eight years of their romance. (She had had her heart set especially on a visit to New Orleans: "Would it have cost him all the earth, sometime in all those years, to take her to New Orleans for a week?") Jake remains, ultimately, a vague presence in the background. His importance is clear, but his character and personality remain thoroughly problematic.

Many of the other characters, brief as their bit appearances are, shine vividly on the page, but none of them takes on full flesh and blood.

Themes and Meanings

In an impressionistic collage of prose vignettes, Adler airs her views on social and political issues as well as mulling over such mundane topics as bad drivers and the possible evolution of the convention according to which a football quarterback wipes his hands on a towel draped from the hind parts of the center in front of him. Much of her political and social commentary presumably emanates from her personal experience in the 1960's, and her conservative slant is thinly veiled. The law profession is probed and condemned with a special vengeance that is closely connected with her alienation from Jake, as she seeks to rationalize a way to escape their futile love affair. She comments viciously on the legal system: "Here, on the other hand, with an ingenuity that should take an entrepreneurial schemer's breath away, there has evolved the following proposition: that a legal job no sooner comes into existence than it generates, immediately and of necessity, a job for a competitor. I can think of no other line of work where this is true."

Adler's main theme, however obliquely presented, is love, especially the love of a mistress for a married man. Her comments on this topic are poignant. "Is it always the same story, then?" she asks. It is always the case that "somebody loves and somebody doesn't." Sadly, she concludes that "someone is a good soul and someone a villain." It is obvious that in her own case Kate Ennis has cast herself in the role of the "good soul" and Jake in that of "the villain." She repeatedly asks, "But can we live this way?" She finally decides—or has decided at the novel's opening—that the answer is no, that the crumbs are not enough sustenance. It is then that she tries to make her escape. This prompts the repeated refrain, "Did I throw the most important thing perhaps, by accident, away?"

Critical Context

Critical response to Adler's style has been mixed. Like *Pitch Dark*, her first novel, *Speedboat* (1976), consists of a sequence of disconnected passages which force the reader to impose a pattern from his own imagination. Such a work is hardly a novel in the conventional sense of the term, but critical reaction to *Speedboat* was quite favorable on the whole. Adler's volume of essays *Toward a Radical Middle* (1970) also received excellent notices, and much of the commentary in her fiction should probably be related to her journalistic work. *Speedboat* had the advantage of being new, and its methods enjoyed the attention that attends on novelty, but in *Pitch Dark* her approach had to sway by its own innate virtues. Just how much pleasure a reader takes in these novels will depend finally on how much pleasure from conventional narrative continuity he is willing to sacrifice in return for Adler's freshness and distinct talent for the impressive quick sketch.

Sources for Further Study

Conant, Oliver. "A Novelist's Lonely Song," in *The New Leader*. XVII (January 23, 1984), pp. 17-18.

Epstein, Joseph. "The Sunshine Girls," in *Commentary*. LXXVII (June, 1984), pp. 62-67.

Shattuck, Roger. "Quanta," in *The New York Review of Books*. XXXI (March 15, 1984), p. 3.

Tyler, Anne. "End of a Love Affair," in *The New Republic*. CLXXXIX (December 5, 1983), pp. 27-28.

Len McCall

PLAINS SONG, FOR FEMALE VOICES

Author: Wright Morris (1910-   )
Type of plot: Domestic realism
Time of plot: The early 1900's to the late 1970's
Locale: Madison County, Nebraska, and Chicago
First published: 1980

> *Principal characters:*
> CORA ATKINS, a Nebraska farmwife
> EMERSON ATKINS, her husband
> ORION ATKINS, his brother
> BELLE ROONEY ATKINS, Orion's wife
> MADGE ATKINS KIBBEE, the daughter of Cora and Emerson
> SHARON ROSE ATKINS, daughter of Belle and Orion, a music
> teacher in Chicago and at Wellesley College

The Novel

Plains Song, for Female Voices contrasts the lives of two women of the Nebraska plains who seemingly have completely different ways of looking at the world. Cora Atkins comes west from Ohio in the early twentieth century to be a farmwife for Emerson Atkins and learns to accept the limitations of such an existence. Sharon Rose Atkins, Cora's niece, is appalled by the plains life and heads east to discover herself. The lives of four generations of Atkins women are interwoven in this plotless treatment of changes in a way of life.

Sharon's mother, Belle, is an Ozark hillbilly whose verbosity conflicts with the stoic silence of Cora, Emerson, and Orion, her husband and Emerson's brother. Belle's emotional isolation on the Atkins farm ends when she dies giving birth to her second daughter, Fayrene. Cora has only one child, Madge, the result of the first and last sexual act between her and Emerson.

The outgoing Sharon and the passive Madge develop a close relationship, but when Madge marries Ned Kibbee, Sharon feels betrayed by the cousin whose sole function has been to witness her accomplishments: "She was like a calf, bred and fattened for the market, and the buyer had spoken for her." A music scholarship in Chicago allows Sharon to escape such a fate.

Sharon later tries to save Blanche, Madge's oldest daughter, from the slavish life she associates with the plains and Cora, but Blanche turns out to be even more sluggishly passive than her mother. Meanwhile, after Emerson dies, Cora descends into madness, finally paying for years of labor and emotional abstinence; Madge becomes an invalid after a stroke and is cared for by Blanche.

When Cora dies, Sharon, now a teacher at Wellesley College, returns to

Nebraska for the first time in thirty-three years to discover that she is considered a heroine by some Atkins women. Madge's daughter Caroline tells her, "we don't get married anymore unless we want to. We all had your example." Sharon sees that Cora's farm is nothing but a field of tree stumps and is frightened by the bleak emptiness, feeling more than ever her obligation to answer the questions Cora was never able—or willing—to ask.

The Characters

Cora and Sharon are the most fully developed females characters in Morris' fiction. On the surface, they are complete opposites, but they share some qualities. Perhaps recognition of these is part of what frightens Sharon.

The six-foot, humorless Cora accepts all the duties of a farmwife but one, biting through her hand on her wedding night, her scar becoming representative of the emotional distance between her and her bewildered husband and of her particular individuality and independence. As with the most complex Morris characters, Cora's strengths and weaknesses merge to become almost indistinguishable.

Cora is not very affectionate toward her daughter and the nieces she must rear after Belle's death. Unable to cope with emotional complications, Cora imposes order on her life by reducing it to a simple level that she can control: "Cora had little desire to see more than she had already seen, or feel more than she had already felt." She convinces herself that her life makes sense, that it is what God intends her to have: "Chickens, people, and eggs had their appointed places, chores their appointed time, changes their appointed seasons, the night its appointed sleep." All this, however, does not stop her from experiencing a strange sense of guilt for having peace of mind.

In Chicago for the 1933 World's Fair, she cannot bring herself to visit Sharon as there is no possibility of exerting control over her niece on her own ground. Cora's effort to live her life, limited though it may be, on her own terms ultimately gives her a considerable degree of dignity.

Sharon is admirable for the same reasons, though her life is hardly limited. She learns to overcome what Cora merely accepts. Sharon makes something of herself by breaking with her roots but has mixed emotions about the "half-conscious people so friendly and decent it shamed her to dislike them." She wants to understand why the people of the plains, especially the women, are as they are, how they can settle for so little, how they, like Madge, can find happiness in such a life.

The answer lies in the compromises made by all people, including Sharon. She forsakes some of the emotional attachments, such as relations with the opposite sex, that humans are supposed to need, but unlike her relatives, she is aware of what she has sacrificed. Her self-knowledge sets her apart from the other characters, creates her independence, her true escape from the emotionally barren plains. This self-knowledge makes it possible for Sharon to see beneath the surface differences between her and Cora. Sharon even defends her when Caroline says that Cora has been less than an animal for not complaining about her life: "She *could* have . . . but she simply *wouldn't*."

The main male characters are less fully realized as they are not of primary importance in the lives of the Atkins women. Emerson feels superior to Cora although she has many talents that he lacks: reading, writing, understanding how to order from catalogs, making their chickens productive, covering the kitchen floor with linoleum. The narrow-minded Emerson is not a negative creation, getting along well with all the other Atkins women, but as a husband, he assumes the passive role traditionally associated with wives. Orion, who understands Cora much better than his brother does and admires her, is capable of greater emotion as well; his wife's early death nearly destroys him.

Themes and Meanings

Plains Song, for Female Voices has been called a feminist novel; it is that and more. It presents, in Sharon, a woman of principles who forges her own identity, never even considering the conventional existence into which she could so easily settle, yet the novel avoids the clichés of sexual politics. Morris' women are recognizable human beings, not types illustrating this pathetic, or that heroic, behavior.

Morris, the least didactic of novelists, is especially interested in all his books with the relationship of place and character. The Ohio-born Cora becomes the essence of the Nebraska plains; she and her farm are inseparable entities. The farm molds her personality just as much as she controls it. Sharon, on the other hand, rejects the plains because it dominates its inhabitants: "It seemed incomprehensible to Sharon that people continued to live in such places. Numbed by the cold, drugged by the heat and the chores, they were more like beasts of the field than people."

The home place, however, is an intrinsic part of an American's character and can never be completely ignored because of the tenacious hold of the past on American lives. At the end of the novel, Sharon realizes how much the past is a part of her: "Whatever life held in the future for her, it would prove to reside in this rimless past, approaching and then fading like the gong of a crossing bell." The inescapable influence of the past adds some irony to Morris' portrayal of Sharon's independence, for it is her plains upbringing which has created her desire to be different.

Failed and compromised American dreams are a frequent concern in Morris' fiction. Emerson and Orion pursue the dream west but fail to realize it. Even with Cora's help, they make but a minimal living from their farm, succeeding only in producing daughters who produce granddaughters to whom their agrarian heritage is meaningless. Only Sharon successfully pursues the American Dream, ironically by moving farther and farther east.

Critical Context

Morris' devoting his twentieth novel to a consideration of what it means to be a woman in twentieth century America is somewhat surprising, given the secondary status of women in most of his fiction. Women are presented as dominating their men in such works as *Man and Boy* (1951) and *The Deep Sleep* (1953), but beginning with *One Day* (1965), Morris' women gradually start to establish their distinctive qualities, developing a logical progression to Sharon Rose Atkins. He creates Cora and Sharon because he understands women better than he did previously, not because he wants to write a feminist tract. With the exception of *Love Among the Cannibals* (1957), a rather sexy book by Morris' standards, he eschews the fashionable.

The ninth of his novels to be set at least partially in Nebraska, *Plains Song, for Female Voices* completes Morris' vision of the plains as a place with a profound grip on the emotional lives of its natives, these practical but passionless American dreamers. The Atkinses' failure recalls that of Will Brady, the doomed egg dealer of *The Works of Love* (1952). Despite his criticisms of the deficiencies of the American character, both male and female, Morris always finds something admirable in his protagonists' quests, as when Will Brady dies offering love to an indifferent world. Cora's endurance in a world of loneliness and alienation is no small achievement.

Plains Song, for Female Voices joins *The Works of Love*, *The Huge Season* (1954), *The Field of Vision* (1956), *Ceremony in Lone Tree* (1960), and *Fire Sermon* (1971) as one of Morris' most notable novels, primarily through his portrait of Sharon and his celebration of her individuality. The choice between living a reasonably safe, conventional existence, and one involving challenges and independence—or degrees of independence—is a difficult one for any inhabitant of Wright Morris' America.

Sources for Further Study

Arnold, Marilyn. "Wright Morris' *Plains Song*: Woman's Search for Harmony," in *South Dakota Review*. XX (Autumn, 1982), pp. 50-62.

Bird, Roy K. "Wright Morris: Through a Flaw in the Window of Fiction," in *Mid-American Review*. III (Spring, 1983), pp. 145-166.

Waldeland, Lynne. "*Plains Song*: Women's Voices in the Fiction of Wright Morris," in *Critique*. XXIV (Fall, 1982), pp. 7-20.

Wydeven, Joseph J. "Wright Morris, Women, and American Culture," in *Women and Western American Literature*, 1982.

Michael Adams

PLAY IT AS IT LAYS

Author: Joan Didion (1934-   )
Type of plot: Nihilistic black comedy
Time of plot: The late 1960's
Locale: Southern California and Las Vegas
First published: 1970

> *Principal characters:*
> MARIA WYETH, the protagonist, an unemployed actress
> CARTER LANG, a film director, Maria's husband
> BZ, Carter's producer and Maria's friend, a homosexual
> LES GOODWIN, Maria's lover and the probable father of her
>   unborn child
> IVAN COSTELLO, Maria's former lover, a sadist
> JOHNNY WATERS, a conceited young actor who goes to bed
>   with Maria
> KATE, Maria and Carter's brain-damaged daughter
> BENNY AUSTIN, the business partner of Maria's late father

The Novel

The first thing that one notices about *Play It As It Lays* is its strange physical appearance. Joan Didion has said that her technical intention in the novel was to write "a book in which anything that happened would happen off the page, a 'white' book to which the reader would have to bring his or her own bad dreams." She accomplishes this goal by dividing her 214-page book into eighty-seven short chapters (some as short as a single paragraph). The fast, even violent, pace of the novel and the accumulation of many nearly blank pages instill a sense of vertigo in the reader.

Play It As It Lays tells the story of a young, third-rate film actress named Maria Wyeth. When Maria is introduced, she is remembering the events of the novel from the perspective of a mental institution. A native of Silver Wells, Nevada (a former mining community that is now the site of a nuclear test range), Maria is separated from her obnoxiously cruel husband, Carter Lang, and from her brain-damaged daughter, Kate. (Although Maria feels genuine maternal love for Kate, the child's condition makes it nearly impossible for that love to be demonstrated or returned.) When Maria once again becomes pregnant (probably not by her husband), Carter pressures her into having an abortion by threatening that he will otherwise prevent her from seeing the institutionalized Kate. Following her abortion, and other, lesser traumas, Maria finds herself in bed with Carter's producer, BZ. The purpose, however, is not love but death. BZ (who is a homosexual and thus not erotically interested in Maria) swallows a handful of Seconal and dies in

Maria's comforting arms. Rather than follow his example, she keeps on living.

Unlike BZ, Maria is averse to examining life, philosophically or otherwise. (At the outset of the novel she says: "What makes Iago evil? some people ask. I never ask.") She tells the reader that she keeps on living because she hopes someday to get Kate back and go someplace where they can live simply. Maria will do some canning and be a mother to her child. This "hope" is encouraging, however, only if there is a chance of its being realized, and by the end of the novel, one understands that Maria's dream is, in fact, hopeless. Viewed in this light, the closing lines of *Play It As It Lays* seem ironic indeed. Maria says: "*I know something Carter never knew, or Helene, or maybe you. I know what 'nothing' means and keep on playing. Why, BZ would say. Why not, I say.*"

Maria may actually believe that she is living for Kate. The truth, however, as Didion's narrative perspective forces the reader to see it, is that Maria continues to live because she does not even share BZ's faith that freedom comes with death. Albert Camus once said that suicide was the only truly serious philosophical problem, because it comes down to judging whether life is worth living. BZ has answered the question in the negative. Maria, however, believes that there are no serious philosophical problems.

Although the novel begins with first-person accounts by Maria and two other characters (Carter and BZ's wife, Helene) and ends with a final word from Maria, the bulk of the story is told from a third-person-limited point of view. At its best, this technique allows Didion to move back and forth between a close identification with Maria and an ironic distance from her. Alfred Kazin has argued, however, that when her control becomes too obvious, Didion turns herself into a kind of literary director-auteur.

Upon first reading *Play It As It Lays*, one is likely to be struck by its spare, bleak, nihilistic tone. What becomes evident with successive readings, however, is the crucial function that irony and humor serve in this novel. One of the most hideously black comic scenes in *Play It As It Lays*, the contact between Maria and the man who is to take her to an abortionist, is also one of the most memorable in contemporary fiction. Maria meets her contact, a moral zombie in white duck pants, under the big red "T" at the local Thriftimart. To pass the time he hums "I Get a Kick Out of You" and begins to make inane small talk. Speaking of the neighborhood through which they are passing, he says: "Nice homes here. Nice for kids." He then asks Maria whether she gets good mileage on her car and proceeds to compare the merits of his Cadillac with those of a Camaro that he is contemplating buying: "Maybe that sounds like a step down, a Cad to a Camaro, but I've got my eye on this particular Camaro, exact model of the pace car in the Indianapolis 500."

Because Maria has strong maternal instincts, her abortion is the cause of much guilt and anxiety. It can also be seen as a symbol of the breakdown of the family and of traditional standards of morality. Yet what makes the episode of the abortion unforgettably grotesque is the image of that cretin in white duck pants babbling about the mileage that Maria gets on her car. Throughout *Play It As It Lays*, Didion employs just such comic touches to undercut the sentimental, self-pitying nihilism inherent in Maria's story.

The Characters

In many respects Maria Wyeth is a typical Didion woman—weak, confused, eccentric, and morbidly nostalgic for a traditional society with strong and loving fathers. Her only present link to that world comes in intermittent encounters with her father's old business partner, Benny Austin. None of the men with whom she is sexually involved is strong (they range from weak to brutal), and none could be described as either loving or paternal. Indeed, what Didion depicts is a kind of sexual conflict that pervades American literature. In *Love and Death in the American Novel* (1960), Leslie Fiedler speaks of the schizophrenia that informs American perceptions of sexual identity. He argues that just as women are frequently viewed as either virgin or whore, Earth Mother or bitch goddess; so too are men often depicted in terms of two extremes—as being either gentleman or seducer, rational suitor or demon lover. Accordingly, the protagonist in each of Didion's novels is torn between Apollonian and Dionysian lovers. In *Play It As It Lays* the author has given her single Apollonian figure three Dionysian rivals.

One of the most harrowing scenes in the novel occurs when Maria encounters an egocentric young actor named Johnny Waters at a typically decadent Hollywood party. Waters is the sort of individual who plays "Midnight Hour" repeatedly on the tape deck of his car, mistakenly calls Maria "Myra," and suggests that she "do it with a Coke bottle" when she rejects his sexual advances. Later, when he does get his way with her, he breaks an amyl nitrite popper under his nose just prior to orgasm, tells Maria not to move, and orders her to wake him in three hours—"with your tongue."

Another of Maria's Dionysian lovers is the vaguely demonic Ivan Costello. Because he lives in New York, Ivan is mostly a memory or a voice on the telephone. (He is in the habit of calling Maria up at night to say: "How much do you want it....Tell me what you'd do to get it from me.") If anything, Maria's relationship with her husband, Carter, is even worse. Like Johnny Waters and Ivan Costello, Carter is a self-centered hedonist who treats Maria solely as an object. He has directed the only two films in which she has appeared, and when he thinks of her, it is invariably in cinematic terms. Remembering his life with Maria, Carter says: "I played and replayed these scenes and others like them, composing them as if for the camera, trying to find some order, a pattern. I found none."

As Didion's name typing would imply, Les Goodwin is a better but weaker man than Maria's other lovers. After aborting her unborn child (Les is probably the father), Maria fantasizes an idyllic life in which she and Les and Kate live in a house by the sea. In her waking moments, however, she realizes that such a life can never be. When she finally does get away for a weekend with Les, even that experience proves empty. Although they never mention it, the memory of their aborted child creates a permanent strain between them.

Next to Maria herself, the most important character in the novel is BZ. At the most superficial level, he is an example of the decadence of Hollywood. (While he is secretly indulging in sexual perversions, his mother pays his wife to stay married to him.) Gradually, however, the reader comes to see him as primarily a victim. He cares more for Maria than any of the other men do. When he tries to persuade her to join him in suicide, he is motivated by love, not malice. Also, in his attitude toward life and death, he serves as a necessary foil to Maria.

Themes and Meanings

If there is any positive theme in this otherwise nihilistic novel, it is suggested by Didion's title. *"Always when I play back my father's voice,"* Maria says, *"it is with a professional rasp, it goes as it lays, don't do it the hard way. My father advised me that life itself was a crap game: it was one of two lessons I learned as a child. The other was that overturning a rock was apt to reveal a rattlesnake. As lessons go those two seem to hold up, but not to apply."*

In expecting to find a snake under every rock, Maria is symbolically acknowledging the pervasiveness of evil in an essentially hostile universe. (She has suggested earlier that it is a universe in which one cannot even count on Darwinian logic to prevail.) So, how does one live in such an environment? By playing it as it lays, by never taking the hard way in anything. Although Maria has learned this lesson in childhood and continues to live by it, she concedes that such stoic acceptance (if that is what it is) does not really work. It is simply one arbitrary method among many for dealing with the void in which humanity is doomed to live. It is a lesson that seems to hold up *"but not to apply."*

Critical Context

When *Play It As It Lays* was first published, John Leonard wrote: "There hasn't been another writer of Joan Didion's quality since Nathanael West." This comparison is appropriate for several reasons. First, *Play It As It Lays* is a classic Hollywood novel in the tradition of West's *The Day of the Locust* (1939). The introduction of sound into motion pictures in the late 1920's and early 1930's created a need for dialogue that lured many talented writers to the West Coast. Several (like West) went on to write bitter, satiric novels about the decadence and meretriciousness of Tinsel Town. *Play It As It Lays* seems to be part of that tradition.

To categorize *Play It As It Lays* as merely another anti-Hollywood novel, however, is somehow inadequate. The action of the novel occurs less in Southern California than in an existential void (the white space off the page). Something more fundamental than Hollywood is the cause of BZ's despair and Maria's catatonic resignation. (Indeed, in several of her essays Didion has ridiculed writers who propagate the image of "Hollywood the Destroyer.") At least in this one novel, Didion's pessimism surpasses both the defiant humanism of Camus and the apocalyptic cynicism of West. Maria Wyeth is too passive a character to choose the ritualistic death of suicide or (like West's characters) go berserk at a Hollywood riot. She has been reduced to a state of moral and spiritual paralysis, in which even death seems a sentimental cop-out. Going beyond the comparison to West, Leonard finds an even more suggestive parallel when he notes that Didion's vision in *Play It As It Lays* is "as bleak and precise as Eliot's in *The Waste Land*."

Sources for Further Study
Geherin, David J. "Nothingness and Beyond: Joan Didion's *Play It As It Lays*," in *Critique: Studies in Modern Fiction*. XVI (1974), pp. 64-78.
Henderson, Katherine Usher. *Joan Didion*, 1981.
Leonard, John. "The Cities of the Desert, the Desert of the Mind," in *The New York Times*. CXIX (July 21, 1970), p. 33.
Winchell, Mark Royden. *Joan Didion*, 1980.

Mark Royden Winchell

PLUM BUN

Author: Jessie Redmon Fauset (1882-1961)
Type of plot: Social realism
Time of plot: From 1900 to the 1920's
Locale: Philadelphia and New York City, specifically Greenwich Village and Harlem
First published: 1929

> *Principal characters:*
> ANGELA MURRAY, the central figure, a young black woman who can pass as white and who changes her name to Angèle Mory
> VIRGINIA (JINNY) MURRAY, her younger sister, who has brown skin
> Roger Fielding, a rich white man who, thinking that Angela is white, wants her to be his mistress
> ANTHONY CROSS, a sensitive black man who can pass as white but chooses not to, and who is in love with Angela
> RACHEL POWELL, a young black woman who is a fellow art student of Angela
> MARTHA BURDEN, a young white woman who is a friend and fellow art student of Angela
> JUNIUS and
> MATTIE MURRAY, the parents of Angela and Virginia; the father is dark-skinned; the mother can pass as white; both die early in the novel

The Novel

Most of the narrative focuses on the life of Angela Murray, from her early childhood in a black, working-class area of Philadelphia to her late twenties, when she achieves some success as an artist in New York City. The novel is divided into five parts, each part based on one portion of the well-known children's verse: "To Market, to Market/ To buy a Plum Bun;/ Home again, Home again,/ Market is done."

In the first part, "Home," the Murray family is introduced: a father, a mother, and two daughters, living on Opal Street in Philadelphia, a residential area of small, cramped houses. The race of the family immediately becomes an issue as the focus moves to Angela, the older daughter, who feels at a very young age the constraints placed upon her life by the fact of the family's color. Angela, like her mother, has a "creamy complexion" and can pass as white; Virginia, like her father, is dark. Angela's youthful yearning is for freedom, and she very soon realizes that she and her mother, when

in the city alone, have access to the rewards of life, the glamours and pleasures of the marketplace, that are closed to her father and to Virginia.
Mattie Murray often plays at being white and finds it a pleasant pastime,
but she always professes her color when principle demands it. Angela, however, is keenly aware of the disadvantages of color and deeply hurt by the
rejection of her white friends when they learn that she is black. The family
is a close and caring one, but the tensions brought on by color are only
relieved on Sunday afternoons, when they are alone and isolated from the
color-conscious world of the city.

The two sisters are left truly alone, however, when both parents die
within weeks of each other. The father dies of a heart attack, seemingly
brought about by a racial confrontation in which he has to deny his
husbandly relationship to Mattie. Mattie dies shortly thereafter, her heart
more with her husband than with the tribulations of the world. Angela's
inheritance, three thousand dollars, is, she believes, her golden opportunity
for freedom; she flees Philadelphia for the glamour and promise of New
York City; Virginia decides to stay with her inheritance, the parents' home,
in Philadelphia.

In part 2, "Market," Angela becomes an art student in New York City,
changes her name, establishes herself in Greenwich Village, and, after some
inner debate, determines, as she did in Philadelphia, that to refrain from
announcing her race will afford her the freedom to reach for the riches and
pleasures of life. In New York City, she can rely on the fact that nothing will
betray her race; she can even hope to marry a rich white man who can give
her the entrance into the good life she so desires.

Angela is drawn to the simplicity and the values of the other art students,
particularly Martha Burden and Anthony Cross; she is especially fascinated
by a young black woman, Rachel Powell, who quietly and persistently develops her art. The entrance of a rich young white man, Roger Fielding, is
more alluring, however, and Angela determines to make him her husband.
Roger is attracted to Angela and pursues her, but only with the intention of
seducing her: He is not about to marry a girl out of his own class, even
though she may be white. The climax of this section occurs when Virginia
decides to come to New York; Angela, caught between Roger and her sister, denies the sisterly bond, initiating an estrangement with Virginia that
will last until the closing section of the narrative. Virginia is always a reminder to Angela that, unlike her mother, Angela does not acknowledge
her race when principle is involved.

In part 3, "Plum Bun," Angela appears to be well on her way to achieving her goals—she has taken Roger as her lover with the hope of future
marriage; she is persuading herself that she loves Roger and he her; she is
succeeding in her art. Yet the life of her friends and her sister persists in
intruding—Anthony Cross, who is in love with Angela, attracts her because

of his sensitivity and his sympathy with the struggles of black people; Martha Burden offers her a straightforward, sensible view of the world, an open, honest friendship; Rachel Powell reflects a pride in race and in talent that in Angela's own self has been submerged; Virginia's delight in the life of Harlem, the sustenance and joy she draws from living among blacks, presents Angela with the reality of the happiness possible within the black community, a reality that Angela has evaded since her childhood. Roger grows restless under Angela's possessiveness, and the third section of the novel closes with the end of their affair and Angela's growing awareness of the superficiality of her desire to be white and rich and free.

In part 4, "Home Again," Angela attempts a reconciliation with her sister and tries to recapture the closeness and the caring of their earlier life together. Angela is awakened, by a series of incidents involving her friends and Virginia, to the fact that she in her self-absorption has been blind to the developing selves of the others. Hoping to regain Anthony's love, she learns, by his confession, that he is "colored," and that he and her sister are engaged. This relationship has evolved over a period of time and has, as Anthony tells Angela, been partially a result of his own struggle to overcome the temptations of "passing" as white. Anthony, still thinking that Angela is white, is unaware of her relation to Virginia. Anthony's confessions prompt an empathetic confession from Angela—she, too, is "colored."

Angela's awareness of the ironies of her life, her decision never to see Anthony again, her recognition of the strength of her race, as evidenced not only in Anthony, Virginia, and Rachel but also in her new perceptions of blacks who have moved briefly through her life, lead into the last section, "Market Is Done." Here, Angela confronts her own racial consciousness and announces her heritage publicly, primarily to defend Rachel, who has been refused an art scholarship because of her color. Angela realizes how much her own scholarship was a matter of color and not simply of talent and so identifies herself with those who have been rejected, ostracized, and humiliated because of race. After a series of acknowledgments by all the major figures, Anthony and Angela are reunited, and Virginia returns to her first love, Martin, and to Philadelphia. There is common agreement that happiness cannot be achieved by a denial of one's race and cultural heritage.

The Characters

The continuing focus on Angela allows the development of the duality in her character—her inner sympathy with her race, her external rejection of it. The characterization allows, on one hand, for the reader's questioning of Angela's materialistic external values and, on the other, for the reader's understanding of the inner evolution of Angela's self-esteem and race identification. Most of the other figures are, in some way, parallel with Angela, and they serve symbolically as reflections of various, often contradictory, aspects of Angela's self. Mattie Murray, for example, is the Angela who can pass as white; Mattie has achieved a balance between this external "white" self and the black self she really is—Angela's progress throughout the novel is to achieve that same kind of balance, only in a more complex world than that of her mother. Virginia is the external reminder to Angela of that black self that should be publicly acknowledged; Angela's warring with Virginia is symbolic of the war between her own white and black selves. Anthony's struggle with his racial consciousness parallels Angela's, and his emotional confrontations with his own actions bring to life authentic passions in Angela. Thus, the black Anthony and the white Roger represent the conflict within Angela between a true expression of love for others and a false passion based on selfish ends. Rachel is symbolic of the unity possible between self and art, a unity that Angela must struggle to achieve. Angela's are cannot be true until she is true to herself and to her race.

The characters are all established in realistic settings, in the context of descriptions of their homes, their clothing, and their physical interaction with the varied events and things of the marketplace. This depiction of the external world reinforces those aspects of character that are formed by physical and social realities. For example, Junius and Mattie's withdrawal to their home and their eventual deaths reflect their decision to isolate themselves as much as possible from the pain that the larger society provides. The descriptions of Harlem and of the people actively and intensely involved in that bustling community help to reinforce the characterization of Virginia, who accepts her race and finds within it joy and affirmation. Throughout the novel, Angela's developing character is reflected in the homes and apartments in which she lives—her sense of being cramped is reflected in the smallness of her room at home; the apartment rented by Roger is filled with material objects that have no human connection. The realistic description in the novel reflects how much the characters, and Angela particularly, are tied to the external world. Angela, Anthony, Virginia, and Rachel all achieve a sense of freedom and of freedom of choice once they have confronted truthfully the realities of a larger society that has defined their limitations and constricted their movement.

Themes and Meanings

One of the major themes of the novel and the one concept that Angela has much difficulty in accepting is that color is a matter of paramount importance in the American social system. The characters are caught in a fallacious social construct that stretches appearance far beyond being. To appear white is more important to the marketplace than any quality of being, so friendship for whites, for example, can be created only if the participants are white or are willing to pass as white. Angela could maintain her friendship with her white childhood friends only for as long as she "appeared" white; once the appearance was assaulted by the truth of being, the friendships ended.

This book, like others of the Harlem Renaissance, touches not only on the racial prejudices of white America but also on the color-prejudice involved in denying one's race, as Angela does, because she can pass as white. Through Angela, Fauset shows how those who deny their race also deny their own being; they are both victims of the social system that sanctifies appearance and victimizers of their blood sisters and brothers who do not have the "safety" of a white appearance. Moreover, those who pass as white lose the opportunity to do good for the entire race; Angela can defend Rachel against the injustices of the system only after she decides to announce publicly her own racial bond.

Fauset also suggests that society as a whole can claim its identity if it can reject the powerful myths of the white social system. The myths of the marketplace tempt and seduce Angela. She creates and re-creates her identity only after she overcomes the belief that the pleasures of the white world are more satisfying than the life that can be created on the foundation of values not dependent on appearance. The life of Harlem and the life that Virginia creates come from a love of human worth, diversity, and talent, not from the myth that initially attracted Angela—that the combination of white skin and wealth will provide happiness and freedom.

Critical Context

Plum Bun is generally considered to be one of Fauset's best novels. Fauset, however, has been valued more for her social and journalistic contributions to the Harlem Renaissance than for the considerable literary and cultural value of her fiction. Her fiction has also been misjudged by those who claim that, as an upper-middle-class black woman, she had more sympathy for white American values than for the values of black Americans. A careful reading of *Plum Bun* reveals that Fauset is, indeed, in sympathy with black American values. Her point is that blacks in cities such as New York can find their identity only when they can work through the myths and social constructs of the dominant white culture. Fauset chose Angela rather than Virginia as her protagonist, not because she wanted to promote the values of the marketplace but because she wanted to depict both the internal and the external struggle that is often necessary in order to achieve black pride.

With the recent emphasis on feminist criticism, Fauset's work is receiving the comprehensive attention it deserves. She is no longer dismissed as a writer who wanted, through the novel of manners, to promote the values of a white, class society. By focusing more on the techniques that Fauset used to present the struggle of her major women figures, contemporary critics can separate Fauset's views from those of her characters—for example, no longer is there the simplistic assumption that Fauset validates such beliefs as Angela articulates through most of the narrative. What Angela does admire and value at the end—authentic emotional expression, the bonds of sisterhood and talent, the enhancement of a culture through the vitality of its members—is humanistic values that are not class-dependent, nor are they very evident in the white society that dominates Angela's life. These values are, however, as in the community of Harlem, able to have their impact on cultural growth, both within the black community and perhaps, with even more struggle, within the entire American culture.

Sources for Further Study

Christian, Barbara. *Black Women Novelists: The Development of a Tradition, 1892-1976*, 1980.

McDowell, Deborah E. "The Neglected Dimension of Jessie Redmon Fauset," in *Conjuring: Black Women, Fiction, and Literary Tradition*, 1985.

Sato, Hiroko. "Under the Harlem Shadows: A Study of Jessie Fauset and Nella Larsen," in *The Harlem Renaissance Remembered*, 1972.

Rosalie Hewitt

PNIN

Author: Vladimir Nabokov (1899-1977)
Type of plot: Fictitious biography
Time of plot: 1950 to 1955
Locale: Waindell College, New England, and a nearby mountain resort
First published: 1957

> *Principal characters:*
> TIMOFEY PAVELOVICH PNIN, the protagonist, fifty-two years old, a professor of Russian and a naturalized citizen of the United States
> DR. LIZA WIND, his former wife, a psychologist
> VICTOR WIND, fourteen years old, her son by Dr. Eric Wind
> DR. HAGEN, the head of the German Department and Pnin's boss
> THE NARRATOR, a Russian scholar

The Novel

Timofey Pavelovich Pnin has taught Russian at Waindell College for several years; his odd ways, his restlessness, his difficulty with the nuances of the English language, and his gnomelike features make him the brunt of endless cruel anecdotes and imitations. The story laid out for the reader, however, is one refashioned after the fact from these unkind stories, by the narrator, a scholar who replaces Pnin at Waindell College and who makes of the anecdotes a sympathetic biography of a true humanist, in love with the infinite variety of life and its ability to give pain, in love with his simple surroundings, constantly changing, and impervious to cynicism and incapable of ill will.

The novel follows a series of displacements as Pnin moves from dwelling to dwelling in the college community, first displaced by a returning landlady's daughter, again by a mistaken sense that permanency is on the horizon, and finally by loss of his position at Waindell, when he is replaced by the narrator, who assembles from a residue of anecdotes a portrait of Pnin himself. Pnin's restlessness is an externalization of his own inability to adjust to any circumstance, an outward sign of an inner discomfort with his situation. Having begun his adulthood with exile and emigration, Pnin seems destined to continue it past the novel's last page.

Three incidents give the novel a structure based on human contacts made and broken: Pnin's former wife Liza returns to him briefly but turns down his timid offer to regain their lost affection, breaking Pnin's heart once again. Her son Victor, by another marriage, visits Pnin and establishes a relationship despite the clumsiness of Pnin's efforts to anticipate his pleasures. Pnin's final separation from his friends and colleagues, stemming from his loss of his position, ends the novel on a depressing note; the reader learns in Nabokov's *Pale Fire* (1962) that he finally earned tenure at another college. A bucolic interlude at The Pines, a retreat for Russian immigrants in the mountains, shows a different side of Pnin, a side that, had his ingrained restlessness not taken him away, would have given the reader a happier, more successful story to hear; swimming with friends, Pnin is self-confident, even brave, and on the croquet course he is a force to be reckoned with. His return to the American college atmosphere returns him to timidity. A "house-heating," as Pnin calls it, turns sour when Dr. Hagen, his superior, informs him of his release; the unnamed narrator comes to the campus only in time to see Pnin drive out of town in a wreck of a car.

The Characters

Pnin is an Old World scholar misplaced in a New World academic community; his charming scholarly habits go unappreciated among his colleagues, most of whom are inadequate to their tasks (the head of the French Department cannot speak French and believes that Chateaubriand was a great chef). It is a mistake, however, to label Pnin as a typical absentminded professor. The narrator describes him as overconscious of his surroundings, attentive to details, inconveniencing only himself as he struggles to adjust to the bewildering world of reality. His digressions on details of information constitute an attempt to be helpful, and despite his confusion over the American idiom, he knows intuitively when his help is needed.

His former wife, Liza Wind, every bit as restless as he, moves from husband to husband as Pnin moves from place to place, living a desperate version of romance, possibly begun by a brief affair with the narrator in their youth. On the surface unworthy of Pnin's affection, she is equal to his ardor because her quiet intensity, aimless but complete, echoes Pnin's own aimlessness and intensity. It is appropriate that her son by the man who stole her from Pnin should appear, like a gift, in Pnin's life just when it is most inappropriate and, at the same time, touching.

Young Victor, unsporty, part-orphan, awkward in Pnin's presence, shy and gracious at the same time, shares an uncanny resemblance to Pnin without sharing blood, as though they were related by mutual disappointment. Victor sends Pnin a delicate crystal bowl, a pointless gift that is as accidental and wonderful as his visit; in the most poignant scene in the novel, Pnin drops a nutcracker into some soapy suds and hears a heartrending crack. Has the beautiful crystal bowl broken? It has not, just as Victor's fragile link to Pnin is not shattered by their separation.

Of the faculty at Waindell, Dr. Hagen comes closest to wisdom, although he gives Pnin the bad news of his termination with more insensitivity than one might expect. Regretting the necessity of dismissing Pnin, he offers to keep him on through the spring as the least painful severance procedure, an offer which Pnin declines. Hagen's own change of venue ironically signals Pnin's next, forced exile. The narrator, about whom very little biographical information is given, presents himself modestly; he is apparently a more responsible scholar and a rather more celebrated figure, a neutral observer whose life touched Pnin's at undramatic moments and whose final tribute is the linguistically adroit rearrangement of the cruel anecdotes into the story of Pnin's life.

Themes and Meanings

"Displaced" by the circumstances of his youth, Pnin spends his life trying to find a little corner where he can be comfortable with his books, his eccentricities, his loneliness. Nabokov indicts much of the academic community in this portrait (he was a professor at Cornell University when he wrote the novel), sparing individuals who harbor Pnin from moment to moment, but exposing the callousness and political self-preservation of the majority.

Oddness is never popular, but in theory a liberal arts institution should have a corner or two for the more fragile souls who seek refuge in the academic world. Nabokov's delightful sensitivity to words gives the reader a metaphor for Pnin's more universal difficulty with communications of all kinds; he can understand a squirrel's needs, but not his own. Among the recurring motifs is the presence of a squirrel on certain occasions of Pnin's loneliness, a symbol, according to some scholars, of his lost love, a victim of the German concentration camps. One particular squirrel anecdote adds a special clarification to the reader's understanding of Pnin's dilemma. He holds the water fountain faucet down so that a squirrel can take a drink. The squirrel drinks and goes off without gratitude, and that detail speaks for the thematic thread of Pnin's life: The nurturing and nourishing Pnin finds only ingratitude from those whose thirsts he tries to quench. Every time Pnin looks at an out-of-date timetable, shoves the wrong notes into his pocket, or otherwise relies on an unreliable permanence, the theme of miscommunication that runs through the novel is reinforced. Even Pnin's anguish is untranslatable: "Emitting what he thought were international exclamations of anxiety and entreaty," he lives his life from misunderstanding to misunderstanding, until it is knit together by the narrator.

Nabokov's narrative style is uncommonly complex. Eschewing the simple omniscient narrative form, the narrator assumes, gathers evidence, projects possibilities, and invents isolated incidents based on conjecture, in a complicated style that complements the themes of the novel itself. The author's own remarkable control of the English language, a language he learned under circumstances similar to Pnin's, adds a final layer of irony and pathos.

Critical Context

Although Nabokov's reputation rests in large measure on the successful publication of *Lolita* two years before he published *Pnin*, the later novel offers special pleasures to his readers that the more self-conscious and lustier best-seller lacks. Termed a "fictitious biography" by critic H. Grabes, who discusses the English novels of Nabokov independently of his novels in Russian (which Nabokov himself later translated into English), *Pnin* is distinguished by a narrative strategy that can be traced to the eighteenth century novel, though Nabokov gives it a modern twist. The narrator of *Pnin* falls between the omniscient narrator of traditional fiction and the so-called unreliable narrator of William Faulkner and his imitators; by inserting his own character into Pnin's story, the narrator deliberately limits his knowledge of the man and, unlike a true biographer, selects from truth and fancy those elements that seem to illuminate his subject without undue attention to accuracy. By depicting Pnin as a concentration of central traits, the narrator seeks to show the "real life" of Pnin rather than the true one. While almost all biographers claim accuracy and neutrality regarding their subject, a fictitious biographer is bound by no such stricture, and can paint in whatever strokes and colors best present his fictitious invention.

The reviews of Nabokov's novel about the life of the exiled professor did not accord Nabokov unqualified praise. Some critics thought *Pnin* a slight accomplishment after *Lolita*. *Pale Fire*, on the surface a more ambitious work, followed close after and gave the character Pnin a tenured position as "professor of Russian." In time, however, it has become apparent that the novel's charms, like the those of Pnin himself, are more enduring than the attractions of some of Nabokov's flashier books, which gained a cult following for reasons unrelated to their own literary excellence. Close textual studies of *Pnin* have turned up all manner of obscure literary and personal references, etymological oddities, hidden allusions to other novels, and the like, but no amount of superficial "scholarship" of the kind Pnin both practiced and transcended can obfuscate the book's basic charm and grace.

Sources for Further Study

Bader, Julia. *Crystal Land: Patterns of Artifice in Vladimir Nabokov's English Novels*, 1973.

Clancy, Laurie. *The Novels of Vladimir Nabokov*, 1985.

Grabes, H. *Fictitious Biographies: Vladimir Nabokov's English Novels*, 1977.

Pifer, Ellen. *Nabokov and the Novel*, 1980.

Rampton, David. *Vladimir Nabokov: A Critical Study of the Novels*, 1984.

Thomas J. Taylor

PORTNOY'S COMPLAINT

Author: Philip Roth (1933-   )
Type of plot: Comic monologue
Time of plot: The 1930's to the 1960's
Locale: Newark, New Jersey, and New York City
First published: 1969

> *Principal characters:*
> ALEXANDER PORTNOY, a liberal Jewish man obsessed with sex, self, and shame
> SOPHIE PORTNOY, his stereotypical, smothering Jewish mother
> JACK PORTNOY, his downtrodden and ineffectual father
> MARY JANE REED (THE MONKEY), an Appalachian female who is the fulfillment of his sexual fantasies
> KAY CAMPBELL (THE PUMPKIN), his girlfriend at Antioch College
> NAOMI (THE HEROINE), a Jewish woman with whom he is unsuccessful in his sexual exploits
> SARAH ABBOTT MAULSBY (THE PILGRIM), another woman in his life
> SMOLKA, an envied boyhood classmate

The Novel

Although *Portnoy's Complaint* is a full-length novel, the reader is asked to accept it as an extended dramatic monologue spoken by Alexander Portnoy while in analysis with his psychoanalyst, Doctor Spielvogel. The book is prefaced by a definition of "Portnoy's Complaint," a textbook term coined by Spielvogel for a disorder in which "strongly-felt ethical and altruistic impulses are perpetually warring with extreme sexual longings, often of a perverse nature." Although this definition may be a clinical summation of the dramatic conflict that preoccupies Portnoy, it does not come close to indicating the confessional intensity and bawdy hilarity of Roth's novel.

The book is divided into connected, but somewhat independent, sections focusing on Portnoy's parents (particularly his mother, "the most unforgettable character" he has ever met); his endless adolescent experience with masturbation; his youthful sexual experiences, especially with Gentile girls; his varied sexual experiences with "the Monkey," a high-fashion model from the hills of West Virginia; and his pilgrimage to Israel. All of these adventures are punctuated by rebellious outcries against the guilt that he feels for his sexual obsessions, as he continues to try to be "Mommy's best little boy."

Indeed he is a "good boy"—that is, in public, making all A's in school, becoming a good Jewish liberal, even to being appointed New York's Assistant Commissioner of Human Opportunity. Nevertheless, it is his sexual fantasies and adventures and his shame about them which dominate the book, and if the reader can overcome his or her reactions to explicit sexual descriptions and four-letter words, both Portnoy's escapades and his disproportionate guilt are riotously funny. No summary can convey the absurdist humor of Portnoy's voice in recalling his adolescent preoccupation with his penis and the genitals of every female he encounters.

Dominated by his well-meaning but smothering mother, Portnoy yearns for the masculinity represented by a Turkish bath that he visits with his father, an all-male preserve. Yet, as much as he is obsessed with sex, he is also dominated by the repression he believes is characteristic of his Jewish childhood. Although the book is thoroughly Jewish in its idiom and cultural background, the dilemma Portnoy describes is also characteristic of American Puritan culture in general. No American male can fail to identify with his real but comic anguish.

The novel depicts one long quest in which Portnoy uses sexuality as a weapon to rebel against repression, even as he is victimized by sexuality itself. Caught by what Sigmund Freud calls "The Most Prevalent Form of Degradation in Erotic Life," Portnoy cannot unite the two currents of feeling—the affectionate with the sensuous. Only when his sexual partner is degraded can he freely feel his sensual feelings—which explains his preoccupation with, and his ultimate rejection of, shiksas, or Gentile women. When he meets the Monkey, who seems the complete embodiment of his adolescent sexual fantasies, he ridicules and humiliates her until he drives her away—for he can neither accept her as a real woman nor be satisfied with her as a sexual fantasy.

Throughout the novel, Portnoy recounts his obsessive masturbation, his constant preoccupation with a pornographic fantasy object whom he calls Thereal McCoy, and his unsuccessful romantic and sexual experiences with various Gentile women. In addition, however, he devotes as much of his confessional monologue to his complaints against the repressions placed on him by his parents and his Jewish culture in general—which primarily amounts to the constant message that "life is boundaries and restrictions if it's anything, hundreds of thousands of little rules laid down by none other than None Other." Finally, when he goes to Israel on a sort of pilgrimage to atone for his transgressions and to come to terms with his cultural roots, he meets and tries to have sex with a Jewish woman, only to discover that he is impotent with her. The novel ends with Portnoy's drawn-out howl at what he calls the disproportion of the guilt he feels, followed by a "punch line," Dr. Spielvogel's only words in the novel, "Now vee may perhaps to begin Yes?"

The Characters

In a way the entire novel *is* Portnoy's character, for he not only is its central and entirely dominating figure but also is its only narrator. Because of his Jewish childhood, particularly his desire to please his mother, Portnoy says at one point that his occupation is "being good." He wants to be a good little boy, but he cannot control the demands of his own physical body as a child, and thus suffers disproportionate guilt for his masturbation and for his adolescent sexual fantasies about every female whom he meets. Portnoy is the living embodiment of what Freud defines as "civilization and its discontents"—a walking personification of the Oedipus complex. Moreover, he is representative of what many refer to as the "self-hating" Jew, which is what the Jewish woman Naomi calls him in the novel's final section. He presents himself throughout as both the teller of and the butt of an extended Jewish joke. He is intelligent enough to know himself well, to know who and what he is, but he is not strong enough to free himself from his dilemma of being torn between his desire to be good and his obsessive sexual desires.

Portnoy's mother and father, Sophie and Jack, are less real people than they are stereotypes of the Jewish mother and father in America, with Sophie complaining to her friends that she is "too good," and warning Portnoy about eating Gentile junk food, and Jack complaining about his constant constipation, both literally and metaphorically. Portnoy sees them both as the greatest packagers of guilt in society. Having read Freud, Portnoy sees the Jewish woman, Naomi, with whom he unsuccessfully tries to have sex, as a mother-substitute; he then cries out to Doctor Spielvogel, "This then is the culmination of the Oedipal drama, Doctor? More farce, my friend! Too much to swallow, I'm afraid! *Oedipus Rex* is a famous tragedy, schmuck, not another joke!" Although Portnoy wishes that he could have nourished himself on his father's vulgarity instead of always searching for his mother's approval, even that vulgarity has become a source of shame—"every place I turn something else to be ashamed of."

The Monkey also is less a real character than she is the embodiment of Portnoy's adolescent fantasy of the sexual woman, the "star of all those pornographic films" he produces in his own head. Uneducated hillbilly turned high-fashion model, she is an aggressively sexual creature instead of the reluctant, puritan Gentile women he has known before. Although she has her own needs, Portnoy can focus on the needs of no one but himself. Kay Campbell (the Pumpkin), Portnoy's girlfriend at Antioch College, represents his yearning for Protestant middle-American values, while Sarah Abbott Maulsby (the Pilgrim) embodies New England respectability. Still, as Portnoy himself recognizes, he does not want these women so much as he wants what they represent.

Themes and Meanings

The most basic thematic interest in the novel centers on the Freudian tension between human desires for controlled civilized behavior and the discontent that results from having to give up impulsive behavior to establish civilization. Portnoy is the extreme embodiment of the modern man self-consciously caught in this war between necessary control and desired freedom. Such a description, however, is surely misleading, for the novel, serious as its theme may be, is one of the great comic masterpieces of American literature. It is hard to take seriously the Portnoy voice agonizing about locking himself in the bathroom to engage in masturbation while his mother stands outside asking him not to flush so she can examine his stool. Portnoy describes his penis as his "battering ram to freedom," and cries out, "LET'S PUT THE ID BACK IN YID. Liberate this nice Jewish boy's libido, will you please?" Although Portnoy longs for the uninhibited sexual attitude of his boyhood classmate Smolka, at the same time, he asks, "How would I like my underwear all gray and jumbled up in my drawer, as Smolka's always is?" What Portnoy cannot tolerate is the fact that he cannot have both the cookies and milk which his mother supplies and the sexual experiences that Smolka enjoys.

Since sexuality is the central taboo impulse which civilization seeks to control to assure its own stability, the nature of sexuality itself is a primary theme of the novel. "What a mysterious business it is," says Portnoy, "with sex the human imagination runs to Z, and then beyond." Because sexuality itself is so inextricably bound up with fantasy, the very style and tone of the book combines the realism of Portnoy's experience with the surrealism of his sexual fantasies. The fact that he is Jewish is less important in its own right than as an embodiment of the extreme insistence on "self-control, sobriety, sanctions" which society says is the "key to human life." The goyim, or non-Jews, whom Portnoy often envies are in fact subject to restrictions and recriminations no less banal and crippling than the values which his Jewish heritage attempts to instill. Thus, the primary themes of the book are both psychological and social, but the medium for both themes is the hilarious self-satirizing voice of Portnoy, which is alternately sophomoric in its humor and sharply critical of social absurdity.

Critical Context

Portnoy's Complaint was somewhat of a cultural milestone in the fiction of the 1960's, for, although its obsessive focus on sexuality and its constant use of taboo words seemed to align it with many of the conventions associated with pornography, it was a serious novel with a serious theme. Consequently, its publication forced many cultural critics to reevaluate their previous assumptions about sexually explicit literature. It was hailed by many reviewers, made the best-seller list, and became a topic of cocktail-party conversation in an era in which "pop porno" became acceptable. Not since the works of Henry Miller had autobiographical fiction and explicit sexuality been so forthright and engaging.

Although much of the criticism of the book has focused on its Jewishness, many have argued that Roth's novel is as typically American as Mark Twain's *The Adventures of Huckleberry Finn* (1884) or J. D. Salinger's *The Catcher in the Rye* (1951)—a comic masterpiece of the cultural and personal conflicts of growing up in American society.

Portnoy's Complaint catapulted Roth into fame and controversy and assured his literary status after the early promise of his National Book Award winner, *Goodbye, Columbus* (1959). After its publication, he in a sense tried to live down its notoriety in a series of three semiautobiographical novels about a fictional character, Nathan Zuckerman, who also has written an autobiographical and scandalous book. It is as though *Portnoy's Complaint* were a personal demon that Roth sought to exorcise—one which continues to dominate his work.

Sources for Further Study
McDaniel, John N. *The Fiction of Philip Roth*, 1974.
Pinsker, Sanford. *The Comedy That "Hoits": An Essay on the Fiction of Philip Roth*, 1975.
_____, ed. *Critical Essays on Philip Roth*, 1982.
Rodgers, Bernard F., Jr. *Philip Roth*, 1978.
Roth, Philip. *Reading Myself and Others*, 1975.

Charles E. May

PRAISESONG FOR THE WIDOW

Author: Paule Marshall (1929-   )
Type of plot: Social realism
Time of plot: The late 1970's
Locale: A cruise ship in the Caribbean; Grenada; and Carriacou
First published: 1983

> *Principal characters:*
> AVEY JOHNSON, the protagonist, an affluent widow
> JEROME JOHNSON, her deceased husband
> LEBERT JOSEPH, an old native of Carriacou

The Novel

The primary action in the novel lies in the recapturing of identity and the achievement of self-actualization by Avey Johnson, who is recovering from the death of her husband, Jerome, four years earlier. In an effort to heal herself of her grief, she goes on a Caribbean cruise with two friends at the urging of two of her daughters and over the objections of the third. While on the cruise, she experiences persistent physical discomfort and emotional disquietude and is tormented by a recurring, disturbing dream of her childhood summers on Tatem Island in the South Carolina tidewater at the home of her great-aunt Cuney. Haunted by this experience, she abandons the cruise in Grenada with the intention of returning to her home in White Plains, New York, on the next available flight. Her return to New York is not immediate, however, for from Grenada she makes an excursion to the island of Carriacou, where she participates in the annual Big Drum ritual. Through this experience, she is able to achieve a physical and emotional healing as she probes her personal past and becomes reacquainted with her identity as "Avatara," who, as a child under the firm insistence and guidance of her great-aunt Cuney, was fully in tune with her essential self and the rich mythology of the black American heritage. In addition, her participation in the Big Drum ceremony precipitates her further discovery of her roots in the Arada people of Carriacou and in turn motivates her decision to sell her house in White Plains and to move to Tatem for at least part of the year so that she, like her great-aunt, can assume the role of the griot—the elder responsible for transmitting the people's history, mythology, and values to the younger generations.

Inextricably linked with this line of action is the story of Avey's marriage, which represents success as it is defined in traditional American terms and which epitomizes the realization of the American Dream. One learns the details of this marriage through Avey's flashbacks. From their origins in the tiny apartment on Halsey Street in Brooklyn to the spacious and costly house in the suburb of White Plains, the reader is able to trace the course of their marriage and, ultimately, Avey's need to find herself.

The Characters

Avey Johnson, the protagonist, is one of the most positive and finely portrayed characters in Afro-American literature. As opposed, for example, to the characters Pauline Breedlove and Eva Peace in Toni Morrison's novels *The Bluest Eye* (1970) and *Sula* (1973), Avey is free of the pathology that warps the mother-nurturer figure and renders her monstrous. Also, while as a nurturing figure she is not as spiritually evolved and as cosmically in tune as Minnie Ransom, the legendary healer in Toni Cade Bambara's *The Salt Eaters* (1980), she nevertheless possesses a secure sense of self and enough expertise and sophistication to prevent her from perceiving herself as a victim. She is a strong, self-directed, and insightful woman.

This insight becomes clear in her interactions with the women in the world of the novel. It is first perceived in her relationship with her three daughters. Because of her solidly middle-class definition of herself and her strong respect for upward mobility, she communicates effectively with Sis and Annawilda, who are themselves traditional American success stories. Her relationship with Marion, her third daughter, however, is strained because of Marion's worldview and her powerful Afrocentric allegiances. Further evidence lies in her decision to abandon the cruise to the great annoyance of her overbearing friend Thomasina Moore and the cowering dismay of her second traveling companion Clarice. By revealing Avey's indifference to their concerns and the shallowness of their thinking, Marshall foreshadows the spiritual regeneration that Avey will experience by the end of the novel, a regeneration that will prepare her to follow in the tradition of her great-aunt Cuney.

On the other hand, Marshall carefully manipulates how the reader sees Avey and her development through skillful juxtaposition of the two extreme male influences in her life. First, there is her husband, Jerome, known affectionately as Jay during the early years of their marriage. Spontaneous, fun-loving, and thoroughly in tune with the richness of his African and Afro-American past, he is without the trappings of middle-class life but is authentic in his response to himself, his family, and his larger environment. Nevertheless, as he assimilates into the mainstream of American life and becomes a black Horatio Alger, his ambition dulls the sparkle of his personality and diminishes his ethnic sensibilities and loyalties. Indeed, Jerome the high achiever and eminently successful entrepeneur gradually replaces Jay, with all that such a transition implies.

Diametrically opposed to Jerome yet also significant to Avey's well-being is Lebert Joseph, the aged native of Carriacou whom Avey meets in his small bar in Grenada. To the reader, it becomes clear that Lebert Joseph is what Jerome might have become had he been less dogged in his pursuit of the American Dream. Lebert, having enjoyed a long life, continues to maintain a strong sense of tradition and ethnicity; in describing the Big Drum ceremony to Avey, he is careful to stress the importance of respect for ancestral spirits to personal success. As a result of his urging and provision for accommodation, she makes the native excursion to Carriacou for the ceremony that ultimately leads to her spiritual awakening. If, then, Jerome has provided for her all of the physical comforts, Lebert provides for her what Jerome's hierarchy of values cannot—the gifts of salvation and a viable link with the past, gifts which enable her to redefine the present and thus lay the foundation for a positive and healthy future. One might say, then, that Lebert gives her the true gift of life.

Themes and Meanings

The principal theme in the novel is the quest for identity, out of which arise all other questions posed by the novel. Certainly, this quest is alluded to in one of Avey's flashbacks when she recalls her great-aunt Cuney's instruction that she tell people that her name is Avey, short for Avatara. It is only when Avey has come to terms with exactly who she is—after abandoning the cruise and making the correct assessment of what was virtuous in her life with Jerome—that her name holds true significance for her. Her quest is beset with ironies that become increasingly clear as the reader follows Avey's progress through each of the four sections of the novel. Like the persona in Robert Hayden's poem "Runagate Runagate," from which the first section of the book takes its name, Avey too pursues a type of freedom. Unlike the slave in the poem, however, Avey has not correctly defined her goals.

As the reader follows the workings of her mind through the course of the novel, one sees her as a manifestation of the tension between two warring value systems. Like the runaway slaves, Avey has fled the South for freedom of personhood, which she finds in the affluent sophistication of the urban North. Ironically, however, salvation or emancipation for her lies not in the American Dream and the traditional success story, but instead in what she has left behind: the healing and integrating properties of the traditional black South, which clearly have beckoned to her at various points in her life. As long as Avey is committed to the American Dream, she resists the pull of traditional black values (symbolically represented in the recurring dream about Aunt Cuney). It is only after she is able to divorce herself from the American Dream that she is able to achieve affirmation through her exposure to traditional black values.

The irony of Avey's quest is one of the great and recurring ironies in Afro-American fiction and governs the plot structure of many other novels. In short, while the protagonist seeks affirmation and fulfillment through upward social and economic mobility, he or she ultimately discovers that a descent is necessary in order to experience self-actualization. Similar experiences are depicted, for example, in the life and motion of the protagonist in Ralph Ellison's *Invisible Man* (1952) and in that of Janie Crawford in Zora Neale Hurston's *Their Eyes Were Watching God* (1937). Ellison's invisible man achieves insight only after he abandons his pursuit of the American Dream of success and physically descends to his habitat under the streets of New York. The plot of Janie Crawford's story also involves a descent motif: She marries affluence and success and thus moves up the social ladder, yet it is only after she marries Vergible "Tea Cake" Woods, a gambler and a drifter, and physically moves down into the land of muck and itinerant workers that she achieves emotional fulfillment and escalation. So it is also with Avey. In the novel, she has physically moved down from White Plains, New York, to the Caribbean. There she has to shed the trappings of her upper-middle-class identity—for example, once in her recurring dream Aunt Cuney is trying to strip away Avey's fur coat. In addition, when she is in Grenada, on the boat to Carriacou, and in Carriacou, her care is in the hands of people who are beneath her own social class. Lebert Joseph, in particular, although central to her existence, is by no means the social and economic success that her husband, Jerome, was. Yet it is only in moving down geographically, even below Tatem Island in the South Carolina tidewater, and in making the accompanying downward social motion, that Avey is able to evolve spiritually, resolving to take her rightful place in American society.

Important also to the central theme and structure of the novel are the subsidiary death and rebirth motif and the special role of bonding patterns among women. The reader is aware that in the acquisition of success and the good life, Avey and Jerome have died spiritually. It is only after Jerome has physically died as a result of a stroke (perhaps because of overwork) that Avey is ultimately able to achieve life. Before Avey's rebirth, one notes that Marion, whose birth she had tried to abort, but who is the most socially and spiritually alive of her daughters, is her least favorite. One notes further that while Avey is still locked into mainstream values, Aunt Cuney is her antagonist. When Avey reaches her crisis, succumbing to seasickness and losing control of her bowels (symbolic of her throwing off the decay and excess of her former life-style), she is nurtured through the experience by the women of Carriacou, who are reminiscent of the church mothers of her childhood. In addition, her bath after she awakens is administered by Rosalie Parvay, Lebert Joseph's daughter. The bath itself assumes the ritual symbolism of baptism, which at its core is anchored to the cycle of death and rebirth. A cleansed Avey is now prepared to participate in the Big Drum ritual, the various stages of which Mildy, Rosalie Parvay's maid, explains to her. Only thus rejuvenated can Avey reassess her relationship with the women in her life, acknowledging the true worth of Marion and Aunt Cuney and fully appreciating their centrality to her new sense of mission.

Critical Context

Upon its publication, *Praisesong for the Widow* was a critical success. The Book-of-the-Month Club carried it as an alternate, and it became the subject of scholarly discussion. As a writer, Marshall has been hailed both in the Caribbean and in the United States, although she has had to struggle against the barriers of sexism and racism. Her works have been widely published, and some have been reissued. *Praisesong for the Widow* was the fourth novel in her career as a serious fiction writer, which began with the publication of the novel *Brown Girl, Brownstones* (1959). Central to all of Marshall's fiction is the individual's desire for self-actualization and affirmation—a desire which, for the most part, her protagonists achieve. In contrast to many contemporary novels, *Praisesong for the Widow* celebrates life and hope.

Sources for Further Study

Christian, Barbara T. *Black Feminist Criticism: Perspectives on Black Women Writers*, 1985.

_____. "Paule Marshall," in *Afro American Fiction Writers After 1955*, 1984. Edited by Thadious M. Davis and Trudier Harris.

Carol P. Marsh

PYLON

Author: William Faulkner (1897-1962)
Type of plot: Modernist realism
Time of plot: Mid-Depression, during Mardi Gras
Locale: Primarily New Valois, Franciana, a transparent reference to New Orleans, and Ohio
First published: 1935

Principal characters:
LAZARUS, the reporter who covers the air show and becomes the book's major protagonist
ROGER SHUMANN, a pilot and the leader of a flying team
LAVERNE, a companion of Roger Shumann and a member of the team
THE BOY, LaVerne's son
JACK HOLMES, a member of the team and a parachutist
JIGGS, an airplane mechanic
HAGOOD, a newspaper editor

The Novel

Pylon was William Faulkner's eighth novel; he wrote it at the height of his powers, just before *Absalom, Absalom!* (1936) and not long after *Light in August* (1932). The novel is, above all, about flying and the motivation of those who fly. The "pylon" of the title is the tower or steel post around which a pilot must turn as he competes in a race at an air fair. The term figures prominently in the jargon of competing pilots; they "turn pylons" with their planes on each lap—they "take that pylon" and try to "fly the best pylon." Because of its subject matter, the novel is less well known than other novels Faulkner wrote during this period, yet it would be a mistake to think that it is "just about flying"; many of the themes closest to Faulkner's heart receive full, complex treatment in this neglected novel. *Pylon* is also one of Faulkner's most exciting books, set near and in New Orleans during the week of Mardi Gras.

The plot of the novel can be summarized quite simply: A flying team composed of a pilot, a "jumper," or parachutist, and a mechanic, accompanied by a woman and her son, are desperately short of money and hope to win at least one of the purses at an air show. They live only on their winnings, which means that often they have no place to stay, little to eat, and no money for transportation within a city. They resemble circus performers, and some of the themes in the book are remarkably close to those of Ingmar Bergman's film *The Naked Night* (1953). Although the book is about the "romance" of flying, the hard physical conditions of the performers are kept firmly in the foreground. Onlookers, newspaper reporters, and members of the audience speculate on their motivation: Do they fly for money or for another reason? Are they "human" and "like us" (or a Holy Family)? If one supposes that they do not do it for money, he quickly learns that they are driven by material needs. At the same time, money cannot account for their motivation. The exploration of this conflict is central to the book. It throws considerable light on Faulkner's theme of "survival," explored in other novels and referred to in his Nobel Prize address; as *Pylon* reveals, this survival is never a purely materialistic necessity but is balanced against ideals and other claims, often extremely irrational. The book also develops Faulkner's concept of psychological necessity, that men and women must do what they are driven to do by their most profound inner motivations. This is explored through solid, complex characters who differ widely from one another and who come from a very broad variety of social strata.

One of the strangest, most unexpected relationships in the book gradually develops as it proceeds. The reporter who covers the air show becomes fascinated by Roger Shumann's flying team; he makes their acquaintance and tries to help them. This desire appears to be completely altrustic, with no self-interest. He becomes increasingly involved in the action, and, inadvertently, it is he who is responsible for the team's destruction. He devises a scheme that will permit them to buy a new, more powerful plane which will win the final trophy race that has the biggest purse. This, he thinks, will solve their financial problems once and for all. The reporter is partly in love with the female member of the team, LaVerne, but he is equally concerned about the welfare of the child and the team as a whole. His intention is like that of Gregers Werle in Henrik Ibsen's *The Wild Duck* (1884), the busybody who tries to do good but ends up creating only destruction—this is what George Bernard Shaw called "the quintessence of Ibsenism," and Faulkner's treatment of the theme in *Pylon* is masterful.

The powerful plane which the reporter contrives to buy has several defects; the reporter learns about them at an early stage and so does Shumann, but they persevere in their plan, caught up in the desire to win. A safety expert refuses to certify the plane, but they persuade other authorities to overrule him. It becomes increasingly clear that the plane has serious flaws—Faulkner beautifully handles the hurried, panicky attempts of the flying team to compensate for them and ignore their seriousness. During the final, tense race, the plane does not perform and comes apart in the air; the pilot is killed in a lake. At the end of the novel, the group disbands.

The Characters

The major characters in *Pylon* are complex. Indeed, there are few "flat" or simplified characters in the book, and they appear only in chance encounters. Some difficulty is caused by names—when a major character appears in the course of the narrative, Faulkner frequently fails to name him, and the reader is often given a phrase like "the boy" or "the woman." Keeping the characters straight is often as confusing as in a Russian novel, when the reader is given only a first name or patronymic—if anything, it is even more difficult with Faulkner. This difficulty has a rationale: Faulkner usually follows the point of view of a specific character very closely, and if that character does not think in terms of a name, then Faulkner does not provide that name. The reporter knows LaVerne only from a distance, so for him she is never LaVerne, only "she" or "the woman."

On the other hand, the characters are highly dramatic—Faulkner describes almost all of them with a heightened physical presence and various meaningful accompanying objects. For example, Jiggs the mechanic has the boots he is buying as the novel opens. These are his prized, most valuable possession, and they acquire enormous significance as the action proceeds. At the close of the novel, he pawns them. Jiggs is one of Faulkner's most successful creations: Poor, totally irresponsible, sly, and predatory, he is the cause of the first accident in the story—instead of pulling the valves from the motor and inspecting their stems, he gets drunk; the plane performs badly as a result, and the parachutist almost breaks his leg. In Faulkner's words, Jiggs is a "vicious halfmetamorphosis between thug and horse." He is a memorable addition to Faulkner's gallery of extremely harmful, evil characters, whom he succeeds in portraying not only from the outside but also from the inside, from their own point of view—an astonishing feat, of which few other novelists are capable.

In the course of the book, the reporter's name is given only once, in passing. As if to compensate for this, Faulkner endows him with a unique appearance. He is extremely thin, referred to as a scarecrow, a lath, a "person made of clothes and bones," "a cutglass monkeywrench or something."

> He did not speak loudly, and with no especial urgency, but he emanated the illusion still of having longsince collapsed yet being still intact in his own weightlessness like a dandelion burr moving where there is no wind. In the soft pink glow his face appeared gaunter than ever, as though following the excess of the past night, his vital spark now fed on the inner side of the actual skin itself, paring it steadily thinner and more and more transparent.

Perhaps the nature of his personality explains why he is almost never named; he becomes consumed by his reportorial function, a "fly on the wall" who comes to live vicariously in the lives of those he observes. He ceases to have any life of his own and even stops being a reporter—he is fired, and he becomes an active agent of the plot, almost a member of the flying team. Despite this peculiar, leechlike psychological mechanism, Faulkner makes clear that he has little understanding of those he is trying to help. Toward the end of the novel, the parachutist advises him, "Only take a tip from me and stick to the kind of people you are used to after this."

What distinguishes Faulkner's characters is, above all, their presentation both from within—from their own subjective point of view—and from without—from the points of view of others. This gives them a unique amplitude and depth. The point of view changes many times in the course of the novel, and the reader will not find the "unified sensibility" of which Henry James wrote—as a consequence he might occasionally be confused. On the other hand, the reader will encounter numerous characters presented in great depth and urgent, compelling life.

Themes and Meanings

Pylon is above all a study of human motivation, of the diverse mechanisms and drives that make people act as they do. These range from concrete, external circumstances to inner desires, compulsions, and obsessions, and they are all brought to bear on the specific character as he thinks, feels, and acts. *Pylon* especially investigates what might be termed the claims of "romance" or romantic glamour. They form an aura that surrounds the activity of flying, above all the competitive flying in air fairs. The principal characters in the book all feel the pull of this nongravitational force, which comes to alter and definitively change their lives. It assumes a different form depending on their specific personalities. With the opportunistic, cynical Jiggs, who counts his pennies, it is nevertheless potent; with Roger Shumann, it takes on an idealistic, aesthetic form; with LaVerne, it is associated with love; with the reporter Lazarus, it assumes the most extraordinary form of all—unbalanced, voyeuristic, totally impractical, and all-consuming.

The primary tool for exploring these complex motivations is the novel's style. With Faulkner, this is often close to the process of free association, but it is not chaotic or purposeless. On the contrary, the style always significantly advances the narrative at the same time that it renders the thought processes of the principal characters. This closeness to actual thought characterized the practice of modernists such as James Joyce and Virginia Woolf during the period between the two world wars, but since 1946, this intimacy has been abandoned by most novelists in favor of a more formal point of view located in the middle distance. In *Pylon* and other novels by Faulkner during the same period, there is an impressive breadth in the presentation of character largely lacking in the post-World War II novel: a thought-for-thought, heartbeat-for-heartbeat intimacy with characters combined with an ability to step back, assume distance and a sweeping perspective, then once again to enter the thoughts of that character or another. Faulkner excels at this combination of amplitude and intimacy.

The technique of jumping in and out of different people's thoughts can have drawbacks. The reader is sometimes lost, missing the firm hand of a considerate guide. Faulkner incorporates much of the complexity and some of the chaos of real life into his narrative; many readers do not seek these when they pick up a book. On the other hand, *Pylon* contains a living and breathing solidity and depth of meaning found in few other novels. After reading Faulkner, numerous readers will wish that other novelists were as daring as he.

Critical Context

Malcolm Cowley's effort to promote Faulkner's literary reputation after the end of World War II was largely successful. The Viking Portable selection from Faulkner's work—edited by Cowley—brought Faulkner once again to the attention of the serious American reading public, and his reputation steadily increased until his reception of the Nobel Prize. Cowley stressed Faulkner's achievement as a regional Southern writer, as "proprietor" of Yoknapatawpha County. Perhaps this was correct; at any rate, Faulkner's "mythical kingdom" seized the imaginations of American readers. *Pylon* has no place in Yoknapatawpha County, and for some that may seem reason enough to exclude it from the canon of Faulkner's finest novels. Yet that would be a mistake. It was written when Faulkner was producing other novels that are among his finest—*Light in August* and *Absalom, Absalom!*—and it has all their élan and creative complexity. It is an urban novel, just as successful as the novels set in his rural "mythical kingdom." It will probably continue to fall victim to critical simplification, yet it will remain one of his half dozen most impressive novels.

Sources for Further Study

Backman, Melvin. *Faulkner: The Major Years, a Critical Study*, 1966.

Blotner, Joseph. *Faulkner: A Biography*, 1974.

Brooks, Cleanth. *William Faulkner: The Yoknapatawpha Country*, 1963.

Cowley, Malcolm. *The Faulkner-Cowley File, Letters and Memories, 1944-1962*, 1966.

Hoffman, Frederick John, and Olga Vickery, eds. *William Faulkner: Three Decades of Criticism*, 1960.

John Carpenter

QUICKSAND

Author: Nella Larsen (1893-1964)
Type of plot: Psychological realism
Time of plot: The 1920's
Locale: Texas, Chicago, New York City, Denmark, and Alabama
First published: 1928

> *Principal characters:*
> HELGA CRANE, the protagonist, a young mulatto woman who
>   leaves her teaching post in Texas to find something more,
>   first in Chicago, then in New York City
> JAMES VAYLE, Helga's fiancé in Texas, who is twice rejected
>   by her
> DR. ANDERSON, the principal at the school for blacks in
>   Texas, who enters Helga's life again in New York City
> MRS. HAYES-RORE, a Chicago matron and lecturer to black
>   women's groups, who employs Helga as her companion
>   and introduces Helga to friends and opportunities in New
>   York City
> ANNE GREY, a young black woman who becomes Helga's
>   friend and later marries Dr. Anderson
> POUL and
> KATRINA DAHL, Helga's uncle and aunt in Denmark
> AXEL OLSEN, an artist who paints Helga's portrait in Den-
>   mark and proposes marriage
> THE REVEREND MR. PLEASANT GREEN, a minister of a small
>   church in a small town in Alabama, who marries Helga

The Novel

The focus of the action throughout the novel is on the literal and metaphoric journeys of Helga Crane, who on her first appearance is planning to leave her teaching job in a small private school for blacks in Texas for the material, social, and cultural advantages which she thinks she wants and deserves. Helga is a mulatto in her twenties, half Danish American, half black, who can "pass" as white. As the narrator enters Helga's consciousness, the disjunction between the attractive, poised exterior self and the dissatisfied, restless interior self is readily apparent. Helga blames the school for its superficiality and hypocrisy, condemns her fiancé, James Vayle, for his conformity and self-satisfaction, and charges Dr. Anderson, the new principal, with coldness and lack of understanding. While there is some basis for her assessments, they primarily reflect Helga's own lack of direction, her loneliness, and her inability to find her own self and her racial identity as a mulatto woman.

Helga's journeys in search of who she is and what she wants lead her to Chicago, to New York City, to Denmark, back to New York City, and finally to a small rural town in Alabama. Helga's dissatisfaction is partially sexual; only after several traumatic encounters is she able to confront her own desires. These encounters involve Vayle, whom Helga meets again in New York City, who again proposes marriage, and who essentially represents to Helga an ineffectual, smug member of the black middle class. Yet Helga's second rejection of Vayle takes place after she has refused the marriage proposal of the sexually aggressive Olsen in Denmark, who represents a self-important cultural superiority that Helga also finds difficult to accept. Helga's revelation about her own sexual desires comes after a series of intense, at times humiliating, encounters with Dr. Anderson.

Helga's first encounter with Dr. Anderson is at the beginning of the novel, on the day that she announces her decision to abandon teaching. There is an unarticulated physical reaction on Helga's part, but at this point she thinks that she is more repulsed by him than attracted; she feels him to be a kind of undefined threat. Paralleling this sexual unease is Helga's racial and cultural unease, but the sexual unease is suppressed while Helga seeks some social stability and fulfillment, first in Chicago, then in New York City, then in Denmark. In each place, however, she is either rejected or rejects—her white relatives in Chicago close the door on her. Helga accepts temporarily the friendship of Mrs. Hayes-Rore, a rich black Chicago matron, but she moves on to seek happiness in the middle-class black society represented by her new friend, Anne Grey.

Helga, content for a while, once again becomes restless. Anne's perfection and her political involvement in the fight for black social equality begin to irritate Helga. Still unsure of herself and not ready yet to declare a racial identity or consciousness, Helga decides to visit her aunt and uncle in Denmark. The visit turns into a two-year stay, results in Olsen's marriage proposal, and ends, once again, with Helga's rejection. Denmark is too racially white for her—she begins to realize that she is tied by blood to the black race, and she longs for Harlem, where she can live with blacks again. Olsen's powerful sexual and artistic presence smothers her, and she cannot agree to her uncle's desire for this socially advantageous marriage—cannot agree, in essence, to become a white, middle-class European wife. It is upon Helga's return to New York City and her resumption of her friendship with Anne, now married to Dr. Anderson, that she is forced to admit to her previously repressed sexual desires.

The major encounter between Helga and Dr. Anderson is at a party where he, having had too much to drink, passionately kisses her. She responds, mistakenly believing that he is declaring his desire for an affair with her. When he arranges a meeting with her to offer his apology, she thinks that he has planned a tryst. Humiliated and still unable to find a release for her feelings, still unable to be comfortable with the ironies and the ambivalences of her life, she again runs away, literally and figuratively. She returns to Harlem, enters a revival meeting, and, in a state approximating a nervous breakdown, gives herself over to the people there and their religious fervor.

The last short section of the novel records Helga's recovery through the solicitude of the Reverend Mr. Pleasant Green, her giving herself over to him, accepting his protection and marriage proposal, living with him in the alien environment of an Alabama town, and bearing him five children with the suggestion that more will follow. In focusing on Helga's consciousness, the emphasis of the narration remains on her discontent and her seeming lack of fulfillment. Yet there is also the suggestion that the sexual, racial, and social identities that she now exhibits to the external world are in some strange, unconscious way what she was seeking all along.

The Characters

The novel is totally dominated by the character and consciousness of Helga Crane. The narrator carries the reader along in Helga's development but does not distance the commentary by overt judgmental assessments of the meaning of her decisions. The reader is forced to share in Helga's dissatisfaction, her alienation, and her struggle for self-esteem without really knowing much more than Helga does about the meaning to attach to the events of her life. Certainly the character of Helga is to be seen in the context of the tragic mulatta figure of earlier nineteenth and twentieth century fiction and nonfiction, but the characterization is so subtle and so disturbing that one cannot easily assign a stereotypical reading of Helga. She is not tragic in any clearly defined way, nor is she clearly self-affirming. Perhaps the most that one can say is that her conscious sense of self has not yet caught up with the meaning which she has given her life. She has definite sexual, racial, and social identities at the end; she is producing several children for the continuing growth of the race; she has accepted her blackness; she has become a lower-middle-class woman in a rural setting.

Most, if not all, of the other characters are set up as contrasts to Helga; they are not fully rounded characters, yet they carry a certain intensity and credibility because they participate in Helga's personal conflicts. Each of the men she leaves—Vayle, Olsen, and Dr. Anderson—represent a social class, a cultural attitude, or a sexual intensity, respectively, that she also rejects. The women, too—Anne and Mrs. Hayes-Rore—reflect selves and social, cultural, and political involvements with which Helga cannot be comfortable. The most puzzling characterization is that of the Reverend Mr. Green. There is very little that is sympathetic or likable about him—he is physically unattractive, he is unattentive to Helga once she becomes his wife, he dominates Helga sexually—yet his social, cultural, and racial sureness is a major strength at the close of the novel.

Themes and Meanings

The themes are not overtly stated, but they might be articulated in terms of Helga's struggle for identity. One major theme is that the mulatto woman is confronted with very difficult circumstances—neither black nor white, she cannot easily choose either identity. In some ways, the choice is thrust upon her by forces stronger than she. There is a naturalistic component to this novel, and Helga's final situation is, to some extent, the result of her nervous breakdown, her inability to work within the dominant white culture and her inability to accept the middle-class black culture of the New York City with which she is most familiar. Regardless of how one reads the ending of the novel, Helga's sanity has been purchased at great personal cost. The quicksand may enclose her—her husband and the children may indeed smother her. There is no doubt, however, that Larsen presents Helga's rejection of the material life and her "affirmation" of her racial and religious bonds as positive.

Critical Context

Nella Larsen has offered a rich psychological study of the mulatto woman who is caught in several social and moral conflicts because of the uncertainties, the ambivalences, and the split identities caused by her racial mixture. In this novel, Larsen achieved what no other writer had achieved before— she appropriated the developments in psychology and in the psychological novel for the experiences of the black woman. Both *Quicksand* and her other novel, *Passing* (1929), have been rediscovered and reread as significant precursors to contemporary fiction by black women writers.

Sources for Further Study

Christian, Barbara. *Black Women Novelists*, 1980.
Cooke, Michael G. *Afro-American Literature in the Twentieth Century*, 1984.

Rosalie Hewitt

THE RABBIT ANGSTROM NOVELS

Author: John Updike (1932-   )
Type of plot: Social chronicle
Time of plot: Rabbit, Run, 1959; *Rabbit Redux,* 1969; *Rabbit Is Rich,* 1979-80
Locale: The fictional towns of Mt. Judge and Brewer, Pennsylvania
First published: Rabbit, Run, 1960; *Rabbit Redux,* 1971; *Rabbit Is Rich,* 1981

> *Principal characters:*
> HARRY "RABBIT" ANGSTROM, a former high school basketball
>   star
> JANICE SPRINGER ANGSTROM, his wife
> NELSON ANGSTROM, the son of Harry and Janice
> REBECCA ANGSTROM, the daughter of Harry and Janice, dead
>   in infancy
> MARTY TOTHERO, Harry's former athletic coach
> RUTH LEONARD, Harry's mistress during 1959
> JACK ECCLES, an Episcopal priest
> FRED SPRINGER, Janice's father, a car dealer
> BESSIE SPRINGER, Janice's mother
> PEGGY GRING FOSNACHT, Janice's friend
> BILLY FOSNACHT, Peggy's son, Nelson's friend
> EARL ANGSTROM, Harry's father, a printer
> CHARLIE STAVROS, a car salesman, Janice's lover during 1969
> JILL PENDLETON, a teenage runaway who is killed in a house
>   fire
> SKEETER, a black militant and fugitive
> MIRIAM ANGSTROM, Harry's younger sister
> ANNABELLE BYER, Ruth Leonard's daughter and possibly
>   Harry's as well
> MELANIE, a college friend of Nelson's
> TERESA "PRU" LUBELL, Nelson's mistress, later his wife
> ARCHIE CAMPBELL, an Episcopal priest

The Novels
  With his sixth novel, *Rabbit Redux,* published in 1971, John Updike resumed the life story of Harry "Rabbit" Angstrom, the antiheroic protagonist of his acclaimed second novel, *Rabbit, Run.* Another decade and several more novels followed before Updike came forth with his third record of Harry's adventures, appropriately entitled *Rabbit Is Rich.* Whether such a sustained chronicle was part of the author's original plan (presumably, if Updike is still active, the 1990's will bring another installment in this open-ended series), the Rabbit Angstrom books provide an accurate, absorbing,

and aesthetically satisfying social history of middle-class North America from the 1950's into the 1980's; taken together, the three novels may well constitute Updike's finest achievement.

Born in 1933, a year later than his novelistic creator, Harry "Rabbit" Angstrom is at times an Everyman of sorts, at other times a kind of holy fool, yet even at his most disgraceful moments he appears to represent the voice of common sense. His mundane adventures, meanwhile, are consistently backlighted by contemporaneous events in political and cultural history, to which they may frequently be seen as a response. The end product of such a technique is an impressive social chronicle, brought close to the reader by the generally amiable, if not always admirable, character of Harry Angstrom himself.

When Harry first emerges on the scene, in *Rabbit, Run*, he is twenty-six years old, a veteran of Stateside service during the Korean War, married not long thereafter to Janice Springer, who happened to be carrying his child. Although demonstrably intelligent, Harry did not attend college and is thus limited in his job prospects: At the start of *Rabbit, Run*, he is employed as a demonstrator of kitchen gadgets, barely managing to support his young son and pregnant wife. His only claim to fame, already growing stale, derives from his erstwhile prowess on the high school basketball court.

Janice, daughter of a rather prosperous used car dealer, has grown lazy and apathetic, with an unfortunate fondness for strong drink. One evening, the sordidness of his domestic scene catches up with Harry and he flees, driving aimlessly about the countryside until daybreak. Unwilling to return to either home or job, he seeks refuge in the garret inhabited by Marty Tothero, his former basketball coach, who has quit his job in disgrace. It is through Tothero that Harry meets Ruth Leonard, moving soon thereafter into Ruth's apartment.

Ruth Leonard, an unemployed secretary of Harry's own age, is perhaps less a prostitute than a "kept" woman with several occasional "keepers." At Harry's urging, however, she soon reserves her attentions for Harry alone, reluctantly falling in love as she does so. To her credit, Ruth is both more affectionate and "better company" than Janice; she is also, in general, a good influence on Harry, allowing him the opportunity to sort out the tangled threads of his life.

It is while he is living with Ruth that Harry is first befriended by Jack Eccles, rector of the Episcopal church attended by Janice's parents. Although ostensibly sent by the Springers to prepare a reconciliation, Jack becomes fascinated by Harry's simple yet strong personal faith and seemingly adopts him as a separate case, unrelated to that of his estranged wife. Soon the two young men are playing golf together, and it is Eccles who finds steady work for Harry in the garden of an elderly widow. Still living with Ruth and working for Mrs. Smith, who adores him, Harry leads an idyllic life that is cut

short only by the birth of his and Janice's baby, a daughter to be named
Rebecca.

Reluctantly recalled by Eccles to face his true responsibilities, Harry
gamely attempts to repair his relationship with Janice, doing most of the
housecleaning himself. Janice, however, has learned little or nothing from
their separation, and it is not long before Harry escapes again, returning to
Ruth's apartment only to find that Ruth is not there. No sooner has Harry
left the flat than Janice begins drinking heavily, recklessly, in an effort to
console herself: Enveloped in an alcoholic haze, her reflexes dangerously
impaired, she accidentally drowns baby Rebecca while attempting to give
the child her bath.

Perhaps inevitably, given their respective personalities, Harry and Janice
will blame each other for Rebecca's death; after all, reasons Janice, the
accident would not have happened if Harry had not walked out on her. As
befits the title *Rabbit, Run*, in keeping also with his athletic conditioning
and background, Harry has spent much of his time running, literally as well
as figuratively. Thus will he flee the scene of Rebecca's funeral, running as if
for his life with Father Eccles in ineffectual pursuit. Deciding thereafter to
resume his affair with Ruth, generally pleased to learn that she is pregnant
with his child, Harry suddenly balks at the thought of divorce and
remarriage, finding himself on the run once again, with no particular destination in sight or in mind as *Rabbit, Run* comes to an end.

Written almost completely in the narrative present tense with occasional
shifts in point of view, exploiting also the "free indirect discourse" borrowed
by James Joyce from Gustave Flaubert, *Rabbit, Run* is notable for its narrative technique as well as for its contribution to the tradition of social realism exemplified by the works of Sinclair Lewis and John O'Hara. In its evocation of rural Pennsylvania and its people, *Rabbit, Run* is, in fact, strongly
reminiscent of O'Hara except in the area of technical innovation, a refine-
ment which O'Hara generally eschewed. At the same time, the novel speaks
eloquently of and for a younger generation both liberated and alienated by
its potential freedom. A decade later, borrowing his Latinate title from the
medical profession, Updike would show Harry Angstrom "led back,"
"recovered," even recuperated by the society that he once sought to flee.

At the start of *Rabbit Redux* the reader learns that Harry, reconciled
with Janice not long after the baby's funeral, has been employed ever since
as a Linotype operator in the same shop where his father still works as a
printer. By 1969, however, both men's jobs are threatened by the imminent
prospect of automation. Also threatened, perhaps even more seriously than
before, is Harry's marriage to Janice: Employed by her father in the office
of his new Toyota dealership, Janice has commenced a torrid affair with one
Charlie Stavros, Springer Motors' top car salesman. No sooner has Harry
confronted Janice with his suspicions than she moves out of the ranch-style

tract home where they now live, ostensibly to clear her head at her parents' summer cottage but in fact to share Stavros' small apartment.

To a greater extent than in the earlier novel, current events loom large in *Rabbit Redux*; prior to Janice's flight, Harry engages Charlie Stavros, a liberal, in a heated discussion of the war in Vietnam; not long thereafter, he reflectively watches the televised landing of American astronauts on the moon. Janice's departure has created a rent in the surface of Harry's presumably well-ordered life, and before long the world rushes in from outside: Alternately fascinated and repelled, Harry finds himself playing host to two representatives of the youthful counterculture: Jill Pendleton, a runaway from an affluent Connecticut family, and the black man known only as Skeeter, a fugitive from justice, possibly the son or brother of one of Harry's coworkers at the print shop. Thirteen-year-old Nelson Angstrom, housed with his father for the unspecified duration of his mother's defection, soon develops a hopeless crush on the eighteen-year-old Jill, even as Jill divides her physical favors between Harry and Skeeter under Nelson's watchful eyes. Skeeter, meanwhile, is determined to raise Harry's middle-American, conservative consciousness with liberal doses of illegal drugs and underground political philosophy, conducting responsive readings from the works of Eldridge Cleaver and others.

Predictably, the cohabitation of Harry and Nelson with a black militant and a white female "hippie" begins to provoke gossip, and worse; on one occasion, Harry is ambiguously threatened by two of his neighbors on his way home from the bus stop. Still, he is reluctant to take action, being somewhat mesmerized by Skeeter, half in love with Jill, and more than a little afraid of them both. Peggy Fosnacht, a longtime friend of Janice and the mother of Nelson's best friend, beckons to Harry from his "own" world, suggesting the desirability of an affair now that both have separated from their spouses. Yielding at last to Peggy's blandishments, Harry is in her apartment when his house burns to the ground with Jill Pendleton still inside, Skeeter having escaped at the last minute to hide in the woods nearby. Later found hiding in the backseat of Harry's car, Skeeter persuades Harry of his innocence and successfully hitches a ride toward freedom. Although no arrests are ever made in the arson and murder, Harry's suspicion naturally falls on the neighbors who had threatened him.

The memory of Jill Pendleton, like that of baby Rebecca, will continue to haunt the Angstroms as a family. Young Nelson, in particular, will carry his grief and resentment well into adulthood, inwardly and at times outwardly accusing his father of allowing Jill to die. In time, Janice and Harry will come back together; Charlie Stavros, it seems, feels consigned to bachelorhood by the same chronic heart ailment that exempted him from military service, free also to enjoy brief "flings" with such people as Harry's sister Miriam, who has flown east from her life on the fringes of the show business and gaming world to pay her respects to the terminally ill Mrs. Angstrom, senior.

Narrated, like its predecessor, in the present tense, with frequent use of free indirect discourse, *Rabbit Redux* continues Harry's saga as if without interruption. Perhaps even more significantly, it provides a most informative and thoughtful chronicle of the turbulent late 1960's, brought fully to life by the credible if outrageous portrayals of Skeeter and Jill. Writing in the affectless third person, the author manages also, before the Watergate case, to express his own heavily ironic views of the Nixon presidency.

In *Rabbit Is Rich*, Harry Angstrom has at last arrived in the bourgeoisie to which he has more or less aspired, thanks mainly to his co-ownership, with Janice and her mother, of the Toyota dealership inherited from her late father. Laid off from his job setting Linotype at the end of *Rabbit Redux*, Harry was hired not long thereafter by Fred Springer as a salesman and potential successor, working without friction in close proximity to Charlie Stavros, who has since become his friend. Unable to rebuild their own house after the fire, Harry and Janice are still living with Mrs. Springer but are planning to buy a house of their own, which they can now easily afford.

Now that he has "arrived," with respectable standing in the community and a regular golf foursome, Harry at forty-six finds himself increasingly concerned with the idea of himself as a father. Nelson at twenty-three is something of a disappointment, unsure of the future, keeping company with one woman while another is carrying his child. Almost in desperation, Harry fixes his attentions upon a ripe young blonde glimpsed by chance at the Toyota dealership, imagining her to be his daughter by Ruth Leonard. This obsession will occupy Harry throughout most of *Rabbit Is Rich*, alternating with his anxieties over Nelson's uncertain future and tangled interpersonal relationships. Harry's relationship with Nelson, always somewhat problematic, has remained seriously flawed since Jill Pendleton's death; his relationship with Janice, meanwhile, has become more stable than ever before, frankly rooted in mutual economic self-interest; she and Harry are now partners in most possible senses of the term.

Throughout *Rabbit Is Rich*, as in *Rabbit Redux*, current events figure prominently in the action: The characters freely discuss President Carter, Afghanistan, and the Iran hostage crisis; Harry, taking advantage of recent changes in United States fiscal policy, grows richer still through shrewd short-term investments in gold and silver coins even as he anticipates possible negative economic influences on the Toyota import trade. Fittingly, the Toyota car itself serves as both the subject and the "vehicle" of some of Updike's most telling observations; the various models and their prospective buyers are described in considerable detail as American tastes turn toward smaller, more fuel-efficient cars. So total is Harry's absorption in his job that the firm's best-known slogans begin to creep into his speech and even into his unspoken monologues.

Nelson Angstrom, an intermittent student at Kent State University some years after the infamous National Guard incident, finds himself torn between his ambitions and his origins; although moderately successful as a student, befriended by the intellectually inclined Melanie, Nelson nevertheless chooses his mistress and consort from the university's secretarial pool, feeling less threatened by his "own kind" of people. Teresa Lubell, known ironically as "Pru" since childhood for her apparent prudery, is a year or two Nelson's senior, generally likable yet hardly better suited to Nelson than Janice once was to Harry. Both Harry and Janice, however, believe that Pru and Nelson should have a proper church wedding before their child is born; Nelson, unwilling to resume his studies, attempts to find himself both a job and a "place" at Springer Motors, the better to support his family.

The tension between Nelson and Harry, hitherto perceived mainly on Nelson's side, erupts into open warfare when Harry consistently blocks Nelson's entry into the firm, against the strong support of Janice and her mother, his coproprietors. Nelson, hoping to impress his father, talks his mother and grandmother into letting him develop, at Springer Motors, an ancillary trade in antique cars; Harry, feeling outmaneuvered, so frustrates Nelson with his opposition that Nelson rams one of his newly acquired old cars with another, thus ruining them both. In the end neither side wins; although Nelson has correctly perceived a market for such cars, the argument with Harry has killed his enthusiasm. After a brief stint at selling Toyotas, failing to meet his father's expectations, Nelson will return to Kent State, leaving Pru behind to bear their baby under the protection of his parents and grandmother. Harry and Janice, meanwhile, have finally bought a house of their own over Mrs. Springer's objections, with enough money left over from Harry's precious-metal speculations to afford a brief winter trip to the Caribbean in the company of Harry's golf companions and their wives.

Not long after the Caribbean trip, highlighted by "discreet" mate swapping, Pru Lubell Angstrom is delivered of a healthy baby daughter. Harry, his paternal instincts aroused once again, sets forth in search of the elusive blonde whom he believes to be his child. A brief encounter with Ruth, recounted in *Rabbit Redux*, has helped to encourage his suspicions; his subsequent encounter, toward the end of *Rabbit Is Rich*, repeats the acrimonious tone of the previous meeting, with Harry's questions left unanswered. In all likelihood, Annabelle Byer is indeed Harry's child, but Ruth Leonard Byer, by now a farm widow with two sons in addition to "Annie," will give Harry no such satisfaction; as a woman wronged, she will even misrepresent her daughter's age in one final effort to rid her life of Harry Angstrom. As *Rabbit Is Rich* draws to a close, Harry sits in his Barcalounger with his infant granddaughter in his lap, pondering in his fashion the mysteries of life and death.

Rabbit Is Rich is perhaps more indebted to Sinclair Lewis than either of the previous novels in the sequence. In a sense, Rabbit has at last become Babbitt, thanks to forces somewhat beyond his control. Trained at an early age toward athletic success, Harry, with the onset of middle age, has at last found employment suited to his competitive skills, albeit with the help of the Springers, from whom he has frequently estranged himself. With all his failures plainly visible behind him, his political outlook tempered by contact with the counterculture, grown even more cautious before the threat of global economic crisis, Harry nevertheless perseveres in his pursuit of "American" values, intent on "conserving" whatever might remain of their validity. Like George Babbitt, he is frequently at odds with his wife and offspring, yet for all his disillusionments he retains a generally positive outlook that will probably sustain him well into, and possibly through, his retirement.

The Characters

Owing something to the schlemiel of the Jewish tradition as well as to the stereotype of the American boy athlete, Harry "Rabbit" Angstrom remains, throughout his questionable adventures, one of the more credible and memorable main characters in recent American letters.

Although confronted with failure, death, and destruction, in part as a result of his own weaknesses, Harry Angstrom retains throughout his life the deep if inarticulate religious faith that evokes the interest of Father Eccles in the chronicle's first volume. Moderate to abstemious in his approach to liquor and tobacco, owing perhaps to his early indoctrination as an athlete, Harry is nevertheless doubly obsessed with sex and with religion from adolescence onward, his sexual fantasies often merging with the solid bedrock of his unquestioning belief to produce a peculiar, honest obstinacy. Harry can rarely look at a woman without disrobing her in his mind's eye (or in fact), yet he endures his tribulations with the patience and prescience of a modern Job, as unquestioning of his sufferings as he is of his belief in an underlying principle of order.

To Updike's credit, the character of Harry Angstrom remains consistent throughout the sequence, developing slowly but plausibly as Harry passes from his twenties into his forties. From volume to volume, the author presents Harry from an angle of compassionate detachment, his restrained irony suggesting that Harry is to be viewed as representative rather than exemplary: Harry may learn from his mistakes, but he never seems to learn quite enough. He remains oddly insensitive to the needs of those around him, even as his experiences should have taught him otherwise.

Among the greater, no doubt intentional, mysteries surrounding Harry Angstrom is his continued attachment to Janice. Although described in physical detail, further revealed through her speech and actions, Janice remains a shadowy figure, more of an enigma to the reader than she apparently is to Harry. At the end of *Rabbit, Run*, Jack Eccles' wife suggests to her husband that perhaps the Angstroms would be better off divorced; her suggestion, although it goes unheeded, continues to reverberate through succeeding volumes of the sequence. Janice, to be sure, is at least the partial cause of Harry's major problems; self-centered and shallow, she never appears to accept her responsibilities toward Harry, nor does she appear deserving of his continued allegiance and support. Apart from a certain physical attraction, intermittently short-circuited by Janice herself, there seems little enough reason for Harry not to leave her. In *Rabbit Is Rich*, however, the union is at last "explained" by economic self-interest, as Janice and Harry are shown as coconspirators against the competition of other auto dealers.

Of the two "other women" in Harry's life, Ruth Leonard is perhaps the more memorable, although it is Jill Pendleton whose early death will cast the stronger shadow. Ruth, although no older than Harry, serves him as a kind of mother figure, strong and commonsensical, with few illusions. The waiflike Jill at first appears to be a stereotypical "flower child," on the run from her comfortable bourgeois surroundings. With Harry, however, she seems about to emerge from stereotype when her life is cut short by the house fire.

Similarly, the angry young militant Skeeter, Jill's fellow "houseguest" in *Rabbit Redux*, gradually emerges from stereotype to stand as one of Updike's more masterful and memorable creations. Restless, intelligent, possessed of manic vital energy, Skeeter reaches into Harry's consciousness at a level achieved by few other characters in the sequence: In thus affecting Harry, he also affects the reader, giving tangible form and shape to the prospect of world revolution.

Like John O'Hara before him, Updike derives no small part of his total effect from the skillful evocation of rural Pennsylvania and its ethnic types, particularly those of German extraction. Janice's parents and even Harry's, despite the Scandinavian surname, provide strong local color with their attitudes and accents. Peggy Gring Fosnacht, a former schoolmate of Harry who later becomes Janice's friend and would like to be Harry's mistress, is likewise a recognizable regional type, as is Charlie Stavros, the Greek-American car salesman whom Janice takes as her lover. Throughout the sequence, Updike's portrayal of such characters is generally compassionate and free of condescension, aimed toward authenticity rather than toward satire.

Indeed, given the tone and scope of the Rabbit Angstrom novels, the satirical tone is surprisingly restrained throughout, with few characters presented in broad caricature. A notable exception, however, is Updike's portrayal of the two Episcopal clergymen who appear in the story. Both, in different ways and for different reasons, turn out to be remarkably ineffective in their chosen mission: Jack Eccles, for all his earnestness, has clearly lost the support of his wife, Lucy, who somewhat reluctantly finds herself attracted to the errant Harry Angstrom. After the death of little Rebecca, Lucy will go so far as to blame her husband for his mismanagement of the situation. Jack's eventual successor, Archie Campbell, called in to officiate at Nelson's wedding, is drawn even closer to caricature, an apparent homosexual given to self-parody in speech, gestures, and attire. Implicitly, both portraits tend to highlight the authenticity of Harry's understated, even touching, religious faith, suggesting that the Almighty might indeed be better served by the laity than by the clergy.

Themes and Meanings

Taken together, the three Rabbit Angstrom novels provide, at the most literal level, a highly accurate and entertaining record of United States history during the years of Harry Angstrom's life. It is perhaps no accident that Harry was born during the same month that saw Franklin D. Roosevelt inaugurated as President of the United States. Harry's childhood and young manhood are closely linked to political events of the time; as he ages, such events begin to take on greater significance, suggesting that Harry is, at least in part, the product of historical forces that he himself perceives only barely, if at all. Although Harry's politics are conservative, it is clear from the outset that the author's are not; the ensuing counterpoint sharpens Updike's social observation to a keen edge, leaving for future generations of readers an unforgettable record of American society in transition.

Like O'Hara before him, Updike is also a keen observer of sexual mores, not excluding sexual activity and practice, described in full detail. By 1960, however, the American reading public was in general more receptive to such description, sparing Updike's work the expressions of shock and outrage that had greeted O'Hara's novels a decade or so earlier. In the case of Harry Angstrom, the prevalence of sexual activity is amply prepared for and justified by character; given Harry's limitations, sex is both an understandable preoccupation and a natural, even logical form of personal expression.

Harry's childlike religious faith, closely related at times to his sexual preoccupation, is deeply embedded in the substructure of all three novels. Updike is careful never to present Harry as a saint, nor to suggest that he is somehow "better" than other mortals: Harry's faith is simply another of his personal characteristics, along with his height and hair color; it does not prevent him from acting stupidly, nor does it afford him any special insight into human character. At the very least, however, it allows him to endure such shocks as the deaths of baby Rebecca and Jill Pendleton, and possibly even to prevail.

Critical Context

With the publication of *Rabbit Is Rich* in 1981, Harry Angstrom emerged at last as Updike's most enduring and memorable fictional creation. Updike's novels exhibit an enormous range, but the success of the third Rabbit novel, consistently on pitch, suggested to some critics that he is at his best when practicing the domestic realism that has also distinguished his finest short stories.

After the death of O'Hara in 1970, Updike remained perhaps the only committed chronicler of small-town America, notable like O'Hara for his short stories as well as for his novels. With Updike, however, the social chronicle gained an added dimension absent from the works of O'Hara, as from those of Sinclair Lewis before him. Updike, an accomplished poet and essayist as well, is a more conscious stylist than either of his predecessors, applying to the social chronicle the technique and polish of elevated literary art. The Rabbit Angstrom novels, in particular, are as notable for the way in which they are told as for the story which they tell.

Sources for Further Study

Detweiler, Robert. *John Updike*, 1972.

Hunt, George W. *John Updike and the Three Great Secret Things: Sex, Religion and Art*, 1980.

Markle, Joyce B. *Fighters and Lovers: Themes in the Novels of John Updike*, 1973.

Uphaus, Suzanne Henning. *John Updike*, 1980.

David B. Parsell

RAGTIME

Author: E. L. Doctorow (1931-   )
Type of plot: Historical fiction
Time of plot: The early twentieth century, from 1906 to approximately 1915
Locale: New York, Massachusetts, Philadelphia, Egypt, Mexico, Alaska, and
    Germany
First published: 1975

> *Principal characters:*
> LITTLE BOY, the narrator
> FATHER, a manufacturer of fireworks and flags, an amateur
>   explorer, and the narrator's father
> MOTHER, the narrator's mother
> MOTHER'S YOUNGER BROTHER, an inventor of fireworks,
>   bombs, and grenades
> TATEH (BARON ASHKENAZY), a pioneer filmmaker
> THE LITTLE GIRL, Tateh's daughter
> SARAH, the mother of an illegitimate baby and a housemaid
> COALHOUSE WALKER, JR., Sarah's lover and the father of her
>   child, a ragtime pianist and murderer

The Novel

   Ragtime chronicles the lives of three families: a white Anglo-Saxon Protestant (WASP) family (composed of the narrator when he is a young boy, Mother, Father, Mother's Younger Brother, and Grandfather); a black family (Sarah, Coalhouse Walker, Jr., and their illegitimate infant); and an immigrant family (Tateh, Mameh, and The Little Girl). At the beginning of the novel these families' existences are entirely segregated from one another, but by the story's end the three families have become one in a uniquely American type of ethnic heterogeneity.

   It is significant that the story begins from an exclusively WASP perspective, told in retrospect by the Little Boy grown to manhood. This perspective, the reader is meant to understand, was America's in the early years of the twentieth century, when Teddy Roosevelt was president and when "Everyone wore white in summer." It is an ideal (and idealized) period, when there "was a lot of sexual fainting. There were no Negroes. There were no immigrants." In such an America, everyone was presumed to be patriotic, for "patriotism was a reliable sentiment in the early 1900's." Father is the model patriot as a maker of flags, buntings, and fireworks; his family is supposed to be a model American family. This, at least, is the status quo when Father, an amateur explorer, leaves with Robert Peary on his third (and ultimately successful) expedition to discover the North Pole. It is 1906, and Father will take part in the actual discovery in 1909. While Father is away, however, his WASP family undergoes a surprising change, only the first of several Americanizing changes he and his family will experience. Mother is the catalyst for this first change.

Mother, a stereotypically Victorian creature with whom Father has always had to make appointments to make love, finds an abandoned black infant half-buried but still alive in her flower garden, then takes the child and its young mother, Sarah (after she is found by the police), into her home as her responsibility. Not only does she take on this responsibility, but also she assumes all the executive responsibilities of Father's business, so that upon his return he discovers that she can "speak crisply of such matters as unit cost, inventory and advertising," and she has expanded the company's sales into California and Oregon. Not the least of the changes that Mother has undergone concerns her reading: She now reads feminist and socialist literature, for example. Father, because he fornicated with Eskimo women while in the Arctic, assumes that the changes in his wife and home are God's "punishments." Another such punishment is that some of his employees have become union members.

Father's home and business are also changed, through Mother's Younger Brother, who lives in the home and works in the business. Having fallen obsessively in love with Evelyn Nesbit (the wife of Harry K. Thaw and lover of Stanford White until Thaw assassinates him), Mother's Younger Brother succeeds in wooing Evelyn for a short time, and as he is doing so he meets and becomes a follower of Emma Goldman, the political radical and revolutionary unionizer. It is through Mother's Younger Brother, in fact, that Father's family is initially (albeit peripherally) connected to the immigrant family of Tateh, Mameh, and The Young Girl—and it is through both Mother and her brother that the WASP family is infiltrated by Emma Goldman: Mother is reading one of Goldman's pamphlets when Father returns from his expedition, his employees are unionizing, and Mother's Younger Brother has already become a political radical. (He will ultimately become a revolutionary who dies in Mexico while fighting for Emiliano Zapata.)

While the life of the WASP family is complicated by Mother's discovery and harboring of the black infant and Sarah, the second story line of the novel is revealed. The third member of this black family is Sarah's former lover, the father of her child, Coalhouse Walker, Jr., a ragtime pianist. Several months after Father's return from the Arctic, Walker drives up to the family's house in a shiny new Model T Ford car; he asks to see Sarah but, by her request, is refused the visit. This happens on a Sunday. On several Sundays thereafter, Walker visits the home, plays the piano for the family, and gradually breaks down Sarah's resistance; they become engaged to be married. Walker becomes a victim of violent racism, however, and after futilely seeking retributive justice from the law—and after Sarah is killed when attempting to approach the vice president of the United States to beg him to help her fiancé receive justice—Walker seeks vengeance on his own terms and kills several of the men who victimized him. While he is being hunted, Walker attracts a few young black followers who become (unlike their leader, who is concerned only with retaliation for the injustice done to him personally) fierce revolutionaries fighting for the rights of all blacks. Significantly, one of Walker's armed "soldiers" is Mother's Younger Brother, filled with the self-consuming desire to fight for the downtrodden, a desire fueled by his association with Goldman and expressed through his creation of grenades and bombs. He transforms Father's patriotic fireworks into weapons for a different kind of patriotism—revolution. Ultimately, Walker is executed and Mother's Younger Brother escapes to Mexico; Sarah and Walker's infant (christened Coalhouse Walker III) becomes the adopted child of Father and Mother.

While the black family's story is directly linked to that of the WASP family from the moment that Mother discovers the infant in her garden, the immigrant family's story develops separately from that of the other two families throughout most of *Ragtime*. Like those immigrants whom Doctorow's narrator describes as setting "great store by the American flag," Tateh, Mameh, and The Little Girl come to America to realize the American dream of comfort, prosperity, and freedom from repression. Instead they find abject poverty in New York. Mameh and The Little Girl sew pants, for seventy cents a dozen, every day, from the time they get up to the time they go to bed, and Tateh sells his paper silhouettes on the streets. Their labor proves insufficient for their survival, their rent becomes delinquent, Mameh reluctantly sells her body for money, and Tateh—banishing his wife from the family because he views her as a whore—sets out with The Little Girl to find a secure home and an escape "from the fate of the working class." They move from New York to Massachusetts to Philadelphia, and it is in the last-named city that Tateh sells his invention ("movie books") and signs a contract for future productions of his creations.

When Father, Mother, and the Little Boy meet Tateh and The Little Girl, it is in Atlantic City, where both families are vacationing (just days before Coalhouse Walker is killed). Tateh has by this time changed his name to Baron Ashkenazy, and he has become a very wealthy entrepreneur in the nascent motion picture business. By the time of the two families' meeting, furthermore, Mother has become disillusioned and bored with Father and their marriage, and while she keeps her attraction to Ashkenazy hidden, the reader is made aware of it. Thus it comes as no surprise when, after Father is killed on the *Lusitania* in 1915, Mother marries Ashkenazy and they move to California. Together, then, they create the "new" American family: Jewish father and daughter, WASP mother and son, and black son. Moreover, it is his interracial family that gives Ashkenazy "an idea for a film" about "a society of ragmuffins, like all of us, a gang, getting into trouble and getting out again." The film will be *Our Gang*, as uniquely American as Doctorow's novel itself.

The Characters

While Doctorow's characters are usually memorable, they are also frequently unbelievable. Derived as they seem to be from a preconceived idea about both what America is and how the author wants to portray it, the characters often seem to be primarily embodiments of various positions in a dialectic. Indeed, Doctorow—called an ideologue by some critics—is a Shavian novelist, developing his fiction the way George Bernard Shaw developed his dramas: Thesis versus antithesis equals synthesis.

Father's exclusively WASP view of America is the ethnocentric and theocentric thesis that Doctorow gives his reader in the first few pages of *Ragtime*. In the Shavian, dialectical approach to fictionalizing, the thesis is presented as a straw man of sorts, inevitably broken down or subsumed by its dialectical opposite, the antithesis. Thus, even though Father remains a character in the story until near the end, his usefulness for the underpinning dialectical tension is exhausted much earlier in the story, and in direct proportion to the increased ascendency of his antithesis. In *Ragtime*, however, the antithesis is two-pronged, for it consists of both Coalhouse Walker's family and Tateh's family, and, significantly, parts of both are combined permanently with Father's family after he has been killed. In short, with Father's complete removal from the story, the dialectical synthesis is realized.

Coalhouse Walker provides an excellent example of how an initially complex and engaging character may be (subject as he is to his creator's intellectual and artistic determinism) reduced to little more than a static puppet with limited purpose. Although it might be argued that Doctorow is attempting to portray mimetically the kinds of limitations that have been traditionally imposed upon blacks by America, such an argument is undercut by Walker's demeanor and his own high self-esteem. For example, he annoys Father because it seems that he "didn't know he was a Negro. . . . Walker didn't act or talk like a colored man." Indeed, Walker refuses to accept the social role assigned to him by an essentially WASP-dominated society, and his sense of his own dignity precludes his expression of any type of deference expected of him because of his skin color. When several white thugs mentally abuse him, and then go several steps further by destroying his new automobile, Walker's hunger for justice—unfed by America's pro-white legal system—becomes an unassuageable passion for vengeance. Significantly, it is not because Sarah is killed that Walker decides to (and does) kill several people; it is, rather, because he wants his automobile restored to its original condition and returned to him. Hence, while

Doctorow draws Walker as a dignified individual and very talented pianist early in the story, he eventually reduces him to a materialistic and monomaniacal madman, willing to sacrifice any and all lives (including his own) for the gleaming cleanness of a new machine.

Yet to say only this is unfair to Doctorow and those characters he succeeds in drawing deeply and completely. Mother and Tateh are two of the most successfully rendered of these characters. While Mother is initially portrayed as a flat character, frigidly Victorian and devoid of any genuinely authentic personality traits, she undergoes a remarkable transformation after the humanizing experience of discovering the abandoned baby in her garden. She becomes thereafter a new woman, a prototypical feminist, as she begins to read intellectual literature and grows to be quite comfortable with her sexuality by the time Father returns from the Arctic. Indeed, he finds her "not as vigorously modest as she'd been. . . . She came to bed with her hair unbraided." Even so, Mother's initial flatness of character may itself seem, to some readers, a rather obvious technique employed by Doctorow so that any change in her character will be artistically easy to accomplish, and, moreover, her later roundness and depth will stand out as remarkable when compared to her earlier stasis.

Tateh is a different matter. Initially proud of being a member of the working class, Tateh suffers immeasurable hardships, the worst of which is his wife's betrayal of him when she reluctantly sells her body for rent money. The situation is more complex than Tateh's denunciation of Mameh would lead one to believe, but his essentially two-valued orientation to the world (as well as his male ego) precludes any forgiveness of her. Nevertheless, Tateh's consequent obsession over saving his daughter from poverty-derived corruption is both poignantly believable and admirable. Likewise, after being beaten and almost losing his daughter to strangers, when Tateh defiantly lifts his head, abandons what he has come to view as an unworkable, essentially socialistic ideology, and then embraces capitalism, his transformation is lifelike and complex: "Tateh began to conceive of his life as separate from the fate of the working class. I hate machines, he said to his daughter." (Yet, his artistic creations depend upon "machines" for mass-marketing, for their success and his.) Nevertheless, though he becomes a "Count" nominally, his working-class origins are reaffirmed by the heterogeneous family he comes to call his own.

Themes and Meanings

The principal theme of *Ragtime* is summed up in Doctorow's description of novelist Theodore Dreiser, who, "suffering terribly from the bad reviews and negligible sales of his first book, *Sister Carrie*, took to sitting on a wooden chair in the middle of [his] room. One day he decided his chair was facing in the wrong direction." He turns the chair several times to the right "to align it properly," but each time he stops and tries to sit in the chair, "it still felt peculiar. . . . Eventually he made a complete circle and still could not find the proper alignment for the chair. . . . Through the night Dreiser turned his chair in circles seeking the proper alignment." Doctorow makes it clear in *Ragtime*, through his portrayal of both fictional characters and actual historical personages, interwoven throughout the story, that America is a country shaped physically and psychologically by people searching obsessively for "the proper alignment," which might better be thought of as a sure and satisfactory sense of place and belonging in the world and the universe. Besides Dreiser, two other actual historical figures whom Doctorow uses to illustrate his theme further are Robert Peary and John Pierpont Morgan.

While Dreiser's futile search for the proper alignment is enacted in a rented room where he finds himself in a nadir of self-doubt and depression, Peary's "lifetime of effort" is to find the exact center of the top of the world; yet, although the boundaries of Peary's search are incomparably wider than Dreiser's in his room, Doctorow describes the Arctic explorer's ultimate predicament as exactly the same as the writer's, as far as a proper alignment is concerned. Having arrived in the general area where he believes the North Pole to be, Peary struggles to find the exact spot of the axis of rotation. Lying on his stomach, he calculates his position but is not satisfied; he walks further along the floe and takes another sighting, but still he is not satisfied: "All day long Peary shuffled back and forth over the ice, a mile one way, two miles another, and made his observations. No one observation satisfied him. . . . He couldn't find the exact place to say this spot, here, is the North Pole. Nevertheless there was no question that they were there." Doctorow makes it clear that there is, in fact, some "question," but the negation of such by Peary exemplifies the extent to which the human ego and need for identity can supersede scientific exactness. Indeed, scientific exactitude itself is called into question in this instance when the narrator notes: "On this watery planet the sliding sea refused to be fixed."

Whereas Dreiser's central focus, expressed through naturalistic fiction, was on the urban American society and the individual's place therein, and whereas Peary's was on his being in a central, geographical position on the earth's globe, Morgan's questing focus is on his place in the eternal universe. Believing that "there are universal patterns of order and repetition that give meaning to the activity of this planet," Morgan (a financier and symbol of monopolistic capitalism) believes that he is the reincarnation of a great Pharoah and the incarnation of "secret wisdom," which he views as an "eternal beneficent force" available only to a select and superior few. He travels to the Great Pyramid of Giza and decides to spend one night in the "heart" of the monument (he wants "to feel in advance the eternal energies he would exemplify when he died and rose . . . to be born again," and he hopes to learn "the disposition" of his soul and physical vitality in the universal patterns). Unfortunately, Morgan's quest for a sure sense of his place in the universe is futile, for during his nocturnal vigil in the pyramid he is bitten by bedbugs and resorts to pacing the great center chamber: "He paced from west to east, from the north to the south, though he didn't know which was which."

With Dreiser, Peary, and Morgan (paradigms of superior achievements in the realms of art, natural science, and economics, respectively), Doctorow draws a bleak—albeit witty—portrait of the human quest for a definite sense of place and purpose in the universe, a quest that he views as absurd and futile as long as the goal of the quest is sought in the material world rather than within the searching individual.

Critical Context

Unquestionably Doctorow's most popular novel, made into a film in 1981, *Ragtime* is one more expression of its author's satiric attempt to re-create American history and thereby create imaginative truth in place of dry, historical facts. Indeed, his fiction is deeply embedded in history, and most of his novels have dealt with a significant time in America's past: *Welcome to Hard Times* (1960) portrays the settling of the West; *The Book of Daniel* (1971) exposes the American heritage of political radicalism and repression, specifically as it is manifested in the postwar era; *Ragtime* chronicles the metamorphosis of American life at the beginning of the twentieth century; *Loon Lake* (1980) describes the traumatic repercussions suffered by Americans as a result of the Great Depression; and *World's Fair* re-creates the 1930's from another angle of vision.

As might be expected, all of Doctorow's fiction is political insofar as he portrays time and again the dichotomy that exists between how America is supposed to be ideally and the way it is actually. Yet the conflict between these two Americas is never resolved in his fiction; instead, in Doctorow's novels America is like the floe-hidden sea on which Peary searches for the North Pole in *Ragtime*: It is in perpetual flux and resists being "fixed." At one point in *The Book of Daniel*, the narrator observes: "Of one thing we are sure. Everything is elusive. God is elusive. Revolutionary morality is elusive. Justice is elusive. Human character." Doctorow makes it quite clear in *Ragtime*, as in his other novels, that America—as it is defined in the Constitution—is itself elusive.

Sources for Further Study
Levine, Paul. *E. L. Doctorow*, 1985.
Trenner, Richard. *E. L. Doctorow: Essays and Conversations*, 1983.

David A. Carpenter

REBELLION IN THE BACKLANDS

Author: Euclides da Cunha (1866-1909)
Type of plot: Factual historical chronicle
Time of plot: The 1870's through the 1890's, especially October, 1896, to October, 1897
Locale: The backlands (*os sertões*) of Northeast Brazil, centered in Bahia state, especially in and around the town of Canudos
First published: Os sertões, 1902 (English translation, 1944)

Principal characters:
ANTONIO VICENTE MENDES MACIEL, "Antonio Conselheiro," a fanatic religious leader of the backlands rebellion
PAJEHÚ, a guerrilla leader of the *sertanejos,* rustic, tough, mixed-race inhabitants of the backlands
LIEUTENANT MANUEL DA SILVA PIRES FERREIRA, the leader of the government's doomed first expedition
MAJOR FEBRONIO DE BRITO, the leader of the government's doomed second expedition
COLONEL ANTONIO MOREIRA CESAR, the leader of the government's doomed third expedition
GENERAL ARTHUR OSCAR DE ANDRADE GUIMARÃES, the leader of the government's fourth expedition
GENERAL CLAUDIO DO AMARAL SAVAGET, the leader of the second column of the fourth expedition
MARSHAL CARLOS MACHADO DE BITTENCOURT, the war minister and eventual commander of the fourth expedition

The Novel

Rebellion in the Backlands is not fiction but rather a factual account of an actual historical event. The event—a rebellion led by a charismatic religious fanatic against the federal government of Brazil—might have sunk into obscurity but for Cunha's account, which does not merely report the event but also defines and interprets its significance. As a result, *Rebellion in the Backlands* has been called Brazil's national epic, and its influence on Brazilian fiction—indeed, South American fiction—has been substantial. The work itself, with its plot buildup, might be said to anticipate the so-called nonfiction novel of later decades.

Cunha does not, however, begin with plot but with extensive essays on the land and the people of the backlands region. Taking up approximately one third of the book and covering geography, geology, rainfall, flora and fauna, race, ethnology, psychology, and other subjects, these two long essays are burdened by outdated nineteenth century theories of environmental influence and race. Cunha draws a daunting picture of the hot, rugged, semidesert *sertão*, periodically stricken by killing droughts, and speculates that the *sertanejo*'s personality has been formed by this harsh environment and by his mixed racial heritage (white, black, and Indian). Whereas the admixture of "superior" and "inferior" racial stocks (as Cunha expresses it) has resulted in universal "degeneration" along the Brazilian seaboard, the *sertanejo*, through isolation in his primitive backlands environment, has become "a retrograde, not a degenerate, type." He is physically robust but morally backward. The *sertanejo*'s atavistic tendencies are superbly represented by his undying devotion to the religious fanatic Antonio Conselheiro, himself a spiritualized version of the backlands mentality. In the *sertanejo*'s simple view, "Anthony the Counselor" is a backlands saint.

These long introductory essays serve to romanticize the subject matter, to set the stage for the narrative of the rebellion. The introductions make clear that the underlying causes of the conflict are cultural differences between the isolated backlands and the developed seaboard. These cultural differences first cause religious friction between the established Catholic Church and Antonio Conselheiro. Later, the Counselor begins preaching against the recently established Brazilian Republic (proclaimed in 1889), whose new taxes and new laws regarding civil marriage and the like offend him. The Counselor's idea of proper government is a vague theocracy, ruled by the law of God rather than civil law. He and his followers label the republic an Antichrist, call its laws "the law of the hound," and rip down its tax notices.

In 1893, a contingent of thirty Bahian policemen comes after the Counselor for preaching insurrection. They catch up with him in Massete, where his band routs them in a shoot-out. Another contingent of eighty soldiers turns back when the Counselor fades into the forbidding backlands. The die now cast, Antonio Conselheiro and his followers withdraw to distant, inaccessible Canudos, where they establish their theocracy and military stronghold. Actually, it is a fairly inadequate theocracy, since the motley backlands population rallying to Canudos includes not only thousands of the religiously devout but also hordes of bandits, who raid the surrounding countryside. Despite such depredations and the Counselor's growing power, the government leaves Canudos alone until October, 1896, when a trivial incident—a dispute between the Counselor and the Joazeiro magistrate over a load of lumber—precipitates the military phase of the rebellion.

With the Counselor's forces threatening to attack Joazeiro, the town's magistrate wires for help from the Bahian governor, who dispatches one hundred troops under Lieutenant Manuel da Silva Pires Ferreira to put down the nuisance. This ridiculous expedition arrives in Joazeiro, sets out for Canudos, and, after marching for days through the backlands heat, encounters perhaps thousands of the Counselor's *jagunços* at Uauá. The encounter is fierce and swift, and the surviving troops escape only because the *jagunços* do not pursue.

The government immediately begins organizing a second expedition, involving more federal troops and artillery. After some organizational delays, the second expedition of 560 men, led by Major Febronio de Brito, sets out for Canudos from Monte Santo. Again, there are days of marching through the torrid heat, this time with the *jagunços*, from the cover of the roadside *caatinga* (tangled scrub forest), sniping and making running attacks on the advancing column. The expedition's provisions give out just as, somewhat demoralized and depleted, it arrives in the vicinity of Canudos. Outside Canudos it runs into an ambush and, the following morning, a full-scale enemy attack. Forced to retreat, to the jeers of the surrounding *jagunços*, the expedition has to fight its way back along the same roads by which it fought its way in. A herd of wild goats frightened into its path proves to be a handy source of food for the men, but of troops arriving back in Monte Santo, not a single one is able-bodied.

Sterner government measures to quell rebels are called for, as well as a forceful leader. The man of the moment is Colonel Antonio Moreira Cesar, a ruthless hero of the Republican wars, whose fame is guaranteed to strike fear into the hearts of the *jagunços*. He is called up from the South to head the third expedition, consisting of thirteen hundred men with artillery.

Colonel Moreira Cesar's aggressive tactics live up to his reputation. From Monte Santo to Canudos, he leads a series of long forced marches through the backlands heat; as a result, his troops arrive quickly and relatively intact, but exhausted. The colonel decides to storm Canudos immediately, sending columns of his troops charging across the dried riverbed into town and expecting to rout the quivering *jagunços*. The results, however, are not as encouraging as expected: The troops who survive the enemy fire can be seen spreading out and disappearing down the narrow alleyways and into the wood-and-mud huts. As the attacking troops continue to be absorbed, Colonel Moreira Cesar decides to lead an inspiring cavalry charge. He himself is shot down, however, and the command falls to timid Colonel Tamarindo. Amid the mounting confusion and faltering attack, Colonel Tamarindo consults with his fellow officers, who decide on a retreat the next day. The planned retreat becomes a panic as the *jagunços* turn and pursue the fleeing troops, who abandon their equipment and wounded along the road. The *jagunços* line the roadsides with soldiers' heads and hang the decapitated corpse of Colonel Tamarindo from a bush to dry and blow in the wind.

Stunned by the defeat, the whole nation panics, with rumors flying of a Monarchist conspiracy behind the backlands revolt. The Republic calls for full mobilization of its military resources, which prove to be embarrassingly limited, but within three months a fourth expedition, commanded by General Arthur Oscar de Andrade Guimarães, is organized. The expedition divides into two columns: The first column, consisting of 1,933 men under General Arthur Oscar, leaves from Monte Santo, while a second column, of 2,350 men under General Claudio do Amaral Savaget, departs from Geremoabo. The second column must fight its way to Canudos, but it arrives in time to rescue the first column, pinned down on the town's outskirts. After the columns link up, a state of siege begins, though sometimes it is difficult to tell who is besieging whom. Since the army has a foothold only on one side of Canudos, the town has easy access to supplies, while the army has trouble getting its supplies through. Meanwhile, the army's casualties are horrendous.

Seeing the supply problem, Marshal Carlos Machado de Bittencourt, the war minister, steps in at this point and takes charge of the situation. He buys one thousand mules, sets up regular supply trains, and sends in troop reinforcements. Saved by mules, the army begins asserting itself: Through various forays and attacks, it extends its line further into and around Canudos, eventually surrounding the city. After that, Canudos is doomed, though the *jagunços* continue to resist strongly and to inflict heavy casualties. The army's artillery bombards the city, starting extensive fires, but somehow the huts absorb the cannonballs and shrapnel. When the army tightens its circle, it must stop the bombardments to avoid endangering its own troops. The center of Canudos resistance must then be taken by close fighting, including hand-to-hand combat. The army tries dynamite bombs briefly, but their effects on the civilian population are so heartrending that, even in this vicious war, they are discontinued. Only one truce is called, to allow some two hundred women, children, and old men to surrender. The remaining defenders of Canudos die to the last man, conveniently falling back into a mass grave that had earlier been dug.

The Characters

The historical personages of *Rebellion in the Backlands* are not developed or viewed from inside as are characters in a novel. Cunha often gives only their names, and even then he shows an aristocratic bias by naming only officers or leaders: The troops and common folk remain anonymous. The most prominent leaders, however, are accorded elaborate analytical introductions.

Cunha devotes his most complete analysis to Antonio Conselheiro, whom he views as a perfect embodiment of the backlands mentality. Coming from a powerful family previously involved in a bloody feud with a rival family, Antonio Maciel seems born to the pattern of violence endemic to the lawless backlands. Yet the crucial event of his life is a personal blow: When he is a young man, his wife deserts him for a policeman, which seems to leave Antonio Maciel permanently deranged. He begins wandering the backlands roads, eventually adopting the life and appearance (flowing beard, blue tunic, and staff) of an early Christian ascetic. Impressionable and superstitious, the backlands population soon accepts him as Antonio Conselheiro, whose confused message is heard as the wisdom of God. The power which this following gives him makes the Counselor a walking time bomb whose fuse is only shortened by religious and civil persecutions. Primarily important as the rebellion's instigator, the Counselor gradually fades into the background, dying during Canudos' last days either from dysentery or from deliberate starvation.

Among the army's commanders, only Colonel Moreira Cesar and Marshal Bittencourt get full-scale introductions. The heroic Colonel Moreira Cesar is notable for his incongruous physical appearance (reminiscent of a squat, froglike Napoleon) and for his epileptic seizures, a few of which interrupt the forced marches to Canudos. Cunha suggests that the progressive disease is eroding the colonel's mental faculties, which might help account for his overly zealous tactics. Contrasting with Colonel Moreira Cesar is Marshal Bittencourt, a plodding bureaucrat whose dullness superbly equips him to manage the logistics of mule trains, supplies, and reinforcements. Also contrasting with Colonel Moreira Cesar is his understudy, Colonel Tamarindo, who stands out despite not receiving a full introduction: Nearing sixty and anticipating a peaceful retirement, he instead loses his head and is hung out to dry.

A number of unnamed *sertanejos* are also memorable, mainly for their toughness—a young boy already hardened in violence, a dried-up old grandmother looking after her wounded grandchild, an old man still fighting even though too weak to lift his gun, the set of dirt-encrusted prisoners. These individual portraits contribute to the collective characterization of the *sertanejos* as a crafty, hardy, and durable mixed breed, like the mules who save the army. In contrast, the military gives an impression of mass incompetence.

Themes and Meanings

Rebellion in the Backlands should be required reading for all military students, since it clearly points out the dangers to a cumbersome army, with outmoded tactics and long supply lines, of fighting a guerrilla war on the guerrillas' home turf. The *sertanejos* utilize classic guerrilla procedures, including local intelligence networks, hit-and-run maneuvers, enticement into ambushes, recycling of captured equipment, and psychological demoralization. Most of all, the *sertanejos* are expert at using their terrain against the army, striking after the troops have marched into exhaustion or cul-de-sacs. Finally, the *sertanejos* illustrate the determination of guerrillas fighting for a fanatical cause or merely their homes.

Notwithstanding Cunha's interest in military lessons, *Rebellion in the*

Backlands is ultimately an antimilitaristic work. Besides showing the military to disadvantage, Cunha was condemning his country for using military power against its own citizens, poor people living in a neglected region which might be termed the Appalachia of Brazil. His condemnation may seem unfair under the circumstances, but Cunha believed that integrating the *sertanejos* into the national culture is a matter of time and education, not military force. Furthermore, Cunha's admiration of the *sertanejos* suggests that such integration does not simply mean conformity of the "backward" *sertanejos* to the "civilized" national culture. How civilized, asks Cunha, is a culture which must prevail through superior brutality? This paradox continues to plague not only Brazil but also the superpowers and "civilization" generally.

Critical Context

Rebellion in the Backlands is Brazil's own *Iliad*, with soldiers and *sertanejos* replacing Greeks and Trojans. A monumental work of the early Brazilian Republic, *Rebellion in the Backlands* contributed to the rediscovery of Brazil's colorful regions, particularly the Northeast, and to the creation of the *sertanejo* myth. Cunha thereby helped lay the groundwork for the modern flowering of the Brazilian novel, dominated by *Nordestino* writers. Cunha's influence can be seen, for example, in such novels as Jorge Amado's *Terras do sem fim* (1943; *The Violent Land*, 1945) and *Gabriela, cravo e canela* (1958; *Gabriela, Clove and Cinnamon*, 1962), with Gabriela as a modern embodiment of the *sertanejo* myth.

Indeed, the influence of *Rebellion in the Backlands* does not stop at Brazil's borders. It inspired, for example, a fictional retelling of the Canudos story, *La guerra del fin del mondo* (1981; *The War of the End of the World*, 1984), by Peruvian novelist Mario Vargas Llosa. More generally, Cunha and other nonfiction writers, particularly sociologists, have helped to define the subject matter of Latin American fiction and have influenced its tendency to incorporate sociology, local color, and other factual material. The bizarre nature of some Latin American fact (especially political fact), as depicted by Cunha and others, has also influenced fictional interest, by novelists such as Argentina's Julio Cortázar and Colombia's Gabriel García Márquez, in the interplay of illusion and reality, fact and fantasy.

Sources for Further Study

Bates, Margaret J. "*Rebellion in the Backlands*," in *The Americas*. I (July, 1944-April, 1945), pp. 387-389.

Frank, Waldo. *South American Journey*, 1943.

Goldberg, Isaac. *Brazilian Literature*, 1922.

Putnam, Samuel. "A Translator's Introduction," in *Rebellion in the Backlands*, 1944.

Stein, Barbara Hadley. *"Rebellion in the Backlands,"* in *Hispanic American Historical Review*. XXIV (February, 1944), pp. 471-473.

Harold Branam

THE RECOGNITIONS

Author: William Gaddis (1922-   )
Type of plot: Social morality
Time of plot: From about 1910 to shortly after World War II
Locale: New York City, Paris, Spain, and Rome
First published: 1955

> *Principal characters:*
> WYATT GWYON, the protagonist, an artist, forger, and
>   adventurer
> ESME, a poet who seeks the truth
> STANLEY, a composer of organ masses
> BASIL VALENTINE, an art critic in a counterfeiting ring with
>   Gwyon
> AUNT MAY, Gwyon's aunt, a devout Calvinist, whose "face
>   wore the firm look of election"
> THE REVEREND GWYON, Wyatt's father, who is the town min-
>   ister but who secretly worships the sun

The Novel

Most of the characters inhabiting William Gaddis' novel *The Recognitions* pretend to be intellectuals in order to attain fame and money. They do not seek the universe's principles, God's laws, like the novel's few true intellectuals. These few, because they struggle to recognize the universe's rules and to obey them, live moral lives. The impostors, on the other hand, do not.

Wyatt Gwyon is the novel's main character and, because he seeks fame, its main dissembler. The book follows his journey from pretense to truth, illuminating the way to discover morality.

The novel begins with Wyatt's childhood. His mother has died, so his father, the Reverend Gwyon, and his live-in relative Aunt May rear him. The two adults battle each other over whose philosophy Wyatt will follow. Gwyon tries to teach his son to think and learn. He lures him with mythology, tales of his travels, and the excitement of discovery. May tries to deaden the boy's mind with blind, unquestioning faith in God. She berates him for being one of Adam's descendants and therefore a sinner who will go to Hell unless he believes in Jesus.

May fears creativity more than anything else because man imitates God when he creates. He tries to become God, she reasons. Therefore, when Wyatt, still a child, shows her his first picture, that of a robin, she asks: "Don't you love our Lord Jesus, after all?" He says that he does. "Then why do you try to take His place? Our Lord is the true creator, and only sinful people try to emulate Him." She goes on to tell him that "to sin is to falsify something in the divine order, and that is what Lucifer did. . . . He tried to become original. . . . And he won his own domain. . . . Is that what you want? Is that what you want? Is that what you want?" From then on, Wyatt "made drawings in secret . . . more convinced as those years passed, and his talent blossomed . . . that he was damned." He buries the paintings in the yard.

Wyatt feels such great guilt for creating as a child that as an adult he ends up painting only reproductions. He becomes good at copying, and because he wants fame and money, he starts forging paintings of fifteenth century artists. Recktall Brown, a rich collector, claims that he finds the paintings in old houses he buys; Basil Valentine, a renowned art critic, first disputes, then concedes their authenticity, allowing Brown to sell them for large amounts of money, which the three men split.

The counterfeiting ring dissolves, however, when Brown dies and Wyatt tries to kill Valentine. The critic reveals to Wyatt that the fifteenth century works and, therefore, Wyatt's copies have too much extraneous detail cluttering them up. He accuses the artist of concentrating on detailed, limited work rather than trying to find "the origins of design," the order of the universe. The criticism negates all that Wyatt has done, making him murderously angry.

He flees to Spain and changes his name to Stephen. There he realizes that Valentine was right. One must not limit oneself to details if one wants to find an orderly universe, for such a universe applies its principles to all things equally. That is why it is ordered, because it has right and wrong. To find rules that apply to all things one must try to study all things; but since that is impossible, one must study a great many things, in order to recognize the rules common to everything.

Artists try to reveal principles in their works, an act that takes great creativity and imagination; for, because one person cannot know everything, he must theorize and struggle to find the rules that God made. Then he imitates them. Wyatt fears to "emulate" God because May's lesson that God punishes those who create has never left him. He has simply buried his creativity, as he buried his original paintings. His bringing the fear to light and overcoming it allows him to start seeking the eternal principles and living a moral life.

The Characters

Wyatt, of all the pretenders, changes to become a truth seeker. Most of the other characters loiter at the right bars, attend fashionable parties, and go sightseeing at the correct places. They gossip, drink, develop their images, and, whenever they can, because they have nothing better to do, antagonize and distract the moral characters. Hannah tells Anselm to "shut up," "go home," and "take a nap" when he and Stanley discuss religion.

Don Bildow asks Stanley for methyltestosterone ("I'm with this girl, see")
and later "the Italian word for contraceptive" when Stanley frantically pursues Esme.

Three other characters besides Wyatt seek the truth in the novel: Esme,
the poet; Stanley, the composer; and Valentine, the art critic. They warrant
the reader's attention because they discover truth.

Gaddis has created a fascinating character in the beautiful Esme. She has
the self-discipline to make herself look beyond details to find the eternal
principles. Her use of the third-person singular when talking about herself
illustrates this asceticism. The use of the third person allows her to think of
herself as she would another person, with the distance necessary to ignore
petty needs and selfish desires. These needs only get in the way of her
broad study, for they are details such as the ones Wyatt has painted for so
long.

Using the third person, Esme says beautiful things. When Stanley gets
her pregnant, she asks him, "Will you marry her... ? For he put it there
and did not take it away as he promised, as he always had done before, as
he promised." When the "damned black androgyne," the epithet that she
gives Father Martin, holds up the cross to exorcise her, she says: "Take him
away, he's hurting her." When she gets the sore on her lip which later becomes infected and kills her, she explains that "something bit her perhaps."

Unlike Esme, Stanley does not believe that man, by himself, can find the
truth. He thinks that God works through prayer and ritual to make man forget the limited and look for the infinite. His efforts to convert others to
Catholicism show his belief in the power of faith. Since he composes a piece
of music good enough "to offend the creator of perfection by emulating his
grand design," he justifies his belief.

Characters in the novel often ask the question, "Should we understand in
order to believe or... believe in order to understand?" Gaddis never gives
an explicit answer. Since both Stanley and Esme find truth, however, perhaps both methods are valid; a character's temperament determines which
alternative is right for him.

Valentine, though a Jesuit priest, never says whether he thinks a person
must have faith to find truth or truth to find faith; but one way or another,
the art critic does find the eternal principles. His trenchant comments to
Wyatt prove that. His ability to discover truth makes him an intriguing character because he lacks genius, unlike Wyatt, Esme, and Stanley. Gaddis,
through Valentine, shows that average people can also look beyond details
and recognize truth; they simply cannot express it as beautifully as artists
can.

Themes and Meanings

Gaddis paints a Zoroastrian world in his novel, one in which good—represented by the natural, honest, alive, loving, moral truth seekers—battles evil—represented by the unnatural, pretentious, deathlike, selfish, immoral fame seekers. Evil seems to conquer good, since the truly wicked survive and even prosper, while most of the people who are wavering toward the good and many of the good themselves die. Death ultimately takes Esme, Stanley, the Reverend Gwyon, and Valentine, leaving only Wyatt to continue the struggle.

Since the evil are the victors, why should people choose the good? The answer to this question is the novel's theme. People should live morally because God exists and has made an orderly universe. He ultimately rewards those who follow His principles and punishes those who do not. Yet He deceives "good people by keeping the path to paradise littered with filth." He makes living a good life difficult by hiding His principles and not seeming to reward His followers who discover them. In this way God makes certain that only the truly good reach Heaven.

Critical Context

The Recognitions first appeared in print in 1955. Very few critics gave favorable reviews because the reader must stumble through 956 pages of obscure analogies, unfinished conversations and sentences, events not explicitly described, interspersed foreign languages, and characters who talk at one another in enigmatic language. Gaddis does give obscure explanations of glossed-over events and supplies some omitted details as the story progresses, so that a reader who uses his imagination and creativity to fill in the blanks can work through the story slowly. Gaddis litters the path so that only those willing to take great effort will finish.

Few people have wanted to struggle enough to uncover the novel's message until recently. The book went out of print in the late 1950's. In 1962, Meridian published it in paperback, and in 1970 another paperback edition came out. More and more people have read it and praised it, so that now numerous critical articles have been devoted to it. Some reviewers even compare Gaddis to James Joyce and T. S. Eliot.

The novel sufficiently rewards the reader who perseveres. The conversations amuse; the analogies, beautiful poetry, and poetic language provoke thought; the mention of arcana fascinates. Finally, in deciding how to live, everyone should know the argument advocating a moral life, even if the argument is ultimately rejected.

Sources for Further Study

Koenig, Peter. "Recognizing Gaddis' *Recognitions*," in *Contemporary Literature*. XVI (Winter, 1975), pp. 61-72.

Moore, Steven. *A Reader's Guide to William Gaddis' "The Recognitions,"* 1982.

Salemi, Joseph. "To Soar in Atonement: Art as Expiation in Gaddis' *The Recognitions*," in *Novel*. X (Winter, 1977), pp. 127-136.

Patrick Wright

THE RECTOR OF JUSTIN

Author: Louis Auchincloss (1917-   )
Type of plot: Social chronicle
Time of plot: Primarily the first half of the twentieth century
Locale: Primarily New York City and New England
First published: 1964

Principal characters:
> FRANCIS (FRANK) PRESCOTT, founder and headmaster (rector)
> of Justin Martyr Academy
> BRIAN ASPINWALL, a young teacher, Frank's would-be
> biographer
> HARRIET PRESCOTT, Frank's wife
> CORDELIA PRESCOTT TURNBULL, the youngest daughter of
> Harriet and Frank
> HORACE HAVISTOCK, Frank's friend since childhood
> DAVID GRISCAM, a Wall Street lawyer and longtime trustee of
> Justin Martyr Academy
> ELIZA DEAN, a former fiancée of Frank
> CHARLEY STRONG, Cordelia's deceased lover
> JULES GRISCAM, David's son, a suicide

The Novel

Outwardly traditional in form, consisting of an assemblage of journal entries, letters, and memoirs, *The Rector of Justin* goes beyond tradition in the skillful characterization afforded each of the several narrators whose testimony combines to produce the novel. The principal narrator of *The Rector of Justin* is Brian Aspinwall, a somewhat old-maidish graduate student who has joined the faculty of Justin Martyr Academy during the eightieth year of the fabled old headmaster's life. From keeping a journal about his life at the school, including his encounters with Dr. Frank Prescott and his ailing wife who soon dies, Aspinwall goes on to project a Prescott biography, interviewing many of the old gentleman's family and friends; in several cases, the interviewees have already written memoirs of their own, which are incorporated within the body of the novel.

Born in 1860 and orphaned at an early age, the Boston-bred Prescott is himself the product of a New England private-school education. From his earliest youth onward, however, he has cherished a dream of the perfect boarding school—unlike the school he himself attended and more on the order of such "competition" as Groton and St. Mark's. With his friend Horace Havistock, with whom he seeks to share the dream, Prescott spends three years at Oxford University, ostensibly to study the British public-school model. Upon his return to the United States, he briefly forsakes his dream for a promising career with the New York Central railroad and is about to marry the vivacious young Californian Eliza Dean when he is suddenly recalled to his earlier vocation in a kind of vision. Eliza, at first willing to join in his changed plans, allows Havistock to persuade her that she is not "cut out" to be a headmaster's wife; in exchange, however, she exacts a promise from Havistock that he will not teach in Prescott's eventual model school; both promises are kept, as neither Havistock nor Eliza sees fit to interfere with Frank's calling.

Leaving the railroad, Prescott enrolls in Harvard Divinity School, if only to acquire the credential needed by such a would-be founder of a church-related school; he is otherwise little interested in theology or in the Episcopalian priesthood. While at Harvard, he meets and marries Harriet, the intellectually derived New Englander with whom he will share nearly sixty years of his life. Thereafter, the facts of Prescott's life become inextricably interwoven with those of the school, which he establishes and develops into prosperity through sheer willpower.

As Aspinwall sifts through the various layers of Prescott's existence, he becomes discomfittingly aware that Justin Martyr, for all its founder's protestations, is little different from any other boys' preparatory school, particularly in the matter of elitism and snobbery; yet Prescott, even in his dotage, continues to cherish the illusion that Justin is somehow far more democratic than the competition, lamenting the philistinism of those "old boys" who, ironically, continue to provide the school with most of its financial support. So great is the force of Prescott's personality, meanwhile, that his associates would sooner lie to him than risk shattering a dream that provides inspiration even to them.

Against the background of World War II in Europe and eventual American involvement, Aspinwall, medically unfit for military service, continues his effort to interpret Frank Prescott's life and career even as he struggles with his own possible vocation toward the Episcopalian priesthood. The documents, both written and verbal, that would provide the material for his biography are often contradictory and baffling; at the time of Prescott's death in 1946, Aspinwall has joined the priesthood and returned to Justin following his studies; the projected biography, however, will in all likelihood remain unfinished, its open questions unresolved.

The Characters

Lacking a plot, save for the events of Frank Prescott's life and career, *The Rector of Justin* derives most of its considerable force through the delineation of its characters, often in their own voices. Notably absent from the list of narrators is Prescott himself, whose implied intent to speak through his actions provides the novel's heavily ironic substructure.

As the various observers among his intimates make clear, Francis Prescott possesses both the talent and the force of character to have succeeded in a number of professions. In *A Writer's Capital, Life, Law and Letters* (1974), Auchincloss readily identifies the model for Prescott as Judge Learned Hand (1872-1956), with whom he was personally acquainted. The reasons for Prescott's particular vocation, barring divine revelation, remain open to question; in any event, the vocation was sufficiently strong that he cut short a promising career in business and allowed his fiancée to abandon him. The irony is that the "unique" institution of secondary education for which Prescott apparently sacrificed so much turns out to be little different from others of the same type, owing to the simple fact that democracy can neither be taught nor fostered in an institution with high tuition and selective admissions policies. To Aspinwall's implied indignation, Prescott states that he has always admitted scholarship students, yet he concedes in the next breath that the school's only Catholics are the sons of Justin alumni who happened to marry women of that faith and that all of its ethnic Jews are in fact professing Christians. The blindness of such a stance, or of his guiding principles, appears never to have occurred to him.

Predictably, such single-mindedness as Prescott's has left frequent casualties in its wake, as Aspinwall will soon discover. Among the major casualties, apart from his former fiancée, Eliza Dean, are his youngest daughter, ironically named Cordelia, and her deceased lover Charley Strong.

Cordelia Prescott Turnbull, although perhaps a rebel by temperament, has good reason to resent a childhood in which her father's family perpetually yielded first place to his students. Her disastrous first marriage was an obvious gesture of revolt, her choice of husband a mild-mannered nonentity whose main virtues, for Cordelia, lay in his Roman Catholic faith and his public-school education—both poles apart from her father's values. A Bohemian by nature, Cordelia in her middle forties has progressed from being an indifferent if talented artist to being a highly knowledgeable critic; still, she will never forgive her father for his treatment of Charley Strong, the terminally wounded World War I veteran with whom she shared a brief idyll in Paris following the collapse of her first marriage. Charley, unique among her various consorts, was a Justin alumnus, and during the last months of his brief, doomed life, her father's psychic hold upon Charley so greatly exceeded her own that Charley's lifework, a novel of some promise, was burned on the day of his funeral, thanks to tacit collusion with Frank Prescott. Cordelia's second husband, although not a Justin graduate, soon estranged himself from her by becoming one of the school's more generous and enthusiastic benefactors. At forty-five, she remains both restless and resentful, even attempting to seduce the callow and most unwilling Aspinwall.

David Griscam, an early alumnus of the school who has become one of its strongest supporters, is a hard-nosed Wall Street attorney whose lifelong devotion to Prescott and his cause often places him in the unenviable position of mediator between Prescott's dream and the harsher realities of human nature. More than once, his chosen position causes him to perjure himself in Prescott's presence. Among Prescott's more notable failures, moreover, is Griscam's own son Jules, who died a suicide in the 1920's after an abortive attempt to destroy Prescott, in part because of Prescott's influence upon his father.

Brian Aspinwall, Auchincloss' choice of principal narrator, is, like Miss Gussie Millinder in *The House of Five Talents* (1960), an oddly neutered narrator whose asexuality makes him a privileged observer. Although not a homosexual, Aspinwall has been ailing for most of his life and voluntarily remains on the sidelines, so to speak, the better to observe the effects of full sexuality in others. In later years, Auchincloss would still employ such narrators with considerable effect: In *The House of the Prophet* (1980), similar in structure to the present novel, the principal narrator is a writer rendered impotent for life by a severe diabetic crisis sustained in early adolescence. Aspinwall, meanwhile, is not without interest as a character in his own right; of all Prescott's intimates, he is perhaps unique in his breadth of knowledge, in his curiosity, and in his instinctive, if seldom articulated, awareness of the ironies that lurk just beneath the surface of Prescott's well-publicized life. To the end, however, he will lack the courage of his convictions, and his biography of Prescott will remain unfinished for want of simple, evident answers to the many questions raised.

Themes and Meanings

Louis Auchincloss, himself a Wall Street attorney and a product of Groton, among the most eminent of American preparatory schools, has often used such schools in his fiction to help delineate the background formation of his characters. Never before or since, however, has he so successfully presented the implicit irony, or even absurdity, of the existence in the United States of an educational alternative frankly based on the elitist British public school yet ostensibly dedicated to the ideals of democracy. Through the character, actions, and career of Frank Prescott, Auchincloss shows both the benefits and the dangers of such a hybrid; the dangers are perhaps most evident to Prescott himself who, perceiving the true nature of his accomplishment at the end of his life, honestly believes that he has failed in his appointed task.

Through his skillful use of multiple narrators and viewpoints, Auchincloss in *The Rector of Justin* also underscores the elusive nature of human truth, necessarily subjective as well as relative, and the inevitable moral blindness implicit in any and all human endeavor. Frank Prescott's ideal of democracy, which he supposes to be doubly grounded in Holy Scripture and the United States Constitution, proves considerably more ephemeral than he might have imagined, given the simple fact that both documents lend themselves to a multiplicity of readings. In the end, Prescott no doubt stands convicted of failure, not because he failed to meet his goals but rather because he failed to sustain the human relationships that he sacrificed in favor of his elusive dream.

Critical Context

The Rector of Justin was Auchincloss' first novel to reach high critical and popular acclaim; by most accounts, it still rates as his finest accomplishment, rivaled only by its immediate successor, *The Embezzler* (1966). In his two preceding novels, *The House of Five Talents* and *Portrait in Brownstone* (1962), Auchincloss had begun to develop the technique of limited-viewpoint, first-person narration as an instrument of social satire, a device that he would use to considerable profit in *The Embezzler* as well. *The Rector of Justin*, however, may well represent the high point of the form, providing as it does the many-sided portrait of an unwittingly complex individual whose own voice is rarely heard, and then only in conversation.

Following the death of John O'Hara in 1970, Auchincloss stood alone as an accomplished American novelist of manners, but the genre thereafter appeared to fall out of favor, kept viable mainly by Auchincloss himself at the approximate rate of one novel per year. In retrospect, his finest period is that of the early to middle 1960's, with *The Rector of Justin* securing his reputation as a major American novelist.

Source for Further Study

Tuttleton, James W. *The Novel of Manners in America*, 1972.

David B. Parsell

THE RED PONY

Author: John Steinbeck (1902-1968)
Type of plot: Story cycle
Time of plot: About 1910
Locale: Salinas Valley, California
First published: 1937, enlarged 1945

> *Principal characters:*
> JODY TIFLIN, a boy about eleven years old
> CARL TIFLIN, his father, a rancher
> BILLY BUCK, a middle-aged ranch hand working for the
> Tiflins
> MRS. TIFLIN, Jody's mother
> GRANDFATHER, Mrs. Tiflin's father and a former wagon-train
> leader
> GITANO, an elderly Chicano laborer

The Novel

These stories present a young boy's entrance into maturity through his encounters with life's harsh realities. Death, disappointment, and the world's stubborn refusal to conform to human ideals break down Jody's childlike certitudes. Yet, though Jody at times is callous or bitter because of these experiences, he ultimately realizes that life holds both disappointment and promise and that acceptance of life with endurance and sympathy is the way of maturity.

In the first story, "The Gift," Mr. Tiflin presents Jody with a red pony which Jody names after the Gabilan Mountains near his home. The pony quickly becomes his chief joy and responsibility, and under Billy Buck's guidance, he prepares Gabilan to be ridden. As the horse is nearing the completion of his training, however, he is caught out in the rain on a day Billy had promised Jody it would not rain. Gabilan catches cold and, despite Billy Buck's constant attention, dies. As Jody watches buzzards descend on Gabilan's body, he kills one of them out of frustration.

Jody's next encounter with the harsh realities of nature occurs in "The Great Mountains," when an old Chicano named Gitano walks onto the Tiflin ranch on his way to the western mountains where he was born and asks to stay at the Tiflins' until it is time for him to die. Mr. Tiflin refuses to grant his request, and Gitano rides off the next morning on an old horse called Easter, but not before Jody sees that Gitano is carrying an old and beautiful rapier, passed down in his family for generations.

"The Promise" and "The Leader of the People" repeat the patterns of the first and second stories, respectively. In "The Promise," Jody receives another colt but only after the colt's mother, Nellie, is killed by Billy when she is having trouble delivering him. Jody's pleasure in his horse is soured by Billy's killing of Nellie. Another old man, Jody's grandfather, visits the Tiflin ranch in "The Leader of the People." Though Jody is eager to hear his grandfather's repetitive stories of his experiences as a wagon-train leader, the old man tells Jody that the value of his work lay not in being leader but in being a part of "westering" the general movement of people into new lands and experiences. He also confides to the boy his belief that the new generation represented by Mr. Tiflin has lost the westering spirit. As *The Red Pony* closes, Jody makes a lemonade for his grandfather to console him, indicating that he has matured enough to care for others.

The Red Pony's plot belongs to the *Bildungsroman* tradition, in which a young person, in this case Jody Tiflin, is initiated into the mysteries of life. Each of the individual stories is part of his education. The loss of Gabilan in "The Gift" reveals to Jody nature's cruelty and man's inability to predict nature accurately. In "The Great Mountains," Jody sees in Gitano both a symbol of human decay and the enduring power of human ideals, since he carries the ancient sword passed down through the generations. In "The Promise," Jody observes the wonder and pain of the reproductive cycle when he sees Nellie and a stud horse copulate violently and assists at the birth of Nellie's colt. Finally, Jody's grandfather teaches him man's special destiny of westering, and Jody's act of kindness shows that he has some perception of this spirit.

The Characters

Jody Tiflin is the main character of the story, and because its main theme is his education, he is largely a passive figure observing events rather than directing them. In the first stories, Jody is described as a "little boy" who is slightly punier than his playmates. His life is regulated almost entirely by his stern father and doting mother, and he readily acquiesces in this, since he cannot imagine anything different. The pony Gabilan is his first real responsibility and a sign that he is leaving childhood, but the pony's death embitters him. This loss of innocence is a fallen state in which he kills or annoys helpless animals, fears but no longer respects adult authority, and regards maturity as the ability to swear.

Yet Jody's disappointments also cause him to speculate on the world outside his own meager experience. When he sees Gitano's sword, he realizes that he must tell no one about it, because to do so would destroy the sword's peculiar truth; thus, Jody makes an important moral decision. In his grandfather, Jody sees that one whom he has idolized has also been disappointed by life and learns the value of sympathy. In his last action, making a lemonade, he becomes a mature and active character, who sees life without glorifying illusions.

Jody's grandfather and Gitano have a similar function in *The Red Pony*: as representations of human frailty and transcendence. Both are very old men, yet they maintain strength and dignity because they carry on a tradition: Gitano, with his ancestral sword; Grandfather, with stories of his wagon-train days. These traditions exemplify man's destiny to move into unknown areas of existence. They are embodiments of westering, whether it is the movement of the conquistadors or the American pioneers. Steinbeck also grounds these figures in physical detail, so that each is a vivid and individual character in his own right. The treatment of both men indicates that the westering spirit has died down in later generations. Jody's parents regard them with mingled pity and scorn. Neither man can fully express himself to them. The taciturn Gitano speaks only in simple, repetitious terms, while Grandfather constantly retells the same stories. Only to Jody do they reveal their true nature, and in his respect for them lies the hope that their spirit will live on.

The Tiflins might be seen as evidence of Grandfather's claim that the younger generation has lost its spirit, but Steinbeck more sensitively portrays them as conventional people who, within their narrow range, function well. Carl Tiflin is an authoritarian father who nevertheless wishes to see his son become a man by giving him the responsibilities of owning a horse. Mrs. Tiflin is a kind and intelligent parent who recognizes that her son is maturing. Yet neither can fully understand the larger world outside their ranch. Carl dislikes both Gitano and Grandfather, while Mrs. Tiflin is sympathetic but does not see their real merits. The Tiflins are good people who do not possess the imagination to respond fully to the natural world.

Billy Buck, however, does have this imagination, and he voices the book's central lesson—that no one knows what the future will bring. The son of a mule packer, Billy is a horse expert, but even he is fallible, as in the episode with Gabilan. Thus, knowing his weaknesses, he can be sympathetic to Jody and respectful to Gitano and Grandfather in a way that Mr. Tiflin, who despises weakness, cannot. Because of this, Billy functions as Jody's friend and teacher, instructing him not only in horsemanship but also in the ways of nature. Billy is Steinbeck's example of a mature human being in *The Red Pony*.

Themes and Meanings

The principal theme of *The Red Pony* is the exploration of man's complex relationship with nature, as presented through Jody's education. For Steinbeck, all nature, including man, is bound together. *The Red Pony* is filled with descriptions of natural phenomena—weather, animals, and plants—reflecting and directing events in the story, as when the rainy season gives Jody an omen of doom and, later, exposure to the rain fatally sickens Gabilan, or when Grandfather compares Jody's planned mouse hunt to the slaughter of the American Indians, showing how human mistreatment of the natural world parallels man's mistreatment of his fellowmen. The unity of nature does not, however, preclude its harshness: The deaths of Gabilan and Nellie, the approaching death of Gitano, and Grandfather's sense of failure show how nature ignores human desires. The titles "The Gift" and "The Promise" are ironic, for these stories reveal that nature makes no gifts and keeps no promises. Nor can even the wisest character in the stories, Billy Buck, alter this situation. Steinbeck is here in the naturalist tradition, which sees the world as indifferent to human notions of right and wrong.

Yet naturalism is only one side of Steinbeck's vision. He also belongs to the Emersonian transcendentalist tradition, which sees nature as mysterious but nevertheless as a bounteous wellspring of hope. Death thus becomes an opportunity for new life, as when the dead body of Gabilan provides food for vultures or Nellie's death allows her colt to be born. All life is seen as interdependent, as are human and animal life, for example, on the ranch. Billy is an expert horseman because he respects horses and is sensitive to their needs. The Tiflins teach Jody that it is wrong to hurt innocent animals. Grandfather recalls how he had to keep hungry pioneers from eating their team oxen. In each of these instances, natural and human life are seen as connected. This vision finds its highest expression in the idea of westering, in which the trek across the wilderness forges the pioneers into a single organism, an organism which embodies the human spirit. Westering also exhibits the violent side of nature in the slaughter of the American Indians, but it is the one way in which dreams can be fulfilled, for it is an educational process for the race, enabling it to attain full maturity just as the events of *The Red Pony* cause Jody to mature. Those characters who display the greatest wisdom, Gitano, Billy, and Grandfather, have all been involved in westering. They can accept personal failure and transcend it, the lesson which Steinbeck has Jody learn in the course of the story cycle.

Steinbeck's symbolism and imagery reflect this union of man and nature. The mysterious mountains to the west of the ranch symbolize the inscrutability of nature, since no one except Gitano knows what lies beyond them. The mountains also represent the connectedness of life and death, since Gitano was born in the mountains and returns there to die. Significantly, he rides toward them on the horse Easter, suggesting a link with the Christian cycle of death and resurrection. Two other symbols are the water tub— which is constantly filled with water from a pipe so that it overflows and creates a permanent spot of green grass around itself—and the ugly black cypress tree near which pigs are slaughtered. These are analogues of the Garden of Eden and the Tree of Knowledge and represent the life-giving and destructive sides of nature, respectively. Jody regards the tub and the cypress as antithetical, but in Steinbeck's vision they are both part of the natural order.

Critical Context

The Red Pony is regarded by critics as one of Steinbeck's finest fictions. With a sure hand he integrates realistic detail of life in Monterey County, which he knew so well, with mystical speculations. The theme of the interconnected quality of all life is developed in greater depth and scope in *The Grapes of Wrath* (1939), but in *The Red Pony* the reader has an excellent introduction to Steinbeck's distinctive combination of naturalism and transcendentalism. The education of Jody Tiflin in this book has been compared with Ernest Hemingway's Nick Adams stories.

Sources for Further Study
Davis, Robert Murray, ed. *Steinbeck: A Collection of Critical Essays*, 1972.
French, Warren. *John Steinbeck*, 1961.
Lisca, Peter. *The Wide World of John Steinbeck*, 1958.

Anthony Bernardo

THE ROBBER BRIDEGROOM

Author: Eudora Welty (1909-   )
Type of plot: Satiric folk/fairy tale
Time of plot: Pioneer days
Locale: Along the Natchez Trace in Mississippi
First published: 1942

> *Principal characters:*
> JAMIE LOCKHART, the robber bridegroom, a gentleman and
>   the leader of a band of bandits
> CLEMENT MUSGROVE, a kindly, innocent planter
> ROSAMOND MUSGROVE, his beautiful young daughter
> SALOME, Rosamond's jealous and possessive stepmother
> MIKE FINK, the legendary river boatman of American
>   folklore
> GOAT, a foolish, interfering creature, the "familiar" of
>   Salome
> BIG HARP and
> LITTLE HARP, bandit brothers
> THE INDIANS, anonymous and mysterious, but important
>   presences

The Novel

This deceptively simple novel is both a bit of American folklore which depicts the rough-and-tumble life of the frontier and a satiric fairy tale which draws from and parodies the tales of the Brothers Grimm. As is typical of fairy tales, the story is highly plotted. It begins when Clement Musgrove, an innocent planter, meets Jamie Lockhart, a bandit, and Mike Fink, the famous folklore figure, at an inn. When Jamie saves Clement from being murdered and robbed by Fink, Clement tells Jamie of his past, when his first wife and his two sons were captured, tortured, and killed by the Indians. Only his daughter Rosamond remains, and he has remarried an ugly woman named Salome, whom the Indians did not kill because they were afraid of her. The relationship between Rosamond and Salome—the beautiful young girl and the evil stepmother—is right out of "Cinderella" and "Snow White": "If Rosamond was as beautiful as the day, Salome was as ugly as the night." Salome harasses Rosamond, who in turn fights this by creating her own fantasy world; even though she means only to tell the truth, lies fall out of her mouth like "diamonds and pearls."

The witch-like Salome has, as witches often do, her familiar, a foolish young man who, because of his habit of butting his way out the door when his mother locks him in, is named Goat. Salome hires Goat to follow

Rosamond and to "finish her off" if he finds the chance. The plot begins in earnest when Jamie Lockhart, dressed as a robber rather than as a gentleman, complete with berry juice stains on his face as a disguise, encounters Rosamond in the woods and robs her of all her clothes, making her go home "naked as a jaybird." When Clement hears of this, he goes to get Jamie to avenge his daughter's honor. In the meantime, Jamie once more carries Rosamond off into the forest and robs her "of that which he had left her the day before"—that is, her virginity. When Clement brings Jamie to his home, Rosamond is so begrimed, in typical Cinderella fashion, that he does not recognize her. Moreover, since he is now the gentleman, with no berry juice on his face, he is not recognized by her. Salome, however, who sees traces of the berry juice, knows everything.

Rosamond tries to find out where Jamie lives, for after he has dishonored her, she feels pity for him. She finds the house of the bandit gang and, like Snow White at the house of the seven dwarfs, sets about cleaning it up. While being kept captive at the bandit hideout, she begs Jamie to wash the berry juice off his face so that she can know who he is. As in the classical Cupid and Psyche story, however, Jamie insists on keeping his other identity a secret.

Being so preoccupied with Rosamond, Jamie neglects Clement's request to find the violator of his daughter, until once again he takes it up and runs into Big Harp and Little Harp. Big Harp is only a decapitated head, having lost his body to an executioner's ax; Little Harp, who knows Jamie the bandit to be also Jamie the gentleman, uses this knowledge to blackmail Jamie and to move into his home. Rosamond returns to her father, telling him of her robber bridegroom, and Salome gives Rosamond a recipe to remove berry stains so that she might know his true identity. Little Harp tells the bandits that he is entitled to the bandit chief's woman, but they get him an Indian girl instead, whom he then brutally rapes and murders. Rosamond catches Jamie asleep, removes the berry stains, and discovers that he is only Jamie Lockhart; at the same time, he knows her to be Clement Musgrove's silly daughter. Because of Rosamond's distrust, Jamie runs away.

In a rapid series of events, Rosamond follows Jamie, Salome goes to the woods to try to find him to cut off his head, and Clement searches for his daughter and Jamie. All are captured by the Indians who seek to avenge the murder of the Indian girl. Goat frees them one by one, and Jamie and Little Harp fight until Little Harp is killed. Salome dies in an unsuccessful attempt to make the sun stand still by her dancing. Rosamond wanders through the woods until she arrives in New Orleans, meets Jamie Lockhart again, and they get married. In the spring, Clement Musgrove goes to New Orleans and finds them where they have everything they could want in the world. Thus, the story ends in typical "They lived happily ever after" fairy-tale fashion.

The Characters

All the characters in the story, with perhaps the exception of Clement Musgrove, are one-dimensional figures drawn from American folklore and the fairy tales of the Brothers Grimm. What makes Clement more complex is his awareness of the changing nature of the frontier and his knowledge of the essential duality of life—both central themes in the story. Clement tells Jamie earlier in the novel that the Indians know their time has come; "they are sure of the future growing smaller always, and that lets them be infinitely gay and cruel." When he discovers that Jamie is both the gentleman he met and the bandit who raped his daughter, he says that all things are double: "All things are divided in half—night and day, the soul and body, and sorrow and joy and youth and age. . . ." Thus, Clement is the central figure, both innocent in the ways of the world and wise in the meaning of that which he discovers.

Jamie, the robber bridegroom, is the central embodiment of the novel's duality; he is both the handsome prince who comes to claim the beautiful daughter, as well as the stereotypical outlaw of the old frontier. Rosamond is the beautiful princess who at first rebuffs and then accepts her captor and violator; she is the fanciful and resilient adolescent heroine of countless fairy tales. Salome, the evil stepmother, not only is jealous of Rosamond's beauty but also is an embodiment of the grasping materialism that gradually destroys the freedom of the frontier, for she continually insists that Clement increase his land holdings and build an empire in the wilderness. The minor characters—Mike Fink, Goat, and the Harp brothers—are the stock figures of folklore and fairy tale. They are both functions of the plot, serving to further the complications of the action, and embodiments of the violence and grotesque humor inherent in folk traditions.

Themes and Meanings

This novel seems so childlike and simple that one is tempted to think it carries no theme at all, but that it is rather merely an extremely well-done satire of fairy tale conventions. Welty herself once said that the story came from "a lifetime of fairy-tale reading." Nevertheless, there are two underlying themes in the work—a cultural one concerning the nature of the inevitably changing American frontier and a psychological one typical of all great fairy tales.

On one level, the story is about the gradual loss of American frontier life; Clement, goaded by his possessive and greedy wife, is a reluctant embodiment of the taming of the wildness of the frontier by the civilizing effect of landowning. The Indians, mysterious and mostly unseen presences in the story, represent both the violence and the innocence of the wilderness; as Clement understands, they know that their time is limited. The central duality of Jamie, who is both a gentleman and a robber, suggests the transition point of the wilderness that the novel attempts to capture, for it takes place at a time in American history which hovers between the freedom of lawlessness and the restraint of civilized society.

Because the story also makes use of fairy-tale conventions as well as those of American folklore, it is not only the innocence, violence, and youth of the country that is depicted but also these same characteristics of the individual, for these are aspects upon which the fairy-tale genre particularly focuses. Thus the youth of America and the youth of the individual are paralleled in the story. Just as this duality dominates the overall story, the tone and the characters of the story also exhibit a duality, for the tale is one of innocence and of violence at the same time. Moreover, just as the characters are caught between their dual selves as well as between the past and the present, so also is the reader caught between fantasy and reality. As is typical of the youth of the nation and the youth of every individual, the two realms of fantasy and reality blend together in such a way that one can never be too sure what realm one inhabits. As Clement says about the duality, "This should keep us from taking liberties with the outside world, and acting too quickly to finish things off." Thus, the story's most basic theme has to do with the elusive nature of reality itself, which is chimerical and ever-changing.

Critical Context

Eudora Welty is better known for her short stories than for her novels, and in this, her first novel, one can appreciate her familiarity with the folktale and fairy-tale conventions that contribute to her own work and to the short-story form in general. When *The Robber Bridegroom* first appeared, many critics admired it for its clever satire and for its pure and sustained and ironic style, but few saw it to be a serious work of fiction with an important theme. Several reviewers thought that it was a tour de force of technique likely to be appreciated by admirers of Welty's short fiction, but to be of little interest to the general reader. Later, however, critics took the story more seriously, exploring its sources in folklore and works of American humor and probing its cultural and metaphysical themes.

Most of Welty's works, both novels and stories, are mythic and fantastic to some degree, although perhaps none is so deeply imbued with fairy-tale conventions as is *The Robber Bridegroom*. Welty is more concerned with what she has called "the season of dreams" than she is with the world of external reality. Thus, her stories are seldom realistic, although she invariably sets them in recognizable places and inhabits them with characters who, although often grotesque, possess human qualities that are easily recognizable.

Welty's best-known stories, many of which are anthologized in short-story textbooks, are from *A Curtain of Green* (1941), *The Wide Net and Other*

Stories (1943), and *The Golden Apples* (1949). All are characterized by her fascination with myth and legend and her blending of the characters and events of archetypal stories with ordinary people of the American South. Eudora Welty is, without doubt, one of the greatest American short-story writers in the twentieth century, and *The Robber Bridegroom*, drawing on her intimate familiarity with folklore, myth, and fairy tale, is a compendium of the sources of her art.

Sources for Further Study
Appel, Alfred, Jr. *A Season of Dreams: The Fiction of Eudora Welty*, 1965.
Desmond, John, ed. *A Still Moment: Essays on the Art of Eudora Welty*, 1978.
Dollarhide, Louis, and Ann J. Abadie, eds. *Eudora Welty: A Form of Thanks*, 1979.
Kreyling, Michael. *Eudora Welty's Achievement of Order*, 1980.
Vande Kieft, Ruth M. *Eudora Welty*, 1962.

Charles E. May

THE ROCK CRIED OUT

Author: Ellen Douglas (Josephine Haxton, 1921-   )
Type of plot: Realism
Time of plot: The 1960's and the 1970's
Locale: Homochitto County, Mississippi
First published: 1979

> *Principal characters:*
> ALAN McLAURIN, the protagonist, a young white man return-
> ing home to Mississippi after spending time in the North
> MIRIAM WEST, Alan's Northern girlfriend who is visiting him
> in Mississippi
> PHOEBE CHIPMAN, Alan's cousin who was killed in an automo-
> bile accident when they were teenagers and who was the
> only true love of Alan's life
> DALLAS BOYKIN, a friend of Alan from childhood who has
> remained in Mississippi working as a laborer and who
> resents Alan's not having fought in Vietnam
> SAM DANIELS, a black man and a good friend of Alan; he
> oversees the family's country place
> LEILA McLAURIN, Alan's free-spirited aunt; she has had an
> affair with Sam

The Novel

Ellen Douglas tells the story of the emergence of a new South. She also tells about a local Mississippi boy who comes home to discover that new South and to discover the truth about the past. The novel opens with Alan McLaurin making his way back home to Mississippi after having spent a number of years in the Northeast. Hitchhiking, he is picked up by a carload of blacks. Marveling at the changes, he explains that he has been away from Homochitto County, Mississippi, for a number of years, but that now he is home to settle down on his family's land in the country. Having quit his job in a sugar refinery and separated from his live-in girlfriend, Miriam West, Alan has left Boston to "live on the land" and write poetry. A conscientious objector who did not serve in the Vietnam War, Alan had left home to go to school in the North. He had left behind a South in racial and social turmoil and now has returned home to discover what is left of the land that he abandoned.

The discovery process provides a framework for the novel's action. Told as a recollection by Alan, the writer, several years after the events in the novel have taken place, the novel moves as a first-person account from the narrator's present back to the events in the novel and even back to the

1960's. The novel is also a discovery process for the reader, for not until the book's end do the pieces of the puzzle fit together.

After arriving at the family place, Alan becomes reacquainted with Sam Daniels, the black caretaker of the family land, and catches up on events in the community. As each character is introduced, there are flashbacks to past events that put the characters in perspective. In Sam's case, she describes him as a stubborn man, living right on the edge of danger during the turbulent 1960's. Sam has been integral to the McLaurin family for years; he has tended the family land, has had a love affair with Alan's Aunt Leila McLaurin, and has driven the car in which Alan's cousin, Phoebe Chipman, was killed. Douglas then goes on to describe Phoebe's accident. Her death haunts Alan throughout the novel and ultimately leads to his own violent action. Furthermore, his present girlfriend, Miriam, bears a striking resemblance to Phoebe. The reader learns at this point in the novel that Phoebe was killed in an accident in which Sam drove with her down a gravel road not far from home. Sam vaguely recollects rocks striking the windshield, temporarily blinding him, and making him run off the road. This one incident sends out tendrils to nearly every other event in the novel. In one sense, the entire book is about Alan's search for the true nature of this accident.

With Sam's help, Alan sets about fixing up an old house on the family place. He plans to live there alone; his parents live in the city and come out to the country only during the summers. Gradually, old friends from the past appear to help Alan with his project. Dallas Boykin, a boyhood friend, shows up one day to help with the house. The reader learns that Boykin served a tour of duty in Vietnam, returned home to settle down, and married a Fundamentalist wife. They live in a house trailer, and Dallas earns his living hauling pulpwood from the pine forests.

After several months of celibacy, Alan invites Miriam, who is in Boston, for a visit, and his liberal, artistic Aunt Leila comes to "chaperone" the couple. At a party, Alan learns from a drunken Leila about her affair with Sam. Also at the party is Lindsey Lee, a local boy turned hippie whom they had met earlier at a general store. Miriam becomes attracted to Lindsey Lee and they form a sort of trio. The three of them, Miriam, Alan, and Lindsey, set out to discover the truth about the new South by interviewing locals, including Sam's eighty-five-year-old father, Noah Daniels. Their tape recordings allow Douglas to unearth another layer of past history, but the precious truth remains elusive.

Meanwhile, Sam and Leila rekindle their romance, while Lindsey Lee and Miriam also become lovers. Tension builds among the trio as Alan, almost an outsider, tries to reconcile his relationship with Miriam. They had promised that they would not possess each other, but Alan cannot give up his claim to her sole affections.

The novel's climax comes in a twenty-five-page monologue in which a distraught Dallas drives wildly all over the county in his truck, talking nonstop on his CB radio. Thinking that he is talking to his wife, Dallas confesses to her—and also to Alan, who is listening on another radio—that he, too, once loved Phoebe. Dallas also tells the real story of her death. Phoebe's death occurred during the most violent time of the civil rights struggle. Several churches were burned down in Homochitto County, including one near the McLaurin family place. Naturally, whites—including members of the Ku Klux Klan—were trying to stop black civil rights progress in this rural Mississippi community. On the day of Phoebe's death, Sam was driving her in the car down a country road. Dallas and some of his friends (including Lindsey Lee) were watching a meeting at a black church through the scopes on their high-powered rifles. They saw Sam's car coming down the road, and for some reason, Dallas explains in his monologue, he fired. That was the shot (Sam thought it was gravel) which made him wreck the car.

Furious that Dallas had killed his beloved cousin, Alan sets out across the county to find him, finally catching the man near a small dam which is about to overflow. As Alan and Dallas fight, the escaping water knocks them down a ravine and Dallas is killed. "I knew he was dead," Alan says. "A horrible pain, unassuageable grief, seized me, worse than any kick in the balls, worse than any ice pick in my liver. I had killed him."

By the end of the novel, Douglas brings the reader full circle to the present Alan McLaurin, who talks about finally settling down to write the truth about the past and about the new South—a truth the reader experiences as *The Rock Cried Out*.

The Characters

Much of Douglas' strength lies in her characterization. She does well writing a first-person account from a male point of view and her skillfully crafted Alan McLaurin grows from a naïve, idealistic youth into a cynical, worldly man. He becomes a metaphor, in some ways, for so many in his generation whose idealism was fueled by a protest against a war in which they did not believe and a struggle to correct a region's racial attitudes, which were clearly oppressive. Then his generation grew up to find a morally ambiguous world. He grows up by searching for the real story of the past and matures as he puts together some of the unpleasant aspects of that painful reality. In the final chapter, Alan McLaurin displays a certain confidence and peacefulness—much like the confidence displayed in his new South as it, too, emerges from a trial by baptism and fire.

Douglas' other characters all exhibit originality. She avoids clichéd Southern characters but still represents all aspects of the South about which she writes. For example, the free-spirited Aunt Leila puts love and compassion ahead of community mores, but she is still a Southerner. She loves Sam Daniels; his being black does not matter.

Dallas Boykin represents the confused, poor Southerner. After fighting for his country in Vietnam and against racial equality in the South, he emerges at the end of the 1970's confused and quietly angry. Feeling guilty for his transgressions, he tries to make amends, yet the new South gives him little, save religion, to hang on to. His wife is the born-again, talking-in-tongues, Southern Fundamentalist who escapes the modern world by living in a religious cocoon. Dallas accepts her, but he does not really find peace in the life that she represents.

To her credit, Douglas takes the stereotypes and molds them into real human beings. Her blacks, for example, become genuine people in a racially confused South. Noah, born of a generation of shuffling old "Uncle Toms," is a witty, spry, three-dimensional character. Perhaps most interesting of all, however, is Sam. He has fought all of his life. Refusing to succumb to the white man, he almost but not quite pushes his independence too far. For example, refusing to say "sir" to white men, Sam "talks around" those kinds of references. Also, he becomes a lover to a white woman. Sam, however, does spend some time in jail for attacking the navy's satellite tracking station (SPASURSTA), which sits on a parcel of McLaurin property rented to the government. He simply got angry one day and crossed the fence with his cows to start destroying the equipment. Stoically, he accepted his punishment.

Other characters also evidence Douglas' skill. There is Lindsey Lee, the local boy turned hippie who goes around the county taping "quaint old black men and local rednecks" for a story that he is going to write for a large East Coast paper. The naïve Miriam West also fits in with the patronizing Lindsey Lee. She comes from the North with her preconceived notions about the South and naturally has an affair with Lindsey.

Themes and Meanings

The essential theme of the novel is the search for what is real in the new South. Alan McLaurin comes home to a land he does not really understand to try to piece together his life and, more specifically, to try to understand Phoebe's tragic death. To separate truth from fiction becomes Alan's mission. A poet at the novel's beginning, he seems to discard art as an organizing principle rather quickly, perhaps partially because his poetry is unsuccessful.

Douglas skillfully leads the reader along Alan's discovery process. By telling the story in the first person, Douglas must reveal to the reader little bits of truth at the same time that she allows Alan to discover them. These revelations—the truth—have a powerful effect on Alan, driving him, a registered conscientious objector, to kill at the novel's end. It is almost as if by finding out the truth about Phoebe's death, Alan also finds out the truth about himself and about the world. This point is evidenced in the novel's title, taken from an old spiritual about trying to escape: "I went to the rock to hide my face./ The rock cried out, 'No hiding place.'/ No hiding place down there."

An attachment to the land, a major theme in many Southern novels, also plays an important part in this work. Alan returns not only to his native South but also to his "old home place." There, living in a rustic old house, he observes nature and the seasons. With SPASURSTA, Douglas makes an obvious comment on the relationship between nature, the new South, and technology. When Sam finally loses all patience with the new technology's invasion of his pastoral life, he attacks the radar station. Douglas seems to be saying that what destroys nature also harms mankind.

This fenced, steel, computer-operated SPASURSTA that sits in the middle of old Mississippi pasture land becomes a symbol for the blending of the old South and the new South. The old South, with its surreptitious miscegenation, its bigotry, violence, and steadfast commitment to the old ways, haunts Alan McLaurin, blinding him to the truth. To discover the truth, he must face and conquer these ghosts while realizing, at the same time, the futility of trying to destroy the machinery of the new, progressive South. The two, Alan learns, must live in harmony.

Critical Context

Douglas' reputation has grown steadily since the publication of her first novel, *A Family's Affairs* (1962). In each succeeding novel, she has managed to transcend the banality of Faulknerian imitations to make fresh statements about the South and about the human condition.

Born in 1921, Douglas is one of a group of writers who, although influenced by the Southern Renaissance, have looked for new meanings in the Southern experience. In *The Rock Cried Out*, Douglas writes a novel for the contemporary reader. While this novel bears a likeness to her earlier work, it also shows that Douglas writes about the modern world; she is not mired in the past. The book also provides a bridge to her next work, *A Lifetime Burning* (1982), another well-received novel about contemporary times.

Sources for Further Study

Dean, Michael P. "Ellen Douglas's Small Towns: Fictional Anchors," in *Southern Quarterly*. XIX (Fall, 1980), pp. 161-171.

Jones, John Griffin, ed. *Mississippi Writers Talking, II*, 1983.

Phillips, Robert L., Jr. "Ellen Douglas," in *Southern Writers: A Biographical Dictionary*, 1979. Edited by Robert Bain.

Prenshaw, Peggy Whitman, ed. *Women Writers of the Contemporary South*, 1984.

John Canfield

RUBYFRUIT JUNGLE

Author: Rita Mae Brown (1944-   )
Type of plot: Picaresque
Time of plot: From the early 1950's to the late 1960's
Locale: Coffee Hollow and Shiloh, Pennsylvania; Fort Lauderdale and
   Gainesville, Florida; and New York City
First published: 1973

Principal characters:
>
> MOLLY BOLT, the protagonist, who grows up clever, proud,
>   illegitimate, female, and gay
> CARRIE BOLT, her uneducated, strong-willed, Southern
>   stepmother
> CARL BOLT, her stepfather
> LEROY DENMAN, her cousin and childhood companion
> LEOTA B. BISLAND, her sixth-grade love
> CAROLYN SIMPSON, her lover and Fort Lauderdale High's head
>   cheerleader
> FAYE RAIDER, her roommate, lover, and partner in expulsion
>   at the University of Florida
> CALVIN, a gay hustler whom Molly meets in an abandoned car
>   shortly after her arrival in New York City
> HOLLY, a kept woman who is Molly's friend and lover
> POLINA BELLANTONI, one of Molly's numerous liaisons

The Novel

Rubyfruit Jungle is a picaresque novel in the tradition of Voltaire's *Candide* (1759) and Henry Fielding's *Tom Jones* (1749). It recounts the escapades of an engagingly roguish hero in a series of humorous or satiric episodes, but on a much smaller scale. Instead of spanning a lifetime, *Rubyfruit Jungle* covers the protagonist Molly Bolt's adventures only from the age of seven to her graduation from college. Rather than being international in scope, all the action takes place in the geographical triangle between Pennsylvania, Florida, and New York. Instead of an Everyman with whom the reader might identify, Molly Bolt is decidedly female, Southern, and gay.

Rubyfruit Jungle opens with an incident which deals with sex and money in a humorous way and is characteristic of many episodes in the novel. Molly Bolt, a precocious first-grader, arranges with a Barnum-like sense of spectacle to exhibit Brockhurst Detwiler's uncircumcised penis to her schoolmates. As she says with her naïve but irrefutable logic: "Look, Broc, money is money. What do you care if they laugh? You'll have money then you can laugh at them. And we split it fifty-fifty." This sort of enterprise and lack of concern for world opinion accounts for much of the book's charm.

Molly's interest in both sex and money continues throughout the novel: She loses her virginity in sixth grade to Leota B. Bisland; she sleeps with her cousin and best friend, Leroy Denman, in the spirit of healthy experimentation; she enjoys a liaison with Carolyn Simpson, head cheerleader at Fort Lauderdale High; she keeps her heterosexual credentials in order with her high school boyfriend Clark; she is seduced by Faye Raider, with whom she eventually shares not only her bed but also her expulsion from the University of Florida; she is introduced to the high life in New York City through Holly, a kept woman; and finally, she enters the unusual fantasy life of medievalist Polina Bellantoni.

When Molly is not erotically engaged, she is busy trying to make a success of her academic life, with an eye to a lucrative and artistically fulfilling career as a film director. She excels in high school; wins a much needed full scholarship, with room and board, to the University of Florida; and when that opportunity is lost, works at odd jobs to support herself in New York City, so that she can attend New York University.

Permeating the entire story is a sense of family, and it is no surprise that at the end of the novel, when Molly is doing her final project for her film degree, she chooses to return home and do a short, and intensely personal, documentary of her stepmother, rocking in her old chair and talking about her roots. Molly's flight from the poverty and ignorance of her childhood ironically, or perhaps fittingly, brings her home again to contemplate the values which have made her, above all, a survivor.

The Characters

Rubyfruit Jungle is clearly semiautobiographical. Like Molly Bolt, Rita Mae Brown was born illegitimately in a small town just outside York, Pennsylvania. She was adopted, and her new parents eventually migrated to Florida in search of better jobs. She attended the University of Florida in Gainesville on a scholarship and was, in fact, asked to leave. She then hitchhiked to New York City and lived in an abandoned car with her cat, Baby Jesus. She went to New York University, and she received a bachelor of arts in English while also earning a certificate in cinematography from the New York School of Visual Arts. Her first publication was a translation of *Hrotsvitra*, the Latin medieval plays mentioned to Molly Bolt by Polina Bellantoni in *Rubyfruit Jungle*.

Throughout the novel, Rita Mae Brown keeps attention focused on the protagonist, Molly Bolt, through Molly's first-person narrative. There are no authorial intrusions. What the reader sees, he sees through Molly's eyes, and Molly has no patience with either prejudices or pretensions. She will not be stereotyped, although it is true that most of the other characters in the novel are rendered with rather broad strokes.

Somewhat ironically perhaps, the most sympathetic characters in *Ruby-fruit Jungle* are men. While Carrie, Molly's stepmother, is shrewish and abusive, her father, Carl, is a gentle if ineffectual man who loves Molly very tenderly, even when she is being her most irascible. Leroy Denman remains her loyal friend, and despite ever-widening differences, he never loses his regard for Molly. Calvin, a charming New York hustler, is genuinely charitable to Molly when she is down and out. Even the men who pick Molly up when she is hitchhiking give her money, encouragement and few problems.

The women in *Rubyfruit Jungle* are more problematical and also more interesting. Leota B. Bisland, Molly's sixth-grade lover, is visited by Molly at the end of the novel and is rather starkly portrayed as a self-limiting, small-town matron. Faye Raider completely crumbles under her expulsion from the University of Florida and returns home to daddy, a life of useless leisure and probable alcoholism. In New York, Holly sells her stunning good looks to the highest bidder, an easy option, which Molly, full of Southern pride, denies herself. Polina Bellantoni spins out extremely unsavory and scatological male fantasies, while Molly, at her worst, fills the jealousy-ridden Rhea Rhadin's desk with dog droppings. Overall, one gets the feeling that the women in *Rubyfruit Jungle* are portrayed so harshly, not because Molly despises them, but because she has such incredibly high expectations for them, expectations no higher than those she has for herself.

Themes and Meanings

Readers, distracted by the novelty of an unrepentant lesbian protagonist, sometimes miss the broader and less obviously political themes of *Rubyfruit Jungle*. A central issue in the novel is the maintenance of a strong sense of personal ethics. When chided by Holly for not taking the easy route through school by becoming a kept woman, Molly explains her position: "I have to do it my way. My way, understand. It has nothing to do with morality, it has to do with me."

Other major tenets of Molly's personal philosophy are the importance of overcoming, not succumbing to, adversity, and the necessity of sustaining a sense of humor. Despite repeated setbacks, Molly manages to rise above her inauspicious beginnings, while never losing her comic perspective. At the end of the novel, the reader revels in, and halfway believes in, Molly's final, triumphant words: "Watch out world because I'm going to be the hottest fifty-year-old this side of the Mississippi."

Critical Context

Rubyfruit Jungle was first published in 1973 by Daughters Inc., a small, independent women's collective. Reviewed by Bertha Harris in *The Village Voice*, it quickly sold seventy thousand copies and became an underground phenomenon. Because its publication coincided with the struggle over gay rights in the women's movement, the novel was originally, and erroneously, seen simply as a lesbian/feminist tract, albeit a very amusing one. The novel was notable for breaking the stereotypic image of gay women as masculine, unattractive, unhappy, and incapable of getting a man. Previous books with lesbian protagonists, such as Radclyffe Hall's *The Well of Loneliness* (1928), had tended to foster this melancholic view of what psychiatrists were then calling "inversion," and so *Rubyfruit Jungle* broke new ground with its resilient protagonist overcoming poverty, gender, and sexual preference with boisterous self-assurance.

In 1977, Bantam Books bought the rights to *Rubyfruit Jungle* and published it in an edition of 250,000 copies, bringing it into the mainstream of American literature and to the attention of a much more diverse audience. Critical reaction has always been mixed.

The book's detractors have pointed out, with considerable clarity, that the book is often preachy; that the rascally Molly Bolt is more lovable as an intractable youngster than as a prankish adult; that the use of Southern epithets, clichés, profanity, and hyperbole becomes tiresome; and that most of the characters suffer from a comic-book two-dimensionality.

On the other hand, *Rubyfruit Jungle* is clearly in the tradition of numerous renowned American novels that received roughly the same criticisms in their day. Novels such as *The Adventures of Huckleberry Finn* (1884), *The Catcher in the Rye* (1951), and *To Kill a Mockingbird* (1960) all deal, like *Rubyfruit Jungle*, with the archetypical problems of coming of age in difficult times. *Rubyfruit Jungle* has been justifiably praised for its Thoreau-like belief in nature and the individual, for its irrepressible and boisterous energy, for its quick wit, and for its unforgettable protagonist, Molly Bolt. *Rubyfruit Jungle* is vintage Rita Mae Brown, hearty and full-bodied, young, and more than slightly acidic.

Sources for Further Study

Fox, Terry Curtis. "Up from Cultdom and Down Again," in *The Village Voice*. XXII (September 11, 1977), p. 41.

Harris, Bertha. "*Rubyfruit Jungle*," in *The Village Voice*. XIX (April 4, 1974), p. 33.

Klemesrud, Judy. "Underground Book Brings Fame to a Lesbian Author," in *The New York Times*. CXXVII (September 26, 1977), p. 38.

Pepe, Barbara. "Up from the Sexual Jungle," in *Crawdaddy*. February, 1978, pp. 13-14.

Turner, Alice, K. "Books," in *New York*. XI (September 18, 1978), pp. 60-61.

Cynthia Lee Katona

RUNNER MACK

Author: Barry Beckham (1944-   )
Type of plot: Absurdism
Time of plot: A time resembling the Vietnam War era of the 1960's
Locale: An Eastern American city and Alaska
First published: 1972

> *Principal characters:*
> HENRY ADAMS, the protagonist, a young black man
> BEATRICE MARK ADAMS, Henry's wife
> RUNNINGTON (RUNNER) MACK, a revolutionary
> "MR." PETERS, the personnel manager at Home Manufacturing Company
> "MR." BOYE, the supervisor at Home Manufacturing Company
> CAPTAIN NEVINS, an officer in the Alaskan War

The Novel

Runner Mack follows Henry Adams through a period in his life during which he moves from confusion and ignorance to a hard-bought understanding. At the beginning of the book, he has brought his new wife, Beatrice, to a Northern city, where he expects to become a baseball star. As the novel proceeds, Henry is beset by all the evils that human nature and American society can devise. As one confusing incident follows another in a world which is never explained to Henry, the dreams of stardom fade and are replaced by dreams of revolution. The revolution fails, however—indeed, it never begins—and at the end of the book, Henry has increased wisdom but diminished hopes.

The novel is divided into three segments. In the first, Henry has a single goal: to support his beloved new wife, Beatrice, while he waits for the big break that will make him a baseball star. Yet even that goal is difficult to realize in an absurd world. Beatrice is miserable in the city apartment where she and Henry live. The ceiling leaks; there is no heat; the neighbors are noisy; the Puerto Rican superintendent is apathetic. When Henry goes to the Home Manufacturing Company to apply for a job, he is hit by a huge truck. Although he gets the job, Henry is branded as a troublemaker; after overhearing a discussion which seems to threaten him, Henry leaves. Meanwhile, his baseball tryout has been unpromising, and his relationship with Beatrice is deteriorating. She is choked by polluting fumes and deafened by the noise of the city, and both she and Henry are terrified after an unexplained raid which soldiers make on their apartment.

In the second segment of the book, the lesser worries are dwarfed by a major crisis: Henry is drafted and shipped to "the war" in Alaska, which seems to involve butchering caribou and seals in order to protect the United States. Here Henry meets the revolutionary Runner Mack, who plans to desert, bomb the White House, and take over the country. Runner Mack and Henry escape in a helicopter and begin a mysterious journey which is supposed to end in revolution and in a remade world.

In the third part of the book, Henry blindly follows Runner Mack's directives as the two travel by train and by car, periodically changing disguises, presumably toward Washington. Somehow they find themselves in Henry's old neighborhood. Leaving Runner Mack briefly, Henry visits Beatrice, only to find that she is deaf. The noise has at last conquered her. When Henry and Runner Mack go to the union hall where the revolutionaries are to meet, they find only eight people. In despair, Runner Mack hangs himself in a toilet stall, and Henry runs out into the street. As the novel ends, a truck is bearing down on him.

The Characters

The name of the protagonist of *Runner Mack* ironically recalls a classic work of American literature: *The Education of Henry Adams* (1907). Barry Beckham's Henry Adams gets his painful education in a world which contains two kinds of people: those who mouth words which they are programmed to say, like the executives at the Home Manufacturing Company and the military officer in Alaska, and those who genuinely communicate their thoughts. It is only through those who view the world with independent minds that Henry can grow in understanding. Although Henry comes to disagree with his father's philosophy of humility, he can at least follow his reasoning: that a really big man does not become angry. Sometimes Henry can talk to Beatrice, but generally he must simply hear her complaints, which do keep him in touch with the real world in which he and she must live. At the Home Manufacturing Company, no one will admit that he does not know what he is doing. Finally, Henry's supervisor, whom neither Henry nor the reader knows as other than "Mr." Boye, communicates with Henry, beginning with baseball talk and ending with the admission that he has never understood what he is doing or even what the plant is making. Later, Boye is reprimanded.

The person who most deeply reveals himself to Henry is Runner Mack, who has learned enough about the world to decide on revolution. Runner Mack can explain to Henry how hollow are many of the promises in which he has believed. Convincing Henry that the road of humility leads nowhere, Mack persuades him that revolution is the only answer. Mack, in Henry's eyes, has become a hero whom all black men should follow. When Mack can fly a helicopter without training, Henry is not even surprised. When Mack's organization provides clothing, transportation, even a picnic lunch from a limousine, Henry comes to believe that Runner Mack, who has read everything and knows everything, has the world under control. Clearly, Mack can perceive reality, for he has interpreted Henry's world and explained its falseness; clearly, he is going to change it. That confidence which Runner Mack has in himself and which Henry has in him does not break until the disaster in the union hall, when only eight people show up for the revolution. At that point, Runner Mack himself realizes that nothing changes, that everything repeats itself, and that there are no answers. No longer believing in his own heroic stature, Mack kills himself.

Henry Adams, whose thoughts lead the reader through the events of the book, has much of his father's ability to accept life. When the truck runs him down, he picks himself up and goes on to the job interview; when he is not told what his company is manufacturing, he waits patiently for a revelation. In this absurd world, Henry waits for understanding, just as he waits for a telephone call from the Stars, the team for which he hopes to play. Run down by a truck, shocked by a wired baseball, raided, drafted, and wounded, Henry is bewildered, not angry. It is only when he returns to Beatrice to find her deaf, forever cut off from him, that he vents his anger by kicking in the television screen. He has ceased to trust an absurd world whose inhabitants only pretend to understand it.

Themes and Meanings

Beckham's world is an absurd one. Superficially, the events of this world seem to be ruled by the laws of cause and effect: If one is good enough at baseball, one can become a major league player; if one works hard at one's job, one can advance in the company; if enough people are discontented with society, they will rebel and change their society. Ultimately, however, the events of the novel, viewed realistically, suggest that there is no logic in human responses or in human institutions. In this world, human beings keep themselves very busy convincing themselves and others that the world is not absurd.

As in every novel of initiation, Henry Adams moves toward understanding, and he does come to understand some truths about the nature of the world. He learns that one cannot depend on human beings: His friend on the baseball team cannot really help him, and the supposed revolutionaries will not turn up for the revolution. Yet although people's words are unreliable, they produce them with great enthusiasm and distrust anyone who questions their relation to fact, as the Home Manufacturing Company staff distrusts Henry. Furthermore, although everyone will talk, very few people will communicate. Mister Boye is reprimanded for talking honestly to Henry, and throughout the novel Beatrice continues in her misery to distance herself further and further from Henry and from the world of which he is a part until at last she is totally deaf. Finally, most people will not protest cruelty, whether it be in the form of a trick baseball or in the government-sanctioned butchery of innocent caribou. Indeed, there is something in man which enjoys killing—a common denominator which reduces Henry to the level of his commanding officer in Alaska.

Critical Context

As a novel of the black experience, *Runner Mack* includes the expected incidents and attitudes: the stereotypes, the denial of dignity, the assertion of authority without explanation, whether in a raid or in military orders. Beckham, however, also dramatizes the plight of modern man in an urban wasteland of filth, pollution, noise, slums, and junkyards. Henry Adams is not puzzled merely because he is black. Therefore, Henry also becomes a modern Candide, surrounded by optimistic Panglosses. Like Candide, he moves from the search for a simple good—for Henry, his Beatrice and his career in baseball—to an inquiry as to whether the search itself can be successful. Yet unlike Candide, who at least can find meaning in work, Henry is left without a goal and with one more truck bearing down upon him.

It should be mentioned that although Beckham's effective use of absurdist techniques in order to dramatize a modern urban black man's perception of his world is his most significant accomplishment in this novel, critics have also been interested in his use of baseball metaphors throughout the book. It is not surprising that Henry, the baseball player, sees life as a baseball game. Evidently, for everyone, a strikeout is inevitable.

Sources for Further Study
English Journal. Review. LXIII (January, 1974), p. 65.
Kirkus Reviews. Review. XL (July 1, 1972), p. 737.
The New York Times Book Review. Review. December 3, 1972, p. 78.
Watkins, M. Review in *The New York Times Book Review.* September 17, 1972, p. 3.

Rosemary M. Canfield

SACRED FAMILIES

Author: José Donoso (1924-   )
Type of plot: Psychological symbolism
Time of plot: The early 1970's
Locale: Barcelona, Spain
First published: Tres novelitas burguesas, 1973 (English translation, 1977)

> *Principal characters:*
>
> > *Chattanooga Choo-Choo*
> > ANSELMO PRIETO, a doctor whose hobby is painting
> > MAGDALENA PRIETO, Anselmo's wife
> > SYLVIA CORDAY, a model
> > RAMÓN DEL SOLAR, an architect married to Sylvia
>
> > *Green Atom Number Five*
> > ROBERTO FERRER, a dentist and painter, about forty years old
> > MARTA MORA, his wife
>
> > *Gaspard de la Nuit*
> > MAURICIO, Sylvia Corday's sixteen-year-old son
> > SYLVIA CORDAY, a model
> > RAMÓN DEL SOLAR, an architect, Sylvia Corday's second
> > > husband

The Novel

Sacred Families comprises three connected novellas about the middle class. The first one, "Chattanooga Choo-Choo," revolves around two couples who have recently met. Their encounter begins as a superficial relationship that becomes more serious when Sylvia Corday, who is married to Ramón del Solar, has an affair with Anselmo Prieto, Magdalena's husband. On the night on which they consummate the affair, Anselmo notices that Sylvia does not have a face or a pair of arms. Upon her request, he provides her with a mouth using red paper. After consummating their affair, Anselmo realizes that a vital part of his male anatomy has disappeared. What follows is a sequence of events that inform the reader that the wives have been playing a game in which they have disassembled their husbands' bodily parts and are keeping them in a briefcase. The women have given special attention to that one vital male part; they keep their husbands' penises in a little velvet bag, and they interchange them frequently.

The second novella, "Green Atom Number Five," unfolds to reveal Roberto and Marta, a middle-aged couple who have purchased a brand-new apartment. The apartment represents the fulfillment of their lifelong dream. They proceed to furnish the dwelling with the finest things: as a finishing touch to the decoration of their home, they compromise in placing Roberto's oil painting, *Green Atom Number Five*, on the wall nearest the front door. After the departure of a visitor, they notice that the painting has disappeared, which puzzles them very much. In a series of circumstances, everything is taken away before their very eyes and they find themselves unable to do anything. After losing everything they become increasingly vicious toward each other, eventually ending up naked and fighting like mad dogs.

The third novella, "Gaspard de la Nuit," pivots around Mauricio, who is coming to visit his mother, Sylvia, for three months. He has been living with his father and grandmother, "Abuelis," since his parents were divorced seven years previously. Mauricio neither likes nor approves of his mother's lifestyle and does not want to become part of the society in which she lives, much to her frustration and dismay. Instead, he goes out every day and spends his time strolling the streets while whistling a Maurice Ravel piece *Gaspard de la Nuit*, and trying to find a soul mate. One day, in a forest, he meets a vagabond about his age whom he teaches to whistle the Ravel piece. He and the vagabond become closely acquainted until a fantastical sort of metamorphosis occurs: Mauricio becomes the vagabond and the latter becomes Mauricio. After that, the situation at home improves greatly, since the new Mauricio accepts all the material things with which his mother has been trying to bribe him in an attempt to keep her son at home. Mauricio's changed attitude makes everyone happy.

The Characters

"Chattanooga Choo-Choo" pits men against women. The husbands, Anselmo and Ramón, regard themselves as the ones who set the rules and dominate the battle of the sexes. That is, however, a very simplistic evaluation. In fact, the women, Sylvia and Magdalena, are the ones who control the situation, in a very efficient and subdued fashion. They pretend to be the victims but are actually the opposite. The men are depicted as business-minded personages who believe that they get what they want when they want it in their dealings with women. The truth is that whether they get something or not, the quality and quantity will depend upon the women.

"Green Atom Number Five" is a thorough study of a couple, Roberto and Marta. They are well-characterized before, during, and after the crisis that tears them apart. Roberto, a very successful odontologist, is a man who knows what he wants in life, is sure about his priorities, and dogmatic and pragmatic to the point of thinking that a change in life must start with a change of address. Now that he has moved into his own place, he thinks that everything will be under control. The only disturbance in his apparently peaceful existence in the foreseeable future is the one empty room in the apartment, where he had planned on installing a studio for painting. His fondness for painting, which has been stimulated by Marta, diminishes when she, under the impulse of an angry reaction, tells him that his painting *Green Atom Number Five* is nothing extraordinary and that her choice of the painting instead of an emerald jewel was motivated more by kindness on her part than by any real talent on her husband's part.

In this novella, as throughout *Sacred Families*, Donoso suggests that identity is unstable. Marta, Roberto's sweet and unselfish wife of many years, who has been unable to bear children, has acted as Roberto's mother as well as wife. She has never argued or protested, yet now she starts changing for the worse. Indeed, both Roberto's and Marta's behavior increasingly worsens, going from love to the most profound hatred. That modification in conduct is achieved slowly. Donoso has proceeded through episodes and incidents, the effects of which have rebounded on the characters. Other supporting characters have merely given a direction to the changes that occur in the main characters.

In the third novella, "Gaspard de la Nuit," the theme is the obsession that affects the people in the story, especially two of them, although to different degrees. This obsession can be seen in Mauricio, the protagonist, in his endless search for identity; in Sylvia, Mauricio's mother, the obsession is evidenced by her insistence on making him a part of her world. There are very few digressions, either in the novella's structure or in Mauricio's mind. Mauricio's continual search runs through the story: When he finds himself, and the metamorphosis takes place, the obsession and the story are both over.

All the characters that appear in the novellas are interrelated in some fashion. The character of Sylvia is presented in two different lights: In "Chattanooga Choo-Choo" she is a plastic, faceless mannequin, while in "Gaspard de la Nuit" she plays a very concerned, flesh-and-blood mother.

Themes and Meanings

In "Chattanooga Choo-Choo," an evident mutual exploitation between men and women is shown. Neither respects the individuality of the other: One woman is all women, one man is all men. This is represented through the mutual disassembly and convenient use of one another without regard for sentiment. To these characters, making love becomes a formula, a mechanical engagement.

The emphasis on makeup shows that people masquerade their real being—everything is changed through cosmetics. The people's behavior at parties illustrates the lack of sincerity in their relationships. Convenience and opportunism are the keys to success: People are used and then disposed of when they are no longer useful.

In "Green Atom Number Five," the apparently happily married couple find their relationship deteriorating when their well-organized material world starts to collapse. There is a sharp contrast between the couple's sweet behavior at the beginning of the story and their savage conduct at the end.

Roberto and Marta have built their happy and harmonious relationship in part on Marta's pretended admiration for her husband's painting. This has been a lie: She considers his talent mediocre. Roberto goes from unconditional devotion to Marta's generosity and love to thinking of her as a selfish woman, doubting her intentions and even her honesty after her disclosure. The nightmarish way in which the objects disappear parallels the increasing deterioration in the couple's relationship.

The theme in "Gaspard de la Nuit" is the obsession of the protagonist, Mauricio, with finding his identity. The obsession is displayed in his continuous whistling, which he uses as an instrument to penetrate other people's intimacy as he tries to find the right person to help him fulfill his search. He whistles on his daily strolls through the streets, which last many hours. While he walks, he also looks at people, attempting to find the long-awaited double who will either implement him or replace him.

He shows his displeasure with the type of life he has been compelled to live with his father and grandmother, and he does not like his mother's way of living either. Yet he refuses his mother's offers of a stereo, a motorcycle, and a tour through Europe. He wants to be left alone to continue his search. His obsession stops when he finds his double and becomes a docile youngster ready to comply with his mother's desires.

The role that nature plays in Mauricio's transformation is important. The Vallvidrera Forest, where Mauricio meets the other boy, is a peaceful place that provides the right setting for Mauricio's music; on the other hand, it can be equated with paradise, where life starts easy but also can turn into the beginning of a life of hardship. When Mauricio leaves the forest, he has already become another person with responsibilities that frame him in a completely different fashion.

Critical Context

Since writing *Coronación* (1957; *Coronation*, 1965), *Esta domingo* (1966; *This Sunday*, 1967), and *El obsceno pájaro de la noche* (1970; *The Obscene Bird of Night*, 1973), among other works, José Donoso has been writing about middle-class people and their fruitless existence. He has depicted this social class as decadent, and as a victim of its conventionality, its blind submission to rules, and its absolute acceptance of whatever is in fashion. *Sacred Families* is no exception: The three novellas revolve around the bourgeoisie and its most negative characteristics. In each case, below the surface action lies the impossibility for the characters to be themselves: Regardless of the fight that some of the characters may put up, they will finally bend to the rules and become part of the society.

Sources for Further Study

Alegría, Fernando. *La literatura chilena del siglo*, XX, 1970.

Goic, Cedomil. "El narrador en el laberinto," in *José Donoso: La destrucción de un mundo*, 1975.

Magnarelli, Sharon. "The Dilemma of Disappearance and Literary Duplicity in José Donoso's *Tres novelitas burguesas*," in *Prismal/Cabral*. III, no. 4 (Spring, 1979), pp. 29-46.

_____. "From *El obsceno pájaro* to *Tres novelitas burguesas*: Development of a Semiotic Theory in the Works of Donoso," in *The Analysis of Literary Texts: Trends in Methodology*, 1980. Edited by Randolph Pope.

Vidal, José. *José Donoso: Surrealismo y rebelión de los instintos*, 1972.

Rebeca Torres-Rivera

SAINT JACK

Author: Paul Theroux (1941-   )
Type of plot: Social morality
Time of plot: 1953-1971
Locale: Singapore, at an unnamed American college
First published: 1973

> *Principal characters:*
> JACK FLOWERS, the protagonist, a water clerk and pimp
> WILLIAM LEIGH, a British accountant from Hong Kong
> EDWIN (EDDIE) SHUCK, a United States government official
> CHOP HING KHENG FATT, the ship chandler and Jack's
>   employer

The Novel

Saint Jack centers on the efforts of Jack Flowers, a middle-aged American expatriate in Singapore, to achieve a success that he believes is almost within his grasp. Jack is an eternal optimist who considers being poor "the promise of success." Jack is ostensibly employed as a water clerk for Hing, a ship chandler, but he uses the contacts he makes through his work for Hing, who pays him little, to conduct his real business: He is a pimp who obtains customers for his "girls" from among sailors, tourists, and the lonely inhabitants of his "tedious little island."

The first section of the novel focuses on Jack's having to escort William Leigh, a British accountant from Hong Kong, who has come to Singapore to work on Hing's books. Leigh is a stuffy dullard who ignores Jack's suggestions about how he could be spending his time. When Leigh realizes that he is a hustler and smugly asks, "How do you stand it?" Jack is upset. He sees pimping as a means to an end, realizes that it is degrading, but tries to carry it out as much as possible within a code of conduct. The ambiguous nature of morality is central to all the actions and themes of *Saint Jack*. The unease which Leigh causes Jack is increased when the accountant suddenly dies of a heart attack, awakening Jack to a sense of his own mortality.

The novel returns, by means of a flashback, to Jack's arrival in Singapore fourteen years earlier, when he "enjoyed a rare kind of happiness, like the accidental discovery of renewal." This sense of or attempt at renewal becomes a pattern in Jack's life. There are then flashbacks to the cause of his exile. At thirty-five, Jack goes to college on the GI Bill and tries to write a novel. When he is charged with possessing drugs without a prescription and procuring drugs for a minor, he flees the United States and becomes a seaman. He intends never to return to America, accepting his exile as final, almost as inevitable.

Prior to his encounter with Leigh, Jack has two opportunities to achieve the big success of which he dreams. He establishes Dunroamin, his own house of prostitution, but is kidnaped by one of the secret societies which control vice in Singapore. The thugs tattoo Chinese obscenities on his arms and burn down his house. Later, he has the tattooed Chinese characters converted into flowers—a symbol of his philosophy of making the best of awkward situations, his never giving in to his frequent bad luck.

His second limited success comes when Eddie Shuck, a shady operator working for the American government, puts Jack in charge of a brothel for servicemen on five-day leaves from Vietnam. (The dubious morality of this enterprise is meant to parallel that of the war in Vietnam.) Jack's good fortune ends abruptly when the army closes the operation, which officially has never existed.

After Leigh's death, Jack experiences a sense of desperation and asks Shuck for help. Shuck involves him in blackmailing Andrew Maddox, a corrupt general, but Jack backs out at the last minute when he realizes that Shuck's corruption is as great as Maddox's, that Shuck is trying to entrap the general in the same way that circumstances have entrapped Jack. The simplicity and shallowness of Shuck's view of the world finally disgusts Jack too much—Jack attains a level of ironic sainthood by refusing to be part of it all.

The Characters

The only major character in the novel is Jack Flowers. Born in 1918 as John Fiori, the second child of Italian immigrants in the North End of Boston, he is a combination of innocence and experience, control and chaos, with similarities to Joseph Conrad's Lord Jim, Jake Barnes in Ernest Hemingway's *The Sun Also Rises* (1926), Saul Bellow's Augie March, Yossarian in Joseph Heller's *Catch-22* (1961), and Mark Twain's Huckleberry Finn. The novel's first-person narrator, he is a complex, multifaceted protagonist who evolves over the course of the action; as he explains at the beginning, "being slow to disclose my nature is characteristic of me." With red hair— what is left of it—big belly, and tattoos, he is "the ultimate barbarian" to some, especially those, such as Eddie Shuck, who accept his surface as the real Jack: "I resented comparisons, I hated the fellers who said, 'Flowers, you're as bad as me!' They looked at me and saw a pimp, a pornocrat, an unassertive rascal marooned on a tropical island, but having the time of his life: a character."

Jack is both searching for and denying his identity. He says that his assumed name is "an approximation and a mask"; he always hides behind one mask or another. Around Yardley, Frogget, Yates, Smale, and Coony, the English expatriates who frequent the Bandung bar and are the closest that Jack comes to having friends, he tries "to give the impression of a cheerful rascal, someone gently ignorant; I claimed I had no education and said 'If you say so' or 'That's really interesting' to anything remotely intelligent." They all despise Leigh, but when he dies, Jack becomes "the grieving person they wanted me to be."

Jack sees Leigh as his double, and the Englishmen's death seems to be a warning about actions and expectations, denying Jack the luxury of not questioning his life: "I could not say . . . that I had arrived anywhere. I was pausing . . . and there was no good reason for any of my movements except the truthful excuse that at the time of acting I saw no other choice." The unease that Jack feels in the face of Leigh's criticism of his life, of Leigh's pathetic death, causes him to write this book, finally to confront the meaning and direction of his life: "Fiction seemed to give me the second chances life denied me."

The other characters are merely reflectors of aspects of Jack's nature. Hing so devotes himself to his work that he has no other life, loses what individuality he ever had. The Bandung Englishmen retreat into their camaraderie, their drinking, their memories of the United Kingdom, their hopes of returning, to try to drown out the hideous silence of their lonely exile. Eddie Shuck is as much a pimp as Jack, manipulating people from behind the scenes, justifying it all because his side will always be the right one.

Themes and Meanings

Through the character of Jack Flowers, *Saint Jack* satirizes certain aspects of the American Dream. Jack longs for "success, comfort, renown," hustles to keep the possibility of the dream alive, but essentially hopes that it will come about suddenly, dramatically, through no direct effort of his own. Someone somewhere will spot some special something in Jack and bestow great wealth and privilege upon him. The irony is that the American Dream is supposed to be the reward for hard work and initiative, and Jack does work hard for long hours. He prides himself on the quality of his pimping, on his charging much less for his prostitutes than he could actually get. He is an honest, industrious man, but where does it get him? He merely survives.

Jack wishes that he could be even more than a president, more than a king: He wants to be a saint. His work on the streets, in the bars, is not hustling but "conscientious shepherding": "It wasn't the money that drove me; I can't call it holy charity, but it was as close to a Christian act as that sort of friendly commerce could be, keeping those already astray happy and from harm, within caution's limits." Jack does not fool himself about the value of the service he provides; he is certain of its necessity. His "unselfish" dedication to his customers protects them from greedy cabbies, secret societies, transvestites, sadists, venereal disease. Jack's world is hardly pure, but it lacks the evasions and self-justifications of that of Eddie Shuck: "I took blame, I risked damnation, I didn't cheat: *A Useful Man*, my tombstone motto would go." He looks after others in the way that he wishes someone would look after him; he is the kind of beneficent angel whom he has long been hoping will visit him.

Theroux and his protagonist recognize the moral ambiguity of a society cluttered by war, pornography, and corruption, but they also realize the individual's responsibility not to make this society any worse than it need be. Such an individual in such a less-than-perfect world can be a kind of saint.

Critical Context

From *Fong and the Indians* (1968) to *The Mosquito Coast* (1982), Theroux has examined the cultures of Third World countries and the interactions of outsiders, usually Americans, with them. Singapore is a most appropriate setting for a Theroux novel: "In such a small place, an island with no natives, everyone a visitor, the foreigner made himself a resident by emphasizing his foreignness." Jack Flowers is a chameleon who can fit himself into any environment; he is proud of the Chinese and Malay touches in his brothel, especially since so much of Singapore has fallen prey to fast food and other Western influences. Other Theroux visitors to the Third World fail to adapt and sometimes die in the attempt.

Jack, however, like so many characters in contemporary American fiction, would be something of an outsider wherever he found himself. He is a picaro, a rogue, a con man, but he is not a comic figure, is not alienated. He is believably complicated, a closet puritan with admittedly old-fashioned attitudes about sex despite his offers to supply "anything" for his customers. His innocence, combined with his self-knowledge and lack of self-pity, makes him a remarkable achievement, almost a Dickensian character with an awareness of Sigmund Freud, a Graham Greene character who will never burn out. Much of Theroux' subsequent fiction and nonfiction has displayed an impatience with human imperfections bordering on misanthropy, but *Saint Jack* is full of unsentimental compassion for the fallibility of man. Jack sees himself as "a person of small virtue; virtue wasn't salvation, but knowing that might be."

Source for Further Study

Coale, Samuel. " 'A Quality of Light': The Fiction of Paul Theroux," in *Critique: Studies in Modern Fiction*. XXII (1981), pp. 5-16.

Michael Adams

SAPPHIRA AND THE SLAVE GIRL

Author: Willa Cather (1873-1947)
Type of plot: Historical realism
Time of plot: From 1856 to c. 1881
Locale: Southwestern Virginia
First published: 1940

> *Principal characters:*
> SAPPHIRA COLBERT, a slave owner and the invalid mistress of
>   Mill House in Back Creek, Virginia
> HENRY COLBERT, Sapphira's husband, a miller
> NANCY, a slave girl in the Colberts' household
> RACHEL BLAKE, the Colberts' daughter, a widow who holds
>   abolitionist views
> MARTIN COLBERT, Henry's nephew, a notorious rake

The Novel

The novel opens on a dinner quarrel. Sapphira Colbert has announced to her husband, Henry, her intention of selling a slave girl, Nancy, to neighbors. Henry refuses to countersign the necessary documents, although the slaves belong legally to Sapphira. "We don't sell our slaves!" is Henry's blunt reply. Sapphira, portrayed as a particularly strong-minded woman, begins to devise other means to rid herself of Nancy, who has lost favor (and an easy job as light maid) because of a perceived favoritism paid to the lovely girl by Sapphira's husband, a favoritism that Sapphira feels (wrongly) is sexual. Her determination to sell Nancy does not sit well with her daughter, Rachel Blake.

Determined to have her way, Sapphira comes up with a plan to force Henry to agree to let Nancy go. Inviting Henry's lecherous nephew, Martin Colbert, to come stay with them, Sapphira hopes to compromise Nancy's morals, a situation that would make Nancy's continued place at the Colberts' unthinkable, according to the slaveholding ethos. When Martin arrives, it looks as though the ploy will work. Sapphira is charmed by the younger man's flatteries and bonhomie. The hardworking Henry, however, is not, and he questions Sapphira when Martin's stay becomes obviously prolonged.

Meanwhile, Nancy has indeed caught Martin's eye, but she knows of no way to deflect his—a white man's—flirtatious suggestions. His persistence and boldness begin to terrify the girl, so Sapphira, feigning concern, arranges for her to sleep in the hallway outside Sapphira's bedchamber (and within easy reach of Martin). One day, Martin finds her while she is picking fruit. Although she attempts to climb the tree, Martin sees her and pulls her down, causing Nancy to scream and alerting nearby field hands who take note, but keep working. Nancy has, by this time, begun to be talked about around the slave quarters.

Rachel Blake, who has opposed her mother's slave owning, devises a plan of her own when it becomes clear that Nancy is being terrorized because of Sapphira's vindictiveness. With the help of local Quakers, who have connections with the Underground Railroad, and with the tacit approval of Henry, she convinces Nancy of the necessity for escape. At first Nancy resists the suggestion, but Martin's pursuit of her forces her to realize that escape is her only solution. At length, Nancy flees to Canada. Meanwhile, Rachel, who has been banned from Sapphira's house, loses a daughter, Betty, to diphtheria, and the two women are finally reconciled through mutual grief.

An epilogue, "Nancy's Return," takes place twenty-five years later. Nancy's return to Virginia is witnessed through the eyes of a child who is identified as Cather. Although Nancy has grown into an agreeable, handsome woman, there is a poignancy to her character that comes from exile. That this is perceived through a child's eyes—as much of this dream has been seen through Nancy's—concludes the novel on a note of unexpected continuity.

The Characters

Certainly the most striking character in the novel is Sapphira Colbert. Cather presents Sapphira as "entirely self-centered" and stubborn, feeling that she has a right to do with her slaves as she pleases. She is also, unfortunately, capable of vindictiveness and cruelty. Her determination to rid herself of Nancy sends profound reverberations throughout the household and the larger social environment. At the same time, Sapphira is also capable of isolated acts of magnanimity, as in her tender solicitousness toward Tansy Dave, a youth deranged after an unhappy love affair.

By contrast, Henry Colbert is a gentle soul troubled by the immorality of slavery, against which he can find no explicit condemnation in the Bible, which he reads feverishly each night. He is genuinely fond of Nancy but does little to protect her from Martin's designs. His assistance in Nancy's escape takes the form of a feeble gesture: He leaves some money for her in an overcoat. Tellingly, he keeps his bed at the mill and ventures forth to meet Sapphira only at mealtime.

Nancy's affection for Henry Colbert is entirely innocent, and yet the punishments to which she is submitted begin to make even her fellow slaves cast a doubtful look at her. As Nancy believes (at first) that she is unable to escape, her fear of Mrs. Colbert—and later of Martin Colbert—reaches the level of hysteria, giving her plight a nightmarish quality. Despite the degree and nature of her victimization, her decision to escape is not an easy one to make. After all, her entire world is circumscribed by the Colbert household.

Meanwhile, Rachel Blake has long been at odds with her mother over the issue of slavery. The feeling of resentment is compounded with the fact that she feels she has also been a disappointment to her mother. Because of this resentment, it is Rachel who arranges for Nancy's escape. A widow, Rachel herself once felt rescued by Michael Blake, who "dropped from the clouds . . . to deliver her from the loneliness." Nancy's troubles reinforce the memory of that deliverance and help motivate Rachel to act.

Martin Colbert, a suave, former military man, entertains the Colbert household with his tales of derring-do and exotic places. His surface sophistication and mild flirtations amuse Sapphira but quickly leave Henry at a loss for anything to say. Martin's chief characteristic, however, is his unappeasable lechery. As intended, he quickly spots the demure and pretty Nancy and resolves on a course of relentless pursuit with a view to making her one of his conquests.

Themes and Meanings

Sapphira and the Slave Girl is a novel about the evils of private ownership, in this case, the ultimate crime of owning other human beings. Individual ownership and the right of the owner to do with his property exactly as he saw fit, regardless of how low his tastes and motivation might be, were forms of anarchy that Cather saw as inimical to ordered, civilized life—the basis of peaceful human existence.

Although the Civil War plays no part in the novel, the sundering of relationships that were to take place within a decade are prefigured in the Colbert family, which is broken by the fact of slavery itself. The desire to possess and control determines both character and plot. Sapphira's determination to sell Nancy brings her husband's opposition. Faced with a dilemma, she hatches a wicked plan of sexual harassment to force the issue. Martin's obsessive desire to possess Nancy results in the desperate and dangerous plan to escape. The very fact of slavery produces rifts that can only be healed over time. In the reader's last glimpse of Sapphira and Henry, Sapphira remarks forgivingly: "We would all do better if we had our lives to live over again."

Yet the spirit of reconciliation is more metaphorical than real. Nancy's return in the epilogue, after Sapphira and Henry are long dead, has a dreamlike aura around it. One suspects that Sapphira and Henry have survived in the child's mother and father. The narrator's mother dominates the household just as Sapphira did, and the father, like the passive Henry, is not present when Nancy returns.

Moreover, part of the drama of this novel derives from the fact that Sapphira and Henry do not let their differences show explicitly (except in the opening scene). Bitter feelings are hidden by manners and an atmosphere of domestic tranquillity. Nancy's dilemma is thus set in relief against these mores, which provide the Colberts a defense which the slave girl cannot possess.

Critical Context

Cather's last novel brings the author's career full circle by dealing with her Virginia origins. While most of her work concerns life in the West. *Sapphira and the Slave Girl* deploys characters based on her earliest memories of family life to dramatize her lifelong opposition to the increasing materialism of American life. The epilogue suggests that the story of Sapphira and the slave girl, Nancy, may well represent Cather's own fundamental psychological drama, that of the well-meaning but ineffectual father, the domineering mother, and the orphaned protagonist. Be that as it may, the work is Cather's final statement in the novel form concerning the question of what America will finally become and her hope that the tide would finally turn against the forces of materialism—as represented by the abuses of private ownership. This novel of slavery and division argues in an elemental way against that tide and its attendant mentality with an authority that comes only with long experience.

Sources for Further Study

Daiches, David. *Willa Cather: A Critical Introduction*, 1951.
Edel, Leon. *The Paradox of Success*, 1960.
Gerber, Philip. *Willa Cather*, 1975.
Stouck, David. *Willa Cather's Imagination*, 1975.

David Rigsbee

SAVE ME THE WALTZ

Author: Zelda Fitzgerald (1900-1948)
Type of plot: Autobiographical romance
Time of plot: The 1920's
Locale: Alabama, New York, France, and Italy
First published: 1932

> *Principal characters:*
> ALABAMA BEGGS, the youngest and wildest of the Beggs
> daughters, but a thoroughbred
> DAVID KNIGHT, Alabama's artist husband
> BONNIE KNIGHT, the daughter of Alabama and David
> JUDGE AUSTIN BEGGS, Alabama's father, a living fortress of
> security
> "MISS MILLIE" BEGGS, Alabama's mother, whose "fixation of
> loyalty. . . achieved in her life a saintlike harmony"
> DIXIE BEGGS, the oldest daughter of Judge and Mrs. Beggs,
> who moved to New York and married an Alabama man
> "up there"
> JOAN BEGGS, the middle daughter, who "was so orderly she
> made little difference"
> JACQUES CHEVRE-FEUILLE, a French aviator
> MADAME, a Russian ballet mistress

The Novel

Save Me the Waltz, according to its author, derives its title from a Victor record catalog, and it suggests the romantic glitter of the life which F. Scott Fitzgerald and Zelda Sayre Fitzgerald lived and which Scott's novels have so indelibly written into American literary and cultural history.

Divided into four chapters, each of which is further divided into three parts, the novel is a chronological narrative of four periods in the lives of Alabama and David Knight, names that are but thin disguises for their real-life counterparts. The four chapters loosely follow four distinct phases of the author's life up to the death of her father: her childhood filled with romantic dreams of escape from the increasingly stifling family; her exciting escape via marriage to a painter and their early life together in Connecticut, New York, France, and Switzerland; the increasing emptiness of that life; and a final escape into ballet training, concluding with the return to Alabama for her father's final illness.

These four phases conclude with a party given by the Knights in Alabama, at which once more David is the idol of the evening and once more Alabama and David are envied for their exciting and glamorous lives. The talk at the party, for Alabama, "pelted her consciousness like the sound of hoofs on a pavement," an effect evocative of the remoteness and boredom in lines from T. S. Eliot's "The Love Song of J. Alfred Prufrock": "In the room women come and go/ Talking of Michelangelo."

The tragic events of Zelda's reverse fairy tale remained to be played out in real life in the devastating effects that she and her husband had on each other: his alcoholism, her many bouts with insanity, and finally, in 1948, her death in a fire at a mental institution. To the end, neither seemed to understand the other. Nicole Diver in *Tender Is the Night* (1934) and David Knight in *Save Me the Waltz* are graphic demonstrations of the masculine and feminine defenses, respectively, that each built against the other.

The Characters

The novel begins with a description of Judge Austin Beggs as a living fortress who provides his family with security. Equally strong is his "detached tenderness," his bulwark against the disappointments of life, the most important of which is the loss of an only son in infancy. His anger and outraged sense of decency take over from time to time when additional disappointments invade his concentration on the "origins of the Napoleonic code" and on his attempts to provide financially for his family of three socially frivolous daughters. His handling of situations is direct, as when he "brusquely grabbed the receiver" of the telephone "with the cruel concision of a taxidermist's hands at work" to ask a beau never to attempt to see Dixie, his eldest daughter, again.

"Miss Millie" Beggs, Alabama's mother, on the other hand, possesses a "wide and lawless generosity," "nourished from many years of living faced with the irrefutable logic of the Judge's fine mind." Because her sense of reality was never very strong, she could not "reconcile that cruelty of the man with what she knew was a just and noble character. She was never again able to form a judgment of people, shifting her actualities to conform to their inconsistencies till by a fixation of loyalty she achieved in her life a saintlike harmony." Her strategy in life consists of avoiding or preventing difficult situations, so that when Alabama tells her that she does not want to go to school any longer and her mother can react only with a faintly hostile surprise, Alabama merely switches the subject to save her mother the difficulty of listening to an explanation that she cannot comprehend. Millie's major battles are fought over dresses remade for one daughter from an older sister's clothes.

Alabama's older sisters, Joan and Dixie, the belles of Montgomery society and the envy of their younger sister during her childhood, eventually settle into conventional patterns of life in New York and Connecticut. Alabama finds the social whirl exciting at first and then suffocating; her pattern for life is established early, when her first escape arrives one day in the person of a handsome military officer from the north, David Knight. He is, indeed, the knight come to release his princess, as he refers to her in his letters. He even expresses a wish to keep her in his ivory tower for his "private delectation." What Alabama realizes much later is that despite all the initial excitement of the escape, the disillusioning sense of entrapment eventually sets in. She leaves her father's fortress for the ivory tower of her husband's success and popularity as a painter. The need to create her own destiny and identity always lurks beneath the fairy-tale surface of her life. Her affair with a handsome French flyer and the constant adoration of her husband by women and by their daughter, Bonnie, only serve to intensify the emptiness of her glamorous, Bohemian existence.

In desperation, Alabama, at an age at which most ballet dancers have matured, begins achingly long days of lessons with a Russian ballet mistress. She spends less and less time with husband and daughter as her obsession with the ballet consumes her totally. This latest escape is aborted when she undergoes foot surgery in Naples, where she has been dancing in her first professional role. Shortly thereafter, she returns to the emptiness of a life without a purpose.

When she, David, and Bonnie return to Alabama on the occasion of her father's death, she is aware of the pattern that their lives have taken. David continues to be a successful artist; she finds her old feelings of uselessness returning. He is still the idol of guests at a party they give, and their glamorous lives still draw the envy of local society. At that party it is the forms and shapes of things that hold Alabama captive as "the talk pelted her consciousness." Scolded by David for not being the proper hostess, Alabama responds that her premature dumping of the ash trays is expressive of herself, that she simply lumps "everything in a great heap which I have labelled 'the past,' and having thus emptied this deep reservoir that was once myself, I am ready to continue."

In real life, Alabama (Zelda) went on to compete with David (Fitzgerald) in his own chosen art form (writing). In *Save Me the Waltz*, the next escape has not yet taken shape.

Except for one major event in the novel, that of Alabama's professional ballet engagement in Naples—Zelda never danced professionally—the real life of the Fitzgeralds is only thinly disguised. Like Alabama, Zelda was twenty-two years of age when she met the man who was to become her husband. The Southern childhood of Alabama is Zelda's own. Millie Beggs, as Nancy Milford points out in her biography of Zelda, is given a name that combines the names of Zelda's and Fitzgerald's mothers, Minnie and Mollie, respectively. Like Millie Beggs, Zelda's mother provided the quiet and harmony necessary to Judge Sayre and the attention to the practical needs of their daughters. Zelda's older sister Rosalind wrote society columns for the local newspaper, as does Alabama's older sister Dixie. Zelda's and

Fitzgerald's daughter Scottie and their Japanese servant Tanaka are the Bonnie and Tanka of the novel. Events in the Knights's odyssey from Montgomery to the New York area, the Riviera, Paris, and Switzerland— then back to Alabama—follow closely those of the Fitzgeralds. Especially significant are the portraits of Zelda's father and of her husband. Judge Sayre symbolized both security and inaccessibility, and her husband, as surrogate father, became both. The contradictory impulses of authority on the one hand and freedom on the other are the poles between which the pendulum of her life swung and between which Zelda could find no stable point.

A major difference between Zelda's self-portrait and that which her husband paints of her as Nicole Diver in *Tender Is the Night* is one of the most intriguing revelations of the novel. Nicole is an irrationally jealous wife whose unpredictable tantrums create marriage problems. Alabama Beggs, on the other hand, although jealous of the attention her idolized husband receives, is in her own words an empty, deep reservoir that she tries desperately to fill. It is from these irreconcilable views that the two companion novels draw their central characters.

Themes and Meanings

It is inevitable that the major theme of the novel is seen as an intense attempt on the part of the wife of one of America's most famous novelists to reorder and shape her own destiny by writing about her attempt to do so. The novel was written during the early stages of a series of mental breakdowns that became the pattern in the remaining years of Zelda's life. It was written also during the time that her husband was working on his own novel, *Tender Is the Night*, in which the two leading roles of Alabama and David Knight are depicted (from a masculine point of view) in the characters of Nicole and Dick Diver.

Although traditional prerogatives of a male society had been broken down by some gains in women's rights during the early years of the twentieth century, it remained for those freedoms to become a reality for most women. Zelda wrote magazine articles on the subject during the 1920's and attempted to achieve that reality for herself. For ten years or so, between her marriage and her schizophrenic attacks, she worked toward this goal, ironically realizing it eventually, not in her ballet dancing, but in the same artistic medium as that of her husband: writing a novel that, although not the aesthetic equal of her husband's work, is an important book in its own right. From the vantage point of more than fifty years after the novel's publication, the novel thus has for its major theme the identity crisis of a woman for whom the ideal of the American Dream seems only to turn to ashes, like those cigarette ashes that Alabama impolitely dumps before all of her guests have left the party.

It is no mere literary convention that Zelda begins and ends the novel with events at the center of which is her father. Like Judge Beggs, her own father—Judge Sayre—represented a fortresslike security that merely changed form in the ivory tower that her husband seemed to her. Both father and husband were, as in the case of Alabama Beggs, ultimately inaccessible. The fictive account of Zelda, however, allowed for the heroine's realization of some personal success in an actual ballet performance in Naples. In this respect, the writing of the novel had some therapeutic, even if temporary, effect on the real-life dancer who never had this opportunity. The fragility of a romantic upbringing and events such as the foot injury conspired to abort Alabama's attempt to shape her own life and to realize fully the newly won feminist freedoms.

Critical Context

Save Me the Waltz makes fascinating reading for a student of literary history in several ways. First, there is the matter of the novel's being read by one of the most famous twentieth century editors, Maxwell Perkins, who liked it well enough to give it serious consideration. Fitzgerald, however, also read the novel and made many changes, against the wishes of Zelda, although she eventually agreed to them. He had been working on his own novel about their marriage, *Tender Is the Night*, at the time, and had his way regarding matters he wished deleted or changed in the original manuscript of *Save Me the Waltz*. Together, Harry Dan Piper states, "these two chronicles of the same marriage seen from the wife's and the husband's points of view, form one of the most unusual pairs of novels in recent literary history."

In a later edition (1960), the novel includes a preface by Harry T. Moore, a note on the text by Matthew J. Bruccoli, a set of emendations, and "an exact type transcript of the typescript opening of Chapter 2 in the form originally set in galleys."

Scholars and critics have shown interest in the novel primarily because of the prominent position occupied by F. Scott Fitzgerald in American literary history. Consequently, critical concern has focused on autobiographical insights rather than on the aesthetic merits of *Save Me the Waltz*. Most critics, however, have mentioned the turgid prose and overblown metaphors in parts of the novel, especially at the outset. One in particular has been noted: "Incubated in the mystic pungence of Negro mammies, the family hatched into girls. From the personification of an extra penny, a street-car ride to whitewashed picnic grounds . . . the Judge became, with their matured perceptions a retributory organ, an inexorable fate. . . . Youth and age: a hydraulic funicular, and age, having less of the waters of conviction in its carriage. . . ." Yet as the action of the novel develops, the self-consciousness of the writing settles down, as in the description of Alabama's sick father:

"The noble completeness of the life withering on the bed before her moved her to promise herself many promises." In the final paragraph of the novel, the linguistic awkwardnesses disappear, as Alabama and David sit in the "pleasant gloom of the late afternoon," and amid "the silver glasses, the silver tray, the traces of many perfumes," they watch "the twilight flow through the calm living room that they were leaving like the clear cold current of a trout stream."

Beyond the interest that important scholars have taken in the novel, beyond its autobiographical value, and in spite of its embarrassingly self-conscious language, Zelda's fictive autobiography slowly catches even the discriminating reader in a rhythmic involvement in the feminist imagination and feminine psychology that have a fascination all their own.

Sources for Further Study

Bruccoli, Matthew J. "A Note on the Text," in *Save Me the Waltz*, 1967.

Milford, Nancy. *Zelda: A Biography*, 1970.

Moore, Harry T. "Preface," in *Save Me the Waltz*, 1967.

Piper, Henry Dan. "Save Me the Waltz: 1932," in *F. Scott Fitzgerald: A Critical Portrait*, 1965.

Turnbull, Andrew. *Scott Fitzgerald*, 1962.

Susan Rusinko

THE SECOND COMING

Author: Walker Percy (1916-   )
Type of plot: Philosophical comedy
Time of plot: The late 1970's
Locale: The affluent rural community of Linwood in North Carolina, especially the golf course and its adjacent wild countryside
First published: 1980

Principal characters:

WILL BARRETT, the protagonist, a middle-aged, prosperous lawyer who is recently widowed

ALLISON (ALLIE) HUGER, a young woman who escapes from a mental hospital

LESLIE BARRETT, Will's grown daughter, a fiercely religious, fundamentalist Christian

LEWIS PECKHAM, the golf pro, one of the few unbelievers in this religious community, who appreciates classical music and good books

THE ELDER BARRETT, Will's father, who committed suicide when Will was twelve years old and may have tried to kill his son as well in a hunting "accident"

EWELL McBEE, a small-town businessman and longtime bully who poaches deer on Barrett's land

JACK CURL, a complaisant chaplain of the nursing home built by Will's late wife's money

KATHERINE (KITTY) VAUGHT HUGER, Allie's mother, an old girlfriend of Will

The Novel

The Second Coming is a seriocomic tale in which a wealthy, middle-aged man who is contemplating suicide and a young woman who has recently escaped from a mental hospital save each other from depression and psychosis and win their freedom from conniving relatives. It is not the usual kind of love story, in which the primary conflict is some obstacle in a romantic pursuit. Each is engrossed in a very private struggle with the crippling emotions peculiar to his or her own past. Their encounter is a happy accident—or perhaps the grace of God extended to two social misfits who cannot make it alone.

Will Barrett seems to have everything: money, social position, friends, early retirement, and a good golf game. In abstract, metaphysical terms, his main adversary is the meaninglessness of his life, even though he and his late wife had been much involved in "good works." The more immediate antagonist, however, is his skeptical father, who shot himself when Will was a boy and intimated that someday his son would follow his example. Much of Will's mental life is spent recapturing in minute detail the reality of his relationship to his father and his legacy of death. Therefore, much of the action, though comical in itself and infused with satiric observations about American, especially Southern, society, still has a somber undertone of self-analysis.

Allison Huger's problem is also psychological, though its sources in the past are not so clear. While Will suffers from obsessive memories, Allie struggles from extreme withdrawal and forgetfulness, the latter exacerbated by repeated electroshock treatments. She manages, nevertheless, to escape the sanatorium and take possession of an abandoned greenhouse, which she inherited from an aunt. Her intention is to prove that she can survive in the world without the help of the psychiatrist and the parents who committed her to the mental hospital.

Will becomes a part of Allie's life when he literally falls into her green-house potting shed. He embarks on an insane religious quest, trying to determine once and for all if God exists. Will, like his father, is an unbe-liever, but he is surrounded by religious fanatics. He decides to hide away in a local cave and starve until God gives him a sign of his presence. If God does so, he will emerge and repudiate his father's cynicism and atheism. If God is silent, he will starve to death and thus fulfill the destiny he inherited from his father.

As usual, God does not oblige with a sign—unless the excruciating tooth-ache that Will develops is a gift of the Almighty. The pain and nausea drive all metaphysical speculations from his mind and set him blundering for the exit. He stumbles, drops his flashlight, loses his way, and falls into an un-explored shaft that plunges him headfirst through tangled vines straight into Allie's greenhouse, where he knocks himself out on the cement floor. The former owner had used the constant temperature of cave air to moderate the climate of the greenhouse. Thus Will, who could not be a born-again Christian like his daughter, is ironically born again from the mountain and nursed back to health by a young woman who has been judged incompetent to conduct her own life.

Will and Allie ultimately outwit the doctors and the assorted relatives and self-seeking friends who try to gain control over their lives and, not in-cidentally, their financial assets. When Will determines to marry Allie, he rises in the night, retrieves his father's German Luger and the shotgun with which he killed himself, and throws them into the gorge. Thus, he repudi-ates his father's cynicism and resolves to give life another chance.

Moreover, he and Allie plan to rescue several other lost souls they know: an old gardener, two physically handicapped but knowledgeable builders, and a former bookkeeper who needs emotional support. Will met the first three in the retirement home in which his daughter had tried to place him for safekeeping when he was diagnosed as having a rare form of epilepsy. The last is a woman friend of Allie, a patient in the mental hospital. Taking off the shelf these still valuable persons discarded by society, they hope to develop Allie's neglected property, beginning with her cave-air-ventilated greenhouse. The story suggests a vision somewhat analogous to the ending of Voltaire's *Candide* (1759), wherein a group of wounded people pool their efforts to compensate for individual limitations in order to "cultivate their garden" in an absurd world.

The Characters

The Second Coming has a large cast of distinctive characters who are cleverly delineated, though not in great depth. This is partly because they are seen through the ironic consciousness of Will Barrett. He is unusually perceptive about fakery or seeming inconsistencies in human behavior, including his own. It bothers him, for example, that his daughter Leslie, so insistent about the joy of her personal relationship to Jesus, is continually frowning. He asks the chaplain Jack Curl point-blank if he believes that God exists and perceives in Jack's confusion and double-talk the paucity of his religious knowledge. He intuits the meaning of Allie's poetic and nonidiomatic speech, recognizing that she tries to express the truth of experience. Most of his acquaintances speak in jargon and trite phrases which have no precise meaning.

Yet Will's experience of other people may be colored by the peculiar sickness of his soul. Certain characters seem to represent facets of Will's own personality, his shadow selves, so to speak, whom he must exorcise in order to be sane. The most conspicuous of these, without doubt, is his father, whose preference for death has infected his very soul. There are others, however, such as his friend Lewis Peckham, who seems to represent the intellectual, or perhaps pseudointellectual, as ruined "natural man." Lewis turns for meaning to classical music and great books, yet he seems curiously empty of any conviction. A more comic shadow self is Ewell McBee, a vulgar bully out of Will's past who seems to represent his more bestial nature.

Will's character remains something of a mystery to himself, to other people, and to the reader, an enigmatic combination of genial tolerance and inner coldness, at once curiously wise and hopelessly naïve, suspecting the worst, yet yearning for the best that human imagination can devise.

Themes and Meanings

This ironic story of mental and emotional regeneration from the edge of insanity has psychological, philosophical, and religious overtones. It is full of ambiguous symbols, yet they are never obtrusive. Even Will's symbolic death and rebirth, covered with the slime of cave clay, has a concreteness of detail that gives it a comic plausibility. Similarly, Allie's ingenious recovery of a huge, nineteenth century cookstove from an old burned-out house on her property is perfectly natural, yet almost a miracle. The stove had fallen through the floor into the basement and thus was saved from destruction in a fire long ago. She takes it apart piece by piece, cleaning each part as she goes, lifts the heavy pieces with block and tackle, moves them on creepers borrowed from an auto store, and reassembles the huge wood and coal stove in her greenhouse to provide heat in the winter. The stove is almost brand new, waiting to be reclaimed from the rubbish of the past. It, too, becomes a symbol of regeneration, and the two marginally sane people fall in love in the genial warmth of its presence.

One of the implications of this story, even though it seems to satirize religious believers, is that there is a saving kernel of truth in the Christian message. Will ironically combines some of the qualities of an absurd, blundering Christ and a modern Job, harried by a disembodied devil-father until he demands an audience with the Lord. Will complains that there are only two classes of people: those who believe anything, indiscriminately but frivolously, and those like his father who believe nothing. He questions both extremes.

Will is surrounded by Episcopalian do-gooders, born-again Baptists, Scientologists, Jehovah's Witnesses, ardent astrologers, married Catholic priests of a reformed church, true believers of every stripe who are all, nevertheless, devoted to the hedonistic pursuit of pleasure, sometimes feebly disguised as good works. The peak of achievement for the American, upper-middle-class male of whatever persuasion seems to be playing golf. Both the psychological and religious quests of *The Second Coming* might be expressed as escaping the golf course, which features prominently in the novel's fictional geography. Playing golf is not intrinsically evil; it simply seems inadequate as the be-all and the end-all of human existence. As the golf pro, Lewis Peckham admits, "You and I know that golf is not enough."

The golf pro, one of the few unbelievers in the community, claims that he and Will are alike because they are both once-born in a society of twice-born and must make their way without "Amazing Grace." Will is appalled, however, at the aridity of Peckham's unbelief. Nevertheless, Lewis is the person who shows Will the secret back entrance to the cave in the tangled patch of wilderness that borders the golf course. To switch from a religious to a psychological metaphor, Peckham acts, all unknowingly, like the Jungian Shadow who points the way to the subconscious and a new understanding of the self. Thus, while unobtrusive on the realistic level, (caves are a common feature of Southern geography), the cave is rich in traditional symbolic associations of womb, tomb, subconscious mind, eternal return to the source of being, and so on.

Percy is not playing with signs and symbols as mere literary decoration, but as an integral part of the philosophic meaning of the novel. The story demonstrates man's propensity as a symbol-making creature to interpret or perhaps to distort objective reality in order to create a subjective meaning. The world is not actually solipsistic but it is continually colored by institutionalized preconceptions or private need. Human beings need to choose their symbols wisely.

Will and Allie are not only acting out elaborate psychodramas but also trying desperately to see and understand the real world. The way men choose to symbolize the world and reflect that reconstructed reality in language defines the nature of society and the relative happiness or meaninglessness of human life. If the world began with God's Word, human society begins with man's word, the language he uses to describe it, which is all too often frivolous and misleading.

Critical Context

Percy has always been concerned in his fiction with the mental and spiritual health of persons in a society that sends confusing, distorted signals about reality. In Percy's *Love in the Ruins* (1971), science and psychology received the brunt of his satire, while in this novel the excesses of Southern religiosity are more prominent, but both novels have an underlying theme of the quest for sanity, truth, and spiritual renewal.

Percy himself is familiar with the intellectual situation of having a foot in the camps of both science and religion. He is a converted Catholic and identifies himself as a Christian novelist. He is also educated as a physician, specifically as a pathologist. Thus, his criticism of institutional biases is, to some extent, from the inside.

The Second Coming demonstrates Percy's interest in semiotics, the study of signs, and probably in phenomenology. Allie's difficulty with speech seems to have something to do with the attempt to express phenomenological reality. This effort to speak truth might theoretically, at least, be aided by a loss of memory for familiar ways of evading truth with borrowed, trite interpretations. Percy has been very interested in existential thought, especially the work of Søren Kierkegaard, with his insistence on the nonrational leap of faith.

Like other Southern writers, Percy often treats the South as a microcosm of American experience. The South was the last region of the country to undergo modernization and industrialization, and the process was accordingly accelerated; thus, one finds jammed together in the South both archaic prejudices and up-to-the-minute amoral commercialism, a combination which, from the viewpoint of a satirist, may offer the worst of two worlds. Nevertheless, it is still a place where the religious quest can be seriously pursued.

Sources for Further Study

Kazin, Alfred. "The Pilgrimage of Walker Percy," in *Harper's Magazine*. CCXLII, no. 1453 (June, 1971), pp. 81-86.
Luschei, Martin. *The Sovereign Wayfarer: Walker Percy's Diagnosis of the Malaise*, 1972.

Katherine Snipes

SEIZE THE DAY

Author: Saul Bellow (1915-   )
Type of plot: Realistic comic novel
Time of plot: The 1950's
Locale: New York City
First published: 1956

> *Principal characters:*
> TOMMY WILHELM, the central character through whose point
> of view this story of suffering and compassion is told
> DR. TAMKIN, an elderly psychologist, a fellow "speculator,"
> who spends much of his time lecturing Tommy on every-
> thing from the stock market to sex
> DR. ADLER, Tommy's father, a cold, unloving parent who
> views his son as a failure
> MARGARET, Tommy's former wife, who constantly nags him
> for money

The Novel

Like a Greek tragedy, *Seize the Day* is a tight, compact work examining one day in the agonized life of Tommy Wilhelm. Set in the Gloriana Hotel on Broadway during one morning and in the commodities exchange on Wall Street later in the day, this short novel opens with Tommy's descent from the twenty-third floor to the lobby for breakfast. The descent is symbolic as well as literal, for Tommy has also descended in the world, coming down from the security of marriage and a promising career at Rojax Corporation to find himself at middle age on the fringe of respectability, without a wife, a job, or a future. His father, Dr. Adler, a well-respected physician who lives at the Gloriana, has given up on his son, stopping short of calling him a bum, but nevertheless making his disdain part of Tommy's agony. Tommy is uncomfortable with his dad, embarrassed and angry, and he has turned to another father figure for consolation. Yet Dr. Tamkin, also a resident of the hotel, merely uses Tommy. A spiritual swindler, Tamkin convinces Tommy to lend him his last few hundred dollars for investment in futures on the commodities exchange, promising Tommy quick profits.

Tommy's agony, reflected in the disarray of his personal life, is illustrated in this central scene, during which he anxiously watches the exchange board for signs of profit while his mentor, Tamkin, preaches about money-making as aggression. In the end, Tommy is wiped out and tries to conceal his horror at yet another failure. Desperate, he turns at last to his father. Ironically, the old man is enjoying a luxurious rubdown, while Tommy, penniless, grovels before him. Dr. Adler assumes his usual "I told you so" attitude and refuses to have anything to do with a son whom he considers a fool, too easily trusting in human nature. Calling him a slob, Adler spurns him and Tommy leaves, making his final descent to the street. Here he fruitlessly looks for Tamkin, but the con man is already gone.

Finally, Tommy calls his ex-wife, Margaret, asking for an extension on the child-support payments, pleading for her understanding. Margaret, however, like his father, is indifferent to Tommy's hurt and insensitive to his need for compassion. She, too, dismisses him. Overwhelmed, burdened with life's disappointments, Tommy wanders into a funeral chapel. Here, unknown to the mourners, he weeps aloud for the dead, symbolizing his own dead end and suggesting his deeper, personal grief over the death of love and human values among those nearest him.

The Characters

Tommy Wilhelm is a questioner; at middle age he realizes that there is more to life than working at a job he despises, and yet he knows that he cannot survive in the world without playing the game. Caught in this middle region between commitment and freedom, between worldly responsibility and personal integrity, Tommy is a kind of latter-day Hamlet. The world is out of joint, yet the world has demands of its own that must be met. Like Hamlet, Tommy must lay to rest the ghost, that spirit of doubt and uncertainty about the meaning of life. His sensitive nature impels him to seek answers among the people nearest him.

Such answers are not forthcoming from his father, Dr. Adler. Adler is a satanic figure, cold, indifferent, heartless. A well-respected physician who is living on his reputation and a snug savings account, Adler despises Tommy. The closer Tommy tries to get to his father, the more Adler tries to put distance between them. Not wanting to get involved, he scolds his son, accusing Tommy of trying to give an old man "another cross" to bear. One wonders if Adler's indifference to his son's plight is a result of Adler's total accommodation to the world, a commitment to physical well-being; or whether his heartlessness is a façade, concealing Adler's fear of being like Tommy, of having to confront the truth about human feelings and needs. Certainly the old man's insistence on being left alone makes him an unappealing figure. "Adler" in German means "eagle," and, in truth, Dr. Adler behaves in that coldly regal manner denoting the predator: lofty, aristocratic, fierce. Adler's complacency, his smugness about the value of his own success in life, is curiously akin to mid-twentieth century America's image of itself—a goal-oriented society, measuring success in terms of wealth. The American eagle and Dr. Adler have become symbolically entwined, a noble predator who has become ignoble by divorcing himself from feeling and love.

For all of Adler's emotional distance, however, he is at least predictable; Tommy and the reader know exactly where Adler stands. The same cannot be said of Dr. Tamkin. A character of dark complexity, Tamkin is clearly a con man, a fast talker who often lights on the truth through a continuous barrage of words. To Tommy he preaches the value of dignity and love, yet his obvious attempt to make a killing on the market shows his greed, and thus puts him in a moral stance similar to Adler's. Throughout the novel, Tamkin proves his ability as a manipulator, using Tommy while risking nothing of his own. Like all good con men, Tamkin knows his mark. Like Roger Chillingworth in Nathaniel Hawthorne's *The Scarlet Letter* (1850), Tamkin uses his knowledge of Tommy's character to his own advantage, ultimately destroying his victim.

Tamkin's pious preachings, his bromidic espousals of "things that mattered" in the midst of his own aggressive pursuit of the dollar, make him one of the great hypocrites in modern literature. He himself characterizes the hypocritical nature of American society. On the one hand, Tamkin is a philosopher, a cynic, a latter-day Henry David Thoreau, contemptuous of the world's material goods while upholding the ideals of humanity; on the other hand, he is a realist who knows that he must "seize the day" to live, that he must pay homage to Success to survive.

Themes and Meanings

Tommy Wilhelm is a classic representative of the typical Jewish American hero: the long-suffering, sensitive victim who, despite life's hardships, remains basically noble and integral in a fragmented world. The title characters of other Bellow novels clearly bear a relationship to Tommy and his problem. Both Joseph in *Dangling Man* (1944) and Asa Leventhal in *The Victim* (1947) suffer from an inability to cope with the harsher, even sometimes mundane affairs of life, yet they survive with their dignity intact.

Tommy's plight is darkly comic—the poor soul who succumbs to the wiles of a fast-talking con man and who is ultimately bereft of everything. His situation is analogous to the old vaudeville skit in which the country bumpkin comes to the big city and gets battered and bashed and otherwise deceived by the initiated. It is a theme that recurs in serious American literature from Hawthorne to Horatio Alger.

For Alger, the country boy makes good by luck and pluck. Alger's books were gospels of faith in the American ethos of success. For Bellow, the theme of Tommy's plight is not an affirmation but a lament, a form of kaddish for the death of idealism, which Tommy performs at the end of the novel.

The novel's title provides further irony. The *carpe diem* theme—literally, "to seize the day"—was a classical pronouncement that urged man to make the most of his time, to extract from each moment that joy of life which time was ever silently stealing from him. Ironically, Tommy cannot subscribe to this idea. Though he quits his job, though dissatisfaction gnaws at him, he cannot live for the moment. His investment in futures, though feckless, is an ironic statement on Tommy's need to live beyond the day, beyond the commercial grind. Tommy dangles, living between two ideas, subscribing to neither: Though he is a speculator, he is still sensitive enough to perceive that the most important speculation is about the meaning of life.

Critical Context

Following closely on the sprawling, picaresque novel, *The Adventures of Augie March* (1953), *Seize the Day* can be viewed as the perfect introduction to Bellow's work; it brilliantly crystallizes the major themes that have preoccupied Bellow's writings. All of Bellow's major characters share with Tommy Wilhelm an ambivalent attitude toward success: ambition tempered by doubt, by the desire to identify what it is to be human in a world callous to human needs and values. Tommy Wilhelm is not as cerebral as Moses Herzog, for example (*Herzog*, 1964), a college professor who writes letters in an attempt to keep his sanity. Yet he is a Herzog in miniature—a middle-class lowbrow who seeks to open meaningful communication with the world.

Seize the Day is a work of rich allusiveness. Typical of Bellow's deep knowledge of literature (in the late 1930's, Bellow supported himself by working on the Great Books Series later published by *Encyclopedia Britannica*), the novel shows a use of traditional forms and material to express contemporary concerns. The character of Tamkin is illustrative of the use of character types already well-established in nineteenth century American literature. The fast talker is derived in part from the tradition of the stage Yankee, a shrewd wheeler-dealer who often worked his game at the expense of the pompous, the rich, the undemocratic. The character-type is also part of the Western tradition of the tall tale in which the straight-faced narrator spins a comically improbable yarn at the expense of the conservative and somewhat priggish listener. (This was a vein which Mark Twain worked well.)

Yet both these traditions are basically comic. *Seize the Day* overturns the pattern: The fast-talking Tamkin is a villain who exploits a sensitive man's grief over the loss of moral values in American life. Thus, the traditional pattern is adapted to contemporary concerns.

Sources for Further Study

Clayton, John. *Saul Bellow: In Defense of Man*, 1968.
Dutton, Robert. *Saul Bellow*, 1982.
Kegan, Robert. *The Sweeter Welcome: Voices for a Vision of Affirmation, Bellow, Malamud and Martin Buber*, 1976.

Rodrigues, Eusebio. *Quest for the Human: An Exploration of Saul Bellow's Fiction*, 1981.
Trachtenberg, Stanley, ed. *Critical Essays on Saul Bellow*, 1979.

Edward Fiorelli

A SEPARATE PEACE

Author: John Knowles (1926-   )
Type of plot: Psychological naturalism
Time of plot: Summer and fall, 1942, and 1957
Locale: The Devon School, a boys' prep school in New Hampshire, and
    Boston
First published: 1960

> *Principal characters:*
> GENE FORRESTER, a Southern sixteen-year-old student at the
>   Devon School
> PHINEAS (FINNY), Gene's best friend and rival at the Devon
>   School
> BRINKER HADLEY, a conservative student leader at the Devon
>   School
> ELWIN "LEPER" LEPELLIER, an eccentric, romantic Devon
>   student

The Novel

The entire story of *A Separate Peace* is narrated by the main character, Gene Forrester. Every action in the novel is presented through his eyes, as Forrester looks back upon the summer and fall of 1942 from the perspective of 1957. Gene Forrester, therefore, is a thirty-one-year-old man looking back at the year 1942, when he was sixteen years old at the Devon School.

Gene Forrester has come to Devon from the South, although Knowles never specifically identifies Forrester's home state. At Devon, Forrester is exposed to a distinctly New England environment as personified by three characters at the school: Brinker Hadley, Elwin "Leper" Lepellier, and Phineas (called "Finny," with no last name given). There is not much action in *A Separate Peace*, as the novel primarily explores the highly complex psychological bond that is established between Forrester and Finny. Whereas Forrester is an exemplary student, Finny is indifferent to his classroom activities and does not envy Forrester's superiority in his studies. Finny is, however, a superior athlete, and Forrester is clearly envious of, yet attracted to, his friend's physical prowess.

The first four chapters of *A Separate Peace* are perhaps the most important in the novel. While he is drawn to Finny, especially as Finny possesses a carefree attitude toward everything around him, Forrester feels compelled to compete with his friend: Finny wins the Galbraith Football Trophy and the Contact Sports Award, so Forrester aims at becoming the head of his class on graduation day, winning the Ne Plus Ultra Scholastic Achievement Citation. Vying with Finny in this way, and in many others, Forrester is still not content. He wishes to be Finny's athletic equal, which leads him to abandon his studies (the day before a critical examination) for an unexcused trip to the beach. This kind of competition also takes Forrester up into a tree, out of which he jumps into a river, at Finny's dare.

The tree is at the center of the novel's action. At the end of chapter 4, while Finny is preparing for his own jump into the river, Forrester deliberately jostles the limb on which Finny is standing (in an earlier part of the novel, Forrester slipped on this same limb and almost fell; he was saved, however, by Finny). Finny falls and severely breaks his leg; his athletic career is over, and while he convalesces at home, Forrester tries to account for his actions. At one point during the summer he visits Finny's home and tries to tell Finny that he made him fall on purpose, but Finny refuses to believe that Forrester intentionally harmed him.

When school resumes at Devon, Finny is still recuperating, so Forrester must find other allegiances at the school; at the same time, a new development begins to dominate the atmosphere of Devon: Enlistments are beginning for World War II. All the boys are eager to enlist; all do enlist before the novel ends, but Forrester is last because, on the day he intends to join, Phineas returns to the Devon School.

Thinking that Finny needs him for an effective recovery, Forrester temporarily abandons his enlistment plans. This allows Knowles to introduce two key episodes. First, the eccentric Lepellier sneaks out of Devon to enlist immediately for the war; quickly, however, he suffers an emotional breakdown in boot camp and is discharged in a state of shock. This is the first indication that the reality awaiting the Devon School boys is not an attractive one. A second and more important event occurs when Brinker Hadley initiates a mock trial of Forrester, to enquire if Forrester maliciously caused Finny's accident. Although Hadley is not truly serious, Finny reacts violently to the episode: He runs away from the trial, falls a second time, and, again, breaks his leg. This injury leads to a second confrontation between Forrester and Finny, in which Finny admits that he knows Forrester deliberately caused his fall. During the second operation, Finny dies.

At the novel's end, something also dies inside Gene Forrester; some evil or uncontrollable part of his nature disappears with Finny's death. Forrester finds that he is finally at peace with himself (thus the novel's title), but he is not a happy individual. As he describes it, his life after the war is a monotonous routine.

The Characters

Gene Forrester is a character whose worst enemy is himself. Although he is a capable athlete and an excellent student, Forrester is unable to prevent the dark side of his inner self from perverting and distorting his enjoyment of the world and the people around him. As Forrester admits to himself in chapter 7, he always finds something bad in the things around him; or, if he does not find it, he invents it. This proclivity, clearly the product of a subconscious force, results in paranoia. At one point in the novel, Forrester entertains the absurd idea that Finny is deliberately trying to destroy his scholastic success (even though Finny is obviously unconcerned). Forrester's personal insecurity is such that it drives him toward somehow getting even with Finny, which he eventually does by causing Finny's fall from the tree. Even though Finny's accident and subsequent death liberate Forrester from his dark interior impulses, something vital inside him also dies.

Finny may symbolize the kind of person Forrester wishes he could be; Finny is an almost complete opposite of Forrester, a natural athlete and a complete individualist, interested in immediate and innocuous personal pleasures. Against the confining background of the Devon School strictures, Finny constructs his own world out of his imagination: It is Finny who invents new games to play; it is Finny's idea to jump from the tree into the river. Whereas Forrester is all calculation, Finny is all spontaneity. Like Forrester, Finny represents an extreme. Forrester's eccentricity is built on his inability to cope with his dark subconscious mind; Finny's way of dealing with the world is geared toward completely ignoring unpleasant realities of any kind. At the end of *A Separate Peace*, Finny is forced to confront a world he cannot physically dominate or imaginatively reshape. Thus, he flees from Hadley's trial of Forrester, refusing to deal with Hadley's emphasis on facts; similarly, he refuses (for as long as possible) to acknowledge Forrester's deliberate injury to him. Dealing with such realities seems to break Finny's will at the novel's end, which may be one reason that he dies during his second operation.

The other characters in the novel are simple foils to Forrester and Finny, although both Brinker Hadley and Leper Lepellier represent two other ways of coping with oneself and the external world. Hadley is a walking personification of a conservative, law-abiding mentality. He monitors the order at Devon School and always does things logically: For example, when the Devon term is over, he will enlist because that is the correct path of action. For a time, during Finny's absence, Forrester aligns himself with Hadley's way of acting. Significantly, however, when Finny reappears at Devon, Forrester immediately gravitates toward his old friend and all the complex things that Finny represents to him.

Leper Lepellier is an even less influential character, whose dominating personal characteristic is a romantic form of eccentricity. A passive creature, Leper derives his pleasures through such pursuits as snail collecting, sketching outdoor scenes, or awakening in the place where the sun first shines on the continental United States. At Devon, Leper's urge is to become a part of the quiet, natural world around him. Then, when the war fervor changes the nature of the outside world, Leper is the first to enlist. He pays a significant price for his impulsive brand of romanticism; at boot camp, he suffers a nervous breakdown from which he does not fully recover in the novel. Still, it is Leper who forces the boys at Devon to acknowledge the harsh realities awaiting them outside the walls of the Devon School.

Themes and Meanings

At its most meaningful level, *A Separate Peace* presents a thoughtfully executed psychological study of its main character, Gene Forrester. Forrester's sense of himself is an extremely dark and critical one, provoking feelings of insecurity particularly when he is in the company of Finny. Knowles explores the dual directions these feelings take: On one level, Forrester desires to get even (to outperform) Finny, he therefore resents Finny's superior athletic skills. On another level, Forrester also wishes to be like Finny, to share his carefree, selfless attitudes and actions. In fact, Forrester clearly is most happy when he is at peace with Finny. At the end, however, Forrester's dark side wins this psychological conflict; the final "peace" that is established between the two occurs after Forrester causes Finny's fall, from which Finny never recovers. This action, in a psychological sense, eliminates Finny as Forrester's rival and allows Forrester to feel less anxious about himself.

Yet less anxious does not mean good. At the conclusion of *A Separate Peace*—when Finny finally asks Forrester why he caused the fall—Forrester replies that he did not do it out of any personal hatred of Finny. Instead, Forrester is fighting himself—out of blindness and ignorance, as he himself admits—and Finny ultimately understands, before he dies, how he has been victimized by Forrester's own psychological conflict. Essentially, then, Finny is simply an object (albeit a very important object) playing a part in Forrester's personal battles. The finishing touch to Knowles's psychological study occurs with Finny's burial, when Forrester cannot cry because he has the feeling that part of himself is being buried with his friend. Thus, when Forrester eventually enlists and goes off to World War II, he does so without any genuine animosity. He has symbolically killed the enemy inside himself, and so he has no further need to find another person to symbolize his dark interior self.

Knowles's exploration of how people are controlled by psychological forces which they do not understand far surpasses the war theme that is worked into *A Separate Peace*. This theme involves Forrester's attempt to find a way to cope with World War II, a different kind of reality that awaits the Devon School boys after their school year. Different ways of dealing with the exterior world are offered by Finny (who ignores it, for as long as he can), Hadley (who approaches everything logically and reasonably), and Leper (whose romanticism fails to prepare him for the violence of enlistment and military service).

Once Forrester's psychological battle with himself is over—it ends with

Finny's death—these themes are quickly dropped in *A Separate Peace*. Readers do not find out what happens to the secondary characters, nor does Knowles reveal what Forrester did during his military service. Forrester reveals that he did not do any fighting during the war, but that is all he has to say about it, and Knowles does not provide any information on Forrester's life after the war, either. The basic theme of *A Separate Peace* concerns Forrester's reconciliation with himself—the peace he establishes "separate" from the war—but the price he pays is a severe one since Forrester is far from being a happy or fulfilled individual at the novel's end. The other themes of the novel—involving the other main characters and also the basic contrast between Forrester (as a Southerner) and Finny (as a typical Bostonian)—simply vanish at the novel's end.

Critical Context

A Separate Peace is acknowledged to be, by far, the best piece of writing produced by John Knowles. In 1960 it won the first William Faulkner Award for a writer's first novel, as well as the 1960 Rosenthal Award of the National Institute of the Arts. By 1976, *A Separate Peace* had sold more than four million copies, and it continues to be one of the most widely read postwar American novels, particularly popular with teenage readers. *A Separate Peace* illustrates Knowles's ability to penetrate and explore the workings of the interior mind with the skillful precision and objectivity necessary for a successful study of human psychology.

Sources for Further Study

Ellis, James. "*A Separate Peace*: The Fall from Innocence," in *English Journal*. LIII (1964), pp. 313-318.

McDonald, James L. "The Novels of John Knowles," in *Arizona Quarterly*. XXIII (Winter, 1967), pp. 335-337.

Sarotte, Georges-Michel. *Like a Brother, Like a Lover*, 1978.

Christopher J. Forbes

SETTING FREE THE BEARS

Author: John Irving (1942-   )
Type of plot: Comic realism
Time of plot: Spring and summer of 1967, with flashbacks to the years 1938-1955
Locale: Primarily Austria (especially Vienna) and Yugoslavia
First published: 1969

Principal characters:
HANNES GRAFF, a failed university student
SIEGFRIED (SIGGY) JAVOTNI, a university dropout, motorcycle salesman, and adventurer
HILKE MARTER, Siggy's mother
GALLEN, a country girl and Hannes's girlfriend
ZAHN GLANZ, Hilke's boyfriend before the war
GRANDFATHER MARTER, Hilke's father
ERNST WATZEK-TRUMMER, a chicken farmer and an Austrian patriot
VRATNO JAVOTNIK, an apolitical Yugoslav survivor and Siggy's father
GOTTLOB WUT, a German soldier, head of a motorcycle unit in Yugoslavia

The Novel

Setting Free the Bears is divided into three parts. The first, titled "Siggy," is narrated in the first person by Hannes Graff, one of the principals in the book. The second part contains Siggy's notebook, with entries alternating between his "Zoo Watches," in which he spies on the guards and animals at the Heitzinger Zoo outside Vienna preparatory to freeing the animals, and his "Pre-History," in which is recounted the personal history of Siggy against a background of World War II, particularly during the *Anschluss* and with the partisans in the mountains of Yugoslavia. The third section, again narrated by Hannes Graff, relates the zoo break which Hannes stages with the help of his girlfriend, Gallen, in order to fulfill the fantasy of his now dead companion, Siggy.

The narrative begins when Graff, who has recently failed an important university examination, meets a strange young man whom he has been watching in the Rathaus Park. Together they purchase a seven-hundred-cubic-centimeter, vintage Royal Enfield motorcycle to take to Italy, where they plan to enjoy the spring. After a stop at the Heitzinger Zoo, where Siggy explains that he plans to free the animals, the two heroes ride into the Austrian countryside, declaring that they will live off the land. They pick up

Gallen, a young country girl who is on her way to work for her aunt, who owns an inn. Hannes burns his legs on the exhaust pipes of the motorcycle, and the two young men lay over at the hotel owned by Gallen's aunt. Siggy assaults the local milkman, whom he sees beating his draft horse, and is pursued by the police as he flees back to Vienna to prepare for the zoo escapade. A few days later, he returns to rescue Hannes from Gallen and her aunt but dies while trying to elude the local police when he slides under a truck loaded with bee hives and is stung to death.

Hannes discovers Siggy's diary, and the second section of the narrative is made up of entries from it. Alternating between Siggy's notes on the guards at the zoo, especially O. Schrutt, and the tales of his ancestry, the notebook passages fill in the details of Siggy's past and explore some of the horrors of World War II as it was experienced by Siggy's mother, Hilke Marter, and her family and her boyfriend, as they witness the humiliation of the German *Anschluss* of Austria during the early spring of 1938. The family flees Vienna for the relative safety of Kaprun, near Kitzbühel, in the Alps, in the taxi of Hilke's boyfriend, Zahn Glanz, who has turned from his studies at the University of Vienna to demonstrate against the Nazi takeover of his homeland. Zahn disappears while smuggling an anti-Hitler newspaper editor out of the country and is never heard from again. The narrative, Pre-History II, switches to Siggy's father, Vratno Javotnik, and his role, or nonrole, amid the brutal internecine fighting among the various partisan bands in the mountains of Yugoslavia during the war.

Vratno Javotnik is politically uncommitted and wants only to survive the hostilities, but he finds himself unavoidably allied with an Ustashi terrorist group, and he is assigned to kill a German officer, Gottlob Wut, the leader of a motorcycle unit. The reasons for killing Wut are extremely vague but have something to do with Wut having been suspected of tampering with the motorcycle of the Italian entry in the Grand Prix of 1930, thereby winning pots of money for himself and for those who knew of the sabotage. Javotnik likes Wut and prolongs his life, only to have Wut killed in the urinal of a nightclub by a rival political group. Vratno escapes from the nightmare of Yugoslavia on Wut's 1933 Grand Prix racing motorcycle, arriving in Vienna in 1945, at the time of the Soviet liberation of the city, where he meets Hilke, and, after it is discovered that she is pregnant by him, the two marry. Siggy's father dies at the hands of some former Yugoslav soldiers while celebrating the death of Stalin in 1953. Hilke abandons her family in 1956, shortly after they move back to Kaprun, and the section closes with the death of Hilke's father, Grandfather Marter.

The concluding section of the novel details the zoo break and its tragic aftermath. Hannes talks Gallen into helping him carry out Siggy's fantasy of freeing the animals, but the results are disastrous, with most of the beasts, being captured immediately after their release. The novel concludes, however, on a hopeful and enigmatic note. Hannes retreats to the country to talk over the failure of the gesture of freeing the creatures with Ernst Watzek-Trummer, and there, alone in the woods, he sees the two "Rare Spectacled Bears" wandering together down a forest road and recognizes that his effort has not been totally wasted. His vision in the woods provides him with a sense of accomplishment and self-knowledge, suggesting that his journey has not been in vain and that the lessons of history will help him to understand his own mortality and what life has in store for him.

The Characters

Setting Free the Bears is peopled by an eccentric collection of historical and fictional characters. The background of history is manipulated and controlled by actual figures such as Kurt von Schuschnigg, Chancellor of Austria, who replaces the previous head of state when he is assassinated by Nazi sympathizers. While Hitler, Hermann Göring, and the Austrian Nazi Artur von Seyss-Inquart plan the *Anschluss*, Ernst Watzek-Trummer, a chicken farmer who lives on the outskirts of Vienna, dons a homemade suit of pie plates covered with feathers in order to protest the coming of the German troops by appearing as the Habsburg eagle in downtown Vienna. Gottlub Wut, leader of the scout outfit, Motorcycle Unit Balkan 4, helps Siggy's father escape from the clutches of the Slivnica family: Dabrinka, the fair; Julka and Baba, the sulky and the squat; Bijelo, the eldest; Gavro and Lutvo, the idiot twins; and Todor, the leader. The names and characters are as loony as the events which make up the adventures which beset Siggy's father as he wanders his way north out of Yugoslavia toward his meeting with Siggy's mother in Vienna.

In the midst of this collection of hapless and often crazy people, the novel focuses on Hannes Graff, a conventional but historyless university dropout who is fascinated and finally seduced by the antics of Siegfried (Siggy) Javotnik, who supplies through his journal the central portion of the narrative and who plans the zoo break which Hannes eventually carries out after Siggy's death. It is Siggy who is preoccupied by history, both his own and the history that has formed the world into which he was born. His journal entries become the most engaging portion of the book and present the reader with the characters that are most memorable both for their eccentricities and their thoughts. In comparison to the Pre-History sections, the protagonists Siggy and Hannes seem to be pale, one-dimensional figures. In fact, it could be easily demonstrated that the most engaging character of the book is Vratno Javotnik, whose adventures during the war provide an instructive point of comparison with the adventures of his son and Hannes.

The rest of the novel is rounded out by the Marter family, Grandfather and Grandmother, Hilke, and Ernst, who joins them as an adjunct member of their household when they leave Vienna during the Nazi takeover. All the characters become living, or, more often, dead witnesses to the irrationality and whims of history as one by one they disappear or meet unexpected, often violent, deaths at the hands of those who haunt them from the past. They carry forward their own delusions about themselves, about their personal myths, and about history, which keeps surprising them with its randomness and cruelty.

Themes and Meanings

The heart of the novel concerns the quest for freedom which is pursued by the characters, both major and minor, as they struggle to escape the trap of history and their sense of helplessness in the face of historical necessity. The two main historical events of the novel reflect this lack of control. The *Anschluss* demonstrates the impotence of the remnants of the Austro-Hungarian world, with its historical preeminence, in the face of the modern and superior force of the Nazi military machine. Equally powerless are the citizens of the various Serbo-Croatian regions of modern-day Yugoslavia, who also collapse in the face of the political and military chaos wreaked by the contending forces of Fascism and Communism as the Germans and Soviets and their local minions battle for control of the Balkans. In the midst of this repression, murder, and corruption, ordinary people try to get on with their lives, rearing families, occupying meaningful jobs, striving for personal dignity, struggling to be free from the shackles of the past. The extended metaphor of freeing the zoo animals forms the controlling image of the book in spite of its obvious impracticality. That Hannes Graff feels called upon to carry out the zoo break to its conclusion by actually setting the bears free, becomes an acknowledgment of the impossibility of his idealism and a gesture of Graff's indebtedness to his friend for his tutelage. Still, however misdirected Siggy's intentions may have been, the presence of the two spectacled bears at the end of the book provides a final vision for Hannes to take with him on his further travels.

Critical Context

Setting Free the Bears was well received for a first novel, garnering complimentary reviews in such publications as *The New York Times Book Review* and *Saturday Review*. The flaws in the novel detected by those early reviews, however, have not really diminished with the passing of time. The novel is still criticized for being a little short on characterization, especially that of the two main protagonists, Siggy and Hannes, and the critics still complain about the division of the novel into three uneven parts. What has happened as John Irving's reputation has grown with his subsequent novels is that the themes and figures of his first book now can be seen in the context of his subsequent fiction, which clarifies some of the material thought confusing on first reading. Seen from this perspective, it is apparent that even with the book's faults, it is the work of a major talent. The distinctive narrative voice and the humor and inventiveness which have characterized Irving's later novels are all present, if in embryonic form, in this first work. The world of Hannes Graff contains the beginnings of the world of T. S. Garp, whose adventures have brought his creator sufficient recognition to be considered a literary force in postwar American fiction.

Sources for Further Study

Marcus, Griel. "John Irving: The World of *The World According to Garp*," in *Rolling Stone*. December 13, 1979, pp. 68-75.

Miller, Gabriel. *John Irving*, 1982.

Ruppersburg, Hugh M. "John Irving," in *American Novelists Since World War II, Second Series*, 1980. Edited by James E. Kibler, Jr.

Williams, Thomas. "Talk with John Irving," in *The New York Times Book Review*. LXXXII (April 23, 1978), pp. 26-27.

Charles L. P. Silet